Bloom's Shakespeare Through the Ages

Bloom's Shakespeare Through the Ages

THE SONNETS

Edited and with an introduction by
Harold Bloom
Sterling Professor of the Humanities
Yale University

Volume Editor
Brett Foster

BLOOM'S
LITERARY CRITICISM
An imprint of Infobase Publishing

Bloom's Shakespeare Through the Ages: The Sonnets

Bloom's Literary Criticism
An imprint of Infobase Publishing
132 West 31st Street
New York NY 10001

Library of Congress Cataloging-in-Publication Data
The sonnets / edited and with an introduction by Harold Bloom ; volume editor : Brett Foster.
    p. cm. — (Bloom's Shakespeare through the ages)
 Includes bibliographical references and index.
 ISBN 978-0-7910-9597-3 (alk. paper)
 1. Shakespeare, William, 1564-1616. Sonnets. 2. Sonnets, English—History and criticism. I. Bloom, Harold. II. Foster, Brett.
 PR2848.S64 2008
 821'.3—dc22   2008012830

Series design by Erika K. Arroyo
Cover design by Ben Peterson

Printed in the United States of America

Bang EJB 10 9 8 7 6 5 4 3 2 1

This book is printed on acid-free paper.

CONTENTS

❧

SERIES INTRODUCTION

Shakespeare Through the Ages presents not the most current of Shakespeare criticism, but the best of Shakespeare criticism, from the seventeenth century to today. In the process, the volumes also chart the flow over time of critical discussion of particular works. Other useful and fascinating collections of historical Shakespearean criticism exist, but no collection that we know of contains such a range of commentary on each of Shakespeare's greatest works and at the same time emphasizes the greatest critics in our literary tradition: from John Dryden in the seventeenth century, to Samuel Johnson in the eighteenth century, to William Hazlitt and Samuel Coleridge in the nineteenth century, to A.C. Bradley and William Empson in the twentieth century, to the most perceptive critics of our own day. This canon of Shakespearean criticism emphasizes aesthetic rather than political or social analysis.

Some of the pieces included here are full-length essays; others are excerpts designed to present a key point. Much (but not all) of the earliest criticism consists only of brief mentions of specific works. In addition to the classics of criticism, some pieces of mainly historical importance have been included, often to provide background for important reactions from future critics.

These volumes are intended for students, particularly those just beginning their explorations of Shakespeare. We have therefore also included basic materials designed to provide a solid grounding in each work: a biography of Shakespeare, a synopsis, a list of characters, and an explication of key passages. In addition, each selection of the criticism of a particular century begins with an introductory essay discussing the general nature of that century's commentary and the particular issues and controversies addressed by critics presented in the volume.

Shakespeare was "not of an age, but for all time," but much Shakespeare criticism is decidedly for its own age, of lasting importance only to the scholar who wrote it. Students today read the criticism most readily available to them, which means essays printed in recent books and journals, especially those journals made available on the Internet. Older criticism is too often buried in out-of-print books on forgotten shelves of libraries or in defunct periodicals. Therefore, many students, particularly younger students, have no way of knowing that some of the most profound criticism of Shakespeare's works was written decades or centuries ago. We hope this series remedies that problem, and more importantly, we hope it infuses students with the enthusiasm of the critics in these volumes for the beauty and power of Shakespeare's poetry.

INTRODUCTION BY
HAROLD BLOOM

The most striking quality of Shakespeare's astonishing Sonnets is the uncanny *detachment* of the voice that speaks them. This voice performs its utterances *as* a poet and *as* an actor, but *not* as a dramatic inwardness or character in a play. Shakespeare, unlike his protagonists, declines self-overhearing. Like the Fair Young Man, the Dark Lady, and the Rival Poet, he is another conscious fiction.

Hamlet and Falstaff are richer fictions, since their inwardness apparently is infinite, but the speaker of the Sonnets is merely a voice. As such the voice is endlessly flexible and has no rival among lyric voices in the language. But Shakespeare maintains his curious impersonality, as though all the humiliations, disappointments, betrayals are being suffered by someone else.

John Hollander remarks upon the difference between traditional sonnet sequences, addressed to idealized female Muses, and Shakespeare's, which invokes an unnamed young man and a fatal woman, who may or may not be actual personages. I would add that neither the man nor the woman is at all idealized, setting aside the man's beauty and the woman's dangerous allure. Indeed the male beloved is something of a self-centered, narcissistic monster, while the woman appears to be an insatiable waste of shame. Neither is ever presented in judgmental terms, nor does the speaker ever *morally* condemn himself, though he seems to accept the societal view that to be an actor-dramatist is a kind of degradation.

It was G. K. Chesterton who observed that Chaucer's ironies were too large to be seen. The ironies of the Sonnets are both palpable and invisible, a paradox I cannot resolve. Shakespeare knows everything he is doing, but we do not. Our optics are impeded by his transparency. We are not presented with any perspectivism, tragic or comic, as we are in the plays. Would we necessarily know that the author of the Sonnets wrote the best tragedies and comedies ever composed if we had read only the Sonnets? Yes and no, no and yes, depending upon how we read.

The Sonnets were made from the early 1590s on to 1609, yet do not give the impression of so extended a time of composition. No one would expect 154 poems to be of equal achievement, yet only a handful or two are discardable as aesthetic artifacts. Dante, Petrarch, Sidney and Spenser—great poets all—do not maintain so high a level, perhaps by design. Here is number 122 of Shakespeare's Sonnets, one of the least renowned, but a poem I cannot forget:

> Thy gift, thy tables, are within my brain
> Full charactered with lasting memory,
> Which shall above that idle rank remain
> Beyond all date, even to eternity;
> Or, at the least, so long as brain and heart
> Have faculty by nature to subsist;
> Till each to razed oblivion yield his part
> Of thee, thy record never can be missed.
> That poor retention could not so much hold,
> Nor need I tallies thy dear love to score;
> Therefore to give them from me was I bold,
> To trust those tables that receive thee more.
>   To keep an adjunct to remember thee
>   Were to import forgetfulness in me.

The ostensible subject is giving away a notebook in which sonnets were inscribed, but the crucial line here is: "Nor need I tallies thy dear love to score," which may have suggested Whitman's use of "tally" as his prime image of voice. Sonnet 122's contrast between outer and inner inscription is simplistic, and may be ironic. Is the poem an apologia for proclaiming one's love by yielding up the notebook? "Bold" suggests a lover's reproof at divulgence. Yet I hear a subtler self-reproach in the sequence of "idle rank," "razed," "missed," "tallies," "score," "bold," "trust." However the legible sonnets are subordinated to their memory, they retain a value beyond keepsake. How glad we would be to possess one of those notebooks now!

The ordering of the Sonnets is arbitrary but sometimes revelatory. Just before is a savage masterpiece, no. 121:

> 'Tis better to be vile than vile esteemed
> When not to be receives reproach of being,
> And the just pleasure lost, which is so deemed
> Not by our feeling but by others' seeing.
> For why should others' false adulterate eyes
> Give salutation to my sportive blood?
> Or on my frailties why are frailer spies,
> Which in their wills count bad what I think good?
> No, I am that I am; and they that level

At my abuses reckon up their own:
I may be straight, though they themselves be bevel;
By their rank thoughts my deeds must not be shown,
    Unless this general evil they maintain:
    All men are bad, and in their badness reign.

The peculiar shock of this is its audacious quotation of Yahweh naming himself to Moses from the burning book: *ehyeh asher ehyer*, "I am that I am," punning upon the four-letter YHWH. Like God, Shakespeare asserts presence but denies blame. "I may be straight though they themselves be bevel": can this be strongly misread (perhaps) as one of the many Shakespearean anticipations of a later usage of "straight"? In such a misprision, a current reader can wonder if the "sportive blood" insinuates homoeroticism that Shakespeare ironically denies.

Sonnet 121 stands back from its own savagery of tone, and Shakespeare subtly maintains distance even where he has been impugned. I scarcely know what the general stance of the Sonnets could be called: "Detachment" is not precise enough. Sonnet 94 is one of the subtlest of apparent distancings:

They that have power to hurt, and will do none,
That do not do the thing they most do show,
Who, moving others, are themselves as stone,
Unmovèd, cold, and to temptation slow –
They rightly do inherit heaven's graces
And husband nature's riches from expense;
They are the lords and owners of their faces,
Others but stewards of their excellence.
The summer's flower is to the summer sweet,
Though to itself it only live and die;
But if that flower with base infection meet,
The basest weed outbraves his dignity:
    For sweetest things turn sourest by their deeds;
    Lilies that fester smell far worse than weeds.

This disturbing portrait of the Fair Young Man ends with a proverbial line that appeared in *Edward III* (1596), a history play that Shakespeare *may* have written (I myself doubt this). Shakespeare's patron-friend presumably read this Sonnet and perhaps was its intended audience. Mutual sophistication hardly could surpass either Sonnet 94 or its likely situation. In teaching the poem I ask students to brood on the word "rightly" in line 5, as it contains what would be a universe of bitterness in any poet or person but Shakespeare. Yet how shall we interpret "rightly" here? It transcends irony and intimates a reality in which what is not given nevertheless famishes the would-be recipient. Here the narcissism of the young nobleman verges upon the abyss of sado-masochism.

To be the steward of another's excellence is to be no more than an upper servant of a will not one's own. What is Shakespeare's tone here? I find this question even more unanswerable than before. Distance has edged into an intimate proximity that allows no intimacy. Whether this is the Earl of Southampton or of Pembroke, he is at the least a vicious personage, with a decadence prophesying a Wildean exquisite of three centuries later.

The contrast to Sonnet 94 is, for me, the strongest of the sequence, the great outcry from an erotic season in hell that is Sonnet 129, a stunning negative tribute to the Dark Lady:

> Th' expense of spirit in a waste of shame
> Is lust in action; and, till action, lust
> Is perjured, murd'rous, bloody, full of blame,
> Savage, extreme, rude, cruel, not to trust;
> Enjoyed no sooner but despisèd straight;
> Past reason hunted, and no sooner had,
> Past reason hated as a swallowed bait
> On purpose laid to make the taker mad:
> Mad in pursuit, and in possession so;
> Had, having, and in quest to have, extreme;
> A bliss in proof, and proved, a very woe;
> Before, a joy proposed; behind, a dream.
>> All this the world well knows, yet none knows well
>> To shun the heaven that leads men to this hell.

The antithesis of the Fair Young Man's husbanding "nature's richness from expense" in Sonnet 94 is the explosive opening of 129: "Th' expense of spirit in a waste of shame / Is lust in action." So powerful is this drumroll of a lyric that I have never found this kinetic energy of release in any other poem, in any language I know. "Spirit" here is Shakespeare's semen, and its expenditure is judged a loss in vitality. "Hell" in Elizabethan slang was the vagina, and a revulsion is expressed far more complexly than Lear's or Edgar's similar recoils from female sexuality. None of the clearly homoerotic Sonnets have anything like the drive of Sonnet 129. Shakespeare, as we should know from the plays, was as ferociously heterosexual as Robert Browning or W. B. Yeats. What we need to know more of (and never will) is the erotic power of the Dark Lady. My late friend Anthony Burgess persuaded me that this enkindling woman was Lucy Negro, London's leading East Indian sex-worker. I recommend strongly Burgess's Shakespeare novel, *Nothing Like the Sun*.

After 129, any other sonnet might seem anticlimactic, but I want to conclude here with two marvelous poems, 86 and 87. Here is Sonnet 86, the hyperbolical invocation of the Rival Poet, who seems to me Christopher Marlowe rather than George Chapman:

Was it the proud full sail of his great verse,
Bound for the prize of all-too-precious you,
That did my ripe thoughts in my brain inhearse,
Making their tomb the womb wherein they grew?
Was it his spirit, by spirits taught to write
Above a mortal pitch, that struck me dead?
No, neither he, nor his compeers by night
Giving him aid, my verse astonishèd.
He, nor that affable familiar ghost
Which nightly gulls him with intelligence,
As victors of my silence cannot boast;
I was not sick of any fear from thence:
        But when your countenance filled up his line,
        Then lacked I matter; that enfeebled mine.

Again highly sophisticated and certainly ironic, this agonistic vision of Marlowe's ghost, or of a Marlowe-Chapman composite, is uttered with a very broad smile. Like Marlowe's Faustus, the Rival Poet channels spirits and daemons in order to achieve "his great verse." But Marlowe is gulled or fooled with false notions, and Shakespeare gracefully indicates his own lack of fear. Instead, he charmingly suggests an inhibition through jealousy, not of superior poetic powers, but of encountering the Fair Young Man's portrait in a rival's verses.

Sonnet 87 is a work of immense richness in brief compass:

Farewell, thou art too dear for my possessing,
And like enough thou know'st thy estimate.
The charter of thy worth gives thee releasing;
My bonds in thee are all determinate.
For how do I hold thee but by thy granting,
And for that riches where is my deserving?
The cause of this fair gift in me is wanting,
And so my patent back again is swerving.
Thyself thou gav'st, thy own worth then not knowing,
Or me, to whom thou gav'st it, else mistaking;
So thy great gift, upon misprision growing,

Comes home again, on better judgment making.
　　Thus have I had thee as a dream doth flatter,
　　In sleep a king, but waking no such matter.

In the Introduction to the Second Edition of my treatise, *The Anxiety of Influence*, I confess indebtedness to this Shakespearean version of the influence process, whether in love or literature. "Swerving," "mistaking," "misprision" are the three crucial emblems, all of which I stole for my own theory of influence. Sonnet 87's legalistic language emanates strong ironies that give this poem mixed tonalities, mingling alienation and lost desire: "too dear," "possessing," "estimate," "charter of thy worth," "releasing," "bounds," "granting," "gift," "patent." The giving has famished the taker, but Shakespeare remains Shakespeare, keenly aware of reality's greater light dimming the dream of eros.

BIOGRAPHY OF
WILLIAM SHAKESPEARE
☙

WILLIAM SHAKESPEARE was born in Stratford-on-Avon in April 1564 into a family of some prominence. His father, John Shakespeare, was a glover and merchant of leather goods who earned enough to marry Mary Arden, the daughter of his father's landlord, in 1557. John Shakespeare was a prominent citizen in Stratford, and at one point, he served as an alderman and bailiff.

Shakespeare presumably attended the Stratford grammar school, where he would have received an education in Latin, but he did not go on to either Oxford or Cambridge universities. Little is recorded about Shakespeare's early life; indeed, the first record of his life after his christening is of his marriage to Anne Hathaway in 1582 in the church at Temple Grafton, near Stratford. He would have been required to obtain a special license from the bishop as security that there was no impediment to the marriage. Peter Alexander states in his book *Shakespeare's Life and Art* that marriage at this time in England required neither a church nor a priest or, for that matter, even a document—only a declaration of the contracting parties in the presence of witnesses. Thus, it was customary, though not mandatory, to follow the marriage with a church ceremony.

Little is known about William and Anne Shakespeare's marriage. Their first child, Susanna, was born in May 1583 and twins, Hamnet and Judith, in 1585. Later on, Susanna married Dr. John Hall, but the younger daughter, Judith, remained unmarried. When Hamnet died in Stratford in 1596, the boy was only 11 years old.

We have no record of Shakespeare's activities for the seven years after the birth of his twins, but by 1592 he was in London working as an actor. He was also apparently well known as a playwright, for reference is made of him by his contemporary Robert Greene in *A Groatsworth of Wit*, as "an upstart crow."

Several companies of actors were in London at this time. Shakespeare may have had connection with one or more of them before 1592, but we have no record that tells us definitely. However, we do know of his long association with the most famous and successful troupe, the Lord Chamberlain's Men. (When James I came to the throne in 1603, after Elizabeth's death, the troupe's name changed to the King's Men.) In 1599 the Lord Chamberlain's Men provided the financial backing for the construction of their own theater, the Globe.

The Globe was begun by a carpenter named James Burbage and finished by his two sons, Cuthbert and Robert. To escape the jurisdiction of the Corporation of London, which was composed of conservative Puritans who opposed the theater's "licentiousness," James Burbage built the Globe just outside London, in the Liberty of Holywell, beside Finsbury Fields. This also meant that the Globe was safer from the threats that lurked in London's crowded streets, like plague and other diseases, as well as rioting mobs. When James Burbage died in 1597, his sons completed the Globe's construction. Shakespeare played a vital role, financially and otherwise, in the construction of the theater, which was finally occupied sometime before May 16, 1599.

Shakespeare not only acted with the Globe's company of actors; he was also a shareholder and eventually became the troupe's most important playwright. The company included London's most famous actors, who inspired the creation of some of Shakespeare's best-known characters, such as Hamlet and Lear, as well as his clowns and fools.

In his early years, however, Shakespeare did not confine himself to the theater. He also composed some mythological-erotic poetry, such as *Venus and Adonis* and *The Rape of Lucrece*, both of which were dedicated to the earl of Southampton. Shakespeare was successful enough that in 1597 he was able to purchase his own home in Stratford, which he called New Place. He could even call himself a gentleman, for his father had been granted a coat of arms.

By 1598 Shakespeare had written some of his most famous works, *Romeo and Juliet*, *The Comedy of Errors*, *A Midsummer Night's Dream*, *The Merchant of Venice*, *Two Gentlemen of Verona*, and *Love's Labour's Lost*, as well as his historical plays *Richard II*, *Richard III*, *Henry IV*, and *King John*. Somewhere around the turn of the century, Shakespeare wrote his romantic comedies *As You Like It*, *Twelfth Night*, and *Much Ado About Nothing*, as well as *Henry V*, the last of his history plays in the Prince Hal series. During the next 10 years he wrote his great tragedies, *Hamlet*, *Macbeth*, *Othello*, *King Lear*, and *Antony and Cleopatra*.

At this time, the theater was burgeoning in London; the public took an avid interest in drama, the audiences were large, the plays demonstrated an enormous range of subjects, and playwrights competed for approval. By 1613, however, the rising tide of Puritanism had changed the theater. With the desertion of the theaters by the middle classes, the acting companies were compelled to depend more on the aristocracy, which also meant that they now had to cater to a more sophisticated audience.

Perhaps this change in London's artistic atmosphere contributed to Shakespeare's reasons for leaving London after 1612. His retirement from the theater is sometimes thought to be evidence that his artistic skills were waning. During this time, however, he wrote *The Tempest* and *Henry VIII*. He also wrote the "tragicomedies," *Pericles*, *Cymbeline*, and *The Winter's Tale*. These were thought to be inspired by Shakespeare's personal problems and have sometimes been considered proof of his greatly diminished abilities.

However, so far as biographical facts indicate, the circumstances of his life at this time do not imply any personal problems. He was in good health and financially secure, and he enjoyed an excellent reputation. Indeed, although he was settled in Stratford at this time, he made frequent visits to London, enjoying and participating in events at the royal court, directing rehearsals, and attending to other business matters.

In addition to his brilliant and enormous contributions to the theater, Shakespeare remained a poetic genius throughout the years, publishing a renowned and critically acclaimed sonnet cycle in 1609 (most of the sonnets were written many years earlier). Shakespeare's contribution to this popular poetic genre are all the more amazing in his break with contemporary notions of subject matter. Shakespeare idealized the beauty of man as an object of praise and devotion (rather than the Petrarchan tradition of the idealized, unattainable woman). In the same spirit of breaking with tradition, Shakespeare also treated themes previously considered off limits—the dark, sexual side of a woman as opposed to the Petrarchan ideal of a chaste and remote love object. He also expanded the sonnet's emotional range, including such emotions as delight, pride, shame, disgust, sadness, and fear.

When Shakespeare died in 1616, no collected edition of his works had ever been published, although some of his plays had been printed in separate unauthorized editions. (Some of these were taken from his manuscripts, some from the actors' prompt books, and others were reconstructed from memory by actors or spectators.) In 1623 two members of the King's Men, John Hemings and Henry Condell, published a collection of all the plays they considered to be authentic, the First Folio.

Included in the First Folio is a poem by Shakespeare's contemporary Ben Jonson, an outstanding playwright and critic in his own right. Jonson paid tribute to Shakespeare's genius, proclaiming his superiority to what previously had been held as the models for literary excellence—the Greek and Latin writers. "Triumph, my Britain, thou hast one to show / To whom all scenes of Europe homage owe. / He was not of an age, but for all time!"

Jonson was the first to state what has been said so many times since. Having captured what is permanent and universal to all human beings at all times, Shakespeare's genius continues to inspire us—and the critical debate about his works never ceases.

SUMMARY OF
THE SONNETS
ॐ

The twentieth-century Irish poet Louis MacNeice writes in his poem "Snow": "World is suddener than we fancy it. // World is crazier and more of it than we think, / Incorrigibly plural." Peeling a tangerine, the speaker feels the "drunkenness of things being various." Suddener. Plural. Various. These are excellent words with which to prepare readers for the wonders of division and diversification that parade amid William Shakespeare's *Sonnets*. Taken together, these poems display an astonishing range of voice, image, situation, crisis, meditation, and resignation. Two quick clarifications are in order. First, *The Sonnets* is the collective title, and has been since the sonnets first appeared in print in 1609, for Shakespeare's 154 14-line lyric poems. Second, the word "division" is used above in at least two senses: the poetic or musical, as when Shakespeare writes of "ravishing division" in *1 Henry the Fourth*, and the psychological, as in self-division, that introspective, examining fearlessness that sets Shakespeare's poems apart from nearly all of their counterparts. For four centuries readers have admired (but have not *always* admired, as we will soon see) the technical and rhetorical accomplishments in these condensed and memorable lyric poems. And they have also endeavored to locate that more profound lyrical originality in *The Sonnets*—an originality of voice, of recognizable thought and feeling, somehow rendered in all of their complexities in the early modern English language and in the formal confines of the sonnet. Some have even argued that Shakespeare in these sonnets invented a new kind of subjectivity, a new way by which the "I" that speaks in lyric poetry could assess itself and come forth to us, as if risen warmblooded and three-dimensional from the black ink of the text.

Despite his innovations, Shakespeare was by no means the first writer to produce a long sequence of sonnets. On the contrary, he was composing near the end of more than two centuries of sonnet writing in Europe and also during a strong literary fad for sonnets in English in Elizabethan England in the 1590s. Francesco Petrarch, a Florentine humanist, diplomat, and poet, elevated the sonnet to an influential literary form with his sequence known as the *Canzoniere* or *Rime sparse* ("Scattered rimes"). Petrarch's preferred poetic form in this collection was the sonnet, a 14-line lyric that often expressed stages of meditation or argumentative reasoning. The form was suited to such mental or emotional activity due to the built-in "turns" at different points in the poem that advanced, rejected, repeated, or complicated the present point. Petrarch's literary predecessors in Florence, including the great epic poet Dante Alighieri, frequently wrote sonnets, as did Sicilian poets at the imperial court before them. Many of those poets were also court lawyers, and this may be why the sonnet has always had a nimble, argumentative movement. Petrarch's sonnets in the *Rime* are predominantly love poems or poems that ruminate on the exaltations and heartaches of love. His beloved addressee and main subject is Laura, a distant, chaste, fair woman. The speaker celebrates Laura, he cries to her for mercy, and he is generally obsessed by her beauty, her virtue, and sometimes what he perceives to be her cruelty. In part inspired by Dante's great heroine Beatrice, Laura proved the more influential female persona in European lyric poetry.

The sonnet was not imported into English writing till the early sixteenth century, less than 50 years before the birth of Shakespeare. Court poets serving England's first great Renaissance monarch, Henry VIII, adopted the writing of sonnets as one of several sophisticated, Italianate habits. These innovators were not writers professionally but aristocrats, courtiers, or diplomats, whose literary activity gave a "civil grace" to their various attainments in languages, music, hunting, and sport. Thomas Wyatt was the most important Henrician sonnet writer, and he translated several of Petrarch's sonnets found in his *Rime*. He also retained the "Petrarchan" or Italian sonnet form, comprising an octave, or eight lines in a rhyme scheme of abbaabba, followed by a "turn" to the sestet, the final six lines that rhymed cdecde, or featuring some variation of this pattern. Each line had 10 syllables, often in iambic pentameter (five pairs of syllables in unaccented-accented order), and this type of line has remained a key feature of sonnets up to our own day. Henry Howard, earl of Surrey, was a fellow sonnet writer during Henry VIII's reign, and his frequent choice of a different sonnet form would influence Shakespeare's habits more obviously.

Howard reoriented Petrarch's sonnet form into a more symmetrical, repetitive scheme, one that was more accommodating of the fewer rhymes in the English language: abab cdcd efef gg. Sometimes poets might repeat the same two rhymes in the second or third quatrain (or stanzas of four lines), but the possible use of more rhymes gave them more flexibility. Howard's alteration also introduced two other striking formal differences: There was no longer one main "turn," as in the Petrarchan move from the octave to the sestet, and the ending was now punctuated by the concluding couplet, or pair of lines linked by one rhyme. Howard might echo the Petrarchan model and redirect the sonnet after his eighth line or at the end of the second quatrain. But suddenly more structural options were available: The same idea could be repeated, with variations or different emphases, in each of the three quatrains and then in the couplet be rounded off . . . or utterly renounced. Shakespeare almost always uses this more flexible sonnet form, likely because it gave him more opportunities for shifts of voice or dramatic developments. This form, comprising three quatrains and a couplet, became known as the "English" sonnet or, in homage to its greatest practitioner, the "Shakespearean" sonnet. Of Shakespeare's 154 sonnets, the only ones that diverge from this English model are sonnet 99, which has an extra line; sonnet 126, which has only 12 lines, in couplets; and sonnet 145, whose lines have only eight syllables.

Wyatt's and Howard's sonnets were read mainly at court and circulated in manuscript. They were first printed, and framed in a more general fashion that the common reader might appreciate, in 1557, when they appeared in a poetry anthology called *Songs and Sonnetts*, known today as *Tottel's Miscellany*. The one great sonnet writer between these Henrician poets and Shakespeare is Philip Sidney, the Elizabethan courtier, soldier, and author of the sonnet sequence *Astrophil and Stella*. To borrow a line from *Hamlet*, Sidney was the "glass of fashion" in the 1580s. His writings inspired his circle of friends, and his early death on a battlefield in the Netherlands made him a national hero. The more than 100 sonnets in his sequence were popular because of the reputation of their creator but also because of the courtly love intrigues they coyly half-concealed. Some readers must have known that the secret relationship dramatized in *Astrophil and Stella* in actuality involved Sidney and Penelope Rich, a prominent lady of the court. Sidney puns on the name "Rich" in the sequence, and with a wink he also hides his own name, Philip, in the title character of "Astrophil." Relying on his Greek and Latin learning for trilingual puns, Sidney gave his protagonists names that meant "star lover" and "star."

Because these poems served as "screens" for possibly real-life amorous activities at court, and because like other court writers he preferred to distribute his poems in manuscript, neither Sidney nor his family deigned to publish *Astrophil and Stella*. Yet a pirate printer was happy to do so, and the unauthorized appearance of Sidney's sonnet sequence in 1591 created a literary craze that lasted for more than a decade, and that led to countless other sonnet sequences by poets of varying talents. Shakespeare's many poems were among them. Paul Innes, in *Shakespeare and the English Renaissance Sonnet*, admirably fills out these broad strokes of sonnet activity in Renaissance England, as well as Shakespeare's relationships to his many predecessors. And there were many, including significant poets such as Thomas Watson, Michael Drayton, and Edmund Spenser. Their activity and the popularity of their sonnets are reflected in the lengthy lists of English sonnet sequences in works by Peter Hyland and Katherine Duncan-Jones. Shakespeare's *Sonnets*, so divergent, ambitious, and memorable, stands preeminently above his peers'. "He is our best sonnet-writer," John Masefield flatly declares, and most critics at least since the early nineteenth century have agreed.

When did Shakespeare begin composing his own sonnets? Scholars' opinions differ widely on this matter. In 1971 Andrew Gurr argued that sonnet

145 was the earliest of Shakespeare's many poems, for it contained in the line "'I hate' from hate away she threw" a pun on Shakespeare's eventual wife, Anne Hathaway. Gurr thought Shakespeare, not yet beyond his teenage years, may have written this in the early 1580s. The poem's shorter, four-beat lines (unlike every other poem in the sequence) and its lack of any particular artfulness were other reasons to support the theory of its early composition.

Traditionally, however, scholars believe Shakespeare wrote the majority of his sonnets in the early to mid-1590s. He was in London at that point, writing for the public theaters, and many find as evidence for this dating various parallels of language and image between *The Sonnets* and Shakespeare's early plays. We also know that Shakespeare was writing two narrative poems in 1593 and 1594, likely because the plague in London closed the theaters. Those two poems, *Venus and Adonis* and *The Rape of Lucrece*, were quickly printed and were very popular during Shakespeare's own day, especially compared with the early, lukewarm reception of his sonnets in the early seventeenth century. More intriguingly, Shakespeare wrote flattering prefaces to both of these narrative poems, which he dedicated to Henry Wriothesley, the earl of Southampton. These dedications suggest that the young earl was likely a patron of Shakespeare, that is, a nobleman who lent his good name and his financial resources to broke, disreputable types such as poets and acting companies. Others have argued for later dates for at least some of the sonnets, either because of historical references inferred in certain poems or because darker, more cerebral moments in certain sonnets invite comparisons with plays from the middle or later phases of Shakespeare's career as a playwright. In any case, the latest date for their composition is 1609, when Thomas Thorpe published a quarto, or small book, of *The Sonnets*. The edition contained no preface by Shakespeare himself, and so critics have henceforth debated whether or not this publication was authorized by Shakespeare. Whatever the case, it was an incredibly important moment in the history and reception of *The Sonnets*, and Thorpe's edition remains the base text for modern editors today.

We should never forget that these sonnets were written by the same author who was writing *A Midsummer Night's Dream*, *Romeo and Juliet*, and *Hamlet*, and being able to imagine *The Sonnets* as a series of dramatic utterances, of mini-monologues, is a valuable critical habit. As you will see in the essays ahead, arguments have always raged about how autobiographical Shakespeare's poems were—are these feelings about love, so passionately expressed, Shakespeare's own, or are the poems spoken by just one more dramatic creation of a great writer? The speaker here is not named Benedict, or Othello, or Lear, but the "I" who speaks forth in lyric poems can be deceptive and may very well be just as fictive as any stage creation. The sheer emotional force of the speaker or persona in *The Sonnets* has led many to believe that these poems record Shakespeare's heartfelt utterances. For example, Ralph Waldo Emerson believed Shakespeare revealed (like Sidney's "screens" before him) "under masks that are no masks to the intelligent, the lore of friendship and of love." Yet many others have questioned this simple one-to-one historical identification. On the contrary, the "I" in a lyric poem can become an even more sophisticated fictive creation, since the lyric genre provides a far more subtle screen than any actor enjoys when he plays a character on a stage. We will assume for convenience's sake, both in this summary and in the sections ahead, that the "speaker" of these sonnets is repeatedly identifiable as such. We will assume him to be a single figure about whom we can say certain things, with some expectation that our comments will apply consistently from one sonnet to the next. But if even this is an assumption, finally, then it is a far greater assumption to think that in *The Sonnets'* use of "I" we are hearing the genuine biographical Shakespeare.

To complicate this matter one degree further, the poet and critic John Hollander points us to the self-conscious, literary qualities of the *The Sonnets'* speaker and the sequence as a whole. "In *The Sonnets*," Hollander explains, "there is a sense of ambivalence in speaking as a sonnet writer at all, at having to speak in a first person. . . . " So, as it turns out, the more subtle and complex lyrical mode is still not complex enough; Shakespeare may still have felt limited by the lyric "I," by what he could typically say at the latter end of a sonnet-writing tradition that was full of clichés and by literary representation in general. For these reasons Hollander and other critics have found the reliability and efficacy of representation—symbolized by images of mirrors, shadows, portraits, cosmetics, acting and theater, dreams, books—to be one of the central concerns recurring throughout Shakespeare's *Sonnets*. Thus these sonnets become, among many other things, great art that meditates on the making of art, both on its limitations that even the greatest poets cannot overcome and on its capacity to bestow immortality on these great poets and those they favor.

We should not be surprised, therefore, to see Shakespeare pushing against, complicating, or subverting other conventions of sonnet sequences, ones that look back all the way to Petrarch. For example, Shakespeare's most daring alteration is to make the addressee of the majority of his sonnets not a virtuous beloved, like Laura, but a young man. This change begs all sorts of questions: Are the two men friends only, or romantically involved, or committed to a sublimated love? Often the speaker praises the Young Man in terms not unlike Petrarch's idealizing awe of his virtuous beloved, but other times the Young Man seems mainly capricious and unfaithful. The bitterness at times expressed in *The Sonnets* surprises some readers, but that tone can also be found in Petrarch, if typically with more self-pity and delicacy. (Philip Sidney mockingly spoke of "Petarch's long-deceaséd woes.") The harsher tones of Shakespeare's speaker are more clearly heard in the love complaints of his English precursor Thomas Wyatt. The speaker's and Young Man's several differences, however, are more original—the older speaker versus the young addressee, the trials and disgraced fortune of the speaker versus the youth's privilege and good estimation, the speaker's low social standing compared with the young man's likely status as a nobleman, and, relatedly, the explicit professional relationship of patron-poet between these two men, which sometimes lends economic and artistic anxieties to the immediate tensions of strained romance or friendship.

If these contrasts were not innovative enough, Shakespeare does introduce an expected woman into these sonnets as well, but she is very different from Petrarch's Laura and her many bland derivatives in later sequences. Shakespeare's woman or "mistress," traditionally known as the Dark Lady, possibly enters the sequence in sonnets 40–42, but she becomes an obsessive centerpiece of the subsequence that concludes *The Sonnets*. Unlike Petrarch's Laura, this mistress is "as black as hell, as dark as night," and this darkness is not only physical but also a signifier of her deeds and moral character. Anything but a paragon of virtue, we learn that the speaker's relationship with the Dark Lady has been consummated (and then some), and he also reveals that their relationship is an extramarital one. *The Sonnets'* world of desire is a far more complex one compared with earlier sequences, as it unflinchingly presents betrayal, romantic despair, and sexual fulfillment, delusion, and compulsion. We also encounter mixed or competing relationships. Shakespeare's sonnets differentiate themselves from earlier sequences by dramatizing not single relationships of two people but rather triangles of personas and the angers, jealousies, competitions, and humiliations that ensue. In between these destabilizing appearances by the Dark Lady (or two different mistresses), Shakespeare creates another triangle, this time causing professional and artistic distress, between his poet-speaker and a Rival Poet, who vies for, and seems to win, the Young Man's favor at the expense of the older, less poetically fashionable speaker.

These, then, are the main personas and their basic relationships shown in Shakespeare's *Sonnets*. The sequence opens on a note of appeal, as the speaker urges the Young Man to marry and have a child as a way of passing on his beauty before Time (an allegorical enemy in several of the poems) devours his youth or, even worse, takes his life. These first 17 sonnets, all roughly on this same topic, are often called the Procreation sonnets, yet there remains some debate as to how many poems precisely constitute this opening subsequence. This ultimate lack of certainty about these groupings of poems, or the exact story they narrate, should give us proper pause. We must prevent ourselves from looking too assuredly and simplistically for a "story" in *The Sonnets*, as we might in a Tolstoy novel or a short story by Raymond Carver. If we cannot finally identity the "I" as the same voice in each sonnet, we are even less likely to find throughout the sonnets a cohesive, consistent, and chronological narrative. E. A. J. Honigmann points out that the sonnets' ultimate arrangement, and the story perceived therein, was very likely inconceivable by their earliest readers, who would have encountered the poems in a manuscript "singly or in small groups." Honigmann even posits that the particular youth, dramatized in the poems as the Young Man, would have read them in this incomplete, provisional way. His reactions to the few he encountered may very well have influenced the tone of Shakespeare's later efforts. Philip J. Martin provides an unusually poised assessment of the poems taken individually and as a collective arrangement, one with varying levels of narrative cohesion:

> Speaking generally we may say that each sonnet in the sequence is final and yet *not* final, that some sonnets (such as "Let me not to the marriage of true mindes") can be read apart from the rest with neither gain nor loss, and that a large number, as it were *provisionally* self-sufficient, are modified or heightened by others, whether in close proximity or not, and perhaps by the sequence as a whole.

In other words, Martin is open to meaning-making at all levels: within the individual poem, read in isolation; in proximate groups of poems; and across the entire sequence as well, as words or images recur and retrospectively reshape earlier moments. This interpretive openhandedness is arguably the best approach to a sequence composed by the likes of William Shakespeare.

Certainly there are groups of poems—broadly defined, such as the Procreation sonnets, or in smaller pairs, such as sonnets 64–65 or 67–68— that seem to share a consistency of thought, a formal character, or a dramatic situation, a prominent example of the last sort being the Rival Poet group (sonnets 78–86). Paul Edmondson and Stanley Wells, in their excellent introduction to *The Sonnets* in the Oxford Shakespeare Topics series, identify multiple poems linked by theme or even a single keyword, and their small groups range from two sonnets only to six or eight poems in a more definable subsequence. Readers wishing for a greater sense of continuity amid these many sonnets should consult Edmondson's and Wells's table of these groupings (33); Dympna Callaghan, in her recent introduction to *The Sonnets*, includes a similarly helpful appendix on the "matter" of *The Sonnets*, consisting of brief paraphrases of the information or argument each poem expresses or enacts. Once again, though, readers are discouraged from too easily formulating a strict narrative or too avidly identifying the sequences' personas with their presumed historical doppelgangers. To read in this way is to simplify the rich ambivalences and multiplicities of meaning and event that lyric poetry makes possible. Recent essays by James Schiffer and Georgia Brown will give readers a fuller appreciation of complexities of genre and literary identity regarding *The Sonnets'* patterns, narratives, and displays of time and movement. Both authors will keep readers from the greatest temptation posed by Shakespeare's poems—the kind of reductive reading described above, which also compromises the diversity of effect for which these sonnets are most praised. For example, consider this comment by George Rylands, praising Shakespeare's and John Donne's lyric poems:

> These two poets before all others have expressed the many different shades of feeling, the varied and complex experiences and attitudes of the lover; the idealism and realism, the *Odi et Amo*, the constancy and jealousy, the daydreams and disillusion, the selfless dedication and the torments of lust.

If *The Sonnets* themselves are so "varied and complex" in their feelings, experiences, and attitudes, then it follows that Shakespeare's great masterpieces of lyric poetry will have encountered diverse critical reactions and creative appropriations during the past four centuries. The essays and readings that follow all attest to this logic and provide the reader a thorough overview of the inexpressible breadth and richness of these reactions.

Although these reactions tend toward the editorial and literary critical developments through the ages, readers should rest assured that even today the speaker's promise to the Young Man in sonnet 55—"You live in this, and dwell in lovers' eyes"—is repeatedly being carried out in many creative contexts, on many continents, and through many media. The mysteries of *The Sonnets* are explored in different, more speculative ways in the frequent novels that seek to reconfigure the original's situations and the characters who inhabit them. Borrowing its title from sonnet 130, Anthony Burgess's *Nothing Like the Sun* (1964) is the supreme example, but in the new century similar works have already been published by Lennard J. Davis and Samuel Park. Christopher Rush's version of *The Sonnets'* story, *Will*, was steamy enough to be a finalist for the *Literary Review*'s 2007 Bad Sex in Fiction Award. More canonically, Virginia Woolf referred to sonnets by Shakespeare in two of her most famous novels, *To the Lighthouse* and *Mrs. Dalloway*, while another modernist giant, Marcel Proust, will forever be associated with Shakespeare, at least to his English readers. C. K. Scott-Montcrieff chose a phrase from sonnet 30, "Remembrance of things past," as the title for his translation of Proust's great novel, *A la recherché du temps perdu*.

Poets, too, continue to draw inspiration from Shakespeare's lyrical achievement. The English poet Wendy Cope wrote a mock sequence called "Strugnell's Sonnets," which whimsically deflated the sonnet conventions of her Renaissance predecessor—"Not only marble, but the plastic toys / From cornflake packets will outlive this rhyme." In the past few years, Peter Cummings has published "Sonnets on Shakespeare's Sonnets," a title whose mirroring effect would likely impress its inspirer, and William Bracy has released sonnets "in a Shakespearean mode" that in effect serve as poetic criticism of his model's sequence. More curiously, Thomas Rangdale is the author of *Nasty Sonnets Descended from Shakespeare*, which is described as a "politically incorrect, literarily deficient, and tastefully disgusting series of sonnets" inspired by Shakespeare.

Perhaps the original poet, his age's greatest writer of comedy as well, would be less offended by these nasty poetic descendants than we might think. Most worthy of mention here is *In a Fine Frenzy: Poets Respond to Shakespeare*, an excellent anthology of contemporary poems in response to all aspects of Shakespeare and his work, including a dozen poems directly related to *The Sonnets*. Of course Shakespeare's poetic influence reaches far beyond the English language. The past few years have seen Bengali and Sicilian translations of *The Sonnets*, and in the previous century some of Europe's greatest poets elevated their own art by facing the challenge of translating Shakespeare's poems. "How was it possible for a translator to find equivalents which can capture the wondrous effects of certain modes of expression particularly notable for their sheer simplicity?" asks the great Italian poet Giuseppe Ungaretti. "How could I do justice to other expressions which were striving to reveal a new and unfettered message of a unique and inimitable nature, by falling back upon traditional forms and time-worn themes?" Ungaretti, to his credit, knew the arduousness of his labors, and he recalls how he "tortured the page for months on end without a whit of progress." More recently, the French poet Yves Bonnefoy has written with similar sensitivity on the great task of translating Shakespeare.

Shakespeare's *Sonnets* continue to bear it out, even to the edge of more living and more modern technologies. The American playwright Tony Kushner's play *Terminating or Sonnet LXXV or "Lass meine Schmerzen nicht verloren sein" or Ambivalence* takes as its epigraph sonnet 75, "So are you to my thoughts as food to life," and one of the play's main characters, Billygoat, recites lines from the poem to his lover, Hendryk, who responds with memorable irritation: "SHUT UP! I hate the sonnets. Boring boring boring." In therapy, Hendryk's later description of Billygoat—"He's beautiful and he has no soul"—makes him sound suspiciously like a certain Young Man, but it is Billygoat who's allowed to express more fully the spirit of Shakespeare's dramas of desire: "Don't let me leave you. I may not have a soul but I'm beautiful so do your soul a favor, hang on tight to me." Film, too, has animated *The Sonnets*, from Derek Jarman's *Fourteen Sonnets for an Epidemic*, which picks up the poems' erotic and aesthetic interconnections, to a recent BBC broadcast, *A Waste of Shame: The Mystery of Shakespeare and his Sonnets*, featuring Rupert Graves as Shakespeare and Zoë Wanamaker as the Countess of Pembroke. The armies of iPod owners may find recordings of *The Sonnets* of interest, and especially recommended is Alex Jennings's eloquent reading of all 154 poems, produced by Naxos Audiobooks. And, of course, the Internet makes available a vast array of resources on *The Sonnets*, with varying degrees of quality and accuracy. Essential sites include The Amazing Web Site of Shakespeare's Sonnets (http://www.shakespeares-sonnets.com) and Mr. William Shakespeare and the Internet (http://shakespeare.palomar.edu)—the latter under "Works" and "The Poetry and Sonnets." Manuscripts, books, CDs, DVDs, MP3s, URLs—Shakespeare almost seems to have envisioned his sonnets assuming new shapes, sounds, interactions, and media identities. "And more, much more, than in my verse can sit," his speaker says in sonnet 103, "Your own glass shows you" (meaning "mirror" then, but today perhaps a TV or computer screen?) "when you look in it."

LIST OF PERSONAS IN
THE SONNETS
ॐॐ

There are four important characters, or personas, who appear throughout Shakespeare's *Sonnets.*

The Speaker
The speaker is a paradoxical persona in Shakespeare's *Sonnets.* He figures to be the most transparent—the one who expresses himself presumably in every poem and sometimes to an incredibly revealing degree—so how could he be anything but straightforward and open to assessment? Yet he (may we even say "he"?) remains an incredibly complicated and elusive voice to judge with literary sensitivity. Too often throughout the history of *The Sonnets*, the speaker has been instantly and simplistically equated with his creator, William Shakespeare. For example, in 1962 Edward Hubler declared that *The Sonnets* concern four people, the first being "Shakespeare, who writes in the first person." Hubler thought the lyrical genre presumed that the "I" speaking in these poems "can be taken to be autobiographical in a degree to which the plays cannot." In truth, the speaker does identify himself as "Will" in a witty pair of sonnets (135–36), but does this suffice to presume such simple identification?

Even if it were accurate (and it is problematic at best), treating Shakespeare himself as an essential, static character, unchanging from the first sonnet to the last, is yet one more assumption critics often make too quickly. The "I" in lyric poetry is never such a simple, one-to-one affair, nor do poetry's greatest goals include filling out the biographical record that so interests admirers of Shakespeare or those merely curious about literary history. Lovers of lyric poetry must not settle for these simpler sorts of "information" or reassurances, especially in a sequence of poems that interrogates issues of subjectivity and self-representation and dramatizes interior meditations on desire like no previous creative work had done.

Once acknowledging the artful, sophisticated construction of *The Sonnets*, their creator and speaker, and the emotional conditions or situations they verbally enact, it would be equally mistaken to evaluate the speaker from the other extreme—utterly impersonal, as the convenient product of a literary

15

exercise, as if Shakespeare were twiddling his thumbs when his quill wasn't scribbling 14-line ditties. The most sensitive and supple readings of these poems suggest some combination of artful design and personal history, whereby the former makes the latter more understandable and enduring. First of all, the formal and conventional qualities surrounding *The Sonnets* are by no means mutually exclusive with biographical details and genuine emotion reflected on the part of the author. Critics throughout the twentieth century, including George Wyndham, G. K. Hunter, and C. L. Barber grasped this well and often better than in prior centuries. Harold Bloom assesses the complex presence of the author in these terms: "Only one human is invented in the Sonnets, and he is not quite a representation of Shakespeare himself. 'Selfsame' with Shakespeare he is not, yet he lingers near Shakespeare, and fascinates us by that proximity."

With this poised position in mind—not "selfsame" yet biographically proximate—what have critics said about *The Sonnets*' speaker, allowing temporarily that he is one speaker and speaks with a fairly consistent voice throughout the sequence? First, he is an older man, for a friend is addressed as "young" repeatedly, and two young men typically do not speak of each other in such a way. We hear in sonnet 62 that the speaker is "Beated and chopped with tanned antiquity," and in sonnets 71 and 73 he broods on the "winter" of his life and contemplates the world after his death, a world in which the Young Man will still live. Does this make him considerably older, or is he using poetic hyperbole in a poem where he recoils from "Sin of self-love" and becomes somewhat self-conscious when beholding in the youth the "beauty of thy days"? Is he facing, in the second examples, a serious illness or the imminent prospect of death, or is he mainly a melancholy lover and possibly struggling with self-pity as well? We are also given the impression of a man who has endured trials in life. We might point to sonnet 29—"When in disgrace with Fortune and men's eyes"—or to sonnet 66—"Tired with all these, for restful death I cry"—or to sonnet 37—"As a decrepit father takes delight / . . . / So I, made lame by Fortune's dearest spite," which seems to combine both these topics of old age and misfortune. Yet note those words "As " and "So," which clearly frame the speaker's statement in figurative terms. Likewise, sonnet 93's phrase "Like a deceived husband" led Edmund Malone, one of Shakespeare's great editors, to presume that Shakespeare's wife, Anne Hathaway, had been unfaithful to him and that was why he was enamored with a youth and sleeping with a Dark Lady. Some sonnets do express the outraged hurt of betrayal, as in sonnets 40–42, or the resigned recognition of falsehood between lovers, as in sonnet 138 or 151, but Malone's inference from a simile is not editorially or logically sound.

Yet once more, in sonnet 23, the speaker alludes to what may possibly be Shakespeare's career as an actor ("As an unperfect actor on the stage"), or he may be using a convenient analogy to describe how tongue-tied his love makes him.

Does he refer to his dramatic career more clearly in sonnets 110 and 111? There his going "here and there" may represent his work as a traveling actor, one who has "made myself a motley to the view" and "thence my nature is subdued / To what it works in, like the dyer's hand." More assuredly, the speaker does make repeated, explicit reference to his identity as a writer or at least to his writing of these very poems that early in the sequence he offers to the Young Man as a kind of antidote against Time's ravishments. He mentions his "Muse," his "pen" and "ink," and his struggles in writing. There also seems to be a genuine anxiety when a Rival Poet appears in the sequence, throughout sonnets 76 to 86. And this leads to questions about a possible patronage relationship between wealthy young man and the poorer, older poet he supports. Does the speaker refer to this more professional writer-patron relationship when he calls himself a "slave," or is that rather a statement of his romantic servility?

These questions of identity and representation do not become less complicated in the final section of the sequence involving the Dark Lady. Is it she who so charms the speaker in sonnet 128 or merely a conventional image of a lady playing the virginal? (Think of a Vermeer painting here or a whole parade of portraits from the Italian Cinquecento.) And the sexual disgust in the following sonnet, 129—do we attribute that to Shakespeare as well or to the speaker with whom we have come to identify at this point in the sequence, or is it merely a literary "heap" of various definitions and effects of the topic of lust? If we begin to see how complicated the genre of lyric poetry makes the identification of characters, or even personas, in these sonnets, then we begin to grasp the opportunities of representational complexity that the supreme dramatist in Shakespeare no doubt savored.

The Young Man

The Young Man is the likely recipient of most—or at least many, if not all—of sonnets 1–126. Most of these address a "thou" in the second person, but a few more narrative poems in the third person may allude to the same person or character, though simply from a different poetic perspective. Relatedly, a few scrupulous critics point out that the traditional division of addressees—the Young Man in sonnets 1–126 and the Dark Lady in 127–154—is only assumed in the case of several sonnets in each series, with no clues whatsoever by way of gendered pronoun. A skeptical reader might also note that there is no distinct, identifying feature that makes the "youth," or "my love," or "fair beauty" and so forth addressed throughout these sonnets the very same person or even same character. We do not know, yet there is an exceptional warmth of address and intensity of situation dramatized in these sonnets, and these qualities have made most readers for four centuries assume, if not an actual, historical recipient behind *The Sonnets* (though no shortage of readers have indeed assumed just that), then at least a carefully crafted, sustained, fictionalized presence to which the speaker declares himself, and this lyrical and arguably dramatic persona has become known as the Young Man.

He is the one to whom the speaker appeals in the first 17 "Procreation" sonnets, and some critics have hypothesized that Shakespeare may have been commissioned by concerned parents to write these poems to convince their son to marry and have children. We hear of his youth as early as sonnet 2, and he is "most rich in youth" and enjoys his "day of youth" in sonnet 15. Sonnet 22 declares that "youth and thou are of one date." Later poems, featuring a more vexed or strained relationship between the speaker and Young Man, refer to his youth as a cause of behavior that pains the speaker or at least becomes a convenient excuse for the younger's actions. Sonnet 41 speaks of chiding the Young Man's beauty and "straying youth," while sonnet 96, opening with the innocuous "Some say," broods on the man's youth being a source of his faults and wantonness, as well as his beauty. Often the Young Man's youth is paired with his beauty, as in sonnet 54's phrase "beauteous and lovely youth." By contrast, the speaker in sonnet 73 lies "on the ashes of his youth," though at times the youth's loveliness or the speaker's desire is enough to give them a shared identity: "our undivided loves are one" (sonnet 36), "my friend and I are one" (41), "thou mine, I thine, eternal Love" (108, and see also sonnets 31, 36, and 39). Sonnet 116's famous defense of the "marriage of true minds" appears by context to be addressed to the male youth. Sometimes the speaker's acknowledgement of the Young Man's age sounds quite affectionate—"sweet boy" (108), "my lovely boy" (126)—and in the unequalled sonnet 20, "A woman's face with Nature's own hand painted," the speaker playfully suggests that the youth has very attractive, feminine features, and he rues that Nature went too far and gave the Young Man a "thing," or penis, for otherwise he would have been the perfect lover. Some readers have found this sonnet on the "master-mistress of my passion" to be shocking, the most explicit statement by the speaker of his sexual relationship with the Young Man. Others, however, infer the exact opposite: Here we have the speaker saying quite plainly that the youth's being a man is the one reason why they are not lovers, fully. They still share a love, but "thy love's use" (i.e., his sexual activity) is meant for women.

How should we define the speaker's relationship with the Young Man exactly? Are they merely friends, even if their Renaissance language of friendship is stronger and seemingly more intimate than is common today? Language aside, are guys today capable of being so dedicated, so praising, of their best friends? Or are the speaker and Young Man romantically involved, and if so, are there any signs that their romance has been consummated and is active physically? Does a poem such as sonnet 20 above shed light on these mysteries? These questions have attracted (or distracted) scholars and critics for centuries. The relationship does seem to have been intense enough that the Young Man's "sweet love" sustains the speaker during hard times (29), and more problematically, the speaker could feel betrayed, or else conflicted, when triangles occur between himself, the Young Man, and another. Thus sonnets 40–42 dramatize a social scandal that many take to be the Young Man's cheating on the speaker with a woman known to them both, who just may be the Dark Lady of the last series of sonnets. The emergence of a Rival Poet likewise pushes the speaker toward despair, as he contemplates a world in which the Young Man's affections or mere attention are lost. It is worth noting that even here, when their relationship is most strained, the speaker is not stingy with praise of his beloved friend: He keeps speaking of the youth's beauty in sonnet 41 with the sort of repetition that borders on obsession or emotional breakdown, and in sonnet 144, where the speaker frames himself as tempted by two loves, it is the youth who is the love of comfort. He is described in warm terms: "the better angel is a man right fair," which looks back to the very opening of the sequence, when the speaker generally explains how we desire "increase" from "fairest creatures" (1.1.).

Moments of praise for the Young Man occur frequently, from the "bright eyes" and the exaggeration of "the world's fresh ornament" in the same opening poem, to the multiple uses of "fair" in nearly all the Procreation sonnets. Similarly, the speaker begs Time not to "carve my love's fair brow" in sonnet 19, and this "fair friend" (sonnet 104), or the speaker's love for him, is described in these terms elsewhere (sonnets 21, 43, 46, 69, 82, 83, 105, and 108). The "beauty" of the Young Man is brought up just as frequently, though sometimes in compromising contexts. For example, the speaker takes pains to discuss the Young Man's beauty in the earliest sonnets because he seeks to warn him that his beauty will not last, and so he should have an heir who will continue his beauteous form. Or, elsewhere, he brings up the youth's beauty to contrast it with ugly falsehood (see sonnet 41 most explicitly). In sonnet 95, the "beauty of thy budding name" is spotted with shame, and the previous sonnet 94 is equally compromised. Yet far more commonly, the speaker composes and operates in the realm of memorializing praise: The speaker will protect "my sweet love's beauty" from the oblivion of Age because "His beauty shall in these black lines be seen" (sonnet 63).

The speaker's penchant for idealizing the Young Man is one key feature that distinguishes his role in the sequence from that of the Dark Lady, where there is almost always a sense of ambivalence (to put it mildly). Sometimes the Young Man seems the Platonic form for lower or more fabricated sorts of beauty, as when sonnet 68 promises that the youth's beauty is made "To show false art what beauty was of yore," or sonnet 106's long "blazon" (or catalogue) of "sweet beauty's best," which ultimately is itemized only to suggest to the Young Man "Even such a beauty as you master now." Additionally, the youth becomes Nature's treasure and serves as a measure to indicate natural abundance. More abstractly, we find "the beauty of thy mind" praised in sonnet 69, while sonnet 101 boldly announces, "Both truth and beauty on my love depends," as does the poet's Muse, yet another idealizing gesture common in courtly lyric poetry dedicated to the exalted beloved. Shakespeare more self-consciously presents the idealizing, and possibly deceptive, element of his artistry when, in sonnet 95, he addresses "thee, / Where beauty's veil doth cover every blot / And all things turn to fair that eyes can see!" This veiling of the blot does not erase it from the wounded speaker's memory, nor does it even remove it; it merely looks fair to those eyes that "can see." But those who know, as the speaker knows, know that this relationship is far more complex, and the Young Man far less ideal, not to mention far less loyal and trustworthy. Even a seemingly transparent address—"Lord of my love" (sonnet 26)—may sound effusively in love or a dark signal of the speaker's feeling of dependence on or enslavement to the beloved (57, 75), either materially, in terms of a patronage relationship between nobleman and poet, or emotionally, as the speaker flails in the nets of a scrutinized love that feels unsure or unrequited.

This insecurity may have a lot to do with the Young Man's apparent social standing, about which much has been written and even more inferred from the sonnets themselves. Clearly the speaker admires the youth for more than physical beauty. Sonnet 37 speaks of "beauty, birth, or wealth, or wit" being "Intitled in thy parts," and later he speaks of "thy glory." (Sonnets 80 and 87 also seem to assume the youth's good reputation in the world's eyes.) Some critics have emphasized the hypothetical construction here, "Whether beauty" and so forth, but that qualification seems intentional, and the list would likely be out of place if those qualities were not generally applicable to the Young Man. Moreover, the word "Intitled" is precisely chosen if the addressee is from the landed aristocracy. The speaker chastises the youth for adding a curse to his "beauteous blessings" in sonnet 84, since he is acting ungentlemanly in "Being fond on praise" or worrying too much about his reputation among the general classes. And certain sonnets do indicate that the Young Man has some public standing. The speaker says the youth need not with "public kindness honor me / Unless thou take that honor from thy name" (sonnet 36), while sonnet 96 may mean "all sorts of ranks of people" when it says the youth's graces and faults "are loved of more and less." This poem also urges him to "use the strength of all thy state!" which likely refers to the privileges of his status. (Sonnets 69 and 95 also imply a youth who spends time in the public eye.) The speaker sounds defensive in sonnet 124—"If my dear love were but the child of state"—and he would likely have no need to disdain "smiling pomp" and "policy" unless he were in danger of being thought an opportunist or sycophant, basking in the glow of the youth's good fortune. The poem's wit, in fact, is heightened by this presumption of social or political standing, for eventually the speaker boasts that his love "all alone stands hugely politic." He means "politic" not in the sense that his accusers would, as in a politically involved minion or favorite, but rather "politic" as prudent or wise, since daily fortunes will not sway his love.

With these clues in mind, it is not surprising that the two historical figures most consistently proposed as patterns for the Young Man have been two young noblemen active in Elizabethan and Jacobean England, the earl of Southampton and the earl of Pembroke. Arguments about their candidacies, and those of many others, will be found in the following essays on *The Sonnets'* critical reception, especially in the introduction to the nineteenth century.

The Dark Lady

The Dark Lady is the woman (presumably just one, but no one can say for sure) to whom Shakespeare's speaker turns after the sonnets to the Young Man. This new addressee surfaces in sonnet 127 and remains through the end of the sequence (again, presumably) or at least till sonnet 152 if the less personal, more derivative sonnets 153 and 154 are judged to be separate—either emblematic epilogues following the Dark Lady poems or an *envoi* that turns from the sonnets as a whole to *A Lover's Complaint*, the long concluding poem in the 1609 quarto edition of *The Sonnets*. Although Shakespeare provides no explicit clues, it is just possible that the Dark Lady enters the sequence in sonnets 40–42, which dramatize a crisis in the speaker's and Young Man's relationship because of the latter's affair with a woman. Is the Dark Lady the object of the "robbery" by the "gentle thief" that is the Young Man? This woman more aggressively "woos" in sonnet 41, and some editors have emended the pronoun in "he hath prevailed" to "she"—that is, the woman becomes the temptress of the Young Man's "straying youth," a role made explicit in line 13. Sonnet 42 resolves this triangle or, more precisely, dissolves it. The speaker admits he loved the woman "dearly" but also admits that he laments the Young Man's unfaithfulness far more. He accuses both of abusing him. In an ending more clever than satisfying, he declares his friend and he are one, and thus, despite the affair, still "she loves but me alone."

When the Dark Lady more formally appears or reappears, toward the end of the sequence, the speaker quickly supplies some of the physical details and characteristics lacking earlier. Having arrived at a kind of closure with "my lovely boy" in sonnet 126, the speaker turns in sonnet 127 to a meditation on the changing measures for beauty. Once things "fair" or light were considered beauty, "But now is black beauty's successive heir / And beauty slandered with a bastard shame." We next hear about his mistress having eyes that are "raven black," and subsequent sonnets speak of her "dun" breasts, the "black wires" of her hair, and her black beauty in general. Usually critics have taken these details as signs of the Dark Lady's dark complexion. Notice that in sonnet 127 the speaker does not admit that blackness is beautiful but only that the present age thinks it so and thus slanders true beauty. It is the first sign of a growing misogyny toward the mistress, and A. D. Cousins nicely points out that the speaker's relationship with the Young Man sometimes celebrates a continuity between past and present (see sonnet 106), but here the Dark Lady presides over a world in decline. The speaker may be decrying cosmetics, which prevented others from knowing if a woman were dark or fair, and he equates that duplicity with the false-seeming eyes of the mistress—"they mourners seem" (a comparison revisited in sonnet 132). Sonnets 128–30 display a breathless range of tone and expression in the span of three short sonnets. The first is a charming poem of physical desire, based on the popular Renaissance tableau of a woman playing the virginal, a piano-like instrument that in the context of the Dark Lady is likely meant with heavy irony. Sonnet 129, one of the most famous of the sequence, reacts to the bodily lightheartedness of the previous poem with a fierce revulsion against the irrational enslavement that is sexual appetite. The tormented speaker frames the woman's sexual attractions paradoxically, as a "heaven that leads men to this hell." This harsh language, and the bitter enchantment behind it, will appear increasingly in the remaining sonnets to the Dark Lady. Yet the Petrarchan parody of sonnet 130, "My mistress' eyes are nothing like the sun," restores some of the jauntiness that sonnet 129 had dashed. Many have taken the couplet, which sets off "my love" from "any she belied with false compare," but this final phrase reintroduces the themes of duplicity, misleading desire, and false representation (whether by cosmetics or by Petrarchan imagery in sonnets) that haunt the speaker in this subsequence.

In the next series of sonnets, the speaker further explores his ambivalent desire for the Dark Lady and reveals the extent of the division within himself. "Thy black is fairest in my judgement's place," he confesses in sonnet 131, but only after he clinically considers how others would not consider the Dark Lady's face worthy of making her the proud, cruel mistress of poetic convention. The speaker, however, feels otherwise, but even he, when alone and speaking to himself, is terribly aware of the "slander" that is his "doting" on this woman, *as if* she were the ideal mistress. Having sketched his own inconsistent and contradictory desire, the speaker introduces the "friend" in sonnet 133 and thus reintroduces a triangle of characters. He and the Young Man are fretfully alike—both, it seems, are romantically enraptured with the Dark Lady. The speaker, by seeing the effects of his desire in another, grows angrier with this harmful woman and her "steel bosom." Moreover, the speaker identifies closely in these sonnets with the Young Man, who is "my next self" and "that other mine" and so forth. The speaker seeks to be a sacrificial stand-in for his friend in 133 but has been manipulated in 134—he has indeed enthralled himself to the Dark Lady, but she has not set free the Young Man from his passion, or vice-versa for that matter: "Him have I lost, thou hast both him and me; / He pays the whole, and yet am I not free." The woman stands accused of double-crossing the male lovers, at both of their expenses. Sonnets 135–137 are some of the bawdiest in all of *The Sonnets*, and by employing so freely the slang meaning for "will" (signifying male or female genitalia, as well as carnal desire generally), the speaker places the Dark Lady and himself in a highly sexualized, brazenly analytical discourse. Apparently the woman can have any guy she wants, and thus "Will in overplus," which perhaps is no big surprise since we're told that her "will is large and spacious." Considering how promiscuous she is, why can't the speaker hide his will in hers, too? Sonnet 136 makes clear the ultimate foundation of the speaker's and Dark Lady's relationship and what is most desired. Neither heart nor soul of ideal lovers, but "Will will fulfil the treasure of thy love, / Ay, fill it full with wills," adds the speaker coarsely. Sonnet 137 continues this tone, speaking of the woman's sex as the "bay where all men ride," and yet the speaker admits this scene fascinates him, falsifies his eyes, and, through them, hooks his judgment. This frustrating sense of hypocrisy is further analyzed in sonnets 139–142, where the speaker justifies and denounces the Dark Lady's unkindness and broods on his eyes and heart. The plateau of his discontent, however, is found in sonnet 138, "When my love swears that she is made of truth." Its catalog of mutual lies, and mutual gratitude for these lies, has been described "as merry as it is vicious," but an altogether different feeling seems primary here—deep resignation at the couple's sexual delusion and their shared need for it.

Driven by an extended simile of mother and child, sonnet 143 implies a situation in which the Dark Lady is now interested in another, who is not so interested in her, all of which leaves the speaker, "thy babe," to chase the woman and beg her to turn back and receive him again. Sonnet 144 clearly reestablishes the triangle the speaker finds himself in with the Dark Lady and Young Man. With no ambiguity he shows his favor to his friend, the love of comfort that is the "better angel," while the woman, "a worser spirit" who is "coloured ill," is the love of despair, tempting the Young Man sexually and thus the speaker to hell. Believing that her "foul pride" will overcome the Young Man's "purity," the speaker ends the poem on a defeated note and one perhaps suggestive of venereal disease. Sonnet 146, a rather exceptional one in the sequence, is a rare example of Shakespeare writing in the vein of religious poetry. Here he wishes to move beyond the confines of the body and its desires and look toward the eternal peace of the soul, beyond Death. Yet this spiritual longing is fleeting. The next four sonnets brood further on the speaker's increasingly infuriating inconsistency and servitude. Sonnet 147 returns to the "irrational" theme of sonnet 129 with a renewed urgency, while the others turn on the "blind lover" motif familiar in sonnets. He accuses his "cunning love" of keeping him in tears, since it prevents his eyes from being "well seeing" and finding her "foul faults." Sonnet 149 is a painful poem, because it acknowledges both the Dark Lady's rejection of him and his nevertheless continuing love for her, however unhealthy and unmerited—"all my best doth worship thy defect," the speaker says. He issues a bitter invitation in his state of blindness: "love, hate on" when it comes to him, and love instead those who see well. Sonnet 150 intensely explores one terrible paradox: why the speaker is increasingly devoted to the woman "the more I hear and see just cause of hate?" It is as if the scale of affection has been completely inverted in the emotionally delusional speaker, who unfortunately retains a dreadful, clinical clarity as to his own ridiculous situation. Sonnet 151 returns to the body-soul concerns of sonnet 146, but in a listless, deflated way. Here the speaker admits his enslavement to his flesh—"I do betray / My nobler part to my gross body's treason"—but quickly the sonnet devolves into a series of erection jokes. The Dark Lady's very name makes the speaker "rise and fall," as if at least one body part were a servant or lieutenant to the sexual captain that is the woman. The last of the Dark Lady poems, sonnet 152, informs us that the Dark Lady is in fact an adulterer. By loving and then rejecting the speaker, she broke a "bed-vow," taken to mean her oath in marriage, and she has also broken her vow of love to the speaker by now "vowing new hate" to him. Yet the subsequence ends on a note of self-recrimination. He has broken twenty oaths to her two, for repeatedly he has perjured his eye (and his own person, his "I" in these tormented sonnets) because "I have sworn thee fair." The concluding image frames the speaker as a victim of blind Cupid, and so fittingly the final two, more impersonal sonnets of the entire sequence are emblematic poems about the "little Love-god."

For centuries scholars have attempted to identify the Dark Lady of Shakespeare's final sonnets with a historical counterpart. Early critics defensive of Shakespeare's honor (and fully assuming the "I" of *The Sonnets* was always he) were quick to associate the woman with the poet's wife, Anne Hathaway. Imagining the woman as a wife in this sequence—fraught with sexual enslavement, betrayal, and love-corrupting hate—hardly provides the social respectability so dear to these critics, and furthermore, the speaker's comment about the broken "bed-vow" makes it fairly clear that his relationship with the Dark Lady was extramarital. Other historical candidates put forward include Elizabeth Vernon, the bride of the earl of Southampton, often thought to be the historical Young Man; Elizabeth I's maid of honor Mary Fitton, who was a popular candidate in the late nineteenth century, until portraits of her surfaced and showed her to be quite light of complexion and lacking the "raven black" eyes of *The Sonnets'* mistress; Queen Elizabeth herself (!); Jane Davenant, whose son William (likely in a case of pathologically deep literary emulation) indeed hinted that he was the illegitimate son of Shakespeare; an African prostitute named Lucy Morgan; and Emilia Lanier, a writer herself and the mistress of the Lord Chamberlain, who sponsored Shakespeare's acting company. As one refreshingly honest and rarely humble critic puts it, "There have been many guesses, but nobody really knows who she was."

Although too old to be even a remote candidate, Penelope Rich has also been mentioned—the inspiration behind Philip Sidney's 1580s sonnet sequence

Astrophil and Stella, an influential source for Shakespeare. Rich raises another important point: literary convention also influenced Shakespeare's choice of characteristics for his mistress. For example, Sidney describes Stella in the seventh sonnet of his sequence in strikingly similar terms:

> When Nature made her chief work, Stella's eyes,
> In colour black, why wrapped she beams so bright?
> . . .
> That whereas black seems Beauty's contrary,
> She even in black doth make all beauties flow?

The presence of this literary tradition should give pause to all historical detectives bent on identifying the characters in *The Sonnets*. Interest in the Dark Lady's presence in Shakespeare's poetry and her various realities—historical, cultural, or lyrical—have often shifted in step with changes of approach in literary criticism. Thus efforts to identify her historical source have waned, while critics interested in more recent New Historicist topics seek different kinds of evidence in the representation of *The Sonnets'* mistress. What did Shakespeare and his early readers envision when imagining the Dark Lady's blackness? Was she African, Mediterranean? Non-English in a general sense, or fully English and simply with dark complexion? What moral qualities did this darkness presuppose? Studies of race and climate theories during the Renaissance have indirectly shown to scholars of *The Sonnets* that Shakespeare's mere choice of color to identify his mistress introduced into his sequence rather complex issues about culture, nationhood, and the other. Recent scholars such as Marvin Hunt and Ilona Bell have shifted their assessment of the Dark Lady into a more consciously literary, theoretical mode, worrying less about questions of history and race and instead considering her role, in Hunt's words, "as a literary sign to which color values have inevitably been attached."

The Rival Poet
The Rival Poet is the least significant of the four personas in *The Sonnets*, yet his brief appearance, from sonnets 78–86, precipitates a series of crises in the speaker's self-confidence—as a poet, as a writer who enjoys the "fair assistance" of a patron's support, and, more personally, as the exclusive favorite of the Young Man and participant with him in a complex relationship dramatized throughout the first 126 sonnets. In this last respect, especially, the Rival Poet plays an important role in filling out another "triangulation" that repeatedly marks Shakespeare's sequence and mars the speaker's peace of mind. Already in the sequence we have heard insinuations of the Young Man's poor behavior and have seen a drama of infidelity as well, perhaps between the Young Man and the Dark Lady, in sonnets 40–42. The "alien pen" of the Rival Poet will

likewise alienate the speaker from the Young Man's affection, thus creating a second, all-male triangle. That said, sonnet 76 indicates a self-doubt in the speaker that the rival's subsequent appearance only heightens. "Why is my verse so barren of new pride," the opening line asks, why is it out of fashion and a stranger to "New-found methods and to compounds strange"? Yet the second half of the sonnet offers a resolution: "You and love are still my argument," the speaker tells the Young Man. He puts a new dressing on old words that reflect the consistency of their relationship. Does this explain the speaker's old-fashioned style, which he seems to be defending here in a roundabout way?

Sonnet 78, traditionally the first of the "Rival Poet" group, still does not reflect a direct competition between poets old and new, but it does acknowledge that the Young Man has inspired and received verses not just from the speaker but from "every alien pen." Notice how, at this point, the speaker defensively introduces a field of poets, figured here as invaders who are vying to take over the speaker's accustomed "use," meaning his poetic activity, or possibly reward, with respect to the young patron. When the sonnet makes a turn, in the third quatrain, the speaker singles himself out as the superior, more loyal poet. He appeals to the Young Man to be "most proud" of him. The Young Man's virtues inspire all of the poets. Yet he augments other poets' verses in merely superficial, stylistic ways, whereas "thou art all my art," the speaker professes. Sonnets 79 and 80 intensify the tensions introduced in the previous poems. Some critics have interpreted the repetition of "alone" in sonnet 79's first two lines as the speaker's emphasis on his being left alone. However, the primary meaning here is his anger at having once been exclusively the Young Man's poet and now having competition, including one particular poet who makes the speaker feel inferior. This Rival Poet is called a "worthier pen" a few lines later and in sonnet 80 becomes "a better spirit." Sonnet 79 is mainly accusatory, implying that the Rival Poet is a fake and even a thief, "robbing" the Young Man's appearance and behavior to offer it up again, as if it were the rival's own gift. This may be a sensitive charge, because any aristocrat would be concerned about servants possibly acting dishonestly in his household. The speaker's inferiority complex grows in sonnet 80, as does his reliance on the Young Man's approval of and preference for him and his poetry. Taken equally, the speaker concedes that the Rival Poet's praise threatens to leave him "tongue-tied," and he judges himself "inferior far" compared with his competitor. Yet if the Young Man wills it, he can make, by his mere favor, the humble seem "as the proudest sail."

If the speaker's criticism of the Rival Poet gives way to an appeal to the Young Man in sonnets 79 and 80, then the colder tone of sonnet 82 may make this second approach less feasible. As with sonnet 116 (which also centers on the idea of marriage), there is a strong impression that the speaker is here responding to a prior criticism by the Young Man. Likely the patron has objected to the speaker's anger or hurt feelings, saying he was not "married," or exclusively united with, the speaker's muse. Indirectly we hear additional information about the Rival Poet: So great is the Young Man's worth, he must "seek anew / Some fresher stamp of the time-bettering days." The rest of the sonnet's lines render the phrase "time-bettering" ironic, yet the fact remains that the patron finds in the rival's poetry something fresher and more fashionable than that of the aging speaker. The older poet finds the rival's attractions dubious, full of "strainéd touches" and "gross painting," and no match for his own "true plain words." Sonnet 83 isolates the triangle still further by mentioning to the Young Man "both your poets."

Sonnets 85 and 86 bring the Rival Poet sequence to a climactic, if dispiriting, close for the speaker. We first hear of his poetic decline. His "tongue-tied Muse" leads him to play a silent, passive role in the face of the "good words" of "that able spirit." The rival has come into his own, with "polished form of well-refinéd pen." Although sonnet 86 features two long questions, a tone of finality leads one to believe that the questions are rhetorical and embittered. Critics have found the opening line—"Was it the proud full sail of his great verse"—to be a clue to the Rival Poet's own style, an apparently high style "above a mortal pitch." John Blades has memorably summarized the opening lines' plosive "b" and "p" sounds as creating a "daringly dramatic beefiness."

In 1874 William Minto first suggested George Chapman as the likeliest candidate for the Rival Poet, and Chapman remains the most valid choice today. (Nearly every writer contemporary with Shakespeare has been put forward, including Christopher Marlowe, Ben Jonson, Samuel Daniel, and Edmund Spenser.) As a translator who rendered Homer's epic poems in long, "fourteener" English lines, he best fits with the speaker's disdainful, defeated appraisal, and Chapman's work *Shadow of Night* may be alluded to in this sonnet's later lines. The drama finally alights on the Young Man, however. It is his "countenance"— the inspiration of his appearance, but most importantly his approval—that has made the Rival Poet's sails "full" and in turn has ensured that the speaker lacked "matter," meaning poetic content, but also a personal deprivation, felt most profoundly. The speaker's painful honesty in these sonnets, about his art and professional standing, his friendship and his love, are significant reasons why so many readers through the centuries have instinctively found *The Sonnets* to be a record of Shakespeare the man.

THREE KEY POEMS FROM *THE SONNETS*

❧

Sonnet 3

Look in thy glass and tell the face thou viewest,
Now is the time that face should form another,
Whose fresh repair if now thou not renewest,
Thou dost beguile the world, unbless some mother.
For where is she so fair whose uneared womb
Disdains the tillage of thy husbandry?
Or who is he so fond will be the tomb
Of his self-love to stop posterity?
Thou art thy mother's glass, and she in thee
Calls back the lovely April of her prime;
So thou through windows of thine age shalt see,
Despite of wrinkles, this thy golden time.
    But if thou live rememb'red not to be,
      Die single, and thine image dies with thee.

Following sonnet 2's hypothesizing and predicting strategy of persuasion ("If thou couldst answer" . . . This were to be new made . . ."), the third sonnet returns to the more direct mood of command, which can be heard in the opening poem (as in its concluding order, "Pity the world" . . .). "Look in thy glass," the speaker says, about to make a more inventive appeal. By imploring the Young Man to look at himself in a mirror, or "glass," the speaker hopes to make him feel beside himself, so to speak—that is, to make him realize how others feel when they see the Young Man's beauty. If he becomes, even to himself and even if momentarily, merely "the face thou viewest," then perhaps he will understand that "Now is the time that face should form another." Colin Burrow points out in his edition of *The Sonnets* that in the most authoritative 1609 text, the first line of this sonnet ends with "an other," which to Burrow further extends the sense that the Young Man is meant to encounter "someone completely new." Seeing himself as if from the outside, maybe he will see how his beauty is fragile and transient. If he does not reproduce and create an heir, which is to say a younger version of himself, he will "beguile the world," which in the Young Man's suddenly bifurcated context (he is both himself but also the separate "face" he sees in the mirror) more easily includes the Young Man himself. Most pronounced is the speaker's concern for the Young Man's individual welfare, which puts this poem in line with the first 17 in this sequence, traditionally known as the Procreation sonnets. Yet this tactic may also represent an attempt by the speaker to make the Young Man not only more concerned for himself but also less reliant on and defined by those traits that *The Sonnets* will sometimes accuse the Young Man of having—namely, thoughtlessness and heartlessness, if not outright cruelty.

The repetition of "now" in lines 2 and 3 adds an urgency to the speaker's appeal and perhaps a subtly ominous undertone as well—as if to say, your features right now enjoy "fresh repair," but now you must concern yourself with renewing them in your offspring, because already you must confront the fact that your freshness, or young beauty, will soon fade. If the Young Man refuses to have children, he will trick or cheat ("beguile") the world and, more personally, will "unbless" (a coinage by Shakespeare) the otherwise fortunate mother who will bear his child. The second quatrain (lines 5–8) picks up this focus on the Young Man's hypothetical mate on a note of argument. Heading off the Young Man's imagined retort or general resistance—"No woman really cares if I have children or not"—the speaker insists that *any* woman would feel this loss just as much as the speaker does, and more so—for obvious physical reasons. No woman, the speaker insists, would turn down a chance to conceive a child with the Young Man. This attention to fertilization explains the agricultural images and metaphors in these lines. Here the speaker equates the woman's "uneared" womb to a cornfield not yet sown and thus lacking ears of corn. An infertile place would welcome the Young Man's "tillage" or ploughing, a metaphor common in Shakespeare's era for the male's insemination of the female. "Husbandry" means farming, thus continuing the metaphor, but of course it also implies that the Young Man should become a good husband as well, one who fulfills his wife by giving her children. The structure of this second quatrain works by contrast, for lines seven and eight point out, rather accusingly, the alternative to this marital fruitfulness. If no woman would reject the Young Man's sexual activity, then surely no man, such as he, would be so dumb as to forgo children or "stop posterity": To do so would be a choice for narcissistic "self-love" and will have deathly consequences; the Young Man's body will become his own tomb, a morbid image Shakespeare also employs in his poem *Venus and Adonis*.

In the third quatrain (lines 9–12), the speaker recasts his argument again, now treating the physical mirror invoked in the opening lines in figurative, and human, terms. You, the speaker says to the Young Man, are in fact a kind of mirror, too, for your mother. Your youthful beauty "calls back" (a verb that nicely captures both the immediate sense of reflection and also an employment of memory) to your mother her spring-like youth, the "lovely April of her prime." Having introduced this old-young dichotomy through the object of the mirror, the speaker ends this section by moving the Young Man hypothetically to his older mother's position: You, too, will one day be old, with wrinkles and diminished eyesight ("windows of thy age," once again continuing the image of glass and mirrors), but if you have children now, then like your mother with you, you will be able to see in your young, beautiful child your own "golden time," a reference to the happy beautiful Golden Age of classical mythology. An implicit threat exists here—you *will* become old—even as the speaker imagines the good outcome of the Young Man taking his advice. The concluding couplet, which contemplates the possibility that the Young Man will reject his advice to marry and conceive, becomes more abrasive in its warning: Go ahead, the speaker seems to say, whether solemnly or mockingly, if you live as if you don't care to be remembered, then stay single. The Young Man would then "die single," of course, but the phrase also carries a sense of "completely" or "wholly" or "ultimately"; you will literally die, but in dying, the memory of you will utterly die, too, since there will be no "image" or derivation or trace to remind people of your mere existence, much less your youthful beauty.

The mirror image, so central to this sonnet, does various work for Shakespeare. In his time the mirror had connotations both of warning, which allows the speaker to reprimand the Young Man, and of ideal appearance, which permits the obvious admiration for him. Some critics have also connected the action of this poem with a passage in St. Paul's second letter to the Corinthians: "For now we see through a glass darkly, but then face to face." Such a connection allegorically converts the speaker's efforts into a drama about self-knowledge, though whereas the apostle anticipates a future clarity that is consoling and beatific, Shakespeare's speaker is more admonishing—if the Young Man continues to see his situation "darkly" or cluelessly, he will soon lose his own fresh face and will have no reflective, consolatory face, in the person of his child, to appreciate.

Sonnet 64

When I have seen by Time's fell hand defaced
The rich proud cost of outworn buried age;
When sometime lofty towers I see down rased,
And brass eternal slave to mortal rage;
When I have seen the hungry ocean gain
Advantage on the kingdom of the shore,
And the firm soil win of the wat'ry main,
Increasing store with loss, and loss with store;

When I have seen such interchange of state,
Or state itself confounded to decay,
Ruin hath taught me thus to ruminate:
That Time will come and take my love away.
    This thought is as death, which cannot choose
    But weep to have that which it fears to lose.

Sonnet 64 is one of the most memorable expressions—and perhaps the climactic one in its sub-narrative—of an emotional crisis often repeated throughout Shakespeare's sequence: a lover's anxiety in confronting *The Sonnets'* ultimately most formidable enemy. That foe is not a capricious Young Man or an unfaithful Dark Lady but Time itself. Time the Devourer, evoked specifically here in the image of the "hungry ocean" (line 5), will eventually consume all things, even young, beautiful, and beloved things. Shakespeare sounds this ominous note early in *The Sonnets*. The metronomic, monosyllabic opening of sonnet 12 ("When I do count the clock that tells the time") serves as a rhythmic stage direction for the entrance of Time as a personified threat against the Young Man. The speaker fears that "thou among the wastes of time must go"—and you're already going there; even as younger things are flourishing quickly, you are dying as fast. The couplet of this poem brings home this grim theme: Nothing can defend itself against Time's scythe, which turns the abstract enemy into a Grim Reaper figure, cutting down all living things. All the Young Man can do is "breed," which becomes a kind of resistance against Time, though still "he takes thee hence." The remarkable sonnet 15 resumes this temporal drama: There the enemy has multiplied, as Time and Decay debate or perhaps conspire as to when the Young Man's life will be extinguished. Yet a new remedy presents itself—the speaker, who is "All in war with time for love of you" and will try to reclaim, through his writing, any diminishment Time causes the friend. In the next sonnet, Time is a "bloody tyrant," and again the poet recommends more than his writing the Young Man's "own sweet skill"—that is, his ability to "draw" himself in the form of his offspring. Sonnet 17 restores a confidence in the poet's rhyme, which he can imagine being read "in time to come," but why stop there? The youth should live twice, through his child and through "my rhyme." "Devouring Time" reemerges in sonnet 19, where the speaker begs, "blunt thou the lion's paw."

After sounding this initial note of conflict, which presumably ends in a standoff, the sequence of the 1609 quarto now turns to other themes and dramas. However, the war with Time returns again in the triumphant sonnet 55. Here the poet's "pow'rful rhyme" will outlast marble and monuments, and these ironically vanquished objects (both marble and monuments, after all, are meant to last into perpetuity!), as well as the poem's opening with these images, signals more explicitly than before Shakespeare's engagement with his classical sources. The Roman poet Horace famously said in his *Odes*, "I have finished a monument more lasting than bronze," by which he meant that his little lyric poem, being recopied through the ages and continuously cherished by readers, will still exist when the sturdy temples and arches of Rome are long fallen. In other words, poetry can make its subject immortal in a way no material commemoration can. This poem is so amazing because, in the short space of its 14 lines, it literally shifts from one grand age to another—it begins on a classical, pagan note but concludes with an eye firmly on the Last Judgment (or "ending doom" in the poem) of the Christian revelation. Mischievously appropriating the Resurrection itself for the sake of his wooing, the speaker says his friend will live in his poetry and in lovers' eyes but only for so long ("till the Judgment"). Because Christians trust in the promise that the body will rise on the last day, the speaker more or less tells the youth that once he rises again, the speaker and he won't have to worry anymore about these less satisfactory mementos. Sonnet 60 opens with an image soon to reappear in sonnet 64—"Like as the waves make toward the pebbled shore"—the incessant crashing of waves that erode the shoreline, even as our minutes pass one by one and erode our remaining life. The next poem expresses a fear for the Young Man's fate at the hands of "injurious Time." Preparing for that devastating moment, the poet seeks to fight against "confounding" age by preserving the youth "in these black lines"—that is, in the poetry lines of this very sonnet. The poet vows to enact the same miracle two sonnets later in the paradox that his love will still shine bright, despite doing so through the "black ink" of the speaker's verse.

Curiously, when John Benson cobbled together the poems included in his 1640 edition of Shakespeare's poems, he combined sonnets 60, 63, 64, 65, and 66 into one long poem titled "Injurious Time." Sonnet 64's central place in this new lyric may be the arbitrary result of a pirateprinter. Nevertheless, it is arguably the most passionate statement among these intense poems against Time and Decay. (Shakespeare revisits this theme of verse and immortality in a later series, in four poems from sonnets 100–107.) Sonnet 64 opens with what the next sonnet calls a "fearful meditation" on the beholding of ruined things once costly or ostentatious—"When I have seen by Time's fell hand defaced." "Fell" means "savage" or "deadly," and Hallett Smith emphasizes the "pounding monosyllables" of the opening line, providing a violent, rhythmic effect. The second line is a gem of Shakespearean compression and implication. Some critics have inferred from the line an ornamental funeral monument (perhaps at London's Westminster Abbey or St. Paul's Cathedral, as Colin Burrow suggests) whose commemoration Time has caused to dilapidate. It has literally been "defaced" or rubbed down, "buried" in dust perhaps, or more figuratively buried by a multitude of exhausted minutes or days. Katherine Duncan-Jones instead takes the line to refer to sumptuous clothing, which tended to be expensive in Elizabethan times, creating from "outworn" the more familiar sense of fabric being worn out and threadbare. The rest of this first quatrain repeats the lesson of ruin but elevates its examples to grander objects. The "lofty towers" in line 3, where "sometime" means "once," are now "down rased," or "razed." The two words together, where one would do, perhaps means to add an intensity of meaning: not just a falling down, but a crashing down spectacularly. Some historically minded critics have seen in this image of fallen towers a reference to the England of Shakespeare's own day. The Dissolution, or destruction of abbeys and monasteries during the reign of Henry VIII, left a lasting, ruinous mark on the post-Reformation English landscape.

The next illustration multiplies its effects thanks to Shakespeare's careful use of syntax. We should likely hear a pause after the phrase "brass eternal" and assume in the phrase a reversal of the typical adjective-noun ordering in English. This syntactical switch mimics a typical Latin construction and so in a timely way (so to speak) brings to mind Horace's aforementioned assertion that his verse is more lasting ("perennius" as in "more perennial") than bronze. Here, in Shakespeare's sonnet, "brass eternal" is not so fortunate or durable but has become a slave to "mortal rage," meaning deadly rage or human destruction or even rage that, in the utter dominance of Time, will also come to an end. Heard another way, brass may be instead an "eternal slave" to rage, that is, once it falls, it is fallen forever, never to be restored. Note, too, how "eternal" and "mortal" bouncing off each other in the same line creates an interesting paradoxical tension. Some critics have seen in this line another image of church monuments, this time commemorative brasses placed in the floors of churches, which would eventually be rubbed down and their messages obliterated by the countless passing of parishioners' feet.

The next quatrain's opening—"When I have seen the hungry ocean gain / Advantage of the kingdom of the shore"—signals to readers perceptive of structure that the greater part of Shakespeare's poem is going to consist of one long periodic sentence. Through variation of example, it recites a list of occasions that make the speaker brood on the central fear of these "Time as Devourer" sonnets, a revelation we will arrive at presently. For right now, notice how Shakespeare places these opening dependent clauses, "When . . . when . . . when . . . when . . . ," across the sonnet form—two in the first quatrain (lines 1, 3), another to begin the second quatrain (5), and another beginning the third and final quatrain (9), the second half of which is dedicated to a confrontation with the speaker's main fear. The couplet, then, comments on "this thought" that has just occurred. The second quatrain develops the emblem for Time's injuries, used elsewhere, of the constant waves eroding a shoreline. Specifically, Shakespeare employs military language ("gain / Advantage"), as if one general were attempting to conquer territory from his foe. The poet may be thinking of another classical source for this image—Ovid's *Metamorphoses* 15. In fact, the following quatrain will echo a contemporary translation of the passage "Even so have places oftentimes / exchangéd their estate, / For I have seen it sea which was / substantial ground alate" in the rendering of Arthur Golding. The "hungry" ocean in the present quatrain invokes another Ovidian figure: "Tempus edax," or Time the Devourer. The quatrain's final line captures with the rhetorical figure of *chiasmus* the give-and-take futility of the battle between sea and shoreline. That movement is captured with "Increasing store with loss, and loss with store," where the ordering moves one way and then, reversed, recedes to turn territory gained ("store") into lost territory. The overall effect is one of cyclical change, beyond human control, and a dizzying sense of transience as well. Shakespeare in his plays also connects Time's power with the limitations of human political stability. In *2 Henry IV*, for example, Hastings says to a group of conspirators, "We are time's subjects, and time bids be gone." Time, as we have heard in a similar sonnet, is a bloody tyrant who oppresses his always moving subjects. G. Wilson Knight and Giorgio Melchiori have pointed to this seesaw passage in sonnet 64 as a central example of the pattern of reversal, or paradox of loss and gain, that for them is the primary pattern of *The Sonnets* as a whole. Others have observed that at this point in the poem, Time's destruction moves from culture to nature: Time will devour the land itself, as well as and as easily as perishable, man-made things like church monuments or towers, however formidable they appear at first. Edmund Spenser may be a source for both sets of images. His sonnet sequence on classical decay, *The Ruines of Rome*, looks ahead to Shakespeare's first examples, while his famous love poem from the *Amoretti*, "One day I wrote her name upon the strand," shares sonnet 64's shoreline setting. However, the poems could not go in more different directions. Spenser's sonnet ends on a note of hope: "Where whenas death shall all the world subdue, / our love shall live, and later life renew." Shakespeare, on the other hand, pushes his observing speaker toward a point of crisis.

The third quatrain speaks more broadly and summarily on "interchange of state," both picking up on the military and political insinuations of the previous quatrain and more fundamentally on the state of being itself ("state itself confounded to decay"): Everything moves from a living, existing state to a state of ruin, death, or nonexistence. Lines 11 and 12 are at the heart of the poem's drama: "Ruin hath taught me thus to ruminate: / That Time will come and take my love away." The ruins witnessed seem to have trespassed upon the very mind of the speaker, a point supported by wordplay (ru-m-inate = ru-in-mate) that early modern typography made even more apparent. To clarify, the speaker has brooded at such length and so intensely on ruins that the word "ruin" has invaded his mental cogitation as "rumination." And this trespass leads the speaker to a fact that, to him, feels shocking and obscene: His young beloved will be kidnapped, as it were, by Time. Since all face death, this abduction is inevitable.

Sonnet 64's couplet is certainly not a frivolous, emotionally detached add-on that mars some of the sonnets, but it does feel anticlimactic after the terribly spare realization that ended the last quatrain. More generously, we might see it, along with George Rylands, as a "dying fall" with which some of these sonnets end. Still, there is something distracting and baroque in these last two lines, which might be paraphrased thus: This thought about all things being ruined can only weep even in the relative bliss of having the Young Man's love, for even as it possesses that love, it must fear its eventual loss. Or maybe the meaning is more ironic: This thought makes the speaker fully aware of the loss and sadness that are inevitable, but nevertheless, it weeps in its desire to have the Young Man, however fragile he is, however transient their love must necessarily be. Whichever the case, the thought—the sonnet's mortal realization—precipitates a kind of death in the speaker, and just maybe this becomes a consolation for the lovers, however grim: They stand together in the face of death—the speaker's present but fortunately figurative (the thought is "as a death"), and the Young Man's quite literal but at least in the future, ominously awaiting him.

Sonnet 116

Let me not to the marriage of true minds
Admit impediments; love is not love
Which alters when it alteration finds,
Or bends with the remover to remove.
O no, it is an ever-fixéd mark
That looks on tempests and is never shaken;
It is the star to every wand'ring bark,
Whose worth's unknown, although his heighth be taken.
Love's not Time's fool, though rosy lips and cheeks
Within his bending sickle's compass come;
Love alters not with his brief hours and weeks,
But bears it out even to the edge of doom.
    If this be error and upon me proved,
    I never writ, nor no man ever loved.

This sonnet merits our attention because its popular reception illustrates nicely how poetic complexities and perplexities remain to be discovered in *The Sonnets*, even within those sonnets that seem best known, constantly quoted, and most overexposed. A greeting-card and wedding-vow favorite, sonnet 116's modern selectors would probably choose not to know the dramatically emotional confrontation that seems to be enacted, and in fact overheard, in this sonnet. Better to stick with the traditional, safer, more celebratory, and more certain reading of the poem, in which the speaker gives a stump-speech, to himself apparently, in order to encourage himself and take comfort in a series of definitions that make love sound faithful, persistent, and, well, cool. This overview does not completely miss the mark of some of the poem's memorable virtues, but it is harmfully simplistic as well, insensitive to the sonnet's lyrical and dramatic dimensions and unable to answer questions that arise if the poem is, indeed, a kind of cheerleading performance of one.

To overcome this "sonnet 116 as pop music" impasse, fortunately we can turn to a few recent editors whose annotations might enable us to approach this outworn poem afresh. For example, Katherine Duncan-Jones and Colin Burrow both highlight the liturgical coordination in the first two lines. Already "admit impediments" is poetically heated, a burst of polysyllables and dental consonants amid two lines of relative monosyllables—"Let me not to the" "of true minds," "love is not love" and so on. These editors draw upon the use of "impediments" in the *Book of Common Prayer*'s "Solemnization of Matrimony" service at that familiar place where the priest asks the assembled if anyone has any reason why the bride and groom should not be married. So, as it turns out, there is a marriage context to this poem, but for dramatic and possibly ironic reasons, considering the context of the speaker and the Young Man at this point in the sonnet sequence. Also with this ongoing, complex relationship in mind, Burrow goes further and suggests that we do not really know *which* two minds the poem has in mind, whether the speaker and youth, or the youth and another, in which case the speaker's opening statement assumes a pitying note or, as Burrow puts it, is "excessive in its self-abnegation." This theory of a triangle, which is more explicit in other sonnets, invites an unusual reading here, but I wish to rely on the openness that Burrow shows, as he thinks of the sonnet as expressing a part of a larger, conflicted relationship. Before continuing, let me offer a few additional points: The marriage meant here is qualified as one "of two minds," which is in keeping with the tendency to idealize that we've seen in the sonnets to the Young Man. Perhaps the hurt speaker is raising the stakes on the unpredictable or lukewarm beloved—what is between us *matters,* he might be saying with this introduction of matrimonial language, and to turn your back on this love will be a kind of profanation, not simply a matter of inevitable change, as you argue. This reading presumes two things: a dramatic confrontation that this poem "overhears," so to speak, and a more traditional view that the poem is a drama between our recognizable speaker and youth.

That said, we can do no better than turn to the sensitive rereading of the poem by Helen Vendler, to whom the present study will be frequently indebted. Instead of a definition of true love, sonnet 116 for Vendler becomes a "dramatic refutation or rebuttal," one reliant on "the fiction of an anterior utterance by another." She shrewdly points to all of the negative words—"nor," "no," "never," "not"—to move beyond the common identification of the sonnet as an affirming, definition poem. Conversely, the speaker seems to be arguing against an excuse already put forward ("pre-poem," as it were) by the addressee. That excuse might sound like this: "Constancy between us would be lovely, but it is unrealistic. Obstacles or impediments will affect our shared commitment. When circumstances change, a person changes. When aspects of a relationship vanish, or when qualities in a lover diminish, then affection in the beloved is lost, too. I loved you once, but you've changed [grown older?], and so I've changed too." To this hypothetical comment, Vendler envisions the speaker of sonnet 116 raising a haughty objection. Objected by the youth's smearing of the "laws of true reciprocity" expressed elsewhere in *The Sonnets,* the speaker takes the high road against the Young Man's vague excuse. Vendler emphasizes the opening iambic foot, which accentuates the second word—"Let ME not . . . admit impediments" (i.e., even though you are quite easily willing to do so). Our "love" (as you call it) is certainly not love if it does these stupid, vague things you attribute to it. Here Vendler hears quotation marks around the following admittedly arch phrases, "alters when it alteration finds" and "bends with the remover to remove." These emotionally impermeable observations bring with them the air of the divorce attorney, as if the Young Man is hiding behind legal explanations or at least material concessions. The speaker will have none of it—"Oh no," he snaps, in a state of firm denial, as the second quatrain begins.

The speaker now matches the youth's evasive abstractions with his own emblem, one that invokes a common image for love and its trials—the lover as a ship wandering the rough seas. Therefore love, to the speaker, is an "ever-fixéd mark" that looks on "tempests" even (so much stronger than the bland "alterations") and still is not shaken, neither altered nor removed. "Ever-fixéd" also announces a stability and constancy missing in the Young Man's earlier comment about "alteration," although the speaker does make a concession of sorts when he describes a "wand'ring" bark, or ship. The adjective introduces a hint of drifting or errancy, but within a framework that will contain this negative wandering. Some readers have taken the "mark" to be a lighthouse, since in *Othello* and *Coriolanus* both feature the phrase "sea-mark" to describe that object. Vendler, however, chooses to see it as the North Star, by which sailors navigate, and so "It is the star" is simply a reiteration of an object already implied at the quatrain's beginning. Line 8 sounds like a direct refutation of the Young Man's own effort to treat their relationship clinically, with its logical space drained of all emotion and its piston-like causality of action and reaction. Here, love is ultimately beyond such assessments—"whose worth's unknown": The youth is presumptuous in his quick prognosis, and there may also be an accusation that he has not really experienced the love that the speaker feels for him, i.e., "No wonder you are saying these things; you've never been into this relationship (its worth is unknown or unexperienced by you) as much as I have been, even though you think you know all the answers." The youth may have his superficial judgments (he has "taken the height" or, in our own idiom, taken the temperature, of their relationship), but he has no idea of the speaker's true feelings, fueled by dedication and equity.

The third quatrain enacts a repetition of argument, as if to suggest the speaker's fierceness—his energetic effort to puncture the bogus logic of the now-distant beloved. "Let me make myself clear," the speaker more or less says at this point. "Love's not Time's fool," he declares, insinuating that the youth's formulation makes love exactly that and nothing more. Yet what follows next is a powerful concession and complicates a poem that up to this point has been built on contrasts—the "alteration" of the first lines versus the steadfastness of the "ever-fixéd mark." Now the speaker modulates his argument. Love may not be Time's fool, but he must admit that Love's "rosy lips and cheeks" are vulnerable to Time's "bending sickle's compass," or swinging arc. The image here is of the Grim Reaper holding his deathly scythe or harvesting blade. Love's outer features will fade, will fall before Time. In a great occasion of compression, Time's literally "bending" sickle (traditionally in a crescent shape) will also be the cause of bending, when its victims are cut down. Notice, too, how the speaker repeats in lines 10 and 11 the key words of the youth's excuse: Yes, those outer features will come within the "bending" sickle, and yet Love is nevertheless not slavishly beholden to Time. Likewise, the "brief hours and weeks" may alter, but Love does not alter as a consequence. Time is minimized here, allowed to alter "brief hours and weeks" but not months, years, ages. Time has no control over true love. Love and its endurance, on the other hand, are associated with the culmination of Time in the Christian outlook—with Doomsday, or the Day of Judgment ("edge of doom"). Love that "bears it out" would have held biblical connotations for Shakespeare's earliest readers. A popular Elizabethan translation of St. Paul's first letter to the Corinthians, the *Geneva Bible*, features the line "Love bears all things," and the liturgical and now eschatological (or world-ending) context ends the third quatrain with a much fuller sense of the speaker's countering definition of love. Other critics, resisting the great expansiveness of this twelfth line, see "doom" as more personally meaning the death of one of the lovers, as in "till death do us part." Doom becomes a "little apocalypse," so to speak, but whichever reading is preferred, the speaker's version is still an exalted one, which intends to show how shallow and ignoble is the youth's version of love.

The defiance of the couplet—"If this be error and upon me proved, / I never writ, nor no man ever loved"—welcomes further this sense of confrontation between the speaker and Young Man. Vendler finds in these last two lines both a further refutation, and also a condemnation. Invoking language of legal contracts and even chivalric challenges, the speaker sounds sure that his version of Love is far more correct. If I am wrong and you can prove it, he says, I never wrote. This in effect makes his argument airtight because obviously he *has* written—we are reading the very thing he has written. Perhaps the speaker is confident that he is right because his version has developed and been modified in the course of the sonnet; it began as an extreme, untouched Platonic emblem—the North Star—and has become something both fragile and powerful. Parts of love will be cut down by time, but if it endures, it will last till the end of time. *If* it endures. The last phrase becomes incredibly poignant in that condition. If "no man" refers to the speaker, then it can be as confidently seen as counter-factual as "I never writ," for of course the speaker has loved and does love. But if the Young Man, after this debate, still thinks the speaker's counter-argument is "in error" (and if the youth does not believe or listen to the speaker, then he has "proved" the speaker's words wrong to his own satisfaction), then the hard realization that awaits the speaker is that "no man ever loved" (me), i.e., the Young Man was not a true lover and, as his formulations threateningly suggest, he was not capable, or willing, to share my high-minded view of love. Such a reading shows how a poem can come to life if it is treated on its own lyric and dramatic terms—not read as an essay governed by a topic sentence, but, in Vendler's words, as a "situationally motivated speech-act," one that initiates further blame and infidelity in the sonnets ahead.

CRITICISM
THROUGH THE AGES
❧

THE SONNETS IN THE SIXTEENTH AND SEVENTEENTH CENTURIES

The earliest printed notice about William Shakespeare and his sonnets appeared just before the seventeenth century and very likely was contemporary with the writing of at least some of the 154 lyric poems in the long, diverse sequence that would soon come to be known as *The Sonnets*. Francis Meres, in his book of literary commonplaces, *Palladis Tamia*, or *Wit's Treasury*, takes great and seemingly exhaustive pleasure in appraising contemporary English authors. He argues proudly that his countrymen accomplish, in the English language and in a variety of genres, the same literary feats as their predecessors in ancient Greece and Rome. Meres's method of cataloging by these ancient/modern pairings marks the book as a product of the English Renaissance. For many of its genres and its sense of literary taste, this period of English literature looked back to classical authors and their aesthetic accomplishments. There is also a patriotic appeal to be heard in Meres, who feels certain late Elizabethan England was experiencing a literary Golden Age, the likes of which had not been seen since the days of Pericles's Athens or Augustus's Rome. Meres's appraisal of Shakespeare, both as a poet and a playwright, is short but justly famous. Bringing up a story about metempsychosis (or the transferral of the soul) related to the ancient philosopher Pythagoras, Meres declares that in similar fashion, the "sweet witty soul" of the Roman love poet Ovid now lives on in "mellifluous and honey-tongued" Shakespeare. Meres offers as proof two of Shakespeare's narrative poems, *Venus and Adonis* and *The Rape of Lucrece*, but also mentions "his sugared *Sonnets* among his private friends." He continues to praise Shakespeare as a writer of both tragedies and comedies, and Meres's subsequent lists of Shakespeare's plays have been a gift to theater scholars for centuries.

The mentioning of Shakespeare's other two poems may seem surprising at first, but for Meres's time, it made perfect sense: These were the two most popular, most frequently reprinted works by Shakespeare during his lifetime. Copies of these narrative poems sold more briskly than any of the plays, and Shakespeare himself, most unusually, included a flattering author's dedication in front of each text. The dedications were addressed to Henry Wriothesley, earl of Southampton, who is also one of the top candidates for the "Young Man" addressed in many of Shakespeare's sonnets. More important, Shakespeare's dedications bespeak a willingness to have these poems publicized and associated with the author—exactly the sort of association that is frustratingly absent when we turn to *The Sonnets*. Meres may in fact hint at Shakespeare's very different intentions with sonnets when he specifies that they are circulating not in print, but "among his *private* friends" (emphasis mine), which is to say, being passed around by a circle of acquaintances (who likely knew the author and perhaps some of the real-life versions of characters or situations in the sonnets) in handwritten, or manuscript, copies.

What did it mean to Meres that the author of *The Sonnets* was "mellifluous and honey-tongued"? Having a sweetly flowing tongue of honey certainly sounds like high praise for a poet, but it was also a phrase commonly connected with lyric poets during Shakespeare's age. "Mellifluous" has classical parallels, which appealed to Meres, and the popular medieval writer Boethius also used the word. Shakespeare himself includes the phrase "honey-tongued" in his play of the mid-1590s, *Love's Labour's Lost*. He would shortly use the same language—"honey-mouthed" or "suck'd the honey"— in the forthcoming plays *Hamlet* and *The Winter's Tale*, but there it implies flattery, duplicity, something cloying; indeed, Meres may have some of these less complimentary connotations in mind, or at the least, these adjectives may properly acknowledge the highly ornate, artificial quality of Shakespeare's early poetry, especially the popular *Venus and Adonis*. Artifice and sweetness also mark many of the poems in *The Sonnets*, but most critics would now say that much more—rhetorically, psychologically, and otherwise—is also at work in this remarkable sequence. There is something new and more complex amid the old, reliable formal virtues of Shakespeare's earliest writing. In any case, it is also important to realize that Meres was not alone in his assessment of Shakespeare's poetic characteristics. A number of other contemporaries spoke of Shakespeare in similar terms: John Weever calls Shakespeare "honey-tong'd," Richard Barnfield speaks of his "hony-flowing Vaine," Thomas Heywood reuses "mellifluous," and an anonymous playwright addresses "O sweet Mr. S," an adjective also used by the young John Milton. Seventeenth-century comments on Shakespeare's *Sonnets* are rare, but occasionally there is evidence of active reading. Sir John Suckling echoes at least six of the sonnets in his tragedy *Brennoralt* (1640), while 30 years later another author refers to them in a preface to his own prose work.

Of course, we have no conclusive evidence that Meres refers to the poems that eventually appeared in Shakespeare's sequence as we now know it. However, in the following year, five of Shakespeare's sonnets appeared in *The Passionate Pilgrim*, an anthology printed three times by William Jaggard. The second edition attributes the whole collection to "W. Shakespeare," although

15 other poems in the collection have nothing to do with our poet. Jaggard seems to have gotten his hands on two of these privately circulating sonnets (numbers 138 and 144), to which he added three sonnets cut from the fourth act of Shakespeare's *Love's Labour's Lost*, plus these other falsely attributed poems. Taken together, he may have hoped to trick the public into thinking his printed collection in fact contained the "Sonnets" by Shakespeare that some had been reading in manuscript and others had been hearing about. The two poems from *The Sonnets* are reprinted here from *The Passionate Pilgrim*: Students can now easily compare these versions with those more critically accepted versions in their textbooks. The frequent variations between the versions lend further support to the notions that Jaggard obtained these before Shakespeare had finished revising them and that Shakespeare had no involvement in the printing of Jaggard's anthology. Furthermore, when Jaggard again attributed *Passionate Pilgrim* to "W. Shakespeare" when a third edition appeared (1612), fellow playwright Thomas Heywood in his *Apologie for Actors* (1612 as well) warned that Shakespeare "was much offended with M[aster]. Jaggard that (altogether unknowne to him) presumed to make so bold with his name." Jaggard, as it turns out, would be the first of many to do so.

A few additional sonnets by Shakespeare deserve a brief mention here as well, although they were not immediately identified as such for good reason—the playwright situated poetry lines in sonnet form within the broader blank-verse horizons of his plays. Most obviously, three characters in *Love's Labour's Lost* recite sonnets, which, as we have seen, even the printer William Jaggard could recognize and thus appropriate for his own anthology. More subtly, Shakespeare includes two sonnets in his early tragedy of young lovers, *Romeo and Juliet*. One serves as a prologue that announces the setting, feuding families, and the "two hours' traffick of our stage," while the other comprises a witty, and deliciously flirtatious, dialogue between Romeo and Juliet about pilgrims' vows and tender kisses. Elsewhere in his dramatic work Shakespeare dramatizes—and parodies— the emotive, sonnet-writing pastimes of young Elizabethan gentlemen, as when Proteus in *Two Gentlemen of Verona* advises the Duke to write "wailful sonnets, whose composed rhymes / Should be full-fraught with serviceable vows." He also employs imagery found in *The Sonnets* for characters' expressions of love and its vagaries; Proteus begins the same play describing his infatuation to his friend Valentine:

> Yet writers say, as in the sweetest bud
> The eating canker dwells, so eating love
> Inhabits in the finest wits of all.

Proteus's discourse brings to mind sonnet 94, among others, and also of interest is Proteus's own awareness of his language as already conventional among sonneteers—"writers say," he begins. Scholars continue to explore this interchange between the better-known sonnets and what Helen Vendler calls the playwright's "extrasequential experiments" with sonnet form and imagery found in the plays.

The most important single text of Shakespeare's *Sonnets*—in fact, the book that gave a collective, lasting literary identity to 154 individual poems— appeared in print in 1609. The Stationers' Register, a record of publishers' intentions to publish new books, features this entry for that year: "20 maii. Thomas Thorpe entred for his copie under the handes of master Wilson and master Lownes warden, a Booke called Shakespeare's *sonnettes*." The first edition was printed soon afterward. Edward Alleyn, one of the most famous actors in Renaissance England, owned a copy: On the back of a letter of June 1609, he wrote an inventory that included "a book Shaksper Sonnetts—5d." Two different booksellers are mentioned on different copies, but Thomas Thorpe was clearly a central figure in bringing Shakespeare's poems into print. He is the "T. T." who signs the incredibly enigmatic dedication to the volume, which, despite its brevity, has fascinated and confounded scholars for centuries with its insinuations and (strategic? unintentional?) evasions. Thorpe addresses, in modern spelling, "the only begetter of these ensuing sonnets." Most readers have taken "begetter" to mean "inspirer," thus referring to the Young Man, and thus almost reflexively identified with the fellow who appears next in Thorpe's text—a "Mr. W. H." (See the "Young Man" entry in the "List of Personas" section for discussion of the most popular candidates for this mysterious identification.) Shakespeare himself is presumably the "ever-living poet," and Thorpe is the investor or "well-wishing adventurer" who is "setting forth" with the for-profit publication of this book. In 1799 George Chalmers muddied these muddy waters further by arguing that "begetter" actually meant "procurer," and thus "Mr. W. H." was no central mystery man, and possibly Shakespeare's male beloved, but merely an acquisitive friend of Thorpe's. Shakespeare himself has also been suggested, and likewise the "well-wishing adventurer," taken objectively, has been identified as the reader about to "set forth" in her reading of the poems.

More to the point, the 1609 text, often referred to as the first quarto, or "Q," collected 154 sonnets and presented them as *The Sonnets*. That said, this too is more complicated than it first appears. There is no proof that Shakespeare authorized the publication of his poems, determined the final form they took (there are actually many misspellings in this volume), or arranged them in their present order. Only 13 copies of this important book exist, a relatively rare number that has led some to argue that Shakespeare actively sought the withdrawal and destruction of this volume. It's hard to say, but Heather Dubrow and Arthur Marotti are among the most eloquent skeptics of Q's de facto authority and the way it shapes critics' presumptions. On the other hand,

Katherine Duncan-Jones, the editor of the latest Arden edition of *The Sonnets*, boldly claims that Shakespeare likely did authorize Thorpe's publication. One of her arguments involves the book as a whole: The sonnet sequence is followed by a narrative poem called *A Lover's Complaint*, which scholars such as John Kerrigan, Katherine Rowe, and Ilona Bell have found worthy of extended critical study. The volume as a whole, as Duncan-Jones argues, is not a random assemblage by an opportunistic printer but rather conformed to standards for poetry books—comprising a sonnet sequence, followed by an interlude (possibly the markedly different sonnets 153 and 154, in Shakespeare's case) and a longer narrative complaint.

Unfortunately, that random assemblage by an opportunistic editor did indeed emerge three decades later, in the form of John Benson's pirated "miscellany" edition of Shakespeare's *Poems*. Even more unfortunately, readers for the next two centuries would be misled by this stew of a collection, full of added "tag" titles ("Injurious Time," "The Glory of Beauty," Love's Cruelty," etc.), sonnets reordered and combined indiscriminately to form longer lyric poems (and some sonnets left out), and strategic pronoun changes, which made Shakespeare's Young Man seem a more traditional female beloved. A 1640 entry in the Stationers' Register reads, "Entred for his Copie under the handes of doctor Wykes and Master Fetherson warden *An Addicion of some excellent Poems to* Shakespeare's *Poems* by other gentlemen." This note provides a clue to another of Benson's damaging ploys: He included, amid Shakespeare's mangled sonnet versions, *A Lover's Complaint* (which was included in the 1609 edition) and "The Phoenix and the Turtle," and other poems by Ben Jonson, Francis Beaumont, Thomas Carew, and Robert Herrick. Moreover, he interspersed additional poems from the 1612 edition of *Passionate Pilgrim* falsely attributed to Shakespeare, so that centuries later the great Romantic poet William Blake would quote lines from a non-Shakespearean poem from this anthology and mistakenly list "Shakespeare" beside them.

As one theory has it, Benson may have added these poems in order to promote his book (wrongly) as the first publication of Shakespeare's sonnets. They did not have the good fortune, he avers in his preface, to receive the "proportionable glory" of his better known "Works"—that is, his plays. Likewise, he may have combined various sonnets to make them less recognizable as such, since the sonnet vogue of the 1590s had long passed by Benson's time. A similar "out-of-fashion" argument has been applied to the 1609 quarto, but critics such as Stephen Orgel and Peter Hyland, by showing that various sonnet sequences were still being published in the 1600s, have tempered that view. (For further information on these early editions of *The Sonnets*, see B. Roland Lewis's *The Shakespeare Documents*, vol. 2.) However suspect Benson's motivations and decisions, his book was the premier edition for the rest of the century.

1598—Francis Meres.
From *Palladis Tamia*, or *Wit's Treasury*

Francis Meres (1565–1647) discusses religion, morality, the arts, and other topics in *Palladis Tamia*. The section in which Shakespeare appears is a survey of Renaissance English writers, associated genre by genre with their classical equivalents.

As the soule of Euphorbus was thought to live in Pythagoras: so the sweete wittie soule of Ovid lives in mellifluous and hony-tongued Shakespeare, witnes his *Venus and Adonis*, his *Lucrece*, his sugred *Sonnets* among his private friends, &c.

As Plautus and Seneca are accounted the best for Comedy and Tragedy among the Latines: so Shakespeare among ye English is the most excellent in both kinds for the stage; for Comedy, witnes his *Gentlemen of Verona*, his *Errors*, his *Loue Labors Lost*, his *Loue Labours Wonne*, his *Midsummers Night Dreame*, and his *Merchant of Venice*: for Tragedy his *Richard the 2*, *Richard the 3*, *Henry the 4*, *King John*, *Titus Andronicus*, and his *Romeo and Juliet*.

As Epius Stolo said that the Muses would speake with Plautus tongue if they would speak Latin: so I say that the Muses would speak with Shakespeares fine filed phrase, if they would speak English.

1599—William Shakespeare. Versions
of sonnets 138 and 144 from William Jaggard's
anthology *The Passionate Pilgrim*

William Jaggard's anthology of poetry is attributed to Shakespeare, but in fact only five of Shakespeare's sonnets appear within its pages, and the two poems from *The Sonnets* appear by their variations from the 1609 quarto to have been unauthorized.

Sonnet 138

When my Love sweares that she is made of truth,
I do beleeve her (though I know she lies)
That she might thinke me some untutor'd youth,
Unskilful in the worlds false forgeries.
Thus vainly thinking that she thinkes me young,
Although I know my yeares be past the best:
I smiling, credite her false speaking toung,

Outfacing faults in love, with love's ill rest.
But wherefore sayes my love that she is young?
And wherefore say not I, that I am old:
O, Love's best habit's in a soothing toung,
And Age in love, loves not to have yeares told.

   Therefore I'le lye with Love, and love with me,
   Since that our faultes in love thus smother'd be.

Sonnet 144

Two loves I have, of Comfort and Despair,
That like two Spirits, do suggest me still:
My better Angel, is a Man (right faire)
My worser spirite a Woman (colour'd ill.)
To win me soone to hell, my Female evill
Tempteth my better Angel from my side:
And would corrupt my Saint to be a Divell,
Wooing his puritie with her faire pride.
And whether that my Angel be turnde feend,
Suspect I may (yet not directly tell:)
For being both to me; both, to each friend,
I guess one Angell in anothers hell:

   The truth I shall not know, but live in dout,
   Till my bad Angell fire my good one out.

━∘∕∘∕∘━   ━∘∕∘∕∘━   ━∘∕∘∕∘━

1609—Thomas Thorpe.
Dedication from *Shake-speares Sonnets*

This first edition of Shakespeare's *Sonnets*, known as the first quarto, or Q, is the basis for all modern editions and the most reliable of early texts of Shakespeare's sequence. Thomas Thorpe's enigmatic dedication has engaged scholars for centuries. For a twentieth-century analysis, see "A Note on the Dedication," by W. G. Ingram and Theodore Redpath (1964), later in this book.

TO. THE. ONLIE. BEGETTER. OF.
THESE. INSVING. SONNETS.
Mr. W.H. ALL. HAPPINESSE.
AND. THAT. ETERNITIE.

PROMISED.
BY.
OVR. EVER-LIVING. POET.
WISHETH.
THE. WELL-WISHING.
ADVENTVRER. IN.
SETTING.
FORTH.

T. T.

1640—John Benson. "Epistle to the Reader," from *Poems: Written by Wil. Shake-speare. Gent.*

John Benson's misleading edition tried to present Shakespeare's son-
nets as newly printed. He combined the 14-line originals into single,
longer poems; gave impersonal titles to them; changed pronouns
within the poems' texts; and added a variety of non-Shakespearean
poetry from *The Passionate Pilgrim* and other sources, thus setting back
readers' appreciation of Shakespeare's actual poems for a consider-
able time.

To the Reader,

I here presume (under favour) to present to your view, some excellent and
sweetely composed Poems, of Master *William Shakespeare*, Which in themselves
appear of the same purity, the Authour himselfe then living avouched; they
had not the fortune by reason of their Infancie in his death, to have the due
accommodation of proportionable glory, with the rest of his everliving Workes,
yet the lines of themselves will afford you a more authentick approbation than
my assurance any way can, to invite your allowance, in your perusall you shall
finde them *Seren*, cleere and elegantly plaine, such gentle straines as shall
recreate and not perplexe your braine, no intricacie or cloudy stuffe to puzzell
intellect, but perfect eloquence; such as will raise your admiration to his praise:
this assurance I know will not differ from your acknowledgement. And certaine
I am, my opinion will be seconded by the sufficiency of these ensuing Lines;
I have been somewhat solicitus to bring this forth to the perfect view of all
men; and in so doing, glad to be serviceable for the continuance of glory to the
deserved Author in these his Poems.

THE SONNETS
IN THE EIGHTEENTH CENTURY
❧

Shakespeare's *Sonnets* were reprinted at various times during the eighteenth century, but it was not till late in this century that a heroic yet underrated Irish scholar, Edmund Malone, restored editorial sanity to one of English poetry's most famous texts. However, before expanding on these printed editions, it is essential that we not overlook completely the poems' earliest means of transmission—the manuscript tradition, or "private" circulation mentioned by Meres—which continued throughout the seventeenth century and into the next. Benson's wrongheaded edition of 1640 may have ruled the printed field till Malone's late-eighteenth-century corrections, but Shakespeare's individual sonnets continued to be recopied and circulated in notebooks and miscellaneous manuscripts.

Surveying manuscript versions of the sonnets, John Kerrigan observes that most stem from the reigns of James I and Charles I, that is, the first half of the seventeenth century. That said, many are clearly copied from printed editions of the sonnets, including Benson's misleading 1640 edition. Thus the typical transmission—from the author's or another's manuscript source to printed edition—can also be reversed. One of Shakespeare's most famous sonnets, sonnet 116, circulated widely in manuscript and was also set to music by the seventeenth-century composer Henry Lawes. The result creates a fascinating echo effect:

Self-blinding error seizeth all those minds
Who with false appellations call that 'love'
Which alters when it alteration finds
Or with the mover hath a power to move— (1–4)

The most frequently recorded poem, sonnet 2, is likewise labeled in one manuscript as "Song," and relatedly those sonnets whose topic is music also appear in manuscript (sonnets 8 and 128 especially). Sonnet 2 is most commonly titled "Spes Altera" (or "Hope changed"), though at times its given title—"To one that would dye a Mayd," "A Lover to his Mistres," "The Benefitt of Mariage"—

51

is meant to identify the addressee as a woman, thus transforming the lyric relationship into something more socially normative, namely, that featuring a male lover and a female beloved. As we have seen, Benson, by changing multiple pronouns, had no qualms doing this in his printed edition.

Having acknowledged this ongoing manuscript presence of Shakespeare's sonnets, let us now return to their fortunes in print in the early eighteenth century. In 1709, Nicholas Rowe achieved a watershed in Shakespeare criticism by completing *The Works of Mr. William Shakespear*, along with the first thorough effort at a biography, in six volumes. The following year, Charles Gildon released a seventh supplementary volume, expressly intended to move Shakespeare's obscured poetry into the warm light of his better-known and more prestigious plays. *The Sonnets*, at least, were indeed obscure. Rowe in his biography makes no mention of them, though he does refer to *Venus and Adonis* and *The Rape of Lucrece*, "the only Piece of his Poetry which he ever publish'd himself." Although his story about the young Shakespeare poaching deer from a Stratford landowner may be legendary, it is interesting that poetry has a role to play. We hear that Shakespeare was prosecuted "somewhat too Severely," so that "he made a Ballad upon" the nobleman, one "so very bitter" that it further aggrieved the prosecution. Was the young poet sounding that bitter, defeated, disgusted note that characterizes some of the sonnets of betrayal, or sexual repulsion, or romantic dissatisfaction? We will never know, but Rowe does call Shakespeare's revengeful ballad the "first Essay of his Poetry," and it was the cause of his fleeing Stratford for his famous, immortalizing future in London.

Unsurprisingly, then, Gildon spends much time in his preface to this seventh, supplementary volume to Rowe's *Works* in a defensive mode: He argues for genuine authorship of these "less known Works of Shakespear," which while admittedly not "all of an equal Excellence," are quite like the plays in their unevenness. Furthermore, he defends Shakespeare's authorship of the poems against the skeptic who might read too much into their being out of print. Mercenary editors and booksellers, Gildon argued, felt no qualms about attributing non-Shakespearean plays to the popular playwright. Excluding the poems, then, was no case of editorial fastidiousness. Each of the poems in this volume, Gildon argues, carries "its Author's Mark, and Stamp upon it," although in fact the volume, dependent as it is on Benson's version, contains several poems not thought to be Shakespeare's. Gildon also raises the biographical flag that will be waved so vigorously later in the century and thereafter. Against skeptics of the sonnets he offers the thesis that some "Mistress" found them to be too personal a record of her and Shakespeare's relationship and thus kept them out of print and the public eye.

One year later, Bernard Lintott published an edition of Thorpe's 1609 quarto, probably less for high-minded editorial reasons and more because he had safer access to this earlier, neglected volume and could thus flank copyright restrictions. He presented his volume as containing "One Hundred and Fifty Four Sonnets, all of them in Praise of his Mistress." Like Gildon, Lintott was either misled by Benson's pronoun replacements, which had effaced the presence of the Young Man in many of the sonnets, or simply could not conceive of the recipient of so many romantic poems being a male. Of course, in both cases these may have been a shrewd editor's or publisher's emphasis; both men hoped for sales of their editions of Shakespeare's less famous poetry, and perhaps they feared a drop in readership if these sonnets were not seen as written to a mistress. Lintott also asserted that Shakespeare's two narrative poems, *Venus and Adonis* and *The Rape of Lucrece*, are "universally allow'd" to be written by Shakespeare: "I have printed them from very old Editions, which I procur'd, as the Reader will find by my keeping close to his Spelling."

George Sewell soon followed in Gildon's editorial footsteps, when in 1725 he provided a supplemental volume of Shakespeare's poetry for an editor (this time Alexander Pope) who had again overlooked the verse in assembling his edition of Shakespeare's *Works*. Sewell referred to Shakespeare's *Sonnets* as "Occasional" poems written early in the writer's career and clearly inspired by a mistress. Again we see a presumption in the sonnets' autobiographical and heterosexual character. In inviting such influence, Sewell places Shakespeare in a traditional line of English poets, including Abraham Cowley and, supremely, Edmund Spenser. Lewis Theobald, an accomplished eighteenth-century editor of Shakespeare, fails to mention *The Sonnets* in his 1734 preface to his edition, although slightly earlier, in a journal devoted to textual corrections, he did deign to make emendations to problematic lines in the poems. For example, the printing of "waste Blacks" in sonnet 77 seemed to him a mistake for "waste Blanks," which fit better the ongoing metaphor of the book ("vacant leaves" earlier in the poem). This change has been generally accepted by modern editors.

In a similarly taciturn spirit, two of Shakespeare's great editors of the second half of the century, George Steevens and Samuel Johnson, have little or nothing to say about the sonnets, or, if little, nothing good to say. Steevens reprinted the 1609 quarto of *The Sonnets* in 1766 but did not include any commentary, as if he were embarrassed to have revisited these poems at all. As we shall see, he just may have been. And as for Johnson, perhaps Shakespeare's greatest critic ever, readers searching among the various modern volumes of "Johnson on Shakespeare" still available will be hard-pressed to find any acknowledgment of the poems among the many timeless insights into the plays. This sort of oversight suggests how critically peripheral Shakespeare's poetry was at this point. Stephen Orgel rightfully says that the rise in *The Sonnets'* reputation is inversely related to the declining reputation of the narrative poems, which were Shakespeare's most popular work in his lifetime but among his least read now. In the eighteenth century, the narrative poems were already overshadowed by the great dramatic works of *Hamlet*, *King Lear*, *Macbeth*, and the like, but *The*

Sonnets were not yet taken seriously. D. Nichols Smith drives this point home in his collection *Eighteenth Century Essays on Shakespeare*, in which "*Sonnets*" is not even an entry in the book's index.

A great if forgotten hero of *The Sonnets*, Edmund Malone began to change all this in 1780 when he issued a *Supplement to the Edition of Shakespeare's Plays published in 1778 by Dr. Samuel Johnson and George Steevens*. Malone was a defender of the sonnets' rightful form and thus rejected Benson's miscellany edition in favor of the best textual predecessor available, which was the 1609 quarto. Adding his considerable linguistic sensitivity and common sense to this judicious choice of source, he established the first critical edition of *The Sonnets*, one that continues to influence modern editors. He also defended the social truths of Shakespeare's poems, however unsavory they were to his critical opponents such as Steevens. This sense of opposition was enhanced by the presentation of opinion, in the shape of a dialogue between the two editors, in the *Supplement* and later editions. One of Malone's major critical achievements was making a distinction that is still accepted by most scholars (Heather Dubrow is one notable, convincing exception)—that the first 126 sonnets are addressed to a Young Man, while sonnets 127 to 154 revolve around a Dark Lady. Steevens did not disagree with this breakdown but was troubled that Shakespeare wrote "a small proportion out of so many" to a woman. Malone also extended the biographical interest of his immediate editorial predecessors and, more important, he retracted Benson's influential generalizing and impersonal context for *The Sonnets* and concentrated it on the "I" of the poetry, who for Malone was one and the same with Shakespeare the poet and historical person. Thus Malone weighs in on possible candidates for the Young Man of this first, long series of poems. He rejected his fellow scholar Richard Farmer's suggestion that the "Mr. W. H." of Thomas Thorpe's preface was Shakespeare's nephew William Harte. (This candidate would have been only 12 years old in 1598, when some sonnets were first heard of.) Altogether more convincing, or at least "not improbable," was his friend Thomas Tyrwhitt's suggestion of W. Hughes, whom he believed is punningly celebrated in sonnet 20: "A man in *hew* all *Hews* in his controlling." Shakespeare's similar word play on his own name "Will" in sonnets 135 and 136 provided a handy corroboration for both scholars.

Steevens vented his disapproval of *The Sonnets* on both formal and moral terms. Unfortunately for Shakespeare and his sequence, many readers in the late eighteenth century found the sonnet generally to be a thoroughly discredited poetic form. Steevens thought of sonnets as mainly "trifles" full of "quaintness, obscurity, and tautology." This detrimental "species of composition" had reduced even the "most exalted poets to a level with the meanest rhimers." Furthermore, he and his contemporary John Monck Mason (for whom *The Sonnets* were similarly "miserable" and "insipid") revealed an anti-Italian bias in their condemnation of the sonnet; the sonnet, they insisted, should have stayed in Italy, and even Shakespeare's earlier editor Gildon regretted that the spirit of Petrarch had "infected" Shakespeare's native wit and passion. To this charge Malone was actually lukewarm in his subject's defense, admitting that *The Sonnets* suffered from a lack of variety and, in so many words, a lack of a female addressee in too many of the poems. Yet they were valuable to study, if for no other reason than their frequently "illustrating obscure passages in the plays." Fortunately Malone had less dependent defenses as well, praising the sonnets' energy and the "many beautiful lines" scattered throughout. The "glowing expressions" of sonnet 29 ("When in disgrace with fortune and men's eyes") alone was enough to protect the sonnets from oblivion or even from Steevens's "indiscriminate censure," and he additionally suggested, in his typically composed manner, that Shakespeare's harshest critics were perhaps excessively narrow in their tastes, too enamored with "blank verse or heroick couplets." Malone developed his support for *The Sonnets* further in 1790 within his own edition of Shakespeare, but that also spurred an even more vitriolic assessment by Steevens (included here) in 1793.

Steevens acknowledged Malone's observant division of addressees between the Young Man and the Dark Lady, but he could not abide the resulting homosocial or even homosexual implications. Sonnet 20, featuring a "master-mistress of my passions," left him with an "equal mixture of disgust and indignation," to which Malone offered up his best justifications: Such language between men was customary in Shakespeare's time and was not "esteemed indecorous," and perhaps that distressing phrase in sonnet 20 merely meant *sovereign* mistress. Malone at times complained of the "overcharged" nature of the denser sonnets, but here in his effort to appease Steevens, he succeeds in removing any charge from one of the sequence's more provocative phrases. The offense may have seemed so great to Steevens and others because Malone's new emphasis on biographical associations between the poems and their writer threatened to dismantle the pedestal upon which Shakespeare was increasingly placed. Already he was considered England's great "national" poet, and for many he was a moral arbiter as well. An anonymous essay from 1748 argues that when it comes to writing "prudential maxim, or moral precept," Shakespeare "seems to stand without equal." Much like our own paradoxical relationship to celebrities, athletes, or political candidates, Shakespeare's late-eighteenth-century readers were curious to know more about their literary hero but were sometimes troubled or alarmed by what they apparently found.

It is fitting to end on a final note of praise in Malone's honor. Truly his work on *The Sonnets*, and its lasting importance for later generations of scholars and readers generally, cannot be overstated. For a while Malone was suspected of borrowing, and failing to attribute, a number of insights into Shakespeare and his poems from an unpublished edition of *The Sonnets* by a contemporary, the Shakespearean scholar Edward Capell. However, among others, Samuel Butler at the end of the nineteenth century consulted with the editors of the Cambridge Shakespeare edition, and their judgment exonerated Malone and renewed the appreciation of his achievement. And let it be clear that his achievement was recognized almost immediately and by his critical adversaries. For example, Steevens praised his fellow scholar, no matter his questionable admiration of *The Sonnets*, for his "attention, diligence, and spirit of enquiry," which had "very far exceeded those of the whole united phalanx of predecessors."

1710—Charles Gildon. From "An Essay on the Rise and Progress of the Stage in Greece, Rome, and England" and "Remarks on the Poems of Shakespear," from *Poems. The Works of Mr. William Shakespear*, vol. 7

Charles Gildon (1665–1724) was an influential English man of letters. He prepared a volume of Shakespeare's poetry to supplement the six-volume edition of Shakespeare's *Works* edited by Nicholas Rowe. His essay on the Greek, Roman, and English stages was an important document of early Shakespeare criticism.

From "An Essay on the Rise and Progress of the Stage in Greece, Rome and England":

"Tho' the Works of SHAKESPEAR have been lately publish'd without the Poems, which now visit the World in a Seventh Volume by themselves; yet the Reader must not imagine, that the Bookseller of those, rejected these as spurious, or doubtful, or as unwilling to shelter under his Name, what was not genuine;" . . . "But out of a good natur'd Principle, agreeable to the Man; he thought it not impolitic to lessen the Towns Expectation of these Poems, because he had no Hand in their Publication. However, I have not only ventur'd to put them to the Press, for the Satisfaction of the Lovers of Shakespear, who have often, with Importunity, demanded them of me; but I doubt not to make it evident that they are genuine, and more perfect in their Kind, than many, if not most, of his Dramatic Performances. I confess, that they are far from being all of an equal Excellence, but there is no more to be drawn from thence to their Disadvantage, than from the Inequality of his other Writings to the Prejudice of his Plays."

From "Remarks on the Poems of Shakespear":

"I Come now to Shakespear's Poems the Publication of which in one Volume, and of a Piece with the rest of the Works, gave Occasion to my Perusal of his other Writings, with so much Attention, that I cou'd not easily be impos'd on by any spurious Copy of that Poet. 'Tis true there may perhaps be a Michel Angelo found, who may copy the Antique so admirably, as to puzzle the greatest

Masters, but then, the very Copy must have the Beauty, and Merit of an Original. Thus I am confident, that tho' the Poems this Volume contains are extreamly distinguish'd in their Excellence, and Value, yet there is not one of them, that does not carry its Author's Mark, and Stamp upon it. Not only the same Manner of Thinking, the same Turn of Thought, but even the same Mode of Dress and Expression, the Decompounds, his peculiar sort of Epithets, which distinguishes his from the Verses of all his Contemporaries or Successors, . . . But to compare all the Poems in this manner wou'd be an endless Work, and make almost as many Volumes as his Plays; and it wou'd be perfectly unnecessary since whoever knows any thing of Shakespear will find his Genius in every Epigram of these Poems in every particular I have mention'd, and the frequent Catachreses; his Starts aside in Allegories, and in short his Versification, which is very unequal; sometimes flowing smoothly but gravely like the Thames, at other times down right Prose. He never touches on an Image in any of them, but he proves the Poem genuine.

"But some, perhaps, who are for undervaluing what they have no Share in, may say that granting them to be Shakespears, yet they are not valuable enough to be reprinted, as was plain by the first Editors of his Works who wou'd otherwise have join'd them altogether.

"To this I answer—That the Assertion is false, or were it not it is more than the Objector knows by his own Judgment, and Understanding, but to prove it false we need only consider, that they are much less imperfect in their Kind, than ev'n the best of his Plays, as will appear from the Rules I shall lay down immediately; in the next Place the first Editors were Players, who had nothing to do with any thing but the Dramatic Part, which yet they publish'd full of gross Mistakes, most of which remains to this Day; nor were they by any means Judges of the Goodness or Badness of, the Beauties or Defects of either Plays or Poems.

"There is next an Objection, that if these Poems had been Genuine, they had been publish'd in the Life time of the Author and by himself, but coming out almost thirty Years after his Death there is no Great Reason to suspect that they are not Genuine.

"To this I answer, that if nothing was to be thought his but what was publish'd in his Life time, much the greater Number of his Plays wou'd be as liable to this Objection as his Poems. Next here is indeed, no weight in the Objection, is there any thing more common, than the Publication of Works of great Men after their Death?"

. . . "Besides these Poems being most to his Mistress, it is not at all unlikely, that she kept them by her till they fell into her Executors Hands or some Friend, who would not let them be any longer conceal'd. But after all there were more in Proportion of these Poems of this Volume, printed in his Lifetime, than of his Plays, as is plain from his *Venus and Adonis*, his *Tarquin and Lucrece*, and several Epigrams and Sonnets."

. . . "Tho' Love and its Effects are often happily enough touch'd in many of these Poems, yet I must confess that it is but too visible, that Petrarch had a little infected his way of thinking on that Subject, yet who ever can admire Mr Cowley's Mistress, has a thousand Times more Cause of Admiration of our Shakespear in his Love Verses, because he has sometimes such touches of Nature as will make Amends for those Points, those Epigrammatic Acumina, which are not or ever can be the Product of a Soul truly touch'd with the Passion of Love."

. . . "How far Shakespear has excell'd in this Way is plain from his Poems before us; but this must be allow'd him, that much of the Beauty and Sweetness of Expression, which is so much contended for is lost by the Injury of Time and the Great Change of our Language since his Time; and yet there is a wonderful Smoothness in many of them, that makes the Blood dance to its Numbers."

1711—Bernard Lintott. From "Advertisement," from *A Collection of Poems . . . by Mr. William Shakespeare*

Bernard Lintott (1675-1736) published an edition of Shakespeare's *Sonnets* based on the more or less forgotten 1609 quarto. His choice of base text was unusual but critically preferable to the popular and more often consulted edition of Benson (1640); however, Lintott may have chosen the earlier, more reliable edition less for scholarly reasons and more to evade copyright restrictions.

The Writings of Mr. Shakespeare are in so great Esteem, that several Gentlemen have subscrib'd to a late Edition of his Dramatick Works in Six Volumes; which makes me hope, that this little Book will not be unacceptable to the Publick."... "I shall not take upon me to say any thing of the Author, an ingenious Person having compil'd some Memoirs of his Life, and prefix'd it to the late above-mention'd Edition . . .

1790—Edmund Malone. From "Preface" to *The Plays and Poems of William Shakespeare in Ten Volumes*

Edmund Malone (1741-1812) is one of the great editors, from any era, of Shakespeare's *Sonnets*. In addition to groundbreaking work on Shakespeare's life and chronology of his writings, Malone produced the first critical edition of *The Sonnets*, which returned scholarly attention to the then-neglected 1609 quarto. His greater interest in biographical readings of the sonnets soon influenced the Romantic readers and writers who followed him.

Though above a century and a half has elapsed since the death of Shakespeare, it is somewhat extraordinary, (as I observed on a former occasion,) that none of his various editors should have attempted to separate his genuine poetical compositions from the spurious performances with which they have been long intermixed; or have taken the trouble to compare them with the earliest and most authentick copies. Shortly after his death a very incorrect impression of his poems was issued out, which in every subsequent edition, previous to the year 1780, was implicitly followed. They have been carefully revised, and with many additional illustrations are now a second time faithfully printed from the original copies, excepting only *Venus and Adonis*, of which I have not been able to procure the first impression.

(. . .)

It is painful to recollect how many of (I had almost said) my coadjutors have died since the present work was begun" [Malone mentions here Samuel Johnson and Thomas Tyrwhitt] "men, from whose approbation of my labours I had promised myself much pleasure, and whose stamp could give a value and currency to any work.

1793—George Steevens. From "Advertisement," from *The Plays of William Shakespeare in Fifteen Volumes . . .* , 4th edition

George Steevens (1736–1800) reprinted the 1609 quarto of *The Sonnets* in 1766, but they received little attention in his editions of Shakespeare's *Works*, produced with Samuel Johnson in 1773 and 1778. He exchanged conjectures and opinions on *The Sonnets* with Edmund Malone in a 1780 *Supplement* and condemned the sequence more harshly in a 1793 reprint of his own edition.

. . . We have not reprinted the Sonnets, &c. of Shakespeare, because the strongest act of Parliament that could be framed, would fail to compel readers into their service; notwithstanding these miscellaneous Poems have derived every possible advantage from the literature and judgement of their only intelligent editor, Mr. Malone, whose implements of criticism, like the ivory rake and golden spade in Prudentius, are on this occasion disgraced by the objects of their culture.— Had Shakespeare produced no other works than these, his name would have reached us as little celebrity as time has conferred on that of Thomas Watson, an older and much more elegant sonnetteer.

THE SONNETS
IN THE NINETEENTH CENTURY
🍃

Nathan Drake's two opposed views on *The Sonnets*, reflecting a significant change of his opinion from 1800 to 1817, exemplifies well a general critical warming toward Shakespeare's poems in the Romantic era. In his earlier essay, Drake sounded a dismissal of *The Sonnets* still common among his peers, and he specifically praised George Steevens for excluding *The Sonnets* from his more dignified collection of Shakespeare's plays. By 1817, however, he was finding much to admire in Shakespeare's lyrical efforts. We might locate the seed of this approval as early as 1798, when Drake dedicated a section of his *Literary Hours* to the sonnet form, tracing its uses in poets such as Dante, Spenser, and Milton. George Steevens, on the other hand, would have found the form itself beneath such attention. In the same year, William Wordsworth and Samuel Taylor Coleridge revolutionized English verse with the publication of *Lyrical Ballads*; its influential preface soon turned English poetic taste away from the neoclassical polish and mythological lacings of the eighteenth century. Instead, Wordsworth praised poetry for being a "spontaneous overflow of powerful feeling" originating in "emotion recollected in tranquility," and this strong aesthetic divergence ensured a renewed appreciation of Shakespeare's own personally oriented, emotionally intense sonnets.

The Romantics' new attraction to vivid personality—of a man speaking to men, in Wordsworth's phrasing—included both the poetic voice speaking within the poem and also the biographical, historical self of the actual poet. In effect, these two voices were most admired when they seemed most one. Wordsworth praises Shakespeare in his 1815 "Essay, Supplementary" for capturing in the sonnets the feelings of "his own person." To Wordsworth, these poems, unmatched by any other work of Shakespeare's, contain "a greater number of exquisite feelings felicitously expressed." Wordsworth attributed the censure of prior editors to the "too common propensity of human nature to exult over a supposed fall into the mire of a genius." Twelve years later, in his well-known poem "Scorn not the Sonnet," he more boldly validated the formal intricacies of the sonnet form. In a much earlier marginal note, he had criticized Shakespeare's poems for their "tediousness" and "elaborate obscurity," a carp characteristic of the younger Wordsworth, or eighteenth-century Wordsworth, as Jonathan Bate has called him. Now, in the later sonnet, Wordsworth declares that "with this key / Shakespeare unlocked his heart."

Writing nearly a half-century later, as a Victorian rather than a Romantic poet, Robert Browning composed a rebuttal to Wordsworth that has proved just as memorable. "Shall I sonnet-sing you about myself? / Do I live in a house you would like to see?" his poem "House" mockingly opens. "Unlock my heart with a sonnet-key?" As his tone makes abundantly clear, Browning had no intention of doing so, and furthermore—"Did Shakespeare? If so, the less Shakespeare he!" Why was Browning so adamant in his disagreement with Wordsworth's effusions? Why was he made so uncomfortable by the possibility that Shakespeare the person might have been so transparent in his sonnets? For Browning—who was the great poet of dramatic monologues, the great verse ventriloquist—Shakespeare was less a person, and a poet, if he merely poured out his heart into the 14 lines of a sonnet. Browning instead valued Shakespeare's ability to create, as if from nothing, real personality in dramatic terms. (Keats's famous praise of Shakespeare's capacity for "negative capability" in creating such genuine stage characters also comes to mind.) In other words, Shakespeare was more himself, or better expressed his poetic personhood, when Browning could imagine him composing behind the veil of the impersonal artist. Wordsworth, on the other hand, dedicated his great autobiographical poem *The Prelude* to charting the "growth of the poet's mind." Browning's age was not Wordsworth's, and it was Wordsworth's age that became enamored with Shakespeare's "miscellaneous" poems and the person who wrote them.

It should be clear, therefore, that Edmund Malone, with his more intensive biographical approach to Shakespeare, did not single-handedly usher in this new interest in *The Sonnets*. From a different, more current scholarly direction, August Wilhelm Schlegel and Frederick Schlegel influenced Romantic readers. For August Wilhelm Schlegel, *The Sonnets* "paint most unequivocally the actual situation and sentiments of the poet." More intriguingly, they are "remarkable confessions of his youthful errors," and August Wilhelm chastised English scholars for not making use of an obvious biographical resource. Frederick Schlegel more generally praised the "extreme tenderness" of the poet, "so exquisite and so deep," recorded clearly in the sonnets and thus proving how different the sensitive Shakespeare was from his stage creations, drawn from "the world as it stood clearly before him."

The time was poetically ripe as well. Poets such as Wordsworth and Keats could not only appreciate the personal voice of a genius in *The Sonnets* but also were ambitious and passionate enough as to identify in personal ways with their great precursor. Thus Wordsworth imagines Shakespeare sighing over the act of conceiving grand thoughts in solitude, which seems a far more likely thing for a Romantic poet like Wordsworth to sigh over. Similarly, Keats writes in a letter how much it would thrill him to behold Shakespeare—to see how he sat!—as he composed Hamlet's "To be or not to be" speech. That said, Malone's prosaic editorial achievement certainly played a critical role in *The Sonnets*' newly elevated reputation. As Gary Taylor writes in *Reinventing Shakespeare*,

> Malone's editorial recovery of the sonnets was instrumental in transforming Shakespeare from the public dramatic poet of the Restoration and eighteenth century into a private lyric poet who could be embraced, celebrated, and appropriated by the Romantics. . . . Shakespeare remained, of course, primarily a dramatist; but the sonnets and narrative poems—freshly restored to the canon, as yet wholly neglected by critics—gave the Romantics opportunity to enjoy the novelty of their own critical perspective, while claiming Shakespeare as a precursor in their own favored genres.

And claim Shakespeare as a precursor, they did. Wordsworth and Keats both paid the ultimate kind of homage for poets; they echoed and redeployed Shakespeare's lines from *The Sonnets* to give their own poetry more authority and depth. Shakespeare's sonnets influence Wordsworth's sonnet "To Sleep," while his "Prospectus" to *The Recluse* and parts of *The Prelude* borrow phrases from sonnets 107, 116, and others. Keats quotes sonnet 12 approvingly in a letter of 1817, and this poem's imagery appears in Keats' great ode "To Autumn." It also influences Keats' sonnet "When I have fears," as does sonnet 64 in a more structural fashion. As Jonathan Bate has written: "With 'When I have fears that I may cease to be,' the Shakespearean sonnet is actively revived, both formally and tonally, by a major English poet for the first time in two hundred years."

This intense response toward Shakespeare and his poetry could also be unpredictable and contradictory. Some brief comments by two other Romantics, Samuel Taylor Coleridge and William Hazlitt, will show how the age had not completely moved beyond their predecessors' sources of praise or occasions for consternation. Comparatively, Coleridge certainly slighted the poetry for the sake of the greatness of the plays, and even among the poetry, he more frequently praised the vividness and compression of *Venus and Adonis*. One reporter of a lecture describes how Coleridge spoke briefly on both narrative poems, "but he utterly passed over the Sonnets and made no remark on the reception that the poems have met with from modern critics." References to certain sonnets do recur in Coleridge's notebooks, and he clearly admired some poems tremendously and thought very lowly of others. In one lecture he belittles a poem of John Donne's by remarking, "Shakespeare has nothing on this. He is never *positively* bad, even in his Sonnets." Yet in his *Biographia Literaria*, his greatest critical work, he singles out lines from three sonnets to demonstrate how in great poetry images are "modified by a predominant passion." Shakespeare, he continues, "still gives a dignity and a passion to the objects which he presents . . . they burst upon us at once in life and power." Coleridge's lengthiest and most memorable response occurs when he encounters a marginal note of Wordsworth's in a poetry anthology. Mentioned earlier, Wordsworth's comment refers to Shakespeare's later sonnets, addressed to the Dark Lady, as "abominably harsh, obscure, and worthless." He is more generous to the earlier poems, which he finds "warm with passion." Coleridge honors his friend by saying even this little note will be, in times to come, a "reverential relic," but he begs to differ with Wordsworth's opinion, praising *The Sonnets* instead for helping to "explain the mind of Shakespeare" and for being "so full of thought and *exquisitest* diction." (As we have seen, this adjective quickly came to the minds of many when describing these poems and the poet they presupposed.) Coleridge does, however, take great pains to justify the sexual dynamics of *The Sonnets*. His intended future audience, his son Hartley, may shed some light on the peculiar tone here, where he emphasizes the "pure love" Shakespeare must have felt, which is to say he recognized that the Young Man was not a "possible object of desire" in a physical sense.

This perceived tension leads Coleridge to sonnet 20, which speaks of the "master-mistress." For him, its very directness makes clear that Shakespeare never thought seriously about physical consummation, nor feared the recrimination of others for poetically treating the subject. "My sweet Hartley!" Coleridge exclaims, showing a concern for his son's future well-being that is not dissimilar from the poet's concern for Time's threatening the Young Man in *The Sonnets*. It is this fatherly context, perhaps, that makes Coleridge so protective of his ideal vision of Shakespeare the Great Man: "I pray fervently that thou may'st know inwardly how impossible it was for a Shakespeare not to have been in his heart's heart chaste." In his influential essay on "editing as cultural formation," Peter Stallybrass follows Coleridge's ongoing engagement with sonnet 20. In 1833, Coleridge discussed again (a record of which can be found in his *Table Talk*) Malone's early defenses of Shakespeare's male recipient—the Elizabethans commonly spoke of friends in this way, and men valued fashionable Platonic relationships with other men, full of "affection beyond friendship and wholly aloof from appetite." However, this is no longer enough to justify the bisexual bravado of sonnet 20; instead, Coleridge supports the curious formulation that Shakespeare intended to seem a pederast, or boy-lover, as a "purposed blind" to conceal his true love for a certain woman. (One German scholar extended Coleridge's shifty thinking to the 1609 quarto itself, suggesting that Shakespeare had intentionally wished to appear as if he had no involvement in the book's publication, in order to distance himself from its true contents.) At this later date, it is apparent to Coleridge that the genuine feeling in Shakespeare's poetry comes from a "man deeply in love, and in love with a woman."

If more dismissively, William Hazlitt also struggled with the specter of personality amid the beauties of *The Sonnets*. Hazlitt could sometimes acknowledge the virtue of the poems, saying that "many of them are highly beautiful in themselves, and interesting as they relate to the state of the personal feelings of the author." He felt more reservations about personal effusions in verse, and so he often sounds rueful when discussing the poems' biographical dimension. Coleridge at times comes to similar conclusions—"Shakespeare's poetry is characterless," he says—but we have seen just how much issues of biography and personality captivated him. Hazlitt, on the other hand, was less sympathetic. He valued impersonality but also criticized Shakespeare's peculiar brand of it. Reversing earlier critics' efforts of setting the poems beside the plays in order to justify the former, Hazlitt declares bluntly that the comparison only harms the poetry's standing. "In a word, we do not like Shakespear's poems, because we like his plays." Compared with the hot-blooded stage characters that Hazlitt so admired, Shakespeare's narrative poems were "a couple of ice-houses . . . about as hard, glittering, and as cold."

A quick survey of further Romantic reactions will continue to show these divergences of opinion. Percy Bysshe Shelley praised the "pathetic" quality in Shakespeare's sonnet 111 (he meant the term positively), while Walter Savage Landor raised an objection that any student who has struggled to understand a dense, knotted, multivalent passage from *The Sonnets* will appreciate: "They are hot and pothery: there is much condensation, little delicacy: like raspberry jam without cream, without crust, without bread, to break its viscidity." That said, he would still prefer rereading one of Shakespeare's poems to the "musty" poetry of his own "dull season"!

I have surveyed these early-nineteenth-century poets and critics at such length because theirs was a crucial time of revaluation for *The Sonnets'* reputation. Many strengths that contemporary readers find in these poems were first identified during the Romantic period or at least apprehended then. Yet scholarship on *The Sonnets* was also advancing, if not always in ways that seem in retrospect desirable or even useful. Two areas of scholarly focus that grew exponentially during this time were the ordering of the sonnets (specifically whether the 1609 quarto offered a valid arrangement, approved by the author) and real-life identifications of various "characters" in the poems, from "Mr. W. H." of Thorpe's dedication to the Rival Poet and the Dark Lady. Nathan Drake, whom we met earlier, deserves credit for rebutting George Chalmers's turn-of-the-century explanation—that poems *apparently* addressed to a young man were all, in fact, composed for Queen Elizabeth I!—and for suggesting as a substitute a candidate who still remains one of the two most respectable, enduring choices. He felt the most logical Young Man was Henry Wriothesley, earl of Southampton, to whom Shakespeare had dedicated his two narrative poems and who may have been resistant to marriage in the 1590s (hence the possibly commissioned "Procreation" sonnets 1–17) and whose initials reversed, at least, were "W. H." James Boaden in 1832 first offered the other most reliable choice for the young man, William Herbert, earl of Pembroke. (Note his initials.)

Scholars' choices between these two candidates also presume other interpretations, namely, of the dates of composition of the sonnets and, relatedly, conjectures on other members of the sequence's lyrical "cast." For example, Southampton's supporters favor an earlier composition, perhaps as early as the late 1580s, whereas supporters of the younger Pembroke believe Shakespeare wrote most of the sonnets in the mid- to late 1590s and well into the seventeenth century. Both groups could point to sonnet 107 and seize upon one line—"The mortal moon hath her eclipse endured"—to support their posited dates; the line alludes either to the defeat of the Spanish Armada in 1588 or to Queen Elizabeth's sickness or her death in 1603, depending on your predisposition. In the late 1800s, convinced of the Young Man's identification as Pembroke, W. A. Harrison and Thomas Tyler both argued that Mary Fitton, maid of honor to the queen, was the Dark Lady, although a later portrait—of a fair-skinned Fitton—undercut their theory. Charles Armitage Brown, a friend of John Keats, published the first book-length study of the autobiographical dimension of Shakespeare's *Sonnets* in 1838, and the essayist Anna Brownell Jameson matched Brown's detective work around the same time.

Conversely, D. L. Richardson, Charles Knight, and John Halliwell-Phillipps were all nineteenth-century Shakespeareans who in different ways foreshadowed the critical emphases of the next century. Richardson as early as 1835 was squeamish about the rush to identify the sonnets' figures, and he thought it not unlikely that the poems addressed several different individuals, some male and some female, some real and some utterly imagined. His reservation of judgment shows a real appreciation for the fictive complexities of the lyric genre. Knight felt a quick, strict judgment on identifications underestimated the dramatic quality of *The Sonnets* and the similarity of its poetry with that in the plays. Halliwell-Phillipps, on the other hand, rejected too-easy identifications of the Young Man not because he shared earlier critics' moral qualms but simply because he thought Shakespeare's publicizing a real homoerotic or homosexual relationship so dramatically was not sensible and thus unlikely.

These differences of opinion aside, fairly early in the century it was clear to nearly everyone that Shakespeare's *Sonnets* had undergone a considerable critical elevation, whether deserved or not. Thus James Boswell, an editor of an 1821 edition of Shakespeare's works that relied largely on further findings by Malone, could declare that George Steevens's condemnation of *The Sonnets* as "worthless" 40 years ago "had not made a convert of a single reader who had any pretensions to poetical taste." The poems may not match the heights of Shakespeare's great tragedies, he admitted, but they certainly stood up well beside his early comedies. The historian Henry Hallam makes a similar acknowledgment, however begrudgingly. Although Steevens showed them "utmost scorn," *The Sonnets'* beauties are nevertheless exaggerated, "especially among young men of poetical tempers." In truth, Shakespeare engaged more fully than anyone with "this species of poetry," which one quickly infers is rather distasteful to Hallam. In saying "it is impossible not to wish that Shakespeare had never written them," he serves as a conduit for Steevens's earlier condemnation. Fortunately for Shakespeare, later critics tended to be more accepting and even sympathetic. Edward Dowden finds in the sequence a young man who struggles with bitterness; the poems "tell more of Shakespere's sensitiveness than of Shakespere's strength." Swinburne, skeptical of the "preposterous pyramid of presumptuous commentary" that currently marred *The Sonnets*, instead turns back to *The Passionate Pilgrim* for clues. Sidney Lanier sympathizes with Shakespeare and his "connected drama of his unfortunate love" by heightening the Young Man's betrayal as the "most unpardonable crime of crimes." He also makes interesting comparisons between Shakespeare's and Philip Sidney's poetry and between Shakespeare's achievement generally and Beethoven's and Keats's.

Finally, Oscar Wilde and Samuel Butler round out the century with approaches to or creative reimagining of *The Sonnets'* world that would continue to resonate in the century ahead. Butler insists that the final 29 sonnets are misplaced and that most are also addressed to the Young Man. He thus seeks in his "rearranged" edition to restore them, by a sometimes breathtaking reliance on inference, to their rightful places within the first sequence. He applauds Malone but is far looser in his own editorial procedures, looking above all for the story of the sonnets that, according to him, stares every reader in the face. Later scholars such as A. L. Rowse soon followed in Butler's hypothesizing, problem-solving footsteps. Oscar Wilde ultimately brings similar creativity to *The Sonnets*, but calls it such, composing his *Portrait of Mr. W. H.* with typical narrative gusto. Claiming to solve the mystery of *The Sonnets'* dedicatee, Wilde in fact returns to an earlier surmise by Tyrwhitt and Malone. He tells the story of one William Hughes, a young actor in Shakespeare's theater. Wilde overreaches his predecessors by brooding on the effects of art and acting on a relationship between men. Through the lens of Wilde's "creative criticism," the young man's acting talent inspires the poetic and fiction-making ideals of the speaker. Yet the delicate maneuverings of eros are undercut by an outer layer of skepticism: Wilde's narrator is investigating a theory of a friend, who no longer believes his own hypothesis. The critical sketch was enlarged in 1921 and has been frequently reprinted, serving as a vanguard for the rise of late-twentieth-century criticism that is newly attuned to issues of desire and sexuality, secret or otherwise.

1803—Samuel Taylor Coleridge.
From *Marginalia*

Samuel Taylor Coleridge (1772-1834) was one of the great poets of
the Romantic era, as well as a popular lecturer and respected literary
critic. Influenced by the German Idealists, Coleridge imported this
Continental thinking into the study of English letters and particu-
larly of Shakespeare. He is still considered one of the great readers of
Shakespeare. He perceptively treats the dramatic works in recorded
lectures and in his key text of literary criticism, *Biographia Literaria*, but
his more peripheral comments on *The Sonnets* occur in his marginal
writings in books, as well as in his conversations recorded in *Table Talk*
(see later in this section for an excerpt from 1833). The excerpt below
contains a written note by Wordsworth and then Coleridge's reply.

[WORDSWORTH]

These sonnets beginning at CXXVII to his mistress, are worse than a puzzle-peg.
They are abominably harsh, obscure, and worthless. The others are for the most
part much better, have many fine lines and passages. They are also in many places
warm with passion. Their chief faults—and heavy ones they are—are sameness,
tediousness, quaintness, and elaborate obscurity.

[COLERIDGE]

I can by no means subscribe to the above pencil mark of W. Wordsworth;
which, however, it is my wish should never be erased. It is *his*: and grievously
am I mistaken, and deplorably will Englishmen have degenerated if the being
his will not in times to come give it a value, as of a little reverential relic—the
rude mark of his hand left by the sweat of haste in a St. Veronica handkerchief!
And Robert Southey! My sweet Hartley! if thou livest, thou wilt not part
with this book without sad necessity and a pang at heart. Oh, be never weary
of reperusing the four first volumes of this collection, my eldest born! Today
thou art to be christened, being more than seven years of age, and with what
reluctance and *distaste* have I permitted this unchristian, and in its spirit and
consequences anti-christian, foolery to be performed upon *thee*, Child of free
Nature. On thy brother Derwent and thy sister Sara, somewhat; but chiefly on
thee. These sonnets thou, I trust, if God preserve thy life, Hartley! thou wilt
read with a deep interest, having learnt to love the plays of Shakespeare, co-
ordinate with Milton, and subordinate only to thy Bible. To thee, I trust, they
will help to explain the mind of Shakespeare, and if thou wouldst understand
these sonnets, thou must read the chapter in Potter's *Antiquities* on the Greek
lovers—of whom were that Theban band of brothers over whom Philip, their
victor, stood weeping; and surveying their dead bodies, each with his shield

over the body of his friend, all dead in the place where they fought, solemnly cursed those whose base, fleshly, and most calumnious fancies had suspected their love of desires against nature. This pure love Shakespeare appears to have felt—to have been in no way ashamed of it—or even to have suspected that others could have suspected it. Yet at the same time he knew that so strong a love would have been made more completely a thing of permanence and reality, and have been blessed more by nature and taken under her more especial protection, if this object of his love had been at the same time a possible object of desire—for nature is not soul only. In this feeling he must have written the twentieth sonnet; but its possibility seems never to have entered even his imagination. It is noticeable that not even an allusion to that very worst of all possible vices (for it is wise to think of the disposition, as a *vice*, not of the absurd and despicable act, as a *crime*) not even any allusion to it [occurs] in all his numerous plays—whereas Jonson, Beaumont and Fletcher, and Massinger are full of them. O my son! I pray fervently that thou may'st know inwardly how impossible it was for a Shakespeare not to have been in his heart's heart chaste. I see no elaborate obscurity and very little quaintness—nor do I know any sonnets that will bear such frequent reperusal: so rich in metre, so full of thought and *exquisitest* diction. S.T. Coleridge. Greta Hall, Keswick, Wed. morning, half past three, Nov. 2, 1803.

1817—John Keats. From *Letters*

One of the great younger poets of the Romantic era, John Keats (1795-1821) was an enthusiastic reader of Shakespeare and actively modeled his own literary efforts on the various achievements of his admired predecessor. With Wordsworth, he was responsible for reviving respectability in the sonnet as an English poetic form. Some of his poems feature clear echoes of Shakespeare's *Sonnets*.

To J. H. Reynolds, 22 November 1817
. . . Why dont you, as I do, look unconcerned at what may be called more particularly Heart-vexations? They never surprize me—lord! a man should have the fine point of his soul taken off to become fit for this world—I like this place very much. There is Hill & Dale and a little River—I went up Box hill this Evening after the Moon—you a' seen the Moon—came down—and wrote some lines. Whenever I am separated from you, and not engaged in a continued Poem—every Letter shall bring you a lyric—but I am too anxious for you to enjoy the whole, to send you a particle. One of the three Books I have with me is

Shakespear's Poems: I neer found so many beauties in the Sonnets—they seem to be full of fine things said unintentionally—in the intensity of working out conceits. Is this to be borne? Hark ye!

> When lofty trees I see barren of leaves
> Which erst from heat did canopy the herd,
> And Summer's green all girded up in sheaves,
> Borne on the bier with white and bristly beard.

He has left nothing to say about nothing or anything: for look at Snails, you know what he says about Snails, you know where he talks about "cockled Snails"—well, in one of these sonnets, he says—the chap slips into—no! I lie! this is in the Venus and Adonis: the Simile brought it to my Mind.

> Audi—As the snail, whose tender horns being hit,
>   Shrinks back into his shelly cave with pain
>   And there all smothered up in shade doth sit,
>   Long after fearing to put forth again:
>   So at his bloody view her eyes are fled,
>   Into the deep dark Cabins of her head.

He overwhelms a genuine Lover of Poesy with all manner of abuse, talking about—

>   "a poet's rage
> And stretched metre of an antique song."

Which by the by will be a capital Motto for my Poem,—won't it?—He speaks too of "Time's antique pen"—and "aprils first born flowers"—and "deaths eternal cold"—By the Whim King! I'll give you a Stanza, because it is not material in connection and when I wrote it I wanted you to—give your vote, pro or con.—

1821—James Boswell. "Preliminary Remarks," from *The Plays and Poems of William Shakespeare*, vol. 20

James Boswell was the son of the more famous James Boswell who was Samuel Johnson's great biographer. He is remembered by his 1821 edition of Shakespeare's works, in 21 volumes, which is often called "Boswell's Malone" because of Boswell's ongoing collaboration with, and continuation of the work of, the eighteenth-century scholar Edmund Malone.

It would, I apprehend, be unnecessary to assign any other reason for reprinting the following poems, than that the editor who undertakes to publish Shakespeare, is bound to present the reader with all his works. Mr. Steevens has, indeed, spoken of them with the utmost bitterness of contempt; but in the course of about forty years, the period which has elapsed since they were first described by that critick as entirely worthless, I will venture to assert that he has not made a convert of a single reader who had any pretensions to poetical taste. That these youthful performances might have been written without those splendid powers which were required for *Othello* and *Macbeth* may be readily admitted, but I question if they would suffer much in a comparison with his early dramatick essays, the *Two Gentlemen of Verona*, *The Comedy of Errors*, or *Love's Labour's Lost*. If they had no other claims to our applause, than that which belongs to their exquisite versification, they would, on that ground alone, be entitled to a high rank among the lighter productions of our poetry. The opinions of Mr. Malone and Mr. Steevens on this subject, will be found as they originally appeared in various parts of this volume; and I have no doubt as to the decision of the public, who, I am satisfied, will gladly welcome an accurate republication of poems glowing with "orient hues" of our great poet's youthful imagination. BOSWELL.

⸺✽⸺ ⸺✽⸺ ⸺✽⸺

1827—William Wordsworth. "Scorn not the Sonnet"

William Wordsworth (1770-1850), along with his dear friend Samuel Taylor Coleridge, was the great introducer of Romantic poetic values to his country's poetry. His reactions to Shakespeare's *Sonnets* were decidedly mixed, but he identified intensely with Shakespeare the poet, and in the sonnet reprinted here, he (as Keats did) defends the sonnet form against earlier critics, calling it a noble vehicle for personal emotion.

Scorn not the Sonnet; Critic, you have frown'd,
 Mindless of its just honours; with this key
 Shakespeare unlock'd his heart; the melody
Of this small lute gave ease to Petrarch's wound;
A thousand times this pipe did Tasso sound;
 With it Camöens sooth'd an exile's grief;
 The Sonnet glitter'd a gay myrtle leaf

Amid the cypress with which Dante crown'd
His visionary brow: a glow-worm lamp,
    It cheer'd mild Spenser, call'd from Faery-land
To struggle through dark ways; and when a damp
    Fell round the path of Milton, in his hand
The Thing became a trumpet; whence he blew
Soul-animating strains—alas, too few!

1833—Samuel Taylor Coleridge. From *Table Talk*

Samuel Taylor Coleridge (1772-1834) was one of the great poets of
the Romantic era, as well as a popular lecturer and respected literary
critic. Influenced by the German Idealists, Coleridge imported this
Continental thinking into the study of English letters, and particularly
of Shakespeare. He is still today considered one of the great readers
of Shakespeare. He perceptively treats the dramatic works in recorded
lectures and in his key text of literary criticism, *Biographia Literaria*, but
his more peripheral comments on *The Sonnets* occur in his marginal
writings in books, as well as in his conversations recorded in *Table Talk*
(see later in this section for an excerpt from 1833). The excerpt below
contains a written note by Wordsworth and then Coleridge's reply.

I believe it possible that a man may, under certain states of the moral feeling,
entertain something deserving the name of love towards a male object—an
affection beyond friendship, and wholly aloof from appetite. In Elizabeth's
and James's time it seems to have been almost fashionable to cherish such a
feeling; and perhaps we may account in some measure for it by considering
how very inferior the women of that age, taken generally, were in education and
accomplishment of mind to the men. Of course there were brilliant exceptions
enough; but the plays of Beaumont and Fletcher—the most popular dramatists
that ever wrote for the English stage—will show us what sort of women it
was generally pleasing to represent. Certainly the language of the two friends
Musidorus and Pyrocles in the Arcadia is such as we could not now use except
to women; and in Cervantes the same tone is sometimes adopted, as in the
novel of the Curious Impertinent. And I think there is a passage in the New
Atlantis of Lord Bacon in which he speaks of the possibility of such a feeling,
but hints the extreme danger of entertaining it, or allowing it any place in a
moral theory. I mention this with reference to Shakespeare's sonnets, which
have been supposed, by some, to be addressed to William Herbert, Earl of

Pembroke, whom Clarendon calls the most beloved man of his age, though his licentiousness was equal to his virtues. I doubt this. I do not think that Shakespeare, merely because he was an actor, would have thought it necessary to veil his emotions towards Pembroke under a disguise, though he might probably have done so if the real object had perchance been a Laura or a Leonora. It seems to me that the sonnets could only have come from a man deeply in love, and in love with a woman; and there is one sonnet which, from its incongruity, I take to be a purposed blind. These extraordinary sonnets form, in fact, a poem of so many stanzas of fourteen lines each; and, like the passion which inspired them, the sonnets are always the same, with a variety of expression,—continuous, if you regard the lover's soul—distinct, if you listen to him, as he heaves them sigh after sigh.

These sonnets, like the *Venus and Adonis*, and the *Rape of Lucrece*, are characterised by boundless fertility and laboured condensation of thought, with perfection of sweetness in rhythm and metre. These are the essentials in the budding of a great poet. Afterwards habit and consciousness of power teach more ease—*praecipitandum liberum spiritum*.

1842—Henry Hallam. From *Introduction to the Literature of Europe in the Fifteenth, Sixteenth, and Seventeenth Centuries*

Henry Hallam (1777-1859) was a popular man of letters and proponent of English and Continental literature in his own day, though his writing feels rather outdated to contemporary readers. He is significant in this context as a later detractor of the perceived moral failings in Shakespeare's *Sonnets*, and in this way he is a critical offspring of the editor George Steevens.

The sonnets of Shakspeare—for we now come to the minor, that is, the shorter and more lyric, poetry of the age—were published in 1609, in a manner as mysterious as their subject and contents. They are dedicated by an editor (Thomas Thorpe, a bookseller) "to Mr. W.H., the only begetter of these sonnets."[1] No one, as far as I remember, has ever doubted their genuineness; no one can doubt that they express not only real, but intense emotions of the heart; but when they were written, who was the W.H. quaintly called their begetter, by which we can only understand the cause of their being written, and to what persons or circumstances they allude, has of late years been the subject of much curiosity. These sonnets were long overlooked; Steevens spoke of them with the utmost scorn, as productions which no one could read; but a very different suffrage is generally given by the lovers of poetry, and perhaps there is now a tendency, especially among young men of poetical tempers, to exaggerate the beauties of these remarkable productions. They rise, indeed, in estimation as we attentively read and reflect upon them; for I do not think that, at first, they give us much pleasure. No one ever entered more fully than Shakspeare into the character of this species of poetry, which admits of no expletive imagery, no merely ornamental line. But, though each sonnet has generally its proper unity, the sense, I do not mean the grammatical construction, will sometimes be found to spread from one to another, independently of that repetition of the leading idea, like variations of an air, which a series of them frequently exhibits, and on account of which they have latterly been reckoned by some rather an integral poem than a collection of sonnets. But this is not uncommon among the Italians, and belongs, in fact, to those of Petrarch himself. They may easily be resolved into several series according to their subjects;[2] but, when read attentively, we find them relate to one definite, though obscure period of the poet's life; in which an attachment to some female, which seems to have touched neither his heart nor his fancy very sensibly, was overpowered, without entirely ceasing, by one to a friend; and this last is of such an enthusiastic character, and so extravagant in the phrases that the author uses, as to have thrown an unaccountable mystery over the whole work. It is true that, in the poetry as well as in the fictions of early ages, we find a more ardent tone of affection in the language of friendship than has since been usual; and yet no instance has been adduced of such rapturous devotedness, such an idolatry of admiring love, as the greatest being whom nature ever produced in the human form pours forth to some unknown youth in the majority of these sonnets.

The notion that a woman was their general object is totally untenable, and it is strange that Coleridge should have entertained it.[3] Those that were evidently addressed to a woman, the person above hinted, are by much the smaller part of the whole, but twenty-eight out of one hundred and fifty-four. And this mysterious Mr. W.H. must be presumed to be the idolized friend of Shakspeare. But who could he be? No one recorded in literary history or anecdote answers the description. But if we seize a clew which innumerable passages give us, and suppose that they allude to a youth of high rank as well as personal beauty and accomplishment, in whose favour and intimacy, according to the base prejudices of the world, a player and a poet, though he were the author of Macbeth, might be thought honoured, something of the strangeness, as it appears to us, of Shakspeare's humiliation in addressing him as a being before whose feet he crouched, whose frown he feared, whose injuries, and those of the most insulting kind—the seduction of the mistress to whom we have alluded—he felt and bewailed without resenting; something, I say, of the strangeness of this humiliation, and at best it is but little, may be lightened and, in a certain sense, rendered intelligible. And it has been ingeniously conjectured within a few years, by inquirers independent of each other, that William Herbert, earl of Pembroke, born in 1580, and afterward a man of noble and gallant character, though always of a licentious life, was shadowed under the initials of Mr. W.H. This hypothesis is not strictly proved, but sufficiently so, in my opinion, to demand our assent.[4]

Notwithstanding the frequent beauties of these sonnets, the pleasure of their perusal is greatly diminished by these circumstances; and it is impossible not to wish that Shakspeare had never written them. There is a weakness and folly in all excessive and misplaced affection, which is not redeemed by the touches of nobler sentiments that abound in this long series of sonnets. But there are also faults of a merely critical nature. The obscurity is often such as only conjecture can penetrate; the strain of tenderness and adoration would be too monotonous were it less unpleasing; and so many frigid conceits are scattered around, that we might almost fancy the poet to have written without genuine emotion, did not such a host of other passages attest the contrary.

NOTES

1. The precise words of the dedication are the following:

"To the only Begetter
Of these ensuing sonnets
Mr. W. H.,
All Happiness
And that eternity promised
By our ever-living poet
Wisheth the
Well-wishing Adventurer
In setting forth
T. T.

The titlepage runs: "Shakspeare's Sonnets, never below imprinted, 4to, 1609. G. Eld for T. T."

2. This has been done in a late publication, Shakespeare's Autobiographical Poems, by George Armitage Brown (1838). It might have occurred to any attentive reader, but I do not know that the analysis was ever so completely made before, though almost every one has been aware that different persons are addressed in the former and latter part of the sonnets. Mr. Brown's work did not fall into my hands till nearly the time that these sheets passed through the press, which I mention on account of some coincidence of opinion, especially as to Shakespeare's knowledge of Latin.

3. "It seems to me that the sonnets could only have come from a man deeply in love, and in love with a woman; and there is one sonnet which, from its incongruity, I take to be a purposed blind."—TableTalk, vol. ii., p. 180. This sonnet the editor supposes to be the twentieth, which certainly could not have been addressed to a woman; but the proof is equally strong as to most of the rest. Coleridge's opinion is absolutely untenable; nor do I conceive that any one else is likely to maintain it

after reading the sonnets of Shakspeare; but to those who have not done this the authority may justly seem imposing.

4. In the Gentleman's Magazine for 1832, p. 217, *et post*, it will be seen that this occurred both to Mr. Boaden and Mr. Heywood Bright. And it does not appear that Mr. Brown, author of the work above quoted, had any knowledge of their priority.

Drake has fixed on Lord Southampton as the object of these sonnets, induced probably by the tradition of his friendship with Shakspeare, and by the latter's having dedicated to him his Venus and Adonis, as well as by what is remarkable on the face of the series of sonnets, that Shakspeare looked up to his friend "with reverence and homage." But, unfortunately, this was only the reverence and homage of an inferior to one of high rank, and not such as the virtues of Southampton might have challenged. Proofs of the low moral character of "Mr. W. H." are continual. It was also impossible that Lord Southampton could be called "beauteous and lovely youth," or "sweet boy." Mrs. Jameson, in her "Loves of the Poets," has adopted the same hypothesis, but is forced, in consequence, to suppose some of the earlier sonnets to be addressed to a woman.

Pembroke succeeded to his father in 1601: I incline to think that the sonnets were written about that time, some probably earlier, some later. That they were the same as Meres, in 1598, has mentioned among the compositions of Shakspeare, "his sugred sonnets among his private friends," I do not believe, both on account of the date, and from the peculiarly personal allusions they contain.

[Much has been written lately on the subject of Shakspeare's sonnets; and a natural reluctance to admit any failings in such a man has led some to fancy that his mistress was no other than his wife, Ann Hathaway, and others to conjecture that he lent his pen to the amours of a friend. But I have seen no ground to alter my own view of the case, except that possibly some other sonnets may have been meant by Meres.—1842.]

1872—Edward Dowden.
From *Shakspere: A Critical Study of His Mind and Art*

Edward Dowden (1843–1913) was an influential Victorian literary critic who wrote memorably on Shakespeare and also edited a popular edition of his works. Continuing his generation's interest in the *Sonnets'* biographical significance, he at least showed sensitivity to what he felt was a sensitive soul recorded by Shakespeare in his poems.

Were there in the life of Shakspere certain events which compelled him to a bitter yet precious gain of experience in the matter of the wrongs of man to man, and from which he procured instruction in the difficult art of bearing oneself justly towards one's wrongers? If the Sonnets of Shakspere, written many years before the close of Shakspere's career as dramatist, be autobiographical, we may perhaps discover the sorrow which first roused his heart and imagination to their long inquisition of evil and grief, and which, sinking down into his great soul, and remaining there until all bitterness had passed away, bore fruit in the most mature of Shakspere's writings, distinguished as these are by serene pathetic strength and stern yet tender beauty.[1]

The Sonnets of Shakspere were probably written during those years when as dramatist he was engaged upon the substantial material of English history, and when he was accumulating those resources which were to make him a wealthy burgher of Stratford. This practical, successful man, who had now arrived at middle age, and was growing rich, who had never found delight, as Marlowe, Nash, Greene, and other wild livers had, in the flimsy idealism of knocking his head against the solid laws of the world, was yet not altogether that self-possessed, cheerful, prudent person, who has stood with some writers for the veritable Shakspere. In the Sonnets we recognise three things—that Shakspere was capable of measureless personal devotion; that he was tenderly sensitive, sensitive above all to every diminution or alteration of that love his heart so eagerly craved; and that when wronged, although he suffered anguish, he transcended his private injury, and learned to forgive. There are lovers of Shakspere so jealous of his honour that they are unable to suppose that any grave moral flaw could have impaired the nobility of his life and manhood. Shakspere, as he is discovered in his poems and his plays, appears rather to have been a man who by strenuous effort, and with the aid of the good powers of the world, was saved, so as by fire. Before Shakspere zealots demand our attention to ingenious theories which help us to credit the immaculateness of Shakspere's life, let them prove to us that his writings never offend. When they have shown that Shakspere's poetry possesses the proud virginity of Milton's poetry, they may go on to show that Shakspere's youth was devoted, like the youth of Milton, to an ideal of moral elevation and purity. When we have been convinced that the same moral and spiritual temper which gave rise to the "Comus" gave rise to the "Venus and Adonis," we shall think it probable that Shakspere could have uttered the proud words about his unspotted life that Milton uttered.

Assuredly the inference from Shakspere's writings is not that he held himself with virginal strength and pride remote from the blameful pleasures of the world. What no reader will find anywhere in the plays or poems of Shakspere is a cold-blooded, hard, or selfish line; all is warm, sensitive, vital, radiant with delight, or a-thrill with pain. And what we may dare to affirm of Shakspere's life is that whatever its sins may have been, they were not hard, selfish, deliberate, cold-blooded sins. The errors of his heart originated in his sensitiveness, in his imagination (not at first inured to the hardness of fidelity to the fact), in his quick consciousness of existence, and in the self-abandoning devotion of his heart. There are some noble lines by Chapman, in which he pictures to himself the life of great energy, enthusiasms, and passions, which for ever stands upon the edge of utmost danger, and yet for ever remains in absolute security:—

> Give me the spirit that on this life's rough sea
> Loves to have his sails fill'd with a lusty wind
> Even till his sail-yards tremble, his masts crack,
> And his rapt ship ran on her side so low
> That she drinks water, and her keel ploughs air;
> There is no danger to a man that knows
> What life and death is,—there's not any law
> Exceeds his knowledge; neither is it lawful
> That he should stoop to any other law.[2]

Such a master-spirit, pressing forward under strained canvas, was Shakspere. If the ship dipped and drank water, she rose again; and at length we behold her within view of her haven, sailing under a large, calm wind, not without tokens of stress of weather, but if battered, yet unbroken by the waves. It is to dull, lethargic natures that a moral accident is fatal, because they are tending nowhither, and lack energy and momentum to right themselves again. To say anything against decent, lethargic vices, and timid virtues, anything to the advantage of the strenuous life of bold action and eager emotion, which necessarily incurs risks, and sometimes suffers, is, we shall be told, "dangerous." Well, then, be it so; it is dangerous.

The Shakspere whom we discern in the Sonnets had certainly not attained the broad mastery of life which the Stratford bust asserts to have been Shakspere's in his closing years. Life had been found good by him who owned those lips, and whose spirit declares itself in the massive animation of the total outlook of that face.[3] When the greater number of these Sonnets were written Shakspere could have understood Romeo; he could have understood Hamlet; he could not have conceived Duke Prospero. Under the joyous exterior of those days lay a craving, sensitive, unsatisfied heart, which had not entire possession of itself, which could misplace its affections, and resort to all those pathetic frauds, by which misplaced affections strive to conceal an error from themselves. The friend in whose personality Shakspere found a source of measureless delight—high-born, beautiful, young, clever, accomplished, ardent—wronged him. The woman from whom Shakspere for a time received a joyous quickening of his life, which was half pain—a woman of stained character, and the reverse of beautiful, but a strong nature, intellectual, a lover of art, and possessed of curious magnetic attraction, with her dark eyes which illuminated a pale face—wronged him also. Shakspere bitterly felt the wrong—felt most bitterly the wrong which was least to be expected, that of his friend. It has been held to be an additional baseness that Shakspere could forgive, that he could rescue himself from indignant resentment, and adjust his nature to the altered circumstances. Possibly Shakspere may not have subscribed to all the items in the code of honour; he may not have regarded as inviolable the prohibited degrees of forgiveness. He may have seen that the wrong done to him was human, natural, almost inevitable. He certainly saw that the chief wrong was not that done to him, but committed by his friend against his own better nature. Delivering his heart from the prepossessions of wounded personal feeling, and looking at the circumstances as they actually were, he may have found it very natural and necessary not to banish from his heart the man he loved. However this may have been, his own sanity and strength, and the purity of his work as artist depended on his ultimately delivering his soul from all bitterness. Besides, life was not exhausted. The ship righted itself, and went ploughing forward across a broad sea. Shakspere found ever more and more in life to afford adequate sustenance for man's highest needs of intellect and of heart. Life became ever more encircled with presences of beauty, of goodness, and of terror; and Shakspere's fortitude of heart increased. Nevertheless, such experiences as those recorded in the Sonnets could not pass out of his life, and in the imaginative recurrence of past moods might at any subsequent time become motives of his art. Passion had been purified; and at last the truth of things stood out clear and calm.[4]

The Sonnets tell more of Shakspere's sensitiveness than of Shakspere's strength. In the earlier poems of the collection, his delight in human beauty, intellect, grace, expresses itself with endless variation. Nothing seems to him more admirable than manhood. But this joy is controlled and saddened by a sense of the transitoriness of all things, the ruin of time, the inevitable progress of decay. The love expressed in the early Sonnets is love which has known no sorrow, no change, no wrong; it is an ecstasy which the sensitive heart is as yet unable to control:

> As an unperfect actor on the stage
> Who with his fear is put beside his part,
> Or some fierce thing replete with too much rage,
> Whose strength's abundance weakens his own heart,
> So I, for fear of trust, forget to say
> The perfect ceremony of love's rite,
> And in mine own love's strength seem to decay,
> O'ercharged with burden of mine own love's might.

The prudent and sober Shakspere—was it he who bore this burden of too much love, he whose heart was made weak by the abundance of its strength? He cannot sleep: he lies awake, haunted in the darkness by the face that is dear to him. He falls into sudden moods of despondency, when his own gifts seem narrow and of little worth, when his poems, which yield him his keenest enjoyment, seem wretchedly remote from what he had dreamed, and in the midst of his depression he almost despises himself because he is depressed:

> Wishing me like to one more rich in hope,
> Featured like him, like him with friends possessed,
> Desiring this man's art, and that man's scope,
> With what I most enjoy contented least.[5]

He weeps for the loss of precious friends, for "love's long-since-cancelled woe;" but out of all these clouds and damps the thought of one human soul, which he believes beautiful, can deliver him:

> Haply I think on thee, and then my state,
> Like to the lark at break of day arising
> From sullen earth, sings hymns at heaven's gate.

Then comes the bitter discovery,—a change in love that had seemed to be made for eternity; coldness, estrangement, wrongs upon both sides; and at the same time external trials and troubles arise, and the injurious life of actor and playwright—injurious to the delicate harmony and purity of the poet's nature— becomes more irksome:

> And almost thence my nature is subdued
> To what it works in, like the dyer's hand.

He pathetically begs, not now for love, but for pity. Yet at the worst, and through all suffering, he believes in love:

> Let me not to the marriage of true minds
> Admit impediments. Love is not love
> Which alters when it alteration finds.

It can accept its object even though imperfect, and still love on. It is not in the common acceptation of the word prudential—but the *infinite* prudence of the heart is indeed no other than love:

> It fears not Policy, that heretic
> Which works on leases of short-numbered hours,
> But all alone stands hugely politic,
> That it nor glows with heat, nor drowns with showers.

He has learnt his lesson; his romantic attachment, which attributed an impossible perfection to his friend, has become the stronger love which accepts his friend and knows the fact; knows the fact of frailty and imperfection; knows also the greater and infinitely precious fact of central and surviving loyalty and goodness: and this new love is better than the old, because more real:

> Oh benefit of ill! now I find true
> That better is by evil still made better;
> And ruined love, when it is built anew,
> Grows fairer than at first, more strong, far greater.

And thus he possesses his soul once more; he "returns to his content."

Such, briefly and imperfectly hinted, is the spirit of Shakspere's Sonnets. A great living poet, who has dedicated to the subject of friendship one division of his collected works, has written these words:

> Recorders ages hence?
> Come, I will take you down underneath this impassive exterior,—
> I will tell you what to say of me;
> Publish my name, and hang up my picture as that of the tenderest lover.

And, elsewhere of these Calamus poems, the poems of tender and hardy friendship, he says:

> Here the frailest leaves of me, and yet my strongest-lasting:
> Here I shade and hide my thoughts—I myself do not expose them,
> And yet they expose me more than all my other poems.

These words of Whitman may be taken as a motto of the Sonnets of Shakspere. In these poems Shakspere has hid himself, and is exposed.

NOTES

1. I shall not enter into the controversy as to the interpretation of the Sonnets. The principal theories held with respect to them may be classified as follows: I. They are poems about an imaginary friendship and love; Dyce, Delius, H. Morley. II. They are partly imaginary, partly autobiographical; C. Knight, H. von Friesen, R. Simpson (On the Italian love-philosophy see Simpson's interesting "Philosophy of Shakespeare's Sonnets," Trübner, 1868). III. They form a great allegory; Dr Barnstorff ("Schlüssel zu Shakspere's Sonnetten," 1860. Mr W. H. = Mr William Himself!), Mr Heraud ("Shakspere's Inner Life." The young friend = Ideal Manhood), Carl Karpf. IV. They are autobiographical; (a) Mr W. H. = Henry Wriothesley (the initials reversed), Earl of Southampton:—Drake, Gervinus, Kreyssig, and others; (b) Mr W. H. = Mr William Herbert, Earl of Pembroke:—Bright, Boaden, A. Brown, Hallam, H. Brown. V. They were partly addressed to Southampton;

other sonnets were written in his name to Elizabeth Vernon; other some, to South-ampton in E. Vernon's name; and subsequently the Earl of Pembroke engaged Shakspere to write sonnets on his behalf to the dark woman, Lady Rich. Of part of this theory the first suggestion was given by Mrs Jameson. It was elaborated by Mr Gerald Massey in the *Quarterly Review*, April 1864, and in his large volume "Shakspeare's Sonnets, and his Private Friends." The peculiarity of Mr Henry Brown's interpretation ("The Sonnets of Shakespeare Solved." J. R. Smith. 1870.) is, that he discovers in the sonnets an intention of Shakspere to parody or jest at the fashionable love-poetry and love-philosophy of the day. See on this subject the articles by Delius and by H. von Friesen in Shakespeare Jahrbücher, vols. i. and iv.; the chapter "Shakspere's episch-lyrische Gedichte und Sonnette" in H. von Friesen's "Altengland und William Shakspere" (1874); and "Der Mythus von Wil-liam Shakspere," by N. Delius (Bonn, 1851), pp. 29–31. Critics whose minds are of the business-like, matter-of-fact, prosaic type cannot conceive how the poems could be autobiographical. Coleridge, on the other hand, found no difficulty in believing them to be such; and Wordsworth emphatically declares them to express Shakspere's "own feelings in his own person."

2. Byron's Conspiracy, *Act* iii. *Scene* 1 (last lines).

3. This is the more remarkable, because the original of the bust was almost certainly a mask taken after death; and the bust betrays the presence of physical death, over which however life triumphs.

4. All that refers in the above paragraph to the supposed facts, which underlie the Sonnets, may be taken with reserve. Only, if this portion of "the mythus of Shakspere" be no myth but a reality, the interpretation of events in their moral aspect given above is the one borne out by the Sonnets and by Shakspere's subse-quent life.

5. From its connection, we may infer that this last line refers to Shakspere's poems and plays.

1876—Robert Browning. "House"

Robert Browning (1812–1889), along with Alfred, Lord Tennyson, is arguably the greatest of Victorian poets, and he is unmatched by his contemporaries as one of English literature's most prolific and influ-ential poet-critics. In "House," Browning famously takes issue with Wordsworth's assumptions of transparent authorial personality in *The Sonnets*. Most famous for his diverse dramatic monologues, Browning had a vested interest in asserting the impersonality that he thought most admirable in Shakespeare's sequence.

1

Shall I sonnet-sing you about myself?
  Do I live in a house you would like to see?

Is it scant of gear, has it store of pelf?
  "Unlock my heart with a sonnet-key?"

   2

Invite the world, as my betters have done?
  "Take notice: this building remains on view,
Its suites of reception every one,
  Its private apartment and bedroom too;

   3

"For a ticket, apply to the Publisher."
   No: thanking the public I must decline.
A peep through my window, if folk prefer;
  But, please you, no foot over threshold of mine!

   4

I have mixed with a crowd and heard free talk
  In a foreign land where an earthquake chanced;
And a house stood gaping, naught to balk
  Man's eye wherever he gazed or glanced.

   5

The whole of the frontage shaven sheer,
  The inside gaped: exposed to day,
Right and wrong and common and queer,
  Bare, as the palm of your hand, it lay.

   6

The owner? Oh, he had been crushed, no doubt!
  "Odd tables and chairs for a man of wealth!
What a parcel of musty old books about!
  He smoked—no wonder he lost his health!

   7

"I doubt he bathed before he dressed.
  A brazier?—the pagan, he burned perfumes!
You see it is proved, what the neighbours guessed:
  His wife and himself had separate rooms."

   8

Friends, the goodman of the house at least
  Kept house to himself till an earthquake came:

'Tis the fall of its frontage permits you feast
   On the inside arrangement you praise or blame.

9

Outside should suffice for evidence:
   And whoso desires to penetrate
Deeper, must dive by the spirit sense—
   No optics like yours, at any rate!

10

"Hoity toity! A street to explore,
   Your house is the exception! 'With this same key
Shakespeare unlocked his heart,' once more"
   Did Shakespeare? If so, the less Shakespeare he!

—⁓⁓— —⁓⁓— —⁓⁓—

1879—Algernon Charles Swinburne.
From *A Study of Shakespeare*

Algernon Charles Swinburne (1837-1909) was a popular Victorian poet and critic, one most remembered today for his formal intricacies, highly ornate style, and energetic "poet's" life. Though his works have gone in and out of critical favor, some of his verse volumes have been more constantly regarded.

Considering that his two attempts at narrative or rather semi-narrative and semi-reflective poet belong obviously to an early stage of his earliest period, we may rather here than elsewhere take notice that there are some curious points of coincidence for evil as for good between the fortunes of Shakespeare's plays and the fortunes of his poems. In either case we find that some part at least of his earlier and inferior work has fared better at the blind hands of chance and the brutish hands of printers than some part at least of his riper and more precious products. His two early poems would seem to have had the good hap of his personal supervision in their passage through the press. Upon them, at least since the time of Coleridge, who as usual has said on this subject the first and the last word that need be said, it seems to me that fully sufficient notice and fully adequate examination have been expended; and that nothing at once new and true can now be profitably said in praise or in dispraise of them. Of *A Lover's Complaint,* marked as it is throughout with every possible sign suggestive of a far later date and a far different inspiration, I have only space or need to remark that it contains two of the most exquisitely Shakespearean verses ever vouchsafed to us by Shakespeare, and two of the most execrably euphuistic or dysphuistic lines ever inflicted on us by man. Upon the Sonnets such a preposterous pyramid of presumptuous commentary has long since been reared by the Cimmerian speculation and Boeotian "brain-sweat" of sciolists and scholiasts, that no modest man will hope and no wise man will desire to add to the structure or subtract from it one single brick of proof or disproof, theorem or theory. As yet the one contemporary book which has ever been supposed to throw any direct or indirect light on the mystic matter remains as inaccessible and unhelpful to students as though it had never been published fifteen years earlier than the date of their publication and four years before the book in which Meres notices the circulation of Shakespeare's "sugared sonnets among his private friends." It would be a most noble and thankworthy addition to a list of labours beyond praise and benefits beyond price, if my honoured friend Dr. Grosart could find the means to put a crown upon the achievements of his learning and a seal upon the obligations of our gratitude by the one inestimable boon long hoped for against hoping, and as yet but "a vision in a dream" to the most learned and most loving of true Shakespearean students; by the issue or reissue in its full and perfect likeness, collated at last and complete, of *Willobie his Avisa*.[1]

It was long since more than time that the worthless and impudent imposture called *The Passionate Pilgrim* should be exposed and expelled from its station at the far end of Shakespeare's poems. What Coleridge said of Ben Jonson's epithet for "turtle-footed peace," we may say of the label affixed to this rag-picker's bag of stolen goods: *The Passionate Pilgrim* is a pretty title, a very pretty title; pray what may it mean? In all the larcenous little bundle of verse there is neither a poem which bears that name nor a poem by which that name would be bearable. The publisher of the booklet was like "one Ragozine, a most notorious pirate"; and the method no less than the motive of his rascality in the present instance is palpable and simple enough. Fired by the immediate and instantly proverbial popularity of Shakespeare's *Venus and Adonis*, he hired, we may suppose, some ready hack of unclean hand to supply him with three doggrel sonnets on the same subject, noticeable only for their porcine quality of prurience: he procured by some means a rough copy or an incorrect transcript of two genuine and unpublished sonnets by Shakespeare, which with the acute instinct of a felonious tradesman he laid atop of his worthless wares by way of gilding to their base metal: he stole from the two years published text of *Love's Labour's Lost*, and reproduced with more or less mutilation or corruption, the sonnet of Longavile, the "canzonet" of Biron, and the far lovelier love-song of Dumaine. The rest of the ragman's gatherings, with three most notable exceptions, is little better for the most part than dry rubbish or disgusting refuse; unless a plea may haply be put in for the pretty commonplaces of the lines on a "sweet rose, fair flower," and so forth; for the couple of thin and pallid if tender and tolerable copies of verse on "Beauty" and "Good Night," or the passably light and lively stray of song on "crabbed age and youth." I need not say that those three exceptions are the stolen and garbled work of Marlowe and of Barnfield, our elder Shelley and our first-born Keats; the singer of Cynthia in verse well worthy of Endymion, who would seem to have died as a poet in the same fatal year of his age that Keats died as a man; the first adequate English laureate of the nightingale, to be supplanted or equalled by none until the advent of his mightier brother.

NOTES

1. Since this passage first went to press, I have received from Dr. Grosart the most happy news that he has procured a perfect copy of this precious volume, and will shortly add it to his occasional issues of golden waifs and strays forgotten by the ebb-tide of time. Not even the disinterment of Robert Chester's "glorified" poem, with its appended jewels of verse from Shakespeare's very hand and from others only less great than Shakespeare's, all now at last reset in their strange original framework, was a gift of greater price than this.

———

1879—Sidney Lanier.
From *Shakspere and His Forerunners*

A soldier in the American Civil War and a native of the South, Sidney Lanier (1842-1881) was also a popular musician, poet, and lecturer at Johns Hopkins University.

In passing on to Shakspere's sonnets, I present you with another type of the lover, differing wholly from those who have gone before.

You all recollect that the body of poems published under the general title of Shakspere's Sonnets consists of two distinct series, one of which is addressed to the man that he loved, and the other to the woman that he loved. To-day I place before you only a few of the first-named series: for of course I will not attempt any general treatment of the subject in this space. These incomparable poems are of such suggestiveness to me that if I should have been lecturing to you on them for a whole year previously I should still be in just as much want of space to finish what should be said of them—by which I mean simply that they seem to me inexhaustible incentives to thought.

The principle of selection upon which I have arranged such sonnets as I read is the setting forth of something like a connected account of Shakspere's affection for the man who inspired this first series. You will remember we found five sonnets of Drummond's which made a sort of connected drama of his unfortunate love. Let us see how Shakspere fared along the thorny path of friendship.

For a special purpose, let me say in advance that he fared but ill. You will see, as I read, that the man upon whom William Shakspere lavished his heart, in such love as few other men could give and in such poetry as no other man could write, basely betrayed him. He committed against Shakspere the most unpardonable crime of crimes, in taking advantage of their friendship to supplant him in the favour of the woman that he loved. You will see—and this the main point to which I am bringing you—that Shakspere forgave this bitter sin, voluntarily, freely, even inventing gentle excuses for it, with a magnificence of generosity to be compared with nothing but the generosity of this earth, which, the more we wound it with our ploughs and scarify it with our many-toothed harrows and rakes, so much the more returns us its immeasurable exuberance of corn for our bodies and of flowers for our souls. You will see how it was with this same immeasurable exuberance that Shakspere loved, that he praised, that he suffered, that he forgave.

And let me further remind you that we are presented with a precisely parallel set of facts in the life of Beethoven. You will probably remember with what wonderful clinging affection Beethoven pertinaciously cherished his nephew for so many years; and how the nephew was all the time but a graceless scamp, who wasted in riotous living the hard-earned money which came in for the immortal symphonies and sonatas, until at last the poor deaf old musician, whom nature and man seemed to have conspired to torment, lay down in his bleak lodgings and breathed out the breath of the most consummate artist this world has yet known. Does not, by the way, this piteous history of these two geniuses, who stand, so far, alone, each upon his own height of excellence, set us to pondering whether the sunlight and springtime are not, after all, less fruitful than darkness and winter? Passing by our astonishment that any human being could have despised the friendship of William Shakspere, that any human being could have set his contemptuous foot upon the faithful love of Ludwig van Beethoven, is it not wonderful that after shredding away from these two men's lives all that was merely incidental, or that stood for connective tissue simply, we find sorrow to have been the main fibre of their being? Is it, then, that not only the cruelty of the coy Delia or Diana inspires the sonnet, but that the cruelty of that other, more coy lady, Happiness, inspires all the works of genius? Must we say that sorrow is the nourisher of poetry and music, and that she stands—a veiled figure—ever by the germs of art, to mulch them with the ashes and dead leaves of hope, and to water them with her tears? Is art like that peculiar lily of the East Indies, of which I have read, that will only grow when watered with ice-water? Does the star of inspiration come out only when trouble has brought on the night of the soul? Are the poets and the musicians a sort of nightingales of time, who can sing only when it is dark?

He is a braver man than I who will attempt a categorical answer to these questions. But it is not merely to leave them unanswered that I have asked them. I wished that you might have them in your mind while we are studying these sonnets, to the end that I may return to them again, when I have finished, and draw from them at least one lesson which I think all of us here will find practically useful in our hurrying modern life.

Hear Shakspere, then, beginning to set forth his love for this extraordinary young man who had so taken his heart. This sonnet, and several of those immediately following it, are particularly interesting to me as revealing the man Shakspere. Our love and admiration yearn for a definite personality; we long to see him and kiss his hands. Here, then, we behold some traits of him: we find, for example, that he thinks of his own verses, and that he anticipates immortality for them; we find him longing for his friend, wretched in absence, brooding upon death, fixing ideals of constancy, loving, suffering, forgiving.

I begin with Sonnet XVIII. It is addressed to his young friend:

Shall I compare thee to a summer's day?
Thou art more lovely and more temperate:
Rough winds do shake the darling buds of May,
And summer's lease hath all too short a date:
Sometime too hot the eye of Heaven shines,
And often is his gold complexion dimm'd;
And every fair from fair sometime declines,
By chance, or nature's changing course untrimm'd;
But thy eternal summer shall not fade,
Nor lose possession of that fair thou owest;
Nor shall Death brag thou wander'st in his shade,
When in eternal lines to time thou growest;
    So long as men can breathe, or eyes can see,
    So long lives this, and this gives life to thee.

In the next sonnet Shakspere makes a beautiful extension of this central thought. Here he tells his young friend that not only shall he live to all time in this verse, but he shall live *young*: for the verse paints him at that time of life, so that what posterity shall read will be the record of his youth. This must remind us of the exquisite way in which John Keats has used a similar idea in his *Ode on a Grecian Urn*.

You remember that the urn which he addresses bears on its sides sculptured representations of a Greek youth in loving pursuit of a maiden and almost in the act of embracing her. Keats first brings out the melancholy thought that the youth, sculptured in the stone as he is, can never catch the maiden, but must always stand there, with outstretched arms, upon the very point and sweet verge of bliss. Immediately, however, the poet calls up the happier fancy that as these figures are sculptured young, they must ever remain so:

> Bold Lover, never, never canst thou kiss,
> Though winning near the goal—yet, do not grieve
> She cannot fade, though thou hast not thy bliss,
> For ever wilt thou love, and she be fair!

Shakspere says in Sonnet XIX:

> Devouring Time, blunt thou the lion's paws,
> And make the earth devour her own sweet brood;
> Pluck the keen teeth from the fierce tiger's jaws,
> And burn the long-liv'd phoenix in her blood;
> Make glad and sorry seasons, as thou fleet'st,
> And do whate'er thou wilt, swift-footed Time,
> To the wide world and all her fading sweets;
> But I forbid thee one most heinous crime
> O carve not with thy hours my love's fair brow
> Nor draw no lines there with thine antique pen;
> Him in thy course untainted do allow,
> For beauty's pattern to succeeding men.
> Yet, do thy worst, old Time; despite thy wrong,
> My love shall in my verse ever live young.

In the next sonnet the poet entirely departs from that employment of unbounded hyperbole which is usually regarded as the special prerogative of the sonnet-writer. He announces his intention to praise his young friend truly and soberly, and in the last line insinuates that he is led to this course by remarking that men who praise their wares overmuch usually do so with the intention of *selling* them. As he does not intend to sell his love, he will not "praise," using that term here in the sense of overpraising.

The word "rondure" in this sonnet you will recognise as coming from the same root as *round*, and means here the circumference, implying also the spheric contents, of the atmosphere which embraces everything on the surface of the earth.

XXI

So is it not with me as with that muse,
Stirr'd by a painted beauty to his verse;
Who heaven itself for ornament doth use,
And every fair with his fair doth rehearse,

Making a couplement of proud compare
With sun and moon, with earth and sea's rich gems,
With April's first-born flowers, and all things rare,
That heaven's air in this huge rondure hems.
O! let me, true in love, but truly write,
And then believe me, my love is as fair
As any mother's child, though not so bright
As those gold candles fixed in heaven's air:
      Let them say more that like of hearsay well;
      I will not praise that purpose not to sell.

1889—Oscar Wilde. "The Portrait of Mr. W. H.," from *Blackwood's Magazine*

Oscar Wilde was one of the great writers of the Victorian age and one of the greatest wits in all of English literature. Accomplished in both playwriting and poetry like Shakespeare before him, Wilde felt he had "solved" the mystery surrounding Shakespeare's *Sonnets* in his *Portrait of Mr. W. H.* In fact, he had mainly taken up a hypothesis first addressed in the previous century by Thomas Tyrwhitt and Edmund Malone.

I had been dining with Erskine in his pretty little house in Birdcage Walk, and we were sitting in the library over our coffee and cigarettes, when the question of literary forgeries happened to turn up in conversation. I cannot at present remember how it was that we struck upon this somewhat curious topic, as it was at that time, but I know that we had a long discussion about Macpherson, Ireland, and Chatterton, and that with regard to the last I insisted that his so-called forgeries were merely the result of an artistic desire for perfect representation; that we had no right to quarrel with an artist for the conditions under which he chooses to present his work; and that all Art being to a certain degree a mode of acting, an attempt to realise one's own personality on some imaginative plane out of reach of the trammelling accidents and limitations of real life, to censure an artist for a forgery was to confuse an ethical with an aesthetical problem.

Erskine, who was a good deal older than I was, and had been listening to me with the amused deference of a man of forty, suddenly put his hand upon my shoulder and said to me, 'What would you say about a young man who had a strange theory about a certain work of art, believed in his theory, and committed a forgery in order to prove it?'

'Ah! that is quite a different matter,' I answered.

Erskine remained silent for a few moments, looking at the thin grey threads of smoke that were rising from his cigarette. 'Yes,' he said, after a pause, 'quite different.'

There was something in the tone of his voice, a slight touch of bitterness perhaps, that excited my curiosity. 'Did you ever know anybody who did that?' I cried.

'Yes,' he answered, throwing his cigarette into the fire,—'a great friend of mine, Cyril Graham. He was very fascinating, and very foolish, and very heartless. However, he left me the only legacy I ever received in my life.'

'What was that?' I exclaimed. Erskine rose from his seat, and going over to a tall inlaid cabinet that stood between the two windows, unlocked it, and came back to where I was sitting, holding in his hand a small panel picture set in an old and somewhat tarnished Elizabethan frame.

It was a full-length portrait of a young man in late sixteenth-century costume, standing by a table, with his right hand resting on an open book. He seemed about seventeen years of age, and was of quite extraordinary personal beauty, though evidently somewhat effeminate. Indeed, had it not been for the dress and the closely cropped hair, one would have said that the face, with its dreamy wistful eyes, and its delicate scarlet lips, was the face of a girl. In manner, and especially in the treatment of the hands, the picture reminded one of François Clouet's later work. The black velvet doublet with its fantastically gilded points, and the peacock-blue background against which it showed up so pleasantly, and from which it gained such luminous value of colour, were quite in Clouet's style; and the two masks of Tragedy and Comedy that hung somewhat formally from the marble pedestal had that hard severity of touch so different from the facile grace of the Italians—which even at the Court of France the great Flemish master never completely lost, and which in itself has always been a characteristic of the northern temper.

'It is a charming thing,' I cried, 'but who is this wonderful young man, whose beauty Art has so happily preserved for us?'

'This is the portrait of Mr. W.H.,' said Erskine, with a sad smile. It might have been a chance effect of light, but it seemed to me that his eyes were quite bright with tears.

'Mr. W.H!' I exclaimed; 'who was Mr. W.H.?'

'Don't you remember?' he answered; 'look at the book on which his hand is resting.'

'I see there is some writing there, but I cannot make it out,' I replied.

'Take this magnifying-glass and try,' said Erskine, with the same sad smile still playing about his mouth.

I took the glass, and moving the lamp a little nearer, I began to spell out the crabbed sixteenth-century handwriting. 'To the onlie begetter of these insuing sonnets.'. . . 'Good heavens!' I cried, 'is this Shakespeare's Mr. W.H.?'

'Cyril Graham used to say so,' muttered Erskine. 'But it is not a bit like Lord Pembroke,' I answered. 'I know the Penshurst portraits very well. I was staying near there a few weeks ago.'

'Do you really believe then that the Sonnets are addressed to Lord Pembroke?' he asked.

'I am sure of it,' I answered. 'Pembroke, Shakespeare, and Mrs. Mary Fitton are the three personages of the Sonnets; there is no doubt at all about it.'

'Well, I agree with you,' said Erskine, 'but I did not always think so. I used to believe—well, I suppose I used to believe in Cyril Graham and his theory.'

'And what was that?' I asked, looking at the wonderful portrait, which had already begun to have a strange fascination for me.

'It is a long story,' said Erskine, taking the picture away from me—rather abruptly I thought at the time—'a very long story; but if you care to hear it, I will tell it to you.'

'I love theories about the Sonnets,' I cried; 'but I don't think I am likely to be converted to any new idea. The matter has ceased to be a mystery to any one. Indeed, I wonder that it ever was a mystery.'

'As I don't believe in the theory, I am not likely to convert you to it,' said Erskine, laughing; 'but it may interest you.'

'Tell it to me, of course,' I answered. 'If it is half as delightful as the picture, I shall be more than satisfied.'

'Well,' said Erskine, lighting a cigarette, 'I must begin by telling you about Cyril Graham himself. He and I were at the same house at Eton. I was a year or two older than he was, but we were immense friends, and did all our work and all our play together. There was, of course, a good deal more play than work, but I cannot say that I am sorry for that. It is always an advantage not to have received a sound commercial education, and what I learned in the playing fields at Eton has been quite as useful to me as anything I was taught at Cambridge. I should tell you that Cyril's father and mother were both dead. They had been drowned in a horrible yachting accident off the Isle of Wight. His father had been in the diplomatic service, and had married a daughter, the only daughter, in fact, of old Lord Crediton, who became Cyril's guardian after the death of his parents. I don't think that Lord Crediton cared very much for Cyril. He had never really forgiven his daughter for marrying a man who had not a title. He was an extraordinary old aristocrat, who swore like a costermonger, and had the manners of a farmer. I remember seeing him once on Speech-day. He growled at me, gave me a sovereign, and told me not to grow up "a damned Radical" like my father. Cyril had very little affection for him, and was only too glad to spend most of his holidays with us in Scotland. They never really got on together at all. Cyril thought him a bear, and he thought Cyril effeminate. He was effeminate, I suppose, in some things, though he was a very good rider and a capital fencer. In fact he got the foils before he left Eton. But he was very languid in his manner, and not a little vain of his good looks, and had a strong objection to football. The two things that really gave him pleasure were poetry and acting. At Eton he was always dressing up and reciting Shakespeare, and when we went up to Trinity he became a member of the A.D.C. his first term. I remember I was always very jealous of his acting. I was absurdly devoted to him; I suppose because we were so different in some things. I was a rather awkward, weakly lad, with huge feet, and horribly freckled. Freckles run in Scotch families just as gout does in English families. Cyril used to say that of the two he preferred the gout; but he always set an absurdly high value on personal appearance, and once read a paper before our debating society to prove that it was better to be good-looking than to be good. He certainly was wonderfully handsome. People who did not like him, Philistines and college tutors, and young men reading for the Church, used to say that he was merely pretty; but there was a great deal more in his face than mere prettiness. I think he was the most splendid creature I ever saw, and nothing could exceed the grace of his movements, the charm of his manner. He fascinated everybody who was worth fascinating, and a great many people who were not. He was often wilful and petulant, and I used to think him dreadfully insincere. It was due, I think, chiefly to his inordinate desire to please. Poor Cyril! I told him once that he was contented with very cheap triumphs, but he only laughed. He was horribly spoiled. All charming people, I fancy, are spoiled. It is the secret of their attraction.

'However, I must tell you about Cyril's acting. You know that no actresses are allowed to play at the A.D.C. At least they were not in my time. I don't know how it is now. Well, of course Cyril was always cast for the girls' parts, and when *As You Like It* was produced he played Rosalind. It was a marvellous performance. In fact, Cyril Graham was the only perfect Rosalind I have ever seen. It would be impossible to describe to you the beauty, the delicacy, the refinement of the whole thing. It made an immense sensation, and the horrid little theatre, as it was then, was crowded every night. Even when I read the play now I can't help thinking of Cyril. It might have been written for him. The next term he took his degree, and came to London to read for the diplomatic. But he never did any work. He spent his days in reading Shakespeare's Sonnets, and his evenings at the theatre. He was, of course, wild to go on the stage. It was all that I and Lord Crediton could do to prevent him. Perhaps if he had gone on the stage he would be alive now. It is always a silly thing to give advice, but to give good advice is absolutely fatal. I hope you will never fall into that error. If you do, you will be sorry for it.

'Well, to come to the real point of the story, one day I got a letter from Cyril asking me to come round to his rooms that evening. He had charming chambers in Piccadilly overlooking the Green Park, and as I used to go to see him every day, I was rather surprised at his taking the trouble to write. Of course I went, and when I arrived I found him in a state of great excitement.

He told me that he had at last discovered the true secret of Shakespeare's Sonnets; that all the scholars and critics had been entirely on the wrong tack; and that he was the first who, working purely by internal evidence, had found out who Mr. W.H. really was. He was perfectly wild with delight, and for a long time would not tell me his theory. Finally, he produced a bundle of notes, took his copy of the Sonnets off the mantelpiece, and sat down and gave me a long lecture on the whole subject.

'He began by pointing out that the young man to whom Shakespeare addressed these strangely passionate poems must have been somebody who was a really vital factor in the development of his dramatic art, and that this could not be said either of Lord Pembroke or Lord Southampton. Indeed, whoever he was, he could not have been anybody of high birth, as was shown very clearly by the 25th Sonnet, in which Shakespeare contrasts himself with those who are "great princes' favourites," says quite frankly—

Let those who are in favour with their stars
Of public honour and proud titles boast,
Whilst I, whom fortune of such triumph bars,
Unlook'd for joy in that I honour most.

and ends the sonnet by congratulating himself on the mean state of him he so adored:

Then happy I, that loved and am beloved
Where I may not remove nor be removed.

This sonnet Cyril declared would be quite unintelligible if we fancied that it was addressed to either the Earl of Pembroke or the Earl of Southampton, both of whom were men of the highest position in England and fully entitled to be called "great princes"; and he in corroboration of his view read me Sonnets CXXIV and CXXV, in which Shakespeare tells us that his love is not "the child of state," that it "suffers not in smiling pomp," but is "builded far from accident." I listened with a good deal of interest, for I don't think the point had ever been made before; but what followed was still more curious, and seemed to me at the time to entirely dispose of Pembroke's claim. We know from Meres that the Sonnets had been written before 1598, and Sonnet CIV informs us that Shakespeare's friendship for Mr. W.H. had been already in existence for three years. Now Lord Pembroke, who was born in 1580, did not come to London till he was eighteen years of age, that is to say till 1598, and Shakespeare's acquaintance with Mr. W.H. must have begun in 1594, or at the latest in 1595. Shakespeare, accordingly, could not have known Lord Pembroke till after the Sonnets had been written.

'Cyril pointed out also that Pembroke's father did not die till 1601; whereas it was evident from the line,

You had a father; let your son say so,

that the father of Mr. W.H. was dead in 1598. Besides, it was absurd to imagine that any publisher of the time, and the preface is from the publisher's hand, would have ventured to address William Herbert, Earl of Pembroke, as Mr. W.H.; the case of Lord Buckhurst being spoken of as Mr. Sackville being not really a parallel instance, as Lord Buckhurst was not a peer, but merely the younger son of a peer, with a courtesy title, and the passage in *England's Parnassus*, where he is so spoken of, is not a formal and stately dedication, but simply a casual allusion. So far for Lord Pembroke, whose supposed claims Cyril easily demolished while I sat by in wonder. With Lord Southampton Cyril had even less difficulty. Southampton became at a very early age the lover of Elizabeth Vernon, so he needed no entreaties to marry; he was not beautiful; he did not resemble his mother, as Mr. W.H. did—

Thou art thy mother's glass, and she in thee
Calls back the lovely April of her prime;

and, above all, his Christian name was Henry, whereas the punning sonnets (CXXXV and CXLIII) show that the Christian name of Shakespeare's friend was the same as his own—*Will.*

'As for the other suggestions of unfortunate commentators, that Mr. W.H. is a misprint for Mr. W.S., meaning Mr. William Shakespeare; that "Mr. W.H. all" should be read "Mr. W. Hall"; that Mr. W.H. is Mr. William Hathaway; and that a full stop should be placed after "wisheth," making Mr. W.H. the writer and not the subject of the dedication, Cyril got rid of them in a very short time; and it is not worth while to mention his reasons, though I remember he sent me off into a fit of laughter by reading to me, I am glad to say not in the original, some extracts from a German commentator called Barnstorff who insisted that Mr. W.H. was no less a person than "Mr. William Himself." Nor would he allow for a moment that the Sonnets are mere satires on the work of Drayton and John Davies of Hereford. To him, as indeed to me, they were poems of serious and tragic import, wrung out of the bitterness of Shakespeare's heart, and made sweet by the honey of his lips. Still less would he admit that they were merely a philosophical allegory, and that in them Shakespeare is addressing his Ideal Self, or Ideal Manhood, or the Spirit of Beauty, or the Reason, or the Divine Logos, or the Catholic Church. He felt, as indeed I think we all must feel, that the Sonnets are addressed to an individual,—to a particular young man whose personality for some reason seems to have filled the soul of Shakespeare with terrible joy and no less terrible despair.

'Having in this manner cleared the way as it were, Cyril asked me to dismiss from my mind any preconceived ideas I might have formed on the subject, and to give a fair and unbiassed hearing to his own theory. The problem he pointed out was this: Who was that young man of Shakespeare's day who, without being of noble birth or even of noble nature, was addressed by him in terms of such passionate adoration that we can but wonder at the strange worship, and are almost afraid to turn the key that unlocks the mystery of the poet's heart? Who was he whose physical beauty was such that it became the very cornerstone of Shakespeare's art; the very source of Shakespeare's inspiration; the very incarnation of Shakespeare's dreams? To look upon him as simply the object of certain love-poems is to miss the whole meaning of the poems: for the art of which Shakespeare talks in the Sonnets is not the art of the Sonnets themselves, which indeed were to him but slight and secret things—it is the art of the dramatist to which he is always alluding; and he to whom Shakespeare said—

Thou art all my art, and dost advance
As high as learning my rude ignorance,

he to whom he promised immortality,

Where breath most breathes, even in the mouths of men,—

was surely none other than the boy-actor for whom he created Viola and Imogen, Juliet and Rosalind, Portia and Desdemona, and Cleopatra herself. This was Cyril Graham's theory, evolved as you see purely from the Sonnets themselves, and depending for its acceptance not so much on demonstrable proof or formal evidence, but on a kind of spiritual and artistic sense, by which alone he claimed could the true meaning of the poems be discerned. I remember his reading to me that fine sonnet—

How can my Muse want subject to invent,
While thou dost breathe, that pour'st into my verse
Thine own sweet argument, too excellent
For every vulgar paper to rehearse?
O, give thyself the thanks, if aught in me
Worthy perusal stand against thy sight;
For who's so dumb that cannot write to thee,
When thou thyself dost give invention light?
Be thou the tenth Muse, ten times more in worth
Than those old nine which rhymers invocate;

And he that calls on thee, let him bring forth
Eternal numbers to outlive long date—

and pointing out how completely it corroborated his theory; and indeed he
went through all the Sonnets carefully, and showed, or fancied that he showed,
that, according to his new explanation of their meaning, things that had seemed
obscure, or evil, or exaggerated, became clear and rational, and of high artistic
import, illustrating Shakespeare's conception of the true relations between the
art of the actor and the art of the dramatist.

'It is of course evident that there must have been in Shakespeare's company
some wonderful boy-actor of great beauty, to whom he intrusted the presentation
of his noble heroines; for Shakespeare was a practical theatrical manager as well
as an imaginative poet, and Cyril Graham had actually discovered the boy-actor's
name. He was Will, or, as he preferred to call him, Willie Hughes. The Christian
name he found of course in the punning sonnets, CXXXV and CXLIII; the
surname was, according to him, hidden in the eighth line of the 20th Sonnet,
where Mr. W.H. is described as—

A man in hew, all *Hews* in his controwling.

'In the original edition of the Sonnets "Hews" is printed with a capital letter
and in italics, and this, he claimed, showed clearly that a play on words was
intended, his view receiving a good deal of corroboration from those sonnets
in which curious puns are made on the words "use" and "usury." Of course I
was converted at once, and Willie Hughes became to me as real a person as
Shakespeare. The only objection I made to the theory was that the name of Willie
Hughes does not occur in the list of the actors of Shakespeare's company as it is
printed in the first folio. Cyril, however, pointed out that the absence of Willie
Hughes's name from this list really corroborated the theory, as it was evident from
Sonnet LXXXVI that Willie Hughes had abandoned Shakespeare's company to
play at a rival theatre, probably in some of Chapman's plays. It is in reference to
this that in the great sonnet on Chapman Shakespeare said to Willie Hughes—

But when your countenance filled up his line,
Then lacked I matter; that enfeebled mine—

the expression "when your countenance filled up his line" referring obviously
to the beauty of the young actor giving life and reality and added charm to
Chapman's verse, the same idea being also put forward in the 79th Sonnet—

Whilst I alone did call upon thy aid,
My verse alone had all thy gentle grace,

But now my gracious numbers are decayed,
And my sick Muse does give another place;

and in the immediately preceding sonnet, where Shakespeare says,

Every alien pen has got my *use*
And under thee their poesy disperse,

the play upon words (use = Hughes) being of course obvious, and the phrase
"under thee their poesy disperse," meaning "by your assistance as an actor bring
their plays before the people."

'It was a wonderful evening, and we sat up almost till dawn reading and
re-reading the Sonnets. After some time, however, I began to see that before
the theory could be placed before the world in a really perfected form, it was
necessary to get some independent evidence about the existence of this young
actor, Willie Hughes. If this could be once established, there could be no possible
doubt about his identity with Mr. W.H.; but otherwise the theory would fall
to the ground. I put this forward very strongly to Cyril, who was a good deal
annoyed at what he called my Philistine tone of mind, and indeed was rather
bitter upon the subject. However, I made him promise that in his own interest
he would not publish his discovery till he had put the whole matter beyond
the reach of doubt; and for weeks and weeks we searched the registers of City
churches, the Alleyn MSS. at Dulwich, the Record Office, the papers of the Lord
Chamberlain—everything, in fact, that we thought might contain some allusion
to Willie Hughes. We discovered nothing, of course, and every day the existence
of Willie Hughes seemed to me to become more problematical. Cyril was in a
dreadful state, and used to go over the whole question day after day, entreating
me to believe; but I saw the one flaw in the theory, and I refused to be convinced
till the actual existence of Willie Hughes, a boy-actor of Elizabethan days, had
been placed beyond the reach of doubt or cavil.

'One day Cyril left town to stay with his grandfather, I thought at the time,
but I afterwards heard from Lord Crediton that this was not the case; and about
a fortnight afterwards I received a telegram from him, handed in at Warwick,
asking me to be sure to come and dine with him that evening at eight o'clock.
When I arrived, he said to me, "The only apostle who did not deserve proof
was S. Thomas, and S. Thomas was the only apostle who got it." I asked him
what he meant. He answered that he had not merely been able to establish the
existence in the sixteenth century of a boy-actor of the name of Willie Hughes,
but to prove by the most conclusive evidence that he was the Mr. W.H. of the
Sonnets. He would not tell me anything more at the time; but after dinner he
solemnly produced the picture I showed you, and told me that he had discovered
it by the merest chance nailed to the side of an old chest that he had bought at

a farmhouse in Warwickshire. The chest itself, which was a very fine example of Elizabethan work, he had, of course, brought with him, and in the centre of the front panel the initials W.H. were undoubtedly carved. It was this monogram that had attracted his attention, and he told me that it was not till he had had the chest in his possession for several days that he had thought of making any careful examination of the inside. One morning, however, he saw that one of the sides of the chest was much thicker than the other, and looking more closely, he discovered that a framed panel picture was clamped against it. On taking it out, he found it was the picture that is now lying on the sofa. It was very dirty, and covered with mould; but he managed to clean it, and, to his great joy, saw that he had fallen by mere chance on the one thing for which he had been looking. Here was an authentic portrait of Mr. W.H., with his hand resting on the dedicatory page of the Sonnets, and on the frame itself could be faintly seen the name of the young man written in black uncial letters on a faded gold ground, "Master Will. Hews."

'Well, what was I to say? It never occurred to me for a moment that Cyril Graham was playing a trick on me, or that he was trying to prove his theory by means of a forgery.'

'But is it a forgery?' I asked.

'Of course it is,' said Erskine. 'It is a very good forgery; but it is a forgery none the less. I thought at the time that Cyril was rather calm about the whole matter; but I remember he more than once told me that he himself required no proof of the kind, and that he thought the theory complete without it. I laughed at him, and told him that without it the theory would fall to the ground, and I warmly congratulated him on the marvellous discovery. We then arranged that the picture should be etched or facsimiled, and placed as the frontispiece to Cyril's edition of the Sonnets; and for three months we did nothing but go over each poem line by line, till we had settled every difficulty of text or meaning. One unlucky day I was in a print-shop in Holborn, when I saw upon the counter some extremely beautiful drawings in silver-point. I was so attracted by them that I bought them; and the proprietor of the place, a man called Rawlings, told me that they were done by a young painter of the name of Edward Merton, who was very clever, but as poor as a church mouse. I went to see Merton some days afterwards, having got his address from the printseller, and found a pale, interesting young man, with a rather common-looking wife—his model, as I subsequently learned. I told him how much I admired his drawings, at which he seemed very pleased, and I asked him if he would show me some of his other work. As we were looking over a portfolio, full of really lovely things,—for Merton had a most delicate and delightful touch,—I suddenly caught sight of a drawing of the picture of Mr. W.H. There was no doubt whatever about it. It was almost a *facsimile*—the only difference being that the two masks of Tragedy and Comedy were not suspended from the marble table as they are in the picture, but were lying on the floor at the young man's feet. "Where on earth did you get that?" I said. He grew rather confused, and said—"Oh, that is nothing. I did not know it was in this portfolio. It is not a thing of any value." "It is what you did for Mr. Cyril Graham," exclaimed his wife; "and if this gentleman wishes to buy it, let him have it." "For Mr. Cyril Graham?" I repeated. "Did you paint the picture of Mr. W.H.?" "I don't understand what you mean," he answered, growing very red. Well, the whole thing was quite dreadful. The wife let it all out. I gave her five pounds when I was going away. I can't bear to think of it now; but of course I was furious. I went off at once to Cyril's chambers, waited there for three hours before he came in, with that horrid lie staring me in the face, and told him I had discovered his forgery. He grew very pale and said—"I did it purely for your sake. You would not be convinced in any other way. It does not affect the truth of the theory." "The truth of the theory!" I exclaimed; "the less we talk about that the better. You never even believed in it yourself. If you had, you would not have committed a forgery to prove it." High words passed between us; we had a fearful quarrel. I daresay I was unjust. The next morning he was dead.'

'Dead!' I cried.

'Yes; he shot himself with a revolver. Some of the blood splashed upon the frame of the picture, just where the name had been painted. By the time I arrived—his servant had sent for me at once—the police were already there. He had left a letter for me, evidently written in the greatest agitation and distress of mind.'

'What was in it?' I asked.

'Oh, that he believed absolutely in Willie Hughes; that the forgery of the picture had been done simply as a concession to me, and did not in the slightest degree invalidate the truth of the theory; and that in order to show me how firm and flawless his faith in the whole thing was, he was going to offer his life as a sacrifice to the secret of the Sonnets. It was a foolish, mad letter. I remember he ended by saying that he intrusted to me the Willie Hughes theory, and that it was for me to present it to the world, and to unlock the secret of Shakespeare's heart.'

'It is a most tragic story,' I cried; 'but why have you not carried out his wishes?'

Erskine shrugged his shoulders. 'Because it is a perfectly unsound theory from beginning to end,' he answered.

'My dear Erskine,' I said, getting up from my seat, 'you are entirely wrong about the whole matter. It is the only perfect key to Shakespeare's Sonnets that has ever been made. It is complete in every detail. I believe in Willie Hughes.'

'Don't say that,' said Erskine gravely; 'I believe there is something fatal about the idea, and intellectually there is nothing to be said for it. I have gone into the whole matter, and I assure you the theory is entirely fallacious. It is plausible up to a certain point. Then it stops. For heaven's sake, my dear boy, don't take up the subject of Willie Hughes. You will break your heart over it.'

'Erskine,' I answered, 'it is your duty to give this theory to the world. If you will not do it, I will. By keeping it back you wrong the memory of Cyril Graham, the youngest and the most splendid of all the martyrs of literature. I entreat you to do him justice. He died for this thing,—don't let his death be in vain.'

Erskine looked at me in amazement. 'You are carried away by the sentiment of the whole story,' he said. 'You forget that a thing is not necessarily true because a man dies for it. I was devoted to Cyril Graham. His death was a horrible blow to me. I did not recover it for years. I don't think I have ever recovered it. But Willie Hughes? There is nothing in the idea of Willie Hughes. No such person ever existed. As for bringing the whole thing before the world—the world thinks that Cyril Graham shot himself by accident. The only proof of his suicide was contained in the letter to me, and of this letter the public never heard anything. To the present day Lord Crediton thinks that the whole thing was accidental.'

'Cyril Graham sacrificed his life to a great idea,' I answered; 'and if you will not tell of his martyrdom, tell at least of his faith.'

'His faith,' said Erskine, 'was fixed in a thing that was false, in a thing that was unsound, in a thing that no Shakespearian scholar would accept for a moment. The theory would be laughed at. Don't make a fool of yourself, and don't follow a trail that leads nowhere. You start by assuming the existence of the very person whose existence is the thing to be proved. Besides, everybody knows that the Sonnets were addressed to Lord Pembroke. The matter is settled once for all.'

'The matter is not settled!' I exclaimed. 'I will take up the theory where Cyril Graham left it, and I will prove to the world that he was right.'

'Silly boy!' said Erskine. 'Go home: it is after two, and don't think about Willie Hughes any more. I am sorry I told you anything about it, and very sorry indeed that I should have converted you to a thing in which I don't believe.'

'You have given me the key to the greatest mystery of modern literature,' I answered; 'and I shall not rest till I have made you recognise, till I have made everybody recognise, that Cyril Graham was the most subtle Shakespearian critic of our day.'

As I walked home through St. James's Park the dawn was just breaking over London. The white swans were lying asleep on the polished lake, and the gaunt Palace looked purple against the pale-green sky. I thought of Cyril Graham, and my eyes filled with tears.

II

It was past twelve o'clock when I awoke, and the sun was streaming in through the curtains of my room in long slanting beams of dusty gold. I told my servant that I would be at home to no one; and after I had had a cup of chocolate and a *petit-pain*, I took down from the book-shelf my copy of Shakespeare's

Sonnets, and began to go carefully through them. Every poem seemed to me to corroborate Cyril Graham's theory. I felt as if I had my hand upon Shakespeare's heart, and was counting each separate throb and pulse of passion. I thought of the wonderful boy-actor, and saw his face in every line.

Two sonnets, I remember, struck me particularly: they were the 53rd and the 67th. In the first of these, Shakespeare, complimenting Willie Hughes on the versatility of his acting, on his wide range of parts, a range extending from Rosalind to Juliet, and from Beatrice to Ophelia, says to him—

> What is your substance, whereof are you made,
> That millions of strange shadows on you tend?
> Since every one hath, every one, one shade,
> And you, but one, can every shadow lend—

lines that would be unintelligible if they were not addressed to an actor, for the word 'shadow' had in Shakespeare's day a technical meaning connected with the stage. 'The best in this kind are but shadows,' says Theseus of the actors in the *Midsummer Night's Dream*, and there are many similar allusions in the literature of the day. These sonnets evidently belonged to the series in which Shakespeare discusses the nature of the actor's art, and of the strange and rare temperament that is essential to the perfect stage-player. 'How is it,' says Shakespeare to Willie Hughes, 'that you have so many personalities?' and then he goes on to point out that his beauty is such that it seems to realise every form and phase of fancy, to embody each dream of the creative imagination—an idea that is still further expanded in the sonnet that immediately follows, where, beginning with the fine thought,

> 'O, how much more doth beauty beauteous seem
> By that sweet ornament which *truth* doth give!'

Shakespeare invites us to notice how the truth of acting, the truth of visible presentation on the stage, adds to the wonder of poetry, giving life to its loveliness, and actual reality to its ideal form. And yet, in the 67th Sonnet, Shakespeare calls upon Willie Hughes to abandon the stage with its artificiality, its false mimic life of painted face and unreal costume, its immoral influences and suggestions, its remoteness from the true world of noble action and sincere utterance.

> Ah! wherefore with infection should he live,
> And with his presence grace impiety,
> That sin by him advantage should achieve,
> And lace itself with his society?
> Why should false painting imitate his cheek

And steal dead seeming of his living hue?
Why should poor beauty indirectly seek
Roses of shadow, since his rose is true?

It may seem strange that so great a dramatist as Shakespeare, who realised his own perfection as an artist and his humanity as a man on the ideal plane of stage-writing and stage-playing, should have written in these terms about the theatre; but we must remember that in Sonnets CX and CXI Shakespeare shows us that he too was wearied of the world of puppets, and full of shame at having made himself 'a motley to the view.' The 111th Sonnet is especially bitter:—

O, for my sake do you with Fortune chide,
The guilty goddess of my harmful deeds,
That did not better for my life provide
Than public means which public manners breeds.
Thence comes it that my name receives a brand,
And almost thence my nature is subdued
To what it works in, like the dyer's hand:
Pity me, then, and wish I were renewed—

and there are many signs elsewhere of the same feeling, signs familiar to all real students of Shakespeare.

One point puzzled me immensely as I read the Sonnets, and it was days before I struck on the true interpretation, which indeed Cyril Graham himself seems to have missed. I could not understand how it was that Shakespeare set so high a value on his young friend marrying. He himself had married young, and the result had been unhappiness, and it was not likely that he would have asked Willie Hughes to commit the same error. The boy-player of Rosalind had nothing to gain from marriage, or from the passions of real life. The early sonnets, with their strange entreaties to have children, seemed to me a jarring note. The explanation of the mystery came on me quite suddenly, and I found it in the curious dedication. It will be remembered that the dedication runs as follows:—

TO · THE · ONLIE · BEGETTER · OF ·
THESE · INSUING · SONNETS ·
Mr · W.H. ALL · HAPPINESSE ·
AND · THAT · ETERNITIE ·
PROMISED ·
BY ·
OUR · EVER-LIVING · POET ·
WISHETH ·
THE · WELL-WISHING ·

ADVENTURER · IN
SETTING ·
FORTH.
T. T.

Some scholars have supposed that the word 'begetter' in this dedication means simply the procurer of the Sonnets for Thomas Thorpe the publisher; but this view is now generally abandoned, and the highest authorities are quite agreed that it is to be taken in the sense of inspirer, the metaphor being drawn from the analogy of physical life. Now I saw that the same metaphor was used by Shakespeare himself all through the poems, and this set me on the right track. Finally I made my great discovery. The marriage that Shakespeare proposes for Willie Hughes is the 'marriage with his Muse,' an expression which is definitely put forward in the 82nd Sonnet, where, in the bitterness of his heart at the defection of the boy-actor for whom he had written his greatest parts, and whose beauty had indeed suggested them, he opens his complaint by saying—

I'll grant thou wert not married to my Muse

The children he begs him to beget are no children of flesh and blood, but more immortal children of undying fame. The whole cycle of the early sonnets is simply Shakespeare's invitation to Willie Hughes to go upon the stage and become a player. How barren and profitless a thing, he says, is this beauty of yours if it be not used:—

When forty winters shall besiege thy brow,
And dig deep trenches in thy beauty's field,
Thy youth's proud livery, so gazed on now,
Will be a tattered weed, of small worth held:
Then being asked where all thy beauty lies,
Where all the treasure of thy lusty days,
To say, within thine own deep-sunken eyes,
Were an all-eating shame and thriftless praise.

You must create something in art: my verse 'is thine, and *born* of thee'; only listen to me, and I will '*bring forth* eternal numbers to outlive long date,' and you shall people with forms of your own image the imaginary world of the stage. These children that you beget, he continues, will not wither away, as mortal children do, but you shall live in them and in my plays: do but—

Make thee another self, for love of me,
That beauty still may live in thine or thee!

I collected all the passages that seemed to me to corroborate this view, and they produced a strong impression on me, and showed me how complete Cyril Graham's theory really was. I also saw that it was quite easy to separate those lines in which he speaks of the Sonnets themselves from those in which he speaks of his great dramatic work. This was a point that had been entirely overlooked by all critics up to Cyril Graham's day. And yet it was one of the most important points in the whole series of poems. To the Sonnets Shakespeare was more or less indifferent. He did not wish to rest his fame on them. They were to him his 'slight Muse,' as he calls them, and intended, as Meres tells us, for private circulation only among a few, a very few, friends. Upon the other hand he was extremely conscious of the high artistic value of his plays, and shows a noble self-reliance upon his dramatic genius. When he says to Willie Hughes:

> But thy eternal summer shall not fade,
> Nor lose possession of that fair thou owest;
> Nor shall Death brag thou wander'st in his shade,
> When in *eternal lines* to time thou growest;
> So long as men can breathe or eyes can see,
> So long lives this, and this gives life to thee;—

the expression 'eternal lines' clearly alludes to one of his plays that he was sending him at the time, just as the concluding couplet points to his confidence in the probability of his plays being always acted. In his address to the Dramatic Muse (Sonnets C and CI), we find the same feeling.

> Where art thou, Muse, that thou forget'st so long
> To speak of that which gives thee all thy might?
> Spend'st thou thy fury on some worthless song,
> Darkening thy power to lend base subjects light?

he cries, and he then proceeds to reproach the mistress of Tragedy and Comedy for her 'neglect of Truth in Beauty dyed,' and says—

> Because he needs no praise, wilt thou be dumb?
> Excuse not silence so; for 't lies in thee
> To make him much outlive a gilded tomb,
> And to be praised of ages yet to be.
>   Then do thy office, Muse; I teach thee how
>   To make him seem long hence as he shows now.

It is, however, perhaps in the 55th Sonnet that Shakespeare gives to this idea its fullest expression. To imagine that the 'powerful rhyme' of the second line refers to the sonnet itself, is to entirely mistake Shakespeare's meaning. It seemed to me that it was extremely likely, from the general character of the sonnet, that a particular play was meant, and that the play was none other but *Romeo and Juliet*.

> Not marble, nor the gilded monuments
> Of princes, shall outlive this powerful rhyme;
> But you shall shine more bright in these contents
> Than unswept stone besmeared with sluttish time.
> When wasteful wars shall statues overturn.
> And broils root out the work of masonry,
> Nor Mars his sword nor war's quick fire shall burn
> The living record of your memory.
> 'Gainst death and all-oblivious enmity
> Shall you pace forth; your praise shall still find room
> Even in the eyes of all posterity
> That wear this world out to the ending doom.
> > So, till the judgment that yourself arise.
> > You live in this, and dwell in lovers' eyes.

It was also extremely suggestive to note how here as elsewhere Shakespeare promised Willie Hughes immortality in a form that appealed to men's eyes— that is to say, in a spectacular form, in a play that is to be looked at.

For two weeks I worked hard at the Sonnets, hardly ever going out, and refusing all invitations. Every day I seemed to be discovering something new, and Willie Hughes became to me a kind of spiritual presence, an ever-dominant personality. I could almost fancy that I saw him standing in the shadow of my room, so well had Shakespeare drawn him, with his golden hair, his tender flower-like grace, his dreamy deep-sunken eyes, his delicate mobile limbs, and his white lily hands. His very name fascinated me. Willie Hughes! Willie Hughes! How musically it sounded! Yes; who else but he could have been the master-mistress of Shakespeare's passion,[1] the lord of his love to whom he was bound in vassalage,[2] the delicate minion of pleasure,[3] the rose of the whole world,[4] the herald of the spring[5] decked in the proud livery of youth,[6] the lovely boy whom it was sweet music to hear,[7] and whose beauty was the very raiment of Shakespeare's heart,[8] as it was the keystone of his dramatic power? How bitter now seemed the whole tragedy of his desertion and his shame!—shame that he made sweet and lovely[9] by the mere magic of his personality, but that was none the less shame. Yet as Shakespeare forgave him, should not we forgive him also? I did not care to pry into the mystery of his sin.

His abandonment of Shakespeare's theatre was a different matter, and I investigated it at great length. Finally I came to the conclusion that Cyril

Graham had been wrong in regarding the rival dramatist of the 80th Sonnet as Chapman. It was obviously Marlowe who was alluded to. At the time the Sonnets were written, such an expression as 'the proud full sail of his great verse' could not have been used of Chapman's work, however applicable it might have been to the style of his later Jacobean plays. No: Marlowe was clearly the rival dramatist of whom Shakespeare spoke in such laudatory terms; and that

Affable familiar ghost
Which nightly gulls him with intelligence,

was the Mephistopheles of his *Doctor Faustus*. No doubt, Marlowe was fascinated by the beauty and grace of the boy-actor, and lured him away from the Blackfriars Theatre, that he might play the Gaveston of his *Edward II*. That Shakespeare had the legal right to retain Willie Hughes in his own company is evident from Sonnet LXXXVII, where he says:—

Farewell! thou art too dear for my possessing,
And like enough thou know'st thy estimate:
The *charter of thy worth* gives thee releasing;
My *bonds* in thee are all determinate.
For how do I hold thee but by thy granting?
And for that riches where is my deserving?
The cause of this fair gift in me is wanting,
And so my patent back again is swerving.
Thyself thou gavest, thy own worth then not knowing,
Or me, to whom thou gavest it, else mistaking;
So thy great gift, upon misprision growing,
Comes home again, on better judgment making.
    Thus have I had thee, as a dream doth flatter,
    In sleep a king, but waking no such matter.

But him whom he could not hold by love, he would not hold by force. Willie Hughes became a member of Lord Pembroke's company, and, perhaps in the open yard of the Red Bull Tavern, played the part of King Edward's delicate minion. On Marlowe's death, he seems to have returned to Shakespeare, who, whatever his fellow-partners may have thought of the matter, was not slow to forgive the wilfulness and treachery of the young actor.

How well, too, had Shakespeare drawn the temperament of the stage-player! Willie Hughes was one of those

That do not do the thing they most do show.
Who, moving others, are themselves as stone.

He could act love, but could not feel it, could mimic passion without realising it.

> In many's looks the false heart's history
> Is writ in moods and frowns and wrinkles strange,

but with Willie Hughes it was not so. 'Heaven,' says Shakespeare, in a sonnet of mad idolatry—

> Heaven in thy creation did decree
> That in thy face sweet love should ever dwell;
> Whate'er thy thoughts or thy heart's workings be,
> Thy looks should nothing thence but sweetness tell.

In his 'inconstant mind' and his 'false heart,' it was easy to recognise the insincerity and treachery that somehow seem inseparable from the artistic nature, as in his love of praise, that desire for immediate recognition that characterises all actors. And yet, more fortunate in this than other actors, Willie Hughes was to know something of immortality. Inseparably connected with Shakespeare's plays, he was to live in them.

> Your name from hence immortal life shall have,
> Though I, once gone, to all the world must die:
> The earth can yield me but a common grave,
> When you entombed in men's eyes shall lie.
> Your monument shall be my gentle verse,
> Which eyes not yet created shall o'er-read,
> And tongues to be your being shall rehearse
> When all the breathers of this world are dead.

There were endless allusions, also, to Willie Hughes's power over his audience,— the 'gazers,' as Shakespeare calls them; but perhaps the most perfect description of his wonderful mastery over dramatic art was in *The Lover's Complaint*, where Shakespeare says of him:—

> In him a plenitude of subtle matter,
> Applied to cautels, all strange forms receives,
> Of burning blushes, or of weeping water,
> Or swooning paleness; and he takes and leaves,
> In either's aptness, as it best deceives,
> To blush at speeches rank, to weep at woes,
> Or to turn white and swoon at tragic shows.

So on the tip of his subduing tongue,
All kind of arguments and questions deep,
All replication prompt and reason strong,
For his advantage still did wake and sleep,
To make the weeper laugh, the laugher weep.
  He had the dialect and the different skill,
  Catching all passions in his craft of will.

Once I thought that I had really found Willie Hughes in Elizabethan literature. In a wonderfully graphic account of the last days of the great Earl of Essex, his chaplain, Thomas Knell, tells us that the night before the Earl died, 'he called William Hewes, which was his musician, to play upon the virginals and to sing. "Play," said he, "my song, Will Hewes, and I will sing it to myself." So he did it most joyfully, not as the howling swan, which, still looking down, waileth her end, but as a sweet lark, lifting up his hands and casting up his eyes to his God, with this mounted the crystal skies, and reached with his unwearied tongue the top of highest heavens.' Surely the boy who played on the virginals to the dying father of Sidney's Stella was none other but the Will Hews to whom Shakespeare dedicated the Sonnets, and whom he tells us was himself sweet 'music to hear.' Yet Lord Essex died in 1576, when Shakespeare himself was but twelve years of age. It was impossible that his musician could have been the Mr. W.H. of the Sonnets. Perhaps Shakespeare's young friend was the son of the player upon the virginals? It was at least something to have discovered that Will Hews was an Elizabethan name. Indeed the name Hews seemed to have been closely connected with music and the stage. The first English actress was the lovely Margaret Hews, whom Prince Rupert so madly loved. What more probable than that between her and Lord Essex's musician had come the boy-actor of Shakespeare's plays? But the proofs, the links—where were they? Alas! I could not find them. It seemed to me that I was always on the brink of absolute verification, but that I could never really attain to it.

From Willie Hughes's life I soon passed to thoughts of his death. I used to wonder what had been his end.

Perhaps he had been one of those English actors who in 1604 went across sea to Germany and played before the great Duke Henry Julius of Brunswick, himself a dramatist of no mean order, and at the Court of that strange Elector of Brandenburg, who was so enamoured of beauty that he was said to have bought for his weight in amber the young son of a travelling Greek merchant, and to have given pageants in honour of his slave all through that dreadful famine year of 1606–7, when the people died of hunger in the very streets of the town, and for the space of seven months there was no rain. We know at any rate that *Romeo and Juliet* was brought out at Dresden in 1613, along with *Hamlet* and

King Lear, and it was surely to none other than Willie Hughes that in 1615 the death-mask of Shakespeare was brought by the hand of one of the suite of the English ambassador, pale token of the passing away of the great poet who had so dearly loved him. Indeed there would have been something peculiarly fitting in the idea that the boy-actor, whose beauty had been so vital an element in the realism and romance of Shakespeare's art, should have been the first to have brought to Germany the seed of the new culture, and was in his way the precursor of that *Aufklärung* or Illumination of the eighteenth century, that splendid movement which, though begun by Lessing and Herder, and brought to its full and perfect issue by Goethe, was in no small part helped on by another actor—Friedrich Schroeder—who awoke the popular consciousness, and by means of the feigned passions and mimetic methods of the stage showed the intimate, the vital, connection between life and literature. If this was so,—and there was certainly no evidence against it,—it was not improbable that Willie Hughes was one of those English comedians (*mimae quidam ex Britannia*, as the old chronicle calls them), who were slain at Nuremberg in a sudden uprising of the people, and were secretly buried in a little vineyard outside the city by some young men 'who had found pleasure in their performances, and of whom some had sought to be instructed in the mysteries of the new art.' Certainly no more fitting place could there be for him to whom Shakespeare said, 'thou art all my art,' than this little vineyard outside the city walls. For was it not from the sorrows of Dionysos that Tragedy sprang? Was not the light laughter of Comedy, with its careless merriment and quick replies, first heard on the lips of the Sicilian vine-dressers? Nay, did not the purple and red stain of the wine-froth on face and limbs give the first suggestion of the charm and fascination of disguise—the desire for self-concealment, the sense of the value of objectivity thus showing itself in the rude beginnings of the art? At any rate, wherever he lay—whether in the little vineyard at the gate of the Gothic town, or in some dim London churchyard amidst the roar and bustle of our great city—no gorgeous monument marked his resting-place. His true tomb, as Shakespeare saw, was the poet's verse, his true monument the permanence of the drama. So had it been with others whose beauty had given a new creative impulse to their age. The ivory body of the Bithynian slave rots in the green ooze of the Nile, and on the yellow hills of the Cerameicus is strewn the dust of the young Athenian; but Antinous lives in sculpture, and Charmides in philosophy.

III

After three weeks had elapsed, I determined to make a strong appeal to Erskine to do justice to the memory of Cyril Graham, and to give to the world his marvellous interpretation of the Sonnets—the only interpretation that thoroughly explained the problem. I have not any copy of my letter, I regret to say, nor have I been able to lay my hand upon the original; but I remember that I went over the whole ground, and covered sheets of paper with passionate reiteration of the arguments and proofs that my study had suggested to me. It seemed to me that I was not merely restoring Cyril Graham to his proper place in literary history, but rescuing the honour of Shakespeare himself from the tedious memory of a commonplace intrigue. I put into the letter all my enthusiasm. I put into the letter all my faith.

No sooner, in fact, had I sent it off than a curious reaction came over me. It seemed to me that I had given away my capacity for belief in the Willie Hughes theory of the Sonnets, that something had gone out of me, as it were, and that I was perfectly indifferent to the whole subject. What was it that had happened? It is difficult to say. Perhaps, by finding perfect expression for a passion, I had exhausted the passion itself. Emotional forces, like the forces of physical life, have their positive limitations. Perhaps the mere effort to convert any one to a theory involves some form of renunciation of the power of credence. Perhaps I was simply tired of the whole thing, and, my enthusiasm having burnt out, my reason was left to its own unimpassioned judgment. However it came about, and I cannot pretend to explain it, there was no doubt that Willie Hughes suddenly became to me a mere myth, an idle dream, the boyish fancy of a young man who, like most ardent spirits, was more anxious to convince others than to be himself convinced.

As I had said some very unjust and bitter things to Erskine in my letter, I determined to go and see him at once, and to make my apologies to him for my behaviour. Accordingly, the next morning I drove down to Birdcage Walk, and found Erskine sitting in his library, with the forged picture of Willie Hughes in front of him.

'My dear Erskine!' I cried, 'I have come to apologise to you.'

'To apologise to me?' he said. 'What for?'

'For my letter,' I answered.

'You have nothing to regret in your letter,' he said. 'On the contrary, you have done me the greatest service in your power. You have shown me that Cyril Graham's theory is perfectly sound.'

'You don't mean to say that you believe in Willie Hughes?' I exclaimed.

'Why not?' he rejoined. 'You have proved the thing to me. Do you think I cannot estimate the value of evidence?'

'But there is no evidence at all,' I groaned, sinking into a chair. 'When I wrote to you I was under the influence of a perfectly silly enthusiasm. I had been touched by the story of Cyril Graham's death, fascinated by his romantic theory, enthralled by the wonder and novelty of the whole idea. I see now that the theory is based on a delusion. The only evidence for the existence of Willie Hughes is that picture in front of you, and the picture is a forgery. Don't be carried away by mere sentiment in this matter. Whatever romance may have to say about the Willie Hughes theory, reason is dead against it.'

'I don't understand you,' said Erskine, looking at me in amazement. 'Why, you yourself have convinced me by your letter that Willie Hughes is an absolute reality. Why have you changed your mind? Or is all that you have been saying to me merely a joke?'

'I cannot explain it to you,' I rejoined, 'but I see now that there is really nothing to be said in favour of Cyril Graham's interpretation. The Sonnets are addressed to Lord Pembroke. For heaven's sake don't waste your time in a foolish attempt to discover a young Elizabethan actor who never existed, and to make a phantom puppet the centre of the great cycle of Shakespeare's Sonnets.'

'I see that you don't understand the theory,' he replied.

'My dear Erskine,' I cried, 'not understand it! Why, I feel as if I had invented it. Surely my letter shows you that I not merely went into the whole matter, but that I contributed proofs of every kind. The one flaw in the theory is that it presupposes the existence of the person whose existence is the subject of dispute. If we grant that there was in Shakespeare's company a young actor of the name of Willie Hughes, it is not difficult to make him the object of the Sonnets. But as we know that there was no actor of this name in the company of the Globe Theatre, it is idle to pursue the investigation further.'

'But that is exactly what we don't know,' said Erskine. 'It is quite true that his name does not occur in the list given in the first folio; but, as Cyril pointed out, that is rather a proof in favour of the existence of Willie Hughes than against it, if we remember his treacherous desertion of Shakespeare for a rival dramatist.'

We argued the matter over for hours, but nothing that I could say could make Erskine surrender his faith in Cyril Graham's interpretation. He told me that he intended to devote his life to proving the theory, and that he was determined to do justice to Cyril Graham's memory. I entreated him, laughed at him, begged of him, but it was of no use. Finally we parted, not exactly in anger, but certainly with a shadow between us. He thought me shallow, I thought him foolish. When I called on him again his servant told me that he had gone to Germany.

Two years afterwards, as I was going into my club, the hall-porter handed me a letter with a foreign postmark. It was from Erskine, and written at the Hôtel d'Angleterre, Cannes. When I had read it I was filled with horror, though I did not quite believe that he would be so mad as to carry his resolve into execution. The gist of the letter was that he had tried in every way to verify the Willie Hughes theory, and had failed, and that as Cyril Graham had given his life for this theory, he himself had determined to give his own life also to the same cause. The concluding words of the letter were these: 'I still believe in Willie Hughes; and by the time you receive this, I shall have died by my own hand for Willie Hughes's sake: for his sake, and for the sake of Cyril Graham, whom I drove to his death by my shallow scepticism and ignorant lack of faith. The truth was once revealed to you, and you rejected it. It comes to you now stained with the blood of two lives,—do not turn away from it.'

It was a horrible moment. I felt sick with misery, and yet I could not believe it. To die for one's theological beliefs is the worst use a man can make of his life, but to die for a literary theory! It seemed impossible.

I looked at the date. The letter was a week old. Some unfortunate chance had prevented my going to the club for several days, or I might have got it in time to save him. Perhaps it was not too late. I drove off to my rooms, packed up my things, and started by the night-mail from Charing Cross. The journey was intolerable. I thought I would never arrive. As soon as I did I drove to the Hôtel d'Angleterre. They told me that Erskine had been buried two days before, in the English cemetery. There was something horribly grotesque about the whole tragedy. I said all kinds of wild things, and the people in the hall looked curiously at me.

Suddenly Lady Erskine, in deep mourning, passed across the vestibule. When she saw me she came up to me, murmured something about her poor son, and burst into tears. I led her into her sitting-room. An elderly gentleman was there waiting for her. It was the English doctor.

We talked a great deal about Erskine, but I said nothing about his motive for committing suicide. It was evident that he had not told his mother anything about the reason that had driven him to so fatal, so mad an act. Finally Lady Erskine rose and said, 'George left you something as a memento. It was a thing he prized very much. I will get it for you.'

As soon as she had left the room I turned to the doctor and said, 'What a dreadful shock it must have been to Lady Erskine! I wonder that she bears it as well as she does.'

'Oh, she knew for months past that it was coming,' he answered.

'Knew it for months past!' I cried. 'But why didn't she stop him? Why didn't she have him watched? He must have been mad.'

The doctor stared at me. 'I don't know what you mean,' he said.

'Well,' I cried, 'if a mother knows that her son is going to commit suicide—

'Suicide!' he answered. 'Poor Erskine did not commit suicide. He died of consumption. He came here to die. The moment I saw him I knew that there was no hope. One lung was almost gone, and the other was very much affected. Three days before he died he asked me was there any hope. I told him frankly that there was none, and that he had only a few days to live. He wrote some letters, and was quite resigned, retaining his senses to the last.'

At that moment Lady Erskine entered the room with the fatal picture of Willie Hughes in her hand. 'When George was dying he begged me to give you this,' she said. As I took it from her, her tears fell on my hand.

The picture hangs now in my library, where it is very much admired by my artistic friends. They have decided that it is not a Clouet, but an Ouvry. I have never cared to tell them its true history. But sometimes, when I look at it, I think that there is really a great deal to be said for the Willie Hughes theory of Shakespeare's Sonnets.

NOTES

1. Sonnet XX, 2.
2. Sonnet XXVI, 1.
3. Sonnet CXXVI, 9.
4. Sonnet CIX, 14.
5. Sonnet I, 10.
6. Sonnet II, 3.
7. Sonnet VIII, 1.
8. Sonnet XXII, 6.
9. Sonnet XCV, 1.

━◁◊▷━ ━◁◊▷━ ━◁◊▷━

1899—Samuel Butler.
From *Shakespeare's Sonnets Reconsidered*

As a writer, Samuel Butler (1835–1902) served as a bridge between the late Victorian and modern literary eras. His novel *The Way of All Flesh* is often regarded as a masterpiece of early-twentieth-century fiction. As a critic, Butler was capable of both memorable and foolhardy assertions. Subsequent editors of Shakespeare's *Sonnets* have mainly rejected his overconfident reordering of the 1609 quarto's arrangement.

ON THE ORDER IN WHICH THE SONNETS WERE WRITTEN, AND ON THE STORY WHICH THEY REVEAL.

A casual reader of the Sonnets as numbered in Q and in almost all modern editions, will be apt to conclude as Malone did, that the first 126 were addressed to a man and the last 28 to a woman; and unless he concentrates his attention on the whole series for a considerable time, he is likely enough to remain, as Malone appears to have done, in this opinion. He will, in fact, divide the Sonnets into two main groups, of (to use the Q numbering) 1–126 and 127–154.

I believe I have shown . . . that only nine sonnets of the second group can be correctly held to have been addressed by Shakespeare to a woman. I believe, moreover, that most readers will agree with me in thinking that 126 Q should be considered not as the last of the first group, but as the first of the second. Let alone its change of form—which seems to forbid its having been an *envoi* to a series of 125 sonnets all of them in another form—it comes after 125 as a May morning after a November afternoon; it is redolent with the spirit in which the earlier sonnets were written, but presents no affinity with the later ones; I imagine, therefore, that it was an occasional piece, written, perhaps, for some one to speak to Mr W.H. when he was playing the part of Cupid, in some mask now lost; but it would by no means necessarily follow from this that Mr W.H. was an actor by profession. Nothing would surprise me less than to find that this sonnet had been originally the first of the whole series, and had been transferred to the beginning of what we should consider as an appendix collection, on the score of its being in a different form from those that follow; and also less attractive as an opening sonnet. But whatever may have been the circumstances under which 126 Q was written, and wherever it may have originally stood, it has no connection with the story of the sonnets.

I turn now to the question whether Q gives us the Sonnets in the order in which they were written. As regards the first 125 (of course, of Q) all of which, I would repeat, appear to have been addressed directly or indirectly to Mr W.H., I can only find two, i.e. 35 and 121, which I believe to have got misplaced. Of the remaining 29 sonnets, several suggest themselves as written (*inter se*) in the order in which we have them, but some are obviously misplaced, while others are irrelevant to the series. For example, 144 Q, in which Shakespeare cannot determine whether or no Mr W.H. has enjoyed his mistress, cannot come after 134 Q, in which he confesses that Mr W.H. is now his mistress's property. The same holds good with 143 Q, from which it appears that though Shakespeare's mistress is doing her best to catch Mr W.H., she has not yet caught him. Furthermore, as Mr Wyndham has more than once justly insisted, the greater number of these sonnets should be intercalated among some of the earlier ones. Speaking of the second series (which he opens with 127 Q) Mr Wyndham says:—

> Most of the numbers were evidently written at the same time as the numbers of group C (xxxiii.–xlii.) and on the same theme.[1]

I am convinced that those which belong to the series at all belong to 40–42 Q, as also does 35 Q, to which I will return shortly. Shakespeare would not write 125 sonnets to Mr W.H., four of the earlier of which refer to an intimacy between him and Shakespeare's mistress—which is never in these 125 sonnets touched upon after 42 Q, though the friendship between Mr. W.H. and Shakespeare seems to have been continued for two or more years afterwards—and then after breaking with him, write some 20 additional sonnets, returning with apparent warm interest to this long discarded theme. An explanation, therefore, must be sought for the fact that these and a few other sonnets or so-called sonnets appear where we find them in Q.

I can discover none more simple than to suppose that Thorpe (for Mr W.H. would have known how to avoid some of the misplacements which we find in Q) intended to keep all the sonnets addressed to Mr W.H. in one group, and in the original sequence, in which Mr W.H. had either kept or rearranged them.

In a second category he placed, with less care about their due order, the sonnets which I have given as appendices A–F, all the sonnets to or about a woman, all sonnets which were not either directly or indirectly addressed to Mr W.H., and four which, as I have explained . . ., were addressed to Mr W.H., but which reflected upon him so severely that Thorpe determined to place them where they might be taken as having been addressed to Shakespeare's mistress. These four sonnets (147–150 Q) appear to have been taken out *en bloc*, and we may be thankful that they were so taken, for had they been dispersed it would have been impossible to guess what they really were. The not inconsiderable traces of order which can be detected in the last 29 sonnets are probably due not to design but to Thorpe's having never quite lost the original order, even when seriously interfering with it—to luck, in fact, not cunning.

*　*　*

I will now go through the first 125 sonnets as they stand in Q, and see how far they bear out the view that we have them, with only two exceptions, in their right order. It would indeed be almost sufficient to refer the reader to the brief headings which I have prefixed to each sonnet, but he will perhaps be glad to have these headings brought together with what few additional remarks may seem likely to assist his judgement.

The first 17 sonnets present every appearance of being in their right order, and have, I believe, been generally considered to be so. They all of them turn upon the same theme, i.e. the urging (obviously *bonâ fide*) Mr W.H. to marry and leave children. After the end of sonnet 17 this theme is abandoned, for good and all, not, I imagine, because Shakespeare had it any the less at heart, but more probably because Mr W.H. showed signs of impatience at being so persistently urged to marry when he had no wish to do so.

I can find nothing in sonnets 18–25 Q, to compel the belief that we have them in their right order, but neither can I find anything to suggest the contrary. Speaking of sonnets 26–32, Mr Wyndham says, as it seems to me quite justly, that they are,

> a continuous poem on absence, dispatched it may be in a single letter
> since it opens with a formal address and ends in a full close (p. cx.).

Of these sonnets, 27 and 28 are certainly in their right order *inter se*; so also are 30 and 31; 26 and 32 appear to be the opening and close of the series; there is nothing to suggest that the noble sonnet 29 ("When in disgrace," &c.) is out of order; I have no hesitation, therefore, in holding that in these seven sonnets, as in the first 17, the original order has been undisturbed. Surely in the absence of anything to suggest the contrary we must admit a strong presumption that sonnets 18–25 are also in their right order.

Sonnets 1–25 Q seem to have been written while Shakespeare was within easy reach of his friend, whereas 26–32 indicate, as we have seen, a time of absence, and also of deep depression. On his return—we may suppose to London, though there is nothing in the Sonnets which fixes London as the place in which Shakespeare and Mr W.H. were then residing—a trap was laid for him, into which sonnet 23 had shown that he would be only too ready to fall. I think no ill of sonnet 20, considering the conventions of the time, but it is impossible not to see that in sonnet 23 Shakespeare was in a very different frame of mind to that in which he had been when he wrote sonnets 1–17—for there can be no question that "looks" should be read in line 9, and not "books" as given in Q—I find it also impossible to believe that the change in Shakespeare's mental attitude evidenced in sonnet 23 would have been effected unless Mr W.H. had intended to amuse himself by effecting it. Shakespeare's "looks" would never have become "eloquent," unless he had believed Mr W.H.'s to have already been so. Mr W.H. must have lured him on—as we have Shakespeare's word for it that he lured him still more disastrously later. It goes without saying that Shakespeare should not have let himself be lured, but the age was what it was, and I shall show that Shakespeare was very young.

Between sonnets 32, therefore, and 33 Q , I suppose that there has been a catastrophe. The trap referred to in the preceding paragraph I believe to have been a cruel and most disgusting practical joke, devised by Mr W.H. in concert with others, but certainly never intended, much less permitted, to go beyond the raising coarse laughter against Shakespeare. I do not suppose that the trap was laid from any deeper malice than wanton love of so-called sport, and a desire to enjoy the confusion of any one who could be betrayed into being a victim; I cannot, however, doubt that Shakespeare was, to use his own words, made to "travel forth without" that "cloak," which, if he had not been lured, we may be sure that he would not have discarded. Hardly had he laid the cloak aside before he was surprised according to a preconcerted scheme, and very probably roughly handled, for we find him lame soon afterwards (sonnet 37, lines 3 and 9) and apparently not fully recovered a twelve-month later. Cf. 109 (89, Q) line 3.

The offence above indicated—a sin of very early youth—for which Shakespeare was bitterly penitent, and towards which not a trace of further tendency can be discerned in any subsequent sonnet or work during five and twenty years of later prolific literary activity—this single offence is the utmost that can be brought against Shakespeare with a shadow of evidence in its support.

I cannot pretend to certainty, or even confidence, but am inclined to think that the lines in sonnet 110 (90, Q),

Ah, do not when my heart hath scaped this sorrow,
Come in the rearward of a conquered woe,

refer to the matter now in question, as though some eight or nine months after the occurrence[2] Shakespeare had begun to find that people held him to have been more sinned against than sinning. So also in 115 (95, Q) we read,

> That tongue that tells the story of thy days,
> Making lascivious comments on thy sport,
> Cannot dispraise but in a kind of praise,

If the same matter is here referred to it would seem that it was generally regarded as blackguard sport rather than as deliberate malice.

(. . .)

Having now satisfied myself, and I trust the reader, that the Sonnets were printed in Q in the order in which Shakespeare wrote them with the exception of 35 and 121, Q ,—and with the further exception that the last 29 sonnets were taken out of the series, so that they should be replaced as far as possible by one who would read the Sonnets in the order in which Shakespeare left them—I shall assume that sonnet 107 Q is in due order, and shall not argue further on this head. This point being established I can go on to the question of the dates when the Sonnets were written.

But before I do so I would ask the reader to consider whether any other arrangement than the one we find (with the exceptions already noted) in Q could be made to show any thing like so coherent a story as the one indicated in this chapter. Let him take Benson's medley, and see what he can make of that. Let him shuffle the Sonnets into any order he pleases and see whether he can make any story out of them at all. It may be asked why have a story, when the one which Q alone permits is throughout painful and in parts repulsive? Many, indeed say, "Read the Sonnets if you like, but do not go below their surface; let their music and beauty of expression be enough." I do not write for these good people, nor are they likely to read me; I therefore pass them by at as wide a distance as I can, and confine my attention to those who will not read anything that fell from such a man as Shakespeare without doing their best to fathom it.

No such persons can even begin to read the Sonnets without finding that a story of some sort is staring them in the face. They cannot apprehend it, but they feel that behind some four or five sonnets there is a riddle which more or less taints the series with a vague feeling as though the answer, if found, would be unwholesome. There the Sonnets are; there is no suppressing them; they are being studied yearly more and more, and will continue to be so, in spite, *pace* Steevens, of the strongest act of parliament that can be framed to prevent people from reading them. Therefore they should be faced for better or worse, and until they are restored approximately to the order in which Shakespeare wrote them and until they are approximately dated, it is impossible to face them. Their date is the very essence of the whole matter; for the verdict we are to pass upon some few of them—and these colour the others—depends in great measure on the age of the writer. And furthermore, what we think of Shakespeare himself must depend not a little on what we think of the Sonnets.

If we date them early we suppose a severe wound in youth, but one that was soon healed to perfect wholesomeness. If we date them at any age later than extreme youth, there is no escape from supposing what is morally a malignant cancer. If the evidence points in the direction of the cancer, we must with poignant regret accept it. I submit, however, that it will be found to point with irresistible force in the direction of the mere scar.

It is a pious act to show that it does so; for the man is not dead. The true life of a man is not that which he leads in himself, but the one he leads in others, and of which he knows nothing. Shakespeare is more living in that life of the world to come by virtue of which he entered after death into the lives of millions, than he ever was in that vexed body to which his conscious life was limited. But enough of this.

Those who pass the riddle of the Sonnets over in silence, tacitly convey an impression that the answer would be far more terrible than the facts would show. Those who date the Sonnets as the Southamptonites, and still worse the Herbertites do, cannot escape from leaving Shakespeare suffering as I have said from a leprous or cancerous taint, for they do not even attempt to show that he was lured into a trap, and if they did, he was too old for the excuse to be admitted as much palliation. Those who regard the Sonnets as literary exercises would have us believe that in the naughtiness of his heart, Shakespeare, with a world of subjects to choose from, elected to invent sonnet 23, and to imagine a situation which required the writing of sonnets 33–35 of my numbering. This is the most degrading view of all; but these four ways of treating the Sonnets are the only ones now before the public, and they are all of them alike slovenly and infamous. True, however early the Sonnets are dated a scar must remain; but who under the circumstances will heed it whose moral support is worth a moment's consideration?

I grant that the story is a very squalid one, but from all we can gather Shakespeare's first few years in London were passed in very squalid surroundings. Furthermore, any one who reads the Sonnets carefully will note that it was not Mr W. H.'s mere good looks which so powerfully attracted Shakespeare. From first to last it is plain that Shakespeare assumed that these were but the outward and visible signs of an inward and spiritual grace. He could not believe that any evil spirit should have so fair a house, and it was the good spirit within, and not the house itself, of which Shakespeare was in truth enamoured; this appears over and over again, and when he has become convinced that his friend's looks are better than his character, he declares the good looks to be like Eve's apple.

Considering, then, Shakespeare's extreme youth, which I shall now proceed to establish, his ardent poetic temperament, and Alas! it is just the poetic temperament which by reason of its very catholicity is least likely to pass scatheless through what he so touchingly describes as "the ambush of young days"; considering also the license of the times, Shakespeare's bitter punishment, and still more bitter remorse—is it likely that there was ever afterwards a day in his life in which the remembrance of that "night of woe" did not at some time or another rise up before him and stab him? nay, is it not quite likely that this great shock may in the end have brought him prematurely to the grave?—Considering, again, the perfect sanity of all his later work; considering further that all of us who read the Sonnets are as men who are looking over another's shoulder and reading a very private letter which was intended for the recipient's eye, and for no one else's; considering all these things—for I will not urge the priceless legacy he has left us, nor the fact that the common heart, brain, and conscience of mankind holds him foremost among all Englishmen as the crowning glory of our race—leaving all this on one side, and considering only youth, the times, penitence, and amendment of life, I believe that those whose judgement we should respect will refuse to take Shakespeare's grave indiscretion more to heart than they do the story of Noah's drunkenness; they will neither blink it nor yet look at it more closely than is necessary in order to prevent men's rank thoughts from taking it to have been more grievous than it was.

Tout savoir, c'est tout comprendre—and in this case surely we may add—*tout pardonner*.

NOTES

1. See Mr Wyndham's "Poems of Shakespeare," Methuen, 1897, p. 325, cf. also Mr Wyndham's Preface pp. cx, cxi.

2. See the dates with which I have headed each sonnet in my text.

THE SONNETS
IN THE TWENTIETH CENTURY
❧

Near the beginning of the twentieth century, in the short space of two years, two serious readers of Shakespeare's *Sonnets* used strikingly ominous images—dark caves, labyrinthine paths, skeletons—to express their exasperation with the state of scholarship on the sonnets and the (to them) questionable biographical directions it had taken in preceding decades. Reviewing a 1904 edition of *The Sonnets*, the biographer and man of letters Lytton Strachey speaks of any bold man who "sets out in quest of the key" that will unlock the mysteries of Shakespeare's sonnets once and for all. The walking is heavy, he warns, and syllables of men's names "lure the unwary traveller at every turn into paths already white with the bones of innumerable commentators." Fascination draws one on, but a "deeper oblivion" awaits the scholar who intends to explore the sonnets in this fashion. The scholar Walter Raleigh assessed his discipline's efforts at understanding *The Sonnets* with a similarly wry dismissal, and one with similarly lethal imagery:

> There are many footprints around the cave of this mystery, none of them pointing in the outward direction. No one has ever attempted a solution of the problem without leaving a book behind him; and the shrine of Shakespeare is thickly hung with these votive offerings, all withered and dusty.

Books on Shakespeare's *Sonnets* proliferated at an even faster rate throughout the twentieth century, but as these two quotations show, there were at least regular efforts to push scholarship beyond the work of literary detection and into more structurally, psychologically, and historically interesting realms. A procession of different critical methods and topical interests became briefly current and then receded into the literary background, but in nearly every case the sonnets as literature, and as a written text, were never quite so obscured as they were in the previous century, which preferred to identify the poems' characters and contemplate the native genius of Shakespeare the poet. As Hallett Smith memorably remarked in praise of George Wyndham and his 1898 edition of the sonnets, for the first time someone was reading the sonnets as poetry, or "Verbal Melody," to use Wyndham's own phrase.

Sidney Lee showed one possible direction away from the intellectual marshland that biographical criticism had become. He chose to read *The Sonnets* in a kind of conversation with other lyrical poetry—classical poetry, the Continental poetry of the Middle Ages and Renaissance, and English writing contemporary with Shakespeare's own. He ultimately found the "story" told in the poems to be less than original, since so many of the sequence's expressions of incidents could in fact be located in influential sources or in the work of Shakespeare's peers, English, Italian, or French. These analogies made Lee insist that Shakespeare was hardly personal and far from revealing in *The Sonnets* but was in fact conventional, varying and restating a large number of familiar topics from European lyric poetry. For example, Ovid's *Metamorphoses* influenced *The Sonnets'* philosophical thought, Lee argues, and in the essay included here, he treats the many correspondences between Shakespeare and Ovid, the Roman poet whom our later Englishman would have read in his Stratford grammar school. Lee was not silent, however, on the biographical questions surrounding *The Sonnets*, though his constant shift of views is reminiscent of Nathan Drake's about-face with respect to Shakespeare's poetry exactly one century earlier. In 1889, Lee's work on the *Dictionary of National Biography* make it clear that he thought the earl of Pembroke was the Young Man in the sonnets. Eight years later, and without explanation, he completed a dictionary entry on Shakespeare that argued that the earl of Southampton was the one whom Shakespeare addressed. In the same year, for American editions of the *DNB*, Lee altered his view once more, this time denying that either identification mattered, since *The Sonnets* were definitely not autobiographical.

Nevertheless it would be a mistake to think that Lee's focus on poetic conventions and Shakespeare's place within the lyric tradition had no bearing on the biographical reception of the poet. Lee was emphasizing that Shakespeare's gestures of desire seemed, as it turned out, to be more the products of the study than affairs of the heart, and in effect his approach became the latest means by which squeamish English readers could come to terms with *The Sonnets'* explicit homoerotic content. Nearly a century ago, the editor James Boswell exonerated the poet he admired by speaking of the fanciful imagination everywhere visible in the poems. Like Lee later, Boswell also offered convenient classical parallels, particularly ones (such as in Virgil's *Eclogue* 2) that made the awkward male-male relationship seem more like a literary exercise and less an erotic confession. The strategy of many critics in the second half of the nineteenth century was to acknowledge the relationship between the speaker and Young Man but then to idealize it in the most high-minded, ethereal, Platonic terms, which only a "demigod" or "superhuman" or "impressive spiritual presence" such as Shakespeare could sustain. The French critic Hippolyte Taine judged *The Sonnets'* creator to be "one of those delicate souls which, like a perfect instrument of music, vibrate of themselves at the slightest touch." Less delicately, one German critic thought it was his "moral duty" to protect Shakespeare's reputation and convince readers that *The Sonnets* reflected this brand of Renaissance Platonism, this celebration of the true and beautiful. Just so, Lee performed similar kinds of justification by pointing readers to poetic conventions and social speech that were awkward to contemporaries but perfectly appropriate then. Consequently, "our" Shakespeare could remain one of the guys. More esoteric, allegorical readings would be propagated, in which the Young Man was the Messiah and the Dark Lady his church, or in which the "master-mistress" was wine and *The Sonnets* a record of Shakespeare's struggle with alcoholism. And later in the century, critics such as Leslie Hotson and A.L. Rowse would continue to undertake more straightforward biographical detective work.

A few early-twentieth-century commentaries act as harbingers, to those of us with the benefit of hindsight, of the general turn to formal criticism that began to flourish in the New Critical atmosphere of the 1930s. Raymond M. Alden announced in his 1916 Variorum edition of *The Sonnets* that new external evidence was needed before critics could add anything useful to the biographical conversation, and T.G. Tucker's edition eight years later showed a more pronounced interest in the poems' formal elements. And in the following decade, yet another editor, George Kittredge, would point to the form as an explanation to all the previous biographical speculation—"a good sonnet appears to be a confession," he claims, but that impression is merely one supported by a strong handling of the form itself. The influential dramatist George Bernard Shaw belittled the biography hunters in his own inestimable way. He wrote a play, *The Dark Lady of the Sonnets*, that presented as Shakespeare's mistress Mary Fitton, whom as we've seen was a popular late-nineteenth-century candidate for the mystery woman. In his preface, however, Shaw takes her main proponent to task, suggests another candidate, and generally makes it clear that the whole question of her identity interests him very little.

L.C. Knights and William Empson deserve credit for inaugurating a new kind of criticism of *The Sonnets*, an approach more attentive to the poems' formal qualities and technical effects (such as their displays of rhetoric or image clusters) and showing new interest in Shakespeare's stylistic tendencies and in his bigger thematic questions. In a 1934 essay in the journal *Scrutiny*, Knight declared that even correct biographical details did nothing to help readers better appreciate Shakespeare's sonnets as *poems*, and he directed readers to the experience enacted in the poetry and the language that articulated it, for which Shakespeare's personal history was only a possible source. Knights also saw *The Sonnets* as a valuable means to understand better the development of Shakespeare's blank verse. Once again, this focus on prosody, or the poet's subtle use of poetic meter, differed vastly from earlier interest in Elizabethan lovers' intrigues. *The Sonnets* played a role in two seminal books by William Empson, who remains one of the great close readers of the twentieth century. He opened his *Seven Types of Ambiguity* (1930) by considering lines from Shakespeare's sonnet 73, but his more extended, and more famous, critical investigations occur in *Some Versions of Pastoral*, where he posits "4096 possible movements of thought" amid the "grave irony" of sonnet 94, "They that have pow'r to hurt, and will do none." By scrutinizing the varied connotations of the poem's words and phrases, as well as the several different tones in the line's spoken delivery, Empson like no one before him explained the sonnet's deeply divided assessment of the Young Man and how it both lauds and accuses its subject all at once. For Empson, the flower imagery foregrounded in the sonnet's conclusion makes this yoking of extreme attitudes possible.

The American poet and critic John Crowe Ransom published a controversial essay three years later, and it remains one of the century's most negative evaluations of Shakespeare's sonnets. Driven by New Critical principles, Ransom criticized Shakespeare for his "careless" writing and his loosely "associationist" method of composition, whereby the imagery and metaphors in the sonnets were "pretty" and full of feeling but lacking in serious thought and ultimately vague. Ransom's attack on Shakespeare's predictable logic and monotony of image betrays this critic's own strong preferences—for Shakespeare's contemporary John Donne and the Metaphysical school of poetry he represented, both of which were, in Ransom's day, in the critical ascendant. In light of Ransom's criticism, Arthur Mizener in 1940 produced the most direct defense of Shakespeare's method. Mizener claimed that Ransom's demand that Shakespeare write like a Metaphysical was patently unfair, since the poet of *The Sonnets* was clearly not of that school, whose artistic effects relied on different, and sometimes opposing, aesthetic values. Shakespeare, Mizener argued, valued many layers of figuration, and so the vagueness criticized by Ransom, or "soft focus" in Mizener's phrase, was necessary to keep these several varying meanings in play for readers and to maintain the satisfying sense of the poems' complexity overall. Mizener proved his case with a close reading of sonnet 124, while another pair of critics, Roman Jakobsen and L. G. Jones, responded explicitly to Ransom and his denial that sonnet 129 could even be called a sonnet in the strictest terms.

Sonnet 129 inspired a number of fine critical examinations in the twentieth century. This poem, one of unique ferocity and revulsion, treats the topic of lust with a rhetorical mastery and intensity that has perhaps never been matched in any shorter lyric poem. It received a breadth of critical attention in a 1926 essay by the famous poets Robert Graves and Laura Riding, an essay that was later revised by the authors and frequently reprinted. Their essay demonstrates just how seriously the editing of punctuation and typography in Thorpe's 1609 quarto could affect the many meanings of such a tightly complex poem. Thomas M. Greene reads the same sonnet with hermeneutical claims and impasses in mind. Greene's sophisticated, poised reading is a fine product of a 1980s critical mode that put a new value on placing traditional texts within new theoretical frameworks.

The polemical battles incited by Ransom gave way in the 1950s to different kinds of critical approaches that were able to take for granted *The Sonnets'* general literary worth. In *The Mutual Flame*, G. Wilson Knight transferred his unique critical emphases usually reserved for Shakespeare's plays to the writer's narrative poems and sonnets. Knight focused on "poetic symbolism" to isolate universal associations in *The Sonnets*, including flowers, the sun, jewels, gold, and kingship. M. M. Mahood accentuated Shakespeare's wordplay and its role in creating dramatic irony and regulating thought throughout the demands of sonnet form. One approach that has had recurring influence upon later generations of scholars is that of G. K. Hunter. In "The Dramatic Technique of Shakespeare's Sonnets," reprinted here, Hunter sought not to discredit the many previous attempts to glean biographical truths from the poems but to understand better how the materials of poetry could set up in readers "an overwhelmingly biographical reaction." Hunter thus argues that critics often lose themselves in a critical wilderness when attempting to evaluate Shakespeare the lyric poet, or storyteller, or metaphysician, or progeny of Italy's Petrarch. In fact, *The Sonnets* are most poetically rich when readers treat them as the writings of, unsurprisingly, a *dramatist*. Edward Hubler showed similar interest in a connection whose importance Hunter strongly implies—that between Shakespeare's plays and poems. For example, in helpfully arguing for an evolution of the character of the speaker throughout Shakespeare's sequence, Hubler compares this development with the "spiritual progress of Lear." He continues: "The sonnets of deepest revulsion present an agony. . . . It is an awareness which must change because it cannot bear to be itself." Here Hubler equates the pain of self-examination, which *The Sonnets* so frequently express or dramatize, with the violent clarity made possible through the suffering of Shakespeare's tragic heroes. These kinds of interconnections between dramatic and lyric achievements continue to this day, from comparisons of *The Sonnets'* language with the early comedies to perceived elements that suggest simultaneous composition, as between the poems and *Hamlet*, *All's Well That Ends Well*, or *Cymbeline*. It remains a deep fountain at which critics will continue to drink far into the present century.

Hubler also produced an edition of Shakespeare's *Songs and Poems*, and in 1962 he published an influential collection of new essays titled *The Riddle of the Sonnets*. Conveniently reprinting Oscar Wilde's "The Portrait of Mr. W. H.," this collection also featured essays by prominent critics and poets such as R. P. Blackmur, Stephen Spender, and Northrop Frye, whose practice of archetypal criticism provided a way of thinking freshly about the long divide between biographical and formal criticism. Reading *The Sonnets* as "transcripts of experience" was, rather counterintuitively, not to read them realistically at all, but rather allegorically, as "riddles" they were not originally intended to be. When one looks for a real person in Shakespeare's incomparable poetry, it means the poet has lavished some of the "greatest sonnets in the language on an unresponsive oaf as stupid as a doorknob and as selfish as a weasel." What produced these sonnets, Frye summarizes, "is not an experience like ours, but a creative imagination very unlike ours." If Frye seeks in his way to estrange Shakespeare's poems for readers who treat them in too pedestrian and non-literary a fashion, other developments in the 1960s and '70s in fact did much to assist readers, both general and scholarly alike. Gerald Willen's and Victor B. Reed's *A Casebook on Shakespeare's Sonnets* (1964) was another important essay collection, making widely available the aforementioned work by Graves and Riding, L. C. Knights, Ransom, Mizener, Hubler, and G. Wilson Knight. The next decade would bring a similarly cumulative collection, Peter Jones's *Shakespeare: The Sonnets*, this time a volume in Macmillan's Casebook series.

Two generation-defining editions of *The Sonnets* also appeared during this period, although mention should first be made of what is perhaps the most important edition of Shakespeare's elusive poems in the history of their publication. In 1944, Hyder Edward Rollins released the massive, two-volume *The Sonnets: A New Variorum Edition*, which replaced Alden's 1916 Variorum volume and made accessible for the first time a wealth of essays and commentaries on individual poems by authors ranging from famous to obscure, erudite to lunatic. W. G. Ingram's and Theodore Redpath's edition of *The Sonnets*, published in 1964, soon became the essential edition for the current generation of scholars. It benefited from Rollins's thoroughness but also achieved a more manageably thorough text and apparatus all its own. (User-friendly editions by Martin Seymour-Smith and Barbara Herrnstein Smith also appeared during this decade.) The influence of this edition would have lasted longer, and it would be more frequently used today, if not for the appearance a little more than a decade later of Stephen Booth's grand edition of *The Sonnets*, featuring a 400-page "analytical commentary" compiled in the semantically exhaustive spirit of William Empson. Booth's resistance to the typical editorial paraphrase of theme looks ahead to Helen Vendler's more recent lyric-sensitive subtleties of reading, and he instead valued a scrupulous accumulation of possible and overlapping meanings for nearly every word of each individual sonnet. At once enlightening and a little overwhelming, Booth's edition remains essential for any serious consultation of a sonnet's possibilities of meaning, even though a handful of scholarly editions have appeared since his was published more than 30 years ago. Booth's book-length *An Essay on Shakespeare's Sonnets* (1969) is full of fine observations made by a reader who was even then hard at work on his magisterial edition, yet more often quoted by readers is his "Facts and Theories About Shakespeare's Sonnets," one of the most pithy essays ever appended to a dense critical edition. Not caring to hide his own lack of interest in others' biographical curiosities, Booth quipped, "William

Shakespeare was almost certainly homosexual, bisexual, or heterosexual. The sonnets provide no evidence on the matter."

The undeniable rise and multiple applications of literary theory, from post-structuralist treatments in the 1980s to the growing interest in the 1990s in more historically and culturally oriented readings, ensured that fresh voices, producing new and provocative critical readings, would usher in a new phase of critical reception for *The Sonnets*. First, certain critics revisited older areas of study with a new critical rigor. For example, Anne Ferry's "Shakespeare and Sidney" follows earlier studies by Joan Grundy and M.C. Bradbrook on the influence of Philip Sidney and other Elizabethan sonneteers upon Shakespeare's sonnet writing. What results is a lengthy comparative study that is as close to the last word as we are likely to get on the affinities between these two giants of English Renaissance poetry. Ferry's method is as rigorous as her taste as reader and writer is exquisite. Joel Fineman's "Shakespeare's Perjur'd Eye" did for Shakespeare's sequence, in terms of theory, what Booth's edition had accomplished editorially in the previous decade; it ushered these poems into a new world of complex academic discourse, all the while showing how capable was Shakespeare's thought and writing to standing up to the most sophisticated of critical-theoretical applications. Applying methods of deconstruction and Jacques Lacan's theories based on psychoanalysis, Fineman seeks to uncover Shakespeare's efforts at constructing a "poetic subjectivity," as it occurs at various stages throughout *The Sonnets*. Fineman takes his title from sonnet 152's concluding couplet—"For I have sworn thee fair: more perjured eye, / To swear against the truth so foul a lie," and the poet's pun on "eye"/"I" resonates throughout Fineman's intellectually dense study, as he moves from the speaker's struggles with narcissism (a topic also treated fruitfully in the 1980s by Janette Dillon), heterosexual *différance*, and an agonized subjectivity or "inwardness," all hammered on the anvil of psychological and sexual conflict. In an essay-length version of his argument presented here, Fineman concludes by considering how Shakespeare wrestled in his sonnets with the problem of *belatedness*. That is, Shakespeare was writing sonnets toward the end of a long tradition of such writing, and as a consequence the language of sonneteering was nearly exhausted. The poet was keenly aware of his problematic position, and his effort to solve that problem led, for Fineman, to an exceptional discovery: "Shakespeare's own response to secondariness introduces, I have suggested, a subjectivity altogether novel in the history of lyric." Fineman's essay is arguably the most cited work in scholarship on Shakespeare's *Sonnets* today. A single editorial development during the 1980s also deserves mention: John Kerrigan's Penguin edition of *The Sonnets*, itself novel because of the editor's new insistence on reading Shakespeare's sonnets along with the longer poem *A Lover's Complaint*. Kerrigan's edition provides the closet thing to what seventeenth-century readers would have encountered when reading Thorpe's 1609 quarto.

In the 1990s, the best readings of Shakespeare's *Sonnets* continued to evolve. The influential work by Bruce R. Smith and Margreta de Grazia, however different their specific areas of interest, exhibited the emergence of cultural materialism and New Historicism as the dominant modes of literary criticism during the 1990s. These new modes reacted against the "sealed vacuum" approaches of earlier structuralist and post-structuralist criticism, which overlooked authorial and cultural questions in favor of revealing the self-referential verbal systems within literary works. Cultural materialists argued that these works could not truly be understood when artificially separated, or quarantined, from the complex matrices of cultural formation that greatly influenced both authors and their texts. De Grazia shows a new interest in culture's role in creating literature by approaching *The Sonnets* as a product of printers' bibliographic decisions and subsequent generations' tastes in reception. Arthur Sherbo has dedicated much of his scholarship to eighteenth-century appropriations of Shakespeare's texts, and Arthur Marotti has done similar work at the pre-print level, that of coterie writing and manuscript circulation. Marotti is interested in how socially situated literary practices, not to mention patronage networks, help to create the sonnets we have, as well as the meaning we ascribe to them. "My real interest is not in factual error," explains de Grazia, after briefly considering the questionable tactics of the printer John Benson, "but in the kinds of cultural imperatives that motivate such errors." In other words, de Grazia's object of study is as much "Shakespeare criticism" as it is Shakespeare himself.

On the other hand, Smith's focus in his book *Homosexual Desire in Shakespeare's England* represents a mode of criticism committed to exploring how Renaissance texts reflect their age's development of social identity. Notice how the focus in the title of the book is not on Shakespeare's poems but rather the country in which the poems are conceived and composed; one of its predecessors was Joseph Pequigney's *Such Is My Love* (1985), a bold study that presupposes a homosexual relationship between the speaker and the Young Man. Pequigney was accused of returning wholeheartedly to the shadowy lands of biographical criticism, but his study already reflects the more sensitive outlook of these later critics of social identity. Pequigney was not seeking to answer those longstanding questions about Shakespeare the man or sonnets' speaker who was his stand-in. Rather, he was newly interested in the *relationships* between characters in *The Sonnets* and how influences in literary representation, as well as in authors' social worlds, made them possible and shaped early readers' understanding of them. For this reason, Smith subtitles his study a "cultural poetics," and he is one of several critics doing fruitful work on *The Sonnets* from the perspective of gender and queer studies. Others include Eve Kosofsky Sedgwick, whose essay "Swan in Love: The Example of Shakespeare's Sonnets," remains a seminal, exploratory work in this critical field, as well as Marjorie Garber's and Valerie Traub's studies of bisexual expressions and homosocial desire in Shakespeare's poems.

The final two essays round out this section in a satisfyingly broad way. Helen Vendler's *The Art of Shakespeare's Sonnets* (1997) has been called one of the best commentaries of a classic work of literature during the past century. Vendler's evident rhetorical, structural, and linguistic sensitivities are never permitted to drive to the periphery a winsome admiration for lyric poetry, and the artful persons who lend it their voices, in all of its dramatic complexity. One criticism of Vendler is that she finds Shakespeare's genius everywhere, as if each line of each sonnet were a beehive awaiting its harvester of lyrical honey. The poet W. H. Auden, on the other hand, thought that only a fraction of the sonnets were great works, while many others were workaday efforts at best. But then again, Shakeseare's *Sonnets* were called "mellifluous" when first noticed in print in 1598, and their author was referred to as "honey-tongued." This is a criticism that Vendler, with her expansive and sensitive esteem of the sequence as a whole, will handily sustain. Jonathan Bate's chapter on *The Sonnets* from his acclaimed book, *The Genius of Shakespeare*, reflects the several virtues of this critic. It is written in a lively way, moving along swiftly but always clearly as well, and he brings the considerable learning drawn from his past studies—on Ovid's influence on Shakespeare, on Shakespeare's relationship with his contemporary Christopher Marlowe, and his later influence on the Romantics—to bear in this helpful overview of *The Sonnets'* initial dramas and poetic achievements and the many visions and revisions of those poems in the four centuries since their first circulation and publication.

1909—Sir Sidney Lee. "Ovid and Shakespeare's Sonnets," from *Elizabethan and Other Essays*

In 1891, Sidney Lee (1859–1926) succeeded Sir Leslie Stephen as the editor of the *Dictionary of National Biography*, for which he contributed nearly a thousand entries. He was an influential biographer of Shakespeare and also wrote other books on the Renaissance era.

For full eighteen centuries the *Metamorphoses* led in the race among Ovid's works for popular favour. Probably the vogue waxed greatest from the thirteenth to the seventeenth century. For those four hundred years generation vied with generation in proofs of admiring interest. The highest honours were steadily accorded to this spacious storehouse of myth and poetry, alike by laity and clergy through medieval western and southern Europe. The book was translated not only into French and Italian, but also into German and medieval Greek—languages then on the confines of culture. Separate fables, like those of Narcissus or Orpheus, Pyramus or Philomela, grew popular everywhere in vernacular renderings into verse. Dante in his treatise on rhetoric (*De vulgari eloquentia*) applauded both the poetic diction of the *Metamorphoses* and its allegorical value. Of the many medieval moralizations of classical poetry over which Rabelais made merry, the most popular were two allegorical interpretations of Ovid's poem—one by Dante's disciple, Giovanni del Virgilio, the fourteenth-century champion of scholarship, and the other by the French Dominican, Pierre Berçuire, who lived in friendly intercourse with Petrarch at Vaucluse. The Italian humanists of the late fifteenth and early sixteenth centuries, Politian and Bembo for example, accepted the *Metamorphoses* as a poetic model of indisputable primacy, and the prolific vernacular poets, Lodovico Dolce, the Venetian, and Clément Marot, the Norman, began new literal translations before the sixteenth was far advanced. The French scholar printer, Stephanus, saluted the author of the *Metamorphoses* as 'the poet of painters'. Tintoretto and Titian sought in Ovid's pages inspiration for their brush. At the bidding of Francis I, Primaticcio and Rosso adorned the walls of the palace at Fontainebleau with scenes of Ovid's fables.

Meanwhile the most artistic of the early printers and engravers of Paris, Venice, and Bologna applied their skill to fine editions of the book. At Paris the first impressions of text or paraphrase bore the significant title 'La Bible des Poètes', for which was substituted in later issues the more sonorous designation 'Le Grand Olympe des histoires poétiques, du prince de poésie, Ovide Naso'. Both formulas bore witness to the vastness of the book's influence on contemporary literary effort. Tudor England shared the continental enthusiasm. Caxton turned the work into his own tongue so early as 1480. Near the opening of Queen Elizabeth's reign, two Englishmen, Thomas Peend and Arthur Golding, simultaneously and independently set to work on new translations into English verse. Peend withdrew from the competition in Golding's favour after publishing a single fable. Golding carried his enterprise through, and in 1567 he completed his publication of the fifteen books of the poem in English ballad metre. Golding's version held the field for half a century. During Shakespeare's lifetime seven editions enjoyed wide circulation; and, when the book's vogue was decaying, its place was filled by the rendering of George Sandys, whom Dryden described as 'the best versifyer of the former age'. Dryden himself was, at a later period, one of the 'most eminent hands' who laboured lovingly at the same oar. The *Metamorphoses* were acknowledged to be the poet's bible in seventeenth-century London no less than in sixteenth-century Paris.

Ovid's *Metamorphoses* appealed to readers of all ages. Boys delighted in its story-telling charm, while their seniors recognized its perfection of style and diction. Its usefulness as an educational manual was acknowledged universally from the medieval era downwards; and no school or college of western Europe in the sixteenth century excluded the work from its curriculum. Montaigne, who graphically presented the dominant literary sentiment of European youth in his epoch, describes in the following words an experience which every contemporary of culture might have echoed:

> 'The first taste or feeling I had of books was of the pleasure I took in reading the fables of Ovid's *Metamorphoses*; for, being but seven or eight years old, I would steal and sequester myself from all other delights, only to read them; forsomuch as the tongue wherein they were written was to me natural; and it was the easiest book I knew; and, by reason of the matter therein contained, [it was] most agreeing with my young age.'[1]

The differences of nationality caused no variation in the affection which Ovid's *Metamorphoses* excited in the budding intellect of Renaissance Europe.

Shakespeare's familiarity with Ovid's *Metamorphoses* was in inevitable conformity with the spirit of his age. The Latin text was part of the curriculum of his grammar school education. Golding's English translation was universally accessible during his boyhood and manhood. There is no straining of the evidence in the assumption that, had Shakespeare left a record of the literary influences of his youth, he would have described a personal infatuation with the *Metamorphoses* no smaller than that to which Montaigne confesses in his autobiographical reminiscences. There is in the Bodleian Library an Aldine edition of the Latin poem which came out at Venice in 1502, and Shakespeare's initials are scribbled on the title-page. Whether these letters be genuine or no, a manuscript note of unquestioned authenticity states that the volume was believed, as early as 1682, to have been owned by Shakespeare. At any rate, no Renaissance poet's work offers fuller or clearer testimony than Shakespeare's of the abiding impression which the study of Ovid's *Metamorphoses* made on poetic genius.

Shakespeare's earliest play, *Love's Labour's Lost*, introduces Ovid as the schoolboy's model for Latin verse (IV. ii. 127): 'Ovidius Naso was the man: and why, indeed, Naso, but for smelling out the odoriferous flowers of fancy, the jerks of invention?' Elsewhere Shakespeare jests familiarly with the unhappy fate of 'the most capricious poet, honest Ovid', who died in exile among the barbarians (*As You Like It*, III. iii. 8). In another early play, *Titus Andronicus*, the book of Ovid's *Metamorphoses* is brought on the stage; and from it the tale of Philomel is quoted. But the proof of Shakespeare's minute knowledge of the *Metamorphoses* does not rest on specific mention of the poem or of its author. With exceptional vividness and completeness Shakespeare's writing assimilates numberless stirring passages of Ovid's mythological treasury. Nor does this bond mark the full limit of Shakespeare's indebtedness. Evidence which has been hitherto overlooked can be adduced to prove that the *Metamorphoses*' sporadic excursions into cosmic and metaphysical philosophy riveted the dramatist's thought with no slighter potency than the poetic figures and fables.

The phraseology of Golding's translation so frequently reappears in Shakespeare's page, especially by way of subsidiary illustration, as almost to compel the conviction that Shakespeare knew much of Golding's book by heart. At the same time it is clear that the Latin text of his schooldays recurred at times to his memory. In *King John* (v. vii. 26, 27) there is a curious verbal echo of Ovid's Latin at the opening of the *Metamorphoses* (i. 7), where 'chaos' is described as 'rudis indigestaque moles'. Shakespeare, in schoolboy fashion, when he speaks of England reduced by King John to chaos, reproduces Ovid's 'rudis indigestaque' as 'that *indigest . . .* so shapeless and so *rude*'. Golding merely renders Ovid's phrase by 'a huge rude heap'. None can mistake the source of Shakespeare's apax legomenon, the substantive 'indigest' (i.e. chaotic mass) with its epithet of 'rude' (i.e. the Latin *rudis*). Again, Ovid twice confers on Diana, in her character of goddess of groves, the name Titania (*Metamorphoses*, iii. 173, and vi. 346). In both places Golding omits this distinctive appellation, and calls Diana by her accustomed title. Ovid's Latin text alone accounts for Shakespeare's designation of his fairy queen as Titania, a word which he first introduced into English poetry. A Latin quotation in *Titus Andronicus* (iv. iii. 4), from the *Metamorphoses* (i. 150), 'terras Astraea reliquit', may have a like bearing on the same issue.

But it is on the translation of the *Metamorphoses* that Shakespeare levies his heaviest loan. No commentator has yet done justice to the full extent of Shakespeare's dependence on Golding's version. Most of them have contented themselves with instancing, as an isolated feature of his plays, the close similarity of language between Prospero's recantation of his magical powers in the *Tempest* (v. i. 33 *seq.*):

Ye elves of hills, brooks, standing lakes, and groves, &c.,

and Medea's incantation when making her rejuvenating potion in Golding's Ovid (*Metamorphoses*, vii. 197 *seq.*):

Ye Elues of Hilles, of Brookes, of woods alone, of standing lakes, &c.

This kinship of phrase, far from being unique, admits of almost endless illustration. The strange and revolting ingredients which Medea, in the same passage of Ovid, flings into her miraculous cauldron, gave the witches of *Macbeth* many cues for their unholy compound.

It is perhaps in his easy allusiveness to Ovid's mythological personages and to the traits with which the Latin poet invests them, that Shakespeare attests the completeness with which the *Metamorphoses*, in Golding's version, swayed his mind. When in the Induction to the *Taming of the Shrew* (Sc. ii. 59–61), the Lord's servant promises the tinker Sly sight of a picture of

> Daphne roaming through a thorny wood,
> Scratching her legs that one shall swear she bleeds;
> And at that sight shall sad Apollo weep,

Shakespeare merely paraphrases Apollo's remorseful apostrophe of the irresponsive nymph in the *Metamorphoses* (i. 508–9) as he chases her through the woods:

> Alas, alas, how would it grieve my heart
> To see thee fall among the briers, and that the blood should start
> Out of thy tender legs, I wretch the causer of thy smart.

There is no more delightful tale in Ovid's work than that of Baucis and Philemon, rustic patterns of conjugal fidelity and simple hospitality, who, in their thatched cottage, 'their shed of straw', entertain unawares Jove himself when travelling on the earth in human shape. The story, doubtless, had a Greek origin, but none has been found; and Ovid is the virtual parent of the delightful fable. The episode fastened itself on Shakespeare's imagination. Twice does he airily employ its detail in metaphor. 'My visor is *Philemon's roof; within the house is Jove*,' remarks Don Pedro, in *Much Ado* (ii. i. 100), at the masked ball when he introduces himself to the lady Hero; the latter playfully caps the allusion with the words: 'Why, then, your visor should be *thatched.*' To like purport is Jaques's comment on Touchstone's affectation of learning in *As You Like It* (iii. iii. 10, 11): 'O knowledge ill-inhabited, worse than *Jove in a thatched house.*'

It is needless to accumulate evidence that Shakespeare's mind was steeped in the mythology of the *Metamorphoses* as Golding rendered it. A final reference deserves citation because it conclusively shows how literal could be Shakespeare's dependence on the English version. Frequently does the dramatist figuratively employ Ovid's touching story of the ardent hunter Actaeon, who, for spying on Diana in the bathing pool, was transformed by her into a stag, and was slain by his own hounds. In *The Merry Wives of Windsor* (ii. i. 122) Pistol likens Master Ford to 'Sir Actaeon', and his patron Falstaff to '*Ringwood*', a mysterious hound in pursuit. Ovid gives names to Actaeon's hounds, calling the last 'Hylactor'. That word Golding arbitrarily and perplexingly renders 'Ringwood'. It is difficult to question the inference to which Shakespeare's use of the same appellation points.

There is good reason to believe that Shakespeare's narrative poems, *Venus and Adonis* and *Lucrece*, were designed in very youthful days, before the poet's ambition centred in drama. In the former he not merely reflects Ovid's phrase and thought, with a completeness unparalleled elsewhere, but he casts the whole piece in an Ovidian mould. The plays freely assimilate Ovid in metaphor and allusion; but the poems reproduce the moving form and spirit of Ovid's work. *Venus and Adonis* bears on the title-page a couplet (from Ovid's *Amores*, I. xv. 35, 36) in which the poet prays Apollo for a draught of the pure Castalian stream. The work is as loyal a tribute to the Ovidian conception and fashion of poetry as any in the range of Renaissance literature. The theme of *Venus and Adonis* comes direct from the *Metamorphoses*, though Shakespeare has woven together more than one thread of story. Ovid's fable of Venus' pursuit of Adonis is fused with the Latin poet's vivid picture of the nymph Salmacis' wanton appeal to the coy and passionless youth Hermaphroditus; while the boar who slays Adonis in the hunt is described by Shakespeare in the language which Ovid uses of the Calydonian boar killed by Meleager. The triple skein is vivified by a voluptuous fervour, a graphic imagery, and a luxuriant diction, which echo the Latin poem with signal fidelity.

French and Italian sixteenth-century writers were prolific in more or less literal adaptions of Ovidian fables in their own tongues. The mythical adventures of Narcissus, Phaethon, and Pyramus had been poetized many times by Shakespeare's predecessors and contemporaries in France, Italy, and Spain. Ovid's tale of Venus and Adonis thrice underwent the ordeal in Italy between 1545 and 1561. English poets, at a little later date, turned to like purpose Ovid's characteristic tales of Glaucus and Scylla, of Cephalus and Procris, of Salmacis and Hermaphroditus. But Shakespeare's earliest publication, *Venus and Adonis*, catches more fully than any foreign or domestic effort the glow of the Ovidian fire. In that poem Shakespeare made his entry on the Elizabethan stage of literature as the best endowed and most ardent of Ovid's disciples.

Shakespeare's second poem *Lucrece* is in scarcely less degree an offspring of Ovidian study, although he does not therein lay the *Metamorphoses* under contribution. The story comes from Ovid's *Fasti*; and the philosophic embroidery, which mainly presents the varied activity of Time, is an echo of the *Tristia*. Neither in subject nor in style does the English poem stray far beyond Ovidian boundaries.

The only other separate volume of poetry of Shakespeare's authorship, apart from *Venus and Adonis* and *Lucrece*, is his familiar collection of sonnets. No critic has yet detected there any extensive trace of definite Ovidian influence. The source of two or three lines has been traced to the *Metamorphoses*. Even the significance of that small reconnaissance has been underrated. Many times in the Sonnets does Shakespeare develop with poetic fervour the classical conceit that the poet's verse resists Time's ravages and preserves eternally the name of him whom the poet commemorates. Ovid, at the close of the *Metamorphoses*, boldly adopts the proud vaunt, after the manner of Horace's ode, 'Exegi monumentum aere perennius', which itself owes much to Pindar. The classical conceit, as Ovid and

Horace handled it, fired the imagination of all the Renaissance poets of western Europe. Ronsard was probably its most enthusiastic exponent. Shakespeare, in his fifty-fifth sonnet, presents the classical boast in gorgeous phrase, which draws directly on Ovid's peroration to the *Metamorphoses*. Shakespeare claims that his verse has so eternized his hero's fame, that

> Nor Mars his *sword* nor war's quick *fire* shall burn
> The living record of your memory.
> *'Gainst death* and all-oblivious enmity
> Shall you pace forth; your praise shall still find room
> Even in the eyes of *all posterity*
> That wear *this world out to the ending doom.*

These words reflect the closing flourish of the *Metamorphoses* (xv. 871 *seq.*), which the Elizabethan translator Golding rendered thus:

> Now have I brought a work to end which neither Jove's fierce wrath
> *Nor sword nor fire nor fretting age*, with all the force it hath,
> Are able to abolish quite. . . . And *all the world* shall never
> Be able for to quench my name. . . . And *time without all end* . . .
> My life shall *everlastingly* be lengthened still by fame.

Under the same inspiration Shakespeare styled his Sonnets 'eternal lines' (xviii. 12), and told his friend (lxxxi. 9–12):

> Your monument shall be my gentle verse,
> Which eyes not yet created shall o'er-read,
> And tongues to be your being shall rehearse,
> When all the breathers of this world are dead.

The Sonnets' classical and conventional claim to eternity has been misread as an original tenet of Shakespeare's poetic creed; and even those who have recognized the likeness between Shakespeare's and Ovid's presentment of the fancy have treated the parallelism in isolation. Yet the many signs elsewhere of affinity between Shakespeare's and Ovid's poetic temperaments offer *a priori* evidence that the Sonnets absorb more Ovidian sentiment than this single turn of thought. There is, too, a piece of contemporary external testimony which points to a more extensive debt. When Shakespeare had reached the midmost stage of his working career, Francis Meres, keen-witted schoolmaster and acute observer of literary activity, wrote of the great dramatist in his *Palladis Tamia* (1598) thus: 'As the soul of Euphorbus was thought to live in Pythagoras, so the sweet witty soul of Ovid lives in mellifluous and honey-tongued Shakespeare;

witness his *Venus and Adonis*, his *Lucrece*, his sugared sonnets among his private friends,' &c.

The critical preceptor gives many proofs of close acquaintance with Ovid's *Metamorphoses*, whence he borrows with precision his allusion to Euphorbus and Pythagoras (xv. 161). Meres plainly detected in Shakespeare's Sonnets, no less than in the two narrative poems, a liberal touch of the Ovidian spirit. A closer comparison of the Sonnets with the *Metamorphoses* than seems to have been yet essayed proves the truth of Meres' verdict. The last lines of the last book of Ovid's long poem gave Shakespeare a cue for his vaunt of eternal fame. A mass of earlier lines in the same book presents a series of subtle conceptions about Time and Nature which Shakespeare's Sonnets absorb no less distinctly.

Tales of enchantment, wherein men and women undergo magical transformation into animals, flowers, trees, rocks, and fountains, fill a great part of the fifteen books of the *Metamorphoses*; and to the graphic energy with which these narratives are invested, Dante paid a lasting tribute in the *Inferno* (xxv. 97). The fables belong for the most part to Greek mythology, and were largely derived by Ovid from cognate Greek miscellanies compiled near his own time at Alexandria. Ovid was a borrower on a liberal scale, and on his Alexandrian canvas he embroidered reminiscences of Homer, of the Greek tragedians, and even of Latin contemporaries like Catullus and Virgil. Yet he can claim originality for his skill in weaving his scattered material into a homogeneous poetic panorama. At the same time mere story-telling did not exhaust Ovid's aim. Along with his tales of magic he seeks to satisfy, parenthetically, two extraneous purposes, one of which concerns politics and the other philosophy. In the penultimate and the last books he vaguely traces the political fortunes of the eternal city from Romulus' miraculous foundation to the death of Julius Caesar, whose metamorphosis into a star brings to a conclusion his records of transformation. His philosophic digressions are more widely distributed. At the opening as well as at the close of the poem, many hundred lines are devoted to speculation on 'the causes of things'. Ovid's work may be almost said to be framed in a philosophic setting. The proem deals with cosmology; it declares the world to be originally an emanation of chaos, and to have been first inhabited by a heroic race of humanity, who passed from the age of Gold to that of Iron, and left behind a colony of giants. These mysterious beings are reported to have made war upon the gods in heaven, who, to avert ruin, decreed a universal flood. A single pair of human beings is credited with having survived the Deluge, and they finally repeopled the earth by flinging stones, to be miraculously changed into men and beasts.

This strange thread of cosmological theory is abruptly suspended by the first series of metamorphic tales, and is kept out of sight until the poet has wellnigh exhausted his metamorphic themes. In the last book Ovid balances his cosmological exordium by a far more complex philosophical pronouncement. There he introduces the Greek philosopher, Pythagoras, as instructing the reputed progenitor of Roman law, Numa Pompilius, in the meaning of life and death. Through more than four hundred lines Pythagoras occupies Ovid's pulpit. The speaker is not content with explaining the orthodox Pythagorean doctrines of metempsychosis and vegetarian asceticism. He soon digresses into an energetic discourse, impregnated with metaphysical subtlety, on the essential imperishability of matter, of which only the outward forms undergo change. These principles of being are shown to serve a perpetual process of rotation among all the phenomena of Nature. The universe of matter is, on Ovid's hypothesis, an ever-turning wheel, which suffers nothing to be either new or old; the appearances of constant change or innovation are due to the effect of a regularly gyrating recurrence. So abstruse a solution of the mysteries of Nature is no part of the creed which is traditionally assigned to the Pythagoras of ancient Greek philosophy. Ovid ignores the mystical mathematical axiom that the essence of all things is number, which is the centre of the original Pythagorean philosophy. The so-called Pythagorean creed which Ovid presents is in fact a recent philosophic development of Alexandria, which, though called Neo-Pythagoreanism, had small right to that title. It was fundamentally based on the Stoic platform, and was nearly akin to Neo-Platonism.

The last of the Stoic philosophers, Marcus Aurelius, summed up Ovid's doctrine in such sentences as 'all the occurrences in this world are the same from age to age and come round in a circle'; 'changes and vicissitudes roll on like one wave upon another'; 'all things were intended by Nature to change, to be converted into other forms, and to perish, so that other things may be produced in perpetual succession'. The ancient beliefs in metempsychosis and the virtue of vegetarianism, which Ovid also takes under his wing, were barely recognized by the new Pythagorean dispensation, of which the mainspring was the Stoic theory of universal 'revolution'. Elsewhere, too, Ovid travels beyond his metaphysical text. On his description of the wheel-like operation of nature, which he borrowed from contemporary metaphysicians of Alexandria, he loosely grafts geographical and geological observations, which he derives from more popular scientific manuals or reports of travel.

Ovid was in no sense a systematic philosopher. A worldling of acute intelligence, he accepted with readiness the first plausible solution at hand of metaphysical or physical puzzles. Nevertheless his fluent command of poetic diction lent charm to all he wrote; and careful readers of his *Metamorphoses* were hardly more impressed by his magical faculty of story-telling than by his unmethodized endeavour to unravel the mysterious process of being. Seneca quotes his philosophic dicta as well as his fables. The philosophic and allegorical interpreters of the poem during the Middle Ages had a specious warrant for their labyrinthine modes of exegesis. Many critics of the Renaissance detected in the *Metamorphoses* serious philosophic purpose no less than poetic charm. William Webbe, author of *A Discourse of English Poetry* in 1586, echoed a prevailing sentiment when he attributed to the *Metamorphoses* 'exceeding wisdom and sound judgement'. Golding, the English translator, in some preliminary original comments on the *Metamorphoses*, twice calls his readers' attention to Ovid's invention of Pythagoras' oration, wherein 'discourse' is made of 'dark philosophy' in its 'moral', 'natural', and 'divine' aspects.

No careful reader can overlook the thread of philosophical speculation which is woven dispersedly into the texture of Shakespeare's Sonnets. In varied periphrasis the sonneteer expresses a fear that 'nothing' is 'new'; that 'that which is hath been before'; that Time, being in a perpetual state of 'revolution', is for ever reproducing natural phenomena in a regular rotation; that the most impressive efforts of Time, which the untutored mind regards as 'novel' or 'strange', 'are but dressings of a former sight', merely the rehabilitations of a past experience, which fades only to repeat itself. The metaphysical argument has only a misty relevance to the poet's plea of everlasting love for his friend. The writer vaguely professes a fear that Nature's rotatory processes deprive his passion for the beautiful youth of all flavour of originality. With no very coherent logic he takes refuge from this distasteful reflection in a bold claim on behalf of his friend and himself to personal exemption from the universal law of Nature's and Time's endlessly recurring 'growth' and 'waning'. The reality and individuality of passionate experience are repeatedly admitted to be irreconcilable with the doctrine of universal 'revolution'.

Shakespeare's reasons for grafting these barely relevant philosophic subtleties on a poetic scheme of emotional confession of passion do not lie on the surface. Shakespeare, though a 'natural philosopher' in the general sense of 'a philosopher by light of nature', was no professed metaphysician. The philosophic digression in the last book of Ovid's *Metamorphoses* supplies the key to the riddle. A poetic master's interpretation of Life and Eternity involuntarily claimed the respectful attention of a loyal disciple. Shakespeare in the Sonnets ignores Ovid's association of his metaphysical doctrine with Pythagoras, though in the dramas of early and middle life he plays irresponsibly, in Ovid's manner, with the proverbial 'opinion' of Pythagoras

> That souls of animals infuse themselves
> Into the trunks of men.[2]

Pythagoras' primordial warning (in the *Metamorphoses*)—'forbear your *kinsfolk's ghosts to chase by slaughter*'—seems echoed too in the 'fear' of the Clown in *Twelfth Night* (IV. ii. 64) 'to *kill* a woodcock lest thou dispossess *the soul of thy grandam*'. The worn-out creed of metempsychosis, however, finds no place in the Sonnets. It is solely with Ovid's Stoic or Neo-Pythagorean musings that Shakespeare there embroiders his emotional utterances. The result is something of a patchwork. The warm tones of the diction obscure the philosophic inconsistencies, but do not dissipate them. At any rate Shakespeare levies loans on Ovid's Neo-Pythagorean deliverances with a freedom which fully justifies Meres's citation of the Sonnets as corroborative testimony that 'the sweet witty soul of Ovid lives in mellifluous and honey-tongued Shakespeare'.

The English poet's discipleship to the Latin poet may, with advantage to perspicuity, be first illustrated by the use Shakespeare makes of two of Ovid's vivid physiographic proofs of his central cosmic theory. The ceaseless recurrence of natural phenomena is illustrated by Ovid from the example of the sea-waves' motion. Golding translates the passage thus:

> *As every wave* drives others forth, and *that that comes behind*
> *Both thrusteth and is thrust himself*; even so the times by kind
> Do fly and *follow* both at once and evermore renew.

Shakespeare (Sonnet LX, 1–4) presents the argument less methodically, but he adopts the illustrative figure without much disguise. Sonnet LX opens thus:

> *Like as the waves* make towards the pebbled shore,
> So do our minutes hasten to their end;
> *Each changing place with that which goes before,*
> In *sequent* toil all forwards do contend.

Even more striking is Shakespeare's reproduction of Ovid's graphic description of the constant encroachments of land on sea and sea on land, which the Latin poet adduces as fresh evidence of matter's endless variations, and fortifies by a long series of professed personal observations. In Golding's rendering the passage opens thus:

> Even so have places oftentimes *exchanged their estate*,
> For *I have seen* it sea which was *substantial ground* alate.
> Again, where sea was, *I have seen* the same become dry land.

In Sonnet LXIV Shakespeare assimilates these words with a literalness which makes him claim to 'have seen' with his own eyes the phenomena of Ovid's narration:

> When *I have seen* the hungry ocean gain
> Advantage on the kingdom of the shore,
> And *the firm soil* win of the watery main
> Increasing store with loss, and loss with store;
> When *I have seen* such *interchange of state*.

The driving vigour with which Ovid pursues this corroborative theme of 'interchange' or 'exchange' between earth and ocean is well reflected in the swing of Golding's ballad metre:

> And in the tops of mountains high old anchors have been found,
> Deep valleys have by watershot been made of level ground,
> And hills by force of gulling oft have into sea been worne,
> Hard gravel ground is sometime seen where marish was beforne.

With especial force does Ovid point to the subsidence of land beneath the voracious sea:

> Men say that Sicil also hath been joined to Italy
> Until the sea consumed the bounds between, and did supply
> The room with water. If ye go to seek for Helice
> And Bury, which were cities of Achaea, you shall see
> Them hidden under water; and the shipmen yet do show
> The walls and steeples of the towns drowned under as they row.

The stirring picture so firmly gripped Shakespeare's imagination that he reproduced it in his drama as well as in his Sonnets. Under the Ovidian spell, the desponding King Henry IV passionately exclaims (*2 Henry IV*, iii. i. 45 *seq.*)

> O God! that one might read the book of fate
> And see *the revolution of the times*
> Make mountains level, and the continent,
> Weary of solid firmness, melt itself
> Into the sea! and, other times, to see
> The beachy girdle of the ocean
> Too wide for Neptune's hips.

Shakespeare's treatment of the central tenet of Ovid's cyclical creed may be best deduced from Sonnets LIX and CXXIII. In both these poems the doctrine of Nature's rotatory process is the main topic, although the theme is developed to different purposes. In the first sonnet the poet seriously examines the theory without committing himself to it; in the second he pronounces in its favour, albeit with a smack of irony. The text of Ovid about which Shakespeare's thought revolves in these two poems is rendered by Golding thus:

> Things ebb and flow ... Even so the times by kind
> Do fly and follow both at once, and evermore renew ...
> Things pass perchance from place to place, yet all, from whence they came
> Returning, do unperished continue still the same.

Shakespeare here concentrates all his attention on the hypothesis of 'revolution' in Nature. Sonnet LIX opens with the lines:

> If there be nothing new, but that which is
> Hath been before, how are our brains beguiled,
> Which, labouring for invention, bear amiss
> The second burden of a former child!

'If there be nothing new', if what we call birth or novelty is mere rotating return of an old state of being, then, the poet proceeds to argue, his friend's beauty would have had a former existence, and would have found 'backward' record five hundred years ago. A far older world would have passed its verdict on the present theme. The poet admits that 'five hundred courses of the sun' are conceivably capable of three sequels. Firstly, things and their appearances may progress; secondly, there is possibility of retrogression; thirdly, there may result the identity which is fruit of recurrence or repetition. The poet cannot determine

> Whether we [i.e. the present age] are mended, or whether better they
>   [i.e. former ages],
> Or whether revolution be the same.

Then, somewhat lamely descending to lower levels of thought, he contents himself with the confident assurance that in any case 'wits of former days' spent their eulogy on less worthy objects than his friend. Ovid's creed is that 'revolution' *is* 'the same', and that things and their appearances are constantly returning to the same point whence they have come. Shakespeare, although tempted to assent, stays hesitatingly at the threshold.

In Sonnet CXXIII Shakespeare takes a bolder position, though again his intellectual courage evaporates when in face of the inevitable conclusion, and he weakly makes escape through an emotional commonplace. In the opening lines he apostrophizes Time and its massive structures thus:

> Thy pyramids built up with newer might
> To me are nothing novel, nothing strange;
> They are but dressings of a former sight.

In other words, Time's imposing manifestations merely rehabilitate what has been seen before. Time's apparent innovations, the poet continues, foist 'upon us' what 'is old'; we vainly imagine things to be 'born' afresh 'to our desire', although 'we before have heard them told'. The poet, wiser than his fellows, declares with some aggressiveness that he will henceforth refuse to distinguish between 'the present and the past'. Both the records of history and our own observations are lying deceptions; the variations in natural phenomena, of

which they offer delusive shows, are effects of the unending haste of Time's
revolving wheel.

> For thy records and what we see doth lie,
> Made more or less by thy continual haste.

Here Shakespeare translates into his own vocabulary Ovid's dicta that 'times by
kind do fly and follow both at once and evermore renew'; and that 'things . . .
do unperished continue still the same'. Golding had inquired if 'that *any noueltie
worth wondring* be in' the miraculous birth and death of the recurring phoenix.
Shakespeare, by way of response, describes himself in the present sonnet as 'not
wondering at the present or the past'. When, in the final couplet, Shakespeare
vows constancy of love, 'despite' Time's 'scythe', he ignores his previous
argument, and breezily excuses himself by a conventional tag for indulgence in
metaphysical subtlety. But the preceding quatrains show penetrating insight into
the significance of Ovid's Neo-Pythagorean creed.

Some fifteen sonnets in all reflect Ovid's metaphysical or physical
interpretation of the universe. In Sonnets XLIV and XLV Shakespeare develops
the belief that life is constituted of the four elements, earth, water, air, and fire;
all of which, he tells us, are necessary to 'life's composition'. Earth and water are
described as oppressively 'slow' in action, while 'slight air and purging fire' are
'quicker' and more 'swift'. Here Shakespeare has adapted to his own purpose a
leading principle of Ovid's natural philosophy:

> This endless world contains therein, I say,
> Four substances of which all things are gendered. Of these four
> The earth and water for their mass and weight are sunken lower.
> The other couple, air and fire, the purer of the twain,
> Mount up, and nought can keep them down.

Such a theory of the elements was common knowledge among the medieval
and Renaissance poets; but Shakespeare's mode of contrasting the density of
earth and water with that of fire and air sounds a peculiarly Ovidian note. A
philosophic significance of more recondite nature attaches to Shakespeare's
apostrophe, in Sonnet CXXVI, of '*Nature,* sovereign *mistress* over wrack' [i.e.
decay], whose '*skill*' may Time disgrace'; whose 'skill' may, in other words, arrest
Time's destroying power. Whatever be the poet's final use of the conceit, he here
not only seems to have in mind the triumph over self-destructive Chaos, which
Ovid's cosmological theory at the opening of the *Metamorphoses* assigns jointly
to 'God and Nature', but would also appear to recall the '*cunning hand*' of '*Dame
Nature*' in fostering human life, which figures in the Neo-Pythagorean manifesto
of Ovid's last book.

Shakespeare's raids on the *Metamorphoses* are often too spasmodic or casual to respect the tenour of Pythagoras' complex discourse. He at times accepts at Ovid's hand a felicitous fancy without regard to its setting. Ovid elucidates his theory of 'revolution' by poetic pictures of the daily course of sun and moon, of the procession of the seasons, of the progress of man's life from youth to age, of Time's recurrent ruin and restoration of kingdoms and cities. From many of these vignettes Shakespeare snatches mnemonically a detached phrase or idea which carries little trace of the philosophic atmosphere. 'Tempus edax rerum' (*Metamorphoses*, xv. 234) becomes in Shakespeare's text 'devouring Time', which makes 'the earth devour her own sweet brood' (Sonnet xix). Golding renders the Latin here:

Thou Time, the eater up of things, and age of spiteful teen,
Destroy all things!

Shakespeare develops Ovid's defiant challenge of Time's voracity by a reference to the burning of 'the long-lived phoenix', on which Ovid also waxes eloquent. But here Shakespeare leaves Ovid's tale half told, and ignores his corollary of Time's counterbalancing forces of renewal.

In Sonnets lxiii and lxiv Shakespeare treats again of 'Time's injurious hand' and of 'Time's fell hand', which defaces 'the rich-proud cost of outworn buried age' such, he says, as '*I have seen*'. The 'lofty towers' which he again asserts he has himself *seen* 'down-razed', are the 'towers' of Athens and Thebes and other cities of Greece, 'ruins of whose ancient works' were overgrown with grass according to the Latin poet's glowing verse. Shakespeare's observation was a vicarious experience for a second and third time. Once more, too, Shakespeare misses Ovid's philosophic assurance that this decay is merely the starting-point of new growth:

So see we all things changeable; one nation gathereth strength,
Another weareth weak, and both do make exchange at length.

Yet in almost all his illustrations of Time's ravages he follows Ovid's leadership with characteristic loyalty.

Shakespeare keeps closer to his guide's steps when he adapts Ovid's sympathetic sketch of man's journey from youth to age. In Sonnet lxiii he imagines the day when his love's 'youthful morn' will have 'travell'd on to *age's steepy night*'. Similarly Ovid notes how the boy, 'growing strong and swift, . . . passeth forth the space of youth; and . . . through drooping *age's steepy* path he runneth out his race'. Not merely does Ovid's metaphor of travel correspond with Shakespeare's reflection, but Golding's phrase, '*age's steepy* path', is accepted with very slight modification. The uncommon adjective 'steepy' tells its own tale.

In Sonnet LX, Shakespeare, with an eye on the same passages in Ovid, tells somewhat cryptically how

> Nativity, once in the main of light,
> *Crawls* to maturity.

This is a difficult mode of saying that the newborn babe, when it has once emerged into the full expanse of the day's light, passes on to manhood through a period of crawling. 'The main of light' echoes Golding's 'lightsome sun' and 'daystar clear and bright'. The ambiguity frequently attaching to Shakespeare's habit of using abstract for concrete terms (i.e. 'nativity' for 'newborn babe') is here increased by an insistent reminiscence of Ovid's graphic description, in the same connexion, of the baby's early endeavour to crawl. On the infant's crawling processes the Latin poet lays curious stress in his account of man's progress from infancy. Golding's version runs:

> The child newborn lies void of strength; within a season though
> He, waxing fourfooted, learns like savage beasts to go;
> Then, somewhat faltering, and as yet not firm of foot, he stands
> By getting somewhat for to help his sinews in his hands.

Another instructive verbal echo of Golding is heard in Sonnet xv. The four ages of man are likened by Ovid to the four seasons—to 'spring-tide', which decks 'the earth with flowers of sundry hue', to 'summer waxing strong . . . like a lusty youth', to 'harvest', and to 'ugly winter', which, 'like age, steals on with trembling steps, all bald or overcast with shrill thin air as white as snow'. In Sonnet xv Shakespeare writes, again claiming another's vision:

> I perceive that men as plants increase . . .
> Vaunt in their youthful sap, at height decrease.

Nothing very distinctive can be alleged of such comparisons between human life and nature. But Shakespeare here, with singular precision, goes on to define his presentation of this law of growth, in language of Golding's coinage; he calls it 'the conceit of this inconstant *stay*'. Golding repeatedly adapts a negative periphrasis, of which the word 'stay' is the central feature, when he writes of the Ovidian theory of Nature's unending rotation. Golding's usage, which is none too felicitous, was probably due to exigencies of rhyme. Thus he asserts that 'in all the world there is not that that standeth at a *stay*'. At different points he notes that 'our bodies' and 'the elements *never stand at stay*'. Shakespeare's 'inconstant *stay*' (Sonnet xv, 9) is Golding's clumsy vocabulary. He shows a keener artistic sense, and a better appreciation of Ovid's argument, when he replaces 'this inconstant stay' elsewhere by such variants as 'nature's changing course' (XVIII, 8), 'revolution' (LIX, 12), 'interchange of state' (LXIV, 9), and 'the course of altering things' (CXV, 8). This terminology, which also echoes Golding (e.g. 'the *interchanging course*' and '*exchange*' of 'estate'), does better justice to the lucidity of the Latin poet.

Some of the ideas common to Ovid and Shakespeare are the universal food of poetry. But the majority of the cited parallelisms have individuality; and their collective presence both in the Sonnets and in one short passage of the *Metamorphoses* establishes Shakespeare's debt. He by no means stood alone among Elizabethan poets in assimilating Ovid's Neo-Pythagorean doctrine. Nor is the cyclical solution of Nature's mysteries the exclusive property of Ovid, or of his Neo-Pythagorean tutors; it is shared by the Stoics and the Neo-Platonists. But the poets of Europe first learnt its outlines in Ovid's pages, even if curiosity impelled some of them subsequently to supplement Ovid's information by resort to metaphysical treatises of one or other of the Greek schools and to current Italian adaptations of Neo-Pythagoreanism or Neo-Platonism. Such was clearly the experience of Shakespeare's great poetic contemporary, Edmund Spenser, who twice in his *Faerie Queene* repeats Ovid's account of the processes of Time and Nature in the *Metamorphoses*, but subtilizes it by references to Plato or Plotinus, to Ficino or Bruno. In Spenser's third book, where Adonis personifies the productivity of Nature, and the garden of Adonis is pictured as a treasury of Nature's seeds, the poet champions the doctrine of the imperishability of matter, despite the variations of its forms, in lines like these:

> That substance is eterne and bideth so:
> Ne when the life decays and form does fade
> Doth it consume and into nothing go,
> But changed is and often altered to and fro.

Ovid's influence is more clearly visible in the extant fragments of the seventh book of Spenser's moral epic, the unfinished canto of Mutability. There Spenser depicts the regular rotation of Nature and Time,

> The ever-whirling wheel
> Of Change, the which all mortal things doth sway.

Spenser's and Shakespeare's phrasings of their accounts of the cyclic workings of 'Dame Nature's' activities differ. But there is sufficient resemblance in thought to prove the suggestive energy of Ovid and to confirm the right of the *Metamorphoses* to its French title of 'La Bible des Poètes'.

The cryptic problems commonly associated with Shakespeare's Sonnets lie beyond the scope of this demonstration of the Ovidian temper which colours the Sonnets' philosophy. The new proofs of Shakespeare's dependence on Ovid support the belief that the bulk of the Sonnets came from Shakespeare's pen in his early life, when his memory of the *Metamorphoses* was freshest. In that elegy of Ovid from which Shakespeare drew the motto for his *Venus and Adonis*, the Latin poet pays a noble tribute to Lucretius, the greatest of all poets who made philosophy their theme. Ovid's fine reference to Lucretius must have been familiar to Shakespeare in very early life, and may well have stimulated an effort to fuse lyric emotion with the philosophic speculation of Ovid's own pages.

In any case, an examination of the philosophic sentiment which courses through the Sonnets renders indefeasible the claim of those poems to rank with the richest fruits of the pagan Renaissance. The main themes of the Sonnets are beauty's obligation to propagate itself in offspring, the supremacy of masculine beauty, faith in the immortality of verse and in its capacity to eternize its subject. All these themes belong to the paganism of Greek lyric poetry, which flowed from Greece through Latin literature into the vernacular poetry of the Western Renaissance. But the philosophical reflections which pervade the poems offer the plainest evidence that has yet been adduced of the pagan tone of the poet's voice. The doctrine that, in spite of all appearances to the contrary, Time is an endless rotatory process, and that what seems 'new' is mere recurrence of what has 'been before', is fatal to all Christian conception of the beginning and end of the world, with its special creations at the outset and its day of judgement at the close. No notion of the soul's immortality is quite consistent with the cyclical workings of Time and Nature. There is no possibility of reconciling these pagan cosmic views with Christianity. Such a conclusion is of importance because it brings Shakespeare's spirit into closer kinship with the intellectual development of the European Renaissance than is sometimes acknowledged. But critical lovers of the Sonnets, who recognize in them the flower of poetic fervour, will probably be content to draw, from the fact of Shakespeare's absorption of the Ovidian philosophy, fresh evidence of that miraculous sympathy and receptivity whereby

> all the learnings that his time
> Could make him the receiver of, . . . he took,
> As we do air, fast as 'twas minister'd,
> And in 's spring became a harvest.

NOTES
1. *Essays*, Bk. I, cap. 25.
2. *Merch. of Ven.*, v. i. 131–3.

1910—George Bernard Shaw.
From "Preface" to *The Dark Lady of the Sonnets*

George Bernard Shaw (1856-1950) was one of the great playwrights of the late nineteenth and early twentieth centuries. In addition to *The Dark Lady of the Sonnets*, he wrote *Arms and the Man*, *Major Barbara*, and *Saint Joan*. He was also a journalist, a literary critic, and a promoter of the socialist cause. He was awarded the Nobel Prize in 1925, and his play *Pygmalion* was the inspiration for the musical and film *My Fair Lady*.

How the Play came to be Written

I had better explain why, in this little *piece d'occasion*, written for a performance in aid of the funds of the project for establishing a National Theatre as a memorial to Shakespear, I have identified the Dark Lady with Mistress Mary Fitton. First, let me say that I do not contend that the Dark Lady was Mary Fitton, because when the case in Mary's favor (or against her, if you please to consider that the Dark Lady was no better than she ought to have been) was complete, a portrait of Mary came to light and turned out to be that of a fair lady, not of a dark one. That settles the question, if the portrait is authentic, which I see no reason to doubt, and the lady's hair undyed, which is perhaps less certain. Shakespear rubbed in the lady's complexion in his sonnets mercilessly; for in his day black hair was as unpopular as red hair was in the early days of Queen Victoria. Any tinge lighter than raven black must be held fatal to the strongest claim to be the Dark Lady. And so, unless it can be shewn that Shakespear's sonnets exasperated Mary Fitton into dyeing her hair and getting painted in false colors, I must give up all pretence that my play is historical. The later suggestion of Mr Acheson that the Dark Lady, far from being a maid of honor, kept a tavern in Oxford and was the mother of Davenant the poet, is the one I should have adopted had I wished to be up to date. Why, then, did I introduce the Dark Lady as Mistress Fitton?

Well, I had two reasons. The play was not to have been written by me at all, but by Mrs Alfred Lyttelton; and it was she who suggested a scene of jealousy between Queen Elizabeth and the Dark Lady at the expense of the unfortunate Bard. Now this, if the Dark Lady was a maid of honor, was quite easy. If she were a tavern landlady, it would have strained all probability. So I stuck to Mary Fitton. But I had another and more personal reason. I was, in a manner, present at the birth of the Fitton theory. Its parent and I had become acquainted; and he used to consult me on obscure passages in the sonnets, on which, as far as I can remember, I never succeeded in throwing the faintest light, at a time when nobody else thought my opinion, on that or any other subject, of the slightest importance. I thought it would be friendly to immortalize him, as the silly literary saying is, much as Shakespear immortalized Mr W.H., as he said he would, simply by writing about him.

Let me tell the story formally.

Thomas Tyler

Throughout the eighties at least, and probably for some years before, the British Museum reading room was used daily by a gentleman of such astonishing and crushing ugliness that no one who had once seen him could ever thereafter forget him. He was of fair complexion, rather golden red than sandy; aged between forty-five and sixty; and dressed in frock coat and tall hat of presentable but never new appearance. His figure was rectangular, waistless, neckless, ankleless, of middle height, looking shortish because, though he was not particularly stout, there was nothing slender about him. His ugliness was not unamiable; it was accidental, external, excrescential. Attached to his face from the left ear to the point of his chin was a monstrous goitre, which hung down to his collar bone, and was very inadequately balanced by a smaller one on his right eyelid. Nature's malice was so overdone in his case that it somehow failed to produce the effect of repulsion it seemed to have aimed at. When you first met Thomas Tyler you could think of nothing else but whether surgery could really do nothing for him. But after a very brief acquaintance you never thought of his disfigurements at all, and talked to him as you might to Romeo or Lovelace; only, so many people, especially women, would not risk the preliminary ordeal, that he remained a man apart and a bachelor all his days. I am not to be frightened or prejudiced by a tumor; and I struck up a cordial acquaintance with him, in the course of which he kept me pretty closely on the track of his work at the Museum, in which I was then, like himself, a daily reader.

He was by profession a man of letters of an uncommercial kind. He was a specialist in pessimism; had made a translation of Ecclesiastes of which eight copies a year were sold; and followed up the pessimism of Shakespear and Swift with keen interest. He delighted in a hideous conception which he called the theory of the cycles, according to which the history of mankind and the universe keeps eternally repeating itself without the slightest variation throughout all eternity; so that he had lived and died and had his goitre before and would live and die and have it again and again and again. He liked to believe that nothing that happened to him was completely novel: he was persuaded that he often had some recollection of its previous occurrence in the last cycle. He hunted out allusions to this favorite theory in his three favorite pessimists. He tried his hand occasionally at deciphering ancient inscriptions, reading them as people seem to read the stars, by discovering bears and bulls and swords and goats where, as it seems to me, no sane human being can see anything but stars higgledy-piggledy. Next to the translation of Ecclesiastes, his *magnum opus* was his work on Shakespear's Sonnets, in which he accepted a previous identification of Mr W.H., the "onlie begetter" of the sonnets, with the Earl of Pembroke (William Herbert), and promulgated his own identification of Mistress Mary Fitton with the Dark Lady. Whether he was right or wrong about the Dark Lady did not matter urgently to me: she might have been Maria Tompkins for all I cared. But Tyler would have it that she was Mary Fitton; and he tracked Mary down from the first of her marriages in her teens to her tomb in Cheshire, whither he made a pilgrimage and whence returned in triumph with a picture of her statue, and the news that he was convinced she was a dark lady by traces of paint still discernible.

In due course he published his edition of the Sonnets, with the evidence he had collected. He lent me a copy of the book, which I never returned. But I reviewed it in the Pall Mall Gazette on the 7th of January 1886, and thereby let loose the Fitton theory in a wider circle of readers than the book could reach. Then Tyler died, sinking unnoted like a stone in the sea. I observed that Mr Acheson, Mrs Davenant's champion, calls him Reverend. It may very well be that he got his knowledge of Hebrew in reading for the Church; and there was always something of the clergyman or the schoolmaster in his dress and air. Possibly he may actually have been ordained. But he never told me that or anything else about his affairs; and his black pessimism would have shot him violently out of any church at present established in the West. We never talked about affairs: we talked about Shakespear, and the Dark Lady, and Swift, and Koheleth, and the cycles, and the mysterious moments when a feeling came over us that this had happened to us before, and about the forgeries of the Pentateuch which were offered for sale to the British Museum, and about literature and things of the spirit generally. He always came to my desk at the Museum and spoke to me about something or other, no doubt finding that people who were keen on this sort of conversation were rather scarce. He remains a vivid spot of memory in the void of my forgetfulness, a quite considerable and dignified soul in a grotesquely disfigured body.

(...)

Shakespear's Pessimism

I submit to [Frank] Harris that by ruling out this idolatry, and its possible effect in making Shakespear think that his public would stand anything from him, he has ruled out a far more plausible explanation of the faults of such a play as Timon of Athens than his theory that Shakespear's passion for the Dark Lady "cankered and took on proud flesh in him, and tortured him to nervous breakdown and madness." In Timon the intellectual bankruptcy is obvious enough: Shakespear tried once too often to make a play out of the cheap pessimism which is thrown into despair by a comparison of actual human nature with theoretical morality, actual law and administration with abstract justice, and so forth. But Shakespear's perception of the fact that all men, judged by the moral standard which they apply to others and by which they justify their punishment of others, are fools and scoundrels, does not date from the Dark Lady complication: he seems to have been born with it. If in The Comedy of Errors and A Midsummer Night's Dream the persons of the drama are not quite so ready for treachery and murder as Laertes and even Hamlet himself (not to mention the procession of ruffians who pass through the latest plays) it is certainly not because they have any more regard for law or religion. There is only one place in Shakespear's plays where the sense of shame is used as a human attribute; and that is where Hamlet is ashamed, not of anything he himself has done, but of his mother's relations with his uncle. This scene is an unnatural one: the son's reproaches to his mother, even the fact of his being able to discuss the subject with her, is more repulsive than her relations with her deceased husband's brother.

Here, too, Shakespear betrays for once his religious sense by making Hamlet, in his agony of shame, declare that his mother's conduct makes "sweet religion a rhapsody of words." But for that passage we might almost suppose that the feeling of Sunday morning in the country which Orlando describes so perfectly in As You Like It was the beginning and end of Shakespear's notion of religion. I say almost, because Isabella in Measure for Measure has religious charm, in spite of the conventional theatrical assumption that female religion means an inhumanly ferocious chastity. But for the most part Shakespear differentiates his heroes from his villains much more by what they do than by what they are. Don John in Much Ado is a true villain: a man with a malicious will; but he is too dull a duffer to be of any use in a leading part; and when we come to the great villains like Macbeth, we find, as Mr Harris points out, that they are precisely identical with the heroes: Macbeth is only Hamlet incongruously committing murders and engaging in hand-to-hand combats. And Hamlet, who does not dream of apologizing for the three murders he commits, is always apologizing because he has not yet committed a fourth, and finds, to his great bewilderment, that he does not want to commit it. "It cannot be," he says, "but I am pigeon-livered, and lack gall to make oppression bitter; else, ere this, I should have fatted all the region kites with this slave's offal." Really one is tempted to suspect that when Shylock asks "Hates any man the thing he would not kill?" he is expressing the natural and proper sentiments of the human race as Shakespear understood them, and not the vindictiveness of a stage Jew.

Gaiety of Genius

In view of these facts, it is dangerous to cite Shakespear's pessimism as evidence of the despair of a heart broken by the Dark Lady. There is an irrepressible gaiety of genius which enables it to bear the whole weight of the world's misery without blenching. There is a laugh always ready to avenge its tears of discouragement. In the lines which Mr Harris quotes only to declare that he can make nothing of them, and to condemn them as out of character, Richard III, immediately after pitying himself because

> There is no creature loves me
> And if I die no soul will pity me,

adds, with a grin,

> Nay, wherefore should they, since that I myself
> Find in myself no pity for myself?

Let me again remind Mr Harris of Oscar Wilde. We all dreaded to read De Profundis: our instinct was to stop our ears, or run away from the wail of a broken, though by no means contrite, heart. But we were throwing away our pity. De Profundis was de profundis indeed: Wilde was too good a dramatist to throw away so powerful an effect; but none the less it was de profundis in excelsis. There was more laughter between the lines of that book than in a thousand farces by men of no genius. Wilde, like Richard and Shakespear, found in himself no pity for himself. There is nothing that marks the born dramatist more unmistakably than this discovery of comedy in his own misfortunes almost in proportion to the pathos with which the ordinary man announces their tragedy. I cannot for the life of me see the broken heart in Shakespear's latest works. "Hark, hark! the lark at heaven's gate sings" is not the lyric of a broken man; nor is Cloten's comment that if Imogen does not appreciate it, "it is a vice in her ears which horse hairs, and cats' guts, and the voice of unpaved eunuch to boot, can never amend," the sally of a saddened one. Is it not clear that to the last there was in Shakespear an incorrigible divine levity, an inexhaustible joy that derided sorrow? Think of the poor Dark Lady having to stand up to this unbearable power of extracting a grim fun from everything. Mr Harris writes as if Shakespear did all the suffering and the Dark Lady all the cruelty. But why does he not put himself in the Dark Lady's place for a moment as he has put himself so successfully in Shakespear's? Imagine her reading the hundred and thirtieth sonnet!

> My mistress' eyes are nothing like the sun;
> Coral is far more red than her lips' red;
> If snow be white, why then her breasts are dun;
> If hairs be wire, black wires grow on her head;
> I have seen roses damasked, red and white,
> But no such roses see I in her cheeks;
> And in some perfumes is there more delight

Than in the breath that from my mistress reeks.
I love to hear her speak; yet well I know
That music hath a far more pleasing sound.
I grant I never saw a goddess go:
My mistress, when she walks, treads on the ground.
  And yet, by heaven, I think my love as rare
  As any she belied with false compare.

Take this as a sample of the sort of compliment from which she was never for a moment safe with Shakespear. Bear in mind that she was not a comedian; that the Elizabethan fashion of treating brunettes as ugly woman must have made her rather sore on the subject of her complexion; that no human being, male or female, can conceivably enjoy being chaffed on that point in the fourth couplet about the perfumes; that Shakespear's revulsions, as the sonnet immediately preceding shews, were as violent as his ardors, and were expressed with the realistic power and horror that makes Hamlet say that the heavens got sick when they saw the queen's conduct; and then ask Mr Harris whether any woman could have stood it for long, or have thought the "sugred" compliment worth the cruel wounds, the cleaving of the heart in twain, that seemed to Shakespear as natural and amusing a reaction as the burlesquing of his heroics by Pistol, his sermons by Falstaff, and his poems by Cloten and Touchstone.

Jupiter and Semele

This does not mean that Shakespear was cruel: evidently he was not; but it was not cruelty that made Jupiter reduce Semele to ashes: it was the fact that he could not help being a god nor she help being a mortal. The one thing Shakespear's passion for the Dark Lady was not, was what Mr Harris in one passage calls it: idolatrous. If it had been, she might have been able to stand it. The man who "dotes yet doubts, suspects, yet strongly loves," is tolerable even by a spoilt and tyrannical mistress; but what woman could possibly endure a man who dotes without doubting; who *knows*, and who is hugely amused at the absurdity of his infatuation for a woman of whose mortal imperfections not one escapes him: a man always exchanging grins with Yorick's skull, and inviting "my lady" to laugh at the sepulchral humor of the fact that though she paint an inch thick (which the Dark Lady may have done), to Yorick's favor she must come at last. To the Dark Lady he must sometimes have seemed cruel beyond description: an intellectual Caliban. True, a Caliban who could say

Be not afeard: the isle is full of noises
Sounds and sweet airs that give delight and hurt not.
Sometimes a thousand twangling instruments
Will hum about mine ears; and sometimes voices,

That, if I then had waked after long sleep
Will make me sleep again; and then, in dreaming,
The clouds, methought, would open and shew riches
Ready to drop on me: that when I wak'd
I cried to dream again.

which is very lovely; but the Dark Lady may have had that vice in her ears which Cloten dreaded: she may not have seen the beauty of it, whereas there can be no doubt at all that of "My mistress' eyes are nothing like the sun," &c., not a word was lost on her.

And is it to be supposed that Shakespear was too stupid or too modest not to see at last that it was a case of Jupiter and Semele? Shakespear was most certainly not modest in that sense. The timid cough of the minor poet was never heard from him.

Not marble, nor the gilded monuments
Of princes, shall outlive this powerful rhyme

is only one out of a dozen passages in which he (possibly with a keen sense of the fun of scandalizing the modest coughers) proclaimed his place and his power in "the wide world dreaming of things to come." The Dark Lady most likely thought this side of him insufferably conceited; for there is no reason to suppose that she liked his plays any better than Minna Wagner liked Richard's music dramas: as likely as not, she thought The Spanish Tragedy worth six Hamlets. He was not stupid either: if his class limitations and a profession that cut him off from actual participation in great affairs of State had not confined his opportunities of intellectual and political training to private conversation and to the Mermaid Tavern, he would probably have become one of the ablest men of his time instead of being merely its ablest playwright. One might surmise that Shakespear found out that the Dark Lady's brains could no more keep pace with his than Anne Hathaway's, if there were any evidence that their friendship ceased when he stopped writing sonnets to her. As a matter of fact the consolidation of a passion into an enduring intimacy generally puts an end to sonnets.

That the Dark Lady broke Shakespear's heart, as Mr Harris will have it she did, is an extremely unShakespearian hypothesis. "Men have died from time to time, and worms have eaten them; but not for love," says Rosalind. Richard of Gloster, into whom Shakespear put all his own impish superiority to vulgar sentiment, exclaims

And this word "love," which greybeards call divine,
Be resident in men like one another
And not in me: I am myself alone.

Hamlet has not a tear for Ophelia: her death moves him to fierce disgust for the sentimentality of Laertes by her grave; and when he discusses the scene with Horatio immediately after, he utterly forgets her, though he is sorry he forgot himself, and jumps at the proposal of a fencing match to finish the day with. As against this view Mr Harris pleads Romeo, Orsino, and even Antonio; and he does it so penetratingly that he convinces you that Shakespear did betray himself again and again in these characters; but self-betrayal is one thing; and self-portrayal, as in Hamlet and Mercutio, is another. Shakespear never "saw himself," as actors say, in Romeo or Orsino or Antonio. In Mr Harris's own play Shakespear is presented with the most pathetic tenderness. He is tragic, bitter, pitiable, wretched and broken among a robust crowd of Jonsons and Elizabeths; but to me he is not Shakespear because I miss the Shakespearian irony and the Shakespearian gaiety. Take these away and Shakespear is no longer Shakespear: all the bite, the impetus, the strength, the grim delight in his own power of looking terrible facts in the face with a chuckle, is gone; and you have nothing left but that most depressing of all things: a victim. Now who can think of Shakespear as a man with a grievance? Even in that most thoroughgoing and inspired of all Shakespear's loves: his love of music (which Mr Harris has been the first to appreciate at anything like its value), there is a dash of mockery. "Spit in the hole, man; and tune again." "Divine air! Now is his soul ravished. Is it not strange that sheep's guts should hale the souls out of men's bodies?" "An he had been a dog that should have howled thus, they would have hanged him." There is just as much Shakespear here as in the inevitable quotation about the sweet south and the bank of violets.

I lay stress on this irony of Shakespear's, this impish rejoicing in pessimism, this exultation in what breaks the hearts of common men, not only because it is diagnostic of that immense energy of life which we call genius, but because its omission is the one glaring defect in Mr Harris's otherwise extraordinarily penetrating book. Fortunately, it is an omission that does not disable the book as (in my judgment) it disabled the hero of the play, because Mr Harris left himself out of his play, whereas he pervades his book, mordant, deep-voiced, and with an unconquerable style which is the man.

The Idol of the Bardolaters

There is even an advantage in having a book on Shakespear with the Shakespearian irony left out of account. I do not say that the missing chapter should not be added in the next edition: the hiatus is too great: it leaves the reader too uneasy before this touching picture of a writhing worm substituted for the invulnerable giant. But it is none the less probable that in no other way could Mr Harris have got at his man as he has. For, after all, what is the secret of the hopeless failure of the academic Bardolaters to give us a credible or even interesting Shakespear, and the easy triumph of Mr Harris in giving us both? Simply that Mr Harris has assumed that he was dealing with a man, whilst the others have assumed that they were writing about a god, and have therefore rejected every consideration of fact, tradition, or interpretation, that pointed to any human imperfection in their hero. They thus leave themselves with so little material that they are forced to begin by saying that we know very little about Shakespear. As a matter of fact, with the plays and sonnets in our hands, we know much more about Shakespear than we know about Dickens or Thackeray: the only difficulty is that we deliberately suppress it because it proves that Shakespear was not only very unlike the conception of a god current in Clapham, but was not, according to the same reckoning, even a respectable man. The academic view starts with a Shakespear who was not scurrilous; therefore the verses about "lousy Lucy" cannot have been written by him, and the cognate passages in the plays are either strokes of character-drawing or gags interpolated by the actors. This ideal Shakespear was too well behaved to get drunk; therefore the tradition that his death was hastened by a drinking bout with Jonson and Drayton must be rejected, and the remorse of Cassio treated as a thing observed, not experienced: nay, the disgust of Hamlet at the drinking customs of Denmark is taken to establish Shakespear as the superior of Alexander in self-control, and the greatest of teetotallers.

Now this system of inventing your great man to start with, and then rejecting all the materials that do not fit him, with the ridiculous result that you have to declare that there are no materials at all (with your waste-paper basket full of them), ends in leaving Shakespear with a much worse character than he deserves. For though it does not greatly matter whether he wrote the lousy Lucy lines or not, and does not really matter at all whether he got drunk when he made a night of it with Jonson and Drayton, the sonnets raise an unpleasant question which does matter a good deal; and the refusal of the academic Bardolaters to discuss or even mention this question has had the effect of producing a silent verdict against Shakespear. Mr Harris tackles the question openly, and has no difficulty whatever in convincing us that Shakespear was a man of normal constitution sexually, and was not the victim of that most cruel and pitiable of all the freaks of nature: the freak which transposes the normal aim of the affections. Silence on this point means condemnation; and the condemnation has been general throughout the present generation, though it only needed Mr Harris's fearless handling of the matter to sweep away what is nothing but a morbid and very disagreeable modern fashion. There is always some stock accusation brought against eminent persons. When I was a boy every well-known man was accused of beating his wife. Later on, for some unexplained reason, he was accused of psychopathic derangement. And this fashion is retrospective. The cases of Shakespear and Michel Angelo are cited as proving that every genius of the first magnitude was a sufferer; and both here and in Germany there are circles in which such derangement is grotesquely reverenced as part of the stigmata of

heroic powers. All of which is gross nonsense. Unfortunately, in Shakespear's
case, prudery, which cannot prevent the accusation from being whispered, does
prevent the refutation from being shouted. Mr Harris, the deep-voiced, refuses
to be silenced. He dismisses with proper contempt the stupidity which places an
outrageous construction on Shakespear's apologies in the sonnets for neglecting
that "perfect ceremony" of love which consists in returning calls and making
protestations and giving presents and paying the trumpery attentions which men
of genius always refuse to bother about, and to which touchy people who have
no genius attach so much importance. No leader who had not been tampered
with by the psychopathic monomaniacs could ever put any construction but
the obvious and innocent one on these passages. But the general vocabulary of
the sonnets to Pembroke (or whoever "Mr W.H." really was) is so overcharged
according to modern ideas that a reply on the general case is necessary.

Shakespear's alleged Sycophancy and Perversion

That reply, which Mr Harris does not hesitate to give, is twofold: first, that
Shakespear was, in his attitude towards earls, a sycophant; and, second, that the
normality of Shakespear's sexual constitution is only too well attested by the
excessive susceptibility to the normal impulse shewn in the whole mass of his
writings. This latter is the really conclusive reply. In the case of Michel Angelo, for
instance, one must admit that if his works are set beside those of Titian or Paul
Veronese, it is impossible not to be struck by the absence in the Florentine of that
susceptibility to feminine charm which pervades the pictures of the Venetians.
But, as Mr Harris points out (though he does not use this particular illustration)
Paul Veronese is an anchorite compared to Shakespear. The language of the
sonnets addressed to Pembroke, extravagant as it now seems, is the language of
compliment and fashion, transfigured no doubt by Shakespear's verbal magic,
and hyperbolical, as Shakespear always seems to people who cannot conceive
so vividly as he, but still unmistakable for anything else than the expression of a
friendship delicate enough to be wounded, and a manly loyalty deep enough to
be outraged. But the language of the sonnets to the Dark Lady is the language of
passion: their cruelty shews it. There is no evidence that Shakespear was capable
of being unkind in cold blood. But in his revulsions from love, he was bitter,
wounding, even ferocious; sparing neither himself nor the unfortunate woman
whose only offence was that she had reduced the great man to the common
human denominator.

In seizing on these two points Mr Harris has made so sure a stroke, and placed
his evidence so featly that there is nothing left for me to do but to plead that
the second is sounder than the first, which is, I think, marked by the prevalent
mistake as to Shakespear's social position, or, if you prefer it, the confusion
between his actual social position as a penniless tradesman's son taking to the
theatre for a livelihood, and his own conception of himself as a gentleman of

good family. I am prepared to contend that though Shakespear was undoubtedly sentimental in his expressions of devotion to Mr W.H. even to a point which nowadays makes both ridiculous, he was not sycophantic if Mr W.H. was really attractive and promising, and Shakespear deeply attached to him. A sycophant does not tell his patron that his fame will survive, not in the renown of his own actions, but in the sonnets of his sycophant. A sycophant, when his patron cuts him out in a love affair, does not tell his patron exactly what he thinks of him. Above all, a sycophant does not write to his patron precisely as he feels on all occasions; and this rare kind of sincerity is all over the sonnets. Shakespear, we are told, was "a very civil gentleman." This must mean that his desire to please people and be liked by them, and his reluctance to hurt their feelings, led him into amiable flattery even when his feelings were not strongly stirred. If this be taken into account along with the fact that Shakespear conceived and expressed all his emotions with a vehemence that sometimes carried him into ludicrous extravagance, making Richard offer his kingdom for a horse and Othello declare of Cassio that

> Had all his hairs been lives, my great revenge
> Had stomach for them all,

we shall see more civility and hyperbole than sycophancy even in the earlier and more cold-blooded sonnets.

(. . .)

Shakespear and the British Public

I have rejected Mr Harris's view that Shakespear died broken-hearted of "the pangs of love despised." I have given my reasons for believing that Shakespear died game, and indeed in a state of levity which would have been considered unbecoming in a bishop. But Mr Harris's evidence does prove that Shakespear had a grievance and a very serious one. He might have been jilted by ten dark ladies and been none the worse for it; but his treatment by the British Public was another matter. The idolatry which exasperated Ben Jonson was by no means a popular movement; and, like all such idolatries, it was excited by the magic of Shakespear's art rather than by his views. He was launched on his career as a successful playwright by the Henry VI trilogy, a work of no originality, depth, or subtlety except the originality, depth, and subtlety of the feelings and fancies of the common people. But Shakespear was not satisfied with this. What is the use of being Shakespear if you are not allowed to express any notions but those of Autolycus? Shakespear did not see the world as Autolycus did: he saw it, if not exactly as Ibsen did (for it was not quite the same world), at least with much of Ibsen's power of penetrating its illusions and idolatries, and with all Swift's horror of its cruelty and uncleanliness.

Now it happens to some men with these powers that they are forced to impose their fullest exercise on the world because they cannot produce popular work. Take Wagner and Ibsen for instance! Their earlier works are no doubt much cheaper than their later ones; still, they were not popular when they were written. The alternative of doing popular work was never really open to them: had they stooped they would have picked up less than they snatched from above the people's heads. But Handel and Shakespear were not held to their best in this way. They could turn out anything they were asked for, and even heap up the measure. They reviled the British Public, and never forgave it for ignoring their best work and admiring their splendid commonplaces; but they produced the commonplaces all the same, and made them sound magnificent by mere brute faculty for their art. When Shakespear was forced to write popular plays to save his theatre from ruin, he did it mutinously, calling the plays "As *You* Like It," and "Much Ado About Nothing." All the same, he did it so well that to this day these two genial vulgarities are the main Shakespearian stock-in-trade of our theatres. Later on Burbage's power and popularity as an actor enabled Shakespear to free himself from the tyranny of the box office, and to express himself more freely in plays consisting largely of monologue to be spoken by a great actor from whom the public would stand a good deal. The history of Shakespear's tragedies has thus been the history of a long line of famous actors, from Burbage and Betterton to Forbes Robertson; and the man of whom we are told that "when he would have said that Richard died, and cried A horse! A horse! he Burbage cried" was the father of nine generations of Shakespearian playgoers, all speaking of Garrick's Richard, and Kean's Othello, and Irving's Shylock, and Forbes Robertson's Hamlet without knowing or caring how much these had to do with Shakespear's Richard and Othello and so forth. And the plays which were written without great and predominant parts, such as Troilus and Cressida, All's Well That Ends Well, and Measure for Measure, have dropped on our stage as dead as the second part of Goethe's Faust or Ibsen's Emperor or Galilean.

Here, then, Shakespear had a real grievance; and though it is a sentimental exaggeration to describe him as a broken-hearted man in the face of the passages of reckless jollity and serenely happy poetry in his latest plays, yet the discovery that his most serious work could reach success only when carried on the back of a very fascinating actor who was enormously overcharging his part, and that the serious plays which did not contain parts big enough to hold the overcharge were left on the shelf, amply accounts for the evident fact that Shakespear did not end his life in a glow of enthusiastic satisfaction with mankind and with the theatre, which is all that Mr Harris can allege in support of his broken-heart theory. But even if Shakespear had had no failures, it was not possible for a man of his powers to observe the political and moral conduct of his contemporaries without perceiving that they were incapable of dealing with the problems raised by their own civilization, and that their attempts to carry out the codes of law and to practise the religions offered to them by great prophets and law-givers were and still are so foolish that we now call for The Superman, virtually a new species, to rescue the world from mismanagement. This is the real sorrow of great men; and in the face of it the notion that when a great man speaks bitterly or looks melancholy he must be troubled by a disappointment in love seems to me sentimental trifling.

If I have carried the reader with me thus far, he will find that trivial as this little play of mine is, its sketch of Shakespear is more complete than its levity suggests. Alas! its appeal for a National Theatre as a monument to Shakespear failed to touch the very stupid people who cannot see that a National Theatre is worth having for the sake of the National Soul. I had unfortunately represented Shakespear as treasuring and using (as I do myself) the jewels of unconsciously musical speech which common people utter and throw away every day; and this was taken as a disparagement of Shakespear's "originality." Why was I born with such contemporaries? Why is Shakespear made ridiculous by such a posterity?

1926—Robert Graves and Laura Riding. "A Study in Original Punctuation and Spelling," from *A Survey of Modernist Poetry*

Robert Graves (1895–1985) was an influential poet, novelist, scholar, and translator of classical mythology and history. His *Goodbye to All That* is a classic memoir of the First World War, and his *Claudius* novels remain popular today. Laura Riding (1901–1991) was an American poet and critic who was Graves's partner and collaborator. The pair co-wrote *A Survey of Modernist Poetry* and *A Pamphlet Against Anthologies*. A revised version of their essay on Shakespeare's sonnet 129 appeared in 1949.

The objections raised against the 'freakishness' of modernist poetry are usually supported by quotations from poems by Mr. E.E. Cummings and others which are not only difficult in construction and reference but are printed oddly on the page. The reader naturally looks for certain landmarks in a poem before he can begin to enjoy it: as the visitor to Paris naturally sets his mental map of the city by the Eiffel Tower, and if the Eiffel Tower were to collapse, would have difficulty in finding his way about for a few days. Modernist poets have removed the well-known landmarks and the reader is equally at a loss. The reasons for this removal

are, apparently, that landmarks encourage the making of paths, that paths grow
to roads, that roads soon mean walls and hedges, and that the common traveller
who keeps to the roads never sees any new scenery.

> because
> you go away i give roses who
> will advise even yourself, lady
> in the most certainly (of what we
> everywhere do not touch) deep
> things;
> remembering ever so . . .

This is the beginning of one of Mr. Cummings' poems. The first obvious
oddity is the degrading of the personal pronoun 'I' to 'i.' This has a simple
enough history. The 'upper case' was once used for all nouns and proper names
and the adjectives formed from them; but since the eighteenth century has been
reserved for the Deity; for Royalty (in 'We' and 'Our'); for certain quasi-divine
abstractions such as Mystery, Power, Poetry; sometimes for 'She' and 'Thou' and
so on, where love gives the pronoun a quasi-divine character. Mr. Cummings
protests against the upper case being also allotted to 'I': he affects a humility, a
denial of the idea of personal immortality responsible for 'I.' Moreover, 'i' is more
casual and detached: it dissociates the author from the speaker of the poem.
The use of 'i' is in keeping with his use of 'who,' instead of 'which,' to qualify
the roses; the roses become so personal as to deserve the personal rather than
the neutral relative. His next idiosyncrasy is his denial of a capital letter to each
new line of the poem. Now, if this convention were not so well established, it
would seem as odd and as unnecessary as, for instance, quotation marks seem
in eighteenth-century books when they enclose each line of a long speech. The
modernist rejection of the initial capital letter can be justified on the grounds
that it gives the first word of each line, which may be a mere 'and' or 'or,' an
unnatural emphasis. If for special reasons the poet wishes to capitalize the first
word, the fact that it is capitalized in any case, like all the other initial 'And's' and
'Or's,' makes any such niceness impossible.

Later in the poem a capital letter occurs at the beginning of a new sentence to
call attention to the full stop which might otherwise be missed: but the 'because'
at the beginning of the poem need not be capitalized since it obviously *is* the
beginning. Similarly, the conventional comma after 'lady' is suppressed because
the end of the line makes a natural pause without the need of punctuation.
Commas are used to mark pauses, not merely as the geographical boundaries
of a clause. Mr. Cummings has even inserted one in another poem between
the *n* and *g* of the word 'falling' to suggest the slowness of the falling. Colons,
semicolons and full stops he uses to mark pauses of varying length. To indicate a

still longer pause he leaves a blank line. In the quotation just given, the new line at 'remembering' is to mark a change of tone, though the pause is no longer than a semicolon's worth. He uses parentheses for *sotto voce* pronunciation; or if they occur in the middle of a word, as in:

the taxi-man p(ee)ps his whistle

they denote a certain quality of the letters enclosed—here the sharp whistling sound between the opening and closing (the two *p*'s) of the taxi-man's lips. When this system of notation is carried to a point of great accuracy we find lines like the following:

CA: G
with-ered unspea-king:tWeNtY,f i n g e r s,large

which, if quoted detached from their context, seem to support any charge of irrational freakishness, but in their context are completely intelligible. Moreover, Mr. Cummings is protecting himself against future liberties that printers and editors may take with his work, by using a personal typographical system which it will be impossible to revise without destroying the poem.

He has perhaps learned a lesson from the fate of Shakespeare's sonnets: not only have his editors changed the spelling and pronunciation, but certain very occasional and obvious printer's errors in the only edition printed in Shakespeare's lifetime have been made the excuse for hundreds of unjustifiable emendations and 'modernizations.' Mr. Cummings and Shakespeare have in common a deadly accuracy. It frightens Mr. Cummings' public and provoked Shakespeare's eighteenth-century editors to meddle with his texts as being too difficult to print as they were written. We shall find that though Shakespeare's poems have a more familiar look than Mr. Cummings' on the page, they are more difficult in thought: Mr. Cummings accurately expresses, in a form peculiar to himself, what is common to everyone; Shakespeare expressed, as accurately but in the common form of his time, what was peculiar to himself.

Here are two versions of a sonnet by Shakespeare: first, the version found in *The Oxford Book of English Verse* and other popular anthologies whose editors may be assumed to have chosen this sonnet from all the rest as being particularly easy to understand; next, the version printed in the 1609 edition of the *Sonnets* and apparently copied from Shakespeare's original manuscript, though Shakespeare is most unlikely to have seen the proofs. The alterations, it will be noticed in a comparison of the two versions, are with a few exceptions chiefly in the punctuation and spelling. By showing what a great difference to the sense the juggling of punctuation marks has made in the original sonnet, we shall perhaps be able to persuade the plain reader to sympathize with what seems typographical perversity in Mr. Cummings. The modernizing of the spelling is not quite so serious a matter, though we shall see that to change a word like *blouddy* to *bloody* makes a difference not only in the atmosphere of the word but in its sound as well.

I

Th' expense of Spirit in a waste of shame
Is lust in action; and till action, lust
Is perjured, murderous, bloody, full of blame,
Savage, extreme, rude; cruel, not to trust;
Enjoy'd no sooner but despisèd straight;
Past reason hunted; and, no sooner had,
Past reason hated, as a swallow'd bait
On purpose laid to make the taker mad:
Mad in pursuit, and in possession so;
Had, having, and in quest to have, extreme;
A bliss in proof, and proved, a very woe;
Before, a joy proposed; behind, a dream.
    All this the world well knows; yet none knows well
    To shun the heaven that leads men to this hell.

II

Th' expense of Spirit in a waste of shame
Is lust in action, and till action, lust
Is periurd, murdrous, blouddy full of blame,
Sauage, extreame, rude, cruell, not to trust,
Inioyd no sooner but dispised straight,
Past reason hunted, and no sooner had
Past reason hated as a swollowed bayt,
On purpose layd to make the taker mad.
Made In pursut and in possession so,
Had, hauing, and in quest, to haue extreame,
A blisse in proofe and proud and very wo,
Before a ioy proposd behind a dreame,
    All this the world well knowes yet none knowes well,
    To shun the heauen that leads men to this hell.

First, to compare the spelling. As a matter of course the *u* in *proud* and *heauen* changes to *v*; the Elizabethans had no typographical *v*. There are other words in which the change of spelling does not seem to matter. *Expence, cruell, bayt, layd, pursut, blisse, proofe, wo*—these words taken by themselves are not necessarily affected by modernization, though much of the original atmosphere of the poem is lost by changing them in the gross. Sheer facility in reading a poem is no gain when one tries to discover what the poem looked like to the poet who wrote it. But other changes designed to increase reading facility involve more than changes in spelling. *Periurd* to *perjured*, and *murdrous* to *murderous*, would have meant, to Shakespeare, the addition of another syllable. *Inioyd*, with the same number of syllables as *periurd*, is however printed *Enjoy'd*; while *swollowed*, which must have been meant as a three-syllabled word (Shakespeare used *ed* as a separate syllable very strictly and frequently allowed himself an extra syllable in his iambic foot) is printed *swallow'd*. When we come to *dispised*, we find in the modern version an accent over the last syllable. These liberties do not make the poem any easier; they only make it less accurate. The sound of the poem suffers through re-spelling as well as through alterations in the rhythm made by this use of apostrophes and accents. *Blouddy* was pronounced more like *blue-dy* than *bluddy*; the *ea* of *extreame* and *dreame* sounded like the *ea* in *great*; and *periurd* was probably pronounced more like *peryurd* than *pergeurd*.

But it is the changes in punctuation which do the most damage: not only to the atmosphere of the poem but to its meaning. In the second line a semicolon substituted for a comma after the first *action* gives a longer rest than Shakespeare gave; it also cuts the idea short at *action* instead of keeping *in action* and *till action* together as well as the two *lust*'s. A comma after *blouddy* makes this a separate characterization and thus reduces the weight of the whole phrase as rhythmic relief to the string of adjectives; it probably had the adverbial form of *blouddily*. Next, several semicolons are substituted for commas; these introduce pauses which break up the continuous interpenetration of images. If Shakespeare had intended such pauses he would have used semicolons, as he does elsewhere. Particularly serious is the interpolation of a comma after *no sooner had*, which confines the phrase to the special meaning 'lust no sooner had *past reason* is hated past reason.' Shakespeare did not write in the syntax of prose but in a sensitive poetic flow. The comma might as well have been put between *reason* and *hated*; it would have limited the meaning, but no more than has been done here. On the other hand a comma is omitted where Shakespeare was careful to put one, after *bayt*. With the comma, On *purpose layd*—though it refers to *bayt*—also looks back to the original idea of *lust*; without the comma it merely continues the figure of *bayt*. In the original there is a full stop at *mad*, closing the octave; in the emended version a colon is used, making the next line run on and causing the unpardonable change from *Made* to *Mad*. The capital 'I' of *In* shows how carefully the printer copied the manuscript. Evidently, Shakespeare first wrote the line without *Made*, and then, deciding that such an irregular line was too dramatic, added *Made* without troubling to change the capital 'I' to a small one. In any case *Made* necessarily follows from *make* of the preceding line: 'to make the taker mad, made (mad)'; but it also enlarges the mad-making bayt to the generally extreame-making lust. The change from *Made* to *Mad* limits the final *so* of this line to *Mad* and provokes a change from comma to semicolon—'Mad in pursuit and in possession so (mad)'—whereas *mad* is only vaguely echoed in this line from the preceding one. The meaning of the original line is: 'Made In pursut and in possession as follows,' and also: 'Made In pursut and in possession as has been said.'

The comma between *in quest* and *to have extreame* has been moved forward to separate *have* from *extreame*. This line originally stood for a number of interwoven meanings:

1. The taker of the bait, the man in pursuit and in possession of lust, is made mad: is so made that he experiences both extremes at once. (What these extremes are the lines following show.)

2. The *Had, having and in quest*, might well have been written in parentheses. They explain, by way of interjection, that lust comprises all the stages of lust: the after-lust period (*Had*), the actual experience of lust (*having*), and the anticipation of lust (*in quest*); and that the extremes of lust are felt in all these stages (*to have extreame*—i.e. to have in extreme degree).

3. Further, one stage in lust is like the others, is as extreme as the others. All the distinctions made in the poem between *lust in action* and *till action lust*, between lust *In pursut* and lust *in possession* are made to show that in the end there are no real distinctions. *Had, having and in quest* is the summing up of this fact.

4. *Had* and *having* double the sense of *possession* to match the double sense of action implied by *Th' expence of Spirit in a waste of shame*; and *in quest* naturally refers to *In pursut*, which in turn recalls *till action*.

5. Throughout the poem it must be kept in mind that words qualifying the lust-interest refer interchangeably to the man who lusts, the object of lust and lust in the abstract. This interchangeability accounts for the apparently ungrammatical effect of the line.

With the emended punctuation the line has only one narrow sense, and this not precisely Shakespeare's; the semicolon placed after *so* of the preceding line, cuts the close co-operation between them. The shifting of the comma not only removes a pause where Shakespeare put one, and thus changes the rhythm, but the line itself loses point and does not pull its weight. In this punctuation the *whole* line ought to be put into parentheses, as being a mere repetition. The *to have* linked with *in quest* is superfluous; *extreme* set off by itself is merely a descriptive adjective already used. Moreover, when the line is thus isolated between two semicolons, *Had, having*, etc., instead of effecting a harmony between the interchangeable senses, disjoints them and becomes ungrammatical. *Mad in pursuit, and in possession so* refers only to *the taker mad*. The next line, *A blisse in proofe and proud and very wo*, should explain to *have extreame*; it is not merely another parenthetical line as in the emended version. To fulfil the paradox implied in *extreame* it should mean that lust is a bliss during the proof and after the proof, and also *very wo* (truly woe) during and after the proof. The emended line, *A bliss in proof, and proved, a very woe*, which refers only to lust in the abstract, not equally to the man who lusts, means that lust is a bliss during the proof but a woe after the proof—and thus denies what Shakespeare has been at pains to show all along, that lust is all things at all times.

Once the editors began repunctuating the line they had to tamper with the words themselves. A comma after *proof* demanded a comma after *provd*. A comma after *provd* made it necessary to change *and very wo* so that it should apply to *provd* only. Another semicolon which they have put at the end of this line again breaks the continuity of the sense: the succeeding line becomes only another antithesis or rhetorical balance ('a joy in prospect, but a dream in retrospect,' to repeat the sense of 'a bliss during proof but woe after proof'), instead of carrying on the intricate and careful argument that runs without a stop through the whole sestet. The importance of the line is that it takes all the meanings in the poem one stage further. Lust in the extreme goes beyond both bliss and woe: it goes beyond reality. It is no longer lust *Had, having and in quest*; it is lust face to face with *love*. Even when consummated, lust still stands before an unconsummated joy, a proposed joy, and proposed not as a joy possible of consummation but as one only to be known through the dream by which lust leads itself on, the dream behind which this proposed joy, this love, seems to lie. This is the over-riding meaning of the line. It has other meanings, but they all defer to this. For example, it may also be read: 'Before a joy can be proposed, it must first be renounced as a real joy, it must be put behind as a dream'; or: 'Before the man in lust is a prospect of joy, yet he knows by experience that this is only a dream'; or: 'Beforehand he says that he proposed lust to be a joy, afterwards he says that it came as involuntarily as a dream'; or: 'Before (in face of) a joy proposed only as a consequence of a dream, with a dream impelling him from behind.' All these and even more readings of the line are possible and legitimate, and each reading could in turn be made to explain precisely why the taker is made mad, or how lust is *to have extreame*, or why it is both *a blisse* and *very wo*. The punctuated line in the emended version, cut off from what has gone before and from what follows, can mean only: 'In prospect, lust is a joy; in retrospect, a dream.' Though a possible contributory meaning, when made the *only* meaning it presents as the theme of the poem that lust is impossible of satisfaction, whereas the theme, as carried on by the next line, is that lust as lust *is* satisfiable but that satisfied lust is in conflict with itself.

The next line, if unpunctuated except for the comma Shakespeare put at the end, is a general statement of this conflict: the man in lust is torn between lust as he well knows it in common with the world and lust in his personal experience which crazes him to hope for more than lust from lust. The force of the second *well* is to deny the first *well*: no one really knows anything of lust except in personal experience, and only through personal experience can lust be known *well* rather than 'well-known.' But separate the second *well* from the first, as in the emended version, and the direct opposition between *world* and *none*, *well knowes* and *knowes well* is destroyed, as well as the word-play between *well knowes* and *knowes well*; for by the removal of the comma after the second *well*, this becomes an adverb modifying *To shun* in the following line—*well* now means merely 'successfully' in association with *To shun*, instead of 'well enough' in association with *knowes*. This repunctuation also robs *All this* of its significance, since it refers not only to all that has gone before but to the last line too: 'All this the world well knowes yet none knowes well' the moral to be drawn from the character of lust (i.e. to shun the heaven that leads men to this hell). The character and the moral of lust the whole world well knows, but no one knows the character and the moral really well unless he disregards the moral warning and engages in lust: no one knows lust well enough to shun it because, though he knows it is both heavenly and hellish, lust can never be recognized until it has proved itself lust by turning heaven into hell.

The effect of this emended punctuation has been to restrict meanings to special interpretations of special words. Shakespeare's punctuation allows the variety of meanings he actually intends; if we must choose any one meaning, then we owe it to Shakespeare to choose at least one he intended and one embracing as many meanings as possible, that is, the most difficult meaning. It is always the most difficult meaning which is the most nearly final. No prose interpretation of poetry can have complete finality, can be difficult enough. Shakespeare's editors, in trying to clarify him for the plain man, weakened and diluted his poetry and in effect deprived him of clarity. There is only one way to clarify Shakespeare: to print him as he wrote or as near as one can get to this. Making poetry easy for the reader should mean showing clearly how difficult it really is.

Mr. Cummings safeguards himself against emendation by setting down his poems, which are not complex in thought, so that their most difficult sense strikes the reader first. By giving typography an active part to play he makes his poems fixed and accurate in a way which Shakespeare's are not; but in so doing he forfeits the fluidity that Shakespeare kept by not cramping his poems with heavy punctuation and by placing more trust in the reader—a trust that may have been merited in his own day, though betrayed later. It is important to realize that the *Sonnets* were first circulated in manuscript 'among his private friends' and not intended for popular publication; the 1609 edition is now generally regarded as a piracy. The trouble with Mr. Cummings' poems is that they are too clear, once the reader sets himself to work on them. Braced as they are, they do not present the eternal difficulties that make poems immortal; they merely show how difficult it is for Mr. Cummings or for any poet to stabilize a poem once and for all. Punctuation marks in any poem of his are the bolts and pins that make it a foolproof piece of machinery requiring common sense rather than poetic intuition for its working. The outcry against his typography shows that it is as difficult to engage the common sense of the reader as his imagination. A reviewer of Mr. Cummings' recent book *is 5*, writes:

> I know artists are always saying that a good painting looks as well upside down as any other way. And it may be true. The question now arises: does the same principle apply to a poem? But it is not necessary to answer the question; if a poem is good, people will gladly stand on their heads to read it. It is conceivable, if not probable, that the favourite poetic form of the future will be a sonnet arranged as a cross-word puzzle. If there were no other way of getting at Shakespeare's sonnets than by solving a cross-word puzzle sequence, I am sure the puzzles would be solved and the sonnets enjoyed. But what about Mr. Cummings? Can his poems surmount such obstacles? Well, perhaps if they cannot survive as poems they can survive as puzzles.

This may be the immediate verdict on Mr. Cummings' typography, but he can be sure of one thing which Shakespeare could not: that three centuries hence his poems if they survive (and worse poets' have) will be the only ones of the early twentieth century reprinted in facsimile, not merely because he will be a literary curiosity but because he has edited his poems with punctuation beyond any possibility of re-editing. The Shakespeare to whose sonnets this reviewer makes a rhetorical appeal is the popular Shakespeare of the anthologies and not the facsimile Shakespeare. How many of our readers have ever before seen the original version quoted here? So few, surely, that it is safe to conclude that no one is willing to stand on his head to understand Shakespeare, that everyone wants a simplified Shakespeare as well as a simplified Cummings. Indeed, very few people can have looked at Shakespeare's sonnets in the original since the eighteenth century, when the popular interest in his high-spirited comedies sent a few dull commentators and book-makers to his poems. In 1766 George Steevens printed the *Sonnets* in the original and without annotations, apparently because he thought they deserved none. Twenty-seven years later he omitted the *Sonnets* from an edition of Shakespeare's works 'because the strongest Act of Parliament that could be framed would fail to compel readers into their service.' Edmund Malone, who undertook in 1780 to justify the *Sonnets* to an apathetic public by simplifying the difficult originals, was considered by Steevens to be 'disgracing his implements of criticism by the objects of their culture.' Steevens' view was the general one. Chalmers reaffirmed it as late as 1810, and if Malone had not defied the general critical opinion of the *Sonnets* by emending the texts and presenting them, well-filleted, to the plain man of the eighteenth century, the plain man of the twentieth would be unaware of their existence. Unlike Mr. Cummings' poems, Shakespeare's *Sonnets* would not even have 'survived as puzzles.'

Thus far does a study of Shakespeare's typography take one: to the difficulties of a poet with readers to whom his meanings are mysteries and for the most part must remain mysteries. A modernist poet like Mr. Cummings handles the problem by trying to get the most out of his readers; Shakespeare handled it by trying to get the most out of his poem. Logically the modernist poet should have many readers, but these with an elementary understanding of his poems; Shakespeare only a few readers, but these with an enlarged understanding of his poems. The reverse, however, is true because the reading public has been so undertrained on a simplified Shakespeare and on anthology verse, that modernist poetry seems as difficult as Shakespeare really ought to seem.

Only a few points of the original sonnet have been left uncovered by our typographical survey, and these occur principally in the first few lines, which suffer from fewer emendations than the rest of the poem. The delicate inter-relation of the words of the two opening lines should not be overlooked: the strong parallelism between *expence* and *waste* and *Spirit* and *shame* expressing at once the terrible quick-change from lust as lust-enjoyed to lust as lust-despised; the double meaning of *waste* as 'expense' and as 'wilderness,' the *waste* place in which the Spirit is *wasted*; the double meaning of *expence* as 'pouring out' and as the 'price paid'; the double meaning of *of shame* as 'shameful,' i.e. 'deplorable' and as *ashamed*, i.e. 'self-deploring'; the double meaning of *shame* itself as 'modesty' and 'disgrace'; and the double meaning of *lust in action* as 'lust unsuspected by man in his actions because disguised as shame' (in either sense of the word), and as 'lust in progress' as opposed to 'lust contemplated.' All these alternate meanings interacting on one another, and other possible interpretations of words and phrases besides, make as it were an oracle which can be read in many senses at once, none of the senses, however, being incompatible with any others. The intensified inbreeding of words continues through the rest of the poem. *Periurd* is another example, meaning both 'falsely spoken of' and 'false.' Again, *heaven* and *hell* have the ordinary prose meaning of 'pleasure' and 'pain'; but 'heaven,' for Shakespeare, was the longing for a temperamental stability which at the same time he mistrusted; his 'hell' was akin to Marlowe's hell, which

> . . . hath no limits nor is circumscribed
> In one selfe place, for where we are is hell.

The reader who complains of the obscurity of modernist poets must be reminded of the intimate Shakespearian background with which he needs to be familiar before he can understand Shakespeare. The failure of imagination and knowledge in Shakespeare's editors has reduced his sonnets to the indignity of being easy for everybody. Beddoes, an early nineteenth-century imitator of Shakespeare, said:

> About Shakespeare. You might just as well attempt to remodel the seasons and the laws of life and death as to alter one 'jot or tittle' of his eternal thoughts. 'A Star,' you call him. If he was a star all the other stage-scribblers can hardly be considered a constellation of brass buttons.

Few of the modernist poets are Stars, but most of them are very highly polished brass buttons and entitled to protect themselves from the sort of tarnishing which Shakespeare, though a Star, has suffered.

Shakespeare's attitude towards the perversely stupid reorganizing of lines and regrouping of ideas is jocularly shown in the satire in repunctuation given in the prologue of *Piramus and Thisby* in *A Midsummer Night's Dream*:

> QUINCE: If we offend, it is with our good will.
> That you should thinke, we come not to offend,
> But with good will. To shew our simple skill,
> That is the true beginning of our end.
> Consider then, we come but in despight.
> We do not come, as minding to content you,
> Our true intent is. All for your delight,
> We are not heere. That you should here repent you,
> The Actors are at hand; and by their show,
> You shall know all, that you are like to know.
> THESEUS: This fellow doth not stand vpon points.
> . . . . .
> LYSANDER: His speech was like a tangled chaine: nothing impaired, but all disordered . . .

<hr />

1935—William Empson. "They That Have Power," from *Some Versions of Pastoral*

William Empson (1906–1984) was one of the great twentieth-century literary critics. Other critics often cite his semantically sensitive, structurally complex readings, especially his books *Seven Types of Ambiguity* and *Some Versions of Pastoral*. He is sometimes associated with the

American New Critics, but his own eclectic brand of criticism resists this easy identification.

I

It is agreed that *They that have power to hurt and will do none* is a piece of grave irony, but there the matter is generally left; you can work through all the notes in the Variorum without finding out whether flower, lily, 'owner,' and person addressed are alike or opposed. One would like to say that the poem has all possible such meanings, digested into some order, and then try to show how this is done, but the mere number of possible interpretations is amusingly too great. Taking the simplest view (that any two may be alike in some one property) any one of the four either is or is not and either should or should not be like each of the others; this yields 4096 possible movements of thought, with other possibilities. The niggler is routed here; one has honestly to consider what seems important.

'The best people are indifferent to temptation and detached from the world; nor is this state selfish, because they do good by unconscious influence, like the flower. You must be like them; you are quite like them already. But even the best people must be continually on their guard, because they become the worst, just as the pure and detached lily smells worst, once they fall from their perfection'—('one's prejudice against them is only one's consciousness of this fact'—the hint of irony in the poem might be covered by this). It is a coherent enough Confucian sentiment, and there is no very clear hint as to irony in the words. No doubt *as stone* goes intentionally too far for sympathy, and there is a suggestive gap in the argument between octet and sestet, but one would not feel this if it was Shakespeare's only surviving work.

There is no reason why the subtlety of the irony in so complex a material must be capable of being pegged out into verbal explanations. The vague and generalised language of the descriptions, which might be talking about so many sorts of people as well as feeling so many things about them, somehow makes a unity like a crossroads, which analysis does not deal with by exploring down the roads; makes a solid flute on which you can play a multitude of tunes, whose solidity no list of all possible tunes would go far to explain. The balance of feeling is both very complex and very fertile; experiences are recorded, and metaphors invented, in the Sonnets, which he went on 'applying' as a dramatist, taking particular cases of them as if they were wide generalisations, for the rest of his life. One can't expect, in writing about such a process, to say anything very tidy and complete.

But one does not start interpreting out of the void, even though the poem once partly interpreted seems to stand on its own. If this was Shakespeare's only surviving work it would still be clear, supposing one knew about the other

Elizabethans, that it involves somehow their feelings about the Machiavellian, the wicked plotter who is exciting and civilised and in some way right about life; which seems an important though rather secret element in the romance that Shakespeare extracted from his patron. In any case one has only to look at the sonnets before and after it to be sure that it has some kind of irony. The one before is full of fear and horror at the hypocrisy he is so soon to recommend; and yet it is already somehow cuddled, as if in fascination or out of a refusal to admit that it was there.

> So shall I liue, supposing thou art true,
> Like a deceiued husband, . . .
> For ther can liue no hatred in thine eye
> Therefore in that I cannot know thy change, . . .
> How like *Eaues* apple doth thy beauty grow,
> If thy sweet vertue answere not thy show.

So the *summer's flower* may be its apple-blossom. His virtue is still sweet, whether he has any or not; the clash of fact with platonic idealism is too fearful to be faced directly. In the sonnet after, with a blank and exhausted humility, it has been faced; there remains for the expression of his love, in the least flaunting of poetry, the voice of caution.

> How sweet and louely dost thou make the shame, . . .
> Take heed (deare heart) of this large privilege.

The praise of hypocrisy is in a crucial and precarious condition of balance between these two states of mind.

The root of the ambivalence, I think, is that W.H. is loved as an arriviste, for an impudent worldliness that Shakespeare finds shocking and delightful. The reasons why he treated his poet badly are the same as the reasons why he was fascinating, which gives its immediate point to the profound ambivalence about the selfishness of the flower. Perhaps he is like the cold person in his hardness and worldly judgment, not in his sensuality and generosity of occasional impulse; like the flower in its beauty, vulnerability, tendency to excite thoughts about the shortness of life, self-centredness, and power in spite of it to give pleasure, not in its innocence and fertility; but the irony may make any of these change over. Both owner and flower seem self-centred and inscrutable, and the cold person is at least like the lily in that it is symbolically chaste, but the summer's flower, unlike the lily, seems to stand for the full life of instinct. It is not certain that the owner is liable to fester as the lily is—Angelo did, but W.H. is usually urged to acquire the virtues of Angelo. Clearly there is a jump from octet to sestet; the flower is not like the owner in its solitude and its incapacity to hurt or simulate;

it might be because of this that it is of a summer only and may fester; yet we seem chiefly meant to hold W.H. in mind and take them as parallel. As for punctuation, the only full stop is at the end; all lines have commas after them except the fourth, eighth, and twelfth, which have colons.

> They that haue powre to hurt, and will doe none,
> That doe not do the thing, they most do showe,
> Who mouing others, are themselves as stone,
> Vnmoued, could, and to temptation slow:

They may *show*, while hiding the alternative, for the first couplet, the power to hurt or the determination not to hurt—cruelty or mercy, for the second, the strength due to chastity or to sensual experience, for either, a reckless or cautious will, and the desire for love or for control; all whether they are stealers of hearts or of public power. They are a very widespread group; we are only sure at the end that some kind of hypocrisy has been advised and threatened.

> They rightly do inherit heavens graces,
> And husband natures ritches from expence,

Either 'inherit, they alone, by right' or 'inherit what all men inherit and use it rightly'; these correspond to the opposed views of W.H. as aristocrat and vulgar careerist. There is a similar range of idea, half hidden by the pretence of easy filling of the form, in the pun on *graces* and shift to *riches*. *Heaven's graces* may be prevenient grace (strength from God to do well), personal graces which seem to imply heavenly virtues (the charm by which you deceive people), or merely God's gracious gift of *nature's riches*; which again may be the personal graces, or the strength and taste which make him capable either of 'upholding his house' or of taking his pleasure, or merely the actual wealth of which he is an *owner*. Clearly this gives plenty of room for irony in the statement that the cold people, with their fine claims, do well all round; it also conveys 'I am seeing you as a whole; I am seeing these things as necessary rather than as your fault.'

> They are the Lords and owners of their faces,
> Others, but stewards of their excellence:

It may be their beauty they put to their own uses, high or low, or they may just have poker-faces; this gives the same range of statement. The capital which tends to isolate *lords* from its phrase suggests 'they are the only true aristocrats; if you are not like them you should not pretend to be one.' *Others* may be stewards of their own excellence (in contrast with *faces*—'though they are enslaved they may be better and less superficial than the cold people') or of the cold people's excellence (with a suggestion of 'Their Excellencies'); the less plausible sense is insisted on by the comma after *others*. This repeats the doubt about how far the cold people are really excellent, and there may be a hint of a doubt about how far the individual is isolated, which anticipates the metaphor of the flower. And 'stewards of their own excellence' may be like 'stewards of the buttery' or like 'stewards of a certain lord'; either 'the good things they have do good to others, not to them' (they are too generous; I cannot ask you to aim so high in virtue, because I desire your welfare, not other people's, and indeed because you wouldn't do it anyway) or 'they are under the power of their own impulses, which are good things so long as they are not in power' (they are deceived; acts caused by weakness are not really generous at all). Yet this may be the condition of the flower and the condition for fullness of life; you cannot know beforehand what life will bring you if you open yourself to it, and certainly the flower does not; it is because they are unnatural and unlike flowers that the cold people rule nature, and the cost may be too great. Or the flower and the cold person may be two unlike examples of the limitation necessary to success, one experienced in its own nature, the other in the world; both, the irony would imply, are in fact *stewards*.

There is a Christian parable at work in both octet and sestet; in the octet that of the talents. You will not be forgiven for hoarding your talents; some sort of success is demanded; you must at least use your powers to the full even if for your own squalid purpose. The pain and wit and solemnity of *rightly*, its air of summing up a long argument, depend on the fact that these metaphors have been used to recommend things to W.H. before.

> Natures bequest giues nothing but doth lend,
> And being franck she lends to those are free:
>
> Who lets so faire a house fall to decay,
> Which husbandry in honour might uphold,

Rightly to be free with yourself, in the first simple paradox, was the best saving of yourself (you should put your money into marriage and a son); it is too late now to advise that, or to say it without being sure to be understood wrongly (this is 94; the first sonnet about his taking Shakespeare's mistress is 40); the advice to be generous as natural has become the richer but more contorted advice to be like the flower. Rightly to husband nature's riches, earlier in the sequence, was to accept the fact that one is only steward of them;

> Thou that art now the worlds fresh ornament,
> And only herauld to the gaudy spring,

Within thine owne bud buriest thy content,
And tender chorle makst waste in niggarding:

the flower was wrong to live to itself alone, and would become a tottered weed
(2) whether it met with infection or not.

Though indeed *husbandry* is still recommended; it is not the change of
opinion that has so much effect but the use of the same metaphors with a shift
of feeling in them. The legal metaphors (debts to nature and so forth) used for
the loving complaint that the man's chastity was selfish are still used when he
becomes selfish in his debauchery; Shakespeare's own notation here seems to
teach him; the more curiously because the metaphors were used so flatly in the
earliest sonnets (1, 2, 4, 6, then 13; not again till now), only formally urging
marriage, and perhaps written to order. It is like using a mathematical identity
which implies a proof about a particular curve and then finding that it has a quite
new meaning if you take the old constants as variables. It is these metaphors
that have grown, till they involve relations between a man's powers and their use,
his nature and his will, the individual and the society, which could be applied
afterwards to all human circumstances.

The sommers flowre is to the sommer sweet,
Though to it selfe, it onely liue and die,

The use of *the* summer's flower about a human being is enough to put it
at us that the flower will die by the end of summer, that the man's life is not
much longer, and that the pleasures of the creature therefore cannot be despised
for what they are. *Sweet to the summer* (said of the flower), since the summer is
omnipresent and in a way Nature herself, may mean 'sweet to God' (said of the
man); or may mean 'adding to the general sweetness; sweet to everybody that
comes across it in its time.' It may do good to others though not by effort or may
simply be a good end in itself (or combining these, may only be able to do good
by concentrating on itself as an end); a preparatory evasion of the central issue
about egotism.

Either 'though it lives only for itself' or 'though, in its own opinion, so far as
it can see, it does no more than live and die.' In the first it is a rose, extravagant
and doing good because the public likes to see it flaunting; in the second a violet,
humble and doing good in private through an odour of sanctity. It is the less
plausible sense which is insisted on by the comma after *itself.* Or you may well
say that the flower is neither, but the final lily; the whole passage is hinting at the
lilies of the field like whom Solomon was not arrayed.

This parable itself combines what the poem so ingeniously keeps on
combining; the personal power of beauty and the political power of wisdom;

so as to imply that the political power has in itself a sort of beauty and the personal beauty, however hollow it may be, a sort of moral grandeur through power. But in England 'consider the lilies of the field,' were we not at once told of their glory, would suggest lilies-of-the-valley; that name indeed occurs in the Song of Solomon, in surprising correspondence to the obviously grandiose Rose of Sharon. Shakespeare, I think, had done what the inventor of the name must have done, had read into the random flower-names of the Bible the same rich clash of suggestion—an implied mutual comparison that elevates both parties—as he makes here between the garden flower and the wild flower. The first sense (the rose) gives the root idea—'a brilliant aristocrat like you gives great pleasure by living as he likes; for such a person the issue of selfishness does not arise'; this makes W.H. a Renaissance Magnificent Man, combining all the virtues with a manysidedness like that of these phrases about him. The unlikeness of the cold people and the flowers, if you accept them as like, then implies 'man is not placed like flowers and though he had best imitate them may be misled in doing so; the Machiavellian is much more really like the flower than the Swain is.' And yet there is a suggestion in the comparison to the flower (since only beauty is demanded of it—Sonnet 54 made an odd and impermanent attempt at quelling this doubt by equating truth with scent) that W.H. has only power to keep up an air of reconciling in himself the inconsistent virtues, or even of being a Machiavellian about the matter, and that it is this that puts him in danger like the flower. Or however genuine he may be he is pathetic; such a man is all too 'natural'; there is no need to prop up our ideas about him with an aristocratic 'artificial' flower. So this class-centred praise is then careful half to hide itself by adding the second sense and the humble flower, and this leads it to a generalisation: 'all men do most good to others by fulfilling their own natures.' Full as they are of Christian echoes, the Sonnets are concerned with an idea strong enough to be balanced against Christianity; they state the opposite to the idea of self-sacrifice.

But the machinery of the statement is peculiar; its clash of admiration and contempt seems dependent on a clash of feeling about the classes. One might connect it with that curious trick of pastoral which for extreme courtly flattery—perhaps to give self-respect to both poet and patron, to show that the poet is not ignorantly easy to impress, nor the patron to flatter—writes about the poorest people; and with those jazz songs which give an intense effect of luxury and silk underwear by pretending to be about slaves naked in the fields. To those who care chiefly about biography this trick must seem monstrously tantalising; Wilde built the paradox of his essay on it, and it is true that Shakespeare might have set the whole thing to work from the other end about a highly trained mudlark brought in to act his princesses. But it is the very queerness of the trick that makes it so often useful in building models of the human mind; and yet the power no less than the universality of this poem depends on generalising the trick so completely as to seem independent of it.

> But if that flowre with base infection meete,
> The basest weed out-braues his dignity:
>> For sweetest things turn sowrest by their deedes,
>> Lilies that fester, smell far worse than weeds.

It is not clear how the metaphor from 'meet' acts; it may be like 'meet with disaster'—'if it catches infection, which would be bad luck,' or like meeting someone in the street, as most men do safely—'*any* contact with infection is fatal to so peculiarly placed a creature.' The first applies to the natural and unprotected flower, the second to the lily that has the hubris and fate of greatness. They are not of course firmly separated, but *lilies* are separated from the *flower* by a colon and an intervening generalisation, whereas the flower is only separated from the cold people (not all of whom need be lilies) by a colon; certainly the flower as well as the lily is in danger, but this does not make them identical and equal to W.H. The neighbouring sonnets continually say that his deeds can do nothing to destroy his sweetness, and this seems to make the terrible last line point at him somewhat less directly. One may indeed take it as 'Though so debauched, you keep your looks. Only mean people who never give themselves heartily to anything can do that. But the best hypocrite is found out in the end, and shown as the worst.' But Shakespeare may also be congratulating W.H. on an imperfection which acts as a preservative; he is a son of the world and can protect himself, like the cold people, or a spontaneous and therefore fresh sinner, like the flower; he may safely stain, as heaven's sun, the kisser of carrion, staineth. At any rate it is not of virginity, at this stage, that he can be accused. The smell of a big lily is so lush and insolent, suggests so powerfully both incense and pampered flesh—the traditional metaphor about it is so perfect—that its festering can only be that due to the hubris of spirituality; it is ironically generous to apply it to the careerist to whom hypocrisy is recommended; and yet in the fact that we seem meant to apply it to him there is a glance backwards, as if to justify him, at the ambition involved in even the most genuine attempt on heaven. You may say that Shakespeare dragged in the last line as a quotation from *Edward III* that doesn't quite fit; it is also possible that (as often happens to poets, who tend to make in their lives a situation they have already written about) he did not till now see the full width of its application.

In a sense the total effect is an evasion of Shakespeare's problem; it gives him a way of praising W.H. in spite of anything. In the flower the oppositions are transcended; it is because it is self-concentrated that it has so much to give and because it is undesigning that it is more grandiose in beauty than Solomon. But it is held in mind chiefly for comfort; none of the people suggested to us are able to imitate it very successfully; nor if they could would they be safe. Yet if W.H. has festered, that at least makes him a lily, and at least not a stone; if he is not a lily, he is in the less danger of festering.

I must try to sum up the effect of so complex an irony, half by trying to follow it through a gradation. 'I am praising to you the contemptible things you admire, you little plotter; this is how the others try to betray you through flattery; yet it is your little generosity, though it show only as lewdness, which will betray you; for it is wise to be cold, both because you are too inflammable and because I have been so much hurt by you who are heartless; yet I can the better forgive you through that argument from our common isolation; I must praise to you your very faults, especially your selfishness, because you can only now be safe by cultivating them further; yet this is the most dangerous of necessities; people are greedy for your fall as for that of any of the great; indeed no one can rise above common life, as you have done so fully, without in the same degree sinking below it; you have made this advice real to me, because I cannot despise it for your sake; I am only sure that you are valuable and in danger.'

II

One may point out that the reason so little can be deduced about W.H., the reason that Butler and Wilde (though he had so much sympathy for snobbery) could make a plausible case for his being not a patron but an actor, is that this process of interaction between metaphors, which acts like a generalisation, is always carried so far; the contradictory elements in the relation are brought out and opposed absolutely, so that we cannot know their proportions in real life. It is hard not to go off down one of the roads at the crossing, and get one plain meaning for the poem from that, because Shakespeare himself did that so very effectively afterwards; a part of the situation of the Sonnets, the actual phrases designed for it, are given to Prince Henry, to Angelo, to Troilus, to the Greek army; getting further from the original as time went on. I shall look at the first two. It is only partly true that this untidy process, if successful, might tell one more about the original situation; discoveries of language and feeling made from a personal situation may develop themselves so that they can be applied to quite different dramatic situations; but to know about these might tell one more about the original discoveries. The fact that the feelings in this sonnet could be used for such different people as Angelo and Prince Henry, different both in their power and their coldness, is an essential part of its breadth.

The crucial first soliloquy of Prince Henry was put in to save his reputation with the audience; it is a wilful destruction of his claims to generosity, indeed to honesty, if only in Falstaff's sense; but this is to say that it was a mere job with no feeling behind it. It was a concession to normal and decent opinion rather than to the groundlings; the man who was to write *Henry V* could feel the force of that as well as take care of his plot; on the other hand, it cannot have been written without bitterness against the prince. It was probably written about two years after the second, more intimate dedication to Southampton, and is almost a cento from the Sonnets.

We would probably find the prince less puzzling if Shakespeare had re-written *Henry VI* in his prime. The theme at the back of the series, after all, is that the Henries are usurpers; however great the virtues of Henry V may be, however rightly the nation may glory in his deeds, there is something fishy about him and the justice of Heaven will overtake his son. In having some sort of double attitude to the prince Shakespeare was merely doing his work as a history-writer. For the critic to drag in a personal situation from the Sonnets is neither an attack nor a justification; it claims only to show where the feelings the play needed were obtained.

Sir Walter Raleigh said that the play was written when Shakespeare was becoming successful and buying New Place, so that he became interested in the problems of successful people like Henries IV and V rather than in poetical failures like Richard II. On this view we are to see in Prince Henry the Swan himself; he has made low friends only to get local colour out of them, and now drops them with a bang because he has made money and grand friends. It is possible enough, though I don't know why it was thought pleasant; anyway such a personal association is far at the back of the mind and one would expect several to be at work together. Henry might carry a grim externalisation of self-contempt as well as a still half-delighted reverberation of Southampton; Falstaff an attack on some rival playwright or on Florio as tutor of Southampton as well as a savage and joyous externalisation of self-contempt. But I think only the second of these alternatives fits in with the language and echoes a serious personal situation. Henry's soliloquy demands from us just the sonnets' mood of bitter complaisance; the young man must still be praised and loved, however he betrays his intimates, because we see him all shining with the virtues of success. So I shall now fancy Falstaff as Shakespeare (he has obviously some great forces behind him) and Henry as the patron who has recently betrayed him.

> I know you all, and will a-while vphold
> The vnyoak'd humor of your idlenesse:
> Yet heerein will I imitate the Sunne,
> Who doth permit the base contagious cloudes
> To smother vp his Beauty from the world,
> That when he please again to be himselfe,
> Being wanted, he may be more wondred at,
> By breaking through the foule and vgly mists
> Of vapours, that did seeme to strangle him.

This seems quite certainly drawn from the earliest and most pathetic of the attempts to justify W.H.

> Fvll many a glorious morning haue I seene, . . .
> Anon permit the *basest cloudes* to ride, . . .
> With *ougly* rack on his celestiall face, . . .
>   *Suns* of the world may staine, when heauens sun staineth.

But it is turned backwards; the sun is now to free itself from the clouds by the very act of betrayal. 'Oh that you were yourself' (13) and 'have eyes to wonder' (106) are given the same twist into humility; Shakespeare admits, with Falstaff in front of him, that the patron would be better off without friends in low life. The next four lines, developing the idea that you make the best impression on people by only treating them well at rare intervals, are a prosaic re-hash of 'Therefore are feasts so solemn and so rare,' etc. (52); what was said of the policy of the friend is now used for the policy of the politician, though in both play and sonnet they are opposed. The connection in the next lines is more doubtful.

> So when this loose behaviour I throw off
> And pay the debt I never promised
> By so much better than my word I am
> By so much shall I falsify men's hopes

(He does indeed, by just so much.) This *debt* looks like an echo of the debt to nature there was so much doubt about W.H.'s method of paying; it has turned into a debt to society. At any rate in the sonnet-like final couplet

> I'll so offend, to make offence a skill

('The tongue that tells the story of thy days . . . Cannot dispraise but in a kind of praise') we have the central theme of all the sonnets of apology; the only difference, though it is a big one, is that this man says it about himself.

One element at least in this seems to reflect a further doubt on to the sonnet I have considered; the prince may be showing by this soliloquy that he can avoid infection, or may be an example of how sour a lord and owner can turn in his deeds on Coronation Day. The last irony and most contorted generosity one can extract from the sonnet is in the view that Shakespeare himself is the basest weed, that to meet him is to meet infection, that the result of being faithful to his friendship would be to be outbraved even by him, that the advice to be a cold person and avoid the fate of the lily is advice to abandon Shakespeare once for all.

This interpretation is more than once as firmly contradicted by Falstaff as it will be by my readers. He first comes on in a great fuss about his good name; he has been rated in the streets for leading astray Harry. At the end of the scene we find that this was unfair to him; the prince makes clear by the soliloquy that he is well able to look after himself. Meanwhile Falstaff amuses himself by turning the accusation the other way round.

> O, thou hast damnable iteration, and art indeede able to corrupt a
> Saint. Thou hast done much harme unto me *Hal*, God forgiue thee for
> it. Before I knew thee *Hal*, I knew nothing: and now I am (if a man
> shold speake truly) little better than one of the wicked. I must giue
> ouer this life, and I will giue it over: and I do not, I am a Villaine. Ile
> be damn'd for never a Kings sonne in Christendome.
> PRIN. Where shall we take a purse to morrow, Iacke?

The audience were not expected to believe this aspect of the matter, but there may well be some truth in it if applied to the situation Shakespeare had at the back of his mind. The other aspect is also preserved for us in the Sonnets.

> I may not euer-more acknowledge thee,
> Least my bewailed guilt should do thee shame,
> Nor thou with publike kindnesse honour me,
> Unlesse thou take that honour from thy name:

'I not only warn you against bad company; I admit I am part of it.' One could throw in here that letter about Southampton wasting his time at the playhouse and out of favour with the Queen.

There are two sums of a thousand pounds concerned, so that the phrase is kept echoing through both parts of the history; it seems to become a symbol of Falstaff's hopes and his betrayal. The first he got by the robbery at Gadshill, and the prince at once robbed him of it; supposedly to give back to its owner, if you take his reluctance to steal seriously, but we hear no more of that. He says he will give it to Francis the drawer, and Falstaff pacifies the hostess by saying he will get it back.

> HOSTESS. . . . and sayde this other day, You ought him a thousand
> pound.
> PRINCE. Sirrah, do I owe you a thousand pound?
> FALSTAFF. A thousand pound *Hal*? A Million. Thy loue is worth a
> Million: thou ow'st me thy loue. Part I, iii. iii.

He will pay neither. But Falstaff gets another thousand pounds from Shallow, and the phrase is all he clings to in the riddling sentence at his final discomfiture: 'Master Shallow, I owe you a thousand pound.' This is necessary, to seem calm and reassure Shallow; it is either a sweeping gesture of renunciation ('What use to me now is the money I need never have repaid to this fool?') or a comfort since it reminds him that he has got the money and certainly won't repay it; but it is meant also for the king to hear and remember ('I class you with Shallow and the rest of my friends'). I cannot help fancying an obscure connection between this sum and the thousand pounds which, we are told, Southampton once gave Shakespeare, to go through with a purchase that he had a mind to.

It is as well to look at Falstaff in general for a moment, to show what this tender attitude to him has to fit in with. The plot treats him as a simple Punch, whom you laugh at with good-humour, though he is wicked, because he is always knocked down and always bobs up again. (Our attitude to him as a Character entirely depends on the Plot, and yet he is a Character who very nearly destroyed the Plot as a whole.) People sometimes take advantage of this to view him as a lovable old dear; a notion which one can best refute by considering him as an officer.

> I haue led my rag of Muffins where they are pepper'd: there's not three
> of my 150 left alive, and they for the Townes end, to beg during life.
> Part I. v. iii.

We saw him levy a tax in bribes on the men he left; he now kills all the weaklings he conscripted, in order to keep their pay. A large proportion of the groundlings consisted of disbanded soldiers who had suffered under such a system; the laughter was a roar of hatred here; he is 'comic' like a Miracle Play Herod. (Whereas Harry has no qualities that are obviously not W.H.'s.) And yet it is out of his defence against this, the least popularisable charge against him, that he makes his most unanswerable retort to the prince.

> PRINCE. Tell me, Jack, whose fellows are these that come after?
> FAL. Mine, Hal, mine.
> PRINCE. I never did see such pitiful rascals.
> FAL. Tut, tut; good enough to toss; food for powder, food for powder;
> they'll fill a pit as well as better; tush, man, mortal men, mortal men.

Mortal conveys both 'all men are in the same boat, all equal before God' and 'all you want is slaughter.' No one in the audience was tempted to think Harry as wicked as his enemy Hotspur, who deserved death as much as Lear for wanting to divide England. But this remark needed to be an impudent cover for villainy if the strength of mind and heart in it were not to be too strong, to make the squabbles of ambitious and usurping persons too contemptible.

On the other hand, Falstaff's love for the prince is certainly meant as a gap in his armour; one statement (out of so many) of this comes where the prince[1] is putting his life in danger and robbing him of the (stolen) thousand pounds.

> I haue forsworne his company hourely any time this two and twenty
> yeares, and yet I am bewitcht with the Rogues company. If the Rascal
> haue not giuen me medecines to make me loue him, Ile be hang'd; it
> could not be else; I haue drunke Medecines.

He could continually be made to say such things without stopping the laugh at him, partly because one thinks he is pretending love to the prince for his own interest; 'never any man's thought keeps the roadway' as well as those of the groundlings who think him a hypocrite about it, but this phrase of mockery at them is used only to dignify the prince; the more serious Falstaff's expression of love becomes the more comic it is, whether as hopeless or as hypocrisy. But to stretch one's mind round the whole character (as is generally admitted) one must take him, though as the supreme expression of the cult of mockery as strength and the comic idealisation of freedom, yet as both villainous and tragically ill-used.

Angelo is further from the sonnets than Henry both in date and situation; he is merely an extreme, perhaps not very credible, example of the cold person and the lily; both simply as chaste and as claiming to be more than human, which involves being at least liable to be as much less. He has odd connections with this sonnet through *Edward III*, which may help to show that there is a real connection of ideas. In the following lines he is recoiling with horror from the idea that Isabella has been using her virtue as a temptation for him, which was just what her brother expected her to do (I. ii. 185—she is a cold person but can 'move men').

> Not she: nor doth she tempt; but it is I,
> That, lying by the Violet in the Sunne,
> Doe as the Carrion do's, not as the flowre,
> Corrupt with vertuous season: II. ii. 165–8.

Edward III is also a man in authority tempting a chaste woman, and he too uses the notion that her qualities are a temptation, so that it is half her fault.

> the queen of beauty's queens shall see
> Herself the ground of my infirmity. II. i. 58.

Both Angelo's metaphor and the chief line of this sonnet come from a speech by the lady's father, which contains the germ of most of the ideas we are dealing with.

> The greater man, the greater is the thing,
> Be it good or bad, that he shall undertake . . .
> The freshest summer's day doth soonest taint
> The loathed carrion that it seems to kiss . . .
> Lilies that fester smell far worse than weeds;
> And every glory that inclines to sin,
> The shame is treble by the opposite. II. i. 430–457.

The freshest summer's day is always likely to kiss carrion, and the suggestion from this is that the great man is always likely to do great harm as well as great good. The sun kissing carrion is brought out again both for Falstaff and by Hamlet (*1 Henry IV*, II. iv. 113; *Hamlet*, II. ii. 158); it is clear that the complex of metaphor in this speech, whether Shakespeare wrote it or not, developed afterwards as a whole in his mind.

The obvious uses of the language of the Sonnets about Angelo all come in the first definition of his character by the Duke; once started like this he goes off on his own. The fascination of the irony of the passage is that it applies to Angelo's incorruptible virtues, associated with his chastity, the arguments and metaphors which had been used to urge abrogation of chastity on W.H.; nor is this irrelevant to the play. As in *virtues, torches,* and *fine touches,* its language, here and throughout, is always perversely on the edge of a bawdy meaning; even *belongings* may have a suggestion, helped out by 'longings,' of nature's gift of desire. It seems impossible even to praise the good qualities of Angelo without bringing into the hearer's mind those other good qualities that Angelo refuses to recognise. The most brilliant example of this trick in the play is the continual pun on *sense*, for sensuality, sensibleness (which implies the claim of Lucio) and sensibility (which implies a further claim of the poet). The first use may be unequivocal, as if to force the sexual meaning on our notice.

I. iv. 59.   The wanton stings, and motions of the sence.

II. ii. 141.   ANGELO. Shee speakes, and 'tis such sence
That my sence breeds with it; fare you well.

II. ii. 168.   Can it be
That Modesty may more betray our Sence
Than womans lightnesse?

II. iv. 73.   Nay, but heare me,
                     Your sence pursues not mine: either you are ignorant,
                     Or seeme so craft(il)y; and that's not good.

IV. iv. 27.   He should haue liu'd,
                     Save that his riotous youth with dangerous sence,
                     Might in the times to come have ta'en revenge.

V. i. 225.   MARIANA. As there is sence in truth, and truth in vertue,
                     I am affianced this man's wife, as strongly
                     As words could make vp vowes.

But this sort of thing does not depend on echoes from the Sonnets, and I think
those that occur have a further effect.

        Thy selfe, and thy belongings
Are not thine owne so proper, as to waste
Thy selfe upon thy vertues; they on thee:
Heauen doth with us, as we, with Torches doe,
Not light them for themselves: For if our vertues
Did not goe forth of us, 'twere all alike
As if we had them not: Spirits are not finely touch'd,
But to fine issues: nor nature never lends
The smallest scruple of her excellence,
But like a thrifty goddesse, she determines
Her selfe the glory of a creditour,
Both thanks, and vse;

'All are but stewards of her excellence'—indeed *their* in the sonnet might refer
back to *nature's riches*. Even Angelo is wrong to think he can be a lord and owner,
though he seems the extreme case of those capable of reserve and power. He is
a *torch* whom nature tricks because she destroys it by making it brilliant; it was
because he accepted office and prepared to use his virtues that she could trick
him all but disastrously into using more of them than he intended. For 'virtues'
mean both 'good qualities' and 'capacities' ('a dormitive virtue') whether for good
or ill; the same ambivalent attitude both towards worldly goods and towards
what claim to be spiritual goods is conveyed by this as by the clash between
heaven's graces and *nature's riches*. The same pun and irony on it, with a hint of a
similar movement of thought about *honour*, are used when Isabella takes leave of
Angelo after her first interviews.

Isab. Saue your Honour.
Ang. From thee: euen from thy vertue.

What's this? what's this? is this her fault, or mine?
The Tempter, or the Tempted, who sins most? II. ii. 162–4

It is his virtues and Isabella's between them that both trick him and nearly destroy Claudio. Not of course that this is straightforward satire against virtue in the sense of chastity; the first great speech of Claudio about 'too much liberty' has all the weight and horror of the lust sonnet (129) from which it is drawn; only the still greater mockery of Claudio could so drag the play back to its attack on Puritanism.

The issue indeed is more general than the sexual one; it is 'liberty, my Lucio, liberty,' as Claudio makes clear at once; which runs through pastoral and is at the heart of the clowns. (Lawrence too seems to make sex the type of liberty; Shaw's Don Juan liberty the type of sex.) 'Nature in general is a cheat, and all those who think themselves owners are pathetic.' Yet we seem here to transfer to Nature the tone of bitter complaisance taken up towards W.H. when he seemed an owner; she now, as he was, must be given the benefit of the doubt inseparable from these shifting phrases; she too must be let rob you by tricks and still be worshipped. There is the same suggestion with the same metaphors in that splendid lecture to Achilles to make him use his virtues as a fighter further; whether rightly to *thank* her is to view yourself as an owner or a steward, you must still in the end pay her the compound interest on her gifts, and still keep up the pretence that they are free. This tone of generous distaste for the conditions of life, which gives the play one of its few suggestions of sympathy for Angelo, I think usually goes with a suggestion of the Sonnets. For instance, it is the whole point about Bassanio; more than any other suitor he is an arriviste loved only for success and seeming; his one merit, and it is enough, is to recognise this truth with Christian humility. His speech before the caskets about the falsity of seeming is full of phrases from the Sonnets (*e.g.* 68, about hair) and may even have a dim reference to the Dark Lady. It is not surprising that this sentiment should make Shakespeare's mind hark back to the Sonnets, because it was there so essential; these poems of idealisation of a patron and careerist depend upon it for their strength and dignity. 'Man is so placed that the sort of thing you do is in degree all that any one can do; success does not come from mere virtue, and without some external success a virtue is not real even to itself. One must not look elsewhere; success of the same nature as yours is all that the dignity, whether of life or poetry, can be based upon.' This queer sort of realism, indeed, is one of the main things he had to say.

The feeling that life is essentially inadequate to the human spirit, and yet that a good life must avoid saying so, is naturally at home with most versions of pastoral; in pastoral you take a limited life and pretend it is the full and normal one, and a suggestion that one must do this with all life, because the normal is itself limited, is easily put into the trick though not necessary to its power. Conversely any expression of the idea that all life is limited may be regarded as only a trick of pastoral, perhaps chiefly intended to hold all our attention and sympathy for some limited life, though again this is not necessary to it either on grounds of truth or beauty; in fact the suggestion of pastoral may be only a protection for the idea which must at last be taken alone. The business of interpretation is obviously very complicated. Literary uses of the problem of free-will and necessity, for example, may be noticed to give curiously bad arguments and I should think get their strength from keeping you in doubt between the two methods. Thus Hardy is fond of showing us an unusually stupid person subjected to very unusually bad luck, and then a moral is drawn, not merely by inference but by solemn assertion, that we are all in the same boat as this person whose story is striking precisely because it is unusual. The effect may be very grand, but to make an otherwise logical reader accept the process must depend on giving him obscure reasons for wishing it so. It is clear at any rate that this grand notion of the inadequacy of life, so various in its means of expression, so reliable a bass note in the arts, needs to be counted as a possible territory of pastoral.

NOTE

1. This is a mistake; it must be Poins whom Falstaff accuses of administering the love-philtre. But I think Falstaff is drawn as regularly expressing love for young men who rob for him, without complete insincerity, and as being unusually sincere in the case of the prince.

—————— —————— ——————

1953—G. K. Hunter. "The Dramatic Technique of Shakespeare's Sonnets," from *Essays in Criticism*

G.K. Hunter was a professor of English at Yale University and the author of several books and articles on Shakespeare and Renaissance drama, including *John Lyly: The Humanist as Courtier, Dramatic Identities and Cultural Tradition: Studies in Shakespeare and His Contemporaries*, and *English Drama 1586–1642: The Age of Shakespeare*.

Though most modern critics would accept the fact that Shakespeare's sonnet-sequence has a pervasive poetry with an excellence recognizably Shakespearean, the peculiar quality of this excellence remains undefined. This may be because criticism of the sonnets has been overshadowed by biographical speculation. There have been few aesthetic critics and these have confined themselves to *minutiae*, and have disregarded or noticed only with condemnation the reactions of their biographically-minded fellows. No one seems to have attempted to explain by what means Shakespeare presents traditional materials so that an overwhelmingly biographical reaction is set up in the reader. Neither the accepted categories of lyric or narrative nor the contemporary verse-fashions—Petrarchan, Anti-Petrarchan, Metaphysical, etc.—will account for this unique flavour in the sequence as a whole and for the concentratedly 'Shakespearean' effect of such sonnets as XV, XVIII, XXX, CXXIX. It is not perhaps a coincidence that the critics who accept these categories tend to find Shakespeare's sonnet-technique in some way misdirected, from Keats with his 'full of fine things said unintentionally—in the intensity of working out conceits' to John Crowe Ransom, 'Shakespeare had no University discipline and developed poetically along lines of least resistance'.[1]

I wish to suggest here that it is rather the approach to the Sonnets as lyric, narrative, or metaphysical exercises that is misdirected. Critics who ignore the biographical approach miss a valuable clue to the bias of Shakespeare's technique—a bias which twists the normal Petrarchan line towards the characteristically Shakespearean flavour of

When not to be receives reproach of being . . .
Oh that our nights of woe might have remembered . . .
Never believe that in my nature reigneth . . . .

I contend that when Shakespeare writes like this he is not misdirecting his talent, not being a quaint and elaborate lyrist, a failed and soured Petrarchan, a Metaphysical *manqué*, or a passionate autobiographical poet whose confessions are cut short by his conceits, so much as—what one would expect—a *dramatist*.

Let us consider in this light two sonnets which, without being masterpieces, seem to me to sound the authentic Shakespearean note:

Say that thou didst forsake me for some fault,
And I will comment upon that offence:
Speak of my lameness, and I straight will halt,
Against thy reasons making no defence.
Thou canst not, love, disgrace me half so ill,
To set a form upon desired change,
As I'll myself disgrace; knowing thy will,
I will acquaintance strangle and look strange;
Be absent from thy walks; and in my tongue
Thy sweet beloved name no more shall dwell,
Lest I, too much profane, should do it wrong,
And haply of our old acquaintance tell.
  For thee, against myself I'll vow debate,
  For I must ne'er love him whom thou dost hate.

      (LXXXIX)

Was it the proud full sail of his great verse,
Bound for the prize of all too precious you,
That did my ripe thoughts in my brain inhearse,
Making their tomb the womb wherein they grew?
Was it his spirit, by spirits taught to write
Above a mortal pitch, that struck me dead?
No, neither he, nor his compeers by night
Giving him aid, my verse astonished. [etc.]
(LXXXVI)

The power of these poems does not reside in lyrical utterance; the vision they present is an individual's, and to that extent like lyric, but in them the reader is not concerned with solitary imaginings presented as of universal significance (as in the Odes of Keats and Shelley), but with the relation of one human heart to others. By setting up a system of tensions between forces presented as persons Shakespeare's sonnets engage the reader's interest in a manner akin to the dramatic. Sonnet LXXXIX is presented as a 'still' from a love-drama, a picture in which the gestures not only make up a present harmony, but hint (with subtle economy of means, which reveals the dramatist) at a psychological background, so that a powerful reaction is built up, as if to a history of love. In Sonnet LXXXVI the number of characters involved is greater, but the technique is the same. An emotional state (estrangement) is expressed by means of a pattern of human figures; as a result of the hints at characterization we become involved as if with personalities, and so experience the dramatic impact. The reaction of the commentator who finds in the 'lameness' of LXXXIX proof of a physical defect in the author is an indication of the force of this impact, and the number of 'keys' to the 'sonnet-story' would seem to show that it is fairly constant throughout the sequence.

At this point the reader might object that the dramatic vividness in Shakespeare's sonnets is only a heightened form of a commonplace Elizabethan quality and that the biographical reaction is not produced by technique so much as by natural curiosity about the greatest and most enigmatic of our poets. Comparisons with other Elizabethan poets show, however, that the Sonnets are not only supreme in dramatic effectiveness, but almost unique in the methods by which this effect is obtained. Many of the sonneteers in Sir Sidney Lee's collection are good dramatic 'plotters' i.e. they can organize a set scene so that the figures contrast effectively and carry well the emotional charge that the author has imparted to them. For example:

Oft with true sighs, oft with uncalled tears,
Now with slow words, now with dumb eloquence;

I Stella's eyes assailed, invade her ears:
But this, at last, is her sweet breathed defence.
'That who indeed infelt affection bears,
So captives to his saint both soul and sense;
That wholly hers, all selfness he forbears: [etc.]
(SIDNEY, *Astrophel and Stella*, LXI)

But such scenes are set at a middle-distance from the reader; the effect that is almost unique in Shakespeare is that of immediate contact with the suffering mind. We learn what it felt like to be the lover in such-and-such a situation, and the figures are arranged to increase the poignant immediacy of our apprehension—so that if the beloved is young the lover is represented as old, if the lover is poor the beloved must be high-born, etc. The brilliance of the language makes the context of these emotions so vivid that the reader naturally supplies from his imagination a complete dramatic situation.

Shakespeare's 'plots' differ from those of contemporary sonneteers in that we are seldom given visual descriptions of the persons involved. This difference does not involve him in a modern 'psychological' presentation: when the lover appears before the reader there is no self-dramatization in the sense that he is presented as a significant and interesting individual. When we hear of him

Beated and chopped with tanned antiquity   (LXII)

Desiring this man's art and that man's scope   (XXIX)

As an unperfect actor on the stage   (XXIII)

we are no nearer any conception of his personality. The dramatic power of conveying personal tensions is achieved by patterning the persons, not by analysing them.

Shakespeare uses the conventions of the sonnet *genre* in such a way that he conjures before us the tone and accent of the traditional personages. Thus like other sonnet-heroes Shakespeare's lover suffers from the tyranny of the beloved while welcoming this slavery as a blessed condition:

Being your slave, what should I do but tend
Upon the hours and times of your desire?
I have no precious time at all to spend,
Nor services to do, till you require.

Nor dare I chide the world-without-end hour
Whilst I, my sovereign, watch the clock for you, [etc.]

(LVII)

The verse is charged here with that heartfelt simplicity which gives the
utterance of Shakespeare's greatest dramatic creations their full force. We fully
share the feelings of this slave, seeing the objects described as coloured by his
predominating emotion. Sidney, whose treatment of the Petrarchan situations
can often be compared with Shakespeare's in artistic worth, gives charm to a
parallel description:

> ... now, like slave-born Muscovite,
> I call it praise to suffer tyranny:
>   And now employ the remnant of my wit
> To make myself believe that all is well;
> While with a feeling skill, I paint my hell.

(II)

But the effect here is different in kind from Shakespeare's; the intellect is more
analytical, and the simile has the objective quality of a rational self-criticism,
which Shakespeare's lacks. In Sidney there seems to be a greater distance
between speaker and reader and consequently the reader tends to take a less
implicated and so less biographical view of the situation.[2]

The tradition in which the Sonnets are written did not always provide
material entirely suitable for Shakespeare's dramatic technique; but even in his
treatments of the more mechanically ingenious themes something of the same
quality of imagination emerges. Sonnet XLVI deals with the traditional theme
of a war between the heart and eye; a more commonplace treatment of the same
theme may be seen in Thomas Watson's *Tears of Fancy*:

> My hart accus'd mine eies and was offended,
> Vowing the cause was in mine eies aspiring:
> Mine eies affirmd my hart might well amend it,
> If he at first had banisht loues desiring.
> Hart said that loue did enter at the eies,
> And from the eies descended to the hart:
> Eies said that in the hart did sparkes arise,
> Which kindled flame that wrought the inward smart,
> Hart said eies tears might soone haue quencht that fl[ame]
> Eies said ... [etc.]

(XX)

Compare Shakespeare:

> Mine eye and heart are at a mortal war,
> How to divide the conquest of thy sight;
> Mine eye my heart thy picture's sight would bar,
> My heart mine eye the freedom of that right.
> My heart doth plead that thou in him dost lie,
> A closet never pierced with crystal eyes,
> But the defendant doth that plea deny,
> And says in him thy fair appearance lies.
> To 'cide this title is impanneled
> A quest of thoughts, all tenants to the heart;
> And by their verdict is determined
> The clear eye's moiety and the dear heart's part:
>   As thus; mine eye's due is thine outward part,
>   And my heart's right thine inward love of heart.
>   (XLVI)

Shakespeare's poem is not simply a better example of a conceited sonnet, it is a more affecting poem, and this is because he makes the conceit serve a felt human situation. Watson concentrates on the antithetical litigants to such an extent that he loses sight of the human 'I' and 'thou'. Shakespeare, in spite of the frigidity of many of the images ('conquest', 'picture', 'closet'), manages to animate the legal imagery with a sense of the lover's craving. He never forgets that the poem is a lover's confession, and accordingly it is directed throughout towards the figure of the beloved.

The same pressure of desire in the speaking voice shapes Shakespeare's treatment of another stock theme—the vision of the beloved in a dream—in such a way that the conceits employed are subordinated to the expression of personal emotion:

> When most I wink, then do mine eyes best see,
> For all the day they view things unrespected;
> But when I sleep, in dreams they look on thee,
> And, darkly bright, are bright in dark directed.
> Then thou, whose shadow shadows doth make bright,
> How would thy shadow's form form happy show
> To the clear day with thy much clearer light,
> When to unseeing eyes thy shade shines so! [etc.]
>   (XLIII)

Here 'darkly bright, are bright in dark directed' is not merely a piece of wordplay but also a triumphant dance of words expressing the lover's delight. The emphatic 'thee' in line three and 'thou' in line five impress on us the fact that the poem, for all its conceits, is a love poem directed towards a beloved object. The contrasts between the radiance of dream and the drabness of reality, the brightness of the beloved and the brightness of the sun, remain expressive of an emotional situation. Shakespeare does not pursue the paradox into areas where it is liberated from this dramatic use and acquires the 'metaphysical' interest of seeming to comment on the nature of experience in general. This is the effect of Sidney's treatment of the same theme:

> I start! look! hark! but what in closed up sense
> Was held, in open sense it flies away;
> Leaving me nought but wailing eloquence.
>   I, seeing better sights in sight's decay;
> Called it anew, and wooed sleep again:
> But him her host, that unkind guest had slain.
>   (XXXVIII)

Here the subsidiary antitheses between closed sleep and open sight, between sight and eloquence, between sleep and Stella as host and guest seem concerned to pursue the mystery in the experience rather than to convey the emotional tension involved. The last line has a degree of detachment common in Sidney but rare in Shakespeare. Other treatments of this theme further sharpen our sense of Shakespeare's individual bias. Linche's version (*Diella* XXIV) and Griffin's (*Fidessa* XIV) are dramatically 'plotted', but raise no emotion. These poets are content to bombast out their fourteen lines with vapid repetitions, whereas Shakespeare's words are for ever creating in the mind of the reader *new* relationships.

At the same time he avoids the enlargement of intellectual interest, the refinement of perception, which accompanies the elaboration of similar material in the poems of Donne. Some critics have claimed that 'the . . . sonnets as a performance represent Shakespeare seeking such effects as John Donne . . . was achieving'.[3] I think this is an error. Donne's poem 'The Dreame' (though not Petrarchan and not a sonnet) obviously springs from the convention we have discussed above. Here however we find not the stock contrast between the cruelty of the real lady and the kindness of the phantom, but a more philosophical distinction: the phantom is banished by the coming of the real mistress, but her going again makes the lover question the nature of that reality (in a way not found in any of the previous treatments). The subsidiary antitheses reason/phantasy, fable/history, etc., show us that Donne is not concerned to build up a poignant image of a loving mind; the figure of the beloved in Donne is not the goal of the whole poem, but rather a symbol for the deeper mystery of the things that lovers experience:

> Coming and staying show'd thee, thee,
> But rising makes me doubt, that now,
>   Thou art not thou.

It is the whole problem of identity that is raised by lines like these.[4]

The bias of Shakespeare's style is no less evident in his handling of details of technique than in the general effect of his treatment of stock themes. He uses the rhetorical tricks which were the common property of the sonneteers but in a way which is mainly expressive of an individual's emotion. For example, the paradoxes in the Sonnets are used less to present the piquantly paradoxical quality of the objective Petrarchan situation and more to communicate a paradoxical quality in the lover's emotion. Of course, lines like

> Still losing when I saw myself to win   (CXIX)

can easily be paralleled from other sonneteers—e.g. Drayton's

> Where most I lost, there most of all I wan (*Idea* 62)

but where Drayton and others tend to use such paradoxes to pattern a situation, Shakespeare's are usually expressive—we feel what it is to endure such situations:

> Thou blind fool, Love, what dost thou to mine eyes,
> That they behold, and see not what they see?
> They know what beauty is, see where it lies,
> Yet what the best is take the worst to be.
>   (CXXXVII)

> My love is as a fever, longing still
> For that which longer nurseth the disease;
> Feeding on that which doth preserve the ill,
> The uncertain sickly appetite to please.
>   (CXLVII)

> O, from what power hast thou this powerful might
> With insufficiency my heart to sway?
> To make me give the lie to my true sight,
> And swear that brightness doth not grace the day?
>   (CL)

In such cases it is not the situation that is paradoxical; it is the condition of the lover's being.

Again, this does not mean that the figure has become 'Metaphysical' in Shakespeare, i.e. that it has become a speculative comment on the human condition. When Donne says:

> I must confesse, it could not chuse but bee
> Prophane, to think thee any thing but thee.
> (*The Dreame*)

or

> Since thou and I sigh one anothers breath,
> Who e'r sighes most, is cruellest, and hastes the others death.
> (*A Valediction: of Weeping*)

he uses a paradoxical playfulness to indicate a state of loving but detached emotion; any difficulty in understanding the meaning seems to mirror the intellectual effort of the poet to bring into focus (and almost within comprehension) a truly human but hitherto undescribed situation. Donne's analysis of the state of loving enlarges our appreciation of human richness by its bizarre re-association of elements plucked out of their normal contexts; here, we feel, is a mind thinking its way through an emotional situation; Shakespeare's world is still recognizably a world of 'normal contexts'; the vision is unhackneyed only because he records the intense immediacy of individuals caught in the stock situation:

> Only my plague thus far I count my gain,
> That she that makes me sin awards me pain.
> (CXLI)

Here, as in the dramas, the individual voice transcends and transforms the convention Shakespeare accepted.

In simile, as in paradox, Shakespeare's bias is towards expressiveness. In most of the Sonnets in Sir Sidney Lee's collection the simile is a device either to describe the physical charms of the beloved or to indicate general conditions in the Petrarchan situation:

> Like as a ship, that through the ocean wide,
> By conduct of some star, doth make her way . . .
> So I, whose star, that wont with her bright ray
> Me to direct, with clouds is over-cast,
> Do wander now, in darkness and dismay . . .
> (SPENSER, XXXIV)

As in some countries, far remote from hence,
The wretched creature destined to die;
Having the judgment due to his offence
By Surgeons begged, their Art on him to try . . .
Even so my Mistress works upon my ill . . .

(Drayton, 50)

These (and the many like them) give clarity and force to the poems they adorn, but do not impart that sense of immediate emotional contact which a majority of Shakespeare's similes, drawn from the familiar experience of simple humanity, do give:

Lo, as a careful housewife runs to catch
One of her feather'd creatures broke away,
Sets down her babe, and makes all swift dispatch . . .
So runn'st thou after that which flies from thee,
Whilst I thy babe chase thee afar behind . . .

(CXLIII)

So am I as the rich, whose blessed key
Can bring him to his sweet up-locked treasure . . .

(LII)

In CXLIII the emotional relationships are defined and made immediate by the simile; in LII it is the human emotion implicit in the comparison which makes the chief effect.

Treatments of the same theme—absence—in poems of merit which use simile as the main feature of their construction may be compared, to show in an extended fashion Shakespeare's individual use of this figure.

How like a winter hath my absence been
From thee, the pleasure of the fleeting year!
What freezings have I felt, what dark days seen!
What old December's bareness every where!
And yet this time removed was summer's time;
The teeming autumn, big with rich increase,
Bearing the wanton burthen of the prime,
Like widowed wombs after their lords' decease:
Yet this abundant issue seem'd to me
But hope of orphans and unfather'd fruit;
For summer and his pleasures wait on thee,
And, thou away, the very birds are mute;

Or, if they sing, 'tis with so dull a cheer
That leaves look pale, dreading the winter's near.
(XCVII)

Like as the Culver, on the bared bough,
Sits mourning for the absence of her mate;
And, in her songs, sends many a wishful vow
For his return that seems to linger late:
So I alone, now left disconsolate,
Mourn to myself the absence of my love;
And, wandering here and there all desolate,
Seek with my plaints to match that mournful dove.
No joy of aught that under heaven doth hove
Can comfort me, but her own joyous sight:
Whose sweet aspect both God and man can move,
In her unspotted pleasance to delight.
      Dark is my day, while her fair light I miss,
      And dead my life that wants such lively bliss.
(SPENSER, LXXXVIII)

Spenser's simile is a graceful one and conveys the gentle melancholy of the poem, but it does not make the lover's feelings vivid by conveying them in images universally charged with these emotions. Shakespeare's 'December's bareness' and 'dark days' are stripped back to their bare function as objective correlatives of the emotion between lover and beloved; they do not intrude at all between the reader and this emotion. Spenser's culver on the other hand is intruded deliberately as a symbol to indicate the mood of the poem (rather than the mood of the persons in the poem). Accordingly, Spenser's image has the charm of an idyll; Shakespeare's generates in the reader a reaction more proper to drama.

Further details of Shakespeare's subject-matter and style could be analysed, but enough has no doubt been said to show how far from the fashions of which they were born Shakespeare's sonnets are taken by his dramatically expressive way of writing. The subject-matter and the rhetoric may be that of the Petrarchan tradition, the effect may sometimes seem Metaphysical, but the uniquely Shakespearean quality of the sequence is not to be explained by either of these labels. We have here what we might expect: a dramatist describes a series of emotional situations between persons (real or fictitious) in a series of separate short poems; the Petrarchan instruments turn in his hands into means of expressing and concentrating the great human emotions, desire, jealousy, fear, hope and despair, and of raising in the reader the dramatic reactions of pity and terror by his implication in the lives and fates of the persons depicted.

NOTES

1. 'Shakespeare at Sonnets' in *The World's Body* (New York), 1938, p. 286.

2. The difference here illustrated between Sidney and Shakespeare the sonneteer is exactly the same difference as we find between *Astrophel and Stella* XXXIX and *1st. Henry IV*, III, i, 5–31.

3. JOHN CROWE RANSOM, op. cit., p. 285.

4. Mr. J. B. LEISHMAN in his *The Monarch of Wit* speaks of Metaphysical poetry as 'the dialectical expression of personal drama'. I accept this definition, but it should be understood that in Donne the personal drama is used as the starting-point for an individual exploration of sensibility, whereas in Shakespeare the whole function of the poem is to convey the emotional quality of the drama. In Donne the language aspires towards intellectual clarity, though not without the glow of passion, but Shakespeare's language aims to give maximum impact to his figures without making their precise function clear. I presume that this is what Leishman refers to when he says of Donne's love-poetry, 'we do not feel that it is in any way symbolic of something else as so often when reading Shakespeare's Sonnets' (p. 224).

1964—W. G. Ingram and Theodore Redpath.
"A Note on the Dedication," from *Shakespeare's Sonnets*

This thorough, modern edition of Shakespeare's *Sonnets* was arguably outmoded by Stephen Booth's "analytical" edition a decade later, but it remains one of the key editorial resources for the study of the sonnets. The editors' sensible, concise notes on Thomas Thorpe's dedication are particularly helpful, as others have noted.

This apparently straightforward dedication of a volume of poems, signed with the initials of the publisher (Thomas Thorpe), and seemingly addressed to somebody only indicated by initials, has raised a welter of ingenious speculations and conflicting interpretations. There is no evidence that the Dedication stimulated attention until very late in the eighteenth century, but since then it has been the playground of theorists who have allowed it to distract their interest from the poems as poems. As the late Professor Rollins wrote in 1944: 'No doubt the sonnets would be more often read for their poetry today if Thorpe had discarded his own thirty words!'

The chief enigmas embodied in the wording are as follows:

(1) What is a 'begetter'?

(2) What does 'onlie' mean?

(3) Who was Mr. W. H.?

(4) Who was the Well-wishing Adventurer?

(5) What is the meaning of 'setting forth'?

(6) What does 'promised' mean, and to whom was the 'eternitie' 'promised'?

(7) Who was T. T.?

(8) What is the syntax of the Dedication?

1 *Begetter*] The chief answers have been: (a) 'inspirer'; (b) 'procurer' (i.e. of the manuscript for the publisher).

Linguistic usage favours 'inspirer'. Although the *verb* 'beget' had earlier borne the sense 'to get, to acquire', no example is cited in *OED* after 1393, other than a sentence from Hamlet's advice to the players: 'You must acquire and beget a temperance that may give it smoothness', where the word does not mean *procuring* something external but *engendering* a quality in oneself. A further point is that the examples cited by *OED* always connote acquiring some thing or goods *for oneself.* This would argue against 'begetter' meaning 'procurer *for another person*', though it would still leave *possible* the sense 'procurer for himself'.

The passage from Dekker's *Satiromastix* often cited in support of the sense (of the *verb* 'beget') 'procure for another' is, in fact, as Samuel Butler pointed out, spoken by a Welshman, Sir Rhys Ap Vaughan, who is held up to ridicule throughout the play by his travesties of English speech. The passage reads as follows: 'If I fall sansomely upon the Widdow, I have some cossens German at Court, shall beget you the reversion of the Master of the Kings Revels.' Other words in this very passage make it hardly respectable evidence of correct English usage.

Moreover, the *noun* 'begetter' is only cited by *OED* as having two senses: (i) 'a procreator'; (2) 'the agent that originates, produces or occasions'. This passage is cited under (2), where in all the other examples the word bears a figurative, theological sense, e.g. in Golding, *De Mornay's Work concerning the Trueness of the Christian Religion*, iii. 28: 'The onely one God . . . the Begetter of the Soules of the other Gods'. In no case cited there or elsewhere could the word mean 'procurer'.

Thus, whatever the dedicator may have intended the word to mean, it would not to the contemporary reader have conveyed the meaning 'procurer'. If the dedicator intended such a meaning he would, therefore, have been writing in a cryptic and private language. In any case, however, since he was himself of that time, the probability against his having even *intended* such a meaning is tremendous.

Against the meaning 'inspirer' it has been urged that the *Sonnets* are not all addressed to the same person. In answer, however, it has been pointed out that the first 126 sonnets (or, at all events, almost all of them) seem to be addressed to the same person, and that those addressed to a woman are printed at the end of the book; so that the allusion in the Dedication would be substantially accurate if 'begetter' meant 'inspirer'.

2 *Onlie*] This is taken by almost all commentators to mean 'sole', whether they think the reference is to the 'inspirer' or to the 'procurer'. There is, however, an alternative sense, namely, 'incomparable', 'peerless' (cf. *OED*, sense 5), and, as William Sharp, who has anticipated us in suggesting this meaning, points out (*Songs, Poems and Sonnets of Shakespeare*, Newcastle, 1885; Introduction, p. 23), the word is used in this sense in Sonnet 1, line 10. This meaning would possibly sort somewhat better with 'inspirer' than with 'procurer'.

3 *Mr. W.H.*] What Rollins called the 'guessing contest' about Mr. W.H. was started by Tyrwhitt and Farmer in the late eighteenth century. The chief candidates nominated by commentators for the honour of the designation have been: (a) William Herbert, Third Earl of Pembroke (1580–1630); (b) Henry Wriothesley, Third Earl of Southampton (1573–1624), whose initials would then be reversed; (c) William Hall, a piratical printer; (d) William Hervey, stepfather of the Earl of Southampton; (e) William Hathaway, Shakespeare's brother-in-law; (f) William Hughes (Hewes), who has been variously identified; (g) William Himself. As stated in our Preface, we have no intention of adjudicating between their rival claims.

4 *The Well-wishing Adventurer*] There seems to be pretty general agreement that this was Thomas Thorpe, who, as the publisher of the *Sonnets*, was 'venturing' some capital.

5 *Setting forth*] The high-flown language of the Dedication is characteristic not only of the time but also, in particular, of Thorpe himself. Just as 'adventurer' would have suggested the enterprises of merchant venturers, so 'setting forth' would have suggested the sailing of one of their ships, though it would also have suggested the process of printing and publishing a book.

6 (a) *The meaning of 'promised'*] Two meanings are possible: (i) 'promised in the specific words of the poems' (e.g. in Sonnets 18 and 19); (ii) 'augured by the quality of the poet's work'.

(b) *To whom was the 'eternitie' 'promised'?*] (i) If Mr. W.H. was the *inspirer* it was 'promised' to him in whichever sense is the right one; (ii) if he was not the *inspirer* but only the *procurer*, it was 'promised' to him in sense (a)(ii), not in sense (a)(i), in which, indeed, it was 'promised' only to the *inspirer*.

7 *T. T.*] Undoubtedly Thomas Thorpe, the publisher of the *Sonnets*.

8 *The syntax of the Dedication*] The printing of the Dedication is lapidary, i.e. closely similar to that of many inscriptions in stone. It has a full stop after every word. The pointing, therefore, does not help in determining the syntax. Some scholars have seen 'wisheth' as concluding a sentence, and having 'Mr. W.H.' as its subject. The French scholar Chasles based this view on the leading between the central five lines, but, as Massey has pointed out, this no more divides them

from what follows than from what precedes. It seems, indeed, pretty evident that the subject of 'wisheth' is 'T.T.'.

⁓⁓⁓   ⁓⁓⁓   ⁓⁓⁓

1983—Anne Ferry. From "Shakespeare and Sidney," from *The "Inward" Language: Sonnets of Wyatt, Sidney, Shakespeare, Donne*

A respected critic of Renaissance poetry, Anne Ferry was the author of several books on Philip Sidney, William Shakespeare, John Donne, John Milton, and John Dryden. She also wrote other works of criticism such as *The Title to the Poem* and *Tradition and the Individual Poem: An Inquiry into Anthologies*.

"O let me true in loue but truly write" is the plea of the speaker in Shakespeare's Sonnet 21. The deliberate echo of the opening of *Astrophil and Stella* is verified by the poem as a whole, which assimilates many characteristic means invented by Sidney for representing Astrophil's struggle to show the truth of his love in verse. The issues involved in that effort about the relation of poetic language to inward experience are first raised in Shakespeare's sequence in this sonnet, which is so closely, complexly, and successfully patterned after a characteristic Sidneian model as to prove that Shakespeare there understood the issues in Sidney's terms, and learned his means for exploring them.

In Sonnet 84 Shakespeare again borrows Astrophil's language about writing love poetry, echoing his claim of Sonnet 3 to be a truthful transcriber of love and beauty: "all my deed / But Copying is, what in her Nature writes." Shakespeare's speaker adapts this metaphor to a prescription for the successful love poet:

> Let him but coppy what in you is writ,
> Not making worse what nature made so cleere.

At this point in the sequence, the issues playfully raised in Sonnet 21, and by means apparently learned from Sidney, have become an obsession of Shakespeare's poet-lover, who reinterprets borrowings from Astrophil's language with implications about the relation of poetry to what is in the heart—his own and his friend's—more radical because more bitterly felt.

Shakespeare's Sonnet 21 invites comparison with Sidney's verse by echoing the opening poem of his sequence while also, it will be shown, following in structure and in verbal detail *Astrophil and Stella* 3. That Sidneian model establishes a pattern used again in his own Sonnets 6, 15, 28, 74: a catalogue of courtly styles dismissed for lacking "inward tuch," and then contrasted with the poet-lover's own style of "pure simplicitie," claimed to utter truly what is in his heart. These sonnets, the previous chapter has shown, use the pattern in ways which implicate the speaker himself in the suspect poetic practices he dismisses, casting in doubt his claims to speak in verse with the true voice of passion. By imitating this model in Sonnet 21, Shakespeare there raises questions about the relation of what the lover experiences as "true in loue" to what as poet he may "truly write." They are virtually identical in nature with Astrophil's questioning in the opening sonnet, and in those patterned after Sonnet 3. The fundamental assumption implied, that there exists an inward identity for the speaker not revealed in his language, is the same.

Sonnet 21 is the only poem in Shakespeare's sequence modeled to these ends after the paradigm of Sidney's third sonnet. Shakespeare, in the lower-numbered sonnets of his sequence, is less consistently concerned than Sidney with the questions of how to write truly about what is grounded inward in the heart. Many of the lower-numbered sonnets ignore them for other interests. Some even articulate a very different conception of the nature and power of poetry, one which would rule out questioning of its truth to inward experience. Sonnet 18 ("Shall I compare thee to a Summers day?"), for example, predicates its promise to immortalize the beauty of the speaker's friend on the assumption of poetry's godlike nature and power. It vows to give eternal life by the inspiration of its divine breath. Though nowhere else so triumphant in their claims, there are many other sonnets in the first half of Shakespeare's sequence built on the conventional promise of the poet-lover to immortalize the beloved. Sonnets 15, 55, 60, 63, 65 postulate for poetry miraculous powers to transform timebound nature into an eternal golden world for the fair friend to dwell in. By contrast Astrophil, like Sidney in *An Apologie for Poetrie*, often ridicules associations of poetry with divine inspiration or power, for instance in Sonnet 74:

Some do I heare of Poets' furie tell,
But (God wot) wot not what they meane by it.

He never includes among his persuasions or praise any promise to immortalize Stella, or any prediction of eternal fame for his verse or name. Nor does Sidney in the sequence ever represent poetry as a force that can transform the mutable into a timeless world, although the most famous passage in *An Apologie for Poetrie* seems to state such a view, and in terms close to Shakespeare's in Sonnet 18. For Sidney argues there that Nature's "world is brasen, the Poets only deliuer a golden."[1] If this view is reflected at all in *Astrophil and Stella*, it is in the absence from the sequence of any consideration of time and its passage. Stella is beautiful, Astrophil young and passionate, and no reminders of fleeting time threaten them in the sequence. In all of *Astrophil and Stella*

Sidney shows little interest in the sweets and beauties of nature, none in the ravages of time upon them or his love, and therefore none in the efficacy of poetry to rescue them from sad mortality.

It is perhaps for these reasons that his sonnet sequence has been traditionally believed to have offered little of interest to Shakespeare, beyond a few motifs already established in the sonnet tradition. For many of the sonnets encountered first in a reading of Shakespeare's sequence, those also most often quoted or anthologized, focus on a struggle altogether different from Astrophil's. They portray the poet battling "all in war with Time" to immortalize his fair, young love.[2] These concerns liken them on the one hand to Daniel's sonnets, twenty-eight of which were first printed in the same volume as Sidney's in the 1591 edition of *Astrophil and Stella*. Of these, twenty-three were then revised and reprinted the following year in an expanded collection of fifty sonnets to *Delia*. Daniel's elegiac tributes to the short glories of the morning dew and the blushing rose, used metaphorically to praise and persuade his sweet love, resemble in mood and metaphor Shakespeare's to his fair friend.[3] On the other hand, Shakespeare's sonnets also resemble Spenser's in his *Amoretti*, published in 1595, which radiantly celebrate the eternizing gift of art.[4] Shakespeare's may have been influenced by both these English contemporaries, who themselves borrowed from continental models. Daniel learned especially from Desportes, Spenser from Petrarch (in Marot's version) and DuBellay, whom he translated in experimenting with the sonnet form, and both from Tasso.[5] The presence and power of the sonnets resembling Daniel's and Spenser's in the lower-numbered poems of Shakespeare's collection overshadow his interest there in Sidney's different questions about poetry, which become much more insistent in the higher-numbered half of Shakespeare's sonnets. For the concerns of *Astrophil and Stella* are with the efficacy of poetry exclusively in the human world as it is experienced by the poet-lover simultaneously in his outward social existence, and his inward states. Where Shakespeare shows interest in these issues in his sonnets, and they become a focus for many in the higher-numbered part of the sequence, the poems reveal that he assimilated their concerns directly from *Astrophil and Stella*.

Sidney's portrayal of Astrophil's struggle to write truly about loving raised explicitly for the first time in English verse questions about the adequacy of poetic language to portray what is in the heart. Shakespeare, alone among English writers of love sonnets after Sidney, followed him in making these questions a central concern, assimilating their most far-reaching implications for what amounts to a new conception of human nature. . . .

NOTES

1. Sidney, *An Apologie for Poetrie*, p. 156. Its influence on Shakespeare's plays is the thesis of Alwin Thaler, *Shakespeare and Sir Philip Sidney* (Cambridge, Mass.: Harvard University Press, 1949). Lack of concern with mutability in Sidney's

sonnet sequence is discussed by Connell, *Sir Philip Sidney*, pp. 49–50, citing Kalstone, *Sidney's Poetry*, p. 122; A. C. Hamilton, "The 'mine of time': Time and Love in Sidney's *Astrophil and Stella*," *Mosaic* 13 (1979): 81–91.

2. For extended discussions of the promise to immortalize the friend in Shakespeare's sonnets, see Ferry, *All in War with Time*, pp. 3–63; J. B. Leishman, *Themes and Variations in Shakespeare's Sonnets* (New York: Hillary House, 1961); Lever, *The Elizabethan Sonnet*, pp. 246–72.

3. The widely noticed influence of Daniel's *Delia* on Shakespeare's sonnets is discussed by Paul Ramsey, *The Fickle Glass* (New York: AMS Press, 1979), pp. 52–62.

4. Spenser's sonnets, often discussed as influencing Shakespeare's, are said to be "mysteriously closer to Shakespeare's than to those of any other Elizabethan" by F. T. Prince, "The Sonnet from Wyatt to Shakespeare," *Elizabethan Poetry*, Stratford-upon-Avon Studies 2, pp. 23–24.

5. Among many discussions of Italian and French influences on English sonneteers see Janet Scott, *Les Sonnets Élisabéthains* (Paris: Librairie Ancienne Honoré Champion, 1929); Sells, *The Italian Influence in English Poetry*; D. G. Rees, "Italian and Italianate Poetry," *Elizabethan Poetry*, Stratford-upon-Avon Studies 2, pp. 53–70.

1984—Joel Fineman.
"Shakespeare's Perjur'd Eye," from *Representations*

Joel Fineman was an influential Shakespeare scholar who unfortunately died young, at the age of 42. A professor at the University of California at Berkeley, Fineman applied post-structuralist and Lacanian theories in this essay, which he expanded into the book *Shakespeare's Perjured Eye: The Invention of Poetic Subjectivity in the Sonnets*, awarded the Modern Language Association's James Russell Lowell Award for outstanding book of the year.

In the first portion of his sonnet sequence—in the subsequence of sonnets addressed to a young man—Shakespeare writes a matching pair of sonnets that develop the way in which his eye and heart initially are enemies but then are subsequently friends. The first sonnet of the pair begins: "Mine eye and heart are at a mortal war, / How to divide the conquest of thy sight" (46).[1] In contrast, the second sonnet, relying on a "verdict" that "is determined" at the conclusion of sonnet 46, begins: "Betwixt mine eye and heart a league is took, / And each doth good turns now unto the other" (47).

Taken together and in sequence, the two sonnets compose an argument *in utramque partem*, with their poet placing himself on both sides of a rhetorical question that is a commonplace in the tradition of the Renaissance sonnet.[2]

Despite the conventional opposition, however, the two sonnets confidently argue to what is the same, and equally conventional, conclusion: namely, that their poet's eye and heart do "good turns now unto the other" (47). Thus, in the first sonnet, after meditating on the war between his eye and heart, the poet syllogistically and Neo-Platonically derives the moral that: "As thus: mine eye's due is thy outward part, / And my heart's right thy inward love of heart." In turn, in the second sonnet, from thinking on the amity between his eye and heart, the poet reassuringly discovers that "thy picture in my sight / Awakes my heart to heart's and eye's delight." Taken together and in sequence, therefore, the two sonnets respond to the rhetorical question that they raise by juxtaposing a *concordia discors* and a *coincidentia oppositorum* each against the other. Both sonnets speak to the fact that their poet's eye and heart, however much they differ from or with each other, are equally "delighted." In both sonnets, eye and heart will peacefully "divide the conquest of thy sight," as though, from the ideal perspective shared by the two sonnets, eye and heart are complementary and coordinated aspects of each other.

In a straightforward way, the rhetorical wit of these two sonnets consists of thus hendiadystically arriving, from different starting points, at a common destination, for in this way the two sonnets manage to resolve, or to beg the question raised by, a traditional *débat*. Yet, however witty, the poems take seriously the equivalence of the conclusions that they share. In both cases the relationship of eye and heart, whether initially antipathetic or sympathetic, leads immediately, via complementary antithesis, to a recuperative and benign assessment of yet other differences adduced. In war or peace the sonnets' several binaries combine to generate a clarity of eye and purity of heart whose own discrete proprieties and properties in turn reciprocally establish, or are established by, the integrity and integration of the other categorical oppositions to which the poems refer. In the first sonnet, for example, sonnet 46, the difference between "outward" and "inward" is secured and reconciled because the vision of the eye and the "thinking" of the heart can be harmoniously apportioned between the clear-cut opposition of "The clear eye's moiety and the dear heart's part." In the second sonnet, 47, the absence of the beloved is converted or transmuted into presence because: "So either by thy picture or my love, / Thyself away are present still with me."

This systematic complementarity—whereby opposites either are the same or, as opposites, still somehow go compatibly together—speaks to a general, indeed, a generic, homogeneity subtending both sonnets, something that informs them more deeply than the thematic heterogeneity that the two sonnets only provisionally or momentarily evoke. In the first sonnet it is the difference between eye and heart that establishes the concord between them, whereas in the second sonnet the concord derives from their similarity. But this difference, which is the difference between difference and similarity, turns out not to make much difference. In both sonnets the eye is "clear" and the heart is "dear" by virtue of a governing structure of likeness and contrast, of identity and difference, of similarity and contrariety, that both sonnets equally and isomorphically employ.

What these two young man sonnets, 46 and 47, share, therefore, as Lévi-Strauss might say, is the sameness of their differences: what joins them together is a structural identity, or a structure of identity that is yet more fundamental and more powerful than their apparent opposition. At the level of theme and of poetic psychology, this yields the Petrarchan commonplace in accord with which the poet's eye and heart come instantly to complement each other, moving from war to peace, from antipathy to sympathy, in a progress that constitutes a kind of shorthand summary of the amatory assumptions of ideal admiration, e.g., the way Cupid shoots his arrows through the lover's eye into the lover's heart.[3] This is a specifically *visual* desire, for in both sonnets it is as something of the eye that the young man's "fair appearance lies" within the poet's heart. In both sonnets "thy picture in my sight" indifferently "Awakes my heart to heart's and eye's delight."

Such homogenizing visual imagery, applied to the poet's love, to his beloved, and to his poetry, pervades the sequence of sonnets addressed to the young man, and this imagery is regularly employed, as in sonnets 46 and 47, to characterize a material likeness or sameness that conjoins or renders consubstantial two distinctive yet univocally collated terms: not only the poet's eye and heart, but, also, the poet and his young man (e.g., "'Tis thee (myself) that for myself I praise, / Painting my age with beauty of thy days" [62]), the young man and, in the opening sonnets which urge the young man to procreate, *his* young man (e.g., "Look in thy glass and tell the face thou viewest, / Now is the time that face should form another" [3]), as well as the poet's poetry and that of which the poetry speaks (e.g., "So long as men can breathe or eyes can see, / So long lives this, and this gives life to thee" [18]). In general, the poet identifies his first-person "I" with the ideal eye of the young man—"Now see what good turns eyes for eyes have done" (24)—and then proceeds to identify these both with the "wondrous scope" (105) of his visionary verse: "So till the judgement that yourself arise, / You live in this, and dwell in lovers' eyes" (55).

In all these cases the visual imagery that Shakespeare employs is, of course, nothing but conventional. Indeed, the sonnets addressed to the young man regularly allude to the conventionality of their visual imagery, often characterizing such imagery, as well as that of which it is an image, as something old-fashioned, even antiquated, as in the literary retrospection of sonnet 59:

O that record could with a backward look,
Even of five hundreth courses of the sun.
Show me your image in some antique book,
Since mind at first in character was done!

There are a good many reasons why the young man's poet might "look" in this "backward" way to specifically visual imagery, to imagery of vision, in order, as sonnet 59 goes on to say, to "see what the old world could say / To this composed wonder of your frame." With regard to the poet's ideal desire, which aims to conjoin poetic subject with poetic object—"thou mine, I thine" (108)—the young man's poet can rely upon a familiar Petrarchist motif, derived from Stoic optics, of eroticized *eidôla* or likenesses, intromissive and extromissive, whose very physics establishes a *special* (from *specere*, "to look at") coincidence of lover and beloved, as, for example, when Astrophil, at the beginning of Sidney's sonnet sequence, looks into his heart to write, and finds there pre-engraved or "stell'd" upon it the stylized image or *imago* of the Stella whom he loves. In turn, this physics of the *eidôlon* presupposes an equally familiar and specifically idealist metaphysics of genus and species whereby individual particulars are but subspecies of a universal form or type, declensions of a paradigmatic archetype whose immanent universality is regularly and perennially conceived in terms of light, as in Platonic *eidos*, from *idein*, "to see," or as the end of the *Paradiso*, where Dante sees "La forma universal" in his vision of "luce etterna" and "semplice lume" (in this divine light, we can add, Dante also sees the painted "likeness," the "effige," of himself).[4] Moreover, again in ways that are nothing but conventional, the poetry of idealization, especially as it develops in the self-consciously literary tradition of the Renaissance sonnet, characteristically assimilates such visual imagery, which is its imagery *of* the ideal, to itself, so as thereby to idealize itself as effective *simulacrum*, physical and metaphysical, of that which it admires. As an activity of "stelling,"—e.g., "Mine eye hath play'd the painter and hath stell'd / Thy beauty's form in table of my heart" (24)—such poetry is *Ideas Mirrour*, as Drayton called his sonnet sequence, and it is so precisely because, being something visual and visionary, it can claim to be not only the reflection of, but also the objectification of, its idea of its ideal.[5]

Speaking very generally, it is fair to say that this is the regular force of visual imagery in the tradition of the literature or poetry of praise—a tradition that goes back to the praise of love in the *Symposium* or *Phaedrus*, but one that is especially vital in the particular literary genre of the sonnet, where it goes without saying that the poet is a lover who desires only that which he admires. With regard to poetic procedure or, rather, with regard to what is the common and long-standing understanding of poetic procedure, this is a tradition of specifically visionary poetic likeness, either mimetic likeness, whereby poetry is the simulating representation of that which it presents—"ut pictura poesis," speaking picture—or figural likeness, as when Aristotle defines metaphor (whether based on analogy or commutative proportion) as the capacity "to see the same" (*theôrein homoion*), metaphor being for Aristotle, as for the tradition of rhetorical theory that derives from him, an activity of speculative likening that, quite literally, "theorizes sameness."[6] Correspondingly, with regard to poetic subjectivity, this is a literary tradition in which the poet is a panegyric *vates* or seer who, at least ideally, is the same as that which he sees (e.g. Dante's reflexively reflective "effige"), just as, with regard to poetic semiosis, poetic language, as *eikón*, *speculum*, *imago*, *eidôlon*, etc., is Cratylitically the same as that of which it speaks, for example, the way Dante identifies his own "beatitude" with "those words that praise my Lady," his "lodano" with "la donna," or the way Petrarch puns on "Laura," "laud," and "laurel."[7] These are general themes and motifs by reference to which the poetry of praise characteristically become a praise of poetry itself.[8]

It is possible to get some sense of how very familiar, over-familiar, this received literary tradition is to Shakespeare if we register the formulaic way the young man's poet in sonnet 105 identifies, one with the others, his "love," his "beloved," and his "songs and praises":

> Let not my love be called idolatry,
> Nor my beloved as an idol show,
> Since all alike my songs and praises be.

What joins these three together is the ideality they share, an ideality that establishes a three-term correspondence between the speaking, the spoken, and the speech of praise. "'Fair,' 'kind,' and 'true' is all my argument," says the poet in sonnet 105, and these "Three themes in one, which wondrous scope affords" ("Three themes" that sonnet 105 repeats three times) amount to a phenomenological summary, an eidetic reduction, of a Petrarchist metaphysical, erotic, and poetic Ideal: "Fair" identifies the visibility, the *Sichtigkeit*, of an ideal sight (*idein*, "to see"); "kind" identifies the homogeneous categoriality, the formal elementality, of an ideal essence (Platonic *eidos*); "true" identifies the coincidence of ideal knowledge and knowing (*oida*, which is also from *idein*). It is by reference to such precisely conceived and conceited ideality, an ideality that in effect recapitulates the history of ideas up through the Renaissance, that sonnet 105 manages to identify "my love," "my beloved," and "my songs and praises," each one of these being "'Fair,' 'kind,' and 'true,'" and therefore, by commutation, each one of these being the same and truthful mirror-image of the other two. In the same idealizing way, this is how sonnets 46 and 47 manage to eliminate the difference between their eye and heart, and thereby manage, despite the difference with which they begin, to say the same thing. More generally, we can say that this is how Shakespeare's poetry of visionary praise, because it is a "wondrous scope" and because it is addressed to a "wondrous scope," is always, as sonnet 105 puts it, monotheistically, monogamously, monosyllabically, and monotonously "To one, of one, still such, and ever so." This is an ideological poetry, as sonnet 105 seems almost to complain, whose virtue consists in the way .its copiousness always copies the same ideal sameness—"Since all alike my songs and praises be"—a universal and uni-versing poetic and erotic practice whose very ideality is what renders it incapable of manifesting difference, for, as the poet puts it in sonnet 105:

> Kind is my love to-day, to-morrow kind,
> Still constant in a wondrous excellence,
> Therefore my verse, to constancy confin'd,
> One thing expressing, leaves out difference.

However, as the palpable claustrophobia of sonnet 105 suggests, it would be possible to look more closely at the sonnets addressed to the young man so as to see the way they characteristically resist and conflictedly inflect their most ideal expressions of visionary unity, the way they chafe against the "constancy" to which they are "confin'd," the way that they implicitly "express" the "difference" that they explicitly "leave out." If, as Murray Krieger has suggested, we are supposed to hear the "one" in sonnet 105's "*won*drous scope," then so too do we also hear the "two" in its "T(w)o one, of one, still such, and ever so."[9] So too, the entire sonnet is colored by the ambiguous logic of its opening "Since"—"Since all alike my songs and praises be"—since this concessive particle explains both why the young man is an idol as well as why he is not. Such complications, though they are implicit, have their effect. As complications, they add a reservation or a wrinkle to the poet's otherwise straightforward rhetoric of compliment. In such oblique, yet obvious, ways the young man sonnets will regularly situate themselves and their admiration at one affective and temporal remove from the ideality that they repeatedly and repetitiously invoke, with the peculiar result that in these sonnets an apparently traditionary poetics of ideal light comes regularly to seem what sonnet 123 calls "The dressings of a former sight."

This peculiar retrospection is a consistent aspect of the young man sonnets' imagery of the visual and the visible, imagery that is characteristically presented in the young man sonnets as though it were so tarnished with age that its very reiteration is what interferes with the poet's scopic or specular identification of his poetic "I" with the ideal "eye" of the young man: "For as you were when first your eye I ey'd" (104). In general, the young man's poet, *as* a visionary poet, seems capable of expressing only a love at second sight; his identification of his ego with his ego-ideal seems worn out by repetition, as though it were the very practice by the poet of an old-fashioned poetry of visionary praise that effectively differentiates the poet as a panegyricizing subject from what he takes to be his ideal and his praiseworthy object. We can take as an example the mixed-up deictic and epideictic compact of the couplet to sonnet 62 which has already been cited—"'Tis thee (myself) that for myself I praise, / Painting my age with beauty of thy days"—where the confused identification of the poet's "I" and "thou" effectively identifies the first person of the poet with the youth and age of visionary praise. The same thing goes, however, to take another example, for the "stelling" of sonnet 24. At the beginning of the sonnet the poet remembers how, in the past, "Mine eye hath play'd the painter and hath stell'd / Thy beauty's form in table of my heart." At the end of the sonnet, however, speaking in and for the present, the poet observes: "Yet eyes this cunning want to grace their art. / They draw but what they see, know not the heart" (24).

In this context, we can recall the fact that Shakespeare writes his sonnet sequence, for the most part, after the Elizabethan sonnet sequence vogue has passed, in what we might call the literary aftermath of the poetry of praise, when such Petrarchist panegyric has come to seem, to some extent, *passé*. This is the historical literary context within which the sonnets addressed to the young man—which are conceived long after what even Sidney, at the inaugural moment of the Elizabethan sonnet sequence, called "Poor Petrarch's long-deceased woes"—make a personal issue out of their self-remarked literary belatedness, regularly associating what they themselves characterize as their old-fashioned literary matter and manner with their poet's sense of his senescence.[10] In sonnet 76, for example, the poet asks:

> Why is my verse so barren of new pride?
> So far from variation or quick change?
> Why with the time do I not glance aside
> To new-found methods and to compounds strange?

As the poet first poses them, these are rhetorical questions, questions about rhetoric, but these questions then will press themselves upon the poet's person; they define for him his sense of superannuated self:

> Why write I still all one, ever the same,
> And keep invention in a noted weed,
> That every word doth almost tell my name,
> Showing their birth and where they did proceed?

A good many young man sonnets are concerned with just this kind of literary question, and, as in sonnet 76, in these sonnets it appears as though it is the very asking of the question that turns out to empty out the poet's praising self. It is as though, because he is committed to an ancient poetry of praise, the poet feels himself obliged to pay the debts incurred by a bankrupt literary tradition—as though the poet, as a person, is himself entropically exhausted by the tired tropes with which, according to an old poetic custom, he ornaments himself:

> So all my best is dressing old words new,
> Spending again what is already spent:

For as the sun is daily new and old,
So is my love still telling what is told. (76)

This is significant because it introduces a new kind of self-consciousness into the already highly self-conscious tradition of the Renaissance sonnet. In familiar ways, the poet in sonnet 76 identifies himself with his own literariness. At the same time, however, it is in an unfamiliar way that the poet's subjectivity here seems worn out by the heavy burden of the literary history that his literariness both examples and extends. For what is novel in a sonnet such as 76 is not so much the way the poet takes the ever-renewed sameness of the sun, its perennially revivified vivacity, as a dead metaphor for the animating *energeia* and *enargia* of an ideal metaphoricity. Rather, what is striking, and what is genuinely novel, is the way the visionary poet takes this faded brightness personally, the way he identifies his own poetic person, his own poetic identity, with the after-light of this dead metaphoric sun. Identifying himself with an aged eternity—which is itself the image of an ideal and an unchanging identity—the young man's poet is like a bleached Dante: he is a visionary poet, but he is so, as it were, after the visionary fact, a seer who now sees in a too-frequently reiterated "luce etterna" a vivid image, an *effige* or an *eidôlon*, of the death of both his light and life, as in sonnet 73: "In me thou seest the twilight of such day / As after sunset fadeth in the west, / Which by and by black night doth take away, / Death's second self, that seals up all in rest." This is the peculiarly inflected imagery of light with which the young man's poet assimilates to his own poetic psychology the self-consuming logic of "Spending again what is already spent," for it is with this imagery of after-light that the poet makes his own poetic introspection into something retrospective:

In me thou seest the glowing of such fire,
That on the ashes of his youth doth lie
As the death-bed whereon it must expire,
Consum'd with that which it was nourish'd by. (73)

In terms of what we can think of as the conventional visual imagery of the poetry of praise, it is as though in Shakespeare's sonnets to the young man *Ideas Mirrour* had now become the "glass" of sonnet 62, a "glass," however, that rather horrifyingly "shows me myself indeed, / Beated and chopp'd with tann'd antiquity," with the subjective consequence of this for the poet being that, as sonnet 62 goes on to say, "Mine own self-love quite contrary I read."

There is much more that might be said about this imagery of tired light, or tired imagery of light, for it can be argued that such imagery not only determines the young man's poet's sense of space and time, but also his erotic sensibility as well (consider, for example, "A liquid prisoner pent in walls of glass" [5]). As it is, however, it seems clear that we cannot overlook—as sentimental readings often do—the novel coloring that Shakespeare's young man sonnets give to their visual imagery, to their imagery *of* the visual, for this is responsible, to a considerable degree, for the pathos of poetic persona that these sonnets regularly exhibit. By the same token, however, it would be a mistake to overemphasize this darkness that informs these sonnets' literary, visionary light. If the young man sonnets are suspicious of their visual imagery, this is not a suspicion that they put directly into words. Quite the contrary, whatever reservations attach to the young man sonnets' imagery of vision, these reservations, like those that shade the poet's various characterizations of the ideality of the young man, are implicit rather than explicit, something we read between what the young man sonnets call their "eternal lines to time" (18).

It is important to insist upon this indirection, upon the fact that the young man sonnets do not explicitly speak against their light, because this accounts for the residual idealism with which the young man sonnets always turn, heliotropically, to "that sun, thine eye" (49). At least ideally, the young man sonnets would like to be like the courtly "marigold" of sonnet 25, whose "fair leaves spread . . . at the sun's eye." Like such flowers of fancy, the young man sonnets would like to look exactly like the ideal that they look at, just as the poet would like his "I" to be "as you were when first your eye I ey'd" (104). Hence the nostalgia of the poet's introspection: the poet sees his difference from an eternal visionary sameness, his difference from a visionary poetics that would always be the same because, as Aristotle says of metaphor, it always "see(s) the same." But this insight serves only to make the poet's ideal bygone vision seem all the more ideal, an image of poetic presence that is always in the past, even when this ancient past is the present in the future tense, as in the prospective retrospection of sonnet 104, where the poet tells "thou age unbred: / Ere you were born was beauty's summer dead." This loyally retrospective visuality, a poetry of re-turn rather than of turn, accounts for the complex texture of the young man sonnets' imagery of vision, a complexity that derives from the fact that the young man sonnets never entirely reject the ideality from which they are estranged. If the young man sonnets characteristically distance themselves from their visual imagery even as they employ it, this distanciation possesses poetic force precisely to the extent that such imagery of light continues to retain, specifically in retrospect, at a distance, its originary and traditional ideal connotations.

I stress the vestigial power of such visual ideality in the young man sonnets, its "present-absent" (45) presence, because this both measures and prepares for the difference between the sonnets addressed to the young man and those addressed to the dark lady. As is well known, in the subsequence of sonnets addressed to the dark lady such ideal imagery of light is explicitly—Shakespeare's word here is important—"forsworn" (152). What gives this "forswearing" its power, however, and what distinguishes it, tonally as well as thematically, from the implicit visual reservations informing the sonnets addressed to the young man, is the way the dark lady's poet puts these heretofore unspoken visionary suspicions directly into words. In the young man sonnets, the young man, whatever his faults, is an "image" whose idealization effectively can represent an ideal that is lost, as in sonnet 31: "Their images I lov'd I view in thee, / And thou (all they) hast all the all of me," or the young man is a "shadow" who to the poet's "imaginary sight ... makes black night beauteous, and her old face new" (27). In contrast, in the dark lady sonnets, though as something that is more complicated and more unsettling than a simple opposition, the dark lady has the "power," as in sonnet 149, "To make me give the lie to my true sight, / And swear that brightness doth not grace the day."

We broach here what is often called the anti-Petrarchanism of the sonnets to the dark lady, and it is certainly the case that the dark lady sonnets regularly characterize their literary peculiarity and novelty in terms of the way they differ from the specular ideality of a previous Petrarchist poetics. When the poet looks at the young man, he sees "That sun, thine eye" (49). In contrast, when he looks at the dark lady, what he sees is the way she is unlike the ideal brightness of the young man: "My mistress' eyes are nothing like the sun" (130). On the face of it, this amounts to a straightforward difference, for, on the one hand, there is brightness, whereas, on the other, there is darkness. What makes this difference complicated, however, is that when the poet makes an issue of it, when he gives explicit expression to it, he presents the darkness of the lady as itself the image of this difference, as an image, precisely, of the difference between the black that it is and the light that it is not.

This is why the difference between the lady's stressedly unconventional darkness and the young man's emphatically conventional brightness produces something that is both more and less than a straightforward black and white antithesis of the kind suggested by the "anti-" of anti-Petrarchanism. On the one hand, there is brightness, but, on the other, is a darkness that, in a peculiar or what Troilus calls a "bi-fold" way, is both these hands together both at once.[11] Such is the strangeness of a lady whom the poet alternately praises and blames for being other than what at first sight she appears. As an image of that which she is not, the lady is presented as the likeness of a difference, at once a version of, but at the same time a perversion of, that to which she is, on the one hand, both positively and negatively compared, and that to which she is, on the other, both positively and negatively opposed. For this reason, as she is presented, the lady is, strictly speaking, beyond both comparison and opposition. The lady both is and is not what she is, and because she is in this way, *in* herself, something double, the lady cannot be comprehended by a poetics of "To one, of one, still such, and ever so." As the poet puts it in sonnet 130—this the consequence of the fact that his "mistress' eyes are nothing like the sun"—the lady is a "love," just as she inspires a "love," that is "as rare, / As any she belied with false compare." The irrational ratio of the formula defines the peculiarity of the lady. She is a "she" who is logically, as well as grammatically, both subject and object of "belied with false compare," comparable, therefore, only to the way comparison has failed.

From the beginning, this effective doubleness of the lady, defined in specifically literary terms, i.e., in terms of a new kind of poetics, is what the poet finds distinctive about her, as in the first sonnet he addresses to her:

> In the old age black was not counted fair,
> Or if it were it bore not beauty's name;
> But now is black beauty's successive heir,
> And beauty slander'd with a bastard shame. (127)

What we are supposed to recognize here as officially surprising is that the lady's traditional foul is now characterized as something that is fair, just as in later sonnets this novel fair will be yet more surprisingly foul: "For I have sworn thee fair, and thought thee bright, / Who art as black as hell, as dark as night" (147). In either case, however, whether fair or foul, it is always as images of that which they are not, as something double, fair *and* foul, as something duplicitous and heterogeneous, that the lady and her darkness acquire their erotic and their literary charge.

Thus "black" is "now" "beauty's successive heir," now that "beauty" is "slander'd with a bastard shame." In the context of the sequence as a whole, the force of this unconventional "succession" is that it repeats, but with a difference, the themes of reiterated and legitimately procreated likeness with reference to which the young man at the opening of his subsequence is supposed, as an *imago*, to "prove his beauty by succession thine" (2): "Die single, and thine image dies with thee" (3). Instead of the ideal multiplication of kind with kind, the ongoing reproduction of the visual same, by means of which the young man is supposed to "breed another thee" (6)—a breeding implicitly associated in the young man sonnets with a kind of homosexual usury: "that use is not forbidden usury" (6)—the novel beauty of the lady instead exemplifies a novelly miscegenating "successivity"—novel *because* successive to such Platonized "succession"—whereby black becomes the differential substitute, the unkind "heir," of what is "fair."[12] So too with the blackness of the lady's "raven" eyes, a darkness that replaces at the same time as it thus displaces the brightness it sequentially succeeds:

> Therefore my mistress' eyes are raven black,
> Her eyes so suited and they mourners seem
> At such who, not born fair, no beauty lack,
> Slandering creation with a false esteem. (127)

This, in little, defines the structural and temporal relationship of the dark lady sonnets to the young man sonnets. The second subsequence is a repetition of the first, but it is a discordant and a disturbing repetition because the latter subsequence, stressing itself as a repetition, represents the former (as also the former's themes of visionary presence—"So either by thy picture or my love / Thyself away are present still with me" [47]—in such a way that its memorial repetition explicitly calls up the poignant absence of that which it recalls. To the degree that this articulates the silent reservations that darken the idealism of the young man sonnets, to this extent we register the way in which the "black" of the second subsequence is continuous with the elegaically retrospective visuality of the first. Yet there is also an emphatic difference between the two, a difference that derives precisely from the fact that the dark lady's poet explicitly expresses what the young man's poet preferred to leave implicit. For what the dark lady's poet sees in the darkness of the lady's mourning eyes is the death of ideal visionary presence; her darkness is for him an image or *imago* of the loss of vision. But, according to the poet, it is this very vision of the loss of vision that now thrusts him into novel speech—the discourse of "black beauty"—making him now no longer a poet of the eye, but, instead, a poet of the tongue: "Yet so they mourn, becoming of their woe, / That every tongue says beauty should look so" (127).

As Ulysses says of wanton Cressida, therefore, "There's language in her eye."[13] But what is odd about this language is what is odd about the lady's eye, namely, that it is opposed to vision. The difference between this and the way that language is characterized in the young man sonnets is, of course, considerable, and we may say that this difference at once examples and defines the novelty of the way a poet speaks in a post-Petrarchist poetics. In the young man sonnets the poet ideally speaks a visionary speech, and therefore, when he speaks about this speech he speaks of it as something of the eye: "O, learn to read what silent love hath writ: / To hear with eyes belongs to love's fine wit" (23). In contrast, but again as something that is more complicated than a simple opposition, the poet in the dark lady subsequence will speak about his speech *as* speech, and as something that, for just this very reason, is different from a visual ideal. It is in this "forswearing" way that the dark lady, with the "pow'r" of her "insufficiency," will "make me give the lie to my true sight, / And swear that brightness doth not grace the day" (150). The double way the lady looks is like the double way that language speaks, which is why, for example, when the poet looks at the lady's far too common "common place" (137), a place that is at once erotic and poetic, he tells us how "mine eyes seeing this, say this is not" (137).

Thematized in this way, as something radically discrepant to the truth of ideal vision, as the *voice* of "eyes . . . which have no correspondence with true sight" (148), language is regularly presented in the dark lady sonnets as some thing whose truth consists not only in saying, but in *being*, something false:

"My thoughts and my discourse as madman's are, / At random from the truth vainly express'd: / For I have sworn thee fair, and thought thee bright, / Who art as black as hell, as dark as night" (147). Correspondingly, because no longer something visual, because no longer the iconic likeness or the *eidôlon* of what it speaks about, verbal language now defines itself as its forswearing difference from what is "'Fair,' 'kind,' and 'true'": "For I have sworn deep oaths of thy deep kindness, / Oaths of thy love, thy truth, thy constancy, / And to enlighten thee gave eyes to blindness, / Or made them swear against the thing they see" (152). And, as a further and more personal result, the poet now identifies himself with the difference that his language thus bespeaks. He is no longer a visionary poet who identifies his "I" and "eye." Instead, *because* he speaks, the poet comes to inhabit the space of difference between poetic language and poetic vision, a difference generated *by* the speech he speaks. The poet's subjectivity, his "I," is precipitated in or as the slippage between his eye and tongue. The poet becomes, in the phrase I take as title for this paper, the subject of a "perjur'd eye": "For I have sworn thee fair: more perjur'd eye, / To swear against the truth so foul a lie!" (152).

It is fair to say, therefore, that in the dark lady sonnets we encounter a poetics in which true vision is captured by false language, and that the conflict thus engendered—between sight and word, between being and meaning, between poetic presentation and poetic representation—in turn determines specific variations on, or mutations of, traditionary sonneteering claims and motifs. A poetics of verbal re-presentation, stressing the repetition of the re-, spells the end of the poetics of visual presentation, thereby constituting the Idea of poetic presence as something that is lost. To the extent that this is the case, Shakespeare's sonnet sequence marks a decisive moment in the history of lyric, for when the dark lady sonnets forswear the ideally visionary poetics of the young man sonnets, when poetic language comes in this way to be characterized as something verbal, not visual, we see what happens to poetry when it gives over a perennial poetics of *ut pictura poesis* for (literally, *so as* to speak) a poetics of *ut poesis poesis*, a transition that writes itself out in Shakespeare's sonnets as an unhappy progress from a poetry based on visual likeness—whose adequation to that which it admires is figured by a "wondrous scope" by means of which "One thing expressing, leaves out difference" (105)—to a poetry based on verbal difference—whose inadequate relation to that which it bespeaks is figured by an "insufficiency" that "make(s) me give the lie to my true sight" (150). In the sequence as a whole, this progress from a homogeneous poetics of vision to a heterogeneous poetics of language is fleshed out as a progress from an ideally homosexual desire, however conflicted, for what is "'Fair, 'kind,' and 'true'" to a frankly misogynistic, heterosexual desire for what is fair *and* unfair, kind *and* unkind, true *and* false—a progress, in other words, from man to woman. Here again, however, it is explicitly and literally as a figure of speech that the lady becomes the novel "hetero-" opposed as such to an ideal and a familiar Neo-Platonic "homo-," as when: "When my love swears that she is made of truth, / I do believe her though I know she lies" (138). It is in this way, by making each the figure of the other, that the poet collates his corrupting Eros with his corrupting Logos. When the poet "credit[s] her false-speaking tongue," the result is that "On both sides thus is simple truth suppress'd" (138). But the consequence of this false correspondence, of this traducement of the Cratylism of the poetry of praise—e.g., of the "beatitudinizing" power of Dante's "Beatrice," or of the self-applauding circularities of Petrarch's puns on "Laura," "laud," and "laurel"—is that the poet comes to express, in terms of a specific desire of language, the novel duplicity of a specifically linguistic language of desire: "Therefore I lie with her, and she with me, / And in our faults by lies we flattered be" (138).

Again there is more that might be said about the way the dark lady sonnets thematize their lady's and their poet's speech as speech, and draw from this the moral that such speech is radically excessive to an orthodox poetics of admiration. As with the implicit reservations that inform the young man sonnets' visionary themes, it would be possible to show how Shakespeare's explicitly paradoxical version of a traditional poetics of praise not only affects the poet's expressions of desire—leading him from a homosexual desire for that which is admired to a heterosexual desire for that which is not admired—but, again, his sense of space and time as well. If we could follow this out in sufficient detail we would develop a more textured phenomenology of the psychology of the Shakespearean subject. This would help not only to describe the ways in which poetic person or lyric subjectivity in Shakespeare's sonnet sequence is altogether foreign to the kind of poetic person we find in first-person poetry up through the Renaissance, but also to explain why this novel Shakespearean subjectivity—not only as it appears in Shakespeare's first-person sonnets but also as it manifests itself in Shakespeare's zero-person plays—subsequently becomes (since Shakespeare, which is to say since the decisive conclusion of an epideictic poetics, which is to say since the end of a poetic tradition in which all poetry is a poetry of praise) the dominant and canonical version in our literary tradition of literary subjectivity per se.

For obvious reasons an essay is not the place to develop the details of such an account, an account that necessarily calls for all the particularity and specificity of extended practical and historical literary criticism.[14] However, for the sake of an outline of such an account, one point seems especially important: namely, that this novel Shakespearean subjectivity, for all its difference from that which it succeeds, is nevertheless constrained by the traditional lyric literariness to which it stands as epitaph. In this sense, we might say that "poor Petrarch's long deceased woes" exert a posthumous power, prescribing in advance the details of their own forswearing. This point, too, can only be developed here in a schematic and perfunctory fashion. But it is possible, by looking at the way the dark lady's poet revises the visionary logic and psychologic of the young man's poet's eye and heart, to get some sense of the way Shakespeare's paradoxical invention of a heterogeneous and heterosexual poetics of paradoxical praise amounts to an orthodox mutation of a conventionally homogeneous and homosexual poetics of orthodox idealization:

> Thine eyes I love, and they as pitying me,
> Knowing my heart torment me with disdain,
> Have put on black, and loving mourners be,
> Looking with pretty ruth upon my pain.
> And truly not the morning sun of heaven
> Better becomes the grey cheeks of th' east,
> Nor that full star that ushers in the even
> Doth half that glory to the sober west,
> As those two mourning eyes become thy face.
> O, let it then as well beseem thy heart
> To mourn for me, since mourning doth thee grace,
> And suit thy pity like in every part.
> Then will I swear beauty herself is black,
> And all they foul that thy complexion lack.

As in sonnets 46 and 47, the general conceit of sonnet 123, with its frustrated lover addressing his pitiless, disdaining beloved, is a Petrarchan commonplace, going back beyond Petrarch to the *rime petrose* of Arnault Daniel. Equally common is the intricate development of the imagery of sympathetically erotic vision. In this sense we deal here with the same poetics Shakespeare presupposes in the young man sonnets, where, for example, he can speak familiarly of "that sun, thine eye" (49) precisely because a long-standing tradition of metaphysical and sexual allegory authorizes an iconographic equating of the two. On the other hand, but in an equally insistent way, sonnet 132 further plays upon this convention and these traditional light-sight metaphors when, as a result of comparing the beloved's eyes to the sun, it turns out not that her eyes are lamps, but that the sun to which they are compared is therefore black. This too is, in part, conventional (e.g., Stella's eyes are black), but what concerns us is the stressed contrast to what has come before. In the young man sonnets the morning is "sacred," "new-appearing" (7), "golden" and "green" (33). Here, instead, "the morning sun of heaven" is obscuring complement to "the grey cheeks of the east," shining in the morning like the evening star at night, because it is a brightness in an encroaching darkness of which it is itself the cause and sign. Where in the sonnets addressed to the young man the sun is a "gracious light" (7) to the morning, here, instead, the morning is a "mourning" whose inversion is a darkening "grace"; "Since mourning doth thee grace." This pun on "mo[u]rning," which explains why in the dark lady sonnets "brightness doth not grace the day," is the kind of motivated homophone that Shakespeare is often either faulted or appreciated for, either the sort for which, in Johnson's phrase, he threw away the world, or the sort with which he generates the resonant ambiguities that critics like to list. The point that is emphasized by the sonnet, however, is that the pun, which must be noticed as such for it to work its poetic effect, does in little what the poem does rhetorically as a whole: repeating itself in itself so as to undo itself with its own echo, discovering and producing its own loss at the very moment of calling to our attention the way language, theme, and image displace themselves by folding over upon themselves in paradox. So too, this is precisely the mourning paradox of what is epideictically orthodox for which the poem will sadly say that it was written: "Then will I swear beauty herself is black, / And all they foul that thy complexion lack."

In obvious ways, therefore, all this—morning *and* melancholia—results in something that is much more complex than a simple negation of Petrarchan themes and images, and for this reason the poem possesses a tonality unlike even the most self-consciously witty Petrarchan lovers' complaint. The system of logical oppositions and conventional antitheses into which we might be tempted to organize the sonnet's courtly courtship argument falls to pieces as soon as the sonnet brings antithesis into play. Just as the lady's eyes by turning black express a pity occasioned by her heart's disdain, so too does the poet here thematize the fact that he here expresses his heart's desire with a language of disdain. In the same way that the stain of the lady's eyes is both image of and answer to the disdain of her heart, so too does the poet here amplify the lady's beauty by fouling the conventional images of fairness. The relationship between the lady's eye and the lady's heart, or of the poet to the lady, is a matter, therefore, neither of similarity and contrast nor of pity and disdain, and, for this reason, there is no way either poet or lady might "suit thy pity like in every part." Pity is a figure of disdain just as morning is a version of the night, each of them the homeopathic mirror of the heteropathy of the other. As a result, with likeness emerging as the instance, rather than the antithesis, of difference, with pity the *complement* to disdain, the sonnet forces its reader to deal with oddly asymmetrical oppositions whereby each polarized side or half of every opposition that the sonnet adduces already includes, and therefore changes by encapsulating, the larger dichotomy of which it is a part. With regard to the lady, this means that she cannot treat the poet either with pity or with disdain, or even with an oxymoronic combination of the two. For her "charm" consists precisely of the way these two apparently antithetical modalities, empathy and antipathy, each turn out to be, within their singular propriety, the contrary double not only of its other but also of itself, the two together thus composing a double doubling whose reduplicating logic forecloses the possibility of ever isolating either modality in itself. With regard to the poet, this means that he cannot speak of his lady with a simple rhetoric of similarity and contrast, for his language undercuts the logic of likeness and difference even as it advances complementary contrarieties.[15]

The difference between this and what happens when sonnets 46 and 47 develop their eye-heart topos is pointed enough, a difference now that *makes* a difference. Where the two young man sonnets see both eye and heart as each the figure and occasion of the other, sonnet 132 instead both literally and figuratively describes a desire at odds with itself because at odds with what it sees. Where the two young man sonnets bring out the syncretic identity built into their differences, the dark lady sonnet instead brings out the diacritical difference built into its identities. Where the two young man sonnets develop an ideal logic of sympathetic opposition, the dark lady sonnet gives us instead what is the paradoxical opposite, if we can call it that, to such a logic of sympathetic opposition. In terms of form, of theme, of tone, these are all significant differences. But it is important to realize that these differences derive not only their force but also their specific qualities, their content as well as their contours, from the structurally systematic way in which sonnet 132 understands its language paradoxically to redouble, with a difference, the orthodox dual unities with which it begins—i.e., from the way in which the double doubling of sonnet 132 tropes, re-turns, re-verses, the unifying tropes of an idealizing, homogeneous poetics, this way inverting the reciprocal way that eye and heart in sonnets 46 and 47 "each cloth good turns now unto the other" (47). "Mourning" its "morning," the sonnet puts into words, literally puts *into* words, the duplicity of its speech, and this duplicity, thus bespoken, in turn divides the original bright desire and golden poetics presupposed by the young man sonnets. By means of this remarked duplication, the sonnet undoes both erotic and rhetorical identification, and thereby, *through* its language, justifies the chiasmic inversion of the poet's eye and heart. In sonnet 132 the content of "mourning" *is* the loss of "morning," and this hole built into a double language, this difference sounded in a sameness, is what functions both to blind the poet's eye and to break the poet's heart. Developed in this way, as the forswearing double of a visual ideal, as "morning" *manqué*, language acquires in the sonnet, and at the same time also proclaims, its novel motives and motifs, precisely those that the poet defines, logically and psychologically, as "Then will I swear beauty herself is black."

It is language, therefore, conceived and conceited as something linguistic, as something of the *tongue*, as both like and unlike the vision to which it is opposed and on which it is superimposed, that in the dark lady sonnets describes and names the redoubling of unity that leads to division, the mimic likeness of a likeness that leads to difference, the representation of presentation that spells the end of presence. Writing at or as the conclusion of a tradition of poetic idealism and idealization, when poetic imitation no longer functions as *Ideas Mirrour*, when poetic metaphor no longer "see(s) the same," Shakespeare in his sonnets draws the formal and thematic consequences that follow from the death of visual admiration. In the poetics of the sequence as a whole, at the level of its rhetorical figures, the dark lady sonnets explicitly break the amatory metaphorics of "Two distincts, division none" (*The Phoenix and the Turtle*) by substituting for such a unitary duality a tropic system of triangular, chiasmic duplicity: "A torment thrice threefold thus to be crossed" (133). In the narrative the sequence tells, this figural double duplication, which brings out the difference built into binary identities, is thematically embodied in the ambiguously duplicitous dark lady—darker and older, almost by structural necessity, than the fair young man—and then projected into the double cuckoldry story itself, where the poet is betrayed by both his objects of desire when they couple or cross-couple with each other, and when the sequence as a whole moves from the unity of *folie à deux* to the duality of *ménage à trois*. In terms of the sonnets' own literary self-consciousness, there is an analogous contrast, again thematic, between the traditional poetry of erotic idealization addressed to the young man and the parodic undoing of that tradition by means of the radically *para-*, not *anti-*, Petrarchanism addressed to the dark lady, which repeats, but with a difference, the "sameness" of traditional idealizing themes. Finally, because the self-conscious tradition of the poetry of praise assumes that the language of poetic desire is itself identical to the object of poetic desire—which is why an orthodox poetry of love characteristically writes itself out as a love of poetry—Shakespeare's paradoxical version of the poetry of praise brings out even the difference built into the identity of literary and sexual admiration, which is how the dark lady sonnets describe a poetic desire whose Eros and Logos are themselves thematically out of joint.

It would be possible, of course, to find literary precedents for what seems novel in Shakespeare's sonnets. The kind of chiasmic (not oxymoronic) figurality that governs so many of Shakespeare's sonnets, the darksome light of the young man sonnets and their conflicted response to idealism, the general sense of literary belatedness that runs through the sequence as a whole—such features are already present in Dante, and they are yet more insistently and urgently emphatic in Petrarch, where the intractably heterogeneous relation of poetic signifier to poetic signified defines, to some extent, the central worry of the "scattered" songs to Laura. (In *The Secretum*, Petrarch's private and unpublished imaginary dialogue with Saint Augustine, Augustine accuses Petrarch of having fallen in love with Laura only on account of her name.) So too, we could readily trace the way the Renaissance sonnet grows increasingly arch in its presentation of the Cratylitic correspondence of signifier to signified. This archness develops in so smooth and continuous a way as to suggest an unbroken line linking Beatrice, through Laura, through Stella (and through others) to, finally, what Shakespeare in several voluptuary sonnets calls his "Will."[16] So too, we could correlate the development of such literary self-consciousness with the increasingly intentional artificiality of the later "golden" sonnet, the way such sonnets strive, quite frankly, to present the conventionally reflexive reflections of orthodox epideixis as something *merely* literary, for prime example, the over-written way that Astrophil looks deep into his heart and in this way underwrites his introspective astrophilia. Even more obviously, we could find in the Renaissance vogue for the mock encomium, in the widespread enthusiasm for comically paradoxical praises of that which is low, not only the hyper-rhetorical temperament that Shakespeare's sonnets presuppose, but, also, a regularly reiterated interest in the specific themes that Shakespeare develops in the sonnets to the dark lady—e.g., the paradoxical praise of blindness, darkness, nymphomania, cuckoldry, false language, and so forth.[17]

The existence of such precedents is evidence of the fact that what Shakespeare "invents" in his sonnets is what he "comes upon" in a literary tradition and a literary history of which he is well aware and to which his sonnets are, again in a conventional way, intended as response. Yet it is important to recognize the genuine novelty that Shakespeare introduces into this literary tradition when he puts into words, as I have put it, his suspicions—truly, *sub-spicere*—of the visual and visionary poetics of idealism. For when Shakespeare thus outspokenly articulates, thematically as well as formally, the "insufficiency" that "make[s] me give the lie to my true sight" (150), when he makes his language literally as well as figuratively "mourn" the "morning," he manages, on the one hand, to render explicit reservations that in the orthodox Renaissance sonnet are serious but always implicit, just as, on the other, he manages to take seriously what in the tradition of the paradoxical mock encomium is explicit but always merely comic. He can do so because the thematic innovation has more than thematic consequence. By "expressing" the "difference" that the idealizing and homogeneous Renaissance sonnet necessarily "leaves out," the peculiar matter of Shakespearean paradox finds itself instantiated, exampled, by the corresponding paradox of Shakespearean poetic manner. Language thus speaks for its own gainsaying. The result is a new kind of Cratylism, a second degree of Cratylism, that, like the Liar's Paradox Shakespeare often flirts with in his sonnets—"Those lines that I before have writ do lie" (115), "When my love swears that she is made of truth" (138)—is proof of its own paradoxicality. In this gainsaying way—a speech acquired on condition that it speak against itself—Shakespeare accomplishes a limit case of the correspondence of signifier to signified. As the self-belying likeness of a difference, language becomes in Shakespeare's sonnets the true icon of an idol. Shakespeare's poetics of the word in this way acquires the "power" of its "insufficiency" (150), for every word the poet speaks effectively presents, is demonstration of, the loss of his ideal.[18]

With regard to Shakespearean subjectivity, two points follow from this, one practical, the other theoretical. First of all, the poet who speaks such a "forswearing" speech is no longer the speaking "eye" of the traditional sonnet. As a result, the poetic persona of Shakespeare's sonnets can no longer elaborate his subjectivity in accord with the ideal model of a self composed of the specular identification of poetic ego and poetic ego-ideal, of "I" and "you," or of eye and eyed. Instead, identifying himself with the heterogeneous look of the lady, or with the duplicity of her speech, the poet identifies himself with difference, with that which resists or breaks identification. The result is that the poet's identity is defined, by chiasmic triangulation, as the disruption or fracture of identity: "Me from myself thy cruel eye hath taken, / And my next self thou harder hast engrossed" (133). In terms of poetic erotics, we can say that this is why the poet of Shakespeare's sonnet sequence possesses a doubly divided desire—"Two loves I have of comfort and despair" (144)—and why the one is purchased dialectically, measure for measure, at the expense of the other, as "Th' expense of spirit in a waste of shame" (129). Speaking more generally, we can say that such a poetic self identifies himself with an inescapable, because constitutive, "insufficiency." Built up on or out of the loss of itself, its identity defined as its difference from itself, a hole opens up within the whole of poetic first-person self-presence. This "hole" within the "whole" (and also without, see sonnet 134: "He pays the whole, and yet am I not free") inserts into the poet a space of personal interiority, a palpable syncope, that justifies and warrants poetic introspection. This accounts for the strong personal affect of Shakespeare's lyric persona, what is called its "depth." By joining the rhetorical form of triangular chiasmus to the thematic heartbreak of a "perjur'd eye" (a phrase that, for this reason, we can think of as a "Shakespeareme," i.e., the smallest minimal unit of Shakespearean self), Shakespeare's sonnets give off the subjectivity effect called for by a post-idealist literariness. This is also how Shakespeare produces subjectivity in his plays, where, to take a simple example, the cross-coupling of pairs of lovers, their "star-cross'd" fate regularly explained in terms of a thematic disjunction between vision and language, characteristically generates what are taken to be Shakespeare's deeply realized, psychologistically authentic, dramatic personae. Moreover, to the extent that the characterologies of these characters continue to retain their specifically characterological or subjective appeal, to this extent we have evidence of the abiding, though posthumous, power of the idealism and the idealization to which the logic of their unhappy psychologies attest—an ideality all the more powerful for being constituted retrospectively, as a "remembrance of things past," as "th' expense of many a vanish'd sight," as a "fore-bemoaned moan," "Which I new pay as if not paid before" (30).

This leads, however, to a concluding theoretical observation. It has no doubt already been noticed that this reading of Shakespeare's sonnets, perfunctory as it is, has many affinities with various literary theories that have been labeled, somewhat simplistically, Structuralist and Post-Structuralist. My concern with the way the "languageness" of language is stressed by Shakespeare's sonnets is related to accounts of literariness that have been developed by such formalists as Roman Jakobson, Gérard Genette, Michael Riffaterre. My concern with cross-coupling chiasmus is related in very obvious ways to A.J. Greimas's "semantic square," to Paul De Man's discussions of figural chiasmus, and also to Jacques Lacan's "Schema L," which Lacan draws as a quaternary "Z." So too, my discussion of the way in which an idealist homogeneity is disrupted by a supplementary heterogeneity is in many ways like, and is certainly indebted to, Jacques Derrida's various essays in deconstructive phenomenology. Most obviously and most importantly, my account of a subjectivity precipitated by the paradoxical relationship of language to vision, my understanding of a language of desire and a desire of language, is very much influenced by Lacan's psychoanalytic account of what he calls the capture of the Imaginary by what he calls the Symbolic.

It is possible to recognize, therefore, a considerable overlap between certain contemporary literary, and not only literary, theorizations and both the formal and thematic peculiarities of Shakespeare's "perjur'd eye." This suggests either that Shakespeare was very theoretically acute or, instead, that contemporary theory is itself very Shakespearean. However, before choosing between either of these alternatives, we should recall the fact that contemporary literary theory, as it has thought itself out, has enacted a development very similar not only to the development we can discern in Shakespeare's sonnets as they move from the sonnets addressed to the young man to those addressed to the dark lady, but similar also to the larger literary development within which we can locate the historical significance of Shakespeare's sonnet sequence as a whole. Responding to Husserl's Dantesque phenomenology of *Ideas*, to Husserl's concern with eidetic reduction and a transcendental Ego, Sartre developed a psychology of imagination whose logic and metaphors very much resemble the paranoiac visionary thematics of a good many of Shakespeare's sonnets to the young man. The subjective optics of the Sartrian "gaze" and its melodrama of mutually persecutory master–slave relations subsequently receives in the thought of Merleau-Ponty, especially in late works such as *Le Visible et l'Invisible*, an ironically comic revision whose chiasmic marriage of subject and object is reminiscent of more than a few of Shakespeare's most genuinely poignant sonneteering conceits; it was Merleau-Ponty, after all, who introduced "chiasmus" into contemporary critical discourse, as a way to explain the way Cézanne paints the trees watching Cézanne.[19] Lacan, Merleau-Ponty's friend, broke with Merleau-Ponty on just this point, seeing in the fully lived "flesh" and "visibility" of Merleau-Ponty's chiasmus a psychological and a phenomenological sentimentality. Instead, Lacan developed an account of the way subjectivity is born in the place where chiasmus breaks. Lacan's anamorphic "gaze," very different from "*le regard*" of Sartre or of Merleau-Ponty, along with Lacan's account of the way language potentiates and inherits this rupture of the imaginary, rather perfectly repeats the formal as well as the thematic logic of Shakespeare's "perjur'd eye."[20] So too, Derrida's attempt to rupture this rupture, Derrida's putatively post-subjective account of a supplemental *différance*, seems, from the point of view of Shakespeare's sonnets, nothing but another "increase" that "From fairest creatures we desire" (1), assuming we recognize the wrinkle, literally the "crease," that Shakespeare introduces into the perennial poetics of copious "increase."

This is significant because it raises the possibility that current thought works to transfer into a theoretical register a constellated set of literary themes, metaphors, motifs, that Shakespeare introduces into literature, in response to specific literary exigencies, at and as the beginning of the end of the Humanist Renaissance. If so, it is possible that current theorizations are important not because they offer a method or even a point of view with which to look back at Shakespeare, but, instead, because they participate in the very same literary history within which Shakespeare writes his sonnets, emerging now as a symptomatic and epiphenomenal consequence of the way, at the beginning of the modernist epoch, Shakespeare rethinks the literature he succeeds. Putting the question more strongly, we can ask whether, repeating Shakespeare's repetition, it is possible for contemporary theory to do so with a difference.

These are not questions I mean fully either to answer or even to address in this essay. But I would like at least to raise them, for it seems important that such a sense of repetition is itself a distinctive mark of Renaissance sensibility, especially of a good many literary minds for whom the project of their present is to give rebirth to the past. The very great Humanist Leone Ebreo—precursor to Spinoza, and in this way an important influence on Freud—in his dialogue *D'amore e desiderio* distinguishes—the topic is an old one—between love and desire on the grounds that love is an emotion one feels for that which one possesses, whereas desire is the emotion one feels for that which one does not possess.[21] Returning to the subject sometime later, in a dialogue called *De l'origine d'amore*, Ebreo emends his original distinction, reformulating it on the grounds that even that which one possesses, because it is possessed in transient time, carries with it, even at the moment of possession, a sense of loss.[22] This possession of loss, an emotion which is half love and half desire—what we might call a desire for love, but what we cannot call a love of desire—grows increasingly strong when the later and post-Humanist Renaissance returns to rethink a good many other topics relating to the origin of love. In time, in Shakespeare's sonnets, the rebirth of the Renaissance turns into the death of remorse, for in Shakespeare's sonnets "desire is death" (147) *because* "now is black beauty's successive heir" (127).[23]

It is because this is so central a theme in them, because they fully realize their *re-*, that Shakespeare's sonnets possess more than merely local interest. In Shakespeare's sonnets we hear how a literature of repetition, rather than a literature *de l'origine*, explains its desire to itself. With regard to the matter of poetic person, this is important because it allows us to understand how Shakespeare's response to secondariness leads him to introduce into literature a subjectivity altogether novel in the history of the lyric, or, as Shakespeare puts it, "Since mind at first in character was done" (59). For this very reason, however, the constitution of Shakespearean poetic self necessarily recalls the imperatives of a literariness larger even than the Shakespearean:

> If there be nothing new, but that which is
> Hath been before, how are our brains beguil'd
> Which laboring for invention bear amiss
> The second burthen of a former child! (59)

"The second burthen of a former child" very well characterizes the subjectivity fathered in the late Renaissance by the burden of a belated literariness. There is good reason to compare the rebirth of this aborted subject that "invention bear(s) amiss" with "Death's second self, that seals up all in rest" (73). However, to the extent that it is not only Shakespeare who looks, as sonnet 59 puts it, "with a backward look," to see "Your image in some antique book," the revolutionary question raised by such Shakespearean retrospection will continue to retain the ongoing urgency of a perennial and, it seems fair to say, since even Shakespeare now is "nothing new," an increasingly important literary commonplace:

> That I might see what the old world could say
> To this composed wonder of your frame,
> Whether we are mended, or whe'er better they,
> Or whether revolution be the same.
> O, sure I am the wits of former days
> To subjects worse have given admiring praise. (59)

NOTES

1. All Shakespeare references are to *The Riverside Shakespeare*, ed. G. B. Evans, et al. (Boston, 1974). Sonnet numbers are indicated within parentheses.

2. See Lisle C. John, *The Elizabethan Sonnet Sequences: Studies in Conventional Conceits* (New York, 1938), pp. 93–95; J. H. Hanford, "The Debate of Eye and Heart," *Modern Language Notes*, 26:6 (1911), 161–65.

3. Petrarch, 174; compare to 86 and 87; references are to *Petrarch's Lyric Poems: The Rime Sparse and other Lyrics*, ed. and trans. R. M. Durling (Cambridge, Mass., 1976). *Le Roman de la Rose*, ed. F. Lecoy (Paris, 1914), pp. 1684–87; see notes for background of the motif.

4. Dante, *Paradiso*, Canto 33, lines 91–131; references are to *Dante's Paradiso*, ed. and trans. John D. Sinclair (New York, 1977).

5. "Idea" is a sonneteering commonplace: J. W. Hebel, in his edition of *The Works of Michael Drayton* (Oxford, 1961) cites parallels in de Pontoux's *L'Idée*, in du Bellay, Desportes, Daniel; see vol. 5, p. 13. The Quarto prints "steeld"; Stephen Booth summarizes the range of connotations in *Shakespeare's Sonnets* (New Haven, 1977), pp. 172–73. The conflicting ensemble of motifs attaching to "steeld"—visual, metallic, inscriptive, all those also referring to "stolen" and to "styled"—themselves stage the tensions that sonnet 24 develops out of its general visual conceit, especially the sonnet's play on "perspective."

6. Simonides' saying is already a cliché for Plutarch, *De aud. poet.* 3. In *Elizabethan Critical Essays* (London, 1937), vol. 1, pp. 386–87, G. G. Smith cites the many Renaissance parallels. Aristotle, *Poetics* 1459a 5–8: "But the greatest thing by far is to be a master of metaphor. It is the one thing that cannot be learnt from others; and it is also a sign of genius, since a good metaphor implies an intuitive perception of the similarity in dissimilars (*to gar eu metapherein to to homoion theôrein estin*)," *Aristotle on the Art of Poetry*, ed. and trans. I. Bywater (Oxford, 1909), p. 71.

7. "'We beg you to tell us wherein this bliss of yours (*tua beatitudine*) now lies.' And I answered her by saying: 'In those words that praise my lady (In quelle parole che lodano la donna mia)' . . . Therefore I resolved that from now on I would choose material for my poems that should be in praise of this most gracious one." *La Vita nuova* (XVIII), F. Chapelli, ed., *Opere di Dante Alighiere* (Milan, 1967); M. Musa, trans., *La Vita Nuova of Dante Alighieri* (Bloomington, Ind., 1965). Acting on this resolve, Dante composes the first canzone of *La Vita Nuova*, "Donne ch'avete inteletto d'amore*," which later, in *Purg.* 24, 49–63, in conversation with Buonagiunta, will be remembered as marking the beginning of "*le nove rime*" of the "*dolce stil nuovo*." For Petrarch's puns on "Laura," see, for example, *Rime Sparse*, 5, 6, 7, 194, 196, 246, 327, 356.

8. Because the sonnet begins as a poetry of erotic praise, and because praise is also a central thematic issue in the orthodox Renaissance sonnet, the genre is a particularly focused instance of the poetry of praise. This is a significant fact because from antiquity up through the Renaissance, praise or, more generally, the epideictic (praise or blame), is taken to be the master literary genre of literature as such, the single genre under which all other, more particular, literary genres are properly subsumed. This is the basis for the hierarchy of literary genres or "kinds" in Renaissance literary theory, a typology that goes back to Aristotle, who derived all poetry from primal, epideictic imitation: praise of the high and blame of the low. We can identify the idealist assumptions at stake here by recalling the fact that the only poetry Socrates allows into the republic is "praise of gods and virtuous men."

The epideictic bias of traditional poetics—e.g., reading the *Aeneid* as a praise of Aeneas—is usually understood to reflect a concern on the part of the theoreticians with the didactic function of the poetical and the rhetorical; this is to understand the poetical or rhetorical in terms of effective moral persuasion. There is a more formal reason, however, with which traditional poetic theory accounts for the generic importance of the epideictic. Epi-deictic or de-monstrative rhetoric is called such because it is a rhetoric of "show" and "showing forth." The Greek is *epideiknunai*, "to show," "display"; in the middle voice, "to show off," "to display for oneself." The Indo-European root is **deik*, with variant **deig*, "to show," which gives Greek *dikê*, "justice," and the verb *deiknunai*, "bring to light," "show forth," "represent," "portray," "point out," "show," leading to English "deictic," "paradigmatic," "apodeictic," etc. So too, *deiknunai* is also closely related to *deikeilon*, "representation," "exhibition," "reflection," "image," "phantom," "sculpted figure."

Aristotle brings out the significance of this semantic field, the Heideggerean resonance of which is obvious enough, when he distinguishes epideictic rhetoric from the two other kinds, forensic and deliberative, on the grounds that in the former the audience serves as "observer" (*theôron*), whereas in the latter two the audience serves as "Judge" (*kritên*), *Rhetoric*, 1358b2. Aristotle's point, brought out by his distinguishing between a rhetoric addressed to vision and a rhetoric addressed to judgment, is that epideictic or demonstrative oratory, as distinct from the transparent language of the law courts or the assembly, is a rhetoric both of display and self-display, a spectacular speech that we "observe" precisely because its manner calls attention to itself, a pointing "there" that points egocentrically to "here," an objective "showing" that amounts to a subjective "showing-off." This explains why the epideictic is an extraordinary, not an ordinary, language. The point could be put in more contemporary terms by recalling the way Jakobson defines the specifically literary function as that message which stresses itself as merely message. The Renaissance sonnet characteristically amplifies this formal circularity of the language of praise, its recursive reflexivity, through various psychologistic conceits all designed to demonstrate the correlation of admiring subject with admired object. The point to realize is that when Shakespeare gives over the poetry of praise, when he distances himself from a visionary poetics, he not only gives over the themes and imagery of a perennial poetics, but also gives over the semiosis of this profoundly orthodox (and structuralist) literariness.

For the visual imagery employed by Renaissance poetic theory, especially theory of epideixis, see O. B. Hardison Jr., *The Enduring Monument: A Study of the Idea of Praise in Renaissance Literary Theory and Practice* (Westport, Conn., 1962), pp. 51–67. For general background see R. Tuve, *Elizabethan and Metaphysical Imagery* (Chicago, 1947), chaps. 2, 3; R. W. Lee, *"Ut Pictura Poesis*: The Humanistic Theory of Painting," *Art Bulletin* 22 (1940), 197–269; E. H. Gombrich, *"Icones Symbolicae*: The Visual Image in Neo-Platonic Thought," *Journal of the Warburg and Courtauld Institutes* 11 (1948); R. J. Clements, *"Picta Poesis"*: *Literary and Humanistic Theory in Renaissance Emblem Books* (Rome, 1960).

9. Murray Krieger, "Poetic Presence and Illusion: Renaissance Theory and the Duplicity of Metaphor," *Critical Inquiry* 5:4 (1979), 619.

10. *Astrophil and Stella*, No. 15.

11. *Troilus and Cressida*, V.2.144.

12. Dante puts homosexuals and usurers in the same circle of hell, on the grounds that they couple, for sterile profit, kind with kind. For a very plausible explanation of why Brunetto Latini is also included here, see Eugene Vance, "Désir, rhétorique et texte," *Poétique* 42 (April, 1980), 137–55.

13. *Troilus and Cressida*, IV.5.55–57. With regard to the way Shakespeare represents Petrarchism in the plays, compare this with Longaville's sonnet in *Love's Labor's Lost*: "Did not the heavenly rhetoric of thine eye, / 'Gainst whom the world cannot hold argument, / Persuade my heart to this false perjury" (IV.3.58–60), or with Romeo's "She speaks, yet she says nothing; what of that? / Her eye discourses, I will answer it," *Romeo and Juliet*, II.2.12–13.

14. I develop such an account in *Shakespeare's Perjured Eye: The Invention of Poetic Subjectivity in Shakespeare's Sonnets* (forthcoming, University of California Press); this contains a fuller account of visual metaphors in traditional poetics, especially the way such metaphors are employed in the literature of orthodox and paradoxical praise.

15. From Aristotle on, rhetoricians regularly identify comparison as the distinctive, characteristic trope of praise, this because comparison allows a speaker to amplify his referent. It is possible to double the two terms of a comparison so that the four terms thus produced stand to each other in a chiasmic relation. This is what happens to eye and heart in sonnet 132. This kind of chiasmic trope

is especially characteristic of paradoxical, comic praises of that which is low, this because such paradoxical praises present themselves as mimic repetitions of orthodox praise. The technical term for this kind of reduplicating trope—tropes that break, by redoubling, the dual unities of metaphors that "see the same"—is *syneciosis*. Puttenham calls this the "cross-coupler," and associates it with the erotic, unkind mixture of kinds: "Ye have another figure which me thinkes may well be called (not much swerving from his originall in sence) the *Crosse-couple*, because it takes me two contrary words, and tieth them as it were in a paire of couples, and so makes them agree like good fellowes, as I saw once in Fraunce a wolfe coupled with a mastiffe, and a foxe with a hounde," in George Puttenham, *The Arte of Englishe Poesie* (1589), facsimile reproduction (Kent, Ohio, 1970), p. 216.

16. With their puns on "Will" the dark lady sonnets render explicit a good deal of what is left implicit in the young man sonnets. To begin with, the dark lady sonnets play on the fact that in Elizabethan slang "Will" refers to both the male and female genitals: "Wilt thou, whose will is large and spacious, / Not once vouchsafe to hide my will in thine?" (135). This picks up and extends, by doubling, several *doubles entendres* that run through the sonnets addressed to the young man. In the young man sonnets, for example, Shakespeare develops, in various ways, not only sexual, the image of the "pricked prick"—"But since she prick'd these out for women's pleasure, / Mine be thy love, and thy love's use their treasure" (20)—and uses this to characterize a desire which stands somewhere between the homosexual and the heterosexual. It is the same image, really, as "stell'd" in sonnet 24, or the time-marking "dial hand" of sonnet 104, but Shakespeare clearly enjoys the erotic connotations of the "pricked prick"—consider, for example, the fate of Adonis: "And nousling in his flank, the loving swine / Sheath'd unaware the tusk in his soft groin" (*Venus and Adonis*, lines 1115–1116), or the bawdy puns of *Love's Labor's Lost*, e.g., "Let the mark have a prick in't" (IV.1.132), "The preyful Princess pierc'd and prick'd a pretty pleasing pricket" (IV.2.56), or, more elaborately, the way Othello takes as well as "took . . . by the throat the circumcised dog / And smote him—thus" (V2.355–356). In the dark lady sonnets, however, by virtue of the pun on "Will," the poet becomes not only a "pricked prick," but also, again exploiting Elizabethan slang, the "cut cunt" (compare Malvolio in *Twelfth Night*: "These be her very c's, her u's, and her t's, and thus makes she her great P's" (11.5.86–88). This double doubling, whereby "Will" performs the copulation that the poet speaks about, enables Shakespeare explicitly to develop some of the thematic consequences, not only erotic, that the subject of a verbal name *must* suffer. As a "Will," the poet becomes the chiasmic copula between male and female, presence and absence, inside and outside, waxing and waning, showing and hiding, whole and hole, one and none:

> Among a number one is reckon'd none:
> Then in the number let me pass untold,
> Though in thy store's account I one must be,
> For nothing hold me, so it please thee hold
> That nothing me, a something sweet to thee.
> Make but my name thy love, and love that still,
> And then thou lovest me, for my name is Will.
>   (136)

Quite apart from the various themes and images that are thus put into crosscoupling play, the "Will" sonnets are significant precisely because they mark the first person of the poet with a name, not a deictic, for this identifies the person of the poet through a system of representational, not presentational, reference. This is quite different from the kind of immediate reference achieved by deictic, I–you, indication, for, as has often been pointed out (e.g., Bertrand Russell on egocentric particulars, Jakobson on shifters, and E. Benveniste on pronouns and relationships of person in the verb), such egocentric reference requires the presence of the speaker to his speech. In contrast, a name retains a stable referent regardless of who speaks it. In ways which I discuss in *Shakespeare's Perjured Eye*, it can be shown, first, that deixis is the mode of first-person speaking required by an epideictic poetics, second, that a post-epideictic poetry, such as Shakespeare experiments with in the dark lady sonnets, acquires its subjective effects from the contest it stages between self-displaying visual deictics and self-belying verbal names, as in sonnet 151, where "flesh . . . rising at thy name cloth point out thee / As his triumphant prize," but is also obliged "thy poor drudge to be, / To stand in thy affairs, fall by thy side."

There is more to say about these disappointing pointers, but I would like to note here that it was Oscar Wilde who first insisted in a strong way on the importance for Shakespeare's sonnets of this quarrel between verbal name and visual deictic. It was Wilde who, reading between the lines, and picking up an old conjecture (going back to Thomas Tyrwhitt in 1766), named the poet's catamite "Willie Hughes," doing this in order to draw out the important and pervasive Shakespearean pun on double "hue," "view," "use," and "you"—the same double-U whose present-absent presence distinguishes "whole" from "hole" in sonnet 134. These are the signifiers through which Shakespeare thinks the large narrative of the sonnets. By doubling the dual unity of first and second person, Shakespeare introduces, for the very first time, a third person into epideictic lyric. This formally *absent* third person—a "he" or "she" or "it"—who stands in between, as missing connection, the poet's first and second person, is what the poet becomes to himself when he becomes his name. Compare, for example, the progress of Othello from "all in all sufficient" (IV.1.265) to "That's he that was Othello; here I am" (V.2.283). Recognizing this, it becomes possible to understand why Wilde's *Portrait of W. H.* is the only genuinely literary criticism that Shakespeare's sonnets have ever yet received. Wilde's novella narrates the argument between the metaphorics of visual presentation, the "Portrait," and the signifiers of linguistic representation, "W. H." In the same way, Wilde's *The Importance of Being Earnest* acts out the question of what is *in* a Shakespearean name, thereby putting an end to a theatrical tradition that begins, at least in English drama, with *The Comedy of Errors*. I discuss the relation of Wilde to Shakespeare more fully in *Shakespeare's Perjured Eye*. I also discuss Wilde's concern with the issue of specifically literary naming in "The Significance of Literature: *The Importance of Being Earnest*," October 15 (1980), pp. 79–90.

17. For a discussion of the classical mock encomium, see T. C. Burgess, *Epideictic Literature* (Chicago, 1902), pp. 157–66. For discussions of Renaissance praise paradox, see A. E. Mallock, "The Techniques and Functions of the Renaissance Paradox," *Studies in Philology* 53 (1956), 191–203; E. N. Thompson, "The Seventeenth Century English Essay," *University of Iowa Humanistic Studies*,

3:3 (1926), 94–105; A. S. Pease, "Things Without Honor," *Classical Philology* 21 (1926), 27–42; H. K. Miler, "The Paradoxical Encomium with Special Reference to its Vogue in England: 1600–1800," *Modern Philology* 53:3 (1956), 145–78; A. H. Stockton, "The Paradoxical Encomium in Elizabethan Drama" *University of Texas Studies in English* 28 (1949), 83–104; R. E. Bennet, "Four Paradoxes by Sir William Cornwallis, the Younger," *Harvard Studies and Notes in Philology and Literature* 13 (1931) 219–40; W. G. Rice, "The *Paradossi* of Ortensio Landi," *University of Michigan Essays and Studies in English and Comparative Literature* 8 (1932), 59–74; "Erasmus and the Tradition of Paradox," *Studies in Philology* 53 (1964), 191–203; W. Kaiser, *Praisers of Folly* (Cambridge, Mass., 1963); B. Vickers, "*King Lear* and Renaissance Paradoxes," *Modern Language Notes* 63:2 (1968), 305–14; R. Colie, *Paradoxia Epidemica: The Renaissance Tradition of Praise Paradox* (Princeton, N.J., 1966).

18. At stake here is the difference between a rhetorical paradox and a merely logical paradox, for these are not the same, though in the Renaissance they are, of course, very much related. In contemporary philosophical terminology, this is something like the distinction between a real logical paradox (which would carry, if such a thing exists, some of the weight of the rhetorical paradox) and a merely semantic paradox (e.g., The Liar's Paradox).

19. See especially the discussion of *entrelacs* in *Le Visible et l'Invisible* (Paris, 1964), chap. 4.

20. I refer here not only to Lacan's explicit formulations, but also to the development of Lacan's thought, from the early emphasis on visual themes, as in the essay on the "mirror-stage" and accompanying discussions of aggressivity, to the later emphasis on language, anamorphosis, and accompanying discussions of (male) desire, to, finally, as a third term added to the opposition of the Imaginary and the Symbolic, Lacan's emphasis on the "Real," the limits of representation, and accompanying discussions of (female) *jouissance*. Lacan's sense of the Renaissance is colored, however, by a very Catholic and Counter-reformational, a very French, conception of the Baroque: "Le baroque, c'est la régulation de l'âme par la scopie corporelle," *Encore* (Paris, 1975), p. 105, which is why Lacan's direct comments on Shakespeare are often disappointing.

21. Leone Ebreo, *Dialoghi d'amore*, ed. Santino Caramella (Bari, 1929), p. 5, cited by J. C. Nelson, *Renaissance Theory of Love* (New York, 1958), p. 86. Ebreo's distinction remains a strong challenge to subsequent writers on the subject. Consider, for example, "Love, universally taken, is defined to be a desire, as a word of more ample signification; and though Leon Hebraeus, the most copious writer of this subject, in his third dialogue makes no difference, yet in his first he distinguisheth them again, and defines love by desire." Robert Burton, *The Anatomy of Melancholy*, ed. A. Shilleto (London, 1903), Part III, sect. 1, mem. 1, subs. 2; vol. 111, p. 10.

22, Ebreo, *Dialoghi*, p. 207, cited by Nelson, pp. 86–87.

23. That desire is death is of course a commonplace, e.g., Ronsard's "Car l'Amour et la Mort n'est qu'une mesme chose," *Sonnets Pour Hélène*, 11:77, *Oeuvres complètes de Ronsard*, ed. G. Cohen (Paris, 1950). What is important is the specifically double way in which Shakespearean revision revives this dead metaphor.

1986—Thomas M. Greene. "Anti-Hermeneutics: The Case of Shakespeare's Sonnet 129," from *The Vulnerable Text: Essays on Renaissance Literature*

Thomas M. Greene was a longtime professor of comparative literature at Yale University. He also served as president of the Renaissance Society of America and received the first Paul Oskar Kristeller Lifetime Achievement Award from that organization. His many books include *The Vulnerable Text: Essays on Renaissance Literature* and *The Light in Troy: Imitation and Discovery in Renaissance Poetry,* which won prizes from the Modern Language Association and the American Comparative Literature Association.

A scholarly contention has recently rearisen over the editing of Shakespeare's *Sonnets* that focuses conveniently a complex of perennial problems, not only affecting the editing of Shakespeare or any other author but also adumbrating vaster questions of historical understanding. In his useful, important, and exhaustive edition with commentary on the *Sonnets,* Stephen Booth takes vigorous issue with a well-known essay by Robert Graves and Laura Riding, "A Study in Original Punctuation and Spelling." This essay, published in its original form over fifty years ago, argues against the modernization of Shakespeare by comparing the original and reedited texts of a single sonnet, 129, "Th'expense of Spirit in a waste of shame." By explicating the allegedly richer, more open, more polysemous quarto version and by showing the reductive flatness imposed by modernization, Graves and Riding call into question what they call the "perversely stupid" habits of most modern editors. Professor Booth, no mean polemicist himself, labels this essay "an exercise in irresponsible editorial restraint" and devotes more than five large pages to disposing of its arguments. His basic position is that "an editor distorts the sonnet more for a modern reader by maintaining the 1609 text than he would if he modernized its spelling and punctuation."[1]

No one can deny the enduring importance of this contention between, on the one hand, two practicing poets writing a long time ago as radical critics beyond the pale of the scholarly guild and, on the other hand, a gifted contemporary member of the guild, not lacking in professional independence and even irreverence, but in this dispute adopting something close to a hard-line conservative position. But in describing Booth as the conservative one may already falsify the issue, since Graves and Riding would argue that they are the true conservatives, preserving Shakespeare's original words and meaning against the tendentious contaminators of the intervening centuries. Perhaps one useful step toward resolving the quarrel would be to ask which side has the better right to be called conservative in the best, most positive sense.

Clearly this inexhaustible question will not be settled simply by an appeal to
sonnet 129, but a glance at the two versions competing for our attention could
be instructive. Booth provides both the quarto text and, facing it throughout, a
compromise modernization that represents what he calls a "mid-point" between
the punctuation and spelling of the original and modern directive adaptations.

Th'expense of Spirit in a waste of shame
Is lust in action, and till action, lust   2
Is periurd, murdrous, blouddy full of blame,
Sauage, extreame, rude, cruell, not to trust,   4
Inioy'd no sooner but dispised straight,
Past reason hunted, and no sooner had   6
Past reason hated as a swallowed bayt,
On purpose layd to make the taker mad.   8
Made in pursut and in possession so,
Had, having, and in quest, to have extreame,   10
A blisse in proofe and proud and very wo,
Before a ioy proposd behind a dreame,   12
    All this the world well knowes yet none knowes well,
    To shun the heaven that leads men to this hell.   14

Th'expense of spirit in a waste of shame
Is lust in action, and till action lust   2
Is perjured, murd'rous, bloody, full of blame,
Savage, extreme, rude, cruel, not to trust,   4
Enjoyed no sooner but despisèd straight,
Past reason hunted, and no sooner had,   6
Past reason hated as a swallowed bait,
On purpose laid to make the taker mad;   8
Mad in pursuit, and in possession so,
Had, having, and in quest to have, extreme,   10
A bliss in proof, and proved, a very woe,
Before, a joy proposed, behind, a dream.   12
    All this the world well knows, yet none knows well
    To shun the heav'n that leads men to this hell.   14

What are the main differences? Booth supplies a comma after "blouddy" in line 3
and another at the end of line 6 where the quarto has nothing; at the end of line
8 he substitutes a semicolon for the quarto's period; together with virtually all
editors he emends the first word of line 9 from "Made" to "Mad," adds a comma
after "pursuit" in line 9, and shifts the third comma in line 10. In lines 11 and 12
the surgery is radical: in 11 two commas are added and "a" is substituted for "and";

in 12 three commas are added and a period at the end replaces the quarto's only comma. Finally in line 13, a comma is shifted from the end to the middle. The spelling is modernized, with apostrophes inserted in "murdrous" and "heaven." If this text does represent a midpoint in editorial tact, we're left to wonder what further changes are possible, but in fact the text from *The Oxford Book of English Verse* quoted by Graves and Riding is still more freely repunctuated.

This is not the occasion to analyze thoroughly the semantic transformations, some subtle and some obtrusive, effected by the modern version. But if one stands back and contemplates the two texts as a set, a few impressions emerge immediately. The revised version is undeniably more accessible. Assuming with Booth that the Jacobean reader found few obstacles to reading the poem and that the modern reader should be assisted to enjoy a similar facility so far as possible, then unquestionably the revised version does extend us that assistance. It smoothes over almost all the superficial perplexities in this poem of anguish and despair, this terrible sonnet. For example, it attaches the third quatrain to the first two, thus allowing all three to form one coherent sentence, rather than attaching the third quatrain to the couplet as the quarto does, a little mysteriously. The new version helps us to understand the first word of line 9, which here simply echoes the last word of the previous line—"mad"; in the quarto version one's eye has to move further back in line 8 to the verb "to make" and then understand "Made" in the next line as an altered form of it. "Mad" clearly assists the reader, as does the substitution of "a" for "and"; the line in its old version *could* mean, as Graves and Riding point out, that lust is both bliss and woe at once, both "in proof" and "provd," during its gratification and afterward. But that meaning has to be worked for. The revised line 12 imposes a reassuring tidiness on the puzzling original, where we have to struggle to see how lust could be a joy which is "proposed," envisioned, behind a dream. Again the original *could* make sense, but not easily. Throughout, the modern version supplies us with the *facilior lectio*, and if that is what it takes for our reading to approach the Jacobeans', then undoubtedly the quarto text can only be regarded as unsuitable. "In 129," writes Booth, "modern punctuation gains 'sheer facility in reading' and denies a modern reader nothing that Shakespeare's contemporaries would have perceived."[2]

Surely for better or worse the modernization does more than that. It really acts as a shield for the modern reader, a shield extended to protect him from the problematic contingencies of the original. It protects him from worrying whether the punctuation in front of him corresponds to Shakespeare's actual intent or only his compositor's—whether in fact it corresponds to any knowledgeable intent rather than an ignorant man's caprice. The altered text does certainly correspond to a knowledgeable intent, its editor's, and in this certainty we take comfort. We're protected as well from the strenuous effort of groping unassisted for those shifting, floating, ambiguous relations of clause to clause, phrase to phrase, that constitute one of the outstanding rhetorical features of the *Sonnets* and which Booth himself stresses. Thus in the altered text we don't have to grope for the elusive, possibly nonexistent connection between the third quatrain and the couplet that would justify their separation by a mere comma after line 12. But should we really have this protection? Do we truly want it? Don't we ultimately want, or shouldn't we want, the actual mysterious artifact history has handed down to us with all its built-in puzzlements and uncertainties? Some of these surely the Jacobean reader wrestled with also. What *did* he do with that "Made" in line 9? Why should we be spared his perplexities if his experience is the norm we're expected to approach?

Most decisively and significantly the altered text shields us from that curious Renaissance sense of grammar that fails to isolate a self-contained sentence from its successor. Take one of the most assertive and distinct and self-enclosed affirmations in the *Sonnets*: "Let me not to the marriage of true mindes / Admit impediments." That affirmation is denied in the quarto the full stop it deserves according to our logic: " . . . Admit impediments, love is not love . . ." Here at least the practice is too common to blame only on the compositor, and even if it were the compositor's alone, we have no reason to believe that it troubled the Jacobean reader. We are forced to recognize that the sense of syntactic closure, the sense of declarative completeness, the very status of the affirmation during the Jacobean period, violate our grammar and our logic. This troubling recognition would also be spared us if we confined our reading to the altered text. Even if it were true that modern punctuation denies us nothing a Jacobean would have *perceived*, it does deny us something crucial about the presuppositions he brought to the printed page: it denies us something about his mind-set. Modernization in this respect is less conservative because it fails to preserve an important element of Shakespeare's semiotic world. It not only conceals the mysteries, the contingencies, the authentic riddles, truly present for us in the original; it conceals those offenses to our logic that historical distance will always impose.

That distance makes itself felt equally in the puzzles posed by individual words. In sonnet 129 the opening phrase immediately presents a kind of hermeneutic hurdle. The expression "expence of Spirit" sustains the fundamental metaphor of the sequence linking economics with emotion and sexuality. The constant concern with thrift and profligacy organizes the *Sonnets*, and there is nothing a priori in this figural pattern that is necessarily inaccessible to a twentieth-century reader. The metaphor begins to lose us only when the economic implications of "expence" are taken literally at the physiological level. The sexual act is really impoverishing only if one holds the medieval and Renaissance belief that it shortens a man's life. If, in place of the restorative, therapeutic release our post-Freudian society perceives, one attributes to sex a literal expenditure of vitality, then the struggle between the sexes takes on a crude economic reality, and we begin to understand the linkage made by the Wyf of

Bath. She ends her tale by praying for "housebondes meeke, yonge, and fressh abedde" while calling down a plague on "olde and angry niggardes of dispence."[3] In sonnets 1–126 of Shakespeare's sequence, the bourgeois poet speaks for the values of husbandry, as befits his class, in order prudently to correct the failures of this art assigned to that social class of "unthrifts" which includes the friend. In sonnet 129 the young man's profligacy is less at issue than, one presumes, the bourgeois speaker's among others. The phrase "th'expence of Spirit" means several things, including the implication that the speaker has been *unclassed* by lust, that he is now guilty of that aristocratic waste he had attempted in so many preceding poems to moderate. In yielding to lust he is yielding to a literally self-destructive extravagance, which heretofore he has followed tradition in charging to his social superiors.[4] This biological as well as sociological undoing of the self, implicit in Shakespeare's word "expence," remains an abstraction for us even if we catch its resonance. We might begin to recapture that reference to personal ontology by taking seriously the lost implications of such words as "dissolute" and "dissipated."

Modernized spelling also helps to conceal the different status of the word itself in a prelexicographical culture. The quarto calls attention to the word "Spirit" by capitalizing it, a stress modern editors tend to drop. The word is not easily defined in any case. Glosses for "Spirit" suggested by Booth and other editors include "physical vigor," "mental energy," "spiritual essence," "life force," "bodily fluid," "penis erectus," and "the subtle vapor supposed to be contained in the heart and needed for generation." This gives seven distinct glosses which the modern reader experiences as a supersaturated plethora of competing meanings. But it is unlikely that the prelexicographical reader felt this kind of division and subdivision; it is more likely that he or she read the word "Spirit" as a multifaceted unity we can only try to imagine. The polyvalent word before the era of dictionaries could not simply be felt as the sum of an indefinite series of parallel definitions; it must have been apprehended as a veined monolith. It was not yet reducible to a vertical list of semidiscrete equivalents. It must have remained somehow a simultaneous whole which nonetheless presented multiple aspects to be perceived as context indicated. Not only the lost meanings of a word but the very process of their fusion within a single signifier eludes us.

One peculiarly elusive word appears at the openings of lines 2 and 3. One of the most deceptive signifiers in the code of any remote text is the copula: deceptive because to the naked eye it looks to be the most unchanging and the most transparent of all parts of speech. But in fact the copula, underlying implicitly or explicitly most metaphorization and predication, is the part of speech most sensitive to historically shifting intuitions of relationship and reality. It is rooted in each culture's, each era's, metaphysical and epistemological assumptions—not necessarily the assumptions spelled out discursively but those silently shared and invoked in poetry as in ordinary speech. Fully to understand the force of a copula in a given text is to understand a good deal of the text and the semiotic universe that nourished it.

Shakespeare's sonnet 129 is largely controlled by those two copulas appearing at the openings of the second and third lines. The second of these is the more important, since so much of what follows depends on it; it is also the more mysterious. To begin to understand the force of "Is" in line 3, we have to decide whether its subject, "lust," the last word in line 2, is passion working within a given individual; or rather the lustful individual himself; or rather a partially allegorized Lust, a sort of personification out of Spenser; or rather the experience of gratification. If we read "this hell," the last words of the sonnet, to summarize all that has been predicated about lust, then we have to extend the meaning of that word to the object of male desire, since the word "hell" in subsequent sonnets will clearly acquire a specific anatomical reference.[5] "Lust" thus has four or five potential meanings that fade in and out or reinforce each other a little confusingly as the reader moves through the series of participles, nouns, and clauses that maintain the predication apparently through line 12. All the rich, disturbing intricacy of meaning hangs upon that "Is." Is lust "murderous" because it destroys the individual who feels it, or is he led to feel murderous toward the person he desires? Or toward himself? Is lust "cruell" toward other feelings and traits, virtues and vices, in a kind of shadowy psychomachia, or toward human beings? Are we dimly invited to half-imagine some hypostatized embodiment, some furious naked "salvage man" spotted with gore, both hunted and hated? How does that potential predication jibe with lust as bliss and woe in line 11? There the "salvage man" disappears and lust "is" the feelings stemming from the end of its quest.

Is it possible for so many alternative predications to be jammed into one uncertain copula? As we read we have to keep revising or recombining our notions of just how the signifier "lust" is, can be, something. We strain to grasp the mysterious equations implied in that deceptively innocent bridge. Only if we are puzzled by it will we begin to unravel its secrets. Booth's argument against distortion obscures the need for puzzlement. We need to register the actual warping, which from our perspective is there, before we can set out to deal with it. The distortion in the case of the copula is particularly insidious because modernization leaves it untouched.

"No editor," Booth writes, "is likely to succeed perfectly in accommodating a modern reader and a Renaissance text to one another, but that is no reason to do nothing."[6] The question is what one *can* do if one measures the full distance between the two. To do what Booth and most editors do risks a sham accommodation with the past which in fact increases our estrangement from it. How does the editor avoid that trap? To begin to answer this question satisfactorily one really needs a theory of understanding; one has to ask how a reader would evade the trap. One has to bracket the editorial problem and consider the larger problems of hermeneutic theory; one has to reflect on the process of understanding any remote text. The growing body of hermeneutic speculation is by no means irrelevant to the practical decisions of editors, just as the consequences of their decisions are not irrelevant to theory. The crucial question focused by Booth's polemic is not whether we want original or altered texts—both are necessary for different purposes—but rather how and to what degree a modern reader's experience might resemble that of the text's first readers.

No linguist would dissent from Sapir's formulation.

> Language moves down time in a current of its own making. It has a
> drift. . . . Nothing is perfectly static. Every word, every grammatical
> element, every locution, every sound and accent is a slowly changing
> configuration, moulded by the invisible and impersonal drift that is the
> life of language.[7]

This drift was first discovered for the modern world by Dante and the philologists of the Italian Renaissance. Lorenzo Valla insisted on the central dilemma of anachronistic reading with all the energy of his ferocious intelligence. Changing referents require changing terms: *nova res novum vocabulum flagitat*. But referents and words change at varying rates of speed. Language ideally requires a continuity which neither words nor things possess.

The fact of historical estrangement, historical solitude, is doubtless most fully grasped by those like Valla who spend their careers contending with it. The pathos of estrangement has never been evoked more beautifully than by one of the heroes of modern philology, Wilamowitz.

> The tradition yields us only ruins. The more closely we test and examine
> them, the more clearly we see how ruinous they are; and out of ruins
> no whole can be built. The tradition is dead; our task is to revivify life
> that has passed away. We know that ghosts cannot speak until they have
> drunk blood; and the spirits which we evoke demand the blood of our
> hearts. We give it to them gladly; but if they then abide our question,
> something from us has entered into them.[8]

A little of ourselves will always enter into the ghosts we force to speak. If, as Heidegger suggests, we are what we understand to be, then what we understand to be will already be a part of us. The conversation with our classics will always be partial; we can never altogether escape interpretive anachronism. "Which of your Hesterdays Mean Ye to Morra?": that Joycean song haunts the historian of meanings. It haunted Theodore Adorno: "Nothing more is given to philosophy than fleeting, disappearing traces in the riddle-figures of that which exists and their astonishing entwinings."⁹ We can love from the past only that which we have begun by misunderstanding and continue to understand gropingly. Perhaps this is why we love the shard, the ruin, the blurred hieroglyph, as we love those broken, discolored, weather-beaten statues, hieratic and withdrawn, standing at the portal of a cathedral.

One can approach the central hermeneutic problem through the experience of the classroom. The teacher is compelled by his role to perform a kind of activity analogous to textual modernization. He is obliged to translate, to find contemporary equivalents and glosses for his students in order to make a remote text "accessible." He can only present a literary work to them in their terms or in terms they can follow. In doing this the teacher has literally no choice. But if he is at all self-conscious, he knows that his glosses and his explanations are subtly or palpably inaccurate. How will he gloss the word "Spirit" at the opening of sonnet 129? He has no means of conveying the different feeling for syntactic closure of the English Renaissance. And what happens in the classroom is only a heightened imitation of what happens to the solitary reader in his study; he too inevitably translates into his own dialect. He appropriates, anachronizes, no matter how deep his historical consciousness. If we read sonnet 129 in its quarto version, we try to organize its apparent disorder and soften its offenses to our mind-set. To begin to read any unfamiliar text is to try to make it less strange, make it new. In Norman N. Holland's Freudian vocabulary, the act of reading involves "a kind of fusion or introjection based on oral wishes to incorporate."¹⁰

The act of appropriation has been described more than once in hermeneutic theory. Hans-Georg Gadamer calls it *Aneignung*, and Paul Ricoeur uses the French word *appropriation*. In the thought of each it has a positive resonance; ideally for each it leads to self-knowledge. For Ricoeur appropriation occurs when "the interpretation of a text is completed by the self-interpretation of a subject who henceforth understands himself better or differently or even begins to understand himself."¹¹ Gadamer quotes with approval Hegel's statement that *Aneignung*—appropriation or assimilation—"is the fundamental fact of being alive." But his own hermeneutics invests the term with a somewhat different significance. Gadamer's analysis of the entire process of understanding is very rich and sometimes profound. His perception of its historicity, its "situatedness," his critique of nineteenth-century historicism, his analysis of the mutual questioning between reader and text, his quest for a dialogue across time—these and other contributions to hermeneutic thought are welcome and valuable. But other elements of his theory raise doubts about its viability as a whole system.

According to Gadamer, understanding begins when something other, something outside, addresses us. Something, such as a text from the past, asserts its own validity, which is distant from our own. In responding to this stimulus we are led properly to an awareness of our own prejudices and can correct our own preunderstandings through a circular process which is not vicious but productive. The proper goal of the hermeneutic encounter for Gadamer is a blending or fusion of horizons, a *horizontverschmelzung*. This occurs when the interpreter widens his own horizon of experience to include that of the text, reaches an intuitive understanding of the questions the text poses and answers through the common medium of language; he thus enlarges his own personal horizon, perceives it afresh, and gains insight into both worlds now blended into one. This experience is possible because both interpreter and text belong to a single continuous tradition.

> Historical consciousness is aware of its own otherness and hence
> distinguishes the horizon of tradition from its own. On the other hand,
> it is itself . . . only something laid over a continuing tradition, and hence
> it immediately recombines what it has distinguished in order, in the
> unity of the historical horizon that it thus acquires, to become again one
> with itself.[12]

This act of combining followed by a reassuring return to selfhood is so smooth because the tradition for Gadamer is in fact so "continuing"; it seems to be free of all revolts, gaps, leaps, and disjunctures. The concept of tradition becomes an instrument to tame, sweeten, and abstract history, which now appears purely unbroken and unalienating. It is true that Gadamer speaks of a tension between the two horizons. But functionally this tension counts for less than the blending mediation. Distance in time, Gadamer writes, is "not a yawning abyss, but is filled with the continuity of custom and tradition, in the light of which all that is handed down presents itself to us." Elsewhere he speaks of tradition as "an unbroken stream."[13] But tradition as we know it may not be a healing, sacred river but a polluting Love Canal which carries dangerous flotsam. Tradition as a stream has many tributaries, falls, and blockages. It runs less smoothly than this account suggests, and the history of interpretation as we know it reveals the defenses interpreters have had to raise against the threat of tradition.

What if the tension between horizons proves to be intolerable? Allegoresis developed partly as one defense against unwelcome meanings suspected in past texts; we in our day have abandoned allegoresis for a more economical defense, ironization. If a given text, say More's *Utopia*, asserts too emphatically its estrangement from us, we shield ourselves by reading it ironically. Frank Kermode has recently shown the affinities of interpretation not with a fresh openness but with an enclosing institutionalism, with a group of insiders reluctant to open their gateway and reveal their arcane knowledge.[14] Graves and Riding, we remember, wrote very consciously as outsiders against one form of institutional protectionism.

The actual status of the original text emerges from Gadamer's formulation a little blurred.

> The true historical object is not an object at all, but the unity of the one [the object] and the other [true historical thinking taking account of its own historicality], a relationship in which exist both the reality of history and the reality of historical understanding.[15]

If the true object is not an object, then it is difficult to see how it can form half of a higher unity. For Gadamer the text has no existence independent of the tradition in which it is understood; in effect he denies the text an original historical situatedness such as he claims for the interpreter. This denial calls into question the equality of the dialogue as well as the tension between horizons. Essentially the text is robbed of its own particular horizon. The supposed dialogue lacks symmetry because only the interpreter's governing assumptions are called into play, not those of the text. The context of each work is not its original, living semiotic matrix but rather a series of posthumous readings. Gadamer in his own way wants to protect us from our solitude. The resulting concept of appropriation fails to isolate its potential self-deception. His account of understanding blurs a little the central problem of interpretation: language changes, modes of experience change, texts become estranged, and yet the contact with texts in their authentic otherness would provide precious knowledge and self-knowledge, would save us from a hermeneutic narcissism Gadamer himself is eager to avoid.

My own plea would be for a moment in the process of understanding which no hermeneutics has authorized. I would ask for a moment which deliberately tries to frustrate appropriation, which tries to restore the work to its own world of meanings perceived in all their distant strangeness. Simply to draw the work to ourselves, willfully, voraciously, is to dim that clarification which contact with otherness does truly bring. Let us for a moment refuse to appropriate; let us try, however unsuccessfully, to return the work to its own mysterious alienation. Instead of clutching it too quickly, we should recognize its isolation and vulnerability, recognize what deceives our expectations, offends our proprieties, refuses dialogue, will not abide our questions. We need to measure without blinking the pathos of estrangement, the ruptures of history, the blockages of tradition.[16]

It is true that this act of distancing the work is itself subject to the distortions of our historicial moment. But if our distortions are to be progressively corrected, they will not be affected by a bland tradition but by perceived interruptions of tradition. Let us try for a moment to overcome that force which Heidegger calls "averageness" (*Durchschnittlichkeit*) and which, he says, smoothly suppresses every kind of spiritual priority. "Overnight," he writes, "everything that is primordial gets glossed over as something that has long been well known. . . Every secret loses its force."[17] Let us try to recover that sense of the work's forceful secrecy. Let us for a moment refuse to understand.

The response to that moment can take one of two directions. One alternative would be to find a freedom in this impasse, call the rupture radical and total, and play with the flotsam of the past as context-free, neutral counters to be juggled at will. This response would free the interpreter from any responsibility to a vestige of original meaning, which, according to Jacques Derrida, will undergo a loss inherent in the character of all utterances. One can then appropriate with a vengeance, liberated from all constraints; one might even hope with Derrida to take a kind of Nietzschean joy in an endless innocent game of free associations. The one thing excluded from such play would of course be the stimulus of contact as well as the risk; there could be no dangerous impact which would challenge and conceivably clarify. The work interpreted would be an inkblot test in which the interpreter would reveal over and over only his own obsessions without understanding them, lacking any transcendental key to make sense of his private musings. Derrida's own discussions of texts by Plato, Descartes, Leibniz, Rousseau, Hegel, and others do not in fact play with them freely and "innocently," but tend rather to subject these texts to precise and often brilliant analysis which assumes personal time-bound authorship.[18] Everyone doubtless has a right to his own avocations, but some will be moved to ask, as Shakespeare asks his friend: "Why dost thou spend, upon thy selfe thy beauties legacy?" For some, the pleasure of the "profitless usurer" quickly loses its charm.

The alternative to this hermeneutic play with free associations would be much more austere. This course would try to avoid that self-indulgence as it avoided the opposite mirror indulgence that denies the work's estrangement. This hermeneutic would accept estrangement as a given and then search out patiently some bridge, some passage, some common term, which might help to mitigate it. On this basis one would suspect all modernized versions and easy assimilations, one would settle for less than full understanding, but one would accept a responsibility for a partial interpretive correspondence to an intrinsic meaning or complex of meanings. One would think not of appropriating but of working out a reading appropriate to those intrinsic meanings. One would conceive of a text coming to us bearing its own intentionality—not the intentionality of its creator but simply its own patent design for a certain kind of use. A chair exists to be sat on; a text exists to be read and read *appropriately*, within certain limits of potential response. It carries with it coded directions or provocations to the mind, and certain types of mental responses befit a given text more closely than others. The task of the reader is to ascertain the experience or the activity most perfectly corresponding to the text's coded instigations.

In the case of a remote text—and no formula can specify how remote is "remote"—the directions or instigations will always be blurred, but one accepts a need to begin deciphering them. In the case of a mathematical equation one can think of the directions to the mind as *commands* to perform certain operations; in the case of a poem one can think of the directions rather as *orientations*. To interpret, Ricoeur writes suggestively, is to set out toward the *orient* of the text. To think of interpreting as an appropriate response to coded but blurred directions is not to limit the potential wealth of suggestion of a literary work, but it is to rule out the expense of spirit in self-indulgent anachronism. The wealth of significance has to stem from the work's concrete historical situation as we can best divine it.[19] If it does this, then we may gain a small accretion of self-knowledge. In the case of Shakespeare's sonnets, this would include—what can be gathered from most Renaissance poems—the limiting regularity, the hypertrophy of logic in our assumptions about words and syntax; in the case of sonnet 129, this might include an altered view of the pallid, therapeutic sexuality of our post-Freudian era, Eliot's "natural, life-giving, cheery automatism,"[20] which is not of course to be found in Freud. But these crude indications of acquired self-consciousness badly approximate the gradual, profound growth of understanding whereby we slowly and fumblingly come to situate ourselves in history.[21]

The first, simple, and difficult act of reading is to see the remote text as truly remote. To begin to measure its removal from us, to intuit its privacy and specificity, to make out the density of its aura, one has to restore it to its original silence. The text comes to us as a shard, out of its own quietude and distance; by disencumbering it of its secular impediments, by stripping it of its false modernity, we release it to withdraw from us back into its own universe of meanings, cruelly and beautifully back where we can gauge its strangeness. In that strangeness begins true knowledge, the true partial knowledge that history allows us. We can begin to read only after granting the text the seclusion and the particularity of its unique inflection.

NOTES

1. The essay by Graves and Riding first appeared under the title "William Shakespeare and E.E. Cummings," in *A Survey of Modernist Poetry* (London: Heinemann, 1927) and in revised form was later included in Graves' *The Common Asphodel* (London: Hamilton, 1949) under the title "A Study in Original Punctuation and Spelling." The reply to Graves and Riding appears on pp. 447–52 of *Shakespeare's Sonnets*, Stephen Booth, ed. (New Haven: Yale University Press, 1980). The passages quoted appear on p. 447.

2. *Sonnets*, p. 450. Booth explains and defends his editorial policy on p. ix of his preface as follows:

"My primary purpose in the present edition is to provide a text that will give a modern reader as much as I can resurrect of a Renaissance reader's experience of the 1609 Quarto; it is, after all, the sonnets we have and not some hypothetical originals that we value. I have adopted no editorial principle beyond that of trying to adapt a modern reader—with his assumptions about idiom, spelling, and punctuation—and the 1609 text to one another. . . . Both my text and my commentary are determined by what I think a Renaissance reader would have thought as he moved from line to line and sonnet to sonnet in the Quarto. I make no major substantial emendations and few minor ones. It might therefore seem reasonable to reprint the Quarto text alone and simply comment on that, but the effects of almost four centuries are such that a modern reader faced with the Quarto text sees something that is effectively very different from what a seventeenth-century reader saw.

In modernizing spelling and punctuation I have taken each poem individually and tried to find a mid-point between following the punctuation and spelling of the Quarto text (which modern readers, accustomed to logically and semantically directive punctuation and spelling, are inclined to misinterpret) and modern directive spelling and punctuation (which often pays for its clarity by sacrificing a considerable amount of a poem's substance and energy). In each case I have tried to find the least distorting available compromise. Sometimes no compromise is satisfactory, and I describe the probable operation of a line or quatrain in a note."

3. Lines 1258–63. See also "The Shipman's Tale," 7.170ff.

4. The considerable reality behind the nobility's reputation for extravagance is detailed in chapter 10 of Lawrence Stone's *Crisis of the Aristocracy, 1558–1641* (Oxford: Oxford University Press, Clarendon Press, 1965).

5. See, e.g., sonnet 144, line 12.

6. *Sonnets*, p. 448.

7. Edward Sapir, *Language* (New York: Harcourt, Brace and World, 1949), pp. 150, 171.

8. Ulrich von Wilamowitz-Moellendorff, *Greek Historical Writing and Apollo*, G. Murray, tr. (Oxford: Oxford University Press, 1908), p. 26.

9. T. W. Adorno, *Moments Musicaux* (1930), quoted by Susan Buck-Morss, *The Origins of Negative Dialectics* (New York: Free Press, 1977), p. 52.

10. Norman N. Holland, *The Dynamics of Literary Response* (New York: Norton, 1975), p. 104.

11. French text in Paul Ricoeur, "Qu'est-ce-qu'un texte?" in R. Bübner et al., eds., *Hermeneutik und Dialektik*, 2:194–95 (Tübingen: Mohr, 1970).

12. Hans-Georg Gadamer, *Truth and Method* (New York: Seabury Press, 1975), p. 273. German text in Gadamer, *Wahrheit und Methode* (Tübingen: Mohr, 1960), p. 290:

> "Das historische Bewusstsein ist sich seiner eigenen Andersheit bewusst und hebt daher den Horizont der Überlieferung von dem eigenen Horizont ab. Andererseits aber ist es selbst nur . . . wie eine Überlagerung über einer fortwirkenden Tradition, und daher nimmt es das voneinander Abgehobene sogleich wieder zusammen, um in der Einheit des geschichtlichen Horizontes, den es sich so erwirbt, sich mit sich selbst zu vermitteln."

13. Gadamer, *Truth and Method*, pp. 264–65, 262.

14. Frank Kermode, *The Genesis of Secrecy: On the Interpretation of Narrative* (Cambridge, Mass.: Harvard University Press, 1979).

15. Gadamer, *Truth and Method*, p. 267. German text in *Wahrheit und Methode*, p. 283: "Der wahre historische Gegenstand ist kein Gegenstand, sondern die Einheit dieses Einen und Anderen, ein Verhältnis, in dem die Wirklichkeit der Geschichte ebenso wie die Wirklichkeit des geschichtlichen Verstehens besteht."

16. Maurice Blanchot evokes the danger to the literary work judged to be good; it is likely to be "made useful" and exploited. The work judged to be bad on the other hand is preserved by its lack of esteem: "set aside, relegated to the inferno by libraries, burned, forgotten: but this exile, this disappearance into the heat of the fire or the tepidness of oblivion, *prolongs in a certain way the just distance of the work. . . .* The work does not endure; it is" (my italics). French text in *L'espace littéraire* (Paris: Gallimard, 1955), p. 270.

17. Martin Heidegger, *Being and Time*, J. Macquarrie and E. Robinson, tr. (New York: Harper and Row, 1962), p. 165.

18. "This structuralist thematic of broken immediacy is therefore the saddened, *negative*, nostalgic, guilty Rousseauistic side of the thinking of play, whose other side would be the Nietzschean *affirmation*, that is the joyous affirmation of the play of the world and of the innocence of becoming, the affirmation of a world of signs without fault, without truth, and without origin which is offered to an active interpretation." Jacques Derrida, *Writing and Difference*, A. Bass, tr. (Chicago: University of Chicago Press, 1978), p. 272; French text in *L'Ecriture et la différence* (Paris: Seuil, 1967), p. 427. The very allusions to Rousseau and Nietzsche in the sentence quoted imply a knowable, traceable continuity, an identifiable determinacy inherent in the ideas of these two thinkers and resistant to the misunderstandings of history. The "immediacy" of their work would appear not to have been broken. It is unclear finally just how much Derrida concedes to history.

19. It is true, as Stanley Fish has argued, that interpretation is guided by context, but to deny the text (with Fish) *any* priority to interpretation is to be excessively rigid. The literary text when read as literature is precisely of that kind which invites a series of circular adjustments between itself and its interpretive context. This series never ends; it never fully succeeds; but a fitting interpretive context possesses a flexible capacity for revision which Fish is unwilling to recognize. The fact is that interpreters can meaningfully discuss a text, persuade one another, and revise their interpretations without surrendering an entire "set of interpretive assumptions." Revised interpretations within a single "context" are possible because a prior text does exist. See Stanley Fish, "Normal Circumstances, Literal Language, Direct Speech Acts, the Ordinary, the Everyday, the Obvious, What Goes Without Saying, and Other Special Cases," *Critical Inquiry* (1978), 4:625–44.

20. T. S. Eliot, *Selected Essays* (London: Faber and Faber, 1956), p. 429.

21. Wolfgang Iser writes suggestively of the reading process: "The production of the meaning of literary texts . . . does not merely entail the discovery of the unformulated . . . it also entails the possibility that we may formulate ourselves and so discover what had previously seemed to elude our consciousness." *The Implied Reader* (Baltimore: Johns Hopkins Press, 1974), p. 294. But I would not agree that "the convergence of text and reader brings the literary work into existence" (p. 275). To split the text and the work is to court a potentially narcissistic subjectivism.

1991—Bruce R. Smith. "The Secret Sharer," from *Homosexual Desire in Shakespeare's England: A Cultural Poetics*

Bruce R. Smith is a professor of English at Georgetown University, as well as a past president of the Shakespeare Association of America. His books include *Ancient Scripts and Modern Experience on the English Stage, 1500–1700, Homosexual Desire in Shakespeare's England: A Cultural Poetics,* and *Shakespeare and Masculinity*.

In three respects Horace's love lyrics must have startled, bothered, and intrigued Renaissance readers. The Roman poet writes about love, not as an idealistic young suitor eager for ungranted favors and untasted delights, but as a jaded man of the world, someone who has traversed Venus's myrtle groves and come out the other side. Nothing could be less like Petrarch praising Laura or Astrophel gazing upon Stella. Furthermore, Horace writes about sexual desire between males with a matter-of-fact-ness that avoids romanticizing that desire no less than it refuses to be embarrassed by it.[1] He drops all the masks. There, simply, it is. Nothing could be less like Aufidius insinuating his admiration of Coriolanus in ardent metaphors, or Barnfield wooing "Ganymede" in the vestments of pastoral, or Musidorus battling Pyrocles in the disguise of an Amazon, or Sir Voluptuous Beast lusting after goats. Finally, for a Renaissance reader able to buy or to borrow a copy for himself, Horace's love lyrics offered an experience of sexual desire quite unmatched by anything we have encountered so far not only in the intensity of that desire but in its *intimacy*. As texts for private reading, Horace's *Carmina* might seem to invite the same kind of socially licensed fantasizing as romance narratives like Sidney's *Arcadia* and Ovidian *epyllia* like Marlowe's "Hero and Leander." But those texts, after all, are third-person narratives. Storyteller and reader band together in looking at "them." The protagonists of the story exist somewhere else, in a fictional place and time that are home to neither storyteller nor reader. In Beaumont's "Salmacis and Hermaphroditus," the most intimate relationship is not between the lovers or even between the reader and the lovers but between the narrator and the reader. With his sensuous turns of phrase and coy wit Beaumont's persona intrudes between us and the lovers from beginning to end. In lyric poems the intimacy, ostensibly at least, is between poet and lover. The reader, if not an out-and-out eavesdropper, is cast as a secret sharer, a privileged witness to someone else's private life.

All three things that distinguish Horace's *Carmina* distinguish also the love poems that were published in 1609 as *Shake-speares Sonnets. Never before Imprinted.* Verbal echoes of Horace's *Carmina*, heard throughout Shakespeare's plays, suggest that Shakespeare had firsthand acquaintance with the Latin text, probably in one of the editions annotated by Denys Lambin.[2] Echoes of Horace in Shakespeare's sonnets are not so direct as in the plays, but Shakespeare's love poems are unlike any other sonnet sequences written in English during the sixteenth century in the very ways that Horace's love poems also differ: they are focused on what love is like after sexual consummation, not before; many of them (in Shakespeare's case, most of them) are addressed, not to a woman, but to another man; and they are nondramatic, subjective, private. Each of these three features has attracted serious critical notice only in our own day.

Thoroughly unconventional in Shakespeare's sonnets is what amounts to an obsession with sexual experience. Stephen Booth's ingenuity has revealed how charged these poems are—even the most idealistic ones—with sexual puns.[3] It is sexual desire, to be sure, that ignites the freezing fires of Sidney, Spenser, Samuel Daniel, and all the other English disciples of Petrarch, but only in Shakespeare's sonnets does sexual desire remain uncontained by spiritual metaphor. Metaphors connect; puns disjoin. The way in which ideology and power are aligned with feeling in most sonnet cycles of the fourteenth, fifteenth, and sixteenth centuries defines a sexuality that satisfied perfectly the idealistic sensibility of the Renaissance. When we look for the transformations that these poems work on sexual desire, we can see at once why they fascinated Renaissance writers and readers: the scenario of indefatigable male pursuing unattainable female serves to focus, and thus control, sexual desire at the same time that it confirms the structures of power in Renaissance society. By investing the objects of their desire with ideal significance Petrarchan poets manage to deprive sexual energy of some of its frightening power to overwhelm. And by directing that energy into sonnets they confirm, as we shall see, the power of men over women. Amid these well tried ways of harmonizing feeling, ideology, and power Shakespeare, like Horace, sounds a distinctly discordant note.

A second difference in Shakespeare's sonnets concerns the objects of desire. As Horace in his odes, Shakespeare in his sonnets uses erotic images quite indifferently in talking about his affections, whether those affections concern his mistress or the male friend to whom most of the poems are addressed. To Renaissance philologists the homoeroticism of Horace's verses proved even more of a challenge than Ovid's *Metamorphoses* or Virgil's eclogues. Some of the humanists fulminated; some of them philosophized; some of them kept a tactful silence. As the commentators go, Denys Lambin, whose edition of the *Carmina* Shakespeare seems to have read, is remarkably matter-of-fact.

(. . .)

For our purposes here, what is important is not whether particular poems and particular passages "prove" that Shakespeare the man did or did not have sexual relations with a certain other man but how the sonnets as poems insinuate sexual feeling in the bonds men in general made with one another in early modern

England. Shakespeare's speaker articulates that connection, not through what he does or what he says to the friend directly, but through what he thinks and what he says to us as readers. Shakespeare may have made his living as a dramatist, but, as Heather Dubrow points out, his sonnets are surprisingly undramatic compared to the sonnets of Sidney, Spenser, and Daniel.[10] Seldom are they addressed to another person as if he or she were actually present. Almost never do they arise out of a specific, immediate incident. Rather, they are personal reflections on events that have taken place at some indefinite time in the past, events that have an existence primarily in the poet's mind. Like Horace with his dreams of Ligurinus, Shakespeare's speaker evokes friend and mistress not as real presences, but as mental images. In several sonnets the friend figures as a "shadow" who disturbs the poet's sleep. As a discourser about homosexual desire, the persona of Shakespeare's sonnets might in some ways seem to resemble Virgil's Corydon and Barnfield's Daphnis. Are they not also men who struggle with their desires in the solitude of lyric verse? There are, however, subtle but important differences in the audience to which these voices speak. Virgil's Corydon and Barnfield's Daphnis speak directly to Alexis and to Ganymede. Shakespeare's persona speaks to himself. In both cases we as readers are privileged to "overhear," but in Shakespeare's case we share with the speaker a privacy and secrecy different in degree and in kind from the much more public performance that goes on in pastoral monologues.

(. . .)

In looking at Shakespeare's sonnets from the point of view of Renaissance readers we have, then, something much more fluid than the 1609 quarto would suggest. For Renaissance readers these were verses *ad hoc* and *ad hominem* with respect not only to the poet, his friend, and his mistress but to *themselves*. Sixteenth-century manuscripts were "properties" of their owners in both the legal and the psychological senses of the word. In the critical parlance of our own day, Shakespeare's sonnets were constantly being deconstructed and appropriated to the interpretations and the uses of different readers. The history of their dissemination in manuscript and print offers a radical demonstration of how a text, once out of a writer's hands, "belongs" to nobody. *The Passionate Pilgrim* is simply the first of these deconstructions to appear in print. More than any other texts we have considered in this book, Shakespeare's sonnets occupy a highly equivocal position on the border between public and private.

With Shakespeare's sonnets, as with Donne's poems, we should perhaps distinguish *degrees* of privacy. Judging from the number of surviving manuscripts and from the particular poems recurring in them, Arthur Marotti proposes that Donne's satires and elegies enjoyed a much wider circulation in manuscript than did the love lyrics that were collected and printed after his death as *Songs and Sonnets*. Beyond the lady (or ladies) so forcefully addressed in the love poems, only a small coterie of Donne's friends must have seen them and then only in loose sheets, as individual poems, and not as an entire collection.[31] To surmise from the few manuscripts that survive, Shakespeare's "sugred Sonnets among his private friends" must have been very private indeed. *Shake-speares Sonnets. Never before Imprinted*: the subtitle to the 1609 quarto says it all. As a complete group these poems had never been made public, had never been bought and sold, had never passed from one stranger's hand to another in exchange for a coin. From manuscripts limited to Shakespeare's "private friends" to manuscripts containing only one or two of the sonnets to *The Passionate Pilgrim* to *Shake-speares Sonnets* to John Benson's edition of 1640: in that progression we can read a transformation of hand and voice into things. Personal utterances are turned into commercial commodities. Topical immediacy fades into literary distance. Particularity becomes universality. J. W. Saunders's metaphor about sixteenth-century publishing seems right:

> All through the period of manuscript circulation there was a steady expansion of the reading audience outwards from the first circle of intimates. The widening circulation was a continuous process, like the circular ripples on a pond when a stone disturbs the surface, from the poet's intimates at the source to the unconnected enthusiasts and ultimately the printers on the fringes.[32]

If sixteenth-century printers were on the fringes and sixteenth-century purchasers were beyond that, where do *we* stand as twentieth-century readers? To situate ourselves in Saunders's metaphor is to realize what a huge imaginative distance we have to bridge to see Shakespeare's sonnets in their original social context.

(…)

In Shakespeare's first nineteen sonnets, if not in Spenser's Epithalamium, the harmony among ideology, power, and feeling is less settled than it first appears. Discordant questions about power and its relationship to feeling are left unresolved. As gestures of rhetoric, Shakespeare's early sonnets seem to be selfless attempts on the persona's part to convince the young friend of a more experienced vision of sexual desire—a view that sees desire in a wider frame of time than an adolescent can. In that sense each sonnet is a gesture of power directed toward two objects: toward time and toward the friend. The couplet of sonnet 15 nicely catches this complexity: "And all in war with Time for love of you / As he takes from you, I engraft you new" (15.11–12).

Many readers have noted the pun here on "engraft": it suggests the Greek root *graphein*, "to write," at the same time that it sets up the images of horticultural grafting in the next sonnet. Shakespeare's early sonnets are an attempt to impose his vision simultaneously on time and on the friend. Despite the pun, sonnets 15 and 16 keep the two senses of "engraft" entirely separate: the poet creates, the friend procreates. The persona himself keeps his distance from sexual desire. And that is exactly where most editors and critics since Malone have tried to keep him. Then comes sonnet 20:

> A Woman's face with natures own hand painted,
> Haste thou the Master Mistris of my passion,
> A womans gentle hart but not acquainted
> With shifting change as is false womens fashion,
> An eye more bright than theirs, lesse false in rowling:
> Gilding the object where-upon it gazeth,
> A man in hew all *Hews* in his controwling,
> Which steales mens eyes and womens soules amaseth.
> And for a woman wert thou first created,
> Till nature as she wrought thee fell a dotinge,
> And by addition me of thee defeated,
> By adding one thing to my purpose nothing.
>> But since she prickt thee out for womens pleasure,
>> Mine be thy love and thy loves use their treasure.

With this poem four things change dramatically: the ends to which the poet speaks, the language that he uses, the imaginative setting in which he situates himself, and the self-identity he assumes.

Quite suddenly, hortatory verse starts sounding like amatory verse. A reader who is out for secrets is forced to reconsider what he or she has read already. As Pequigney argues, we can see in the first twenty sonnets a progression in which the poet's sexual feelings for the friend, held carefully in check at first, gradually emerge as the poet's real subject. Homosocial desire changes by degrees into homosexual desire. The word "love" first enters the sonnets very obliquely indeed when the poet appeals to the friend's "selfe love" as a motive for begetting progeny (3.8). In sonnet 5 love is still a property of the friend, though more ambiguously so, when the poet remarks "the lovely gaze where every eye doth dwell" (5.2). The personal significance of that word for the poet becomes increasingly clear—and increasingly physical—as he begs the friend to have a child, to create another self "for love of me" (10.13), as he ventures to call him "love" (13.1) and "deare my love" (13.11), as he goes to war with time "for love of you" (15.13), as he defies time to carve wrinkles in "my loves faire brow" (19.9), as he boasts "My love shall in my verse ever live young" (19.14). Is "my love" in this line a name for the friend, or does it refer to the poet's feelings? "Love" and "my love" emerge after sonnet 13 as the poet's favorite epithets for the young man. Speaking to him and speaking about him, the poet refers to the young man by that title more than twenty times. Only seven times does the poet refer to him as his "friend." "Love," "lover," and "lovely," as Booth points out, were ambiguous if not ambivalent in sixteenth-

and seventeenth-century usage. They might or might not suggest sexual desire, depending on the context.[39] The context in Shakespeare's sonnets is, to say the least, equivocal. "Love," on equal terms with "mistress," is likewise how the poet speaks to and about the woman who is the subject of the 27 sonnets printed toward the end in Thorpe's edition. Only once does he call her his "friend." We have, then, two people—and three terms for talking about them. At one extreme is "mistress," with its explicitly sexual reference. At the other extreme is "friend," with its largely nonsexual reference. In between is "love," which can be sexual, or nonsexual, or both. "Two loves I have," declares the poet in sonnet 144,

> of comfort and dispaire,
> Which like two spirits do sugiest me still,
> The better angell is a man right faire:
> The worser spirit a woman collour'd il. (144.1–4)

We do no more than respect an ambiguity in early modern English if we follow Shakespeare's example and refer to the young man, not as the poet's "friend," but as his "love."

Questions about love reach a crisis—for the poet, for his readers, and presumably for the young man—in sonnet 20. The issue here is easy enough to state but not so easy to decide: is sonnet 20 a *denial* of sexual desire, or is it an *avowal?* The *literal sense* of what the poet says certainly indicates denial. "Love" versus "love's use": the terms the poet/speaker uses to draw his distinctions derive from Aristotle's *Nicomachean Ethics. Philia*, the highest of human bonds, is premised on the *equality* of men as one another's peer; *eros*, a lesser bond, thrives on *inequality*, on needs that each partner fulfills for the other. All of the preceding sonnets, we see in retrospect, have been arguments in an implicit debate. In effect, Shakespeare has been addressing the great question in classical ethics that is posed so often in Shakespeare's comedies about courtship: which has the greater claim on a man, friendship with other men or sexual ties with women? The procreational images of the first nineteen sonnets would seem to place the poet/speaker of the first nineteen sonnets squarely with Daphnaeus, the spokesman in Plutarch's dialogue "Of Love" who urges Bacchon to marry. When Daphnaeus says of marriage that there is "no knot or link in the world more sacred and holy," Protogenes, the critic of women and praiser of pederasty, counters with the "higher" values of male friendship:

> This bond in trueth of wedlocke . . . as it is necessary for generation is
> by good right praised by Polititians and law-givers, who recommend

the same highly unto the people and common multitude: but to speake of true love indeed, there is no jot or part thereof in the societie and felowship of women. . . . For amitie is an honest, civill and laudable thing: but fleshly pleasure, base, vile, and illiberal.[40]

Here is just the distinction between "love" and "love's use" that Shakespeare draws in sonnet 20. In Plutarch's dialogue, Bacchon's marriage transpires during the very time the debaters are having their argument, making their conclusion— or rather their lack of one—a moot point.

In sonnet 20 the issue is likewise left unresolved. What Shakespeare's speaker says is above reproach; how he says it has left many readers since George Steevens uneasy, whatever Edmund Malone may have said to reassure them. There is something playfully salacious about those puns on "thing" and "prick" that distinctly recalls Richard Barnfield's poems. Indeed, the whole conceit of sonnet 20, casting a male in the role most sonnets would assign to a female, recalls Barnfield's sonnet 11 ("Sighing, and sadly sitting by my Love, / He ask't the cause of my hearts sorrowing"). In Shakespeare's sonnet 20, as so often in Barnfield, sexual innuendo seems to be working at cross purposes to moral innocence. To lament that the friend has "one thing to my purpose nothing" might seem to imply that friendship and sexual passion, "love" and "love's use," are two separate things. The tone, however, makes one wonder just what the persona's "purpose" is. Does he find other parts of the beloved's anatomy more commodious? If Shakespeare is citing Plutarch, he calls him to witness on both sides of the case.

Shakespeare's speaker may side with Plutarch's Daphneus on the issue of "love" versus "love's use," but he echoes Protogenes, Plutarch's homosexual apologist, when it comes to which kind of beauty is superior, male or female. The diptych that sonnet 20 forms with sonnet 21 is hinged on a contrast between the young man's fresh face "with natures own hand painted" (20.1) and the "painted beauty" (21.2) that inspires the muses of most other poets. The implied contrast *within* both poems is between male and female, as it may be also *between* them. Male beauty is superior to female, according to Plutarch's Protogenes, for just the reasons Shakespeare's speaker cites: "it is not besmered with sweet ointments, nor tricked up and trimmed, but plaine and simple alwaies a man shall see it, without any intising allurements" (fol. 1133). Whatever suspicions a reader may have about the sonnet's tone are encouraged by the capitalizations and italics in Thorpe's edition. "Woman," "Master Mistris," and *Hews* are all tricked out as possible code words, as possible keys to a closely guarded secret that has been hinted at since "beauties *Rose*" in sonnet 1. The tone of sonnet 20, so troubling to modern readers, seems perfectly consonant with the myths we have been exploring in this book. In its social, narrative, and rhetorical contexts, sonnet 20 comes across as an extremely sophisticated version of "Come live with me and be my love."

There is a sense, then, in which the early sonnets are gestures of power not just toward time and toward the friend but toward the poet's own self: they are attempts to convince not only the friend but the persona himself that the cosmic heterosexuality exemplified in Spenser's Epithalamion has highest claims on erotic desire. They argue Elizabethan orthodoxy. For the friend, the early sonnets are poems of persuasion; for the persona, they are poems of renunciation. The whole scenario here seems uncannily similar to Barnfield's eclogues. We encounter the same pair of characters, the same implied setting, the same double sense of time, the same tension between conventional and unconventional sexualities. Like Barnfield's Daphnis toward the end of the eclogues, Shakespeare's persona in the first nineteen sonnets speaks as an older man to a younger, as experience to innocence, as disciplined desire to overpowering beauty. Both speakers counsel marriage. Implicit, perhaps, in Shakespeare's luxuriant images of flowers and trees is the pastoral landscape in which Barnfield plays out his erotic fantasies to their ultimately chaste end. There is the same sharply divided attitude toward time: both poets celebrate the pleasures of morning, of spring, of "this thy golden time," but both are just as keenly conscious of time's destructive power. Finally, both sets of poems turn on the same conflict between male–male attachments and heterosexual passion. That is to say, Shakespeare's early sonnets, like Barnfield's eclogues and sonnets, enact the rites of wooing that make up the Myth of the Passionate Shepherd.

Sonnet 20 may be a poem of courtship, but Shakespeare does not stop there. Like Horace, but unlike most Renaissance poets who write about love, Shakespeare goes on to write about what happens when emotional desire becomes physical act. John Donne's love poems, infamous as they may be in this regard, are all about the before ("Come, Madame, come, ... / Off with that girdle") and the after ("Busie old foole, / unruly Sonne, / Why dost thou thus, / Through windowes, and through curtaines call on us?").[41] They imply the physical and emotional realities of lovemaking, but they do not talk about them directly. Those emotional and physical realities are Shakespeare's very subject in the poems that succeed sonnet 20. Quite in keeping with all the other ways in which the sonnets play off experience itself against the words that would inscribe it, sexual experience in the sonnets resides largely in puns. Many of the puns that Stephen Booth has caught and cataloged occur not just once, in individual sonnets, but are sustained through the whole sequence: "have" (52.14, 87.13, 110.9–12, 129.6), "use" (2.9, 4.7, 6.5, 20.14, 40.6, 48.3, 78.3, 134.10), "will" (for male and female sexual organs as well as for sexual desire: 57.13, 112.3, 134.2, 135. passim, 136. passim, 143.13, 154.9), "pride" (for penis: 64.2, 52.12, 151.9–11), and "all" (for penis, likely by analogy with "awl": 26.8,

75.9–14, 109.13–14). As heard by Booth, the couplet to sonnet 109 embodies something more substantial than sentiment:

> For nothing this wide Universe I call,
> Save thou my Rose, in it thou art my all. (109.13–14)

"All" or "no-thing": when it comes to homosexual puns, most academic readers of Shakespeare's sonnets have insisted on the nothing. Booth gallantly tries to have it both ways, noting the possibility of homosexual double entendres but finding a metaphorical excuse for their presence. Of sonnet 98 ("From you have I beene absent in the spring") he says, for example:

> The language of this sonnet and of sonnet 99 ["The forward violet
> thus did I chide"] is full of unexploited relevance to sexual love. . . .
> All these senses remain dormant throughout the poem; they function
> only to the extent that such a concentration of potentially suggestive
> terms gives a vague aura of sexuality to the poem and thus . . . reinforces
> the persistent and essential analogy Shakespeare draws between the
> speaker's relationship with a beloved and the traditional courtly love
> poet's relationship with a mistress.[42]

Joseph Pequigney will have none of this. The sonnets to the young man trace the course of a sexually consummated love affair, Pequigney argues, and in the sexual puns of the sonnets about the young man, no less than in the sexual puns of the sonnets about the mistress, Shakespeare is talking about the psychological and anatomical realities of sexual love. As a record of a love affair, the sonnets about the young man tell a three-part story, with a beginning (sonnets 1–19, in which the poet falls in love), a middle (sonnets 20–99, in which the poet's passion "finds fruition in sexual acts"), and an end (sonnets 100–126, in which the poet's love wanes).[43]

(. . .)

After the persona's first avowal of sexual desire in sonnet 20, we would expect, according to the progression of myths we have been following in this book, a moral or legal intervention, on the part of the poet's conscience if not from some other person. Even Barnfield, for all his salacious imaginings, lays aside his illicit desires for the "higher" concerns of epic poetry—and for marriage. In Shakespeare's sonnets no such thing happens. We hear nothing about moral reservations. No thought of the law provokes fear. In the course of his self-confessions after sonnet 20 Shakespeare's speaker struggles with problems of authority, to be sure, but those problems have nothing to do with moral philosophy or the law. They concern instead authority in being the lover of another man and authority in writing about homosexual love.

The familiar, even complacent role the poet enjoys in the first nineteen sonnets ends abruptly after sonnets 20/21: to declare homosexual desire—and to act on it—changes everything. Conventional structures of ideology and power explode; the fragile proprieties of the first nineteen poems are shattered. In the early sonnets power is all on the persona's side. His age, his experience, above all his powers as a poet put him in command of the situation at hand. Both the sonnet as a medium and orthodox heterosexuality as the message are firmly under his control. As long as he plays the sage older friend, it is he who is doing the acting; the young friend's role is to react. Admitting his passion changes all that. "I" and "you" no longer have their comfortable separate identity. The poet who doubts his own abilities in sonnet 23 ("As an unperfect actor on the stage") is quite another person from the poet who confidently went to war with time in sonnet 15 ("When I consider every thing that growes, / Holds in perfection but a little moment"). Critics customarily speak of the young man as the poet's "friend," but the perplexed relationship described in the sonnets after 20/21 is anything but Aristotle's *philia*, with its easy mutuality between men who are equals.

(. . .)

"Master Mistris": ambiguities of syntax in that epithet in sonnet 20 are bound up with ambiguities of power in the sonnets as a whole. Are the two words in apposition? Is it "master–mistress" with a hyphen? The line is then a kind of in-joke between persona and friend, as the persona quips about the young man's gender. Is one word subordinated, grammatically and sexually, to the other? Is the young man "the *master* mistress of my passion," as opposed to the persona's "lesser" mistress, the woman of sonnets 127 to 154? The line in that case becomes a witty compliment of the sort the persona has been serving up in the previous nineteen poems, but it also foreshadows the dark jealousies of persona-love-mistress as a *ménage à trois*. If we bite Thomas Thorpe's bait and accept "W.H." as a cipher for the young man addressed in these poems, it is worth remembering that the abbreviation "Mr." in late sixteenth-century orthography more likely stands for "Master" than "Mister."

Whichever way we read the phrase, the word "master" points up the reversal of meaning that has overtaken the word "mistress" since the Middle Ages. In the context of courtly love "mistress" originally designated the lady as a setter of tasks for her servant-knight. By Shakespeare's time, however, the word had taken on the specifically sexual meaning of "a woman who illicitly occupies the place of wife" (OED 11)—and with that meaning all the Judeo-Christian assumptions about the husband as "head" of the wife (Ephesians 5:22–23). The earliest citations in the *Oxford English Dictionary* all occur in contemptuous contexts that see compliant woman as a source of pleasure for predatory man. Mistress Quickly fails to make the OED, but the title fits her perfectly. The difference between the literal and the secondary meanings of the word "mistress" turns, indeed, on whether the lady has granted sexual favors or not. If she holds off, she remains in control, a "mistress" in the original courtly sense; if she gives in to the suitor's desires, she gives up her power and becomes a "mistress" in the secondary sexual sense. Questions of power are neatly decided by the question of sex or no sex.

If *Paradise Lost* celebrates the fortunate fall, Petrarchan sonnets celebrate the fortunate refusal. At first glance, the scenario of suitor prostrate before his mistress would seem to give all the power to the lady. She, after all, has the prerogative of saying no. That much is only natural. Among animals at least, it is females that do the choosing of sexual partners. There is a very good biological reason why that should be the case: in the great scheme of things sperm are plentiful, eggs are scarce. The physical consequences of sexual activity are much more serious for a female animal than for a male. Females have a right to be choosy.[46] From the social games they played if not from the observations they made of animals, Renaissance sonneteers seem to have recognized this basic fact about rituals of courtship. At the very beginning of the sonnet tradition, in Dante's *La Vita Nuova*, we discover a fundamental anomaly: the poet may be firmly in control of his medium, but he is not in control of the lady. The medium becomes, then, a way of extending control from poem to person. A sonnet shows us poetry in just the terms that Renaissance critics like Sidney and Puttenham best understood it: as a species of oratory, an art of persuasion.[47] It is a strategem on the suitor's part to bend the lady's will to his own. It is a male's attempt to defy the dictates of biology. It is Art's revenge on Nature.

The lady may have the prerogative of saying no, but, for the persona at least, her power stops there. In holding off she in fact gives the male speaker just the opportunity he needs to celebrate his own prowess: to make a public display of his feelings, to show off his ingenuity as a poet, to turn the woman with her disconcerting *otherness* into a managable image in a poem. The dramatic conventions of the Renaissance sonnet grant the lady a reality only as an object of the male persona's desires. "Look into thy heart and write": Sidney's advice to himself indicates just where the writer's interest—and the reader's—lies, not on the lady but on the suitor. The poet, not the mistress, is the *subject*, in every sense of the word. Seen in its rhetorical context, a Petrarchan sonnet is a power ploy of speaker over listener; seen in its social context, it is a power-ploy of a man over a woman; seen in its sexual context, it is power-ploy of male over female. Change the gender of the listener from female to male, and all of the delicate alliances of feeling, ideology, and power are called into question. "Master Mistris": Shakespeare's yoking together of those two words reminds us that there is no real equivalent in English for a man as a lover of a man. "Master" comes with all the suggestion of superior power that "mistress" implies, but with none of the suggestion of sexual subjection. In a relationship between two men, of what use are the conventional terms "master" and "mistress"? Who exercises power over whom?

(. . .)

If not friend and friend, if not knight and lady, if not master and minion, if not father and son, who are the lovers to one another? A more complicated tie than all the rest is implied in sonnet 82. Complaining about the rival poet who has threatened his sovereignty since sonnets 20/21, Shakespeare's poet concedes,

> I Grant thou wert not married to my Muse,
> And therefore maiest without attaint ore-looke
> The dedicated words which writers use,
> Of their faire subject, blessing every booke. (82.1–4)

It may, in this instance, be the gender of the poet's muse that inspires an allusion to marriage, but in other sonnets the poet needs no such excuse. "So shall I live, supposing thou art true, / Like a deceived husband" (93.1–2), he confesses in sonnet 93. The poet as husband and his love as wife keep their metaphorical identities through the whole sonnet, until they acquire truly mythic dimensions at the end: "How like *Eaves* apple doth thy beauty grow, / If thy sweet vertue answere not thy show" (93.13–14). In the very next poem the roles are reversed. As a gesture of submission, as an act of obeisance spoken in third person, as a return to the argument of the earliest sonnets in urging the poet's love to "husband natures ritches from expence," sonnet 94 implicitly casts the *love* as husband and the *poet* as wife. Sonnet 97 ("How like a Winter hath my absence beene") seems to do the same, as the poet contrasts "the teeming Autumne big with ritch increase" with his own feelings of sterility and emptiness:

> Yet this aboundant issue seem'd to me,
> But hope of Orphans, and un-fathered fruite,
> For Sommer and his pleasures waite on thee,
> And thou away, the very birds are mute. (97.5–8)

In the metaphors of sonnets 82, 93, 94, and 97 we find overt expression of a subtext that Stephen Booth sees running through the whole sequence. The paradox avowed in sonnet 36 ("Let me confesse that we two must be twaine, / Although our undevided loves are one") and affirmed in the exchange of hearts and the sharing of one identity in sonnets 22, 34, 39, 42, 62, 109, 134, and 135 is the very mystery that makes a sacrament of human marriage. "Ye husbands love your wives, even as Christ loved the Church and hath given himself for it": St. Paul's words in Ephesians 5:25–33 were appointed in the Elizabethan *Book*

of Common Prayer to be read at the end of the marriage rite when there was to
be no sermon.

> For this cause shall a man leave father and mother, and shall be joined
> unto his wife, and they two shall be one flesh. This mystery is great, but
> I speak of Christ and the congregation. Nevertheless, let every one of
> you so love his own wife, even as himself.[49]

St. Paul may have been talking primarily about a religious mystery; the 1559
Book of Common Prayer is quite explicit—much more explicit than its twentieth-
century counterpart—in talking about the mysteries of sex. Matrimony, the
priest says in his greeting,

> is not to be enterprised nor taken in hand unadvisedly, lightly, or
> wantonly, to satisfy men's carnal lusts and appetites, like brute beasts that
> have no understanding, but reverently, discreetly, advisedly, soberly, and
> in the fear of God, duly considering the causes for which matrimony
> was ordained. (p. 290)

Of those three causes—procreation, avoiding fornication, and giving "mutual
society, help, and comfort" (pp. 290–291)—the first two are concerned with
sex. After such a preamble, one can understand why the spiritual metaphor
of "one flesh" in Ephesians 5 would have such physical force, why listeners
like Shakespeare would find it easier to remember the fleshly vehicle than the
spiritual tenor. It is Ephesians 5, and "The Form of Solemnization of Matrimony"
in which it is embedded, that provides the context for one of Shakespeare's
most famous sonnets. "Let me not to the marriage of true mindes / Admit
impediments": sonnet 116 is an implicit answer to what the priest is instructed
to say before anything else to the man and the woman who have presented
themselves for marriage:

> I require and charge you (as you will answer at the dreadful day of
> judgment, when the secrets of all hearts shall be disclosed) that if either
> of you do know any impediment why ye may not be lawfully joined
> together in matrimony, that ye confess it. (p. 291)

One word of the priest's charge, "impediment," sounds out in sonnet 116. Two
other words, "secrets" and "confess," inspire the sonnets as a whole. Like the
marriage of man and wife in the *Book of Common Prayer*, "The marriage of true
minds" in sonnet 116 may have a physical as well as a spiritual aspect. "True
minds" can mean not only the true "affections" (OED II.15.b) that readers
conventionally find in the phrase, but the true "intentions" (OED 11.14) of

two people who present themselves for marriage before a priest. Only twice in the sonnets addressed to the mistress does Shakespeare's poet make even the remotest allusion to these marriage texts from the *Book of Common Prayer*.[50]

(. . .)

What we can observe in the course of the first 126 sonnets is, then, a constantly shifting attempt on Shakespeare's part to bring structures of ideology and structures of power into the kind of viable alignment with feeling that we find in more conventional love poetry. In the sonnets Shakespeare seeks to speak about homosexual desire with the same authority that Petrarch assumes in speaking about heterosexual desire. In pursuit of that end Shakespeare invokes three different modes of discourse: Horace's language of erotic experience, the traditional language of courtly love, and the language of Christian marriage. On very few points are those three languages in accord. Shakespeare's sonnets to the young man not only record what happens between the speaker and his love; the sonnets also play out the conflicts and inconsistences in the conventional ways the poet has for explaining what happens—to himself, to his love, to us as sharers of his sexual secrets. Shakespeare's sonnets test the limits of the love sonnet as a genre. In the hands of other sixteenth-century poets, sonnets serve to confirm those interlocking structures of power and ideology—and feeling—that define Renaissance heterosexuality. In testing the soundness of those structures Shakespeare tests also the verse form in which the structures that define sexuality are turned into words and are made accessible to the imagination. To take the terms of courtly love and Christian marriage and apply them to a subject to which they do not conventionally belong is to force a reexamination of both the terms and the subject. Society may dictate the terms, but the use to which Shakespeare has put those terms is a radical choice. The result is, or can be, something *new*. In *Shake-speares Sonnets. Never before Imprinted*, we have an exercise in the "conditioned and conditional freedom" held out by Pierre Bourdieu's idea of social *habitus*. Out of the already tried "strategies" open to him as a writer, out of the "matrix of perceptions, appreciations, and actions" that he shared with his contemporaries, Shakespeare improvised a new form of discourse.[51] It will not do to say that Shakespeare's sonnets cannot be about homosexual desire since no one else in early modern England addressed homosexual desire in just these terms.

Using a new imaginative vocabulary to talk about an old subject brings Shakespeare to a conclusion altogether different from that of poets in other sequences of sonnets. Traditional sonnet sequences control sexual desire by transcending it: caught up in an impossible conflict between his own hot desire and the lady's cold disdain, the Petrarchan poet turns desire into art and lover's lust into philosopher's zeal. Only Spenser manages to have it both ways by actually marrying the lady in question. In the matter of closure, as in everything else, Shakespeare's sonnets present an anomaly. How critics read the ending seems to depend very much on how they have been filling in the narrative gaps along the way. C. S. Lewis speaks for older, idealistic critics when he singles out sonnet 144 ("Two loves I have of comfort and dispaire") and sees a psychomachia between Comfort and Despair going on through all the poems. The sequence ends "by expressing simply love, the quintessence of all loves whether erotic, parental, filial, amicable, or feudal."[52] From a psychoanalytical point of view C.L. Barber and Richard P. Wheeler find special significance in sonnet 114 ("Or whether doth my minde being crown'd with you / Drinke up the monarks plague this flattery?") and its articulation of the persona's hard-won "*self-regard*, with all that implies as against entire dependence on the regard of the friend."[53] For Pequigney the sonnets' end is the affair's end. The two pairs of parentheses that take the place of a final couplet in the quarto printing of sonnet 126 ("O Thou my lovely Boy who in thy power, / Doest hould time's fickle glasse[,] his sickle, hower") are, Pequigney proposes, pregnant with meaning. They imply that "the poet is entering upon a course of gradual detachment or falling out of love. The parenthetical message might then be translated, 'the rest is silence.'"[54] Showing how rhetorical devices in the poems serve to communicate psychological states, Heather Dubrow compares the last two poems printed in the quarto, verses whose ultimate inspiration is not Petrarch but Anacreon, with the Epithalamium that Spenser puts at the end of the *Amoretti*. In both cases the reader encounters a shift in genre and a stepping back from the intense emotionality of the earlier poems. But the subject of sonnets 153 ("Cupid laid by his brand and fell a sleepe") and 154 ("The little Love-God lying once a sleepe, / Laid by his side his heart inflaming brand") is "the very impossibility of achieving distance from love and the inaccessibility of any finality, any cure." Perhaps, then, there is no closure.[55]

If, on the other hand, we look at the poems as an attempt to read homosexual experience in the idiom of courtly love and according to the ideals of Christian marriage, the volume of *Shake-speares Sonnets* ends by making us realize, and feel, the void between sexual experience and the metaphors we have to talk about it. "O Thou my lovely Boy": the poet's parting gesture toward the lover whose fickleness has caused him such anguish is to give up the whole enterprise, to fall back on a cant term, to look at sodomy from the outside and to see it as an act of aggression. The fact that Shakespeare's poet takes the power on himself makes the ending all the bleaker. Once he took up arms against Time in defense of the young man's beauty. Now he joins forces with Nature, "soveraine mistress over wrack" (126.5), in envisioning the young man's destruction. "O thou minnion of her pleasure," he sneers as he gives up the struggle and lays down his pen (126.9). Here is anything but the "mutuall render only me for thee" (125.12) that the poet has desired and the lover has refused. The other person, Shakespeare's poet discovers, remains *another* person, forever fugitive from all attempts to fix him in imagination. We come away from the sonnets with a sense that the conflicts of ideology and power are never really resolved. Horatian odes, Petrarchan sonnets, the Christian marriage rite: none of these can tell the whole truth about sex. Out of all the homosexualities studied in this book, the homosexuality inscribed in Shakespeare's sonnets is the most compelling because it is not end-stopped. The enjambment of Shakespeare's lines with life continues even when we have come to the sonnets' end.

What is *not* cast aside at the end of the sonnets is the fact of sexual desire. In this respect the Myth of the Secret Sharer is different from all the other modes of poetic discourse in this book. If these myths do not close with an absolute denial of homosexual desire, as with The Shipwrecked Youth and Knights in Shifts, they end with the isolation of the hero who persists in acknowledging that desire. One thinks of Antonio in the Myth of Combatants and Comrades, of Virgil's Corydon and his English-speaking imitators in The Passionate Shepherd, of Edward II in Master and Minion. "Me neither woman now, nor boy doth move, / Nor a too credulous hope of mutuall love": if by the end Shakespeare's persona finds himself in the position of Horace's urbane lover, he does so not for any of the reasons that isolate the other heroes. It is not structures of power or structures of ideology, social disapproval or moral dogma, that set him apart, but problems of authority. He is alone in his subjectivity. Like Montaigne, Shakespeare remains acutely aware, as none of his English contemporaries seem to be, that sexuality is something we can know only "in circumlocution and picture." It is this self-conscious subjectivity that puts the Myth of the Secret Sharer closest of all six myths to our own experience of sexual desire in the twentieth century.

(...)

NOTES

1. Horace, *Odes* 4.1.29–40, trans. Henry Rider in *All the Odes and Epodes of Horace* (London, 1638), pp. 93–94. Selected odes had been translated and published by John Ashmore in 1621, but the homoerotic poems are not among them. On Horace's reputation and influence in the sixteenth and seventeenth centuries see Gilbert Highet, *The Classical Tradition* (Oxford: Oxford Univ. Press, 1949), pp. 244–250, and Valerie Edden, "'The Best of Lyrick Poets,'" in *Horace*, ed. C.D.N. Costa (London: Routledge & Kegan Paul, 1973), pp. 135–159.

2. T.W. Baldwin reaches this conclusion by noting that Shakespeare's allusions to Horace incorporate elements of Lambin's commentary. See *William Shakspere's Small Latine & Lesse Greeke* (Urbana: Univ. of Illinois Press, 1944), 2:497–525.

3. *Shakespeare's Sonnets*, ed. Stephen Booth (New Haven: Yale Univ. Press, 1977). In addition to a lightly edited text Booth provides a facsimile of the 1609 quarto and a full commentary. In that commentary sexual puns figure prominently.

10. Heather Dubrow, *Captive Victors: Shakespeare's Narrative Poems and Sonnets* (Ithaca: Cornell Univ. Press, 1986), pp. 171–190.

31. Arthur F. Marotti, *John Donne, Coterie Poet* (Madison: Univ. of Wisconsin Press, 1986), pp. 3–24.

32. J. W. Saunders, "From Manuscript to Print: A Note on the Circulation of Poetic MSS in the Sixteenth Century," *Proceedings of the Leeds Philosophical and Literary Society* 6 (1951): 523.

39. Booth, *Shakespeare's Sonnets*, pp. 431–432.

40. Plutarch, *Moralia* 767, trans. Philemon Holland in *The Philosophie* (London, 1603), fols. 1132–1133. Further quotations are cited in the text by folio number. Connections between the sonnets and the plays with respect to the scenario of two male friends parted by a woman are explored in Cyrus Hoy, "Shakespeare and the Revenge of Art," *Rice University Studies* 60 (1974): 71–94.

41. John Donne, Elegy "To his Mistris Going to Bed" and "The Sunne Rising," in *The Elegies and The Songs and Sonnets*, ed. Helen Gardner (Oxford: Clarendon Press, 1965), pp. 14, 72.

42. Booth, *Shakespeare's Sonnets*, pp. 98–99.

43. Pequigney, *Such Is My Love*, pp. 209–210, summarizing the argument he has made in earlier chapters.

46. Heather Trexler Remoff, *Sexual Choice: A Woman's Decision* (New York: Dutton, 1984), pp. 3–11. The same observation about the expendability of males is made by Walter J. Ong, *Fighting for Life: Contest, Sexuality, and Consciousness* (Ithaca: Cornell Univ. Press, 1981), pp. 52–56.

47. Puttenham defines love poetry, like other forms of verse, according to its original use: "There were an other sort, who sought the favor of faire Ladies, and coveted to bemone their estates at large, & the perplexities of love in a certain pitious verse called *Elegie*, and thence were called *Eligiack:* such among the Latines were *Ovid, Tibullus, & Propertius*." *The Arte of English Poesie*, ed. Gladys Doidge Willcock and Alice Walker (Cambridge: Cambridge Univ. Press, 1936), p. 25. Sidney has these origins in mind when he sets up his criterion as to whether a love poem is good or not: "But truly many of such writings as come under the banner of unresistible love, if I were a mistress, would never persuade me they were in love: so coldly they apply fiery speeches, as men that had rather read lovers' writings . . . than that in truth they feel those passions, which easily (as I think) may be bewrayed by that same forcibleness or *energia* (as the Greeks call it)." *Defence of Poetry*, ed. J. A. Van Dorsten (Oxford: Oxford Univ. Press, 1966), pp. 69–70.

49. *The Book of Common Prayer 1559: The Elizabethan Prayer Book*, ed. John E. Booty (Charlottesville: Univ. of Virginia Press, 1976), p. 297. Further quotations are cited in the text. Booth's remarks on Ephesians 5 occur in connection with sonnet 36, pp. 192–195.

50. The reference in sonnet 134, though addressed to the mistress, still concerns the poet's male love: "So now I have confest that he is thine, / And I my selfe am morgag'd to thy will, / My selfe Ile forfeit, so that other mine, / Thou wilt restore to be my comfort still" (134.1–4). The allusion to "one flesh" in sonnet 135 ("Who ever hath her wish, thou hast thy Will") leaves St. Paul and spiritual concerns far behind.

51. Pierre Bourdieu, *Outline of a Theory of Practice*, trans. Richard Nice (Cambridge: Cambridge Univ. Press, 1977), pp. 72–95.

52. C. S. Lewis, *English Literature in the Sixteenth Century Excluding Drama* (Oxford: Clarendon Press, 1954), p. 505.

53. Barber and Wheeler, *The Whole Journey*, p. 195.

54. Pequigney, *Such Is My Love*, pp. 202–207.
55. Dubrow, *Captive Victors*, pp. 221–222.

1994—Margreta de Grazia. "The Scandal of Shakespeare's Sonnets," from *Shakespeare Survey*

Margreta de Grazia, a professor of English at the University of Pennsylvania, is an authority on the eighteenth-century editorial reception of Shakespeare and his works, as discussed in her book *Shakespeare Verbatim: The Reproduction of Authenticity and the 1790 Apparatus.* She is also the author of *Hamlet Without Hamlet* and co-editor of *The Cambridge Companion to Shakespeare* and *Subject and Object in Renaissance Culture.*

Of all the many defences against the scandal of Shakespeare's Sonnets— Platonism, for example, or the Renaissance ideal of friendship—John Benson's is undoubtedly the most radical. In order to cover up the fact that the first 126 of the Sonnets were written to a male, Benson in his 1640 *Poems: Written by Wil Shake-speare. Gent.* changed masculine pronouns to feminine and introduced titles which directed sonnets to the young man to a mistress. By these simple editorial interventions, he succeeded in converting a shameful homosexual love to an acceptable heterosexual one, a conversion reproduced in the numerous reprintings of the 1640 *Poems* up through the eighteenth century. The source for this account is Hyder E. Rollins's authoritative 1944 variorum *Sonnets,* the first edition to detail Benson's pronominal changes and titular insertions.[1] Subsequent editions have reproduced his conclusions, for example John Kerrigan's 1986 edition which faults Benson for inflicting on the Sonnets 'a series of unforgivable injuries', above all 'a single recurring revision: he emended the masculine pronouns used of the friend in 1 to 126 to "her", "hers", and "she"'.[2] With varying degrees of indignation and amusement, critical works on the Sonnets have repeated the charge.

The charge, however, is wrong. Benson did not attempt to convert a male beloved to a female. To begin with, the number of his alterations has been greatly exaggerated. Of the seventy-five titles Benson assigned to Shakespeare's sonnets, only three of them direct sonnets from the first group of the 1609 Quarto (sonnets 1–126) to a woman.[3] Furthermore, because none of the sonnets in question specifies the gender of the beloved, Benson had no reason to believe a male addressee was intended. As for the pronominal changes, Rollins himself within nine pages of his own commentary multiplies the number of sonnets 'with verbal changes designed to make the verses apply to a woman instead of a man' from '*some*' to '*many*'.[4] Rollins gives three examples as if there were countless others, but three is all there are and those three appear to have been made to avoid solecism rather than homoeroticism. In only one sonnet are pronouns altered, though even there not uniformly. In sonnet 101, masculine pronouns are emended to feminine in lines 9, 11, and 13 ('Because *she* needs no praise wilt thou be dumb?'; 'To make *her* much outlive a gilded tomb'; 'To make *her* seem, long hence, as *she* shows now'), but the masculine (or neutral) pronoun is retained in line 5 ('Truth needs no colour with *his* colour fix'd').[5] Benson apparently wished to avoid a possible confusion between Truth and the beloved by altering the gender of the latter. In sonnet 104, 'friend' is emended to the more conventional 'love' but again apparently out of formal rather than moral considerations: the 'fair love' of sonnet 104 is thereby made consistent with the twice repeated 'my love' of sonnet 105, the sonnet with which it is grouped (along with sonnet 106) to form a single poem entitled 'Constant Affection'. The only other alteration may also be stylistic: the emendation of sonnet 108's nonce 'boy' to the frequently repeated 'love' avoided the anomaly of a single sonnet addressed to a boy.[6]

Indeed the 1640 collection hardly seems concerned with covering up amatory poems to males. The very first fourteen lines printed in the 1640 *Poems* contain eleven male pronouns, more than any other sonnet, in celebrating an emphatically male beauty. If Benson had wished to censure homoerotic love, why did he not omit the notoriously titillating master-mistress sonnet (20)? Or emend the glamorizing sonnet 106 that praises the beloved—in blazon style, part by part— as the 'master' of beauty? Or the sexually loaded sonnet 110 that apologizes to a specifically male 'god in love' for promiscuity of a decidedly 'preposterous' cast?[7] The same question applies to the numerous sonnets in which references to a male beloved as 'my love', 'sweet love', 'lover', and 'rose' are retained.

It is not Shakespeare's text, then, that has been falsified by Benson but rather Benson's edition that has been falsified by the modern tradition.[8] The question is, why has so patent an error not been challenged before? Certainly it is not for scarcity of copies: while only twelve copies exist of the original 1609 Sonnets, there are that many of the 1640 *Poems* in the Folger Library alone.

I wish to propose that modern treatments of the Sonnets have displaced onto Benson a singularly modern dilemma: what to do with the inadmissible secret of Shakespeare's deviant sexuality?[9] Benson is described as having put an end to that dark secret in the most radical way imaginable, by altering the sex of the beloved and thereby converting an ignominious homosexual passion into a respectable (albeit still adulterous) heterosexual one. In attributing such an act and motive to Benson, modern criticism curiously assumes—indeed posits—the secret it then reviles Benson for concealing. Quite simply, Benson's alleged act of editorial suppression presupposes something in need of suppression: there *must* be something horrible at the heart of the sonnets—the first 126 of them—to compel such a dire editorial manoeuvre.

I have dwelled on Benson only parenthetically to set the factual record straight. My real interest is not in factual error but in the kinds of cultural imperatives that motivate such errors. I see Benson's error as a glaring instance of the need to bury a shameful secret deep within the Sonnets. The need was not Shakespeare's. It has been rather that of Shakespeare criticism which for the past two centuries has been repeating variants of the repression it obsessively ascribes to Benson. This repression has, as I will proceed to argue, produced the very scandal it would deny. At the same time, it has overlooked the scandal that *is* there, not deep within the text but right on its surface.

I

This has been the case from the time the Sonnets were first edited: by Edmond Malone in his 1780 edition.[10] Or, to be more precise, from the time the Sonnets were first *not* edited: by George Steevens who reprinted the 1609 Sonnets in a collection of early quartos in 1766 but refused to edit them for his 1793 edition of Shakespeare's complete works. While he could justify their publication as documents, he refused to honour them with an editorial apparatus, the trappings of a classic.[11] Though he maintained that it was their literary defects that disqualified them, his response to sonnet 20 points to something more visceral: 'It is impossible to read [it] without an equal mixture of disgust and indignation.'[12] Surely it is this kind of aversion that prompted his condemnation of Malone's decision to edit them: Malone's 'implements of criticism, like the ivory rake and golden spade in Prudentius, are on this occasion disgraced by the objects of their culture'. For Steevens, Malone's attempt to cultivate such soiled objects as the Sonnets defiled the tools of editing. It was Steevens then and not Benson who first attempted to conceal the scandal of Shakespeare's dirty sexuality, not by changing pronouns but by reproducing the Sonnets in the form of a dusty document rather than of a lofty classic.

Malone, by providing the Sonnets with a textual apparatus in 1780 and then by including them in the canon proper in his 1790 edition of Shakespeare's Plays and Poems achieved precisely what Steevens had dreaded: he elevated the Sonnets to the status of literature. But the filth that embarrassed Steevens remained—remained to be covered up. In fact, as we shall see, Malone's major editorial ambition in regard to the Sonnets—to establish the connection between the first person and Shakespeare[13]—made the cover-up all the more urgent: if the Sonnets were in Shakespeare's own voice, what was to be done with the fact that the majority of them expressed desire for a young male?

Malone's driving project of identifying the experience of the Sonnets with Shakespeare's own is evident in all his major editorial interventions. Unlike Benson who expanded their contents to accommodate the experience of all lovers by giving them generic titles, Malone limited them so that they applied exclusively to Shakespeare.[14] His first step was to restrict the Sonnets to two addressees by introducing a division after sonnet 126. With only two beloveds, the task of identifying particulars could begin. First the young man was identified on the assumption that he was the same as the dedication's Mr W.H. Other identifications followed suit: of persons, time, things, circumstances. The dedicator's T.T. was Thomas Thorpe, Spenser was the rival poet, the 'now' of the sonnets was early in Shakespeare's career, the gift referred to in 122 was a table-book given to Shakespeare by his friend, sonnet 111's 'publick means, which publick manners breeds', referred to Shakespeare's own lamentable ties to the theatre, the unfaithful lover of sonnet 93 was Shakespeare's own wife. All of these efforts to give particularity to the Sonnets contributed to Malone's project of personalizing them. His attempts to identify their abundant deictics, what Benveniste has called 'egocentric markers'—their hes and shes, thous and yous, this's and thats, heres and theres—fastened the Sonnets around Shakespeare's 'I'.[15] Thus the experience they recorded could be recognized as that which Shakespeare lived.

The identification proved, as might be anticipated, highly problematic, for there was one connection that could not be allowed: as Malone's own division emphasized, most of the sonnets were addressed to a male. At each of the three points where Malone insisted upon the division at 126, circumlocutions betrayed his unease: although he referred to the addressee of the second group as a 'lady' and 'female', the addressee of the first group was no man or male, but rather 'this person', the majority of the sonnets are '*not* addressed to a female'.[16] The unspeakable, that 126 sonnets were addressed to a *male*, remained literally unspoken; at the same time, the basic division according to the beloved's gender proclaimed it.

Within the text too, Malone had to dodge the implications of his own specification, indeed whenever any of the first 126 sonnets were explicitly erotic or amatory. Footnotes then must strain to distance Shakespeare from their content, as did the note to the notorious sonnet 20: 'such addresses to men, however indelicate, were customary in our author's time, and neither imported criminality, nor were esteemed indecorous' (p. 207). Even more belaboured was Malone's rationalization of Shakespeare's references to himself as the 'lover' of the male youth. Here, too, it is not Shakespeare who offends, but rather the custom of his age: and the customary offence was even then not at the level of conduct but at the level of speech. It was 'Such *addresses* to men', '*expressions* of this kind', as well as 'the general *tenour* of the greater part of them' that were 'common in Shakespeare's time, and . . . not thought indecorous' [my emphasis] (pp. 218–20). For Malone, nothing separated his present from Shakespeare's past more than the 'strange' custom among men of *speaking* of other men as their 'lovers'.[17] The offence was linguistic and literary and not behavioural; to censure the Sonnets would, therefore, be as 'unreasonable' as faulting the plays for violating Aristotle's *Poetics*—an anachronistic *literary* judgement (p. 207). Thus for Malone the greatest difference between his late eighteenth-century and Shakespeare's late sixteenth-century was that in Shakespeare's time, male/male desire was a manner of speaking and not doing, whereas in Malone's more enlightened time it was neither: not done, not even spoken of (hence his repeated euphemisms and circumlocutions).

There is another remarkable instance of how Malone embroils himself in his own editorial commitments. While wanting to read the Sonnets as personal poems, he must impersonalize what his edition foregrounds as their most salient feature: that most of them are addressed to a young male. His longest footnote stretching across six pages pertains to sonnet 93, 'So shall I live supposing thou art true', a sonnet on sexual jealousy. He fastened on this sonnet in full conviction that Shakespeare, in the Sonnets as well as in the plays, wrote with particular intensity on the subject of jealousy because he himself had experienced it; it was his 'intimate knowledge' of jealousy that enabled him to write on the subject 'more immediately *from the heart*' (p. 266). Malone avoids the scandal that Shakespeare experienced sexual jealousy for a boy by a 'Bensonian' changing of Shakespeare's *boy* to Shakespeare's *wife*, thereby violating his own ascription of the first 126 sonnets to a male, or rather 'not a female'. This weird displacement freed Malone to talk comfortably about Shakespeare's sexual experience—in heterosexual (Shakespeare as cuckold) rather than homosexual terms (Shakespeare as pederast). A digression on his wife's infidelity provided the additional benefit of justifying the adulterous liaison that the second group of sonnets recorded—Shakespeare was unfaithful to his wife because she had first been unfaithful to him. Realizing the danger of such inferences, Steevens (in the notes he contributed to Malone's edition) attempted to block it by insisting that the poem reflected not Shakespeare's *experience* but his *observation*, an impersonal rather than a personal relation (pp. 266–8). Malone stuck fast to his position, finding grounds for Shakespeare's experience of jealousy in documents, anecdotes, and the plays themselves.

James Boswell the younger, when he completed Malone's edition of *The Plays and Poems* in 1821, sided with Steevens, ruling Malone's conviction as 'uncomfortable conjecture'.[18] The judgement was unusual for Boswell, for throughout the twenty-one volume edition he rarely contradicted his friend and mentor. Yet his comments on the Sonnets opposed Malone with astonishing frequency. Indeed it would be fair to say that Boswell dismantled all of the connections Malone had worked so hard to forge between the Sonnets and Shakespeare's experience. The reason is clear: Boswell wanted to counteract the impression that Malone's 1780 edition, reissued in 1790, had produced: it is 'generally admitted that the poet speaks in his own person' (p. 219). Boswell, in the preliminary and concluding remarks with which he bracketed Malone's edition, as well as in scattered internal notes, attempted to stifle all autobiographical possibilities, beginning with Malone's opening identification of 'the individual to whom they were principally addressed, and the circumstances under which they were written'. The Sonnets could not have been addressed to any real nobleman for none, according to Boswell, would have tolerated such effeminizing verse. Any 'distinguished nobleman' would have taken offence at the encomiums on his beauty, and the fondling expressions' appropriate only to a 'cocker'd silken wanton' (p. 219). Thus such amorous language could not have been 'customary' between men in Shakespeare's time, as Malone had insisted, for it would have implied that men were effeminate. For Boswell, male desire for males could not have been an acceptable way of even speaking, even back then. For him, male/male desire existed nowhere (in England anyway), not in Shakespeare's past, not in his own present; not in language, not in deed. It was sheer make-believe: what Boswell terms, not unsalaciously, 'effusions of fancy . . . for the amusement of a private circle' (p. 220).

To establish their status as 'fancy', Boswell must sever all the connections Malone had forged between the Sonnets and Shakespeare's life. And so he does, one by one: Shakespeare was as young as thirty-four or at most forty-five when writing the sonnets so how could it be he who is represented as old and decrepit in several sonnets? Of course, it is not the association with old age (or with the theatre) that disturbed Boswell, but the logical extension of *any* connection: 'If Shakespeare was speaking of himself in this passage, it would follow that he is equally pointed at upon other occasions' (p. 220). More specifically, if it was Shakespeare who was old then it was also he who was 'grossly and notoriously profligate', the perpetrator of "'harmful deeds'", whose "'name had received a brand'", and whose reputation suffered from the "'impression which vulgar scandal stamped upon his brow'". Such identifications were, Boswell insisted, absurd, for among the extant biographical materials 'not the slightest imputation [was] cast upon his character'. This is not surprising, for Malone and Boswell in their *New Life of Shakspeare* had rejected as factually inaccurate the numerous scandalous anecdotes that had cast him in the shady roles of poacher, adulterer, and carouser.[19]

If Boswell found any fault at all in Shakespeare, it was for his 'selection of topics', his representation in any form of male/male desire. But Boswell legitimized this choice by attributing it to Shakespeare's altogether admirable 'fondness for classical imitation' (p. 221). Boswell now is at last able to name the unspeakable topic, though only in simultaneously disavowing it: and not in his own words, but in words properly removed from his own by quotation marks and from standard English by sixteenth-century old spelling. The quotation is from Webbe's *Discourse of English Poetrie* that defends Virgil's second eclogue by insisting that the poet 'doth not meane . . . any disordered loue, or the filthy lust of deuillish Pederastice' (p. 221).[20] Boswell keeps a clean distance from the 'filthy' object as if afraid of dirtying his ivory rake and golden spade. Having dismantled all of Malone's connections, Boswell can conclude with a discussion of the Sonnets' literary merits, the only relevant consideration after they have been wrenched from toxic reality and consigned to innocuous fancy.

I have discussed the Malone (1780, 1790) and the Malone/Boswell (1821) editions because it is with them that the modern history of the Sonnets begins, and since no full edition of the 1609 Quarto was printed prior to Malone's, that belated history can be considered their *only* history.[21] They have the further importance of having established the two critical approaches that have repeated themselves for two centuries now—sometimes ingeniously, sometimes hysterically: (1) Malone's—the Sonnets are about Shakespeare but not as a lover of young men or, (2) Boswell's—the Sonnets are not about Shakespeare or anything else, especially not about Shakespeare as a lover of young men. Though these approaches are antithetical and mutually exclusive, it must be stressed that both are motivated by the same urgency to deny Shakespeare's desire for a male.

In this regard the history of the Sonnets' reception provides a stunning example of the phenomenon Jonathan Dollimore has recently identified: the centrality of homosexuality in a culture that denounces it.[22] The denial of homosexuality in the Sonnets has produced the two polarized approaches by which they have been traditionally read for two centuries. Furthermore, what has been denied (by evasions, displacements, circumlocutions, suppressions, abstractions, etc.) has slipped into the text itself producing (as if from the Sonnets themselves) an hermeneutical interior capable of concealing a sin, a crime, a pathology. The unspeakable of Sonnets criticism has thus become the unspoken of the Sonnets—to the exclusion of, as has yet to be seen, what they quite forthrightly say.

II

I now wish to turn to one of Malone's major editorial acts, his division of the sonnets into two gendered groups, 126 to a young man, the remaining twenty-eight to a woman. The division has been generally accepted. It seems, after all, quite obvious: none of the first 126 sonnets are addressed explicitly to a woman and none of the remaining twenty-eight are addressed explicitly to a male. *Explicitly* is the key word, for what Malone's clear-cut division has obscured is the astonishing number of sonnets that do *not* make the gender of the addressee explicit.[23] Shakespeare is exceptional among the English sonneteers (Sidney, Spenser, and Daniel, for example) in leaving the beloved's gender unspecified in so many of the sonnets: about five-sixths of them in the first 126 and just less than that in the collection entire. The uncertainty of the beloved's gender is sustained by other types of ambiguity, most notoriously in the 'master-mistress' sonnet 20, but also in sonnet 53 in which the youth is described as a paragon of both masculine and feminine beauty, of both Adonis and Helen; similarly, a variety of epithets recur that apply to either sex: rose, friend, love, lover, sweet, fair.

The little evidence we have of how the Sonnets were read before Malone strongly suggests that the first 126 sonnets were not read as being exclusively to a male. Benson assumed that the sonnets were to a female unless otherwise specified, as the titles he assigned to his groupings indicate.[24] So too did the numerous eighteenth-century editors who reprinted Benson: Gildon (1723) referred to them as 'being most to his Mistress' and Sewell (1725) believed them to have been inspired by 'a real, or an imaginary Lady'.[25] Independent of Benson, there is further and earlier evidence. Gary Taylor has discussed five manuscript versions of sonnet 2 from the early decades of the seventeenth century with the title 'To one that would die a maid';[26] there is also a 1711 reprint of the 1609 quarto that describes the collection as '154 Sonnets all of them in Praise of his Mistress.'[27] The eighteenth-century antiquarian William Oldys who possessed a copy of the quarto assumed that some of the first 126 sonnets were addressed to a female, and George Steevens defended his logic: 'From the complaints of *inconstancy*, and the praises of *beauty*, contained in them, [the Sonnets] should seem at first sight to be addressed by an inamorato to a mistress'.[28] Malone's preliminary note announcing the division at 126 literally prevented such a 'first sight', precluding the possibility open to earlier readers of assuming the ungendered sonnets to a female.

This is not, however, to say that Malone got it wrong: clearly no sonnets are addressed to a female in the first 126 and none to a male (except Cupid) in the subsequent twenty-eight. Just as clearly, the poet abandons the young man in 126 and declares his allegiance to a mistress in 127 and the formal irregularities (twelve pentameter lines in couplets) may punctuate that shift.[29] Nor is there any reason not to take 144's announcement—'Two loves I have': 'a man right fair' and 'a woman, colour'd ill'—at face value. Some kind of binary division appears to be at work.[30] The question is whether that division is best described in terms—or *only* in terms—of gender difference: in terms, that is, of the object choices that have lent themselves so readily to the modern distinction between homosexuality and heterosexuality.[31]

For that construction of desire—as Foucault's expansive history of sexuality as well as Alan Bray's concentration on the Renaissance have demonstrated[32]— depended on a construal of the body and of the psyche that postdated Shakespeare, like Malone's edition itself, by about two centuries. It may then be that Malone's overly emphatic division of the Sonnets into male/female appears more in keeping with the cultural preoccupations at the turn of the eighteenth century than of the sixteenth. It may be symptomatic of a much later emphasis on sexual differentiation, one that has been fully charted out recently in Thomas Laqueur's *Making Sex: Body and Gender from the Greeks to Freud*.[33]

According to Laqueur, 'Sometime in the eighteenth century, sex as we know it was invented.'[34] What he means by this bold pronouncement is that until then there was essentially one sex rather than two. According to the classical or Galenic model, the female possessed an inverted, interior, and inferior version of male genitalia; as countless anatomical drawings attest, the uterus was imagined as an inverted scrotum, the vagina an inverted penis, the vulva an inverted foreskin. Reproductive processes as well as parts were also on par, so that conception required orgasm from both male and female. Not until the eighteenth century were male and female typically divided into two discrete sexes with distinct reproductive parts and processes: hence the invention of 'sex as we know it'. The shift is reflected in an array of verbal and graphic representations: the construction of a different skeleton for women than for men; anatomical drawings representing incommensurate reproductive structures rather than homologous ones; the division of formerly shared nomenclature into male and female so that once ungendered sperm, testicles, and stones are gendered male and differentiated from female eggs and ovaries. In short, a reproductive biology was constructed based on *absolute* rather than *relative* difference. It is only then, Laqueur notes, that the expression 'opposites attract' is coined, suggesting that 'natural' sexual attraction is between unlikes rather than likes.[35]

As Laqueur points out, this reconstrual removed sexuality from a vast system of metaphysical correspondences based, like society itself, on hierarchical order and situated it firmly in the body or 'nature'. That a woman was previously imagined to possess less perfected versions of male genitalia legitimized her subordination to man. Biology thus upheld social hierarchy. Once difference was grounded in the body rather than in metaphysics, once male and female anatomy was perceived as incommensurate rather than homologous, then sexuality lost its 'social' bearings and became instead a matter of 'nature'. As Laqueur insists repeatedly, and as his characterization of the shift as an *invention* rather than as a *discovery* suggests, the change represents no empirical or scientific advance—'No discovery or group of discoveries dictated the rise of the two-sex model'[36]—but rather a cultural and political reorientation. Malone's division of the Sonnets may best be understood in the context of this reorientation.

There is another shift that strangely corresponds to both Malone's twofold division and biology's two-sex model, and it occurs at roughly the same point in time. In eighteenth-century grammars and discussions of grammar, a new attention to linguistic gender binaries appears. The hierarchy preserved in the one-sex model had also applied in questions of grammatical agreement: male gender prevailed over female because it was the 'more worthy' gender. In his popular rhetoric (1553), Thomas Wilson considered natural order violated when women preceded men in a syntactic construction, since man was clearly the dominant gender. In his official Latin Grammar (1567), William Lyly assumed the same principle in explaining that an adjective describing both a male and female noun must agree with the male ('Rex et Regina Beati') because 'The masculine gender is more worthy than the feminine.'[37] In the eighteenth century, however, this ontological and grammatical hierarchy has ceased to be self-evident. And the reason appears to be that grammar now looks to biology rather than to metaphysics for its lead. New discoveries in biology are brought to bear on grammar, so that it is maintained that the discovery that plants have sexes introduced inconsistency into classical grammar's classification of plants as neuter.[38] In highly gendered languages like German, a general rethinking of conventional grammatical gender occurs. In English that possesses no conventional grammatical gendering, the problem took a more focused form. Towards the end of the eighteenth century, the first call for an epicene or gender-neutral pronoun is heard, in response to what is only then perceived as a problem: what to do with constructions like '*everyone* should go to *his* place' where a female and male antecedent is represented by the male 'his'.[39] As in biology, grammar can no longer assume an hierarchical relation between male and female to justify the predominance of male gender.

It is not only in relation to the third person that hierarchy disappears; in English, it had also by the start of the eighteenth century disappeared from the second person. In standard English, *thee/thou* had been dropped in favour of *you*, collapsing the complexly nuanced range of distinctions based on class relations. It is curious that Malone, who took great pride in noting philological difference in Shakespeare's age, ignored the second person pronoun while focusing on the third. Several recent critics, however, have discussed it, noting that the first 126 sonnets vacillate between *you* and *thou*, while the second twenty-eight consistently stick to *thou*.[40] Their explanations have been varied, contradictory and incomplete; the highly complex code remains unbroken. What can be ventured, however, is that the unwritten rules governing second person usage in the Renaissance were social and hierarchic.[41] They originated in social rank, though clearly complicated by a calculus of differentials that included age, gender, education, experience, race, ethical worth, emotional stake, etc.[42]

This is not to propose a new division, the first 126 to 'you/thou' the next twenty-eight to 'thou'[43]—but rather to suggest that gender difference is not the *only* way to differentiate the Sonnets' 'Two loves'. There are other forms of otherness that the Malonean or modern tradition has ignored. Sexual difference is only one differential category in these poems, class is another, so is age, reputation, marital status, moral probity, even physical availability. In each of these categories, the poet is more like the mistress than like the youth; love of like would, therefore, incline him more to the mistress than the boy. It is because Joel Fineman's awesome *Shakespeare's Perjured Eye: The Invention of Poetic Subjectivity in the Sonnets* limits difference to sexual difference that its argument is so troubling. For more relentlessly and consequentially than any one since Malone, Fineman has emphasized the distinction between male and female; indeed, it is fundamental to his Lacanian account of the constitution of subjectivity. The rupturing transition required by this account occurs, for Fineman, in the move from homosexual love of the same to heterosexual love of the other, from the ideal specularity of the youth to the false linguistics of the mistress, a move that readily translates into the Lacanian break from the imaginary into the symbolic. In short, Fineman bases what may be the vastest claim ever made for the Sonnets—that they invent poetic subjectivity for the western tradition—on sexual difference, on that rupturing but constitutive transition from a like and admired object to an unlike and loathed one.[44] Yet in light of the biological and grammatical phenomena we have been attending, Fineman's construal of sexual difference is premature. The 'Invention of Poetic Subjectivity' he attributes to Shakespeare must await 'the invention of sex' Laqueur sees as an eighteenth-century phenomenon. Until male and female can be seen as two discrete sexes rather than variants on one sex, how can subjectivity be constituted in the break between the two?

It is because Fineman overstresses the gender division at sonnet 126 that his study might be seen as the culmination of the Malonean tradition. Focus on male/female difference lends itself too readily to a psychosexuality that excludes the psychosocial. If social distinctions like class or even age were introduced, for example, the entire Lacanian progression would be turned on its head, for the poet would experience the youth's aristocratic otherness *before* the mistress's bourgeois sameness, his extreme junior *before* his approximate peer. How, then, would it be possible to make the transition Lacanian subjectivity requires from imaginary identification to symbolic dislocation? I've put the burden of two centuries of criticism on Fineman's massively difficult book in order to make a very simple point: tradition has postulated (and concealed) in the Sonnets a sexual scandal that is based in the personal abstracted from the social, on a biology of two-sexes rather than on an epistemology of one-sex, on a division according to a gendered third person rather than a ranked second person. As I will show in the remainder of this paper by turning—at long last—to the Sonnets themselves, this has been a mistake . . . so *big* a mistake that the real scandal has been passed over.

III

The ideological force of the imperious first line of the Sonnets has gone virtually unnoticed: 'From fairest creatures we desire increase.'[45] In the first seventeen poems which have traditionally (and rather preciously) been titled the procreation sonnets, there can be no pretence of *fair* being either an abstract value like the Platonic Good or a disinterested one like the Kantian Beautiful. *Fair* is the distinguishing attribute of the dominant class, not unlike Bourdieu's *taste* that serves both to distinguish the dominant class and, by distinguishing it, to keep it dominant.[46] The first seventeen sonnets urging the fair youth to marry and beget a son have an open and explicit social function: to reproduce, like an Althusserian state apparatus, the *status quo* by reproducing a fair young man, ideally 'ten for one' (6). The preservation of the youth preserves his aristocratic family line, dynasty or 'house': 'Who lets so faire a house fall to decay?' (13). If such houses are allowed to deteriorate, the social formation would itself be at risk: hence the general (and conservative) desire to increase 'fairest creatures' and to convince those privileged creatures that the repair of their 'beautious roofe' should be their 'chiefe desire' (10). Were these houses and roofs unfair, there would be no cultural imperative to maintain them, just as there is none to reproduce *un*fair (homely) persons: 'Let those whom nature hath not made for store, / Harsh featurelesse, and rude, barrenly perish' (ii); while the youth is 'much too faire, / To be deaths conquest and make wormes thine heire' (6), the 'Harsh, featureless, and rude' can return to dust unlamented. 'Increase' is to be desired only from those whom Nature has 'best indow'd' with 'bountious guift' (ii); and those gifts are not simply physical or spiritual riches but the social and material ones that structure society from the top. For this reason, it is only the fair lineaments of fair lineages that should be reproduced for posterity—'Thou shouldst print more, not let that coppy die.'

Underscoring the social concerns of this first group is their origin in pedagogical materials designed to cultivate fair young men. As has long been noted, these sonnets derive from Erasmus' 'Epistle to persuade a young gentleman to marriage', Englished in Thomas Wilson's widely influential 1553 *The Arte of Rhetorique*.[47] The treatise was used in schools as a rhetorical exercise in persuasion. Languet repeated it in a letter to the young Sidney and Sidney in turn echoed it in his *Arcadia*, that consummate expression of aristocratic ethos. The treatise's tropes and arguments attained commonplace status, as is suggested by the seventeenth-century popularity of the sonnet that deploys the most of them, sonnet 2, copies of which survive in twelve early manuscripts.[48] It seems likely, then, that these opening sonnets would have evoked the pedagogical context which prepared fair young men to assume the social position to which high birth entitled them. The 'private friends' among whom according to Francis Meres these sonnets circulated as well as the patron to whom the collection is ostensibly dedicated can be assumed to have recognized this rhetoric as a blueprint for reproducing the fair values of the dominant class.[49]

Shakespeare's 'Two loves' relate to this opening set piece quite explicitly: after sonnet 17, it is through his own poetic *lines* rather than the youth's generational *loins* that fair's lineaments are to be reproduced, fair's lineage extended.[50] The fair line ends, however, at 127 with the shocking declaration that 'now is blacke beauties successive heire'. As if a black child had been born of a fair parent, a miscegenating successor is announced, one who razes fair's lineage ('And Beautie slandered with a bastard shame') and seizes fair's language ('beauty hath no name')—genealogy and etymology. Desire inverts its object at this breaking point: from an embodiment of a social ideal to an embodiment of a social atrocity. In praising the youth's fair lineaments, social distinction had been maintained; in praising the mistress's dark colours, social distinction is confounded. This reverses the modern ranking of the 'Two loves' that has found one unspeakable and the other simply regrettable. For the love of the youth 'right fair' which tradition has deemed scandalous promotes a social programme while the love for the mistress 'collour'd ill' which tradition has allowed threatens to annihilate it.

This is a sign, I think, that there is something misleading about the male/female categories by which Malone divided the collection: they too easily slip into the post-Enlightenment categories of homosexual and heterosexual which provoke responses that are precisely the inverse of what the Sonnets themselves call for. I would like to propose instead that the two groups be reconsidered under rubrics available in the period, appearing in E. K.'s note to the *Shepherdes Calendar* defending Hobbinol's passion for young Colin Clout on the grounds that 'paederastice [is] much to be preferred before *gyne*rastice, that is the love that inflameth men with lust toward womankind'.[51] Unlike homosexual and heterosexual, the terms better correspond with Shakespeare's 'better' and 'worser' loves, his pederastic love of a boy ('my lovely Boy', 126) and gynerastic love of a womb (the irresistible 'waste of shame', 129).[52] As E. K. specifies, pederastic love is 'much to be preferred' over gynerastic, and the Sonnets demonstrate why: because it does not imperil social distinction.

Indeed the poet's main task in the first group is to protect those distinctions, a task that takes the specific form of preserving the youth's lineaments from Time's disfigurations. Shakespeare's 'pupill pen' is in contest with 'Times pensel' (16). In his own verse lines, he would transcribe the youth's fair features before 'confounding Age' unfairs them by cross-hatching his physiognomic lineaments with 'lines and wrincles' (63), cancelling or deleting the youth's fair copy, rendering him thereby 'featurelesse' like those consigned to perish barrenly—as if to make him indistinguishable from the 'Harsh' and 'rude'. In the gynerastic group, however, it is not Time but Lust that threatens distinction. Lust mars not through the sharp incisions of Time's stylus—its pen-knife—but through the obscuring adulterations of 'a woman colour'd ill'. While Time's deadly scriptings disfigure what is seen, Lust's murky adulterations confound what is known. Once a black mistress preempts the fair youth, a whole range of epistemological distinctions collapse: between black and fair (131, 132) to be sure, but also between truth and lies (138); private and public (137); first person and second, first person and third (135–6); past, present, and future (129); is and is not (147), worst and best (150), angel and friend (144). In the first group, though aging himself ('Bested and chopt with tand antiquitie' [62]), the poet sets himself up as Time's adversary, his own glamourizing lines counteracting Time's disfiguring marks; in the second group, however, Lust and Will are familiars rather than adversaries, so much so that Will is literally synonymous with Lust in 135 and 136, and Lust personified blurs into Will's person in 129. Pederasty's 'Pupil Pen' reinscribes the pedagogical ideal with which the Sonnets begin; while the gynerastic 'waste of shame' adulterates even the most black and white distinctions.

This is not to say that love of the youth is altogether 'of comfort'. The majority of the sonnets to him register intense longing, humiliation, loss felt and anticipated, betrayal, and even worse, self-betrayal—all the result, perhaps, of a cultural overinvestment in 'fairest creatures'. Yet the cost is nothing in comparison with what gynerasty exacts.[53] As the promiscuous womb threatens social order, so too gynerasty threatens psychic stability. Will himself takes on the hysterical attributes of the womb that obsesses him, in the breathlessly frantic copulatives of 129, in the semantic confusions listed above which in sonnet 147 he calls 'mad mans' discourse. There could be no more shocking manifestation of his hysteria than sonnet 136 in which every word could be said to signal his desire, homonymically or synonymically.[54] This maniacal repetition is audible in '*Will*, will fulfill the treasure of thy loue, / I fill it full with wils, and my will one', but it is present in all the sonnet's phonetic variables as well, reducing their signification to the tautological deadlock of 'Will wills will'. Nor is Will ever released from this uterine obsession; like all men in sonnet 129, he does not know how to avoid the sulphuric pit (144), how 'To shun the heauen that leads men to this hell' (129); hence the fatal return in the final two Anacreontics to his mistress's genital 'eye', her inflammatory and unquenchable 'Well'.[55]

But the real horror of gynerasty is social and general rather than personal and particular. Edgar in *Lear* contemns Goneril's royal womb adulterated by the bastard Edmund as 'indinguish'd [*sic*] space of Womans will'.[56] It is precisely this failure of discrimination that characterizes the dark lady's sexual capacity, as is evidenced by her indiscrete admission of Wills. In these sonnets it is not only common names that lose distinction, but also proper. Men named Will are indistinguishable: Will Shakespeare would be among them, and perhaps Will of the dedication's Mr W.H., and perhaps the mistress's husband is also Will, but what difference does it make when Will like *Homo* (like 'sausie lackes' too) is a common name to all?[57] Repeatedly in these sonnets the indiscriminate womb is contrasted with that exclusive treasured 'place' or 'viall' (6) in which the youth's purely aristocratic seed would be antiseptically distilled or 'pent in walls of glasse' (5). The 'large and spacious' place that is the focus of desire in the second group is no such discerning 'seuerall plot': it is 'the wide worlds common place' (137) and primarily an incontinently liquid one—'the baye where all men ride' (137) and 'sea all water, [that] yet receiues raine still' (135)—in which all distinctions of blood bleed into one another.

As the law itself under Elizabeth confirmed by more severely prosecuting fornication between men and women than between men, nothing threatens a patriarchal and hierarchic social formation more than a promiscuous womb. By commingling blood-lines, it has the potential to destroy the social fabric itself. The gynecrasty of the Sonnets, then, needs to be considered in terms of the range of sexual practices Alan Bray has foregrounded (among them, bestiality, adultery, rape, and prostitution) that were in the period termed 'sodomy' and associated with such crimes against the state as sorcery, heresy, and treason.[58] There is good reason, therefore, to credit Jonathan Goldberg's recent suggestion that in Renaissance terms, it is Shakespeare's sonnets to the dark lady rather than those to the young man that are sodomitic.[59]

The dark lady's indiscriminate womb images social anarchy no less than Lear's invocation of cosmic cataclysm: 'all germains spill at once'.[60] The germains spill serially in the mistress rather than all at once', but with the same helter-skelter randomness, *including those of the fair youth*, so that his noble seed is intermixed with that of common 'sausie lackes' (128) and of unnumbered intercoursing 'Wills'.[61] The patriarchal dream of producing fair young men turns into the patriarchal nightmare of a social melting pot, made all the more horrific by the fact that the mistress's *black* is the antithesis not just of fair but of *white*. Tradition has been ever slower to entertain the possibility that these poems express desire for a black woman rather than desire for a boy. But the important work that is being done on England's contact with Africa and on its cultural representations of that contact is making it increasingly difficult to dissociate in this period blackness from racial blackness—black from blackamoor—promiscuity from miscegenation, especially in a work that begins by arguing for the perpetuation of pure fair blood.[62]

This paper began with one traditional error and ends with another. The first was minor, an erroneous representation of Benson's publishing efforts. The last, however, is quite major. The scandal in the Sonnets had been misidentified. It is not Shakespeare's desire for a boy; for in upholding social distinctions, that desire proves quite conservative and safe. It is Shakespeare's gynerastic longings for a black mistress that are perverse and menacing, precisely because they threaten to raze the very distinctions his poems to the fair boy strain to preserve. As with the Benson falsification, it is the motive behind the error that is worth thinking about. And I will end by doing so.

Since the eighteenth century, sexuality has been seen in biological and psychological terms rather than social.[63] Perversion, therefore, is seen as pathological rather than subversive. But in a period in which the distribution of power and property depended on orderly sexuality, it remained imperative that sexuality be understood and judged in social terms. The social consequences of sexual arrangements (whether male–female marriages or male–male alliances) and derangements (male–female adultery or male–male sodomy) was too basic to allow them to become merely personal matters—to become, that is, what they have become in modern sexual discourse: the precondition of personal identity. Modern readings of the Sonnets (the only kind we have) have skewed the relation of Shakespeare's 'Two loves' to conform with this classification. The result is quite topsy-turvy: readings of the young man sonnets have concealed a personal scandal that was never there; and readings of dark mistress sonnets have been blank to the shocking social peril they promulgate. A category mistake lies at the bottom of this odd hermeneutic: the Sonnets' 'Two loves' have been misclassified, the 'love of comfort' avoided as abnormal and unnatural and the 'love of despaire' countenanced as normal and natural. This essay has argued that a reclassification is in order according to a different system altogether, one that would replace the personal categories of normalcy and abnormalcy with the social ones of hierarchy and anarchy—of desired generation and abhorred miscegenation.

NOTES

1. *A New Variorum Edition of Shakespeare: The Sonnets*, 2 vols. (Philadelphia, Pa. and London, 1944), vol. 2, p. 20, n. 1. Sidney Lee in his introduction to a 1905 facsimile of the Sonnets noted Benson's changes but without itemizing them or speculating on Benson's motives: *Shakespeare's Sonnets: Being a Reproduction in Facsimile of the First Edition* (Oxford, 1905), pp. 57–8.

2. *The Sonnets and A Lover's Complaint* (Middlesex and New York, 1986), p. 46.

3. Benson gives the title 'Selfe flattery of her beautie' to sonnets 113–15, 'Upon receit of a Table Booke from his Mistris' to sonnet 122, 'An intreatie for her acceptance' to sonnet 125. See Rollins, vol. 2, pp. 20–1 for a list of Benson's titles.

4. Cf. Rollins, pp. 20 and 29.

5. Benson (London, 1640).

6. The only other sonnet referring to the beloved as 'boy' (sonnet 126, 'O thou my lovely boy') was with seven others dropped from the 1640 collection, perhaps by accident.

7. See Stephen Booth's gloss to sonnet 110, lines 9–12, pp. 356–7 as well as to sonnet 109, lines 9, 10, 13, 14, pp. 352–3 in *Shakespeare's Sonnets* (New Haven, Conn. and London, 1977).

8. For accounts of how Benson's printing-house and editorial practices have also been maligned, see Josephine Waters Bennett, 'Benson's Alleged Piracy of *Shakespeares Sonnets* and of Some of Jonson's Works', *Studies in Bibliography*, 21 (1968), pp. 235–48. See also Margreta de Grazia, *Shakespeare Verbatim: The Reproduction of Authenticity and the 1790 Apparatus* (Oxford, 1991), p. 49, n. 1, pp. 163–73.

9. On the hysterical response to this problem in modern readings of the Sonnets, see Peter Stallybrass, 'Editing as Cultural Formation: The Sexing of Shakespeare's Sonnets', *Modern Language Quarterly*, 54, (March, 1993), 91–103.

10. *Supplement to the Edition of Shakespeare's Plays Published in 1778 by Samuel Johnson and George Steevens*, 2 vols. (1780), vol. 2.

11. *Twenty of the Plays of Shakespeare*, 4 vols., ed. George Steevens (1766).

12. Quoted by Rollins, vol. 1, p. 55.

13. See de Grazia, p. 154.

14. See de Grazia, pp. 155–6.

15. For the profusion of deictics in the Sonnets, see Joel Fineman, *Shakespeare's Perjured Eye: The Invention of Poetic Subjectivity in the Sonnets* (Berkeley, Los Angeles, London, 1986), pp. 8–9, p. 311, n. 6.

16. *The Plays and Poems of William Shakespeare*, 10 vols. (1790; facs. rpt, New York, 1968), vol. 10, pp. 191, 265, 294. Subsequent references to this volume will appear in text.

17. On 'lover', see Booth, p. 432.

18. *The Plays and Poems of William Shakespeare* (1821; facs. rpt, New York, 1966), vol. 20, p. 309. Page references to this volume will henceforth appear parenthetically in text.

19. For Malone's invalidation of the inculpatory anecdotes, see de Grazia, pp. 104–7, pp. 135–41.

20. Boswell corrects Webbe for referring to the eclogue as the sixth ('by a slip of memory, or the printer's mistake') when it should be the fourth (p. 221). Bruce R. Smith situates this eclogue in Renaissance pastoral in 'The Passionate Shepherd', *Homosexual Desire in Shakespeare's England: A Cultural Poetics* (Chicago and London, 1991), pp. 79–115.

21. The 1609 Sonnets were reprinted but without an apparatus by Bernard Lintott in 1711 and by George Steevens in 1766.

22. *Sexual Dissidence: Augustine to Wilde, Freud to Foucault* (Oxford, 1991).

23. See Booth's scrupulous account of the division, p. 430.

24. Rollins aligns the 1640 titles with the 1609 sonnet numbers, vol. 2, pp. 21–2.

25. See de Grazia, p. 155, n. 57.

26. 'Some Manuscripts of Shakespeare's Sonnets', *Bulletin of The John Rylands University Library*, 68, 1 (1985), 217.

27. Bernard Lintott, *A Collection of poems in Two Volumes . . . Being all the Miscellanies of Mr William Shakespeare, which were Publish'd by himself in the Year* 1609 . . . , 2 vols.

28. Malone and Boswell, p. 306.

29. In the 1609 quarto, the irregularity is rendered typographically conspicuous by two sets of empty brackets in place of the final couplet.

30. On the possibility that the Sonnets were organized according to a tripartite structure (152 Sonnets, 2 Anacreontics, a Complaint) based on generic rather than gender difference following the model of Daniel, Spenser, Lodge, and others, see John Kerrigan's Introduction to *Sonnets*, pp. 13–14 and the bibliographic references on p. 66.

31. On the taxonomy of 'homo' and 'hetero', see Eve Kosofsky Sedgwick, *The Epistemology of the Closet* (Berkeley and Los Angeles, 1990).

32. Michel Foucault, *The History of Sexuality*, vol. 1: *An Introduction*, trans., Robert Hurley (New York, 1978) and Alan Bray, *Homosexuality in Renaissance England* (London, 1982).

33. (Cambridge, Mass. and London, 1960).

34. P. 149. Laqueur notes the agreement of Michel Foucault, Lawrence Stone, and Ivan Illich in identifying the late eighteenth century as the point at which human sexuality was reconceptualized, p. 5 and n. 14.

35. P. 152.

36. P. 153.

37. *A Short Introduction of Grammar* (London, 1530), p. 47.

38. See Dennis Barron, *Grammar and Gender* (New Haven, Conn., 1986) p. 35.

39. Ibid. pp. 190–1.

40. See G. P. Jones, 'You, Thou, He or She? The Master-Mistress in Shakespearian and Elizabethan Sonnet Sequences', *Cahiers Elisabéthains* 19 (1981), 73–84, and Andrew Gurr, 'You and Thou in Shakespeare's Sonnets', *Essays in Criticism*, 32 (1982), 9–25. Arthur F. Marotti is sensitive to the tonal effects of such positionalities in his discussion of how Shakespeare's artistry can compensate for his inferior social rank, in 'Love is not Love: Elizabethan Sonnet Sequences and The Social Order', *English Literary History*, 49 (1982), 413–16.

41. On the origins of the distinction between *tu/vos* in Latin and thou/you in English, see R. Brown and A. Gilman, 'The Pronouns of Power and Solidarity', in T. A. Sebeok, ed., *Style in Language* (Amherst, Mass., 1960), pp. 253–76.

42. The same perplexing instability of address characterizes another male/male couple divided by rank, not to mention age, experience, and size: Falstaff and Hal, who shift constantly from one form to the other as they uneasily jockey for position in a relationship characterized by jockeying, a relationship in which male/male erotic desire is, as Jonathan Goldberg has recently argued, not entirely absent, 'Hal's Desire, Shakespeare's Idaho', forthcoming in *Henry IV*, ed. Nigel Wood (Open University). I wish to thank him for letting me read the typescript.

43. Sonnet 145 is the sole exception which substitutes 'you' for 'thou', in the interest of preserving rhyme: 'I hate, from hate away she threw, / And sau'd my life saying not you'.

44. The book's overinvestment in gender binaries raises troubling political and hermeneutic questions. Its argument that subjectivity is attained through the renunciation of the imaginary realm of homosexual sameness bears a disturbing resemblance to a pseudo-Freudianism that perceives homosexuality as stunted or incomplete development. It also requires that sonnets 1–126 be read as univocal and 127–52 as equivocal, though Fineman later revises this programme by maintaining that equivocation is present in both groups, though only latently in the first.

45. The Sonnets will henceforth be quoted from the facsimile of the 1609 *Shake-speares Sonnets* printed in Stephen Booth's edition. Lars Engle has recently discussed this first line as inaugurating the Sonnets' concern with 'human value in time', but without noting the specific class inflection of this value, 'Afloat in Thick Deeps: Shakespeare's Sonnets on Certainty', *Publications of the Modern Language Association*, 104 (1989), 832–43.

46. Pierre Bourdieu, *Distinction: A Social Critique of the Judgement of Taste*, trans. Richard Nice (Cambridge, Mass., 1984).

47. For the influence of this epistle on Shakespeare and others, see Rollins, *Variorum* 1, p. 7 and 11, p. 192, T. W. Baldwin, *The Literary Genetics of Shakespeare's Poems and Sonnets* (Urbana, Ill., 1950), pp. 183–5, and Katharine M. Wilson, *Shakespeare's Sugared Sonnets* (London and N.Y., 1974), pp. 147.

48. See Taylor, pp. 210–46.

49. This is not to say that the Sonnets unequivocally reproduce aristocratic value. As Thomas M. Greene points out, the thrift and husbandry urged upon the young man in the first seventeen sonnets is decidedly bourgeois ('Pitiful Thrivers:

Failed Husbandry in the Sonnets', *Shakespeare and the Question of Theory*, ed. Patricia Parker and Geoffrey Hartman (N.Y. and London, 1985, pp. 230–44.) Furthermore, the socially inferior poet (sonnets 25 and 110) by taking on the youth's responsibility for reproducing fair in effect assumes aristocracy's genetic privilege: his inky poetic lines preempt the youth's fair genealogical ones: 'His beautie shall in these blacke lines be seene' (63).

50. For the semantic and homonymic connections between lines and lineaments, see William Empson, *Seven Types of Ambiguity* (New York, 1947), pp. 54–5, cited by Booth, p. xiii. For the line/loin resonances, see Additional Notes to Booth's 1978 edition, p. 579.

51. Kerrigan brings E. K.'s gloss to bear on the Sonnets to conclude that the Sonnets register a 'profound homosexual attachment of a scarcely sensual, almost unrealized kind', p. 51; Stephen Orgel comments briefly on the psychological and legal advantages of 'paederastice' over 'gynerastice' in 'The Boys in the Back Room: Shakespeare's Apprentices and the Economics of Theater', unpublished manuscript. See also Smith's discussion of the quote in relation to Virgil and Spenser, pp. 95–8.

52. On the identification of woman with womb, see Richard Verstegan: 'And as Homo in Latin cloth signifie both man and woman, so in our toung the feminyne creature also hath as we see the same of man, but more aptly in that it is for due distinction composed with womb, *she being that kynde of mann that is wombed*, or hath the womb of conception, which the man of the male kynd hath not', *The Restitution of Decayed Intelligence* (Antwerp, 1605), p. 194.

53. Stephen Orgel, in commenting on the 'all but axiomatic' love of men for boys in the period, refers to the Sonnets as evidence that 'the problem of sex between men involves a good deal less anxiety' than between men and women, 'The Boys in the Back Room: Shakespeare's Apprentices and the Economics of the Theater'.

54. No special case has to be made for 'lone' or 'loue-sute' as synonyms for will, and Booth's commentary supports the equivalence of the sonnet's other nouns ('soule', 'things of great receit', 'stores account', 'treasure', 'number', 'one', 'nothing', and 'none'), pp. 469–73. Verbs also relate to lust: 'come' to climax; 'check' to its deferral; 'knows', 'proves', 'recko'ned' to forms of carnal knowing; 'fulfill' and 'fill' to orgasm; 'is admitted' and 'hold' to sexual entry. Adjectives express sexual desirables—'sweet', 'great', 'blind'—and adverbs modify the sexual act, 'so near', 'thus farre', 'with ease'.

55. On eye as vulva, see Booth, p. 521.

56. *The Tragedie of King Lear*, The Norton Facsimile *The First Folio of Shakespeare*, prepared by Charlton Hinman (New York, 1968), *TLN* 2724.

57. Paul Ramsey notes that 22½ per cent of all Englishmen were named Will at the end of the sixteenth century, *The Fickle Glass: A Study of Shakespeare's Sonnets* (New York, 1979), p. 23.

58. See Smith, esp. pp. 41–53 and Jonathan Goldberg, *Sodometries: Renaissance Texts, Modern Sexualities* (Berkeley, 1992), pp. 18–23.

59. 'Hal's Desire, Shakespeare's Idaho'.

60. *The Tragedie of King Lear*, TLN 1663.

61. The promiscuous dark lady is not unlike Spenser's miscegenating Acrasia ('bad mixture') who razes the estates of her noble lovers in *FQ*, Bk. II, 12.

62. On the racial inflections of fair/dark and black/white in the early modern period, see Ania Loomba, *Gender, Race, Renaissance Drama* (Manchester and New York, 1989), pp. 42–5 and Kim Hall, 'Unacknowledged Things of Darkness', Ph.D. thesis, Univ. of Pennsylvania, 1990.

63. This paragraph owes much to Dollimore, pp. 236–40 et passim.

1997—Helen Vendler. From "Introduction" to *The Art of Shakespeare's Sonnets*

An influential critic of American poetry, Helen Vendler is the writer and editor of more than 30 books. She is the A. Kingsley Porter University Professor at Harvard University, and in addition to Shakespeare, she has written on the poetry of George Herbert, John Keats, Wallace Stevens, and, most recently, William Butler Yeats.

Writing on the Sonnets

Before I begin to describe my own intentions in commenting on Shakespeare's *Sonnets*, I must say a few prefatory words. I intend this work for those who already know the *Sonnets*, or who have beside them the sort of lexical annotation found in the current editions (for example, those of Booth, Kerrigan, or Evans). A brief account of the reception history of the *Sonnets* can be found in these editions, as well as a more comprehensive bibliography than I can offer here. The older reception history in Hyder Rollins' *Variorum Sonnets* is still the most complete—and the most sobering to anyone hazarding a new addition to that history. Perhaps total immersion in the *Sonnets*—that is to say, in Shakespeare's mind—is a mildly deranging experience to anyone, and I cannot hope, I suppose, to escape the obsessive features characterizing Shakespearean sonnet criticism.

How are the *Sonnets* being written about nowadays? And why should I add another book to those already available? I want to do so because I admire the *Sonnets*, and wish to defend the high value I put on them, since they are being written about these days with considerable jaundice.[1] The spheres from which most of the current criticisms are generated are social and psychological ones. Contemporary emphasis on the participation of literature in a social matrix balks at acknowledging how lyric, though it may *refer to* the social, remains the genre that directs its *mimesis* toward the performance of the mind in *solitary* speech. Because lyric is intended to be voiceable by anyone reading it, in its normative form it deliberately strips away most social specification (age, regional location, sex, class, even race). A social reading is better directed at a novel or a play: the abstraction desired by the writer of, and the willing reader of, normative lyric frustrates the mind that wants social fictions or biographical revelations.

Even the best sociopsychological critic to write on the *Sonnets*, Eve Sedgwick, says "Shakespeare's Sonnets seem to offer a single, discursive, deeply felt *narrative* of the dangers and vicissitudes of one male homosocial adventure" [49]; "It is here that *one most wishes the Sonnets were a novel, that readers have most treated it as a novel*, and that we are, instead, going to bring the Sonnets' preoccupation to bear on *real novels*" [46] (italics mine). The persistent wish to turn the sequence into a novel (or a drama) speaks to the interests of the sociopsychological critic, whose aim is less to inquire into the successful carrying-out of a literary project than to investigate the representation of gender relations. It is perhaps a tribute to Shakespeare's "reality-effect" that "one most wishes the Sonnets were a novel," but it does no good to act as if these lyrics were either a novel or a documentary of a lived life.

Other critics (Barrell, Marotti, Kernan) have brought the *Sonnets* into the realm of the social by drawing analogies between the language of the poetry and the language of solicitations addressed to patrons and requesting patronage. This is a reasonable semantic (if not poetic) investigation, and reminds us that lyric language in any given epoch draws on all available sociolects of that epoch. The *Sonnets*, however (as Kernan makes clear), go far outside the originating discourse: no patron was ever addressed *qua* patron in language like that of sonnet 20 (*A woman's face with Nature's own hand painted*). Aesthetically speaking, it is what a lyric *does with* its borrowed social languages—i.e., how it casts them into new permutational and combinatorial forms—that is important. Shakespeare is unusually rich in his borrowings of diction and formulas from patronage, from religion, from law, from courtship, from diplomacy, from astronomy, and so on, but he tends to be a blasphemer in all of these realms. He was a master subverter of the languages he borrowed, and the point of *literary* interest is not the fact of his borrowings but how he turned them inside out. (See, in the commentary, sonnets 20, 33, 105, 135, or 144.)[2] One of Shakespeare's most frequent means of subversion is the total redefinition, within a single sonnet, of a word initially borrowed from a defined social realm (such as *state* in sonnet 33); there is no social discourse which he does not interrogate and ironize.

The sonnets have also been investigated by psychoanalytically minded critics, of whom the most formidable was the late Joel Fineman. Fineman, fundamentally disappointed by the Young Man sonnets, much preferred the Dark Lady sequence, where "difference" (read: the Lacanian Symbolic) replaces "sameness" (read: the Lacanian Imaginary).[3] Anyone who prizes drama above other genres delights in conflict, the structural principle of drama; and for Shakespeareans the Dark Lady sequence is, give or take a few details, a proto-sketch for a drama rather like *Othello*, with its jealousy, its sexuality, its ambiguous "darkness," its betrayals, and so on. It is much harder to imagine the Young Man sequence as a play. Yet, if one judges not by the criteria proper to drama but by those appropriate to lyric—"How well does the structure of this poem mimic the structure of thinking?" and "How well does the linguistic play of the poem embody that structural mimesis?"—Shakespeare's first subsequence is at least as good as (and in my view better than) the second. A psychological view of the *Sonnets* (whether psychoanalytically oriented or not) stresses motivation, will, and other characterological features, and above all needs a story on which to hang motivation. The "story" of the *Sonnets* continues to fascinate readers, but lyric is both more and less than story. And, in any case, the story of the *Sonnets* will always exhibit those "gaps" and that "indeterminacy" [Kuin, 251] intrinsic to the sonnet sequence as a genre. A coherent psychological account of the *Sonnets* is what the *Sonnets* exist to frustrate. They do not fully reward psychological criticism (or gender criticism, motivated by many of the same characterological aims) any more than they do political criticism. Too much of their activity escapes the large sieves of both psychology and politics, disciplines not much concerned to examine the basic means of lyric: subgenre, structure, syntax, and linguistic play.

The true "actors" in lyric are words, not "dramatic persons"; and the drama of any lyric is constituted by the successive entrances of new sets of words, or new stylistic arrangements (grammatic, syntactical, phonetic) which are visibly in conflict with previous arrangements used with reference to the "same" situation. (See, for example, my comments on sonnet 73 or sonnet 116.) Thus, the introduction of a new linguistic strategy is, in a sonnet, as interruptive and interesting as the entrance of a new character in a play. And any internal change in topic (from autumn to twilight to glowing fire in sonnet 73, for instance) or any change in syntactic structure (say, from parallel placement of items to chiastic placement) are among the strategies which—because they mimic changes of mind—constitute vivid drama within the lyric genre. Read in the light of these lyric criteria, the first subsequence is fully as dramatic (in the form proper to lyric) as the second. The art of seeing drama in linguistic action proper (action that may be as simple as the grammatical change in a given passage from nouns to verbals and back again—see sonnet 129) is an art that has lapsed, even in interpreters whose criteria appear to be literary rather than political or psychological.[4]

What, then, am I attempting in the Commentary below? Chiefly, a supplement to the accounts of the *Sonnets* in current editions (Ingram and Redpath, Booth,[5] Kerrigan, Evans) and in the books of the last thirty years (notably those by Leishman, Melchiori, Trousdale, Booth, Dubrow, Fineman, Vickers, de Grazia, Roche, Pequigney, Sedgwick, Weiser, and Martin). These editorial and critical accounts do not, to my mind, pay enough attention to the sonnets as poems—that is, as a writer's projects invented to amuse and challenge his own capacity for inventing artworks. Formal mimeses of the mind and heart in action are of course representative of human reality, but it is not enough to show that the moves of their language "chart . . . the ways we may be affected, morally and emotionally, by our own rhetoric" [Dubrow, 213]. A poem must be beautiful, too, exhibiting the double beauty that Stevens called "the poetry of the idea" and "the poetry of the words." That is, the theme must be freshly imagined, the genre must be renewed, and the words must surprise and satisfy from the point of view of proportion, musicality, and lexical vivacity.

(. . .)

"A Verbal Contraption"

Shakespeare is a poet who matches technique to content in a stunningly exemplary way, and his poems deserve to be asked the two questions formulated by Auden in *The Dyer's Hand*:

> The questions which interest me most when reading a poem are two. The first is technical: "Here is a verbal contraption. How does it work?" The second is, in the broadest sense, moral: "What kind of a guy inhabits this poem? What is his notion of the good life or the good place? His notion of the Evil One? What does he conceal from the reader? What does he conceal even from himself?" [50–51].

Like any poet, Auden knows that the second question cannot be responded to correctly until the first has been answered. It is the workings of the verbal construct that give evidence of the moral stance of the poet. Auden here separates the technical from the moral, and perhaps believes that the answer about the "verbal contraption" must be distinct from the answer about personality, ethics, and what we would now call "unconscious" and "deconstructive" moments in the poem. I believe that the deepest insights into the moral world of the poem, and into its constructive and deconstructive energies, come precisely from understanding it as a contraption made of "words," by which I mean not only the semantic units we call "words" but all the language games in which words can participate. Because many essays on the sonnets attempt moral and ethical discussion without any close understanding of how the poems are put together, I have emphasized in this Commentary the total "contraptionness" of any given sonnet as the first necessary level of understanding. I hope that my comments on the famous "moral" sonnets (such as 66, 94, 116, 129) will not disappoint readers who are looking for Shakespeare's "notion of the good life . . . the Evil One" and so on. As to what Shakespeare may conceal from the reader, or even from himself, such a supremely conscious writer conceals, it seems to me, very little.

I regret the absence, except in occasional cases below, of metrical commentary.[6] I don't doubt that a careful examination of Shakespeare's prosody in the sonnets (which can't be separated from a study of phrasal segmentation in the lines) would reveal repeated patterns of substantial interest. But that would make another book, and one that I (not yet having found an acceptably subtle and yet communicable theory of scansion) am not competent to write. I have tried to notice exceptional moments of prosodic originality that occur outside the common practices of prosodic variation (such as reversed initial feet).

To arrive at the understandings proposed in my Commentary, I found it necessary to learn the *Sonnets* by heart. I would often think I "knew" a sonnet; but then, scanning it in memory, I would find lacunae. Those gaps made me realize that some pieces of the whole must not yet have been integrated into my understanding of the intent of the work, since I was able to forget them. The recovery of the missing pieces always brought with it a further understanding of the design of that sonnet, and made me aware of what I had not initially perceived about the function of those words. No pianist or violinist would omit to learn a sonata by heart before interpreting it in public performance, but the equal habit of knowing poetry by heart before interpreting it has been lost. I first memorized many of the *Sonnets* (from my mother's copy) in the heartfelt way of youth, and I hope I have not lost that "heartfelt" sense of the poems. But I have since learned to love in a more conscious way Shakespeare's elated variety of invention, his ironic capacity, his astonishing refinement of technique, and, above all, the reach of his skeptical imaginative intent. I hope in this Commentary to illustrate these qualities, as well as, from time to time, the pathos, reflectiveness, and moral urgency already well described by previous readers.

Evidence and Import

This Commentary consists primarily of what might be called "evidential" criticism: that is, I wanted to write down remarks for which I attempt to supply instant and sufficient linguistic evidence. This, like all Platonic aims, must be imperfectly achieved, but I've tried to remember it at every point. There must of course be conjecture and speculation in divining the poetic laws which are being obeyed by a particular series of words, but I have given the reasons for my conjectures in as plain a way as I could find. One can write convincing evidential criticism only on fairly short texts (in longer texts, the permutations become too numerous). The *Sonnets* are ideal for such a purpose; and they deserve detailed and particular commentary because they comprise a virtual anthology of lyric possibility—in the poet's choice of subgenres, in arrangements of words, in tone, in dramatic modeling of the inner life, in speech-acts. In every case, I wanted to delineate whatever the given sonnet offered that seemed aesthetically most provocative: if there is an interesting change of address, it will be remarked, while a predictable change of address may not be commented on at all. The presence of unexpected (or inexplicable) words will be dwelt on; other words may go unnoticed. I have tried to point out problems that I have not been able to solve to my own satisfaction.

I come to Shakespeare's *Sonnets* as a critic of lyric poetry, interested in how successful poems are put together, ideationally, structurally, and linguistically; or, to put it another way, what ideational and structural and linguistic acts by a poet result in a successful poem. The brilliant beginnings in this direction by William Empson (on individual words and images), Winifred Nowottny (on formal arrangement), Stephen Booth (on overlapping structures), and Brian Vickers and Heather Dubrow (on rhetorical figuration) suggest that such efforts are particularly rewarding. Inevitably, rather few sonnets have been examined in detail, since critics tend to dwell on the most famous ten or fifteen out of the total 154; in fact, the *Sonnets* represent the largest tract of unexamined Shakespearean lines left open to scrutiny. As A. Nejgebauer remarked in his recapitulation (in the 1962 *Shakespeare Survey*) of work on the *Sonnets*: "Criticism of the sonnets will not stand comparison with that of the plays. . . . It has largely been amateurish and misplaced. . . . As regards the use of language, stanzaic structure, metre, tropes, and imagery, these demand the full tilth and husbandry of criticism" [18]. Nejgebauer's complaint could not be made with quite the same vehemence today, largely because of Stephen Booth's massive intervention with his *Essay on Shakespeare's Sonnets* (1969) and his provocative edition of the *Sonnets* (1977). Yet Booth's critical stance—that the critic, helpless before the plurisignification of language, and overlapping of multiple structures visible in a Shakespearean sonnet, must be satisfied with irresolution with respect to its fundamental gestalt—seems to me too ready a surrender to hermeneutic suspicion.

On the other hand, the wish of interpreters of poems to arrive at something they call "meaning" seems to me misguided. However important "meaning" may be to a theological hermeneutic practice eager to convey accurately the Word of God, it cannot have that importance in lyric. Lyric poetry, especially highly conventionalized lyric of the sort represented by the *Sonnets*, has almost no significant freight of "meaning" at all, in our ordinary sense of the word. "I have insomnia because I am far away from you" is the gist of one sonnet; "Even though Nature wishes to prolong your life, Time will eventually demand that she render you to death" is the "meaning" of another. These are not taxing or original ideas, any more than other lyric "meanings" ("My love is like a rose," "London in the quiet of dawn is as beautiful as any rural scene," etc.). Very few lyrics offer the sort of philosophical depth that stimulates meaning-seekers in long, complex, and self-contradicting texts like Shakespeare's plays or Dostoevsky's novels. In an effort to make lyrics more meaning-full, even linguistically minded critics try to load every rift with ore, inventing and multiplying ambiguities, plural meanings, and puns as if in a desperate attempt to add adult interest to what they would otherwise regard as banal sentiment. This is Booth's path, and it is also that of Joseph Pequigney, who would read the words of the *Sonnets* as an elaborate code referring to homosexual activity. Somehow, Shakespeare's words and images (most of the latter, taken singly, fully conventional) do not seem interesting enough as "meaning" to scholarly critics; and so an argument for additional "ambiguous" import is presented, if only to prop up Shakespeare's reputation. The poet Frank O'Hara had a better sense for the essential semantic emptiness of love lyrics when he represented them (in his poem "Blocks") as "saying" "I need you, you need me, yum yum." The appeal of lyric lies elsewhere than in its paraphrasable statement. Where, then, does the charm of lyric lie? The answers given in this Commentary are as various as the sonnets examined, since Shakespeare almost never repeats a strategy. However, they can be summed up in the phrase "the arrangement of statement." Form is content-as-arranged; content is form-as-deployed.

(. . .)

The Art of the Sonnets, and the Speaker They Create

With respect to the *Sonnets*—a text now almost four hundred years old—what can a commentary offer that is new? It can, I think, approach the sonnets, as I have chosen to do, from the vantage point of the poet who wrote them, asking the questions that a poet would ask about any poem. What was the aesthetic challenge for Shakespeare in writing these poems, of confining himself (with a few exceptions) to a single architectural form? (I set aside, as not of essential importance, the money or privileges he may have earned from his writing.) A writer of Shakespeare's seriousness writes from internal necessity—to do the best he can under his commission (if he was commissioned) and to perfect his art. What is the inner agenda of the *Sonnets*? What are their compositional motivations? What does a writer gain from working, over and over, in one subgenre? My brief answer is that Shakespeare learned to find strategies to enact feeling in form, feelings in forms, multiplying both to a superlative degree through 154 poems. No poet has ever found more linguistic forms by which to replicate human responses than Shakespeare in the *Sonnets*.

Shakespeare comes late in the sonnet tradition, and he is challenged by that very fact to a display of virtuosity, since he is competing against great predecessors. His thematic originality in his *dramatic personae* makes the sequence new in Western lyric. Though the sharing of the speaker by the young man and the lady, and the sharing of the young man by the lady and the rival poet, could in other hands become the material of farce, the "plot" is treated by Shakespeare elegiacally, sardonically, ironically, and tragically, making the *Sonnets* a repository of relationships and moods wholly without peer in the sonnet tradition. However, thematic originality alone never yet made a memorable artwork. Nor did psychological depth—though that is at least a prerequisite for lyric profundity.

No sufficient description exists in the critical literature of how Shakespeare makes his speaker "real." (The speaker is the only "person" interiorized in the *Sonnets*, though there are other *dramatic personae*.) The act of the lyric is to offer its reader a script to say. The words of a poem are not "overheard" (as in the formulations of J. S. Mill and T. S. Eliot); this would make the reader an eavesdropping voyeur of the writer's sensations. Nor is the poet "speaking to himself" without reference to a reader (if so, there would be no need to write the poem down, and all communicative action would be absent). While the social genres "build in" the reader either as listener (to a narrator of a novel) or as audience (to a play), the private literary genres—such as the Psalms, or prayers printed in prayer books, or secular lyrics—are scripted for repeated personal recitation. One is to utter them as one's own words, not as the words of another. Shakespeare's sonnets, with their unequaled idiomatic language-contours (written, after all, by a master in dramatic speech who shaped that speech into what C. S. Lewis called their lyric *cantabile*), are preeminently utterances for us to utter as ours. It is indispensable, then, if we are to be made to want to enter the lyric script, that the voice offered for our use be "believable" to us, resembling a "real voice" coming from a "real mind" like our own.

It is hard to achieve such "realness." Many lyrics are content with a very generalized and transient voice, one of no determinate length of life or depth of memory. In a drama, the passage of time and the interlocking of the web of events in which a character participates allow for a gradual deepening of the constructed personality of even minor characters. But Shakespeare must render his sonnet-speaker convincing in a mere fourteen lines. He is helped, to this end, by the fact that a "thick description" of his speaker accretes as the sequence progresses; but since few readers read the sequence straight through, the demand for evident "realness" in each poem, even were it to stand alone in an anthology, remains. The *Sonnets* cannot be "dramatic" in the ordinary sense because in them, as in every lyric of a normative sort, there is only one authorized voice. True drama requires at least two voices (so that even Beckett's monologues often include an offstage voice, or a tape of a voice, to fulfill this requirement). Some feminist critics, mistaking lyric for a social genre, have taken offense that the women who figure as *dramatis personae* within sonnet sequences are "silenced," meaning that they are not allowed to expostulate or reply. In that (mistaken) sense one would have to see *all* addressees in lyric as "silenced" (God by George Herbert, Robert Browning by E. B. Browning) since no addressee, in normative lyric, is given a counter and equal voice responding to that of the speaker.[7] Since the person uttering a lyric is always represented as alone with his thoughts, his imagined addressee can by definition never be present. The lyric (in contrast to the dramatic monologue, where there is always a listener present in the room), gives us the mind alone with itself. Lyric can present no "other" as alive and listening or responding in the same room as the solitary speaker. (One of

Herbert's witty genre-inventions, depending on this very genre-constraint, was to assert that since God is everywhere, God could be present in the room even in the speaker's "solitariness" and could thus offer a reply, as God the Father does in "The Collar" and as Jesus does in "Dialogue.")

Shakespeare's speaker, alone with his thoughts, is the greatest achievement, imaginatively speaking, of the sequence. He is given "depth" of character in each individual sonnet by several compositional strategies on Shakespeare's part. These will be more fully described and demonstrated in the individual commentaries below, but in brief they are:

1. *Temporal*. The establishment of several retreating "panels" of time, representing episodes or epochs in the speaker's past, gives him a continuous, nontransient existence and a continuity of memory. (See, for example, sonnet 30, *When to the sessions of sweet silent thought.*)

2. *Emotional*. The reflection, within the same poem, of sharply conflicting moods with respect to the same topic (see, e.g., sonnet 148, *O me! what eyes hath love put in my head*). This can be abetted by contradictory or at least nonhomogeneous discourses rendering a topic complicated (see, e.g., sonnet 125, *Wer't aught to me I bore the canopy*). The volatility of moods in the speaker (symbolized by the famous *lark at break of day arising* of sonnet 29) suggests a flexibility—even an instability—of response verbally "guaranteeing" the presence of passion.

3. *Semantic*. The speaker's mind has a great number of compartments of discourse (theological, legal, alchemical, medicinal, political, aesthetic, etc.). These compartments are semipervious to each other, and the osmosis between them is directed by an invisible discourse-master, who stands for the intellectual imagination.

4. *Conceptual*. The speaker resorts to many incompatible models of existence (described in detail in the commentary) even within the same poem; for example, sonnet 60 first describes life as a homogeneous steady-state succession of identical waves/minutes (a stoic model); then as a sharply delineated rise-and-eclipse of a sun (a tragic model); and next as a series of incessant violent extinctions (a brutal model). These models, unreconciled, convey a disturbing cognitive dissonance, one which is, in a philosophical sense, intolerable. The alert and observant mind that constructs these models asserts the "truth" of each for a particular occasion or aspect of life, but finds no "supramodel" under which they can be intelligibly grouped, and by which they can be intelligibly contained. In this way, the mind of the speaker is represented as one in the grip of philosophical conflict.

5. *Philosophical*. The speaker is a rebel against received ideas. He is well aware of the received topoi of his culture, but he subjects them to interrogation, as he counters neo-Platonic courtly love with Pauline marital love (116), or the Christian Trinity with the Platonic Triad (105), or analogizes sacred hermeneutics to literary tradition (106). No topics are more sharply scrutinized

than those we now subsume under the phrase "gender relations": the speaker interrogates androgyny of appearance by evoking a comic myth of Nature's own dissatisfaction with her creation (20); he criticizes hyperbolic praise of female beauty in 130; he condones adultery throughout the "will" sonnets and elsewhere (and sees adultery as less criminal than adulterated discourse, e.g., in 152). This is not even to mention the interrogations of "love" and "lust" in 116 and 129 (sonnets of which the moral substance has not been properly understood because they have not been described in formal terms). No received idea of sexuality goes uninvestigated; and the thoroughly unconventional sexual attachments represented in both parts of the sequence stand as profound (if sometimes unwilling) critiques of the ideals of heterosexual desire, chastity, continence, marital fidelity, and respect for the character of one's sexual partner. What "ought to be" in the way of gender relations (by Christian and civic standards) is represented as an ideal in the "marriage sonnets" with which the sequence opens, but never takes on existential or "realist" lived validation. Shakespeare's awareness of norms is as complete as his depiction, in his speaker, of experiential violation of those norms.

6. *Perceptual.* The speaker is also given depth by the things he notices, from damask roses to the odor of marjoram to a canopy of state. Though the sonnets are always openly drifting toward emblematic or allegorical language, they are plucked back (except in extreme cases like 66) into the perceptual, as their symbolic rose is distilled into "real" perfume (54) or as an emblematic April is *burned* by *hot* June (104). The speaker stands poised between a medieval emblematic tendency and a more modern empirical posture; within his moral and philosophical systems, he savors the tang of the "sensual feast."

7. *Dramatic.* The speaker indirectly quotes his antagonist. Though no one but the speaker "speaks" in a lyric, Shakespeare exploits the usefulness of having the speaker, in private, quote in indirect discourse something one or the other of the *dramatis personae* previously said. Many of the sonnets (e.g., 76 and 116) have been misunderstood because they have been thought to be free-standing statements on the speaker's part rather than replies to the antagonist's implicitly quoted words. Again, I support this statement below in detail; but one can see what a difference it makes to interpretation whether in sonnet 76 the poet-speaker means to criticize his own verse—"Why is my verse so barren of new pride?"—or whether he is repeating, by quoting, an anterior criticism by the young man: "Why [you ask] is my verse so [in your words] 'barren of new pride'?" In the (often bitter) give-and-take of prior-criticism-answered-by-the-speaker (in such rebuttal-sonnets as 105, 117, 151, and the previously mentioned 76 and 116), we come closest, in the sonnets, to Shakespeare the dramatist.

More could be said of the strategies that create a credible speaker with a complex and imaginative mind (a mind which we take on as our own when stepping into the voice); but I want to pass on to the greatest strength of the sonnets as "contraptions," their multiple armatures. Booth sees these "overlapping structures" as a principle of irresoluble indeterminacy; I, by contrast, see them as mutually reinforcing, and therefore as principles of authorial instruction.

Organizing Structures

When lyric poems are boring, it is frequently because they possess only one organizing structure, which reveals itself unchanged each time the poem is read. *If* the poet has decided to employ a single structure (in, say, a small two-part song such as "When daisies pied and violets blue"), then the poem needs some other principle of interest to sustain rereading (in that song, a copious set of aspects—vegetative, human, and avian—of the spring). Shakespeare abounds in such discourse-variety, and that in part sustains rereadings of the sonnets; but I have found that rereading is even better sustained by his wonderful fertility in structural complexity. The Shakespearean sonnet form, though not invented by Shakespeare, is manipulated by him in ways unknown to his predecessors. Because it has four parts—three isomorphic ones (the quatrains) and one anomalous one (the couplet), it is far more flexible than the two-part Italian sonnet. The four units of the Shakespearean sonnet can be set in any number of logical relations to one another:

> successive and equal;
> hierarchical;
> contrastive;
> analogous;
> logically contradictory;
> successively "louder" or "softer."

This list is merely suggestive, and by no means exhaustive. The four "pieces" of any given sonnet may also be distinguished from one another by changes of agency ("I do this; you do that"), of rhetorical address ("O Muse"; "O beloved"), of grammatical form (a set of nouns in one quatrain, a set of adjectives in another), or of discursive texture (as the descriptive changes to the philosophical), or of speech act (as denunciation changes to exhortation). Each of these has its own poetic import and effect. The four "pieces" of the sonnet may be distinguished, again, by different phonemic clusters or metrical effects. Booth rightly remarks on the presence of such patternings, but he refuses to establish hierarchy among them, or to subordinate minor ones to major ones, as I think one can often do.

I take it that a Shakespearean sonnet is fundamentally structured by an evolving inner emotional dynamic, as the fictive speaker is shown to "see more," "change his mind," "pass from description to analysis," "move from negative refutation to positive refutation," and so on. There can be a surprisingly large number of such "moves" in any one sonnet. The impression of an evolving dynamic within the speaker's mind and heart is of course created by a large "law of form" obeyed by the words in each sonnet. Other observable structural patterns play a subordinate role to this largest one. In its Shakespearean incarnation, the sonnet is a system in motion, never immobile for long, and with several subsystems going their way within the whole.

The chief defect in critical readings of the *Sonnets* has been the critics' propensity to take the first line of a sonnet as a "topic sentence" which the rest of the poem merely illustrates and reiterates (a model visible in Berowne's sonnet quoted above). Only in the plays does Shakespeare write nondramatic sonnets in this expository mode. In his lyrics, he sees structure itself as motion, as a composer of music would imagine it. Once the dynamic curve of a given sonnet is perceived, the lesser structuring principles "fall into place" beneath it. See, e.g., my commentary on 129 for a textbook example of a trajectory of changing feelings in the speaker about a single topic (lust); it is the patterns and underpatterns of the sonnet that enable us to see the way those feelings change. If the feeling were unchanging, the patterns would also remain invariable. The crucial rule of thumb in understanding any lyric is that every significant change of linguistic pattern represents a motivated change in feeling in the speaker. Or, to put it differently, if we sense a change of feeling in the speaker, we must look to see whether, and how, it is stylistically "guaranteed." Unless it is deflected by some new intensity, the poem continues by inertia in its original groove.

I deliberately do not dwell in this Commentary on Shakespeare's imagery as such, since it is a topic on which good criticism has long existed. Although large allegorical images (*beauty's rose*) are relatively stable in the *Sonnets*, imagery is meaningful only in context; it cannot be assigned secure symbolic import except with respect to the poem in which it occurs. The point, e.g., of the fire in sonnet 73 (*That time of year*) is that it is a stratified image: the glowing of the fire *lies upon* the ashes of youth. The previous images in the sonnet have been linear ones (*time of year* and *twilight*) referring to an extension in time (a year, a day), rather than superposition in space. By itself, the image "fire" does not call up the notion of stratification, nor does it in the other sonnets in which it appears; but in this poem, because of the poet's desire for variance from a previously established linear structure, the fire is called upon to play this spatial role, by which youth appears as exhausted subpositioned ashes rather than as an idyllic era (*the sweet birds; sunset*) lost at an earlier point in a timeline. Previous thematic commentators have often missed such contextual determination of imagistic meaning.

In trying to see the chief aesthetic "game" being played in each sonnet, I depart from the isolated registering of figures—a paradox here, an antimetabole there—to which the practice of word-by-word or phrase-by-phrase commentary inevitably leads. I wish to point out instead the larger imaginative or structural patterns in which such rhetorical figures take on functional (by contrast to purely decorative) significance. I do not intend, by this procedure, to minimize the sonnets' ornamental "excess" (so reprehensible to Pound); no art is more pointedly ornamental (see Puttenham) than the Renaissance lyric. Yet, Shakespeare is happiest when an ornamental flourish can be seen to have a necessary poetic function. His changes in discursive texture, and his frequent consciousness of etymological roots as he plays on Anglo-Saxon and Latin versions of the "same" meaning ("with my *extern* the *outward* honoring"), all become more striking when incorporated into a general and dynamic theory of the poem. (Rather than invoke the terms of Renaissance rhetoric, which do not convey much to the modern reader, I use ordinary language to describe Shakespeare's rhetorical figuration.)

To give an illustration: I myself find no real functional significance in Shakespeare's alliteration when the speaker says that in *the swart complexioned night, / When sparkling stars twire not, thou [the young man] gildst the even*. Such phonetic effects seem to have a purely decorative intent. But an alliterative "meaning-string"—such as sonnet 25's *favour, fortune, triumph, favourites, fair, frown, painful, famousèd, fight* (an emendation), *foiled*, and *forgot*—encapsulates the argument of the poem in little, and helps to create and sustain that argument as it unfolds. Grammar and syntax, too, can be functionally significant to argument; see, for instance, the way in which 66 uses phrases of agency, or the way in which 129 uses its many verbals. In his edition of the *Sonnets*, Booth leaves it up to the reader to construct the poem; I have hoped to help the reader actively to that construction by laying out evidence that no interpretation can afford to ignore. Any number of interpretations, guided by any number of interests, can be built on the same foundation of evidence; but an interpretation ignoring that evidence can never be a defensible one.

I believe that anyone seriously contemplating the interior structures and interrelations of these sonnets is bound to conclude that many were composed in the order in which they are arranged. However, given the poems' variation in aesthetic success, it seems probable that some sonnets—perhaps written in youth (as Andrew Gurr suggested of the tetrameter sonnet 145, with its pun on "Hathaway") or composed before the occurrence of the triangular plot—were inserted *ad libitum* for publication. (I am inclined to believe Katherine Duncan-Jones's argument that the *Sonnets* may have been an authorized printing.) The more trifling sonnets—those that place ornament above imaginative gesture, or fancifulness above depth (such as 4, 6, 7, 9, 145, 153, and 154)—do seem to be less experienced trial-pieces. The greater sonnets achieve an effortless combination of imaginative reach with high technical invention (18, 73, 124, 138), or a quintessence of grace (104, 106, 132), or a power of dramatic condensation (121, 147) that we have come to call "Shakespearean," even if, as Kent Hieatt (1991) has persuasively shown, they were composed in groups over time.

The speaker of Shakespeare's sonnets scorns the consolations of Christianity—an afterlife in heaven for himself, a Christian resurrection of

his body after death—as fully as he refuses (except in a few sonnets) the
learned adornment of classical references—a staple of the continental sonnet.
The sonnets stand as the record of a mind working out positions without
the help of any pantheon or any systematic doctrine. Shakespeare's speaker
often considers, in rapid succession, any number of intellectual or ideological
positions, but he does not move among them at random. To the contrary: in
the first quatrain of any given sonnet he has a wide epistemological field in
which to play, but in the second quatrain he generally queries or contradicts
or subverts his first position (together with its discourse-field). By the third
quatrain, he must (usually) advance to his subtlest or most comprehensive or
most truthful position (Q_3 therefore taking on, in the Shakespearean sonnet,
the role of the sestet in the Petrarchan sonnet). And the couplet—placed not
as resolution (which is the function of Q_3) but as coda—can then stand in
any number of relations (summarizing, ironic, expansive) to the preceding
argument. The gradually straitened possibilities as the speaker advances in
his considerations give the Shakespearean sonnet a funnel-shape, narrowing
in Q_3 to a vortex of condensed perceptual and intellectual force, and either
constricting or expanding that vortex via the couplet.

(. . .)

Reading the Sonnets

Shakespeare encourages alertness in his reader. Because he is especially
occupied with literary consolidation (resuming the topics, the images, the
consecrated adjectives, and the repertoire of tones of previous sonneteers),
one can miss his subversive moves: the "shocking" elements of the sonnets in
both subsequences; the parodies, by indirect quotation, of Petrarchan praise in
sonnets 21 and 130 (though the latter has been sometimes read as denigration
of the mistress, it is no such thing); the satire on learned language (78, 85);
on sycophantic poets (79) and newfangled poets (76); the revisionism with
respect to Christian views of lust (129) and continence (94) and with respect
to Petrarchan views of love (116); the querying of eternizing boasts (122),
of the Platonic conventions (95), of dramatic plot (144), of enumerative
praise (84), of "idolatry" (105), of the Lord's Prayer (108) and of love-pursuit
(143). That is, readers of the sonnets find themselves encountering—and
voicing—both the most conventional images (*rose, time, fair, stars, love*) and
the most unsettling statements. Many quatrains, taken singly, could well be
called conventional and paraphrases of them by critics make them sound
stultifying. What is *not* conventional is the sonnet's (invisibly predicated) set
of relations—of the quatrains to one another and to the couplet; of the words
and images to one another; of the individual grammatical and syntactic
units to one another. Even though the appearance of logic is often smoothly

maintained by a string of logical connectives (*When . . . When . . . Then*), some disruptive or contradictory force will enter the poem to pull one quatrain in two directions at once—toward its antecedent quatrain by one set of words, toward its consequent by another; toward the couplet by its temporality; toward a preceding quatrain by its spatiality. Since quatrains often participate in several patterns simultaneously, their true "meaning" is chartable only by charting their pattern-sets.

Though antithesis is Shakespeare's major figure for constructing the world in the sonnets, it is safe to say that the ever antithetically minded Shakespeare permitted his antitheses to breed and bring to birth a third thing (see sonnet 66). His second preferred figure, chiasmus, contends in the sonnets against the "natural" formulation of a sentence (linear, temporal, ongoing). Chiasmus refuses to let a phrase or a sentence dilate "naturally": instead, it makes the syntax round on itself. Not "Least contented with what I most enjoy" (the linear or parallel formation), but rather *With what I most enjoy contented least* (the chiastic formulation). The chiastic formulation always implies an analytic moment in the speaker. "Spontaneous" moments say things "naturally"; but when the speaker has had time to think things out and judge them, he speaks chiastically. *Consumed with that which it was nourished by*—where *consumed* and *nourished* bracket *that* and *which*—is a formulation that simply could not occur in Q_1 or Q_2 of 73. The first two quatrains of that sonnet are the epitome of linearity, as phrase follows phrase in a "natural" imitation of life's gradual leakage:

> In me thou seest the twilight of such day
> As after sunset fadeth in the west,
> Which by and by black night doth take away,
> Death's second self that seals up all in rest.

On this narrative of pathos, there supervenes the superb analytic moment of Q_3: the stratified fire does not fade, it glows; and the analytic law of consumption and nourishment refuses a linear statement of itself: "As the fire was nourished by heat, so it is consumed by heat." Between the glowing fire and the physical law, however, there is one line of linear "leakage": *As the death-bed whereon it must expire.* If that were the last line of the poem, the speaker's stoic resolve could be said to have left him, and he would have submitted to a "natural" dying fall. But he pulls himself up from that moment of expiring linearity into his great chiastic law, that we die from the very same vital heat which has nourished us in life. It is (as this example shows) always worth noting whether a Shakespearean statement is being made "linearly," in a first-order experiential and "spontaneous" way, or whether it is being made chiastically, in a second-order analytic way. These represent very different stances within the speaker.

Strategies of Unfolding

One of the strategies making many sonnets odd is that the utterances of the speaker are being generated by invisible strings "behind" the poem—the concurrent deducible actions or remarks of an implied other. Such poems are like the rebuttal sonnets mentioned earlier, except that the invisible prompt is not an earlier speech-act by another but rather a series of actions or speech-acts which are, imaginatively speaking, *in process while* the sonnet is being uttered. (See my comments on 34, which explain why the changes of metaphor in the poem—storm, rain, slave, physic, cross, pearl, ransom—are not inexplicable or unintelligible.) And then there are the "shadow-poems" (as I think of them), where one can deduce, from the speaker's actual statements, what he would really like to say to the young man (in the case of the "slavery" sonnet, 57) or to the mistress (in, say, 138) if he could speak clearly.

Yet another recurrent strategy for Shakespeare is to "mix up" the order of narration so that it departs from the normal way in which such an event would be unfolded. It would be "normal" to say, "He abandoned me; and what did that feel like? It felt like seeing the sun go behind a cloud." In "normal" narration, the literal event is recounted first, and then a metaphor is sought to explain what the narrator felt like. But in sonnet 33 (*Full many a glorious morning have I seen*), the metaphor—not perceived as such because not introduced by "Just as"—precedes the literal event. After seeing the sunny landscape clouded, and thinking we have been admitted to the literal level of the poem, we hear *Even so my sun one early morn did shine*. In order to understand such a poem, we must ask why the poet has rearranged the normal order of narration. In 97, for example, it would be "normal" to state literal perception first, and let an emotional contradiction follow—to say, "It was summertime, *and yet* it seemed like winter to me with you away." Instead, the poet puts the speaker's emotional perception ahead of his sense-perception: "How like a winter hath my absence been / From thee . . . ! / *And yet* this time removed was summer's time." Similarly, the very peculiar order of narration in 62 (*Sin of self-love*) has to be both noticed and interpreted.

I want to say a word here about Shakespeare's fancifulness. It ought not surprise us that the author of *A Midsummer Night's Dream* might also be fanciful in his poems. Modern readers have shown little admiration for the sonnets that play with the convention of the contest between eye and heart (such as 46 or 47) or the sonnet about flowers stealing their odor and hue from the young man (99, *The forward violet*), or the sonnets of elaborate wordplay (43, *When most I wink*), or the more whimsical complimentary sonnets, such as 78 (*So oft have I invoked thee*). Such sonnets may be fanciful, but they are not frivolous, as I hope to have shown in the Commentary. Read from the right angle, so to speak, they can be very beautiful, or at least delightful; and in them, as elsewhere, Shakespeare is inventing some game or other and playing it out to its conclusion in deft and surprising ways.

Shakespeare the Writer

The purpose of my Commentary is to point out strategies of the sort I have been enumerating—strategies that make the speaker credible, that generate an evolutionary dynamic, that suggest interaction among the linguistic ingredients of the lines, that "use" the couplet, that beguile by fancifulness, and so on. There are hundreds of such strategies in the sonnets, since Shakespeare rarely amuses himself the same way twice. He is a poet acutely conscious of grammatical and syntactic possibility as one of the ingredients in "invention," and he routinely, but not idly, varies tense, mood, subject-position, and clause-patterns in order to make conceptual or rhetorical points. These *differentia* contribute to our sense that his mind was discriminating as well as copious. His inventories are sometimes exhaustive (as he reels off the forms of prognostication in sonnet 14, or the forms of social trespass by lust till action in 129) but at other times rigidly repetitive (as in the implication, by the almost invariant organization of 66, that the anatomy of evil is less complex than the world would like to believe). In any given case of enumeration in the *Sonnets*, an implicit table of organization is constructed, frequently through the "places" of logic ("who," "where," "when," "in what manner," "by what means," "with what aid," etc.). Items may then be further accumulated, contrasted, subtracted, and so forth, either from this table of organization or from another organizational grid superimposed on it as a corrective (as love and its obligations are superimposed on the masque of social evil in 66). A formidable intellectual command of phenomena (both physical and moral), of means (both human and cosmic), of categories (both quotidian and philosophical), and of discourses (both learned and popular) lies behind the *Sonnets* in the person of their invisible author. It is this intellectual command which accounts for the *Sonnets'* serene and unfaltering air of poetic resource, even (or perhaps especially) in the moments of the speaker's greatest psychological distraction. Though I cannot hope to have caught all of Shakespeare's strategies, or to have understood them all properly, or to have assigned them their proper weight with respect to one another, I do hope that I will have shown Shakespeare as a poet constantly inventing new permutations of internal form, designed to match what he was recording—the permutations of emotional response.

Sometimes I have not been sure of the "game" of a given sonnet, but I am happy to ask others to try their wits after me. There is always something cryptographic in Shakespeare's sonnet-surfaces—sometimes literally so, as in the anagrams of 7, or as in the play on *vile* and *evil* in 121, but more often merely an oddness that catches the eye and begs explanation. The obviousness of the *Sonnets'* "content"—love, jealousy, time's depredations—simply leaves readers obscurely conscious that their reactions to these poems exceed the rather commonplace matter they have understood. Poetry is not generally in the matter of its utterance philosophical; but it is philosophical insofar as its dynamic (when well constructed) represents in abstract or "geometric" form one or several of the infinite curves of human response. Shakespeare's *Sonnets* are philosophical insofar as they display interrelationships among their parts which, as they unfold, trace a conflict in human cognitive and affective motions. The surface of any poem is what John Ashbery calls its "visible core" ("Self-Portrait in a Convex Mirror"), and I have tried, by examining the surfaces of these poems as a writer would see and interpret them, to make the core visible. And though my main concern has been to show the unifying forces in each sonnet, the whole sequence displays, when taken as a single object, dispersive gaps and uncertainties between its individual units. It is on just such large uncertainties that the smaller certainties of single sonnets float and collide.

(. . .)

NOTES

1. The most recent book considering them in some detail—Christopher Martin's *Policy in Love: Lyric and Public in Ovid, Petrarch and Shakespeare* (Pittsburgh: Duquesne University Press, 1994)—may serve to prove my assertion. Here are some quotations:

On the initial seventeen sonnets: "[The poet's] rigid alignment with a legitimizing community exhausts the technical resources of his discourse as it exposes the emotional sterility of the conventions in which he invests" [134–135].

"While the procreation subsequence's tight focus insures coherence, it simultaneously threatens a monotony that has also taken its toll on the poetry's modern audience. Even Wordsworth . . . was put off by a general 'sameness,' a feature most damagingly concentrated in this introductory series" [145].
"Lars Engle is right to suggest that the initial quatrain:

[From fairest creatures we desire increase,
That thereby beauty's rose might never die,
But as the riper should by time decease
His tender heir might bear his memory . . .]

'might be the voice-over of a Sierra Club film in which California condors soar over their eggless nest'" [148].

"The poet betrays himself [in the early sonnets] as one uneager to focus on human beings in any precise manner, much less upon the potentially messy emotions which join them to one another. . . . Questions of detail make him nervous, and he would just as soon stick to the homey blur of abstracted tradition" [148].

"On sonnets 124 ("If my dear love were but the child of state") and 125 ("Were't aught to me I bore the canopy"): "Posing as sonnets about discovery and liberation, these poems are overtaken by a spirit of persecution and resentment. . . . He resorts to a fantasy isolation. . . He lapses, moreover, by the final couplet's arch renunciation ["Hence, thou suborned informer! A true soul / When most impeached stands least in thy control"], from anxious vigilance to paranoia" [175].

2. Because of Shakespeare's subversion of any discourse he adapts, it seems to me inadequate to suggest, as John Barrell does, that sonnet 29 ("When in disgrace with fortune and men's eyes") "may be actively concealing . . . a meaning that runs like this: 'when I'm pushed for money, with all the degradation that poverty involves, I sometimes remember you, and you're always good for a couple of quid'" [30]. Barrell prefers to conceive of Shakespeare as attempting the language of transcendent love, but unable to achieve it, "because the historical moment he seeks to transcend is represented by a discourse [of patronage] whose nature and function is to contaminate the very language by which that assertion of transcendence must try to find expression. For me, the pathos of the poem—I can repeat here my earlier point—is that the narrator can find no words to assert the transcendent power of true love, which cannot be interpreted as making a request for a couple of quid" [42].

A poet is not quite so helpless before his discourses as Barrell believes. In the first place, the very playfulness of the poem (see my comments below on the chiasmus "most enjoy contented least" and the puns on "state") prevents its being an actual speech-act of either "transcendent love" or "a request for a couple of quid." The sonnet, taken entire, is a fictional speech-act, of which the intent is to mimic the motions of the mind when it rises from low to high. In mimicking, in the octave, the movement of the mind in agitated depression and, in the sestet, the movement of the mind in relieved elation, the sonnet is fulfilling its purpose as a lyric. Shakespeare's skill in such psychological mimicry ensures the continuing power of the poem. A poet (as the contrast between octave and sestet shows) is the master of his discourses, not (as in Barrell's scenario) their helpless performer.

3. According to Fineman's theory, the object of desire as mirror image cannot generate dramatic conflict, and so the poetry of the speaker's same-sex object-relation remains mired in narcissism; but when the object of desire changes gender, and is no longer worshipfully desired but rather is abhorred, a fruitful dissonance arises that generates a new subjectivity. Fineman's more extravagant claims for the historical newness of the subject-position in the Dark Lady sequence have generally not been adopted; but his psychoanalytic criterion of value for poetry—that "difference" is better than "sameness"—has apparently gone unquestioned. It is naturally typical of Shakespeareans to prefer drama to lyric: after all, they became Shakespeareans because they were drawn to drama. And Fineman's book on the *Sonnets* was not fundamentally concerned with lyric, any more than his essay on *The Rape of Lucrece* was about complaint; both were prefatory, in their concern with character and will, to the book on Shakespeare's plays he did not live, alas, to write.

4. One editor of the *Sonnets*, John Kerrigan, betrays his restricted criterion of lyric value—chiefly, that metaphor is necessary for a good poem—as he writes of sonnet 105 that it is "scrupulously and Shakespearianly dull, but it is dull nonetheless. . . . The text is stripped of metaphor. . . . The result is a poem which, for all its charm [unspecified by Kerrigan] (and integrity), lacks the compelling excitement of a metaphoric sonnet such as 60, 'Like as the waves make toward the pebbled shore.' In so far as Shakespeare exceeds the Erasmian *copia*, shunning 'variation' for the sake of tautologous recurrence, his verse palls" [29]. See my commentary on sonnet 105 for a demonstration of how interesting the poem becomes once one admits criteria for lyric excellence besides the presence or absence of metaphor

(though 105 is also one continued metaphor comparing erotic worship to Christian worship, and blasphemously equating them).

To take another instance of Kerrigan's misreading (springing from his lack of interest in linguistic variation), I cite his description of sonnet 129 ("Th'expense of spirit in a waste of shame"). He, like other critics preceding him, takes a single-minded expository view of the poem, as though it were a self-consistent sermon: "While 116 deals with Love complexly, however, questioning the absolute which it erects, 129 describes and enacts with single-minded, though cynically quibbling, forcefulness the distemperature of phallocentric lust. Fitful and fretting, such a passion squanders the moral powers along with the semen, committing both to a 'waste of shame' and 'shameful waist.' . . . It goads men towards satisfaction, yet, once sated in the irrational frenzy of orgasm, it is queasy, woeful, and full of remorse. . . . Lust is fixated by the moment: yearning towards emission, it lies sullied and futile in its wake, sourly foretasting hell, with nothing to hope for but further 'pursuit.' Its imaginative field is vorticose, centripetal, obsessive" [56]. Such a passage allows for no change of mind in the course of the poem—but if there is one thing the poem *does* mimic, it is successive changes of mind in the cycle of desire, changes of mind impossible in a homiletic diatribe such as Kerrigan represents the sonnet to be (see my comments on 129).

5. Every writer on the *Sonnets* owes gratitude to Stephen Booth's giant edition, which spells out in more detail the principles guiding his critical book on the *Sonnets*. Yet in stressing the richness of implication of Shakespeare's language over the firmness of implied authorial instruction, Booth gives up on the possibility of reliable internal guides for interpretation. Of course every interpretive act brings special interests to the poem, so that a psychoanalytic interpretation foregrounds aspects that a historical interpretation may overlook. But any respectable account of a poem ought to have considered closely its chief formal features. A set of remarks on a poem which would be equally true of a prose paraphrase of that poem is not, by my standards, interpretation at all. Commentary on the propositional content of the poem is something entirely different from the interpretation of a poem, which must take into account the poem's linguistic strategies as well as its propositional statements.

The extent of authorial instruction retrievable from a text is also disputed. Yet authorial instruction is embedded, for instance, in the mere fact that one metaphor follows another. Sonnet 73 would have to be interpreted differently if we were given the twilight in quatrain 1, the fire in quatrain 2, and the autumn in quatrain 3. Shakespeare's arrangement of his metaphors is both cognitively and morally meaningful; quatrains cannot be reordered at will. Authorial instruction is also embedded in smaller units of every sonnet. To give one instance, it can be found in the parallels drawn between one part of the poem and another. The grammatical parallel linking the four "moral nouns"—*expense, spirit, waste,* and *shame*—that open sonnet 129 to the four "emotional" nouns—*bliss, woe, joy,* and *dream*—replacing them in its sestet is an "authorial instruction" telling us to notice the contrast between the two sets, and to infer a change of mind in the speaker who is uttering them about one and the same experience.

Any account of a poem ought to contemplate such implicit authorial instructions. Booth gives up too easily on interpretation. Even in the richness of Shakespeare's language, we are not left afloat on an uninterpretable set of "ideational static," not when the formal features of the *Sonnets* are there to guide us. It was her awareness of those formal features that made the late Winifred Nowottny the best guide to the sequence; it is a matter of deep regret to me that she did not complete the Arden edition which she had undertaken, and left only a few brilliant essays as tokens of that effort. It is equally a matter for rejoicing that the new Arden *Sonnets* will soon appear, edited by Katherine Duncan-Jones.

6. The tale of Pound, Bunting, and Shakespeare's *Sonnets* is contained in Massimo Bacigalupo's *Pound in Rapallo*. Bunting's reductions are quoted from a xerox of his copy of Shakespeare's *Sonnets*, kindly sent to me by Professor Bacigalupo of the University of Genoa.

7. The best account of Shakespeare's metrical practice is to be found in George T. Wright, *Shakespeare's Metrical Art*, 75–90; but see my critique of his scansion of 116 in my comments on that sonnet.

1998—Jonathan Bate. "Shakespeare's Autobiographical Poems?" from *The Genius of Shakespeare*

Jonathan Bate is a professor of Shakespeare and Renaissance Literature at the University of Warwick and a governer of the Royal Shakespeare Company. He is the author and editor of many books, including *Shakespeare and the English Romantic Imagination*, *Titus Andronicus* (for the Arden series), *The Genius of Shakespeare*, and *John Clare: A Biography*, which won the Hawthornden Prize. He is a fellow of the British Academy and a reviewer for the BBC.

Brief lives

The first biographies of Shakespeare were anecdotal. In his *Brief Lives*, John Aubrey recorded that the dramatist's father was a butcher and that the boy William used to help him in the family shop, killing calves in a 'high style' to an accompanying dramatic speech. Aubrey also reported that between leaving school and becoming a player in London, William was himself a country schoolmaster. And he said that he had been told that during Shakespeare's working life in London the dramatist returned to his native Stratford once a year, stopping off in Oxford at a tavern owned by a Mr and Mrs Davenant, the latter being a witty and beautiful woman who just might have borne him an illegitimate son who grew up to be Sir William Davenant, Poet Laureate.

Like the anecdotes from Shakespeare's own lifetime, each of these three items of gossip has symbolic meaning. The first attests to his humble and rural origins. It sows the seed for the excesses of later Bardolatry: the butcher's son from provincial Stratford has the same kind of background as the carpenter's son from provincial Nazareth. 'After God,' said the Romantic novelist Alexandre Dumas, author of *The Three Musketeers* and *The Count of Monte-Cristo*, 'Shakespeare created most'. The second anecdote contributes to the long debate about whether Shakespeare's genius was a matter of nature or art. The schoolmastering story had fairly good authority, in that it came from the actor William Beeston, whose father was the actor Christopher Beeston, a member of Shakespeare's company. Aubrey introduced it specifically in order to modify Ben Jonson's 'small Latin and less Greek'. The third piece of gossip serves the dual purpose of suggesting that Shakespeare was a bit of a lad and making him the 'father' of later creative endeavour. Davenant, especially after a few drinks, seems positively to have encouraged the story about his origins: he thought it was worth impugning his mother's good name for the sake of establishing his own poetic pedigree. The royal imprimatur of Davenant's Laureateship is symbolically passed back to Shakespeare, who thus begins his long career as England's National Poet.

After Aubrey came Nicholas Rowe. Though more substantial than anything that had gone before, and formally billed as 'Some Account of the Life of Mr William Shakespear', his biography, prefaced to his 1709 edition of the *Works*, was still anecdotal rather than documentary. Rowe begins by saying that his prime interest is the kind of 'little Personal Story' which brings colour to the life of a great man. This 'Life' gave currency to such memorable anecdotes as the deer-stealing incident—Shakespeare the lad once more—and the casting of William himself as the ghost of Hamlet's father. The latter lays the ground for later readings of Hamlet as the dramatist's most favoured son among all his characters—a reading reinforced by the discovery that Shakespeare really did name his son Hamnet, which appears to be a variant of Hamlet.

The eighteenth century is full of narratives, both historical and fictional, of men who rose from low to high in English society. Rowe's Shakespeare is just such a man. He begins by offending against the Game Laws, which in Rowe's time remained one of the primary means of protecting the property rights of country gentlemen; he is drummed out of town by Sir Thomas Lucy, the local landowner, and, like Dick Whittington or Henry Fielding's Tom Jones, is forced to go to London to seek his fortune. He ends up hobnobbing with the rich and famous:

> He had the Honour to meet with many great and uncommon Marks of Favour and Friendship from the Earl of *Southampton* . . . There is one instance so singular in the Magnificence of this Patron of *Shakespear's*, that if I had not been assur'd that the Story was handed down by Sir *William D'Avenant*, who was probably very well acquainted with his Affairs, I should not have ventured to have inserted, that my Lord *Southampton*, at one time, gave him a thousand Pounds, to enable him to go through with a Purchase which he heard he had a mind to.

He even attracts the attention of the Queen herself:

> Queen *Elizabeth* had several of his Plays Acted before her, and without
> doubt gave him many gracious Marks of her Favour . . . She was so well
> pleas'd with that admirable Character of *Falstaff*, in the two Parts of
> *Henry the Fourth*, that she commanded him to continue it for one Play
> more, and to shew him in Love. This is said to be the Occasion of his
> writing *The Merry Wives of Windsor*.

This tradition of a royal command was first recorded by John Dennis in the
preface to his adaptation of *The Merry Wives of Windsor*, published in 1702. He
added for good measure that the Queen was so keen to see Sir John in love that
she gave Will just ten days to write the play—and he duly obliged.

The anecdote retains its point whether or not the commission came from
the Queen: Shakespeare is imagined to have the gift of dashing off a new play
in less than a fortnight, while Falstaff is made into a larger-than-life character
who bursts the bounds of the play in which he originally appeared. He generates
not only a second part of *Henry IV*, but also *The Merry Wives*. We cannot have
enough of Falstaff, so what better than a play which shows him in love? One of
the first things we want to know about our heroes is who they fell in love with.

Shakespeare unlocks his heart?

What, then, about the love life of Shakespeare himself? Rowe and his successors
among the eighteenth-century Shakespeareans did not take much interest in
the question, though they repeatedly returned to the anecdote about Davenant
being the dramatist's natural son. It certainly did not occur to them to seek in
the plays for hidden clues to Shakespeare's amorous inclinations. They did not
regard literature as encoded autobiography. This was an idea which only emerged
towards the end of the century and which was at the centre of the great cultural
shift that we call the Romantic movement.

The point is crucial and a failure to grasp it has done more than anything else
to create misconceptions and myths about Shakespeare. In a book on Sir Philip
Sidney, John Buxton provides the best summary I know of the cardinal difference
between late sixteenth- and early nineteenth-century poetry:

> The Elizabethans wrote for Penelope Devereux, or Lucy Harington,
> or Magdalen Herbert, for a gentleman or noble person, for the
> court, for the benchers of the Middle Temple. Their audience was
> not vaguely perceived through a mist of universal benevolence: they
> could kiss its hand, or hear the tones of its voice. From this arises
> the paradox that the Romantics, writing for the patronage of the
> unknown man in the bookshop, are much more personal than the

Elizabethans, writing, as often as not, for someone with whom they had dined a few days ago. For the Romantic, with everyone to write for, and therefore with no one to write for, wrote for and about himself in a way 'unprecedented in literary history', as Wordsworth remarked; whereas the Elizabethan tried to produce a poem to suit a particular occasion and a known taste.

'Scorn not the sonnet,' wrote Wordsworth in his sonnet on the sonnet: 'with this key / Shakspeare unlocked his heart'. 'Did Shakespeare?' answered Robert Browning, who knew the habits and conventions of the Renaissance, the arts of *persona* and role-play, rather better. 'If so, the less Shakespeare he!'

When Romantics get their hands on Shakespeare's sonnets, the trouble begins. In 1796 August Wilhelm von Schlegel, a central figure in the German Romantic movement, remarked that the sonnets appeared to have been inspired by real love and therefore gave unique access to the poet's life. In his lectures on drama delivered in Vienna in 1808, he amplified the point:

> It betrays more than ordinary deficiency of critical acumen in Shakspeare's commentators that none of them, as far as we know, have ever thought of availing themselves of his sonnets for tracing the circumstances of his life. These sonnets paint most unequivocally the actual situation and sentiments of the poet; they make us acquainted with the passions of the man; they even contain remarkable confessions of his youthful errors.

In 1838 another German Romantic, Heinrich Heine, confidently proclaimed that the sonnets were authentic records of the circumstances of Shakespeare's life and in particular his misery. Before our eyes Shakespeare becomes a Romantic, making poetry—as Heine himself did—out of his personal misery.

It is to Schlegel and Romanticism, then, that we owe the idea that the sonnets are *Shakespeare's Autobiographical Poems*—a book of this title by Charles Armitage Brown was also published in 1838. Brown had been a close friend of John Keats, whose sonnets most certainly are autobiographical poems. But that Keats inspired Brown and Shakespeare inspired Keats does not mean that Shakespeare's sonnets were like Keats's. Shakespeare was not a Romantic poet like Wordsworth who just sat down and wrote a sonnet when he felt one coming on, or like Keats for whom the sonnet was above all a way of expressing his own intense feelings.

There is some reason to suppose that the order in which the one hundred and fifty-four sonnets appeared in their first Quarto edition of 1609 was carefully thought out. Often a particular sonnet is a continuation of, or a reply to, the one before. Occasionally there seems to be deliberate play between a sonnet's subject matter and its place in the sequence. For instance, the first sonnet on the power of time is number 12 and its first line concerns a 'clock'—which counts in twelves. The climactic sonnet on the same theme, which begins 'Like as the waves make towards the pebbled shores, / So do our minutes hasten to their end', is 60—the number of minutes that are ended by an hour.

But even if we discount the significance of individual placements, the sonnets as a whole unquestionably fall into three discrete groups. The first one hundred and twenty-six appear to be addressed to a youthful 'you'/'thou' who is 'right fair', who seems always to be one and the same person, and who, whenever his sex is identified, is male; the next twenty-six are concerned with a woman, who is 'coloured ill'; the final two sonnets—a pair of vignettes of Cupid—are addressed to neither of them. The break after sonnet 126 might even be marked in the text: uniquely in the collection, that poem has twelve lines instead of fourteen; and it ends with a pair of lines consisting of blanks inside parentheses. Whether the origins of these marks are the author's or the publisher's, they highlight the fact that sonnet 126 is a kind of 'envoy' and they effect a pause before the change of subject represented by 127.

If we read the sonnets in the sequence in which they were printed, the outline of a story is fairly clear. It is not so sequential a narrative as that of Sir Philip Sidney's *Astrophil and Stella*, the most celebrated previous collection of Elizabethan sonnets. By no means every poem fits the pattern—thus for example, numbers 78 to 86 are a discrete group about 'rival poets', yet 81 is an exception. But the grouping of like themes is such that one has a sense of a beginning, a middle, and an end. Charles Armitage Brown's division of the sequence into six phases was the first attempt to summarize it as a narrative, and it remains representative:

1. To his friend, persuading him to marry (1–26)
2. To his friend, who had robbed the poet of his mistress, forgiving him (27–55)
3. To his friend, complaining of his coldness, and warning him of life's decay (56–77)
4. To his friend, complaining that he prefers another poet's praises, and reproving him for faults that may injure his character (78–101)
5. To his friend, excusing himself for having been some time silent, and disclaiming the charge of inconstancy (102–126)
6. To his mistress, on her infidelity (127–152)

Like most readings of the sonnets, this one involves a degree of projection on Brown's part. Subsequent commentators regard the first seventeen sonnets, not the first twenty-six, as the 'marriage-group'—and, strictly, their subject is reproduction rather than marriage. Sonnets 40 to 42 seem to imply that the poet's friend has slept with the poet's mistress, but it is fantasy to make this the matter of all the poems from 27 to 55. Again, phrases like 'reproving' and 'injure his character' owe more to a Victorian notion of gentlemanly conduct than to an Elizabethan patron–client relationship. But it remains true that the sequence begins with seventeen sonnets urging the youth to reproduce his beauty, is focused on time and mortality in the sixties, becomes exceptionally embittered in the nineties, and turns to the 'dark lady' at 127. It is hardly surprising that in a biographical age like the nineteenth century, people started extrapolating Shakespeare's love life from this narrative.

One factor which may have prevented biographical readings of the sonnets from emerging rather earlier was the embarrassing fact that the first one hundred and twenty-six of them were apparently addressed to a young man, not, as was customary in the form, to the poet's lady-love. In 1640 the opportunistic publisher John Benson got round this problem by producing an edition which cheerfully changed some of the pronouns from 'he' to 'she' and 'him' to 'her', but this ceased to be a possible course of action once the eighteenth-century code of editorial responsibility had been carved out. The non-dramatic works were generally excluded from eighteenth-century editions of Shakespeare, such as Dr Johnson's of 1765. When Edmond Malone included them in his 1780 *Supplement* to the revision of the Johnson edition which had appeared two years earlier, George Steevens added notes in which he said that the sonnet form was characterized by 'the highest strain of affectation, pedantry, circumlocution, and nonsense'. Steevens went so far as to say that 'the strongest act of Parliament that could be framed would fail to compel readers into their service'; of sonnet 20, 'A woman's face with nature's own hand painted / Hast thou, the master-mistress of my passion', he wrote 'It is impossible to read this fulsome panegyrick, addressed to a male object, without an equal mixture of disgust and indignation'. This distaste is manifestly moral as well as aesthetic. In the Victorian era, Henry Hallam, father of Alfred Tennyson's dear friend Arthur, was so disturbed by the implied sexual orientation of the sonnets that he wished they had never been written. It was left for a long succession of later commentators to salvage the situation by declaring that the poet's love for the Fair Youth was a matter of pure friendship rather than homosexual desire.

The fortunes of biographical reading

Two great questions have dominated discussion of the sonnets: to whom are they addressed, and are they indeed autobiographical? Who was the beautiful young man whom the poet is urging to marry in the first seventeen sonnets? Since he is the presumed addressee of the next one hundred and nine, did Shakespeare himself fall in love with him? And was he synonymous with the mysterious 'Mr W.H.' described in the publisher's prefatory statement to the 1609 edition as 'the only begetter of these ensuing sonnets'?

The difficulty of answering these questions with any degree of assurance may be seen from the handling of them by Sir Sidney Lee, one of the begetters of the *Dictionary of National Biography* and the author of what was hailed on its publication in 1898 as the fullest and most responsible biography of Shakespeare yet written.

In the early 1890s, Lee contributed entries to the *Dictionary of National Biography* (*DNB*) in which he stated categorically that the dedication to the 1609 Quarto 'is addressed to [the Earl of] Pembroke, disguised under the initials of his family name—William Herbert' and, furthermore, that Shakespeare's young friend 'was doubtless Pembroke himself, and "the dark lady" in all probability was Pembroke's mistress, Mary Fitton. Nothing in the sonnets directly contradicts the identification of W.H .... with William Herbert, and many minute internal details confirm it.' But by 1897 the serially issued biographical dictionary had reached the letter S and thus included Lee's article on Shakespeare (some 40,000 words, the longest entry in the entire *DNB*). Here it was announced that 'There is no evidence that [Pembroke] was in his youth acquainted with the poet, or at any time closely associated with him'. The identification of the fair youth of the sonnets with Pembroke rested 'on wholly erroneous premisses'. As for Mary Fitton, she had proved distinctly unfitting to be the dark lady: in her *Gossip from a Muniment Room*, also of 1897, Lady Newdigate-Newdegate reproduced two portraits which showed that her complexion was fair not dark, her hair brown not black, and her eyes grey not black.

In his *DNB* article on Shakespeare, and the biography into which he expanded it the following year, Lee shifted his allegiance to the other leading candidate for fair youth: the sonnets clearly affirm that the youth is Shakespeare's patron and Shakespeare's only known patron was Henry Wriothesley, third Earl of Southampton. By the time Lee reached the letter W in 1900, he was as convinced of this theory as he had been a decade earlier of the other one: his *DNB* entry on Wriothesley states that 'Southampton doubtless inspired Shakespeare with genuine personal affection'.

In later editions of the earlier entry, the argument that the fair youth was 'doubtless' Pembroke was quietly dropped. As H.E. Rollins put it with the dry humour which characterizes his admirable Variorum edition of the *Sonnets*, 'Of course Lee had a perfect right to move abruptly from one side to another (his doing so speaks well for his open-mindedness); though, in view of the flat contradictions between the 1889 (Fitton) and 1891 (Herbert) volumes and the 1897 (Shakespeare) and 1900 (Wriothesley) volumes of the *DNB*, it might have been fairer to students, and more sporting, if he had mentioned his change of creed'.

The identity of the fair youth matters much more to those who believe that the poems grew from personal experience than to those who believe that they are poetic fictions, influenced more by sonneteering convention than by life. So where did Lee stand on this other great question? When his *DNB* article on Shakespeare was published in London in 1897, readers were given the following categorical statement:

> Attempts have been made to represent [the sonnets] as purely literary exercises, mainly on the ground that a personal interpretation seriously reflects on Shakespeare's moral character. But only the two concluding sonnets (153 and 154) can be regarded by the unbiased reader as the artificial product of a poet's fancy. . . . In the rest of the 'Sonnets' Shakespeare avows, in phraseology that is often cryptic, the experiences of his own heart. Their uncontrolled ardour suggests that they came from a youthful pen—from a man not more than thirty.

But as soon as these words were in print, Lee ordered them to be cut from the dictionary's type-plates. Readers of the New York edition, published a few months later, were informed that the sonnets were 'to a large extent undertaken as literary exercises'—Shakespeare's 'ever-present dramatic instinct may be held to account for most of the illusion of personal confession which they call up in many minds'.

Lee went on to devote a substantial section of his 1898 *Life* to the 'anti-biographical' theory. A chapter entitled 'The Borrowed Conceits of the Sonnets' asserted that most of the poems are 'little more than professional trials of skill' and that to seek a biographical original for the dark lady would be as ridiculous as to suppose that Cleopatra was based upon some dusky woman of Shakespeare's acquaintance and not upon the historical Cleopatra. Two chapters later, Lee turns to 'The Supposed Story of Intrigue in the Sonnets'. Readers might themselves suppose from this chapter title that Lee will argue that the youth's affair with the dark lady is another quasi-dramatic fiction. But at this point the biographer cannot stop himself slipping back to his former position: 'The definite element of intrigue that is developed here is not found anywhere else in the range of Elizabethan sonnet-literature. The character of the innovation and its treatment seem only capable of explanation by regarding the topic as a reflection of Shakespeare's personal experience.' There is something about the sonnets which irresistibly pulls Lee's instincts back to the biographical reading that his reason has rejected.

But the most extraordinary volte-face remains the one whereby Lee passed instantly from the ultra-Romantic position which was first articulated by Schlegel to the ultra-anti-Romantic position which has become dominant among modern scholars. Anti-Romanticism reached its culmination in Stephen Booth's 1977 edition of the *Sonnets*, where it was polemically stated that 'William Shakespeare was almost certainly homosexual, bisexual, or heterosexual. The sonnets provide no evidence on the matter.' Resistance to the biographical approach has even led one critic to argue that since Shakespeare was playing with traditional sonnet-matter, and since in number 130 (and indeed in *Love's Labour's Lost*) he explicitly parodies the conventions of praise so dear to sonneteers, the whole sequence should be read as nothing more than a parody of sonneteering conceived for the delight of his witty friends.

The sonnets have an extraordinary capacity to elicit categorical statements from their interpreters. It is announced that the youth *is* Southampton, the youth *is* Pembroke, the youth *is* nobody, the dark lady *is* Mary Fitton, she *is* Aemilia Lanyer, she *is* nobody, the sonnets *are* based on experience, they are *not* based on experience, the love was *not* homosexual, the love *was* homosexual, the love was a dramatic fiction which had *nothing* to do with Shakespeare's sexuality. Somehow the poems convince each reader that what he or she sees in them is what is really there. But somehow they then sneak up behind you and convince you of something completely different.

They can do this partly because of what they leave out. Sidney's *Astrophil and Stella* consists of one hundred and eight sonnets, each crystallizing a lover's mood, and nine songs in which the 'plot' is carried forward—Astrophil confesses his love to Stella, she rejects him, and so on. Shakespeare left out the songs; all the 'events' take place off stage. Since the poems imply a plot without actually spelling it out, there is room for readers to step in with their version of affairs. As the plays leave interpretive space for the audience—we have to decide whether to side with Hal or Falstaff, we are not *told* how to react—so the sonnets drop hints to draw the reader into their implied narrative, but have a cunning reticence which allows our fantasies to run riot.

This, then, *is* the genius of the sonnets: their power to generate readings. In the nineteenth century, most of those readings were biographical. In the late twentieth-century academy, most of them are linguistic. The Stephen Booth edition came equipped with a four-hundred-page commentary which discovered multiple wordplays in almost every line of every sonnet. This kind of reading had its origin in an essay on sonnet 94 by William Empson which begins as follows:

> It is agreed that *They that have power to hurt and will do none* is a piece of grave irony, but there the matter is generally left; you can work through all the notes in the Variorum [edition] without finding out whether flower, lily, 'owner,' and person addressed are alike or opposed. One would like to say that the poem has all possible such meanings, digested into some order, and then try to show how this is done, but the mere number of possible interpretations is amusingly too great. Taking the

simplest view (that any two may be alike in some one property) any one
of the four either is or is not and either should or should not be like
each of the others; this yields 4096 possible movements of thought, with
other possibilities. The niggler is routed here.

But Empson was a brilliant biographical critic as well as a brilliant linguistic one;
his essay is as shrewd on the poem's implied relationship with its author's patron
as it is on the dazzling wordplay. For Empson it was proper to speculate about
biographical origins, but the problems of the sonnets were by no means 'solved'
by biography.

This seems to me the best position to hold. A story about where the sonnets
came from is necessary for an understanding of their nature, but not sufficient
for an appreciation of their complexity.

The professed aim of Booth's edition, stated in its preface, was to give the
modern reader as much as the editor could 'resurrect of a Renaissance reader's
experience of the 1609 Quarto'. This was a rather curious ambition in view of
the fact that the 1609 Quarto seems to have attracted the attention of hardly
any Renaissance readers. Unlike Shakespeare's two best-selling narrative poems,
Venus and Adonis and *The Rape of Lucrece*, which went through edition after
edition and were praised by dozens of his contemporaries, the 1609 *Sonnets* were
never reprinted and hardly ever referred to. Conceivably the book was actively
suppressed; more probably, it quietly languished and soon died. That some, at
least, of the sonnets circulated in manuscript in the 1590s shows that their
intended Renaissance readers were Shakespeare's 'private friends', who would
by definition have known something of the circumstances of composition. They,
surely, are a more interesting audience to recover than the equally small and even
more hypothetical readership of the 1609 volume. Shakespeare's sonnets were
at least initially written for a specific purpose and a specific reader or coterie
of readers, and we will understand them better if we try to find out who those
readers were.

To establish as best we can the circumstances of composition and initial
consumption is not to fall in with the Romantic biographical fallacy. Consider
the comparable case of Sir Philip Sidney's *Astrophil and Stella*. 'Astrophil' is not
synonymous with Sir Philip, nor 'Stella' with Penelope Devereux, but there is
no doubt that Penelope Devereux was the ideal implied reader of the sequence.
We do not know, and it does not matter much, whether Philip was really in love
with Penelope, but we do know, and it matters a great deal, that in the thirty-
seventh sonnet of the sequence Sidney puns on the name of Lord Rich, to whom
Penelope was unhappily married and whom the poet clearly regarded as unworthy
of her. In other sonnets in the sequence the poet-narrator 'Astrophil' manifestly
alludes to Sir Philip's status at court, his coat of arms, and his father. There is
a character in Sidney's *Arcadia* called Philisides, a name which plays wittily on

Philip and Sidney; by the same account, 'Astrophil' means more than 'lover of Stella' (from Greek, 'astro-', star, and 'Phil-', love)—the name also contains Phil Sidney himself. These facts do not prove the poems to be fully autobiographical, but they do show that Elizabethan sonneteering makes uses of personal material as well as rhetorical convention. Astro-Phil is at some level Sir Philip; so too, 'Will' in sonnets 135, 136, and 143 is at some level William.

Penelope Devereux is and is not 'Stella', but she was the first implied reader of *Astrophil*; the Countess of Pembroke almost certainly is not 'Delia', but she was the first implied reader of Samuel Daniel's sonnet sequence, *Delia*. So too, Shakespeare's potential patron is and is not the 'fair youth', but he was the first implied reader of the sonnets. Furthermore, the gap between the patron as reader and as subject is smaller than in other cases, for—unusually—Shakespeare does not give a mythical name to his subject of praise, along the lines of Stella, Delia, or Ganymede (the name of the lovely lad in Richard Barnfield's overtly homosexual sequence, *The Affectionate Shepherd*).

We may reasonably assume that to begin with there was only one fair youth. It is a further reasonable inference that he was a patron or potential patron: sonnets 26 and 57–8 include words and phrases like 'Lord', 'vassalage', 'written ambassage', 'duty', 'waiting', 'your servant' and 'being at your beck', while the 'rivals poets' sequence only makes sense in the context of a jostle for patronage. For this reason, the only two serious candidates for 'fair youth' are those between whom Lee wavered: William Herbert, third Earl of Pembroke, a noted patron of poets (and one of the dedicatees of the posthumous Folio of Shakespeare's works) who on two occasions in the late 1590s vigorously resisted attempts to marry him off, and Henry Wriothesley, third Earl of Southampton, a noted patron of poets (and the dedicatee of Shakespeare's unquestionably authorized publications, *Venus and Adonis* and *The Rape of Lucrece*), who in the early 1590s vigorously resisted an attempt to marry him off. Either of them is thus a possible candidate as recipient of the first group of sonnets, on the subject of begetting an heir.

The language of this first group—and indeed of many more of the sonnets—is very close to the language both of the two narrative poems which Shakespeare dedicated to Southampton in 1593–4 and of the plays of that vintage, notably *Love's Labour's Lost*. Furthermore, references such as that in sonnet 16 to 'my pupil pen' suggest early work. A starting-date of around 1592–4 favours Southampton, since Pembroke would only have been twelve or thirteen years old at the time. It is also striking that sonnet 26, which makes such extensive use of the language of patronage, reads like a versification of the prose dedication to Southampton which Shakespeare prefixed to *Lucrece* in 1594. The case for Pembroke is much weaker for the simple reason that we have no evidence that Shakespeare—as opposed to his fellow-actors after his death—sought William Herbert's patronage. Many, if not all, of the sonnets were written in the 1590s, yet no Pembrokite has established any link between Shakespeare and Pembroke in the 1590s.

The lovely boy

It is not inconceivable that Shakespeare began writing sonnets to Southampton in the early 1590s, then, when it became clear that the young Earl was not going to be an especially munificent patron, the poet changed course and started addressing sonnets to Pembroke in the late 1590s and early 1600s. Since very few of the sonnets had been published by this time, individual poems could even have been recycled for a new 'ideal reader'. The 1609 Quarto would then have had the effect of collapsing two glamorous aristocrats into one composite lovely boy. The dedicatory address might then be read as a sleight-of-hand: an assurance to Pembroke (W[illiam] H[erbert]) that he was the *only* inspirer of the sonnets, whereas in fact he was one of two male inspirers.

In the absence of new evidence, hypotheses such as this cannot be refuted, but in deciding on the identity of the *original* recipient of the first of the sonnets, we should apply the metaphorical razor of the medieval philosopher William of Occam. Occam's estimable principle was that for purposes of explanation things not known to exist should not, unless it is absolutely necessary, be postulated as existing. *All candidatures for the fair youth with the exception of Southampton's depend on things not known to exist; it is not necessary to postulate any of these things as existing, since the origin of the sonnets can be explained with things we do know to exist.*

Among these things are the following.

The vogue for writing sonnets of praise in an attempt to gain literary patronage belongs to the early 1590s. Of all surviving Elizabethan sonnet-cycles, the closest to Shakespeare's in language and structure is Samuel Daniel's *Delia*, published in 1592. The London theatres were closed, for fear of spreading plague, for much of the period 1592–4. In 1593–4 Shakespeare sought the patronage of the Earl of Southampton by dedicating his two narrative poems to him. Through his mother, Mary Arden, Shakespeare was a distant relative of Southampton. In the period 1591–4 Southampton was notably recalcitrant about marriage. The obvious inference of all this is that Shakespeare began writing sonnets to Southampton in the period 1592–4, probably beginning with a group somehow concerning marriage.

Internal evidence needs to be treated with great caution, but the following could also be numbered among Occam's 'things known to exist'. The sonnets seem to refer to the fair youth's mother as being alive, his father dead: this fits Southampton's case in the early 1590s (and not Pembroke's in the late 1590s). In the nineteenth century, Henry Wriothesley's descendants said that their name was pronounced 'Rosely'; Southampton's most authoritative biographer claims that in the sixteenth century the family name was pronounced 'Rye-ose-ley'. Either way, the word 'Rose' may be audible in the name. Furthermore, Southampton's home at Titchfield was emblazoned with a heraldic representation of roses. Sonnet 1 begins 'From fairest creatures we desire increase, / That thereby beauty's *Rose* might never die'; this *Rose* is one of the few words italicized in the original text, which suggests that it was stressed deliberately. 'Rose' is frequently played on in the sonnets to the youth, for example in sonnet 95, where 'the fragrant rose' is juxtaposed to 'thy budding name'. Additionally, the Southampton family motto was 'one for all, all for one'. Though wordplay on 'one' and 'all' was common in Elizabethan times, it seems almost obsessive in Shakespeare's *Sonnets*—for instance, in sonnet 8 'all in one' occurs in the context of family, and in 53 'all', 'one', and 'none' come into conjunction in the context of a comparison of the fair youth to Adonis, the mythical fair youth of Shakespeare's first poem dedicated to Southampton.

Again, italicization and wordplay give mysterious significance to the word '*Hews*' in sonnet 20, perhaps suggesting a twist on the four initial letters of Henry Wriothesley, Earl of Southampton. 'HEWS' is and is not 'H.W.E.S.', just as in Maria's riddling letter in *Twelfth Night* 'M.O.A.I.' is and is not Malvolio. Insofar as the fair youth is made of language, is a fictional creation, he is not Southampton; but insofar as he has a human original, that original is Southampton and not Pembroke or anyone else.

The first book to be dedicated to Southampton was a Latin poem called *Narcissus*, written in 1591 by John Clapham, a secretary to Lord Burghley. Southampton was Burghley's ward and at this time Burghley wanted him to marry his own granddaughter, Elizabeth de Vere. Southampton refused—with the result that when he came of age he had to pay a substantial fine to Burghley, which crippled him financially. Since Narcissus comes to a watery end as the result of his resistance to womankind, it is likely that Clapham's poem was commissioned by Burghley to put pressure on Southampton in the marriage stakes. Given the similarity of the Narcissus theme to the *Venus and Adonis* one, and the tissue of allusions to Narcissus in the first seventeen sonnets, the so-called 'marriage' group, it seems highly plausible that Shakespeare was aware of what was going on in the Southampton household—though exactly how the sonnets relate to the marriage question is a complicated matter which we will have to pursue further.

It would have been assumed that Southampton would gain control of a considerable fortune once he came of age in 1595 (though because of Burghley's fine this did not in fact prove to be the case), so in 1593–4 we find a number of poets, including Thomas Nashe and Barnabe Barnes, positioning themselves as potential recipients of his patronage by dedicating works to him. This situation provides a reasonable explanation for Shakespeare's sonnets on the theme of rivalry for patronage, though there is no hard evidence to enable us to name the particular poet or poets whom he singles out as his own rivals.

Once all these facts are collected, the case for Southampton as the original patron/youth looks irrefutable. To regard the sonnets as parody, exercise, or pure play is to forget the economic urge which drove Shakespeare to write. He wrote plays to win audiences for his theatre company; when the theatres were closed, he wrote *Venus and Adonis* and *The Rape of Lucrece* to gain the patronage of Southampton. In the 1590s, sonnets were part of a poet's repertoire in the quest for patronage and this is what must initially have drawn Shakespeare to the form. The vast sum of a thousand pounds is hard to credit, but if there is any truth in Rowe's story of Southampton giving Shakespeare financial support, then it looks as if the sonnets might have done the trick.

Bearing this in mind, we must do away with the notion that the first seventeen sonnets were written with the intention of literally urging Southampton to get married. It may have been all very well for John Clapham, under Burghley's protection, to remind the young Earl of the dangers of narcissism, but it is wholly implausible that Shakespeare would have begun his quest for patronage by urging his patron to do the very thing he didn't want to do, namely get married quickly. *Venus and Adonis*, the second book to be dedicated to Southampton, is an essentially comic treatment of the theme of male resistance to woman. It may be regarded as a playful riposte to Clapham that would have been more likely to please Southampton. I suspect that the first few sonnets were conceived in similar terms, perhaps even as a joke at Burghley's expense.

Shakespeare is saying something like the following: 'Burghley wants you to marry, but you're far too smart to be influenced by Clapham's wooden, moralizing Latin poem warning you of the fate of Narcissus; it would be easy to write a more persuasive set of poems on the marriage theme; after all, it's a highly traditional theme (Erasmus wrote a dialogue on it); look, here are all the traditional arguments (that propagation is natural, that it's a way of cheating age and time), but—and here's a twist on convention—the best argument of all is not the traditional one about the need to pass on your *virtue*, but rather it's the need to pass on your *beauty*. We'll begin with Clapham's Narcissus image (sonnet 1: "But thou, contracted to thine own bright eyes"; sonnet 3: "Look in thy glass"), but instead of condemning narcissism, and moralizing about the transience of beauty, we'll positively revel in it.'

Once he started down this line, he quickly saw the next trick: to locate the propagation and immortalization of his subject's beauty not in an heir, but *in the sonnets themselves*. Thus the couplet of 12 reads 'And nothing 'gainst Time's scythe can make defence / Save breed to brave him when he takes thee hence', whereas that of 15 reads 'And all in war with Time for love of you, / As he takes from you I engraft you new'; 17 proposes a double immortality, in a child and in 'my rhyme', but then 18 and 19 make the strongest claims yet for the poet's 'eternal lines' and their power to defeat Time. The initial theme of getting an heir has served its purpose—crudely, that of grabbing the reader's (and especially Southampton's) attention—and we do not hear of it again. Shakespeare has written himself into the most ancient role of the poet: as someone who sings for his supper, immortalizes his master or mistress in return for their patronage.

But now Shakespeare is hooked on writing sonnets arising from this theme. His restless wit and sharp intelligence lead him to press hard upon every word, every idea. Daniel had written his *Delia* to gain the patronage of a great lady, the Countess of Pembroke; his purpose was well served by the two senses of the word 'mistress'—as the idealized fair lady *in* the poems was his mistress in the sense of lover, so the real fine lady *intended to read* the poems was his mistress in the sense of employer. Shakespeare needs a different trick, since he has a male patron and the word 'master' does not contain the same double meaning. He therefore invents in sonnet 20 the double epithet 'Master Mistress'. He playfully, and perhaps tactfully, adds that he does not really want to do with his master what poets traditionally want to do with their mistresses, namely 'use' their beauty in the act of physical lovemaking: thus the 'one thing' with which nature has '*prickt*' the Master out is left for 'women's pleasure'; it is said to be 'to my purpose nothing'.

One cannot, however, go on writing on a subject without thinking oneself deeply into it. If the sonnets are to work on a profounder level than that of the playfulness which characterizes the tone of the first seventeen of them, the poet has to imagine himself really falling in love with the narcissistic youth. In sonnet 53, the youth becomes Adonis, but generally Shakespeare eschews the use of classical names which had characterized the work of his predecessors. He nevertheless retained a controlling classical myth beneath the surface. If the youth is Narcissus, he himself has to be Echo. One meaning of Echo, the girl whose unrequited love for Narcissus causes her to waste away and become a disembodied voice, is that love is by its nature dependent on an Other. Narcissism is a perverted form of love exactly because it denies the Other. To speak words of love and hear them echoed by one's partner is love's lovely requital. But at the same time, an echo does not exist: it is merely a repetition of one's own words. Echo and Narcissus belong in the same story because erotic love itself is a projection of one's own desires and ideals, not an answering to the other. Shakespeare knows that when you look in your lover's eyes, it is a reflection of yourself that you see. Where he had begun sonnet 3 by telling the youth to look in his mirror, he begins sonnet 22 by looking in his own glass. Is love a reception within of the 'thou', the beloved other perceived by the 'eye', or is it a projection outward of the 'I', the voracious self?

Exactly for the reason that the sonnets are about this problem, it is a mistake to make a choice between biographical and anti-biographical readings of them. To make such a choice implies that a love poem must be either fact or fancy. Shakespeare either *really loved* the fair youth or *only imagined* his love. But one of the things that Elizabethan sonnets, Shakespeare's above all others, are very good at showing is that it is simple-minded to envisage such a distinction. Love does not work like that: being in love is very exactly something that happens *in the imagination*. In *A Midsummer Night's Dream*, Theseus says that lunatics, lovers, and poets are of imagination 'all compact'—their mental states lead to kinds of transformed vision whereby they see the world differently from how one sees it when in a 'rational' state of mind. The task of love poets is to find ways of describing this changed vision; their problem is that so many people have tried doing this before that they very quickly start repeating all the clichés of their poetic predecessors.

They start, for instance, to enumerate the beauties of their beloved from top to toe, in a convention known as the blazon. Shakespeare parodies this convention in sonnet 130, 'My mistress' eyes are nothing like the sun', ending by saying that he loves his mistress more truly than those who embellish their mistresses with 'false compare'. Does this mean that he has written a 'sincere' love poem? No, because the anti-blazon was a convention almost as old as the blazon. Does it mean, then, that he has merely written an exercise? Only insofar as all writing is an exercise of the wits, the arts of expressions, as much as it is a record of feeling or experience.

Because they are highly self-conscious about the fact that any kind of recording of feeling or experience is a rhetorical art, Shakespeare's sonnets are peculiarly amenable to the extreme anti-realist practice of deconstruction, which endlessly generates interpretations, always deferring reversion to 'real experience'. But this does not mean that their sole purpose is pure linguistic play or, in the reductive version of this position, that they are 'mere literary exercises' or parodies with no origin in feeling or experience. The tone of those of them that are parodies, notably 'My mistress' eyes are nothing like the sun', is very different from the tone of the rest—I would say that 'My mistress' eyes' was deliberately placed at 130 to lighten the tone after the agonized energies of 129, 'Th'expense of spirit in a waste of shame / Is lust in action'.

Yet in making this distinction, I am projecting, as do all readers of these mesmerizing, puzzling poems. To my ear, the bitterness of tone in certain of the sonnets is incompatible with the idea that they are mere exercises. But it could equally well be argued that Shakespeare knew how to mimic bitterness in his plays—think of Hamlet's soliloquies—and that he may therefore be feigning it in his sonnets. The only solution to this problem is to allow the sonnets to rest in a middle space between experience and imagination. We must not reduce them to their origin, probable as it is that Shakespeare began to write them around the time he was seeking Southampton's patronage by dedicating his two narrative poems to him.

The sonnets are best thought of as *imaginings of potential situations which might have grown* from the initial Southampton situation. We will never know exactly which of them are rhetorical transmutations of actual occurrences and which are rhetorical enactments of potential situations that Shakespeare imagined. *And it is of their essence that they deny us this knowledge*: they do so precisely in order to show us that we cannot know whether love is 'real' or 'imagined'. We do not need to know what happened in the bed, because what the sonnets are interested in is how love happens in the head.

Does love come from the 'I' or the 'eye', is it a 'truth' or is it a 'lie'? The sonnets meditate and pun obsessively on this, until they end (save for their light mythological coda concerning Cupid's bath) with an extraordinary couplet which holds together all four terms, 'I', 'eye', 'truth', and 'lie':

> For I have sworn thee fair—more perjured eye
> To swear against the truth so foul a lie.

The 'thee' addressed here is the 'dark lady', not the 'fair youth'. The introduction of her into the sequence is the inevitable consequence of sonnet 20's invention of the Master-Mistress and its splitting apart of spiritual and sexual love. If the fair youth is to be the idealized object of unrequited desire, physicality and requital must be siphoned off and directed elsewhere: hence the lady's darkness. Sonnet 144 marks the formal division of the two kinds of love:

> Two loves I have, of comfort and despair,
> Which like two spirits do suggest me still.
> The better angel is a man right fair,
> The worser spirit a woman coloured ill.

But the dramatist in Shakespeare recognizes that human beings are not made of such sharp distinctions. His plays are built upon the dissolution of differences, the unravellings whereby we see some soul of good in things evil and vice-versa, whereby we cannot reject the worser spirit of Falstaff just because we admire Hal's transformation into a better angel. Fairness in Shakespeare is always contaminated with foulness, and vice-versa. The sonnets' way of dramatizing this paradoxical alliance is to imagine a liaison between the man right fair and the woman coloured ill. Their relationship is the subject of sonnets 35 (perhaps), 40, 41, 42, 134, and the vicious closing couplet of 144 in which the woman is imagined to 'fire' the man out with venereal disease.

The dark lady

There is no reason to suppose that the sonnets cease to be anchored to Southampton when the dark lady is introduced. The patron remains the first implied reader. Our reconstruction of origins therefore requires us to imagine a situation in which Southampton would have enjoyed reading about himself betraying Shakespeare by going to bed with his mistress. If we are to maintain our principle that the sonnets are imaginings of potential situations which might have grown from the initial Southampton situation, we would do well to locate the dark lady in the same household.

Biographical sleuths have usually looked for Shakespeare's supposed mistress in the wrong place, namely the London acting world. The leading candidates are a notorious dark-skinned Clerkenwell prostitute known as Lucy Negro and a poetess of Italian extraction, Aemilia Bassano (later Lanyer), who was the mistress of Lord Hunsdon, the patron of Shakespeare's acting company. Yet there is nothing to connect either of these women to Southampton in the 1590s, let alone to his household.

When A. L. Rowse made the case for Aemilia Bassano, for whom there is not a scrap of direct evidence, he announced in a wonderfully circular statement that his answers to the problems of the sonnets 'cannot be impugned, for they are the answer', while adding that anyone who disagreed with him was talking 'complete rubbish'. Without anything approximating to this assurance, I would like to propose that our understanding of the sonnets will be assisted if we *suppose*—not if we confidently assert—that they are tied to some rather sordid intrigue in the Southampton household around 1593–4.

The imagined relationship between the poet and the youth grows from routine flattery to intense love to bitter disillusionment and a sense of betrayal. The articulated relationship between the poet and the dark lady veers between mutual sexual use, regarded sometimes casually and sometimes guiltily, and bitterness stemming from the intervention of the fair youth. The element of guilt, and the sexual disgust that explodes in the single extraordinary sentence of sonnet 129's anatomy of desire, may be caused by the fact that the union involves a breach by both parties of what sonnet 152 calls the 'bed-vow', which in Elizabethan English strongly implies marriage vows.

The 'profile' of the dark lady, as a criminal investigator would put it, therefore sounds as if it should be a married woman in or close to the household of Southampton, whom both Shakespeare and Southampton slept with. The 'William the Conqueror' incident discussed in the previous chapter suggests that a married woman's quick wit and willingness would have been sufficient incentive for Shakespeare to sleep with her, but we perhaps need to find some further incentive for Southampton to do so at precisely the time when he was resisting marriage, especially since there was a rumour in the 1590s that he preferred the sexual company of men to that of women.

It seems to me that an Elizabethan earl of possibly homosexual orientation would be more likely to sleep with a married woman of lower social status because he wanted to score off her husband than because he desired her in herself. Suppose that the young Earl's guardian, who wishes to marry him off against his will, places an agent in his household in order to report back on the progress of the marriage suit and related affairs. Suppose that the agent is married. To sleep with his wife would be the most delicious revenge for the man's presumption in reporting intimate matters back to Burghley.

In the period from 1592–4 there was such an agent in Southampton's household. Placed there by Burghley, he acted as the Earl's language tutor. His name was John Florio. His presence in the household seems to have been of considerable importance for the development of Shakespeare's career—it accounts for much of the dramatist's broad, though very patchy, acquaintance with Italian literature and his slight knowledge of the Italian language. It seems to have been immediately after the period of Southampton's patronage during the closure of the theatres that Shakespeare began to make extensive and ambitious use of Italian settings and plots in his plays. Florio was the obvious person to introduce him to his sources for these. In the same period, phrases from Florio's Italian language manual, *First Fruits*, start appearing in Shakespeare's works; it is even possible that the Italian's affected language is parodied in the character of Don Armado and his pedantry in the character of Holofernes in *Love's Labour's Lost*, Shakespeare's sonnet-ridden play of circa 1595. That play's title and subject matter, its merry demolition of stale courtly love-language, are strongly suggested by a passage in *First Fruits*: 'We need not speak so much of love, all books are full of love, with so many authors, that it were labour lost to speak of Love.'

Unromantic as the thought may be, there is no reason why we should not imagine Shakespeare sleeping with Florio's wife as well as pilfering his library and mocking his phrases. Florio himself (born about 1553) was declining into the vale of years and, to judge from his prodigious literary productivity, devoting himself entirely to his work. At the time in question, he was labouring not of love, but at the massive task of single-handedly compiling the first English-Italian dictionary. A spirited and neglected wife, like the young lady of the city in the William the Conqueror story, could easily enjoy a turn in the bed with the witty poet. And she would find it hard to resist the advances of the Earl, knowing that her husband's income and hence her children's well-being depended on his retaining his post.

My dark lady, then, is John Florio's wife, who happens to have been the sister of Samuel Daniel, the sonneteer. It is a pleasing fancy that the dark lady sonnets might be addressed to the sister of a poet who wrote to a more conventionally fair mistress. One could even complicate the plot by proposing Daniel as the 'rival poet'—there is no direct evidence that he sought Southampton's patronage, but the presence of his sister in the household suggests that he might have seen an opening (which might have been closed pretty quickly as a result of the sexual intrigue involving Shakespeare and Southampton which I am supposing).

Florio wrote that in order to be 'accounted most fair' a woman should have 'Black eyes, black brows, black hairs', though we have no way of knowing whether

Mrs Florio lived up to this dark ideal. But to concern ourselves overmuch with literal physical attributes is to miss the point. In Elizabethan love literature, fairness and darkness have a great deal more to do with social status than with actual hair and eye colour. Fairness was regarded as synonymous with aristocratic and courtly elevation, darkness with low origins. A dark woman means a country wench. One thing we do know about Miss Daniel is that she was a low-born Somerset lass.

If genes are to be trusted, we may also surmise that she was witty and talented. Her brother Samuel became one of the most admired poets of the age, whilst another brother, John, became a highly regarded musician and composer. According to Thomas Fuller's *Worthies of England*, the Daniels' father was himself a music master. Miss Daniel's musical ability is a sure bet. In sonnet 128, the dark lady proves herself to be accomplished at the keyboard. The poet envies 'those jacks that nimble leap / To kiss the tender inward of thy hand'. Might the jacks be not only the keys but also the husband, John—which is Jack—Florio? Give husband Jack thy fingers, lover Will thy lips to kiss, the sonnet would then end.

The Florios had four children. A daughter called Aurelia was probably the eldest; another daughter, Joan, was born in 1585, then Edward in 1588 and Elizabeth in 1589. The simile in sonnet 143 whereby 'Will' compares himself to his mistress's 'neglected child' would gain added poignancy if Mrs Florio really were neglecting young Edward and Elizabeth as she lay in bed with Will.

As for Florio himself, he was not a poet but he was in the 'pay and patronage' of Southampton. He states as much in the dedication to *A World of Words*, his Italian dictionary. Shakespeare introduces the theme of rival writers in sonnet 78 with the phrase 'every *Alien* pen'. 'Alien', one of the handful of italicized words in the 1609 Quarto, had a very specific meaning in Elizabethan English: it referred to a foreigner. The Italian Florio was the only writer of Shakespeare's acquaintance who was an 'alien'. Could he have been the initial rival who inspired Shakespeare to imagine a series of greater rivals in the sequence through to 86? (In chapter four, I will suggest the identity of the greatest of them.) And might Shakespeare be tacitly alluding to Florio's other presumed function when in the couplet of sonnet 125 he introduces the figure of a 'suborned informer'?

We do not know Mrs Florio's first name. Our ignorance is tantalizing but fitting. She has hitherto survived in literary history only as 'Daniel's sister' and 'Florio's wife'. To this we may add 'and perhaps Shakespeare's mistress'. She has been made immortal only in terms of her relationships with others: as sister/wife/mistress to a succession of male writers and as mother to the Florio children whose names do survive. The dark lady is always the *addressee*: the fact that we do not know her first name is a token of how we never hear her voice, her side of the story.

We will never know whether Shakespeare and/or Southampton really slept with Florio's wife and the sonnets knowingly allude to actual events, or whether the sonnets are knowing imaginings of possible intrigue. To reiterate, their reticence on this matter is essential to their purpose: we *must* be denied knowledge of the original bed deeds, because the sonnets are interested not so much in who lies with whom as in the paradoxes of eyeing and lying.

My story is and is not a fantasy. To adapt what Oscar Wilde once said of Will Hughes, his candidate for the 'fair youth': you must believe in Mrs Florio—I almost do myself. I began to work on the sonnets with a determination to adhere to an agnostic position on the question of their autobiographical elements. But, like Sidney Lee, I have been unable to hold fast to my unbelief. The sonnets have wrought their magic upon me and forced from me yet one more reading to add to all those which they have generated since the Romantic period. Their genius is still at work.

Master W. H.

Shakespeare did not publish his sonnets with a dedication to Southampton, as he published *Venus and Adonis* and *Lucrece* with such dedications, and as Samuel Daniel published *Delia* with a dedication to the Countess of Pembroke. The reason for this may be mundane: perhaps by the time he got around to contemplating publication, Southampton had been hit with Burghley's fine and Shakespeare realized there wouldn't be much money left for patronage. Perhaps Southampton had already come up with the goods—that gift which, according to Rowe, Davenant knew about. Perhaps the reopening of the theatres in 1594 and the formation of the Chamberlain's Men meant that all Shakespeare's energies went into his playwrighting. Or it may be that the implied narrative of the sonnets was a little too private for publication to be appropriate.

The fact that Shakespeare didn't rush his sonnets into print shows that their purpose wasn't really the immortalizing of his love's name in 'eternal lines' of black ink. Neither the youth nor the lady is overtly named. The only name that is written and thus immortalized is that of Will himself.

Consider sonnet 55:

Not marble nor the gilded monuments
Of princes shall outlive this powerful rhyme,
But you shall shine more bright in these contents
Than unswept stone besmeared with sluttish time.
When wasteful war shall statues overturn,
And broils root out the work of masonry,
Nor Mars his sword nor war's quick fire shall burn
The living record of your memory.
'Gainst death and all oblivious enmity
Shall you pace forth; your praise shall still find room

Even in the eyes of all posterity
That wear this world out to the ending doom.
    So, till the judgement that yourself arise,
    You live in this, and dwell in lovers' eyes.

In a way it is extraordinary that Shakespeare wrote this poem but did not get it printed. Did he really believe that a single sheet of paper with a poem inked on it would outlive marble and gilded monuments? Multiple printed copies would have stood a much better chance. And if the poem is intended to make his love live in the eyes of posterity, why is the 'you' not named? Writing poetry of praise but forgetting to name the person praised is an oxymoronic activity if ever there was one.

But then we stop to think: it is not Shakespeare's 'love' in the sense of his beloved that is at stake here; it is Shakespeare's 'love' in the sense of his capacity to write of love. Who is it that 'dwells in lovers' eyes' when this poem is read? If we read it to our lover, we might imagine that it is him or her. But if we look our lover in the eyes as we recite it, the person we see dwelling in those eyes is ourself. The only person who is immortalized in the sense of speaking beyond the grave, being reanimated, is William Shakespeare.

Once the poems are *published*, then, it is Shakespeare, not the fair youth, who is immortalized. This brings us to what has been the greatest stumbling block in the way of sensible biographical discussion of the sonnets. I mean of course the inscription which the publisher Thomas Thorpe inserted at the beginning of the 1609 text:

TO . THE . ONLIE . BEGETTER . OF . THESE . INSVING .
SONNETS . M^R. W.H. ALL . HAPPINESSE . AND . THAT .
ETERNITIE . PROMISED . BY . OVR . EVER-LIVING . POET
. WISHETH . THE . WELL-WISHING . ADVENTVRER . IN .
SETTING . FORTH. T. T.

All biographical approaches to the sonnets have assumed that 'the only begetter' must mean either the procurer of the manuscript or the inspirer of the poems.

Of the candidates advanced by those who have supposed it refers to whoever passed the manuscript to Thorpe, the least implausible was brought forward in *The Athenaeum* in April 1867. Southampton's father died in his youth, but in 1598 his mother marred Sir William Hervey or Harvey; she died in late 1607 and Hervey remarried the following year. Could he have been the one to pass the sonnets to Thorpe—perhaps while he was clearing out the Southampton effects before his remarriage—and earn the dedication in return? Though he was a 'Sir', knights were sometimes referred to in the period as plain 'Master'. Perhaps Thorpe even knew about Hervey's new young wife and the prospect that Sir William might be eternized through the birth of a son. This is a charming little story. The scholar Mario Praz confessed to 'a partiality for the picture of the widowed husband roaming about the empty house and finding, among dusty family papers, "Shakespeare's Sonnets": it is so delightfully Victorian.' But, alas, there is a severe problem with the case for Hervey or any other procurer: there is not the slightest piece of evidence that in the language of the period the word 'begetter' could refer to a person who 'acquired' something.

The biographers who have had most fun are those who have assumed that 'begetter' means 'inspirer' and that 'Mr W.H.' is therefore the fair youth himself. The candidates are legion, the fantasies a delight—none more so than Oscar Wilde's in his *Portrait of Mr W.H.*, in which we meet a gorgeous boy actor called Willie Hughes. But, though half-seduced by his own theory, Wilde was quite aware that his lovely Willie was a *jeu d'esprit*, invented to help make the case for a homoerotic Shakespeare. Less easily countenanced is the tendency even of reputable critics who remain sceptical of the 'biographical fallacy' to slip into the way of calling the addressee of the sonnets 'Mr W.H.'

W[illiam] H[erbert], the Earl of Pembroke, has the right initials to have been Master W.H., while H[enry] W[riothesley], the Earl of Southampton, has the right initials though in the wrong order. But would Thorpe have identified an earl of the realm as a mere 'Master'? And would he have written such a cursory dedication if its recipient were an earl? Dedicating books to noblemen in the period was a serious business which required a great many ornate sentences, not a few enigmatic words. In certain respects, Thorpe's inscription is not a dedication at all: it makes no appeal for patronage. Nor is there any reason to suppose that Thorpe would have known the identity of the fair youth in the first place. And don't the sonnets have two inspirers, the youth and the dark lady, not an 'only' one?

In Renaissance book dedications, 'begetter' only infrequently meant 'inspirer'. It usually meant 'author'. A poet begets his poems upon his Muse. According to the customary usage, the writer is the father or begetter, while the patron is the sponsor or godfather—this is what Shakespeare calls Southampton in his dedication to *Venus and Adonis*.

Let us assume the customary usage, leave out the mysterious initials, and modernize the wording and word order of Thorpe's statement. It will then read as follows: 'Thomas Thorpe, the well-wishing publisher of the following sonnets, takes the opportunity upon publishing them to wish their only author all happiness and that eternity promised by our ever-living poet.' Had Thorpe not included the initials W.H., would not everyone have assumed that he was addressing Shakespeare? His inscription is not printed like a dedication to a third party; it reads as an acknowledgement to the author himself. If the publication of the sonnets was authorized by Shakespeare, the publisher's statement would have been a word of thanks; if unauthorized, it could have been a kind of apology.

Amidst all the speculation about W.H., two facts about Thorpe's book are often overlooked. First, that it was not the first book to call itself Shakespeare's sonnets. As we saw in the previous chapter, Shakespeare came fully into vogue in 1598–9. In 1599 William Jaggard cashed in on the fashion by publishing *The Passionate Pilgrime by W. Shakespeare*. Elizabethan booksellers advertised their wares by pasting title-pages to posts outside their shops in St Paul's Yard. On the basis of the displayed title, readers purchasing Jaggard's book from W. Leake at the sign of the Greyhound would have gained the impression that they were obtaining a collection of love sonnets by the author of the hugely popular *Venus and Adonis*. It would have looked like a very good buy indeed. Having paid their pence, they would have discovered that Jaggard's tiny volume consisted of twenty sonnets and lyrics. The first was 'When my love swears that she is made of truth', which (with slight alterations) became sonnet 138 in the collection published by Thorpe a decade later; the second was 'Two loves I have, of comfort and despair', number 144 in Thorpe. Two of the next three were sonnets lifted from the text of *Love's Labour's Lost*. But apart from one further lyric from *Love's Labour's Lost*, the rest of the collection contains no more authenticated Shakespeare.

The Passionate Pilgrime by W. Shakespeare in fact had several begetters, including Christopher Marlowe and two lesser poets, Richard Barnfield and Bartholomew Griffin. Jaggard's deception in trying to pass it off as all Shakespeare's makes it highly plausible that Thorpe would have wanted his prospective buyers to know that here was an authentic collection which really did consist entirely of Shakespeare—hence the prefatory claim that W.S. was the *only* begetter.

The second important fact is that Thorpe, as was usual in the period, did not print the book himself. He farmed the work out to the printing shop of George Eld. Some of its misprints suggest that it was poorly proof-read. One of the elaborate Elizabethan secretary-hand forms of capital 'S' closely resembles another secretary form of capital 'H'. Could it have been that in the holograph copy for the prefatory statement Thorpe or an assistant wrote 'Mr W.S.', but that the initials were misread in Eld's shop as W.H.? Might the mysterious Mr W.H., over whom so much ink has been spilt for so long, be no more than an inky slip, the creation of a misprint?

It might be objected that the proof-reader was unlikely to have overlooked an error on the capitalized opening page of the book, but it is surprising how often errors are not picked up on title-pages and in preliminary matter. A careless proof-reader might only start paying serious attention on reaching the main body of the text. Title and dedication-page errors are common in the books of the period. For instance, a play by Thomas Goffe called *The Raging Turke* has its title printed in huge letters—except that in one of the two states of the title-page it appears as THE RANING TURKE.

A further objection to the proposition that W.H. is really W. S. would be that it seems odd for Thorpe to refer to Shakespeare twice, first by initials, then as 'our ever-living poet'. But Thorpe's language is highly wrought: 'wisheth the well-wishing' might be said to be equally redundant. It is quite possible that Thorpe was making an elegant conceit: he wishes earthly happiness and heavenly eternity for the mortal person Master William Shakespeare, just as the immortal poet of the sonnets eternizes the fair youth. If Thorpe had read the sonnets carefully, he would have noticed that they do *not* follow the classical convention of claiming immortality for the poet—they claim immortality for the poet's beloved. Where Horace or Ovid would have written 'So long as men can breathe or eyes can see, / So long lives this, and this gives life to me', Shakespeare writes in sonnet 18, 'So long as men can breathe or eyes can see, / So long lives this, and this gives life to *thee*' (my italics). It is thus left for Thorpe to wish life to Shakespeare.

An alternative explanation is that 'our ever-living poet' does not in fact refer to Shakespeare. 'Ever-living' was an epithet applied to dead poets, not living ones. The point was that they were dead, but they lived eternally through their work. 'Our ever-living poet' might therefore refer to a great dead English poet who had written on the great theme of poetic immortality. Certain poets were so well known that they did not have to be named. In *The Merchant of Venice*, Shakespeare writes, 'Therefore the poet / Did feign that Orpheus drew trees, stones, and floods' (5.1.79–80)—the poet is not named because it is assumed that everyone will know it is Ovid (though some scholars have argued that it is Horace). By the same account, Thorpe's 'our ever-living poet' could refer to Sir Philip Sidney or Edmund Spenser, by 1609 both routinely associated with the idea of poetic immortality. Spenser famously wrote in his *Ruins of Time* that the Muses gave eternity to poets; he ended his translation of Joachim du Bellay's sonnet sequence, *Ruins of Rome*, with an envoy addressed to du Bellay himself, saying that the great dead French poet was 'worthy of immortality' and would 'all eternity survive'. As Spenser promises immortality to du Bellay, so Thorpe imagines Spenser, now immortal, welcoming Shakespeare to the same eternal company.

Of all the candidates for the identity of Master W.H., the misprint seems to me the strongest. But whoever it was that Thorpe really meant, there could be no more appropriate origin for the subsequent history of Shakespeare's *Sonnets*. The metamorphosis of W. S. into W.H. is symbolical of the achievement of the sonnets: they were begotten in Shakespeare's own brain, but they invent 'character' and 'situation' so powerfully that they make us believe in their subject. They perform their work of immortalization so effectively that they have made thousands of readers project that immortalization into the dedication by inventing 'Master W.H.' It is a lovely suppose that Thorpe knew what he was doing: saluting the genius and predicting the immortality of Master William Shakespeare. But I salute George Eld's hypothetical incompetent compositor as an unconscious genius who by substituting W.H. for W.S. allowed Shakespeare to perform in his sonnets the very disappearing act which is always available to a dramatist who loses himself in his characters but which should by rights be impossible for a lyric poet who writes in the first person.

THE SONNETS IN THE TWENTY-FIRST CENTURY: A BRIEF OVERVIEW

❧

The first decade of the twenty-first century has already provided an exciting new post-millennial chapter in the ongoing history of the reception of Shakespeare's *Sonnets*. Some important new scholarly studies have appeared, and continuing editorial projects have risen to a level unseen in recent memory. Moreover, the advent of new technologies has created unexpected platforms for Shakespeare's enduring poems, as striking to readers today as was Thomas Thorpe's 1609 quarto to early-seventeenth-century readers, some of whom may have been still adjusting to the relatively new medium of print. This volume's century-by-century surveys of *The Sonnets* and their influence will conclude with this brief overview of very recent work in this field.

Two works that deserve our initial regard were actually published just before the turn of the twenty-first century, but their importance and usefulness have affected our own decade very positively. Katherine Duncan-Jones released her edition of *Shakespeare's Sonnets* for the usually thorough and authoritative Arden Shakespeare series, and James Schiffer produced a most welcome compilation for Garland's Shakespeare Criticism series, *Shakespeare's Sonnets: Critical Essays*, which reprints the most influential essays from the past decade and 15 new essays on various aspects of *The Sonnets* by prominent scholars. Schiffer's introductory essay, "Reading New Life into Shakespeare's Sonnets," may be the single most informative survey for anyone interested in the complicated reception of these poems. Less than 10 years later, Michael Schoenfeldt has edited a similar volume for Blackwell, *A Companion to Shakespeare's Sonnets*, this time featuring 25 essays by important voices in the field. The section headings suggest well the areas of greatest interest regarding *The Sonnets* today—biographical inquiry, manuscript and print, models of desire, ideas of darkness, memory and repetition, the sonnets and the plays, and the sonnets and *A Lover's Complaint*. Like Schiffer's volume previously, Schoenfeldt's collection is now essential perusal for anyone doing serious, up-to-date research on Shakespeare's *Sonnets*.

Also quite helpful, A. D. Cousins and Peter Hyland produced helpful book-length introductions to both *The Sonnets* and narrative poems earlier this decade, and they have been followed very recently by two similar titles: John Blades's

Shakespeare: The Sonnets, for Palgrave Macmillan's "Analyzing Texts" series, and Dympna Callaghan's *Shakespeare's Sonnets*, for Blackwell's "Introduction to Literature" series. Callaghan's thematic breakdown is more general and intriguing—Identity, Beauty, Love, Numbers, Time—and succeeds in providing a fresh invitation to new and old readers alike. The recently published *Greenwood Companion to Shakespeare* also features relevant introductory writings on *The Sonnets*. Two final books, still of general appeal but perhaps pitched to a slightly more advanced audience, are Robert Montgomery's *The Perfect Ceremony of Love's Rite*, a critical reading of both *The Sonnets* and *A Lover's Complaint*, and Paul Edmondson's and Stanley Wells's *Shakespeare's Sonnets*. Produced for the Oxford Shakespeare Topics series, the latter volume covers a great deal in less than 200 pages. Topics treated include sonnet form and tradition, the publication history of *The Sonnets*, Shakespeare's artistry as a poet, the poems as theater, and, as a significant concluding section, the subsequent reception of Shakespeare's sequence by editors, publishers, writers, and performers. Wells also published, in 2004, *Looking for Sex in Shakespeare*, one chapter of which is titled "The Originality of Shakespeare's Sonnets." The chapter wears its author's considerable learning well, if with a tameness belied by the book's title.

Although one might think their efforts would be exhausted by now, editors have disproved this presumption on multiple occasions during this decade. Colin Burrow published a formidable edition of *The Complete Sonnets and Poems*, featuring a lengthy introduction and frequent annotations, for the Oxford Shakespeare series in 2002. More modestly, Barbara Mowat and Paul Werstine revised the New Folger edition of *The Sonnets*, which includes a valuable "modern perspective" summary of the work by Lynne Magnusson. Penguin published an edition edited by the first-rate scholar Stephen Orgel, with an excellent introduction to Shakespeare, sonnet form, and lyric modes by the poet and critic John Hollander. Orgel also lends a new introduction to the second edition of *The Sonnets* in the New Cambridge series, edited by G. Blakemore Evans. Finally, David West has produced a handsome edition for the general reader, published by Overlook, and Fairleigh Dickinson University Press has just released *Shakespeare's Sonnets: With Three Hundred Years of Commentary*. Edited by Carl D. Atkins, this brand-new volume promises to be a likely more modest but still valuable update to Rollins's magisterial New Variorum edition, which appeared more than 60 years ago.

A few articles on *The Sonnets*, either directly or indirectly, may be of greater than usual interest to someone generally interested in Shakespeare's poems. Burton Raffel provides a warm evaluation of *The Sonnets* as a "touchstone" of sixteenth-century lyric poetry, while Barbara Everett explores the influences of Plato and Erasmus on Shakespeare's sequence and its ordering. (See this volume's bibliography for publication information on all the articles mentioned here.) James Fenton, former Oxford Professor of Poetry, offers a reevaluation of

W. H. Auden's critical treatment of homosocial readings of *The Sonnets*. (The fact that Auden was himself a homosexual is a key point of interest for Fenton.) Katherine Duncan-Jones follows up her editorial work on Shakespeare's *Sonnets* by considering the plague contexts of the poems' likely composition, turning the "playing field" of the sonnet into a "killing field" that vanquishes human beauty. Bruce R. Smith and Valerie Traub both contribute substantial essays on desire and sexuality in Shakespeare's *Sonnets* to a multivolume Blackwell *Companion to Shakespeare's Works*, while Coleman Hutchison boldly revisits a scene that for many scholars is marked off with textual police tape. His investigation of the "Q" text of *The Sonnets* resumes the earlier work of Robert Giroux and the New Bibliographers more recently. And in one of her final essays, Anne Ferry makes an elegant return of her own, picking up in an essay for *Literary Imagination* her previous comparative treatment of Shakespeare and Philip Sidney, this time with specific attention given to rhyme effects in their poetry.

These first years of the new century also saw a striking concentration of more specialized research on *The Sonnets*. In this section's one featured essay, which first appeared in an earlier form in *Shakespeare Quarterly*, Patrick Cheney reacts to the emphasis in the 1990s on the performance of Shakespeare's texts and thus predominantly on Shakespeare the "working dramatist." In *Shakespeare, National Poet-Playwright* (2004), Cheney instead sets Shakespeare the poet alongside the more studied playwright and argues that this comparative focus is mandatory, since the writer himself carried out a "complex meditation" by simultaneously working in both areas at a time when neither printed verse nor public theater enjoyed cultural dominance. A prolific scholar, Cheney has also edited *The Cambridge Companion to Shakespeare's Poetry* (2007), featuring several important essays on Shakespeare's *Sonnets* and several studies of his poetry generally. Lisa Freinkel devotes a chapter to *The Sonnets* in her more broadly ambitious study, *Reading Shakespeare's Will: The Theology of Figure from Augustine to the Sonnets* (2002). Freinkel traces the poetics of *figura* and the theological responses to metaphor in the thought of St. Augustine and Martin Luther, after which she places Shakespeare's *Sonnets* in a necessarily post-Reformation critical milieu. Freinkel's work nicely exemplifies the so-called "turn to religion" taking place recently in Renaissance studies.

Richard Halpern's *Shakespeare's Perfume: Sodomy and Sublimity in the Sonnets, Wilde, Freud, and Lacan* (2002) is similarly broad and transhistorical in its coverage. Finding his originator in St. Paul, Halpern studies the effects of Shakespeare's own conjoining of aesthetics and sexuality in the later works of Oscar Wilde and Sigmund Freud. Effectively representing New Historicism's focus on textual transmission and readers' reception, Sasha Roberts in *Reading Shakespeare's Poems in Early Modern England* (2003) conducts the reader through a fascinating, culturally thick procession of manuscripts, marginalia, commonplace books, and early printed editions. In the case of *The Sonnets*,

Roberts shows how these transgressive poems were slowly turned into "routine poetical utterances." David Schalkwyk's *Speech and Performance in Shakespeare's Sonnets and Plays* (2002) takes up certain time-honored critical traditions related to *The Sonnets*, such as reading the poems in conversation with Shakespeare's plays and analyzing their language as performative rather than descriptive, which naturally led Schalkwyk to revisit the presence (or not) of biography in the sequence. Peter Robinson has also treated the issue of "speech acts" in *The Sonnets*, and it is heartening to find in the *World Shakespeare Bibliography* several essays on performance, or performances outright, of *The Sonnets* by actors, directors, or teachers of drama. This continuing work constitutes a powerful statement that Shakespeare's poems, for all of their interiority and technical virtuosity, remain—as his plays still do—living texts, ones to be spoken and to be outspoken as well.

2004—Patrick Cheney. "'O, let my books be . . . dumb presagers': poetry and theatre in the Sonnets," from *Shakespeare, National Poet-Playwright*

Patrick Cheney, a prolific author and editor, is a professor of English and comparative literature at Pennsylvania State University. In addition to several edited or co-edited volumes, he is the author of *Spenser's Famous Flight: A Renaissance Idea of a Literary Career*, *Marlowe's Counterfeit Profession: Ovid, Spenser, Counter-Nationhood*, and *Shakespeare, National Poet-Playwright*. He is also the editor of *The Cambridge Companion to Shakespeare's Poetry* and is currently at work on a project on Shakespeare's literary authorship.

William Shakespeare is a man of the theatre who wrote a sonnet sequence.

For the English Renaissance, this is an unusual profile. Almost exclusively, the writers who composed sonnet sequences were not the same as those who worked in the theatre. The sonneteers, rather than being professional dramatists, belonged predominantly either to an amateur class of poets (for example, Sir Philip Sidney and Richard Barnfield) or to a laureate class (Edmund Spenser and Michael Drayton).[1] By contrast, the main professional dramatists (from Thomas Kyd to John Ford) did not produce sonnet sequences, even though nearly without exception they wrote in other poetic forms, from love lyric and pastoral to epyllion and satire.[2]

Shakespeare's Sonnets therefore constitute an unusual site for viewing the intersection of poetry and theatre during the English Renaissance. Sonnet 23 illustrates succinctly the discursive form of that intersection, which the sequence as a whole sustains: "O, let my books be then the eloquence / And dumb presagers of my speaking breast" (9–10).[3] While we shall examine Sonnet 23 in detail later, for now we may note simply that these lines intriguingly conjoin the medium of printed books of poetry (editorial tradition suggests *Venus* and *Lucrece*) with that of staged theatre (the dumb show of a play). That these lines turn out to contain a long-standing textual crux could well make the examination more enticing.

In this chapter, we will look further into the Sonnets' sustained conjoining of these two principal forms of production during Shakespeare's career.[4] Such an investigation can prove useful in itself as an analysis of a neglected topic, yet the analysis may prove especially profitable in the current critical conversation about Shakespeare as an early modern author. As we shall see, the Sonnets constitute an unexplored territory for viewing him as inextricably caught in the cultural predicament of conjoining the two forms that engaged him throughout his professional career.

THE CRITICAL AND HISTORICAL CONTEXTS

We can indeed profit from viewing Shakespeare's Sonnets as the product of the world's most famous man of the theatre, the writer or collaborator of forty-two known plays, an actor in a professional company, and a shareholder in a commercial, public theatre. Sometime between the mid-1580s and the early seventeenth century, the famed dramatist wrote 152 sonnets in the Petrarchan tradition, and they were finally published in 1609 (with or without his consent) in a quarto volume titled *Shake-speares Sonnets*. The volume includes two anacreontic sonnets (153, 154) and *A Lover's Complaint*, in what was then a familiar format for a printed volume of verse.[5] Shakespeare did not write his sonnets simply when the theatres closed due to plague in 1592–93; as recent scholarship has demonstrated, he worked on them throughout his career.[6] As we have seen, in 1598 Francis Meres encourages contemporaries to integrate Shakespeare's "sugred Sonnets" centrally into his profession as a public dramatist and a published poet (*Palladis Tamia*, reprinted in *Riverside*, 1970).

Some readers might dispute that Meres refers to sonnets from the 1609 quarto, emphasizing instead the conditions of manuscript circulation and arguing that Shakespeare did not intend the Sonnets for publication.[7] Yet the Meres passage suggests a more complicated cultural milieu, since Meres situates the Shakespearean manuscript sonnets he has read in an authorial practice that includes both printed poems (*Venus*, *Lucrece*) and printed and/or staged plays (quartos began appearing in 1594, and in 1598 Shakespeare's name began to appear on them). Moreover, the recent work by Wendy Wall and Colin Burrow emphasizes how the Sonnets—in Burrow's formulation—"could have been designed to operate more or less exactly on the borderline between the published and the privately concealed": "What makes the volume of *Shake-speares Sonnets* unique is the extent to which its every element can be seen [to] . . . invite from its readers a deliberate interplay between reading the collection for the life as a private manuscript record of a secret love, and reading it as a monumental printed work" (Burrow, "Life," 38, 42). Wall finds the collection periodically brooding over the problem of print publication (*Imprint*, 197). Such criticism is important because it presents a Shakespeare whom critics are increasingly beginning to see: not simply the writer of plays who assiduously avoids print and bookish immortality, but rather the author of both plays and poems whose works as a whole show a fascination with—sometimes also a fear and distrust of—print publication. While acknowledging that the Sonnets are situated on the "borderline between the published and the privately concealed," we might then profit by looking into certain neglected features of the former, especially since recent criticism has emphasized the latter.

In fact, scholars writing on the Sonnets have long emphasized Shakespeare's presentation of himself as a poet—a writer of lyrics—in the very sonnets he is composing.[8] Indebted to Petrarch (and before him, Ovid) as well as his sixteenth-century English heirs (Sidney, Daniel, Spenser), Shakespeare's self-representation appears as the subject of the poet's verse in over twenty-five different sonnets (e.g., 18, 55, 60, 63, 106, 116, 130), including this from Sonnet 60: "to times in hope my verse shall stand" (13). To these sonnets, we need to add the Rival Poet sonnets (78–86), in which this poet-figure presents himself as a rival versifier for the artistic affection of the young man: "Was it the proud full sail of his great verse . . . / That did my ripe thoughts in my brain inhearse" (86.1–3). To these two groups, we can add still other sonnets that refer to the media of printed books or to the literary tradition (11, 25, 53, 59, 77, 117), as represented in Sonnet 59, "Show me your image in some antique book" (7), or in Sonnet 53, which refers to the literary images of both "Adonis" and "Helen" (1–8). We also need to add Shakespeare's use of the vocabulary from the print medium to reflect on sexual experience, as in Sonnet 11 when the speaker advises the young man to marry and procreate: "Thou shouldst print more, not let that copy die" (14). For readers today, as presumably for Shakespeare's first readers, the Sonnets present a speaker who quite literally speaks as a poet, the author of the very sonnets we are reading. As Burrow, Wall, and others help us see, the poet, who calls himself Will in Sonnet 136 (14), situates his own poems on the borderline between print and manuscript.[9] From the perspective of the present argument, he is therefore distinctly compelled by the career of the print poet.

Yet scholars writing on the Sonnets have noted that in at least a few sonnets—most notably, 110, 111, and 112, but also 25, 29, 72, and 87—Shakespeare presents this same poet-figure or sonnet writer as a man of the theatre, as this from Sonnet 110: "I have gone here and there, / And made myself a motley to the view" (1–2).[10] Stephen Booth observes: "If this poem were not by a professional actor, the line would simply say, 'I have made myself a public laughingstock' . . . However, Shakespeare's profession is—and presumably always was—known to his readers (see 111. 3–4), and this line therefore is colored by (and colors the following lines with) its pertinence to the particular circumstances of its author's life. The fact of Shakespeare's profession operates—much as the accident of his first name does in the 'Will' sonnets . . . —to give witty, pun-like extra dimension to statements complete and meaningful in themselves" (Booth, ed., *Sonnets*, 354). We can extend this important principle of representation and reception to other sonnets referring to Shakespeare's theatrical career, as well as to many sonnets that rely on theatrical metaphors (5, 15, 23, 24, 33, 61, 70, 98, 113), which Will often uses to represent erotic experience, sometimes without fanfare or even note: "Mine eye hath play'd the painter and hath [stell'd] / Thy beauty's form in table of my heart" (24.1–2). To these two groups, we can add a large number of sonnets that inscribe Shakespeare's working vocabulary from the theatre, even though in many instances we would be wary to claim a specific theatrical evocation. This vocabulary includes the word "show" (e.g., 5.14); "mask" (33.12); "rehearse" (21. 4); "play" (5.3); "part" (8. 8); "act" (152.3); "action" (65.4); "actor" (23.1); "entertain" (39.11); "shadows" (43.5–6); "mock" (61.4); "trim" (66.3); "case" (108. 9); and, perhaps taking a cue from Sir Philip Sidney, "dumb" (23.10). Shakespeare's insertion of this theatrical discourse into his sonnet sequence, while not surprising, is nonetheless unusual enough during the period to warrant attention.

Despite Shakespeare's inclusion of a discourse of poetry and a discourse of theatre in his Sonnets, critics tend to separate their analyses of poetry and theatre. Most importantly, critics who see Shakespeare worrying about print publication in his Sonnets do not concern themselves much with the theatrical matrix of the sequence.[11] The inventory of both theatrical and poetic matrices, together with the practice among Shakespeare's contemporaries of separating sonnets from plays, pinpoints the historical significance of the Sonnets as lying partly in their unusual representation of the intersection of these two forms at a critical time in English literary history. During the last twenty years, critics have tended to locate the Sonnets' historical significance in terms of Shakespeare's representation of subjectivity and/or sexuality.[12] In a recent, seminal essay, Peter Stallybrass argues that "In the case of the Sonnets . . . we can read the inscription of a new history of sexuality and 'character'" ("Sexing," 92). Stallybrass adds, "But that new history emerges unpunctually, dislocated by its need to write itself over the culturally valued but culturally disturbing body of the Sonnets" (92–93). In Shakespeare's sequence, we can also read the inscription of a new history of authorship and "character," discovering this history to emerge in a similarly unpunctual and dislocated fashion.

According to such a history, Shakespeare's Sonnets are important because they present a new type of European author, memorably represented in the Meres passage: the author who pens both poems and plays. Shakespeare's Sonnets are noteworthy for lots of reasons but especially for their original representation of the interconnection between these two fundamentally nascent literary forms. More specifically, the Sonnets' new history of authorship and authorial character publicizes a cultural clash between printed poetry and the even newer, more socially compromising medium of staged theatre. No other English Renaissance sonnet sequence does so. To represent the clash of media, Shakespeare presents Will in deep introspection suffering a personal dilemma between being a playwright-actor ashamed of his profession and being a poet working hard to be affirmative about his career as a sonneteer.[13]

David Schalkwyk classifies Will as an "actor-poet," presumably because the theatre representations appear to pertain to Shakespeare's role as an actor rather than as a playwright ("Performative," 252). This seems basically right, but we might note two complications: first, it might be difficult, even unwise, to disentangle Shakespeare's theatrical roles as actor and playwright, not least because in the Sonnets a poet is literally writing about his role as an actor; and second, we might come to see one of Shakespeare's major contributions to the representation of authorship during the period to lie in the fact that he presents the author also as an actor.[14] Such a new history emphasizes the homology between the twin but typically separate topics of much recent criticism on Shakespeare's plays and poems: cross-dressing in the plays; and homoeroticism in the Sonnets.[15] Shakespeare, we might say, countered the large-scale European convention of Petrarchism, through which a male poet addressed a sonnet sequence to a female beloved, *because he was a man of the theatre*; this sonnet author experienced the staging of same-sex relationships in costumed disguise as a matter of daily professional practice.[16]

Shakespeare's self-conscious deployment of homoeroticism, theatre, and printed poetry appears to be unique. We might then attribute his "most salient" alteration to the Petrarchan sequence—"that most of them are addressed to a young male" (de Grazia, "Scandal," 38)—not simply to the personal circumstances of his sexual biography, nor even to his characteristically witty and innovative overturning of convention, but also to his singular position in the theatrical world. In his Sonnets, Shakespeare can be seen to transpose the homoerotic gender paradigm from the theatre to the Petrarchan sequence. He is a man of the theatre writing sonnets, and he capitalizes on his unique position in the literary system to present Will precisely as the theatrical man turning his dramatic hand to non-dramatic poetry. It is in this context that we might usefully view Shakespeare's opposing representations of his twin arts, conveyed through Will's public shame over the theatre and his bid for public fame through his poetry.[17] By claiming poetic fame for Will and his subject through his Sonnets, Shakespeare is not simply participating in the long tradition extending from Homer through Virgil, Horace, and Ovid, to Dante, Petrarch, and Spenser: he is simultaneously offsetting a public infamy acquired through his role in the new English theatre. If the Sonnets are "Shakespeare's life's work," we might come to see Shakespeare positioning himself in another European economy besides that of the theatre: the economy of a literary career, designed principally to secure the high cultural authority of poetic immortality.[18]

While we might wish to hold off claiming that the Sonnets constitute an advertisement for Shakespeare's status as a new English and European poet-playwright, his sequence nonetheless constitutes a historically significant meditation on, inscription of, and register for an author who is fundamentally a sixteenth-century invention—or, more accurately, the re-invention of a Roman writer that for Marlowe, Jonson, and Thomas Heywood traces to Ovid (chapters 1 and 2). Recalling Meres' Ovidian comparison, we may understand the conjunction of poetry and theatre in the Sonnets precisely in Ovidian terms: Shakespeare plots Will's aesthetic and subjective struggle for identity amid the triangulated love affair with the young man and the dark lady along a distinctly Ovidian path of amorous poetry and tragedic theatre. Like Ovid in the *Amores* (and Marlowe in his translation), Will stages a narrative of the poet-playwright caught between claims of poetry's power to immortalize and love's power to produce shame. Distinctly, however, Shakespeare shifts the site of shame from love and poetry in the Ovid/Marlowe dynamic to the place of the stage.[19]

It is difficult to determine just how we are to gauge Shakespeare in relation to the Ovid/Marlowe dynamic. For instance, it might seem peculiar that an English Renaissance writer such as Shakespeare could discover in Ovid a model for the poet-playwright, since the great classical writer left a canon decidedly tipped in favor of poetry over drama. Yet in order to take the cue of Marlowe, Jonson, Heywood, and others, we need not insist that Ovid balanced the two; we could simply acknowledge that Ovid achieved his combination in a way that was compelling in the late sixteenth and early seventeenth centuries. Consequently, we might see Shakespeare perfecting an imperfect Ovidian model that Marlowe had instigated yet had left incomplete when he died prematurely in 1593. With their intense interest in classical authors—and especially their shared passion for Ovid—Marlowe and Shakespeare together can be seen to realize a model of authorship that Ovid had advertised but had failed to realize. Although Ovid says he is better "apt" for the "high designs" of "tragedies" than he is for the low designs of love elegy (*Amores*, 2.18.13–18; trans. Marlowe), his chronic disposition for erotic entanglements recurrently impedes the success of this notable dramatic temperament. Effectively, Ovid invents a career path that Marlowe begins to traverse and that Shakespeare is left more fully to chart.

Like Marlowe's other heir, Ben Jonson, Shakespeare may have really "wanted to be a poet rather than a playwright" (Yachnin, *Stage-Wrights*, xii). We might find it striking, however, that Shakespeare does not use his poetry to erase his role in the theatre, but rather makes his shameful theatrical profession a part of his self-presentation. The Sonnets thus stage a kind of crisis: the new English poet-playwright—so popular that in 1599 Jaggard could pirate *The Passionate Pilgrim* under Shakespeare's name—is caught in a compromising predicament with a morally bankrupt young man and an equally bankrupt dark lady. Of this narrative, Michael C. Schoenfeldt has recently observed that Shakespeare's sonnets "Must have struck the 1609 reader as a radical disruption of the conventional narrative of erotic courtship. In the early sonnets, woman is not the idealized recipient of the erotic aspirations of a male speaker but rather a means of biological reproduction, to be frequented so that men may lay claim to the fragile immortality of progeny; in the later poems, woman, now identified with a culturally derogated darkness, is the object of a wasteful, enervating, uncontrollable desire that contrasts markedly with the idealized love of a young man" ("Matter," 240). Schoenfeldt's view of Shakespeare's narrative of sexual physiology and subjectivity corresponds to a striking statistic pertaining to the narrative of authorship and authorial character: with very little exception, Shakespeare confines both his poetic and his theatrical vocabulary to the young-man sonnets (1–126), so that in the dark-lady sonnets (127–52) this vocabulary virtually disappears.[20] Altogether, Shakespeare presents a narrative in which Will, the new Ovidian poet-playwright, loses the voice of his profession to the engulfing swirls of a dangerous, triangulated sexual desire: "desire is death" (147.8). Against such mighty rage, how can poetry hold a plea?[21]

Finally, we might wish to be cautious when gauging Will's authorial self-presentation as definitive of Shakespeare's own view of his career or even of his own personal predicament, because it so clearly resembles Spenser's famous presentation of his persona in the 1579 *Shepheardes Calender*, wherein Colin Clout abandons his career as a poet after Rosalind, his own distinctly rose-tinted Petrarchan mistress, rejects him. Like Spenser, Shakespeare presents a powerful narrative of artistic failure precisely to claim authority as a (national) author.[22] Without recalling Spenser's paradoxical use of his failed, clownish persona to present himself as England's great laureate poet, we might have some difficulty processing Shakespeare's presentation of a rather negative model of authorship that even Ovid (and Marlowe) had presented more positively. Just as we need not confuse Spenser with Colin, so we need not confuse Shakespeare with Will. Thus, we may apply to Shakespeare the principle critics find operating in Spenser's *June* eclogue: the "topos of inability or affected modesty is in effect an indirect tactic of self-assertion."[23] Because the Sonnets are today Shakespeare's best-selling book, and because Shakespeare eventually displaced Spenser as England's "National Poet," we may conclude that in terms of reception history the author of the Sonnets succeeded admirably in substantiating the claim.[24]

Here we might wonder how a work that was basically erased not simply from the First Folio but from the canon itself until the eighteenth century could prove so historically influential. Although we may not be used to viewing the Sonnets the way we are here, they nonetheless record, as countless critics have helped us see (not least Joel Fineman), a large-scale artistic project that matches and even exceeds that of Petrarch's in the *Rime sparse*. Thus, we may not wish to ignore but rather to marvel at just how the Sonnets have undergone a long, extremely complex historical process of reception that finally gets around to recognizing the achievement of this project.[25]

SONNET 15

While many sonnets present Will as a poet and several present him as man of the theatre, a substantial number show him bringing poetry and theatre into conjunction.[26] Let us begin by considering Sonnet 15, long recognized to be important for articulating the central theme of the sequence and for first presenting the art of poetry as a solution to the problem of time and death—those relentless stalkers of the young man's beauty.[27] Sonnet 15 is less often recalled as the first poem to employ a substantive theatrical discourse and thus the first to conjoin theatre with poetry:

> When I consider every thing that grows
> Holds in perfection but a little moment,
> That this huge stage presented nought but shows,
> Whereon the stars in secret influence comment;
> When I perceive that men as plants increase,
> Cheered and check'd even by the self-same sky,
> Vaunt in their youthful sap, at height decrease,
> And wear their brave state out of memory:
> Then the conceit of this inconstant stay
> Sets you most rich in youth before my sight,
> Where wasteful Time debateth with Decay
> To change your day of youth to sullied night,
> > And all in war with Time for love of you,
> > As he takes from you, I ingraft you new.
> > > (Sonnet 15)

This sonnet, a perfect instance of the "Shakespearean sonnet" of three rhymed quatrains and a concluding couplet, is relatively straightforward. Relying on his famous logical pattern, Will tells the young man that "When" he considers the decay and death of all natural things, "Then" he looks on the young man both to discover meaning and to write that meaning into poetry.

Yet Sonnet 15 is also important because it relies on an authorial narrative to represent the central cognitive paradigm of the sequence—what many have seen as the heart of its enduring value: the English Ovidian poet-playwright locates meaning both in the individual's meditation on beauty as a consolation for the tyranny of time and death and in the individual's verse inscription. The cognition itself is hardly new, tracing back to the *Iliad* and receiving famous forms in Virgil, Horace, and Ovid, and later in Dante, Petrarch, and Spenser (among others). Shakespeare certainly brings a rich intelligence and a fresh talent to the topics of subjective perception and poetic fame, but what may make the articulation historically new is the conjunction here of poetry with theatre. If we look carefully at the fiction, Will presents himself as an actor on a stage writing poetry to combat time and death.

In the first quatrain, Will presents his speaking subject, "I," as an actor on a stage performing a cognitive action, as if in soliloquy.[28] The simple syntax of the first line is paradigmatic: "I consider . . . thing." The speaking subject uses his mind to consider material reality—not just any material reality, but one that "grows." Thus, Will considers the natural world in its capacity to change and mature. In line two, his word "but" at the midpoint intimates a problem, as Will considers that natural things retain their perfection for only a "little moment." In line three, he introduces the theatrical metaphor (it is not a simile) to place himself, the perceiver of natural decay, on a "huge stage" that presents nothing but "shows." This is certainly a tautology—but it is worse, a cliché: the trope of the world as a stage presenting man as an actor and life as a show is so popular a formulation during the period—the very motto of the Globe Theatre itself (*Totus mundus agit histrionem*)—that we might intelligently seek to bypass commentary here altogether.[29] Such a bypass, however, would commit us to erasing the historicity of Will's self-presentation, through which he locates intellectual consideration on the stage, his platform for materialist speculations in lines 1–3: the world is nothing but a show, while the show itself merely stages the world.[30] Yet in line 4 Will extends his materialist philosophy to the metaphysical domain, now framing his platform with a sky and its astral bodies, which indeed were displayed on the canopy overarching the stage at the Globe: "Whereon the stars in secret influence comment." For a Christian audience, this line is important and challenging: Will presents the stars "comment[ing]" on the "nought" of the "show" with "secret influence."[31] As Katherine Duncan-Jones observes, Will presents the stars "as audience to the theatre of the world, [which] comment on and guide human life, but in ways that are undiscernible to us (*secret*)" (Duncan-Jones, ed., *Sonnets*, 140). As G. Blakemore Evans reports, however, "Shakespeare's use of 'comment' has caused difficulty, since though spectators at a play may comment, the stars were believed to do much more than 'comment' in a passive sense" (Evans, ed., *Sonnets*, 128). Evans goes on to say that he has "assigned a meaning to 'comment' (with support from the *OED*) which suggests the action of a commentator or reviewer who makes crucial or 'critical' decisions that affect the future of a 'work'" (128; see Booth, ed., *Sonnets*, 286). Thus, Will frames his fiction of an actor on a stage considering the death of nature within a larger setting that includes the religious sphere. The play in which he finds himself is looking like a tragedy, especially one emphasizing the tragic hero's victimization by a metaphysical agent. For Shakespeare's Christian audience, the repercussions must have been—and remain—striking.

In the second quatrain, Will registers the very strike of those repercussions. In line 5, he uses anaphora to consolidate and specify the materialist (and theatrical) consideration of the first quatrain, when he perceives that men "increase" the way "plants" do. In line 6, he metaphysics the subject (to adapt a phrase from the opening of *The Winter's Tale*) in the sonnet's most unsettling line: "Cheered and check'd even by the self-same sky." The line is unsettling because of the (Christian) implications of a single sky performing two opposed actions: this meteorological domain both encourages and rebukes, empowers and impedes, offers hope and takes it away, creates fortune and misfortune equally (cheers "and" checks). If read in the context of the Sermon on the Mount to which Hamlet refers (5. 2. 219–20), or of the Christian tradition from Augustine to Dante to Hooker, the line is not simply unsettling; it is blasphemous. In Will's tragic theatre, unlike in Dante's divine comedy, the sky is not the lucid source of salvation or damnation, nor does it offer a special providence for the fall of a sparrow.[32] Quite literally, the sky overhanging Will has turned cloudy; no longer does the individual perceive the divine clearly, and worse, no longer does the divine communicate clearly to the individual. Once more, Evans helps in understanding the theatrical resonance of the religious representation: "Encourage, solaced (by good fortune), or, possibly, applauded (as in the theatre . . .) and hindered, cut short, reproved (by bad fortune), or cried down, taunted (as in the theatre)."[33] Will's transposition of the cosmic drama to the stage is an important register for the historical context of the Sonnets: the much-discussed advent of science and philosophy and its effects on the truths and authority of Christian teaching (see Cruttwell, *Shakespearean Moment*, 1–38). In Sonnet 15, Shakespeare presents Will as a man of the theatre acting out a tragedy of particular relevance to the early modern audience. As editors note, both lines 7 and 8 retain theatrical imagery in Will's portrait of men who "[v]aunt" in their youth only to "decrease" in their "height" and who "wear their brave state out of memory" (Evans, ed., *Sonnets*, 128). The image catches the sad (yet perhaps slightly humorous) perplexity of this particular tragic individual: he is a young actor who vaunts his voice in splendid costume even as he falls into oblivion, the terrorizing Western alternative to poetic immortality. Moreover, in scripting himself as an actor in a tragedy, Will presents himself simultaneously as the writer of that play. His representation of himself as a playwright is thus identical with his role as a sonneteer.

If the octave uses theatre to represent the material and metaphysical problem of living in an uncertain universe, the sestet thus discovers a solution to lie in the intertwined activities of philosophical vision and written verse. In lines 9–10, Will reports that the "conceit" (both his conception and his literary image) of this murky universe is richly offset by his "sight" of the young man. In lines 11–12, he locates this perception again on the stage, witnessing a "debate" between two other actors in a morality play, "Time and Decay," who struggle over the youth to "change" his "day of youth to sullied night"—to perform an Ovidian degenerative metamorphosis on him. In this tragedic Ovidian theatre, Will imagines Time killing Nature, as Heaven betrays man by passively standing by, simply "comment[ing]" on the hapless protagonist.

Only in the couplet does Will present his poetry as the solution to this tragic predicament: as Time kills the young man, Will "engraft[s] him new"—makes him immortal through his verse. As Bruce R. Smith reports, "Many readers have noted the pun here on 'engraft': it suggests the Greek root *graphein*, 'to write,' at the same time that it sets up images of horticultural grafting in the next sonnet."[34] More locally, poetic ingrafting also solves the problem from the preceding quatrains, where the growing plant increases only to decay; the poet is himself the gardener who can intervene protectively in this process, extending the life of the dying plant. In this sonnet, only the poet-playwright, not any other cultural or cosmic agent, including a real gardener or a real deity, can say to Time what Will says in Sonnet 123: "Thy registers and thee I both defy . . . / I will be true despite thy scythe and thee" (9, 14). In sum, Sonnet 15 presents Will as an actor on the stage writing both drama and poetry to solve the West's most enduring problem, the tragic fact of human mortality. Will's idea of poetry is once again hardly new, but his opposition between poetry with its living fame and theatre with its illusory show is especially fresh and important, at least in the English sonnet tradition.[35]

SONNET 23

The representation of sonneteer and stage appears substantively next in Sonnet 23:

> As an unperfect actor on the stage,
> Who with his fear is put besides his part,
> Or some fierce thing replete with too much rage,
> Whose strength's abundance weakens his own heart,
> So I, for fear of trust, forget to say
> The perfect ceremony of love's [rite],
> And in mine own love's strength seem to decay,
> O'ercharg'd with burthen of mine own love's might.
> O, let my books be then the eloquence
> And dumb presagers of my speaking breast,
> Who plead for love, and look for recompense,
> More than that tongue that more hath more express'd.
> > O, learn to read what silent love hath writ:
> > To hear with eyes belongs to love's fine wit.
> >   (Sonnet 23)

As in Sonnet 15, the general drift here is relatively straightforward. In the first two quatrains, Will employs a theatrical simile designed to explain to the young man why he has forgotten to declare his love to him. In the third quatrain, Will offers a substitute for such a declaration by telling the youth to view his "books" as the "dumb presagers" of his love. Finally, in the couplet Will summarizes this directive by encouraging the young man to learn to read in print what Will has been unable to say in person.

Like Sonnet 15, Sonnet 23 is important for its clear combination of theatre and books. What precisely is that combination? In terms of the literal fiction, Will relies both on a theatrical simile (the actor on a stage) to explain his silence and on a theatrical metaphor (the dumb presagers) to describe the function of his books. In effect, then, he doubles the representation of poetry and theatre, introducing considerable complication: in a sonnet, he likens himself to an actor; and in this sonnet he equates his books of poetry with a play. The complication helps make its own point: Shakespeare's ingrained thinking process both separates and intertwines the two modes of his professional career. Yet, by borrowing Booth's principle from Sonnet 110, perhaps we can see Shakespeare presenting Will as a (clownish) man of the theatre who nonetheless has managed to write poetry of educational value—and is saying so in a Petrarchan sonnet. At the core of Will's educational program is the idea that runs throughout the sequence as a kind of refrain: that true love is silent and does not speak a part. Printed verse, not public theatre, is the fit medium to display the integrity of this faith in silent desire; theatre, by its nature, is a shameful public profession because it violates that integrity.

Yet the combination of theatre and poetry in Sonnet 23 is both more detailed and more complicated than even this preliminary formulation allows, as recent scholarship reveals. The primary problem lies in the textual crux of the word "books" in line 9. In the eighteenth century, George Sewell emended the 1609 quarto's "books" to "looks," mainly because of the problem "books" creates for the meaning of "dumb presagers" in line 10. As Booth explains, the word "presagers" has "not been satisfactorily explained . . . No other instance of 'presager' or any form of 'presage' is known where the reference is not to foreshowing the future" (Booth, ed., *Sonnets*, 172). Evans adds, "since Shakespeare's 'books'" are "already written," they "cannot properly be said to prophesy or foretell" (Evans, ed., *Sonnets*, 136). The word "looks" makes more sense, some editors insist, because "looks" can function as "dumb presagers" of Will's "eloquence."

I confess that I do not understand this line of argument, since a similar thought appears famously in Sonnet 106 (Cheney, "Sonnet 106"). Referring to past writers, Will observes,

> I see their antique pen would have express'd
> Even such a beauty as you master now.

So all their praises are but prophecies
Of this our time, all you prefiguring,
And for they look'd but with divining eyes,
They had not still [or skill] enough your worth to sing.

(Sonnet 106. 7–12)

Here Will engages in a similarly tortuous, hyperbolic writerly thought grounded in impossibility: writers of old wrote works that prophesy the young man; however, because such writers looked only with divining eyes (able to foretell the youth), they lacked the style or skill to sing his worth consciously.[36] In the context of Sonnet 106, the word "books" in Sonnet 23 makes perfect sense: Will asks that his books function as presagers, foreshadowers, of his current poems celebrating the young man. In effect, Will assigns to his own poetry the principle he later assigns to the poetry of others; in both instances, the young man's beauty warrants the time-bending conceit (this turns out to be one of the few things to the youth's credit).

Before turning to the question of which books Will has in mind, we may note something rather curious here; perhaps lines 9–10 construct a fable for modern Shakespearean scholarship: the text's conjunction of printed poetry and staged theatre is precisely what has baffled us. Yet it is such a conjunction that the text presents, and thus we might profitably submit rather than try to erase it. Through theatrical discourse in a sonnet that refers to his printed poems, Will presents himself as a new English Ovidian poet-playwright caught between two interconnected, clashing media, even in his relationship with the young man. This clash is precisely the context for negotiating that relationship.

In the first quatrain, Will likens himself both to an actor in the theatre whose stage fright has compelled him to forget his part and to a wild "thing" (or animal) whose anger has weakened his wrath. As Booth helps us see, the phrasing is more complicated: "Before a reader comes to line 4 and sees that *Or* introduces a parallel construction that presents an alternative for the whole of lines 1 and 2, *Or* can seem to introduce an alternative only to *fear* in line 2, an alternative cause of the actor's lapse of memory" (Booth, ed., *Sonnets*, 171). This reading extends the theatre simile to the whole of the quatrain, making its topic fully professional. Will is identifying either two causes or two alternative causes or perhaps two interlocked causes to the problem he withholds until the second quatrain: the intersection of opposing emotions of fear and desire interferes with his ability to "speak." Facing the young man, Will feels like a fearful actor on the stage (and/or a powerful creature with great energy) unable to act out his desire.

In the second quatrain, line 5 supports the interlock of fear and desire as the emotions Will experiences on the stage, for here the two become one: "So I, for fear of trust, forget to say." *Fear of trust / forget to say*: the loaded line brings to bear on poetry and theatre two ideas central to the Shakespeare canon—the fear of infidelity and the problem of memory and forgetting.[37] Will's fear of trusting the young man, perhaps himself, impedes his ability to write poetry, just as his stage fright impedes his ability to act in the theatre. Will does not cordon his relationship with the young man off from his double life as a poet and dramatist but rather interlocks the two in a complex dynamic. The echo between "*unperfect* actor" in line 1 and poetry's "*perfect* ceremony of love's rite" in line 6—noted by editors—reinforces the structural conjunction between Will's twin professional media, as Evans's gloss helps us see: "word-perfect 'performance' or observance (such as would be given by the 'perfect actor'" on the stage) (Evans, ed., *Sonnets*, 136).

In the third quatrain, Will supplies a solution to his problem: let his "books" speak for him, as the dumb show speaks for the play the audience is about to view. We do not know which books Will has in mind, but editors have turned up three main possibilities: (1) the present sonnets; (2) Shakespeare's past printed books, *Venus and Adonis* and *The Rape of Lucrece*; and even (3) the "written text of a stage play."[38] Each of these possibilities contains an intriguing line of inquiry that we can only sketch in briefly here. Taking the three in reverse order: If the books are Will's written scripts for stage plays, in effect he is encouraging the young man to read Shakespeare's plays as prefigurations of his sonnets, the representation of dramatic characters functioning as presagers for the young man. This reading conjoins poetry and theatre in an important dyad that could lead the historical young man (who ever he was) to view those plays in terms of himself. What would be the effect of carrying out such an interpretive program, even for a single play published before 1609, such as *1 Henry IV* or *Hamlet*? (Has anyone ever devised a sounder strategy for securing patronage? It couldn't hurt box-office receipts either.) If, on the other hand, the books refer to *Venus and Adonis* and *The Rape of Lucrece*, we might ask, What do these poems communicate to that same young man (or even to readers viewing this scenario, such as Shakespeare's "private friends" or his public friends, ourselves)? Plotting the terms of an interpretative program here is easier to perform. *Venus and Adonis* might well encourage the young man to avoid the brutal fate of Adonis' narcissism by listening to the authority of Venus (169–74)—the same authority Will has urged on to the young man in Sonnets 1–17: the young man would free himself from the fatal danger of virginity by marrying and then procreating. By contrast, *The Rape of Lucrece* might entreat the young man to avoid the equally brutal fate of Tarquin's devouring lust—the very bestial desire that Will encounters (albeit with the dark lady's complicity) through the "sensual fault" of Sonnet 35 (line 9; see Sonnet 34). According to this possibility, then, Shakespeare's two minor epics would acquire the status of humanist manifestoes training a young man (and young men generally) in the art of sexual character, in the hopes of turning tragic fate aside. Finally, if the books are the sonnets we are presently reading, Will is simply telling the young man that his sonnets—at the least the first twenty-two—function as presagers of his interior voice: his "speaking breast."

That last phrase deserves a pause, for, as Naomi J. Miller nicely observes, Will employs the discourse of early modern "codes of maternity," and this topic bears intriguingly on our discussion:

> "As an imperfect actor," the speaker fears the responsibility of the
> mother's part, and fears as well the "strength's abundance" of "some
> fierce thing." . . . The nursing metaphor underlying the "speaking breast"
> allows the poet to establish a maternal dumb show, in which the sonnets
> "express" the milk of the poet's love. (N. J. Miller 347, 355)

Although Miller does not engage the theatrical metaphor (from her title), she prepares us to re-imagine Will as that "actor on the stage": he is (also) "play[ing] the mother's part" (143.12), cross-dressed quite.

In the couplet, Will directs the young man to "learn to read" such milky books, for to "hear with eyes belongs to love's fine wit." Here Will finalizes the sonnet's obsessive dichotomy between promulgation and silence, publication and inwardness, speaking and feeling, writing and loving.[39] For his part, Shakespeare turns Will's attempt to explain his lapse in celebrating the young man into a forum on the problem "express[ing]" his twin career as an English Ovidian poet-playwright.

SONNETS 29, 55, 108

In Sonnet 29, one of the most well-known in the sequence, Will appears to locate his public "disgrace with Fortune and men's eyes" (1) in the theatre and his consolation to such disgrace once again in his thought of the young man and in the "hymns" about the youth that he sings at "heaven's gate" (12). Although we do not know for sure the misfortune to which Will alludes, readers often suspect the author's life in the theatre.[40] The opening quatrain, with its portrait of Will "beweep[ing]" his "outcast state" and "troubl[ing] . . . deaf heaven" with his "bootless cries," certainly has the feel of drama, especially tragedy, with its suffering actor strutting on the stage. Therefore, we may wonder whether to detect a pun in "bootless" (perhaps a reference to the *cothurnus* or boot of the tragic actor?).[41] Those who do read theatre into the first quatrain (in particular) would see Will locating "disgrace" in his public role as an actor. Consequently, in the third quatrain, when Will provides the consolation for such misfortune in the thoughts he has of the young man and in the "hymns" he sings, we may once more see Will opposing poetry to theatre: his present practice as a private sonneteer consoles him for his disgraceful public profession.

The details of the antithesis deserve further attention. In the theatre of the octave, Will presents himself as a disgraced sufferer who seeks recourse in "heaven," only to find that high locale "deaf"—as if tragic theatre had no access to Christian grace, bound by the pagan determinism of "fate." In the poetic expression of the sestet, however, Will's "state" of thinking on the young man is "Like to the lark at break of day arising," able to "sing . . . hymns at heaven's gate." Since the lark is the bird that can sing while rising in flight, sixteenth-century writers often used it as a symbol of the individual's intellectual ascent to God.[42] Here Shakespeare uses the lark to evoke Christian resonance for his art, as the word "hymns" confirms. While theatre leaves the individual bootless—in an impotent state of misfortune—poetry puts his soul in touch with the deity. The image of the lark-like hymn singing "at heaven's gate" is pristine in its theological precision, compelling us to situate Shakespeare's claim for poetry in a longer Western continuum that stretches from Virgil and Ovid to Dante and Spenser. Whereas Virgil and Ovid vaunted poetry's power to secure fame along a horizontal axis (on earth, in time, and in the ears of posterity), both Dante and Spenser vaunted poetry's power to secure Christian glory along a vertical axis (in heaven, for eternity, and in the ears of God, Christ, and the saints).[43] By contrast, Shakespeare appears to be claiming an intermediate power for poetry, spatially between Virgilian earthly fame and Dantean Christian glory: Shakespeare's hymn cannot get the individual *into* heaven to secure grace and salvation, but it can get the individual *to* "heaven's gate." The conceit of an art that can sound to the Day of Judgment occurs in a related form throughout the Shakespeare canon, in both poems and plays, including three times in the Sonnets and most importantly in Sonnet 55:

> 'Gainst death and all-oblivious enmity
> Shall you pace forth; your praise shall still find room,
> Even in the eyes of all posterity
> That wear this world out to the ending doom.
>> So till the judgment that yourself arise,
>> You live in this, and dwell in lovers' eyes.
>>> (Sonnet 55. 9–14)

In the history of fame, Shakespeare's tender little words "to" and "till" acquire dramatic significance, segueing the relation between classical Virgilian fame and Dantean Christian glory. Will dramatically writes a verse in which the young man steps forth with great authority in the eyes of posterity "to" the "ending doom"—"till" the "judgment." Shakespeare is not as bold as Dante or Spenser, but he is bolder than Virgil or Ovid.[44] The final *telos* of Shakespearean poetry, we may speculate, is to prepare the individual's soul for this momentous occasion; this may well be the promised end of Shakespearean subjectivity in the Sonnets. In the plays, we witness the same *telos* most powerfully when the

Eastern Star says to Charmian, in her characteristically theatrical way, "I'll give thee leave / To play till doomsday" (*Antony and Cleopatra*, 5. 2. 231–32).

An extended, even technical version of poetry and theatre appears in Sonnet 108:

> What's in the brain that ink may character
> Which hath not figur'd to thee my true spirit?
> What's new to speak, what now to register,
> That may express my love, or thy dear merit?
> Nothing, sweet boy, but yet like prayers divine,
> I must each day say o'er the very same,
> Counting no old thing old, thou mine, I mine,
> Even as when first I hallowed thy fair name.
> So that eternal love in love's fresh case
> Weighs not the dust and injury of age,
> Nor gives to necessary wrinkles place,
> But makes antiquity for aye his page,
> > Finding the first conceit of love there bred,
> > Where time and outward form would show it dead.
> > > (Sonnet 108)

This densely complex sonnet could be the topic of a separate essay. Duncan-Jones notes the significance of the sonnet's number: "Reaching 108, the total number of sonnets in Sidney's *AS* [*Astrophil and Stella*] . . . the poet takes stock of his achievements. He can find no new way of representing either himself or the youth in words, but is compelled to reiterate what he has often said before; in so doing he continually rediscovers his first love and the young man's first beauty, revivified in language though vanished in nature" (Duncan-Jones, ed., *Sonnets*, 326). Sonnet 108 also needs to be situated historically in the context of both Plato and Scripture, as its discourse of philosophy and religion indicates, especially the Platonically precise "eternal love" but also the various echoes of Christian worship: "prayers divine" and "hallowed . . . name."[45] Most obviously, the sonnet is important for its reflection on the seminal challenge of Shakespeare's poetic art: to write "eternal love in love's fresh case"; to present the particular instance or thing of love so that it partakes of the eternal essence, thereby freeing it from the dust of death—in effect, to write verse that allows the young man to prepare for (or participate in) Christian immortality.

Shakespeare's inclusion of a discourse that pertains either to printed poetry or to staged theatre helps support this reading. While the word "show" has clear theatrical resonance, and "antiquity" clear resonance for printed books, most of the words straddle the borderline between the two forms: "character," "figured," "speak," "say," "express," "form."[46] The word "case" is a case in point. John Kerrigan identifies four different meanings for the phrase "love's fresh case": "(1) in the (constantly) fresh circumstances of (truly true) love; (2) contained in affection's sprightly (though *old*) argument (meaning 'my love poetry'); (3) covered by affection's youthful vigour (*case* suggesting 'skin', and thus the *wrinkles* of line 11); (4) clad in affection's sprightly garb (common meaning of *case* in the period)" (Kerrigan, ed., *The Sonnets*, 321). To these four meanings, Evans adds a fifth: "in the case of a newly conceived love" (Evans, ed., *Sonnets*, 219). To these five, we can add a sixth, prepared for by Kerrigan's fourth meaning—one that pertains to the theatre: "case" as dress, costume, as in *Measure for Measure*'s "How often dost thou with thy case, thy habit" (2.4.13), but specifically "case" as theatrical disguise, as in Hal's directive to Poins in *1 Henry IV* during the robbery at Gad's Hill: "Case ye, case ye, on with your vizards" (2.2.53).[47] According to the theatrical meaning of "case," then, Will can be seen to talk not just about an author's expressive challenge but also about the challenge facing a playwright and an actor: the challenge of staging "eternal love" freshly. The emphatic word "show" in the last line compels this theatrical ring for the sonnet as a whole. Characteristically, the verbal play of "show" shifts to where we might expect it—the negative side of the poetry/theatre dialectic, allowing Will to "show" what will die: "outward form."

SONNET 144

Sonnet 144 is the final poem of Shakespeare's Sonnets to bring poetry and theatre into significant alignment. This sonnet is notable not simply because a version of it was published along with a version of Sonnet 138 in *The Passionate Pilgrim*, but also because it is (as we have seen) "one of the strongest sonnets in the volume," and the only one that summarizes the triangulated plot of sexual desire between Will, the young man, and the dark lady.[48] As Duncan-Jones adds, "The sonnet's number in the sequence, 12 x 12, known as a 'gross', may be especially appropriate to this enumeration of the speaker's amorous possessions, which prove to be 'gross' also in the sexual sense" (Duncan-Jones, ed., *Sonnets*, 402). That Shakespeare would conjoin poetry and theatre in such a significant sonnet makes it especially worth entertaining here.

Unlike Sonnet 55 or Sonnet 111, Sonnet 144 contains no explicit reference to either Will's role as a poet or as a playwright, nor does it employ overt poetic or theatrical discourse. Instead, it presents Will as a sonnet writer who deploys a religious metaphor evocative of the morality play tradition, especially as staged famously in Marlowe's *Doctor Faustus*.[49] The effect of the morality play metaphor—and perhaps even of the Marlovian one—is to present Will as a sonneteer staging and rewriting his morality play predicament in terms at once personal and erotic.[50]

The first quatrain stages a dialectic between the young man and the dark lady as types of "love," conveyed through several fields—gender, aesthetics, ethics, theology, and finally personal affect:

> Two loves I have of comfort and despair,
> Which like two spirits do suggest me still:
> The better angel is a man right fair,
> The worser spirit a woman color'd ill.
>   (Sonnet 144.1–4)

Thus the young man is (indeed) a "man," "fair," "better," and an "angel" who brings Will "comfort," while the dark lady is a "woman," "color'd ill," "worser," and a sinister "spirit" who brings him "despair." As Booth observes, "comfort and despair" are "both terms in theology, an area which the poem immediately invades" (Booth, ed., *Sonnets*, 497). Through this dialectic, Will converts his lyric expression into a theatrical event.

The second quatrain puts the dialectic into action:

> To win me soon to hell, my female evil
> Tempteth my better angel from my [side],
> And would corrupt my saint to be a devil,
> Wooing his purity with her foul pride.
>   (Sonnet 144.5–8)

Here we learn that the dark lady has seduced the young man in order to carry out revenge against Will. Critics rightly see Shakespeare rewriting the plot of *Everyman* or *Doctor Faustus*, since the bad angel turns her attention, not to the mortal soul in the middle, but to her mirror opposite, the good angel, effectively cutting Will out of the theological deal. Moreover, lines 6–8 introduce the important blurring of boundaries between the two halves of the dialectic, for the good angel is here subjected to the temptation of the evil angel: Will's "saint" becomes a "devil," the young man's "purity" is wooed by the dark lady's "foul pride." The distinction between masculine and feminine, beauty and ugliness, good and evil, comfort and despair begins to evaporate, to be replaced by a new murkiness that resembles the atmosphere from Sonnet 15.

The third quatrain then shows Will's reaction to this atmospheric murkiness; he loses his ability to see clearly:

> And whether that my angel be turn'd fiend,
> Suspect I may, yet not directly tell,

> But being both from me, both to each friend,
> I guess one angel in another's hell.
>   (Sonnet 144. 9–12)

He can only suspect, not actually determine, whether the young man and the dark lady betray him behind his back. In the end, he is left to "guess," thereby creating a mental fiction in which "one angel [enters] in another's hell." The line is ambiguous, since it does not specify which spiritual creature and which afterlife are which: the dark lady and the young man have become indistinguishable. Will's emphasis here on inwardness ("suspect," "tell," "guess") marks his dramatic progress during the three quatrains, from his formulation of a dialectic, to his representation of a dialectical action, to his own reaction to that action.

In the couplet, Will summarizes his inward condition as one of ignorance, and he gestures toward an end to the (Im)morality play he has been staging: "Yet this shall I ne'er know, but live in doubt, / Till my bad angel fire my good one out." As Booth puts it, he will live in doubt "'Until she gets tired of him and kicks him out' and 'Until he shows symptoms of venereal disease'" (Booth, ed., *Sonnets*, 500). At the close, Will reaches clarity, but only through perceiving the grim effects of a maliciously lustful sexuality.

Will's phrase "live in doubt" is among the most useful in the entire sequence for registering the historical context in which Shakespeare produced his Sonnets. The phrase anticipates Donne's more famous articulation, two years later in the *First Anniversary*: "And new Philosophy calls all in doubt, / The Element of fire is quite put out; / . . . / Tis all in pieces, all coherence gone."[51] While this view of "doubt" during the period is well known, what might be fresh is Shakespeare's portrait of a new kind of author as the mouthpiece to the deeply anxious expression of the age: the English Ovidian poet-playwright.

PASTORAL AND EPIC THEATRE

The presence of Ovidian poetry and theatre in the Sonnets is inflected by the Virgilian career dynamic outlined in earlier chapters. We may take the cue of William Empson, who titles his famous chapter on Sonnet 94 in *Some Versions of Pastoral* "They That Have Power: Twist of Heroic-Pastoral Ideas into an Ironical Acceptance of Aristocracy" (87–115). However influential Empson's essay has been, it remains oblique, so perhaps it should not be surprising to discover that his Virgilian paradigm of epic and pastoral has not taken root in subsequent discussions of either Shakespeare's most discussed sonnet or of the Sonnets generally.

Curiously, Empson's chapter title is the only explicit statement of his thesis, so we may need to recall his special "version of pastoral," emphasized in his larger study: pastoral is an ideological practice of "putting the complex into the simple," the gentleman-courtier into the shepherd-poet. In other words, Empson's famous version "piled the heroic convention onto the pastoral one" (12). While Empson analyzes the intersection of the plant or pastoral imagery and the class or epic imagery in Sonnet 94, he reminds us that such imagery is gathered in from elsewhere in the sequence—from Sonnet 15, for instance, but especially from the memorable "rose" sonnets. Indeed, Shakespeare's sequence opens precisely with this version of pastoral, as Will uses recurrent metaphors from what Empson regards as pastoral simplicity to encourage the young man to marry and procreate: "From fairest creatures we desire increase / That thereby beauty's rose might never die" (1.1–2). Georgio Melchiori well documents these opening sonnets' "concern with concrete principles of good husbandry: ploughing (Sonnet 3), the distillation of perfume from flowers (Sonnet 5 and 6), cattle-rearing (Sonnet 6), harvesting (Sonnet 12), grafting (Sonnet 15), the cultivation of flowers and plants (Sonnet 16)" (*Dramatic Meditations*, 27–28). Bruce R. Smith adds that "The pastoral images of the first twenty sonnets are replaced by chambers and closets (46), beds (27, 142), chests (48, 52, 65), mirrors (63, 77), and clocks (57). The delights of the *locus amoenus* give way to the confidences of the bedchamber" (*Homosexual Desire*, 254). In other words, a pastoral ideal gives way to a courtly one.

By taking these cues and that of Sonnet 94, we can extend Will's "pastoral" and "heroic" concern beyond the Procreation Sonnets in order to see Will, not simply as an Ovidian poet-playwright in the Marlovian vein, but also as a Virgilian pastoral-epicist in the Spenserian vein. Indeed, Will's representation in Sonnet 32 of his "poor rude lines" (4) introduces Spenser's humble pastoral style into the Sonnets.[52] Similarly, Will's representation in Sonnet 106 of "ladies dead and lovely knights" evokes Spenser's epic project:

> When in the chronicle of wasted time
> I see descriptions of the fairest wights
> And beauty making beautiful old rhyme
> In praise of ladies dead and lovely knights.
> (106.1–4)

While each of the first three lines carries Spenserian weight, line 4 is a quite specific *imitatio* of the most important programmatic line in the entire *Faerie Queene*: "And sing of Knights and Ladies gentle deeds" (1. Proem 1). Spenser's line is the first articulation in his romantic epic of his persona as the Virgil of England. As suggested in chapter 2, he opens his epic by relying on a theatrical metaphor that may have interested Shakespeare:

> Lo I the man, whose Muse whilome did maske,
> As time her taught, in lowly Shepheards weeds,

Am now enforst a far unfitter taske,
For trumpets sterne to chaunge mine Oaten reeds,
And sing of Knights and Ladies gentle deeds;
Whose prayses having slept in silence long.

(Spenser, The Faerie Queene, 1. Proem 1)

Here Spenser announces his Virgilian turn from pastoral to epic. If Shakespeare is imitating the penultimate line, he is imitating the very site of Spenser's generic progression. From this brief moment, we can discern that Shakespeare's Sonnets present the author as an Ovidian/Marlovian poet-playwright traveling along the Virgilian/Spenserian path.

Sonnet 102 offers a clear map to this authorial representation:

My love is strength'ned, though more weak in seeming,
I love not less, though less the show appear;
That love is merchandiz'd whose rich esteeming
The owner's tongue doth publish every where.
Our love was new, and then but in the spring,
When I was wont to greet it with my lays,
As Philomela in summer's front doth sing,
And stops [her] pipe in growth of riper days:
Not that the summer is less pleasant now,
Than when her mournful hymns did hush the night,
But that wild music burthens every bough,
And sweets grown common lose their dear delight.
    Therefore like her, I sometime hold my tongue,
    Because I would not dull you with my song.

(Sonnet 102)

As in the previous sonnets we have examined, here we can clearly locate the discourse of both theatre ("show") and poetry ("lays"). Beyond this, however, the form of the conjunction is anything but clear.

In line 4, for instance, the word "publish" might seem to evoke an anxiety over printed poetry (see Burrow, ed., *Sonnets and Poems*, 584), except that Will himself aligns it with the shame of "show" from line 2 (cf. Wall, *Imprint*, 197). As in Sonnet 23, Will distinguishes between the loving poet's silence as a form of integrity and the prospect of over-broadcasting as the mark of only "seeming" to "love." Yet in Sonnet 102 the word "show" describes Will's praise of the young man through the art of poetry: "I love not less, though less the show appear." That is to say, Will's poetry in praise of the young man is a "show," even though it appears less now than it once did. In lines 3–4, Will employs the mercantile terms of both the counting-house and the print shop to distinguish between his reticence in expressing his love and his "merchandiz[ing]" of love through "publish[ing]" it "everywhere." Will does not say "publish" *at all*; he says "publish every where." Thus, in the first quatrain, while the word "publish" shows Shakespeare worrying about print publication, it also associates publication with "show" as a shameful form of publicity violating intimate truth. Unlike other sonnets we have examined, here poetry and theatre are complicit in the economy of shame.

Only in the second quatrain do we begin to acquire more authoritative direction. Line 5, "Our love was new, and then but in the spring," introduces a change from the present of the first quatrain to the past, "When" Will was "wont" to "greet" the spring with his "lays." Even though he no longer praises the young man, in the past he was able to "publish" his love through the "show" of poetry. As in the first quatrain, Will sees poetry as a type of theatre, but here it is not shameful. The simile then comparing Will's writing process with the singing cycle of "Philomela" clarifies a crucial point: just as the nightingale sings in the spring but "stops [her] pipe in growth of riper days"—in late summer—so Will enacts a human process. He does not stop his pipe because he loves the young man "less," but rather because he participates in a natural or seasonal cycle. He compares himself with Philomela to convince the young man that his poetic process is natural rather than merely theatrical.

Yet this is no more than a version of Shakespearean humor, since the author evokes the ancient myth of Philomela. As Evans remarks, the word "'mournful' reflects the tragic events surrounding Philomela," especially as Ovid retold those events in Book 6 of the *Metamorphoses* (424–674), but also as Shakespeare himself had adapted the events in *Titus Andronicus* (Evans, ed., *Sonnets*, 211)— and, we may add, in *The Rape of Lucrece* and elsewhere. While Philomela clearly has the "Ovidian" associations that editors conventionally assign to it, we might recall that both before and after Ovid Philomela appears as the arch-myth for both pastoral and tragedy. For Shakespeare, we might say, unlike for Spenser, the nightingale becomes the quintessential figure for the fusion of theatre with poetry.

In line 8, Will evokes the tradition of Philomela as the myth of pastoral from Theocritus to Spenser: "And stops [her] pipe in growth of riper days." The importance of this line has escaped attention, for it is among the clearest excavations in the English Renaissance of an ancient archaeological artifact: the nightingale as a musical instrument of pastoral poetry.[53] While drawing on an ancient tradition, Shakespeare also situates himself historically. Editors cite Nicholas Breton in Sonnet 1 of his 1604 *The Passionate Shepherd* (Evans, ed., *Sonnets*, 211), Sidney in the *Old Arcadia* (66.13–14; Duncan-Jones, ed., *Sonnets*, 314), Petrarch in Song 311 (Burrow, ed., *Sonnets and Poems*, 584), and Barnabe Barnes in *Parthenophil and Parthenophe* (Burrow, ed., *Sonnets and Poems*, 584). While poet after poet during the period does present him or herself as a type of

Philomela, Spenser's E. K., we have seen, traces English origins to Gascoigne and identifies Spenser himself as the prime inheritor after Gascoigne's death in 1578. If we recall merely that the "Elizabethans, probably influenced by the Philomela story, usually associated the song of the nightingale with the female" (Evans, ed., *Sonnets*, 211), we erase this specific Elizabethan genealogy. Conversely, by recalling that Shakespeare's "*Philomel* resembles a sheperd(ess) playing panpipes in a pastoral landscape" (Kerrigan, ed., *The Sonnets*, 306), we profitably situate Will's pastoral self-representation along Spenser's Virgilian path.[54]

In fact, Will's phrasing in lines 6–8 clearly echoes that of Colin Clout in the *November* eclogue, where Spenser's persona is called "The Nightingale . . . sovereigne of song" (25) and where the shepherd himself refers to "Philomele" steeping her "song with teares" during his Song of Dido (141). Let us place the two sets of lines together:

> When I was wont to greet it with my lays,
> As Philomela in summer's front doth sing,
> And stops [her] pipe in growth of riper days.
> (Shakespeare, Sonnet 102. 6–8)

> The mornefull Muse [Melpomene] in myrth now list ne maske,
> As she was wont in youngth and sommer dayes.
> (Spenser, *November*, 19–20)

Perhaps Spenser's theatrical metaphor, "maske," attracted the theatrical man. In any event, here we discover another Spenserian link between poetry and theatre, pastoral and tragedy. In line 6, Shakespeare's phrase "was wont" is distinctly Spenserian, occurring no fewer than 238 times in his canon (with cognates), often in the context of both pastoral and poetry. Like Will, Colin Clout famously stops his pipe in "growth of riper days" (see *June*, 36).[55]

Thus, in a sonnet conjoining Marlowe's Ovidian discourse of poetry and theatre with Spenser's discourse of pastoral and epic, Shakespeare uses the Philomela myth as a point of intersection between the two literary representations. Effectively, Will presents himself as a pastoral tragedian singing "mournfull hymns." In the third quatrain, he then uses his identity with Philomela to detach himself from rival poets who have also been using "wild music" to "burthen . . . every bough."[56] Here Will justifies "stop[ping]" his poetry through an ornithological process, in which countless birds eventually join with the nightingale in singing their songs. Consequently, in this "riper" season the nightingale-poet ends his song to affirm his distinction as the sovereign of song.

In the couplet, Will confirms his likeness to Philomela. Perhaps his phrasing about "hold[ing] his tongue" and not "dulling" the young man glances at

Philomela's loss of her tongue through the brutality of Tereus. As Wall reveals, Elizabethan poets like Spenser and Gascoigne recurrently cross-dress their voices in the garb of a female, including Philomela, to air their shame over printing their art (*Imprint*, 260–62). While Wall refers to Sonnet 102 only in passing (262), we might extend her analysis about the shame of publication to the twin domains of poetry and theatre, including Shakespeare's pastoral theatre here.

MANUSCRIPT AND PRINT AUTHORSHIP

So far, we have discussed poetry and theatre in terms of the narrative sequence that begins with the young-man sonnets and ends with the sonnets to the dark-lady. Recent textual scholarship, however, suggests that Shakespeare's compositional practice reversed this narrative order: he wrote the dark-lady sonnets first, c. 1591–95; and the young-man sonnets second, c. 1595–1604 (Burrow, ed., *Sonnets and Poems*, 103–11, 131–38). This scholarship has intriguing implications for the present argument, because the discourse of poetry and theatre occurs almost exclusively in the young-man sonnets. While we can follow such critics as Fineman and Margreta de Grazia in formulating a critical narrative based on the structure of the 1609 quarto, foregrounding subjectivity or sexual scandal, we can take the editorial cue of Burrow to see how the Sonnets also register Shakespeare's increasing interest in the twin forms of authorship itself, the conjunction of poetry and theatre, from the mid-1590s through the first years of the seventeenth century. The author did not abandon poetry for theatre but came to see their conjunction as the central form of his art.

Having said so, we might acknowledge the challenge we confront in reconstructing the historical context for the Sonnets, for Shakespeare's collection has long been at the eye of a critical storm over the issue of authorship. On the one hand, the 1609 quarto has been so mysterious that from the perspectives of both the bibliographer and the biographer we would not be unwise to abandon the category of the author altogether. The question was forcefully raised by Duncan-Jones in the title of a seminal essay, "Was the 1609 *Shake-speares Sonnets* Really Unauthorized?" Our answer to this question commits us to a series of critical positions—especially, in the current critical climate, our sense of the relation between a manuscript and a print Shakespeare. Those answering yes to the question, believing the Sonnets unauthorized, are compelled to identify the author as a manuscript rather than a print poet. On the other hand, the bibliographical (and biographical) work done by Duncan-Jones, Kerrigan, and others—those who answer that the Sonnets are indeed authorized—presents us with a radically different Shakespeare: not a private coterie poet in the mold of Donne but a public proto-national poet in the mold of Spenser. In these terms, the Sonnets would become not simply a manuscript poem circulated randomly among private friends but rather a carefully controlled collection that moves from scribal circulation to print publication.

Critics of differing professional temperaments will presumably suit themselves
to whichever position they find comfortable, and few would be so unwise as to
think rational argument could budge anyone either way. One suspects, however,
that the truth lies elsewhere: that Shakespeare is neither Donne nor Spenser;
the Sonnets are neither fully a manuscript-authored nor a print-authored poem.
Presumably, this peculiar reality is why both Shakespeare and his collection have
been so intriguing for so long: here we have an author and his work defying the
binary categories in which we are used to thinking. We are witnessing, then, a
new model of authorship, one that recent scholarship is only now learning to
formulate. Among recent critics, Richard Helgerson most succinctly articulates
this new model, in an evident attempt to reconcile recent historical theories of
social construction with past theories of intentionality, saying of Shakespeare,
"He helped make the world that made him" (*Forms*, 215). While recognizing
Shakespeare's historical complexity in straddling the divide of early modern
authorship—between manuscript and print culture, coterie poet and national
poet, Donne and Spenser—we have attended to the second part of the opposition,
because what seems missing in recent criticism is the kind of close intertextual
work that demonstrates Shakespeare's interest in the Spenserian project.

At least since Charles Gildon and more famously Edmund Malone, critics
have tried to capture the special relation that the Sonnets have to the plays, for
better or for worse. As we have seen, Shakespeare himself *represented* his own
sense of that relation. The Sonnets are surely not theatre, but for that they need
not apologize. Yet neither are they the Elizabethan or Jacobean lyric as usual—as
testified to by so much criticism on their "dramatic" quality, or on their intimate
connection with the inwardness of such plays as *Hamlet*. What is unusual in the
Sonnets is Shakespeare's own self-consciousness about precisely this character
for his historic composition. The Sonnets are poems not merely *by* a practicing
man of the theatre but also *about* a theatrical man who tries to write them. In
this, they may well find their final distinction from so much other great English
Renaissance poetry. Shakespeare's book of sonnets is historically the dumb
presager of his national eloquence.

NOTES

1. For this classification, see Helgerson, *Laureates*. Sonneteers belonging to
the amateur class include Henry Constable, Barnabe Barnes, Giles Fletcher the
Elder, Sir Robert Sidney, Bartholomew Griffin, William Smith, and Sir John
Davies. According to Gabriel Harvey, Spenser wrote *Nine Comedies* (Letter III in
G. G. Smith, ed., *Essays*, 1: 115, while Drayton wrote tragedies, but in both cases
the plays have not survived, and some question whether Spenser's ever existed (see
Oruch, "Works, Lost").

2. Other dramatists who did not write sonnet sequences include John Lyly,
Christopher Marlowe, Robert Greene, Thomas Nashe, George Peele, George
Chapman, Ben Jonson, John Marston, Thomas Dekker, Thomas Middleton,

John Fletcher, Francis Beaumont, and John Webster. On Samuel Daniel, Thomas Lodge, and Fulke Greville as partial exceptions, see Cheney, "Poetry," 222–24.

3. The *Riverside* notes that "books" "may mean these sonnets, or, if the addressee is Southampton, the two poems *Venus and Adonis* and *Lucrece*," and it glosses "dumb presagers" as "presenters, as in the dumb show of a play" (1847).

4. To my knowledge, no one has done so. For different models relating poetry and drama, see Hunter, "Dramatic Technique"; Melchiori, *Dramatic Meditations*; Dubrow, *Victors*, esp. 190; Henderson, *Passion Made Public*; Wright, "Silent Speech," 137; Schalkwyk, "Embodiment," "Performative," *Performance*. While Schalkwyk characterizes Shakespearean self-representation in terms of the Austinian performative, I contextualize it in terms of Shakespeare's historical predicament of being an English author at this time, a man of the theatre who has turned to sonneteering. Schalkwyk looks compellingly at sonnets representing theatre—notably Sonnet 23—but we still lack a detailed investigation into the discursive presence of poetry and theatre in the text of the Sonnets as a whole.

5. See Duncan Jones, "Unauthorized?" and her edition, as well as J. Kerrigan, ed., *The Sonnets*. On the 1580s dating of Sonnet 145, see Gurr, "First Poem."

6. As noted in chapter 1, Burrow, "Life," suggests that we think about the Sonnets "as something approaching Shakespeare's life's work" (17). For further details, see Hieatt, Hieatt, and Prescott "When," 73–74. Duncan-Jones suggests "four probable phases of composition": before 1598; 1599–1600; 1603–04; and August 1608–May 1609 (Duncan-Jones, ed., *Sonnets*, 12–13; see 1–28). In *Ungentle*, she remarks, "Writing, revising and re-ordering sonnets was probably a regular activity throughout his adult life" (214; see 214–16). J. Kerrigan believes that "Shakespeare was consciously shaping a collection when he wrote *A Lover's Complaint* in c. 1602–5" (Kerrigan, ed., *The Sonnets*, 12; see 10–18). Finally, see G. Taylor, "Manuscripts."

7. See, e.g., Love, *Scribal Publications*; Marotti, "Property" esp. 170n30 on Meres. Marotti's essay is invaluable for re-historicizing Shakespearean authorship, yet we need to complicate his thesis, taking his own cue: "Despite the decision to publish two narrative poems early in his career . . . Shakespeare was . . . a professional actor, playwright, and theatrical shareholder" ("Property," 144).

8. For Shakespeare's signature as a poet, see Fineman, *Perjured*, 6. See also Leishman, *Themes and Variations*, 27–91; Muir, *Sonnets*, 30–44, 112–22; Hammond, *Reader*, 61–78, 95–110, 135–49, 195–213. On "Shakespeare's Petrarchism," see the essay of this title by Braden; and on Shakespeare's Ovidianism, see Bate, *Ovid*, 87–100.

9. On the "name" of "Will," see Pequigney, "Sonnets," 298–301; Schalkwyk, *Performance*, 183–88.

10. See H. Smith, *Tension*: "It is traditional to see references to Shakespeare's career as an actor in the little series 110–112" (26; see 26–28). See Hubler, *Sense*, 115–22; Honan, *A Life*, 128, 161.

11. Cf. Wall, *Imprint*, 197n51. Valbuena, "Reproduction," reveals that Shakespeare's language is suffused with the discourse of early modern writing practices.

12. Most famously, Fineman has argued that the Sonnets invent modern subjectivity (*Perjured*; see Ferry). This view has been tempered by such critics as de Grazia, "Motive"; Schoenfeldt, *Bodies*, 74–95. Others, such as B. R. Smith, argue that in the Sonnets "Shakespeare improvised a new form of discourse":

"Shakespeare seeks to speak about homosexual desire with the same authority that Petrarch assumes in speaking about heterosexual desire" (*Homosexual Desire*, 228–70; quotations from 265, 264).

13. Dubrow, "Politics," argues that the Sonnets are best viewed as "internalized meditations unconnected to a narrative line" (123). For a recent rebuttal to Dubrow, see (e.g.) Traub, "Sex," 442.

14. See *The Roman Actor* (1626), wherein Massinger uses the actor as a metaphor for the playwright (see Butler's intro., x). Cf. Honan: "there was a possible tactical advantage, for Shakespeare's actors, in having these elegant lyrics in print in London at a critical time in 1609" (*A Life*, 362). Schalkwyk, *Performance*, demonstrates persuasively that the Sonnets concern themselves with Shakespeare's career as a player-poet; however, by focusing on the Austinian performative, Schalkwyk turns away from (in particular) intertextuality.

15. On theatrical cross-dressing, see Orgel, *Impersonations*. On homoeroticism in the Sonnets, see Pequigney, *Such*; B. R. Smith, *Homosexual Desire*, 228–70, "Politics"; Traub, "Sex." Critics neglect the homology, even though they may discuss the Sonnets and plays (e.g., B. R. Smith, "Politics," 414).

16. One did not need to be an actor to write sonnets addressed to another man, as testified to by Richard Barnfield's twenty sonnets in his 1595 *Cynthia* (Duncan-Jones, *Sonnets*, ed., 47). Unlike Sidney, Daniel, Spenser, and others, however, Barnfield does not include a discourse of theatre. He does present himself as a poet writing in a tradition of English and European poetry in service of fame.

17. See Engle, "Shame"; however, Engle does not situate shame in the theatrical matrix of the Sonnets, even though he reports that "Markets and theaters are, for Shakespeare, the most prominent local instances of such economies" (187).

18. See Duncan-Jones, *Ungentle*, for the assumption that poetic immortality in the Sonnets comes from "the printed book" (177).

19. On this place, see Mullaney, *Place*. On the "presence" of Ovid in the Sonnets, in relation to the "absence" of Petrarch, see Braden, "Ovid, Petrarch," 99. On "shame" in the "Ovidian model," see Brown, "Breaking the Canon," 66–67. For a different view of the *Amores* and Marlowe's translation, see Stapleton, *Harmful*.

20. The only significant uses occur in "compare" at 130.14 and in "play" at 143.12; see Sutphen, "Dateless," 210.

21. On "Desire is Death," see Dollimore.

22. De Grazia borrows her classification for Will's relations with the young man and the dark lady, not from "the post-Enlightenment categories of homosexual and heterosexual," but from E. K.'s note to the *Januarye* eclogue: pederasty and gynerasty, respectively ("Scandal," 46). According to Bednarz, *Poets' War*, "Shakespeare in *Troilus and Cressida* identifies failure as an essential condition of experience" (263).

23. Cain, intro., *June* eclogue, *Shepheardes Calender*, in Oram, et al., eds. *Yale Edition*, 108.

24. For the history of the Sonnets' publication from the seventeenth century onwards, see (in addition to Burrow, "Life," 17–21) de Grazia, *Verbatim*.

25. See N. Frye, "Twain": "Shakespeare's sonnets are the definitive summing up of the Western tradition of love poetry from Plato and Ovid, to Dante and Petrarch, to Chaucer and Spenser" (106).

26. The longer version of this chapter, "Poetry," also discusses Sonnet 54. Others not discussed there or here that *conjoin* poetry and theatre in thought-provoking

ways include Sonnets 5, 8, 17, 21, 26, 38, 53, 76, 103, and 105. All of these, like the ones discussed here, appear in the young-man sequence, except the special case of 144, to be examined presently.

27. Schoenfeldt notes that line 9 contains the "theme that unifies this collocation" (*Bodies*, 89): "this inconstant stay." Evans observes that Sonnet 15 "first sounds the Horatian and Ovidian theme of immortality assured through poetry" (Evans, ed., *Sonnets*, 127; see Rollins, ed., *Variorum: Sonnets*, 1: 41–43). Herman adds that "The thematic emergence of poetry . . . overlaps with the emergence of homoeroticism" ("What's the use," 277).

28. In "Politics," B. R. Smith argues that "'I,' 'he,' and 'she' exist ontologically in these texts exactly as three principal characters might in a theatrical script" (424).

29. The trope was intriguing even to individuals who were not associated with the theatre; see Greenblatt, *Ralegh*.

30. Engle, "Shame," focuses on the treatment of eternity in the Sonnets as social endurance rather than transcendence (186). See his "Certainty," which responds to Bernard's "Platonic" argument.

31. On "nothingness" in Shakespeare, see Bloom, *Shakespeare*, 642–49.

32. Cf. Sir John Cheke, who, says Riggs, "coined the term 'Atheists' to describe people who do not 'care whether there be a God or no, or whether . . . he will recompense good Men with good things, and bad Men with what is Evil'" ("Marlowe's Quarrel," 20).

33. Evans, ed., *Sonnets*, 128. He adds, "Booth notes that Jonson seems to echo the theatrical suggestion of lines 3–6 in his poem 'To the Memory of . . . Shakespeare' in the First Folio (1623), line 78: 'Or influence, chide, or cheere the drooping Stage'" (128).

34. Smith, *Homosexual Desire*, 247. Freinkel, "Rose," traces the grafting image to its religious sources in St. Paul (Romans 11: 19–23) and in Luther (*Lectures on Romans*) (244–45). On husbandry, see Greene, "Thrivers."

35. On fame from classical through modern culture, see Braudy.

36. All editors gloss the textual crux here of "style" versus "skill," but neither reading seriously affects the argument. All three 1997 editions of the complete works—*Riverside*, *Norton*, *Longman*—print "books" and follow up with notes on Shakespeare's reference to his printed poems or works. Moreover, Booth, J. Kerrigan, and Duncan-Jones all print "books," as does Rollins, ed., *Variorum: Sonnets*.

37. Sonnet 23 confirms what Sonnet 152, the last in the Petrarchan part of the sequence, clarifies, that Shakespeare's Sonnets are fundamentally about the problem of infidelity—sexual, marital, philosophical, theological, and of course professional: "new faith torn" (152.3). The problem of memory and forgetting is less often discussed; see Sullivan, "Forgetting."

38. Quoted in Booth, ed., *Sonnets*, 172. For the present sonnets and Shakespeare's two previously printed poems, see Kerrigan, ed., *The Sonnets*, 203; Duncan-Jones, ed., *Sonnets*, 156.

39. For Will's "oscillation" between "subjectivity" and "civic temperament," see Martin, *Policy*, 134–36.

40. See, e.g., Evans, ed., *Sonnets*, 141. Evans also links the reference to bad "Fortune" at 111. 1 with Shakespeare's life in the theatre, citing Sir John Davies' two references to Shakespeare, the theatre, and fortune (Evans, ed., *Sonnets*, 222; see Duncan-Jones, ed., *Sonnets*, 332). Kerrigan glosses line 4 ("And look upon

myself") as follows: "The poet is not navel-gazing but has become the spectator of his own predicament (compare *3 Henry VI*, 2.3. 25–8 . . .)" (Kerrigan, ed., *The Sonnets*, 210).

41. According to the *Oxford English Dictionary*, the word *bootless* can mean both "void of boot or profit" (first entry, def 3) and "Without boots" (second entry), citing *1 Henry IV*, 3. 1. 66–67, when Glendower says he has sent Bullingbrook "Bootless home and weather-beaten back," to which Hotspur rejoins, "Home without boots, and in foul weather too!" The *Oxford English Dictionary* notwithstanding, here Shakespeare brings the two meanings of the word together. In "To the memory of my beloved," Jonson dresses Shakespeare himself in this guise: "to heare thy Buskin tread, / And shake a Stage" (36–37; *Riverside Shakespeare*, 97).

42. See Cheney, *Flight*, 88, 269n11.

43. See Cheney, *Flight*, 7–10.

44. See also Sonnets 116. 2 and 122. 4, as well as *Lucrece*, 924, *Love's Labor's Lost*, 4.3. 270, *Richard III*, 3.1.78, *Henry V*, 4.1.137. Cf. Engle, "Certainty," 837–38 on Shakespeare's commitment to contingency; Greenblatt, who ends *Purgatory* with a note on "the afterlife" in Sonnet 55 (313n1). In "Ovid, Petrarch," Braden traces Shakespeare's use of immortality in the Sonnets to Ovid's *Metamorphoses*, but he misjudges the historic significance of Sonnet 55 when he sees it showing merely "poetry's ability to defy time" (108).

45. Editors emphasize Scripture but neglect Plato. Duncan-Jones glosses "eternal love" as having "strong religious connotations, as in Sidney's *CS* [*Certain Sonnets*], 32: 13–14" (Duncan-Jones, ed., *Sonnets*, 326).

46. On "character" as a print term, see Burrow, "Life," 24–25.

47. See *Romeo and Juliet* 1.4.29–30; *1 Henry IV*, 1.2.179; *Henry V*, 3.2.4.

48. Quoted in Kerrigan, ed., *The Sonnets*, 59. Evans quotes Leslie Fielder, who calls 144 "the thematic key to the entire sequence" (Evans, ed., *Sonnets*, 262).

49. Kerrigan, ed., *The Sonnets*, 375; Evans, ed., *Sonnets*, 262; Duncan-Jones, ed., *Sonnets*, 402.

50. On the morality play in *Doctor Faustus*, see Grantley, "Theatricalism," 234–35.

51. Donne, *First Anniversary*, 205–13. Critics often see Shakespeare in the Sonnets living in doubt (Dubrow, *Victors*, 256–57), and we may wish to lean on his phrase in Sonnet 144 to encapsulate this frame of mind.

52. For details, see Cheney, "Sonnet 106," to which the following discussion is indebted. "Rude" (with cognates) is Spenser's habitual word for his pastoral poetry (*Colin Clouts*, 363, 669, *Januarye*, 67, *June*, 77, *December*, 14; Envoy, 5, *Astrophel*, Proem 12) and for the pastoral poet writing epic (*Fairie Queene* 1.12.23, 3.2.3).

53. See Cheney, *Flight*, 69–70, 265n46; on the panpipe and birds, see 265n45.

54. On Spenserian pastoral and Shakespearean dramatic pastoral, see Alpers, *What is Pastoral?* 185–86.

55. The phrase "mournfull hymns" recalls the "hymne" to Dido sung by Colin, who invokes Melpomene, "mournefulst Muse of nyne" (*November*, 53).

56. Burrow glosses "burthens" by recalling that the "noun 'burden' can mean chorus (*OED* 10)" (Burrow, ed., *Sonnets and Poems*, 584).

BIBLIOGRAPHY

Early Editions and Relevant Texts

Benson, John. "Epistle to the Reader," from *Poems: Written by Wil. Shake-speare. Gent.* London, 1640.

Capell, Edward. Notes in a copy of Lintott's 1711 reprint of Thorpe's 1609 edition, for a planned but never published edition. Trinity College Library, Cambridge University.

Gildon, Charles. "An Essay on the Rise and Progress of the Stage in Greece, Rome, and England" and "Remarks on the Poems of Shakespear," from *Poems.* Vol. 7 of *The Works of Mr. William Shakespear*, edited by Nicholas Rowe. London, 1710.

Lintott, Bernard. "Advertisement," from *A Collection of Poems . . . by Mr. William Shakespeare.* London, 1711.

Malone, Edmund. "Preface" to *The Plays and Poems of William Shakespeare in Ten Volumes.* 1790. Rev. James Boswell et al. London, 1821.

Malone, Edmund, with George Steevens. *Supplement to the Edition of Shakespeare's Plays Published in 1778 by Samuel Johnson and George Steevens.* London: Bathhurst, 1780.

Meres, Francis. *Palladis Tamia,* or *Wit's Treasury.* London, 1598. [Facsimile edition: New York, 1973, edited by Arthur Freeman.]

The Passionate Pilgrim. London: William Jaggard, 1599. [Facsimile editions: Oxford, 1905, edited by Sidney Lee; New York, 1939, edited by Joseph Quincy Adams.]

Shakespeare, William. *A Collection of Poems . . . by Mr. William Shakespeare.* London: Bernard Lintott, 1711.

———. *The Plays of William Shakespeare in Fifteen Volumes . . .* Edited by George Steevens. 4th ed. London, 1793. [Steevens also reprinted the 1609 edition of *The Sonnets,* without commentary, in 1766.]

———. *The Plays and Poems of William Shakspeare.* Edited by Edmund Malone. 1790. Rev. James Boswell et al. London, 1821.

———. *Poems.* Edited by Charles Gildon. London, 1710. Vol. 7 of *The Works of Mr. William Shakespear,* edited by Nicholas Rowe, vols. 1–6, 1709.

———. *Poems: Written by Wil. Shake-speare. Gent.* London: John Benson, 1640.

———. *Shake-speares Sonnets.* London: Thomas Thorpe, 1609. [Facsimile editions: Oxford, 1905, edited by Sidney Lee; and Yale, 1964, edited by J.M. Osborn.]

Thorpe, Thomas. Dedication from *Shake-speares Sonnets.* London, 1609.

Steevens, George. "Advertisement," from *The Plays of William Shakespeare in Fifteen Volumes . . .* , 4th ed. London, 1793.

Modern Editions of *The Sonnets*

Shakespeare, William. *The Complete Sonnets and Poems.* Edited by Colin Burrow. New York: Oxford University Press, 2002.

———. *Poems of Shakespeare.* Edited by George Wyndham. London: Methuen, 1898.

———. *Shakespeare's Poems: A Facsimile of the Earliest Editions.* Edited by J.M. Osborn et al. New Haven: Yale University Elizabethan Club, 1964.

———. *Shakespeare's Songs and Poems.* Edited by Edward Hubler. New York: McGraw-Hill, 1959.

———. *Shakespeare's Sonnets.* Edited by Barbara Mowat and Paul Werstine. Rev. ed. New Folger Shakespeare. New York: Washington Square Press, 2004.

———. *Shakespeare's Sonnets.* Edited by David West. London: Duckworth Overlook, 2007.

———. *Shakespeare's Sonnets.* Edited by Israel Gollancz. London: J.M. Dent, 1898.

———. *Shakespeare's Sonnets.* Arden Shakespeare, third series. Edited by Katherine Duncan-Jones. London: Thomson, 1998.

———. *Shakespeare's Sonnets.* Edited by Samuel Butler. London: Longmans, Green, 1899.

———. *Shakespeare's Sonnets.* Edited by Stanley Wells. New York: Oxford University Press, 1985.

———. *Shakespeare's Sonnets.* Edited by Stephen Booth. New Haven: Yale University Press, 1977.

———. *Shakespeare's Sonnets.* Edited by Tucker Brooke. New York: Oxford University Press, 1936.

———. *Shakespeare's Sonnets.* Edited by W.G. Ingram and Theodore Redpath. London: University of London Press, 1964.

———. *Shakespeare's Sonnets: The Problems Solved.* Edited by A.L. Rowse. New York: Harper & Row, 1973.

————. *Shakespeare's Sonnets: With Three Hundred Years of Commentary.* Edited by Carl D. Atkins. Madison, N.J.: Fairleigh Dickinson University Press, 2007.

————. *Songs and Poems.* Edited by Edward Hubler. New York: McGraw Hill, 1959.

————. *Sonnets.* Edited by A.L. Rowse. Third edition. New York: Palgrave Macmillan, 1984.

————. *Sonnets.* Edited by Barbara Herrnstein Smith. New York: Avon, 1969.

————. *Sonnets.* Edited by C. Knox Pooler. London: Methuen, 1918.

————. *Sonnets.* Edited by E.B. Reed. New Haven: Yale University Press, 1923.

————. *Sonnets.* Edited by Henry Norman Hudson, Israel Gollancz, C.H. Herford, and Sir William Temple. New York: Grosset & Dunlap, 1909.

————. *Sonnets.* Edited by Martin Seymour-Smith. London: Heinemann, 1963.

————. *Sonnets.* Edited by T.G. Tucker. Cambridge: Cambridge University Press, 1924.

————. *Sonnets and A Lover's Complaint.* Edited by John Kerrigan. London: New Penguin, 1986.

————. *The Sonnets.* Edited by Douglas Bush and Alfred Harbage. New York: Penguin, 1985.

————. *The Sonnets.* Edited by Edward Dowden. New York: D. Appleton, 1881.

————. *The Sonnets.* The New Cambridge Shakespeare. 1996. 2nd ed. G. Blakemore Evans. New York: Cambridge University Press, 2006.

————. *The Sonnets.* The New Shakespeare. Edited by John Dover Wilson. 1965. 2d ed. London: Cambridge University Press, 1967.

————. *The Sonnets.* Cambridge School Shakespeare. Edited by Rex Gibson. New York: Cambridge University Press, 1997.

————. *The Sonnets.* Edited by Stephen Orgel. Introduction by John Hollander. New York: Penguin, 2001.

————. *The Sonnets: A New Variorum Edition.* Edited by Hyder Edward Rollins. 2 vols. Philadelphia: Lippincott, 1944.

————. *The Sonnets and Narrative Poems: The Complete Non-Dramatic Poetry. The Sonnets.* Edited by William Burto. New York: Signet, 1989.

————. *The Sonnets of Shakespeare.* Edited by C.L. Barber. The Laurel Shakespeare. New York: Dell, 1960.

————. *The Sonnets of Shakespeare.* Edited by H.C. Beeching. Boston: Athenaeum Press, 1904.

————. *The Sonnets of Shakespeare.* Edited by Raymond M. Alden. Boston: Houghton Mifflin, 1916.

———. *The Sonnets of William Shakespeare and Henry Wriothesley.* Edited by Walter Thomson. Oxford: Blackwell, 1938.

The Sonnets Through the Ages: A General Bibliography

Acheson, Arthur. *Mistress Davenant and the Dark Lady of the Sonnets.* London: B. Quaritch, 1913.

Akrigg, G. P. V. *Shakespeare and the Earl of Southampton.* Cambridge, Mass.: Harvard University Press, 1968.

Alden, Raymond M. "The 1710 and 1714 Texts of Shakespeare's Poems," from *Modern Language Notes* 31 (May 1916): 268–274.

Alger, W. R. "Shakespeare's Sonnets and Friendship," from *Christian Examiner* 73 (November 1862): 403–435.

Allen, Michael J. B. "Shakespeare's Man Descending a Staircase: Sonnets 126–154," from *Shakespeare Survey* 31 (1978): 127–138.

Auden, W. H. *Lectures on Shakespeare,* edited by Arthur Kirsch. Princeton, N.J.: Princeton University Press, 2000: 86–101.

———. "Shakespeare's Sonnets." Introduction to *The Sonnets,* edited by William Burto. New York: Signet, 1963. Repr. *Forewords & Afterwords.* New York: Vintage, 1973. 88–108.

Baldwin, T. W. *On the Literary Genetics of Shakespeare's Poems and Sonnets.* Urbana, Ill.: University of Illinois Press, 1950.

Barber, C. L. "An Essay on the Sonnets," from *The Sonnets of Shakespeare.* New York: Dell, 1960. 7–33.

———. "Shakespeare in His Sonnets," from *Massachusetts Review* 1 (Summer 1960): 648–672.

Barrell, John. "Editing Out the Discourse of Patronage and Shakespeare's Twenty-ninth Sonnet," from *Poetry, Language, and Politics.* Manchester: University of Manchester Press, 1988.

Bate, Jonathan. *The Genius of Shakespeare.* New York: Oxford University Press, 1998.

———. "Ovid and the Sonnets; or, did Shakespeare feel the anxiety of influence?" from *Shakespeare Survey* 42 (1989): 65–76.

———. *Shakespeare and Ovid.* Oxford: Clarendon Press, 1993.

———. *Shakespeare and the English Romantic Imagination.* Oxford: Clarendon Press, 1986.

Bateson, F. W. "Elementary My Dear Hotson," from *Essays in Criticism* 1 (1951): 81–88.

Benckelman, Robert. "The Drama in Shakespeare's Sonnets," from *College English* 10 (1948): 138–44.

Bennett, Josephine Waters. "Benson's Alleged Piracy of *Shakespeare's Sonnets* and Some of Jonson's Works," from *Studies in Bibliography* 21 (1968): 235–48.

Bermann, Sandra. *The Sonnet Over Time: A Study in Sonnets of Petrarch, Shakespeare, and Baudelaire*. Chapel Hill: University of North Carolina Press, 1988.

Berry, Francis. "'Thou' and 'You' in Shakespeare's Sonnets," from *Essays in Criticism* 8 (April 1958): 138–146.

Berryman, John. *Berryman's Shakespeare*, edited by John Haffenden. New York: Farrar, Straus and Giroux. 257–281, 285–291.

Blackmur, R.P. "A Poetics for Infatuation," from *Kenyon Review* 23 (1961): 647–670. Repr. Hubler, ed., 129–161.

Blades, John. *Shakespeare: The Sonnets*. Analyzing Texts series. Houndmills: Palgrave Macmillan, 2007.

Bloom, Harold. *Shakespeare's Poems and Sonnets*. Bloom's Major Poets. Broomall, Pa.: Chelsea House, 1999.

———. *William Shakespeare: Histories and Poems*. Modern Critical Views. New York: Chelsea House, 1986

———. *William Shakespeare's Sonnets*. Modern Critical Interpretations. New York: Chelsea House, 1987.

Boaden, James. *On the Sonnets of Shakespeare*. London: T. Rodd, 1837.

Booth, Stephen. *An Essay on Shakespeare's Sonnets*. New Haven: Yale University Press, 1969.

Boswell, James. "Preliminary Remarks," from *The Plays and Poems of William Shakespeare*, vol. 20. London, 1821.

Bradbrook, Muriel C. "The Fashioning of a Courtier," from *Shakespeare and Elizabethan Poetry*. New York: Oxford University Press, 1952. 141–161.

Braden, Gordon. "Ovid, Petrarch, and Shakespeare's *Sonnets*," from *Shakespeare's Ovid: The* Metamorphoses *in the Plays and Poems*, edited by A.B. Taylor. Cambridge: Cambridge University Press, 2000. 96–112.

Bredbeck, Gregory W. *Sodomy and Interpretation: Marlowe to Milton*. Ithaca: Cornell University Press, 1991.

———. "Tradition and the Individual Sodomite: Barnfield, Shakespeare, and Subjective Desire," from *Homosexuality in Renaissance and Enlightenment England: Literary Representations in Historical Contexts*, edited by Claude J. Summers. New York: Haworth, 1992. 41–68.

Brooks, James. "A Comparison of the 1609 and 1640 Texts of Shakespeare's *Sonnets*," from *Shakespeare Oxford Newsletter* 43, no. 1 (2007): 13–21.

Brown, Charles Armitage. *Shakespeare's Autobiographical Poems*. London: J. Bohn, 1838.

Brown, Georgia. "Time and Nature of Sequence in Shakespeare's *Sonnets*: 'In sequent toil all forwards to contend,'" from *How to Do Things with Shakespeare: New Approaches, New Essays*, edited by Laurie Maguire. Malden, Mass.: Blackwell, 2008. 236–254.

Brown, Henry. *The Sonnets of Shakespeare Solved*. London: J.R. Smith, 1870.

Brown, Richard Danson, and David Johnson. *Shakespeare 1609: Cymbeline and the Sonnets*. London: Macmillan, 2000.

Browning, Robert. "House." 1876. Repr. *The Poems: Volume Two*, edited by John Pettigrew. New Haven: Yale University Press, 1981: 438–439.

Budd, Thomas D. *Shakespeare's Sonnets with Commentaries*. Philadelphia: J. Campbell, 1868.

Butler, Samuel. *Shakespeare's Sonnets Reconsidered*. 1899. London: Longmans Green, 1927.

Callaghan, Dympna. *Shakespeare's Sonnets*. Malden, Mass.: Blackwell, 2007.

Cannan, Paul D. "Early Shakespeare Criticism, Charles Gildon, and the Making of Shakespeare the Playwright-Poet," from *Modern Philology* 102 (2004): 35–55.

Cheney, Patrick. *Shakespeare, National Poet-Playwright*. Cambridge: Cambridge University Press, 2004.

———, ed. *The Cambridge Companion to Shakespeare's Poetry*. Cambridge: Cambridge University Press, 2007.

Coleridge, Samuel Taylor. *Coleridge's Miscellaneous Criticism*, edited by Thomas Middleton Raysor. Cambridge, Mass.: Harvard University Press, 1936.

———. *Coleridge's Shakespearean Criticism*, edited by Thomas Middleton Raysor. 2 vols. Repr. London: J. M. Dent, 1967.

———. *Coleridge's Writings on Shakespeare*, edited by Terence Hawkes. New York: Capricorn, 1959.

———. *Table Talk*. 1833. Repr. London: Murray, 1835.

Colie, Rosalie. *Shakespeare's Living Art*. Princeton: Princeton University Press, 1974.

Cousins, A. D. *Shakespeare's Sonnets and Narrative Poems*. Essex, U.K.: Pearson Education, 2000.

Crosman, Robert. "Making Love Out of Nothing at All: The Issue of Story in Shakespeare's Procreation Sonnets," from *Shakespeare Quarterly* 41 (1990): 470–488.

Cruttwell, Patrick. *The Shakespearean Moment: And Its Place in the Poetry of the 17th Century*. New York: Columbia University Press, 1955: Ch. 1.

de Grazia, Margreta. "Babbling Will in Shakespeare's Sonnets 127 to 154," from *Spenser Studies* 1. Pittsburgh: University of Pittsburgh Press, 1980.

———. "The Motive for Interiority: Shakespeare's *Sonnets* and *Hamlet*," from *Style* 23 (1989): 430–444.

———. "The Scandal of Shakespeare's Sonnets," from *Shakespeare Survey* 46 (1994): 35–49.

———. *Shakespeare Verbatim: The Reproduction of Authenticity and the 1790 Apparatus*. Oxford: Oxford University Press, 1991.

Dobson, Michael, and Stanley Wells, eds. *The Oxford Companion to Shakespeare*. Oxford: Oxford University Press, 2001.

Donoghue, Denis. "Shakespeare in the Sonnets," from *Raritan* 6 (1986): 123–137.

Donow, Herbert S. *The Sonnet in England and America: A Bibliography of Criticism*. Westport: Greenwood, 1982.

Douglas, Alfred. *The True History of Shakespeare's Sonnets*. London: M. Secker, 1933.

Dowden, Edward. *Shakespere: A Critical Study of His Mind and Art*. London: H. S. King, 1872.

Dubrow, Heather. *Captive Victors: Shakespeare's Narrative Poems and Sonnets*. Ithaca: Cornell University Press, 1987: Ch. 3.

———. *Echoes of Desire: English Petrarchanism and Its Counterdiscourses*. Ithaca: Cornell University Press, 1995.

———. "Incertainties now crown themselves assur'd: The Politics of Plotting Shakespeare's Sonnets," from *Shakespeare Quarterly* 47 (1996): 291–305.

Duncan-Jones, Katherine. "Filling the Unforgiving Minute: Modernizing *Shake-speares Sonnets* (1609)," from *Essays in Criticism* 45 (1995): 199–207.

———. "Playing Fields or Killing Fields: Shakespeare's Poems and Sonnets," from *Shakespeare Quarterly* 54 (2003): 127–141.

———. "Was the 1609 *Shake-speares Sonnets* really authorized?" from *Review of English Studies*, new series, 34 (1983): 151–71.

Edmondson, Paul, and Stanley Wells. *Shakespeare's Sonnets*. Oxford Shakespeare Topics. New York: Oxford University Press, 2004.

Empson, William. *Seven Types of Ambiguity*. 1930. Rev. ed. New York: New Directions, 1947.

———. *Some Versions of Pastoral*. 1935. Rev. ed. New York: New Directions, 1968.

Engle, Lars. "Afloat in Thick Deeps: Shakespeare's Sonnets on Certainty," from *PMLA* 104 (1989): 832–843.

Erne, Lukas. *Shakespeare as a Literary Dramatist*. Cambridge: Cambridge University Press, 2003.

Everett, Barbara. "Good and Bad Loves: Shakespeare, Plato, and the Plotting of the Sonnets," from *Times Literary Supplement* (12 July 2002): 13–15.

Felperin, Howard. "The Dark Lady Identified, or What Deconstruction Can Do for Shakespeare's Sonnets," from *Shakespeare and Deconstruction*. New York: Peter Lang, 1988.

———. "Toward a Poststructuralist Practice: A Reading of Shakespeare's Sonnets," from *Beyond Deconstruction*. Oxford: Clarendon Press, 1985.

Fenton, James. "Auden's Shakespeare," from *New York Review of Books* (23 March 2000): 24–28.

Ferry, Anne. *All in War with Time: Love Poetry of Shakespeare, Donne, Jonson, Marvell*. Cambridge, Mass.: Harvard University Press, 1975.

———. *The "Inward" Language: Sonnets of Wyatt, Sidney, Shakespeare, Donne.* Chicago: University of Chicago Press, 1983.

———. "The Sense of Rhyme: Sidney and Shakespeare," from *Literary Imagination* 4 (2002): 163–189.

Fiedler, Leslie. "Some Contexts of Shakespeare's Sonnets," from Hubler, ed., 55–90.

Fineman, Joel. "Shakespeare's Perjured Eye," from *Representations* 8 (Fall 1984): 59–86.

———. *Shakespeare's Perjured Eye: The Invention of Poetic Subjectivity in the Sonnets.* Berkeley: University of California Press, 1986.

———. "Shakespeare's Sonnets' Perjured Eye," from *Lyric Poetry: Beyond New Criticism*, edited by Chaviva Hosek and Patricia Parker. Ithaca: Cornell University Press, 1985. 116–131.

Foster, Donald W. "Master W.H., R.I.P.," from *PMLA* 102 (1987): 42–55.

Freinkel, Lisa. *Reading Shakespeare's Will: The Theology of Figure from Augustine to the Sonnets.* New York: Columbia University Press, 2002.

Frye, Northrop. "How True a Twain," from Hubler, ed., 23–53.

———. *Tables of Identity: Studies in Poetic Mythology.* New York: Harcourt, Brace, & World, 1963.

Fuller, John. *The Sonnet.* London: Methuen, 1972.

Garber, Marjorie. *Vice Versa: Bisexuality and the Eroticism of Everyday Life.* New York: Simon and Schuster, 1995.

Giroux, Robert. *The Book Known as Q: A Consideration of Shakespeare's Sonnets.* New York: Atheneum, 1982.

Goldberg, Jonathan. *Sodometries: Renaissance Texts, Modern Sexualities.* Berkeley: University of California Press, 1992.

Graves, Robert, and Laura Riding. "A Study in Original Punctuation and Spelling," from *A Survey of Modernist Poetry.* 1926. Repr. *The Common Asphodel: Collected Essays on Poetry 1922–1949.* London: Hamish Hamilton, 1949: 84–95.

Green, Martin. *The Labyrinth of Shakespeare's Sonnets.* London: Charles Skilton, 1974.

Greene, Thomas M. "Pitiful Thrivers: Failed Husbandry in the Sonnets," from *Shakespeare and the Question of Theory*, edited by Patricia Parker and Geoffrey Hartman. New York: Methuen, 1985. 230–244.

———. "Anti-Hermeneutics: The Case of Shakespeare's Sonnet 129," from *The Vulnerable Text: Essays on Renaissance Literature.* New York: Columbia University Press, 1986. 159–174.

Grundy, Joan. "Shakespeare's Sonnets and the Elizabethan Sonneteers," from Nicoll, ed. 41–49.

Gurr, Andrew. "Shakespeare's First Poem: Sonnet 145," from *Essays in Criticism* 21 (1971): 221–226.

———. "You and Thou in Shakespeare's Sonnets," from *Essays in Criticism* 32 (1982): 9–25.

Hallam, Henry. *Introduction to the Literature of Europe in the Fifteenth, Sixteenth, and Seventeenth Centuries.* 1842. 4th ed. 4 vols. (in 2). New York: Crowell, 1880: 3:253–256.

Halpern, Richard. *Shakespeare's Perfume: Sodomy and Sublimity in the Sonnets, Wilde, Freud, and Lacan.* Philadelphia: University of Pennsylvania Press, 2002.

Hammond, Gerald. *The Reader and Shakespeare's Young Man Sonnets.* Totowa, N.J.: Barnes and Noble, 1981.

Harbage, Alfred. "Dating Shakespeare's Sonnets," from *Shakespeare Quarterly* 1 (1950): 57–63.

Hardison, Jr., O. B. *The Enduring Monument: A Study of the Idea of Praise in Renaissance Literary Theory and Practice.* Chapel Hill: University of North Carolina Press, 1973.

Hawkes, David. "Sodomy, Usury, and the Narrative of Shakespeare's Sonnets." *Renaissance Studies* 14 (2000): 344–361.

Hayashi, Tetsumaro. *Shakespeare's Sonnets: A Record of Twentieth-Century Criticism.* Metuchen, N.J.: Scarecrow Press, 1972.

Hecht, Anthony. "Shakespeare and the Sonnet." 1996. *Melodies Unheard: Essays on the Mysteries of Poetry.* Baltimore: Johns Hopkins University Press, 2003.

Hedley, Jane. "Since First Your Eye I Eyed: Shakespeare's *Sonnets* and the Poetics of Narcissism," from *Style* 28 (1994): 1–30.

Herrnstein, Barbara, ed. *Discussions of Shakespeare's Sonnets.* Boston: D. C. Heath, 1964.

Hieatt, A. Kent. "Cymbeline and the Intrusion of Lyric into Romance Narrative: *Sonnets*, "A Lover's Complaint," Spenser's *Ruins of Rome*," from *Unfolded Tales: Essays on Renaissance Romance*, edited by George M. Logan and Gordon Teskey. Ithaca: Cornell University Press, 1989. 98–118.

———. "The Genesis of Shakespeare's *Sonnets*: Spenser's *Ruines of Rome: by Bellay*," from *PMLA* 98 (1983): 800–814.

———, C. W. Hieatt, and Anne Lake Prescott. "When did Shakespeare write *Sonnets* 1609?" from *Studies in Philology* 88 (1991): 69–109.

Highet, Gilbert. "Shakespeare in Love," from *The Powers of Poetry.* Oxford: Oxford University Press, 1960.

Honigmann, E. A. J. "The First Performances of Shakespeare's *Sonnets*," from *Shakespeare Performed: Essays in Honor of R. A. Foaks*, edited by Grace Ioppolo. Newark: University of Delaware Press, 2000.

Hopkins, David. *The Routledge Anthology of Poets on Poets: Poetic Responses to English Poetry from Chaucer to Yeats.* New York: Routledge, 1990.

Hotson, Lesley. *Mr. W. H.* New York: Alfred Knopf, 1965.

———. *Shakespeare's Sonnets Dated and Other Essays*. Oxford: Oxford University Press, 1949.

Hubler, Edward. *The Sense of Shakespeare's Sonnets*. New York: Hill and Wang, 1952.

———, ed. *The Riddle of Shakespeare's Sonnets*. New York: Basic, 1962.

Hunter, G. K. "The Dramatic Technique of Shakespeare's Sonnets," from *Essays in Criticism* 3, no. 2 (1953): 152–164.

Hutchison, Coleman. "Breaking the Book Known as Q," from *PMLA* 121 (2006), 33–66.

Hyland, Peter. *An Introduction to Shakespeare's Poems*. New York: Palgrave Macmillan, 2003.

Ingram, W. G., and Theodore Redpath. "A Note on the Dedication," from *Shakespeare's Sonnets*. London: University of London Press, 1964.

Innes, Paul. *Shakespare and the English Renaissance Sonnet: Verses of Feigning Love*. New York: St. Martin's, 1997.

Jackson, Mac D. P. "Punctuation and the Compositors of Shakespeare's *Sonnets*, 1609," from *The Library*, fifth series, 30 (1975): 1–24.

Jakobson, Roman, and Lawrence G. Jones. *Shakespeare's Verbal Art in "Th' Expense of Spirit."* De Propreitatibus Litterarum, Series Practica, no. 35. The Hague: Mouton, 1970.

Jones, G. P. "You, Thou, He or She? The Master Mistress in Shakespearean and Elizabethan Sonnet Sequences," from *Cahiers Elisabéthains* 19 (1981): 73–84.

Jones, Peter, ed. *Shakespeare: The Sonnets*. Casebook Series. Houndmills: Macmillan, 1977.

Joseph, Miriam. *Shakespeare's Use of the Arts of Language*. New York: Columbia University Press, 1947.

Kay, Dennis. *William Shakespeare: Sonnets and Poems*. New York: Twayne, 1998.

Keats, John. *Letters of John Keats*, edited by Robert Gittings. New York: Oxford University Press, 1970.

Kernan, Alvin. "Shakespeare's Sonnets and Patronage Art," from *Shakespeare, the King's Playwright: Theater in the Stuart Court, 1603–1613*. New Haven: Yale University Press, 1995. 169–187.

Klause, John. "Shakespeare's *Sonnets*: Age in love and the goring of thoughts," from *Studies in Philology* 80 (1983): 300–324.

Knight, G. Wilson. *The Mutual Flame: On Shakespeare's Sonnets and The Phoenix and the Turtle*. London: Methuen, 1955.

Knights, L. C. "Shakespeare's Sonnets," from *Scrutiny* 3 (1934): 133–160.

Kott, Jan. "Shakespeare's Bitter Arcadia," from *Shakespeare Our Contemporary*. New York: Norton, 1964. 237–292.

Krieger, Murray. *A Window to Criticism: Shakespeare's Sonnets and Modern Poetics*. Princeton: Princeton University Press, 1964.

Landry, Hilton J. *Interpretation in Shakespeare's Sonnets*. Berkeley: University of California Press, 1963.

———, ed. *New Essays on Shakespeare's Sonnets*. New York: AMS Press, 1976.

Lanier, Sidney. *Shakspere and His Forerunners*. Vol. 1. New York: Doubleday and Page, 1908. Repr. New York: AMS, 1966. From lecture delivered in 1879.

Lee, Sir Sidney. "Ovid and Shakespeare's Sonnets," from *Quarterly Review* 110 (April 1909): 455–476. Repr. *Elizabethan and Other Essays*. Oxford: Clarendon Press, 1929: 116–139.

———. "Shakespeare and the Earl of Pembroke," from *The Fortnightly Review* 69 (February 1, 1898): 210–223.

———. "Shakespeare and the Earl of Southampton," from *Cornhill* 77 (April 1898): 482–495.

Leigh, G. A. "The Rival Poet in Shakespeare's Sonnets," from *Westminster Review* 147 (February 1897): 817–834.

Leishman, J. B. *Themes and Variations in Shakespeare's Sonnets*. 1961. 2d ed. London: Hutchinson University Library, 1963.

———. "Variations on a Theme in Shakespeare's Sonnets," from *Elizabethan and Jacobean Studies*, edited by Herbert Davis and Helen Gardner. Oxford: Clarendon Press, 1960. 112–149.

Lever, J. W. *The Elizabethan Love Sonnet*. London: Methuen, 1956. 162–272.

Levin, Richard. "Shakespeare's Sonnets 153 and 154," from *Explicator* 5 (1994): 11–14.

———. "Sonnet CXXIX as 'Dramatic' Poem," from *Shakespeare Quarterly* 16 (1965): 175–181.

Lewis, B. Roland. *The Shakespeare Documents*. Vol. 2. Stanford, Calif.: Stanford University Press, 1941.

Lewis, C. S. *English Literature in the Sixteenth Century, Excluding Drama*. Oxford: Clarendon Press, 1954. 502–508.

MacInnes, Ian. "Cheerful Girls and Willing Boys: Old and Young Bodies in Shakespeare's Sonnets," from *Early Modern Literary Studies* 6, no. 2 (2000): 1–26.

Magnusson, A. L. "Shakespeare's *Sonnets*: A Modern Perspective," from *Shakespeare's Sonnets*, edited by Barbara Mowat and Paul Werstine, 355–369.

Mahood, M. M. "Love's Confined Doom," from *Shakespeare Survey* 15 (1962): 50–61.

———. *Shakespeare's Wordplay*. London: Methuen, 1957.

Marotti, Arthur F. "Love Is Not Love: Elizabethan Sonnet Sequences and the Social Order," from *ELH* 49 (1982): 396–428.

———. *Manuscript, Print, and the English Renaissance Lyric*. Ithaca: Cornell University Press, 1995.

———. "Shakespeare's Sonnets as Literary Property," from *Soliciting Interpretation: Literary Theory and Seventeenth-Century English Poetry*, edited by Elizabeth D. Harvey and Katherine Eisaman Maus. Chicago: University of Chicago Press, 1990. 143–173.

Martin, Philip J. *Shakespeare's Sonnets: Self, Love, and Art*. Cambridge: Cambridge University Press, 1972.

Masefield, John. *William Shakespeare*. New York: Premier, 1964. 25–28.

Massey, Gerald. "Shakespeare and His Sonnets," from *Quarterly Review* 115 (April 1864): 224–250.

Masten, Jeffrey. *Textual Intercourse: Collaboration, Authorship and Sexualities in Renaissance Drama*. Cambridge: Cambridge University Press, 1997.

Melchiori, Giorgio. *Shakespeare's Dramatic Meditations: An Experiment in Criticism*. Oxford: Clarendon Press, 1976.

Mizener, Arthur. "The Structure of Figurative Language in Shakespeare's Sonnets," from *Southern Review* 5 (1940): 730–747.

Montgomery, Robert L. *The Perfect Ceremony of Love's Rite: Shakespeare's Sonnets and* A Lover's Complaint. Tempe, Ariz.: ACMRS, 2006.

Muir, Kenneth. *Shakespeare's Sonnets*. London: George Allen & Unwin, 1979.

Murry, J. Middleton. *Shakespeare*. 1936. London: Jonathan Cape, 1965. 91–117.

Neely, Carol Thomas. "Detachment and Engagement in Shakespeare's Sonnets: 94, 116, and 129," from *PMLA* 92 (1977): 83–95.

———. "The Structure of English Renaissance Sonnet Sequences," from *ELH* 45 (1978): 359–389.

Nejgebauer, A. "Twentieth-Century Studies in Shakespeare's Sonnets, Songs, and Poems. 2. The Sonnets," from Nicoll, ed. 10–18.

Nelson, Jr., Lowry. "The Matter of Rime: Sonnets of Sidney, Daniel, and Shakespeare, " from *Poetic Traditions of the English Renaissance*, edited by Maynard Mack and George deForest Lord. New Haven: Yale University Press, 1982. 123–142.

Nicoll, Allardyce, ed. *Shakespeare Survey* 15. Cambridge: Cambridge University Press, 1962. [This volume features several essays on the *Sonnets*.]

Nosworthy, J.M. "Shakespeare and Mr. W.H.," from *Library* 18, fifth series, (1983): 294–298.

Nowottny, Winifred M.T. "Formal Elements in Shakespeare's Sonnets, Sonnets I–VI," from *Essays in Criticism* 2 (1952): 76–84.

Padel, John. *New Poems by Shakespeare: Order and Meaning Restored to the Sonnets*. London: Herbert, 1981.

Palmer, George Herbert. *Intimations of Immortality in the Sonnets of Shakespeare*. Boston: Houghton Mifflin, 1912.

Parker, David. "Verbal Moods in Shakespeare's Sonnets," from *Modern Language Quarterly* 30 (1969): 331–339.

Pequigney, Joseph. *Such Is My Love: A Study of Shakespeare's Sonnets*. Chicago: University of Chicago Press, 1985.

Person, Jr., James E., Sandra L. Williamson et al., eds. *Shakespearean Criticism*. Detroit: Gale Research, 1990– . Esp. vols. 10, and 40, 51, 62, 75.

Peterson, Douglas. *The English Lyric From Wyatt to Donne*. Princeton: Princeton University Press, 1967. 212–251.

Petrarca, Francesco. *Lyric Poems* (*Rime sparse*), translated by R.M. Durling. Cambridge, Mass.: Harvard University Press, 1976.

Prince, F. T. "The Sonnet from Wyatt to Shakespeare," from *Stratford-Upon-Avon Studies 2: Elizabethan Poetry*. London: Edward Arnold, 1960: 11–31.

Raffel, Burton. "Shakespeare's Sonnets: Touchstone of the English Lyric Tradition," from *Explorations in Renaissance Culture* 26 (2000): 1–24.

Ramsey, Paul. *The Fickle Glass: A Study of Shakespeare's Sonnets*. New York: AMS Press, 1979.

Ransom, John Crowe. "Shakespeare At Sonnets," from *Southern Review* 3 (1938): 531–553.

Regan, Mariann Sanders. "Shakespeare's Sonnets," from *Love Words: The Self and the Text in Medieval and Renaissance Poetry*. Ithaca: Cornell University Press, 1982. 223–254.

Richmond, Hugh. "The Dark Lady as Reformation Mistress," from *Kenyon Review* 8, no. 2 (1986): 91–105.

Roberts, Sasha. *Reading Shakespeare's Poems in Early Modern England*. New York: Palgrave Macmillan, 2003.

———. "Shakespeare's *Sonnets* and English Sonnet Sequences," from *Early Modern English Poetry: A Critical Companion*, edited by Patrick Cheney, Andrew Hadfield, and Garrett A. Sullivan, Jr. Oxford: Oxford University Press, 2007: 172–183.

Robertson, J.M. *The Problems of the Shakespeare Sonnets*. London: George Routledge and Sons, 1926.

Robinson, Peter. *Poetry, Poets, Readers: Making Things Happen*. Oxford: Clarendon Press, 2002: 113–133.

Roche, Thomas P. *Petrarch and the Elizabethan Sonnet Sequences*. New York: AMS, 1989.

Rosmarin, Adena. "Hermeneutics vs. Erotics: Shakespeare's *Sonnets* and Interpretive History," from *PMLA* 100 (1985): 20–37.

Rostenberg, Leona. "Thomas Thorpe, Publisher of 'Shake-Speare's Sonnets," from *Papers of the Bibliographical Society of America* 54 (1960): 16–37.

Rowse, A.L. *Shakespeare's Sonnets: The Problems Solved*. 2d ed. New York: Harper & Row, 1973.

Rylands, George. "Shakespeare the Poet," from *A Companion to Shakespeare Studies*, edited by H. Granville-Barker and G. B. Harrison. Garden City, N.Y.: Anchor, 1960. 88–115.

Sagaser, Elizabeth Harris. "Shakespeare's Sweet Leaves: Mourning, Pleasure, and the Triumph of Thought in the Renaissance Love Lyric," from *ELH* 61 (1994): 1–26.

Schaar, Claes. *An Elizabethan Sonnet Problem: Shakespeare's Sonnets, Daniel's Delia, and Their Literary Background.* Lund, Sweden: C.W.K. Gleerup, 1960.

Schalkwyk, David. *Speech and Performance in Shakespeare's Sonnets and Plays.* Cambridge: Cambridge University Press, 2002.

Schiffer, James. "The Incomplete Narrative of Shakespeare's *Sonnets,*" from Schoenfeldt, ed., 45–56.

———, ed. *Shakespeare's Sonnets: Critical Essays.* Shakespeare Criticism series, vol. 20. NewYork: Garland, 1999.

Schoenbaum, Samuel. "Shakespeare's Dark Lady: A Question of Identity," from *Shakespeare's Styles: Essays in Honour of Kenneth Muir,* edited by Philip Edwards, Inga-Stina Ewbank, and G.K. Hunter. Cambridge: Cambridge University Press, 1980: 221–239.

———. *Shakespeare's Lives.* 1970. Rev. ed. Oxford: Clarendon Press, 1991.

Schoenfeldt, Michael. "Making Shakespeare's Sonnets Matter in the Classroom," from *Approaches to Teaching Shorter Elizabethan Poetry,* edited by Patrick Cheney and Anne Lake Prescott. New York: MLA, 2000: 239–245.

———, ed. *A Companion to Shakespeare's Sonnets.* Oxford: Blackwell, 2007.

Sedgwick, Eve Kosofsky. "Swan in Love: The Example of Shakespeare's Sonnets," from *Between Men: English Literature and Male Homosexual Desire.* New York: Columbia University Press, 1985: 28–48.

Shaw, George Bernard. "Preface" to *The Dark Lady of the Sonnets.* 1910. Repr. *Misalliance, The Dark Lady of the Sonnets, and Fanny's First Play.* London: Constable & Co, 1914. 203–230.

Sidney, Philip. *The Poems of Sir Philip Sidney,* edited by William A. Ringler, Jr. Oxford: Clarendon Press, 1962.

Simpson, Richard. *An Introduction to the Philosophy of Shakespeare's Sonnets.* London: N. Trubner, 1868.

Smith, A.J. *The Metaphysics of Love: Studies in Renaissance Love Poetry from Dante to Milton.* New York: Cambridge University Press, 1985. 180–186.

Smith, Bruce R. *Homosexual Desire in Shakespeare's England: A Cultural Poetics.* Chicago: University of Chicago Press, 1991.

Smith, Hallett. *Elizabethan Poetry: A Study in Conventions, Meaning and Expression.* Cambridge, Mass.: Harvard University Press, 1952. 131–193.

———. *The Tension of the Lyre: Poetry in Shakespeare's Sonnets.* San Marino, Calif.: Huntington Library, 1981.

Southam, B.C. "Shakespeare's Christian Sonnet? Number 146," from *Shakespeare Quarterly* 11 (1960): 67–71.

Spender, Stephen. "The Alike and the Other," from Hubler, ed., 93–128.

Spiller, Michael G. *The Development of the Sonnet: An Introduction*. London: Routledge, 1992.

Spurgeon, Caroline F. E. *Shakespeare's Imagery and What It Tells Us*. Cambridge: Cambridge University Press, 1935.

Stallybrass, Peter. "Editing as Cultural Formation: The Sexing of Shakespeare's Sonnets," from *Modern Language Quarterly* 54, no. 1 (1993): 91–103.

Stapleton, M. L. *Harmful Eloquence: Ovid's* Amores *from Antiquity to Shakespeare*. Ann Arbor: University of Michigan Press, 1996.

Starkey, David, and Paul J. Willis, eds. *In a Fine Frenzy: Poets Respond to Shakespeare*. Iowa City: University of Iowa Press, 2005.

Stirling, Brents. *The Shakespeare Sonnet Order: Poems and Groups*. Berkeley: University of California Press, 1968.

———. "Sonnets 127–154," from *Shakespeare 1564–1964: A Collection of Modern Essays by Various Hands*, edited by Edward A. Bloom. Providence, R.I.: Brown University Press, 1964.

Swinburne, Algernon Charles. *A Study of Shakespeare*. 1879. London: Heinemann, 1918.

Tannenbaum, Samuel A. and Dorothy R., eds. "Sonnets." 1940. Repr. in *Elizabethan Bibliographies*. Vol. 9. Port Washington, N.Y.: Kennikat, 1967.

Taylor, Gary. *Reinventing Shakespeare: A Cultural History, from the Restoration to the Present*. New York: Weidenfeld and Nicholson, 1989.

———. "Some Manuscripts of Shakespeare's Sonnets," from *Bulletin of the John Rylands University Library of Manchester* 68 (1985): 210–46.

Tyler, Thomas. *Shakespeare's Sonnets*. London: D. Nutt, 1890.

van den Berg, Sarah. "'Mutual Ordering': Subjectivity and Language in Shakespeare's Sonnets," from *Contending Kingdoms*, edited by Marie-Rose Logan and Peter L. Rudnytsky. Detroit: Wayne State University Press, 1991: 173–201.

Vendler, Helen. *The Art of Shakespeare's Sonnets*. Cambridge, Mass.: Harvard University Press, 1997.

Vickers, Brian. *Shakespeare, A Lover's Complaint, and Sir John Davies of Hereford*. Cambridge: Cambridge University Press, 2007.

Wait, R. J. C. *The Background to Shakespeare's Sonnets*. London: Chatto & Windus, 1972.

Waddington, Raymond B. "The Poetics of Eroticism—Shakespeare's 'Master-Mistress,'" from *Renaissance Discourses of Desire*, edited by Claude J. Summers and Ted-Larry Pebworth. Columbia: University of Missouri Press, 1993: 1–12.

Waller, Gary. *English Poetry of the Sixteenth Century*. New York: Longman, 1986.

Weiner, Monica. "Strip Sonnets: An Introduction to Shakespeare," from *Shakespeare* 4, no. 2 (2000): 14–15.

Weiser, David K. *Mind in Character: Shakespeare's Speaker in the Sonnets.* Columbia: University of Missouri Press, 1993.

Wells, Stanley. *Looking for Sex in Shakespeare.* New York: Cambridge University Press, 2004.

———. *Shakespeare for All Time.* Oxford: Oxford University Press, 2003.

White, R. G. "The Sonnets of Shakespeare," from *Westminster Review* 68 (July 1857): 116–137.

Wilde, Oscar. "The Portrait of Mr. W. H.," from *Blackwood's Magazine* 146 (July 1889): 1–21. Repr. *Lord Arthur Savile's Crime, The Portrait of Mr. W. H. and Other Stories.* London: Methuen, 1908: 145–196. [Wilde's essay was significantly enlarged in 1921.]

Willen, Gerald, and Victor B. Reed, eds. *A Casebook on Shakespeare's Sonnets.* New York: Thomas Y. Crowell, 1964.

Wilson, John Dover. *An Introduction to the Sonnets of Shakespeare for the Use of Historians and Others.* Cambridge: Cambridge University Press, 1964.

Wilson, Katherine M. *Shakespeare's Sugared Sonnets.* New York: Barnes & Noble, 1974.

Winny, James. *The Master-Mistress: A Study of Shakespeare's Sonnets.* New York: Barnes & Noble, 1968.

Winters, Yvor. "Poetic Styles, Old and New," from *Four Poets on Poetry*, edited by D. C. Allen. Baltimore: Johns Hopkins University Press, 1959.

Witt, Robert W. *Of Comfort and Despair: Shakespeare's Sonnet Sequence.* Austria: Universitat Salzburg, 1979.

Wordsworth, William. "Scorn not the Sonnet." 1827. Repr. *Poems, Volume II.* London: Penguin, 1977: 635.

Wright, Eugene Patrick. *The Structure of Shakespeare's Sonnets.* Lewiston, N.Y.: Edwin Mellen Press, 1993.

Wright, George T. *Shakespeare's Metrical Art.* Los Angeles: University of California Press, 1991.

———. "The Silent Speech of Shakespeare's Sonnets," from *Shakespeare and the Twentieth Century*, edited by Jonathan Bate, Jill A. Levenson, and Dieter Mehl. Newark: University of Delaware Press, 1998.

ACKNOWLEDGMENTS

Twentieth Century

Lee, Sir Sidney. "Ovid and Shakespeare's Sonnets," from *Quarterly Review* 110 (April 1909): 455–476. Repr. *Elizabethan and Other Essays*. Oxford: Clarendon Press, 1929: 116–139.

Shaw, George Bernard. "Preface" to *The Dark Lady of the Sonnets*. 1910. Repr. *Misalliance, The Dark Lady of the Sonnets, and Fanny's First Play*. London: Constable & Co, 1914. 203–230.

Graves, Robert, and Laura Riding. "A Study in Original Punctuation and Spelling," from *A Survey of Modernist Poetry*. 1926. Repr. *The Common Asphodel: Collected Essays on Poetry 1922–1949*. London: Hamish Hamilton, 1949: 84–95.

Empson, William. "They That Have Power," from *Some Versions of Pastoral*. 1935. Rev. ed. New York: New Directions, 1968: 89–115.

Hunter, G. K. "The Dramatic Technique of Shakespeare's Sonnets," from *Essays in Criticism* 3, no. 2 (1953): 152–164.

Ingram, W. G., and Theodore Redpath. "A Note on the Dedication," from *Shakespeare's Sonnets*. London: University of London Press, 1964: 3–5. © W. G. Ingram. Reprinted by permission.

Ferry, Anne. "Shakespeare and Sidney," from *The "Inward" Language: Sonnets of Wyatt, Sidney, Shakespeare, Donne*. Chicago: University of Chicago Press, 1983: 170–214. © 1983 by The University of Chicago.

Fineman, Joel. "Shakespeare's 'Perjur'd Eye,'" from *Representations* 7 (Summer 1984): 59–86. © 1989 University of California Press. Reprinted by permission.

Greene, Thomas M. "Anti-Hermeneutics: The Case of Shakespeare's Sonnet 129," from *The Vulnerable Text: Essays on Renaissance Literature*. New York: Columbia University Press, 1986: 159–174. Copyright © 1986 Columbia University Press. Reprinted by permission of the publisher.

Smith, Bruce R. "The Secret Sharer," from *Homosexual Desire in Shakespeare's England: A Cultural Poetics*. Chicago: University of Chicago Press, 1991: 228–315. © 1994 by The University of Chicago.

de Grazia, Margreta. "The Scandal of Shakespeare's Sonnets," from *Shakespeare Survey* 46 (1994): 35–49. © 1994 by Cambridge University Press. Reprinted with the permission of Cambridge University Press.

Vendler, Helen. "Introduction" to *The Art of Shakespeare's Sonnets*. Cambridge, Mass.: Harvard University Press, 1997: 1–41. © 1997 by the President and Fellows of Harvard College.

Bate, Jonathan. "Shakespeare's Autobiographical Poems?" from *The Genius of Shakespeare*. New York: Oxford University Press, 1998: 34–64. © 1998 Jonathan Bate.

Twenty-First Century

Cheney, Patrick. "'O, let my books be . . . dumb presagers': poetry and theatre in the Sonnets," from *Shakespeare, National Poet-Playwright*. Cambridge: Cambridge University Press, 2004: 207–238. © 2004 Patrick Cheney. Reprinted with the permission of Cambridge University Press.

INDEX

❧